CORNELL STUDIES IN CLASSICAL PHILOLOGY

EDITED BY

HARRY CAPLAN ★ JAMES HUTTON

G. M. KIRKWOOD

VOLUME XXXV

SOPHROSYNE

*Self-Knowledge and Self-Restraint
in Greek Literature*

By HELEN NORTH

SOPHROSYNE

Self-Knowledge and Self-Restraint

in Greek Literature

By Helen North

CORNELL UNIVERSITY PRESS

ITHACA, NEW YORK

Library of Congress Catalog Card Number: 66-13797

PRINTED IN THE UNITED STATES OF AMERICA

BY THE MAPLE PRESS COMPANY

To C. D. N. and M. C. N.

and to the memory of F. A. D.

Ἀρετῆς καὶ σωφροσύνης ἕνεκα

Preface

WE have had no detailed study of sophrosyne which embraces the entire period of Greek literature. Two brief articles offer useful analyses of the concept in the classical age,[1] and a Göttingen dissertation of 1917, of which only an abstract has been published, studies the period in greater detail.[2] There are many discussions of sophrosyne in recent works on Greek ethics and morality,[3] but nothing on the scale attempted here has been available. My aim has been to trace the development of the concept from its earliest appearance in the Homeric poems to its transformation into a Christian virtue in the fourth century of our era. Although the evidence is found principally in Greek literature, I have also given considerable attention to Roman efforts to naturalize sophrosyne, since its place in Roman thought has proved interesting in itself and clearly affected the form in which it was transmitted to the Latin Fathers. In view of the number and the variety of the authors and

[1] Albrecht Kollmann, "Sophrosyne," *Wiener Studien* 59 (1941), 12–34. G. J. de Vries, "Σωφροσύνη en grec classique," *Mnemosyne*, Series 3, 11 (1943), 81–101.

[2] Ernst Weitlich, *Quae Fuerit Vocis Σωφροσύνη Vis ac Natura apud Antiquiores Scriptores Graecos usque ad Platonem*. Abstract in *Jahrbuch der philosophischen Fakultät der Georg August-Universität zur Göttingen* (1922). An unpublished twenty-five-page essay, "The Meaning of Sophrosyne," by Benedict S. Einarson, submitted for the M.A. degree at the University of Chicago (June 1927), surveys the principal aspects of sophrosyne and illustrates them with passages drawn mainly from classical and Hellenistic sources.

[3] Arthur Adkins, *Merit and Responsibility* (Oxford, 1960); John Ferguson, *Moral Values in the Ancient World* (London, 1958); Werner Jaeger, *Paideia: The Ideals of Greek Culture*, trans. Gilbert Highet (Vol. I, 4th ed.; Oxford, 1954. Vols. II, III; New York, 1943, 1944); Eduard Schwartz, *Ethik der Griechen* (Stuttgart, 1951); Bruno Snell, *The Discovery of the Mind*, trans. T. G. Rosenmeyer (Oxford, 1953). Older standard works that consider sophrosyne at some length include K. F. Nägelsbach, *Die nachhomerische Theologie* (Nürnberg, 1857), and Leopold Schmidt, *Die Ethik der alten Griechen* (Berlin, 1882), I.

periods considered, it may be well to explain the method that I have used.

I was strongly tempted to employ a topical method—that is, to study sophrosyne as a civic virtue, as the *virtus feminarum,* as a topic in rhetoric and a canon in literary criticism, or to discuss it in relation to religion, tragedy, education, and a variety of other subjects with which it is allied throughout the history of Greek thought [4]—but I decided that a chronological approach would be more useful to most readers and would have the additional advantage of enabling one who wished to discover how a given author dealt with sophrosyne to do so without searching through several chapters. Within a chapter my method has also been largely chronological, although in some cases, especially Chapter V (Plato), the advantages of a topical approach seemed particularly compelling. In this case, too, however, I deemed it better, even at the cost of some repetition, to study sophrosyne against the background of individual dialogues, instead of attempting to organize into separate categories a concept whose treatment by Plato is so dependent on its context.

The method followed in the first five chapters, therefore, is to examine the subject in detail, omitting (it is hoped) nothing of significance. The last four chapters, however—which deal with Greek philosophy after Plato, nonphilosophical writing (including inscriptions) of the Hellenistic period and thereafter, Roman adaptations of sophrosyne, and its transition to Christian thought—potentially included so much material that it was necessary to select only the most original developments and the most influential authors. No attempt has been made in chapters VI to IX to offer an exhaustive treatment of the subject; patristic literature in particular received less consideration than it deserved.

My aim throughout has been to identify all the nuances of sophrosyne as they occur, to trace their development, and to suggest, where evidence is available, the reasons for such changes as seem explicable in the light of altered political, social, religious, or economic conditions, or the special interests of a given author. It must be admitted at the outset that I make no attempt in this book to solve the ultimate mystery: the emergence of sophrosyne as a primary virtue among the Greeks and not among other ancient peoples whose background seems in many ways comparable.[5] In default of methods that would enable us to study in

[4] Several of these topics were originally discussed in my doctoral dissertation, "The Concept of Sophrosyne in Greek Thought from Homer to Aristotle" (Cornell University, 1945, unpublished), on which the first five chapters of this book are based.

[5] It is a source of deep regret that we can no longer look forward to enlightenment on this subject from Professor Clyde Kluckhohn, who shortly before his death expressed (in conver-

detail the formative years of the Hellenic people, I am inclined to emulate a writer who says, in connection with an equally baffling problem in Celtic civilization, "There is no other answer than the racial character, with all its virtues and all its weaknesses, that had developed down the centuries. As to what had formed that character nobody will ever know now." [6]

For the early period it seemed imperative to take into account the existence of the *concept* of sophrosyne, even when expressed in other terms. The heroic and the archaic ages afford many examples of the appearance under some other name of what is later recognized as sophrosyne. Among certain persistent themes that are discussed, the most important is the polarity between sophrosyne and the opposing principle—variously called *andreia* ("manliness"), *to eugenes* ("nobility"), *to drastêrion* ("the active principle"), or *megalopsychia* ("greatness of soul") —and the attempts made at various stages of Greek and Roman thought to reconcile the two. This antithesis lies at the very core of Hellenism: it accounts for some of the most perplexing contradictions in Greek attitudes and behavior and may derive ultimately from the most fundamental polarity of all, that between rest and motion, being and becoming. The tension between sophrosyne and the "heroic principle" in the Greek character has often been recognized, but perhaps too much emphasis has been laid on their opposition, too little on their reconciliation.

Moreover—and this is the primary difficulty attending any study of sophrosyne in our time—modern interpreters have generally found it hard to comprehend this quality as a positive force. Even so sympathetic an observer as the classically trained anthropologist Clyde Kluckhohn regarded it as mainly a "negative caution" when he included Discipline versus Fulfillment in a list of polarities devised for the purpose of constructing a cultural profile of the Greeks.[7] But sophrosyne both in its essence and in its most typical manifestations is neither negative nor

---

sation with the writer) his belief that this question is fundamental to anthropology, and proposed to study it with the methods appropriate to that discipline.

[6] Sean O'Faolain, *The Irish: A Character Study* (New York, 1949), 77.

[7] *Anthropology and the Classics* (Providence, R. I., 1961), 50–67. Professor Kluckhohn says in part, "The issue is between safety and adventure, between control and expansion, between adjustment to the culture and internal harmony. Here I think the Greek position was about an equal weighting or balance between the two value systems." Ferguson, *op. cit.*, also emphasizes the negative aspect of sophrosyne and finds parallels in the high regard for moderation expressed by Confucius, Alexander Hamilton, and other spokesmen for middle-class cultures. As will become evident in the course of the present study, many Greeks also emphasized the negative or restrictive aspects of sophrosyne; for example, Thucydides in his portrayal of Spartan sophrosyne and the Cynics in their equation of sophrosyne with frugality and austerity.

merely cautious. Rather it is the harmonious product of intense passion under perfect control, *vis temperata* in the felicitous Horatian phrase. It was this perfect yet precarious control of the most turbulent forces that stamped the inimitable seal of Hellenism on so many aspects of Greek life, producing law in the realm of government, form in art, restraint and proportion in human conduct—diverse results, to be sure, but all the fruits of sophrosyne.[8]

One of the principal aims of this book is to draw attention to the dynamic nature of sophrosyne and to demonstrate that, in the words of Werner Jaeger (referring to the emergence of sophrosyne in the archaic age), it was not "the humdrum doctrine of peace and contentment," but a "strong repression of the new individualistic impulse" to absolute liberty.[9] Or as a political scientist has lately observed, identifying as sophrosyne the dominant quality in the character of President John F. Kennedy, it is "not the product of weakness but of a judicious, disciplined use of very great powers." [10] Not for nothing did the Greeks—from the time of Plato to the end of antiquity, pagan and Christian alike—find the perfect symbol of this excellence in the charioteer guiding and holding in check his spirited horses: sophrosyne "saving *phronêsis*" (as the traditional etymology has it) from the assaults of appetite and passion but at the same time making use of their motive power to reach goals unattainable without them.

Throughout the book I have tried to be aware of the moral and intellectual qualities that are allied with sophrosyne at various stages of its history (*aidôs, eunomia, enkrateia, metriotês, kosmiotês, hagneia, katharotês* in particular), and to suggest the meaning of these shifting alliances, as well as of the fluctuating group of antitheses (*aphrosynê, hybris, andreia, akolasia, anaisthêsia, tryphê*). Another subject that is treated not in one place, but throughout, is the relation of sophrosyne to various expressions of the Greek religious feeling, from the Apolline cult and the Orphic and Pythagorean mysteries to the Platonic doctrine of assimilation to God, which endowed sophrosyne with special value in the eyes of Neoplatonists, pagan and Christian. Exemplars of sophrosyne, divine and human, in myth and history, are kept in view, as reflecting the interpretation of the concept at different periods.

It became evident in the course of my work that the most important

---

[8] J. A. K. Thompson (*Greeks and Barbarians* [London, 1921], 136) describes sophrosyne in these terms.

[9] *Paideia,* 1. 167.

[10] Walter Dean Burnham, *The Commonweal,* December 13, 1963, p. 343.

influences on the development of sophrosyne were the growth of the *polis,* the flowering of tragedy, the rise of philosophy, and the coming of Christianity. Hence I have emphasized the fifth and fourth centuries B.C. and the third and fourth centuries after Christ, when the results of these influences are most readily observed. The length of the chapters has been dictated by the nature and the extent of the material available and therefore varies considerably.

The word sophrosyne has been treated throughout as if it were an English word and has usually been transliterated without italics. Related words, however, are either italicized when transliterated or are rendered in Greek. The singular and plural forms of the adjective (nominative masculine-feminine *sôphrôn, sôphrones,* neuter *sôphron, sôphrona,* accusative masculine-feminine *sôphrona, sôphronas,* neuter *sôphron, sôphrona*) are always distinguished; the adverb is *sôphronôs* (less often *sôphronikôs*), the present infinitive of the corresponding verb *sôphronein.*[11]

As a general rule, classical authors are referred to in the most recent Teubner editions. Important exceptions include the poets edited by Edgar Lobel and D. L. Page in *Poetarum Lesbiorum Fragmenta* (Oxford, 1955) and D. L. Page in *Poetae Melici Graeci* (Oxford, 1962). In Chapter IX, wherever possible, the texts of the Fathers in the *Griechischen christlichen Schriftsteller* (*GCS*) and the *Corpus scriptorum ecclesiasticorum latinorum* (*CSEL*) have been used in preference to the *Patrologia Graeca* and *Latina.*

This book was substantially completed in January 1964, and it has rarely been possible to take into consideration works published since then.

My warm thanks are due to the editors of the Cornell Studies in Classical Philology, who have read the book in manuscript, and who by their advice and criticism have removed at least some of its defects of matter and style. I am indebted above all to Professor Harry Caplan of Cornell University and Professor Friedrich Solmsen, now of the Institute for Research in the Humanities, Madison, Wisconsin, who supervised the doctoral dissertation on which the first five chapters of the book are based, and who subsequently saw it through several stages of revision and expansion. Their wisdom and good judgment have been equaled only by their unfailing kindness over the years in which the book has taken shape.

---

[11] Other cognate words, less often encountered, include the adjective *sôphronikos,* the nouns *sôphronisma* and *sôphronismos* (both mean "discipline, prudent counsel"), *sôphronistês* and *sôphronistêr* ("chastiser, *castigatrix*"), and the verb *sôphronizein* ("to bring to one's senses, to discipline"). Compound verbs such as *synsôphronein* ("to join in being sane or moderate") and *diasôphronein* ("to vie in sophrosyne") are extremely rare.

I am grateful as well to three foundations for assistance of another kind. In 1945–1946 the Phi Beta Kappa Foundation awarded me the Mary Isabel Sibley Fellowship for post-doctoral research, which enabled me to carry my study of sophrosyne into the Hellenistic and Graeco-Roman periods. In 1958–1959 a fellowship from the John Simon Guggenheim Memorial Foundation gave me leisure to begin writing the book, which was completed in 1963–1964 with the help of the Dorothy Bridgman Atkinson Fellowship, awarded me by the American Association of University Women. During 1958–1959 and 1963–1964 Swarthmore College granted me leaves of absence and on several occasions, through its Faculty Research Fund, helped with the cost of typing.

To those friends and colleagues who have read portions of this book in manuscript or who have enlarged my understanding of sophrosyne in the course of many a σωφρονίζων λόγος, I offer my grateful appreciation.

H. N.

Swarthmore College
July 1965

Contents

Bibliography of Abbreviated Titles

Bickel

Ernst Bickel. *Diatribe in Senecae Philosophi Fragmenta.* Vol. I (*De Matrimonio*). Leipzig, 1915.

Commager

Steele Commager. *The Odes of Horace: A Critical Study.* New Haven, Conn., 1962.

Cornford

F. M. Cornford. *The Unwritten Philosophy.* Cambridge, 1950.

CSEL

Corpus Scriptorum Ecclesiasticorum Latinorum. Vienna, 1866– .

Del Grande

Carlo del Grande. *Hybris.* Naples, 1947.

DK

Hermann Diels. *Die Fragmente der Vorsokratiker.* 10th edition, with index, by Walther Kranz. Berlin, 1960–1961.

Dodds

E. R. Dodds. *The Greeks and the Irrational.* Berkeley, 1951.

Düring, *Aristotle and Plato*

Ingemar Düring and G. E. L. Owen. *Aristotle and Plato in the Mid-Fourth Century.* Göteborg, 1960.

Düring, *Protrepticus*

Ingemar Düring. *Aristotle's Protrepticus: An Attempt at Reconstruction.* Göteborg, 1961.

Earl

D. C. Earl. *The Political Thought of Sallust.* Cambridge, 1961.

Finley

John H. Finley, Jr. *Pindar and Aeschylus.* Cambridge, Mass., 1955.

Fraenkel

Eduard Fraenkel. *Horace.* Oxford, 1957.

Gauthier

R. A. Gauthier, O.P. *Magnanimité.* Paris, 1951.

GCS

Die griechischen christlichen Schrifsteller der ersten Jahrhunderte. Berlin, Leipzig, 1897– .

Geffcken

Johannes Geffcken. *Griechische Epigramme.* Heidelberg, 1916.

Gould

John Gould. *The Development of Plato's Ethics.* Cambridge, 1955.

Guthrie

W. K. C. Guthrie. *A History of Greek Philosophy.* Vol. I. Cambridge, 1962.

Hackforth

Richard Hackforth. *Plato's Phaedrus.* Cambridge, 1952.

Hagendahl

Harald Hagendahl. *Latin Fathers and the Classics.* Göteborg, 1958.

Jacoby

Felix Jacoby. *Die Fragmente der griechischen Historiker.* Berlin and Leiden, 1923–1958.

Jaeger, *Aristotle*

Werner Jaeger. *Aristotle: Fundamentals of the History of His Development.* Trans. by Richard Robinson. 2nd English edition. Oxford, 1948.

Jaeger, *Paideia*

Werner Jaeger. *Paideia: The Ideals of Greek Culture.* Trans. by Gilbert Highet. Vol. I, 4th edition, Oxford, 1954. Vols. II, III, New York, 1943, 1944.

Jaeger, *Two Works*

Werner Jaeger. *Two Rediscovered Works of Ancient Christian Literature.* Leiden, 1954.

Kaibel

George Kaibel. *Epigrammata Graeca ex lapidibus conlecta.* Berlin, 1878.

Kaibel, *Com.*

George Kaibel. *Comicorum Graecorum Fragmenta.* Berlin, 1899.

Katzenellenbogen

Adolf Katzenellenbogen. *Allegories of the Virtues and Vices in Mediaeval Art.* Trans. by Alan J. P. Crick. New York, 1964.

Kirkwood	Gordon Kirkwood. *A Study of Sophoclean Drama*. Ithaca, 1958.
Kitto	H. D. F. Kitto. *Greek Tragedy*. 3rd edition. London, 1961.
Kitto, "Idea of God"	H. D. F. Kitto. "The Idea of God in Aeschylus and Sophocles." *La Notion du divin depuis Homère jusqu'à Platon*. Vandoeuvres-Genève, 1952.
Kock	Th. Kock. *Comicorum Atticorum Fragmenta*. Leipzig, 1880–1888.
Ladner	Gerhart B. Ladner. *The Idea of Reform: Its Impact on Christian Thought and Action in the Age of the Fathers*. Cambridge, Mass., 1959.
Laistner	M. L. W. Laistner. *The Greater Roman Historians*. Berkeley, 1947.
Maguire	J. P. Maguire. "Plato's Theory of Natural Law." *Yale Classical Studies* 10 (1947), 151–78.
Mâle	Emile Mâle. *The Gothic Image: Religious Art in France of the Thirteenth Century*. Trans. by Dora Nussey. New York, 1958.
Mattingly	Harold Mattingly. *Coins of the Roman Empire in the British Museum*. Vols. I–III. London, 1923–1936.
Mattingly and Sydenham	Harold Mattingly and E. A. Sydenham. *The Roman Imperial Coinage*. Vol. V. London, 1933.
Merki	Hubert Merki, O.S.B. Ὁμοίωσις Θεῷ *von der platonischen Angleichung an Gott zur Gottähnlichkeit bei Gregor von Nyssa*. Fribourg, 1952.
Musurillo	Herbert Musurillo, S.J. "The Problem of Ascetical Fasting in the Greek Patristic Writers." *Traditio* 12 (1956), 1–64.
Nauck	August Nauck. *Tragicorum Graecorum Fragmenta*. With supplement by Bruno Snell. Hildesheim, 1964.
P.G.	Jacques Paul Migne. *Patrologiae Cursus Completus: Series Graeca*. Paris, 1857–1912.

P.L.	Jacques Paul Migne. *Patrologiae Cursus Completus: Series Latina.* Paris, 1844–1890.
Pohlenz	Max Pohlenz. *Griechische Tragödie.* Göttingen, 1954.
Pöschl	Viktor Pöschl. *Die Dichtkunst Virgils.* Innsbruck, 1950.
P. W.	Pauly-Wissowa-Kroll. *Real-Encyclopädie der classischen Altertumswissenschaft.* Stuttgart, 1893– .
Rambaud	Michel Rambaud. *Cicéron et l'histoire romaine.* Paris, 1953.
Rose	H. J. Rose. *A Commentary on the Surviving Plays of Aeschylus.* 2 vols. Amsterdam, 1957–1958.
Ross	W. D. Ross. *Aristotle.* London, 1937.
Snell	Bruno Snell. "Aischylos und das Handeln im Drama." *Philologus Supplementband* 20 (1928), 1–164.
Solmsen, *Hesiod*	Friedrich Solmsen. *Hesiod and Aeschylus.* Ithaca, 1949.
Solmsen, *Theology*	Friedrich Solmsen. *Plato's Theology.* Ithaca, 1942.
SVF	Johannes Von Arnim. *Stoicorum Veterum Fragmenta.* 4 vols. Leipzig, 1964.
Syme	Ronald Syme. *Tacitus.* 2 vols. Oxford, 1958.
T.L.L.	*Thesaurus Linguae Latinae.* Leipzig, 1900– .
Usener	H. Usener. *Epicurea.* Leipzig, 1887.
Van Marle	Raimond van Marle. *Iconographie de l'art profane au moyen âge et à la renaissance.* The Hague, 1932.
Van Straaten	Modestus van Straaten, O.E.S.A. *Panétius.* Amsterdam, 1946.
Warmington	E. H. Warmington. *Remains of Old Latin.* 3 vols. London, 1935–1938.

Wehrli

Fritz Wehrli. *Die Schule des Aristoteles: Texte und Kommentar.* Basel and Stuttgart, 1944–1959.

Whitman

Cedric Whitman. *Sophocles.* Cambridge, Mass., 1951.

Wilamowitz

Ulrich von Wilamowitz-Möllendorf. *Der Glaube der Hellenen.* Berlin, 1931–1932.

Winnington-Ingram

R. P. Winnington-Ingram. *Euripides and Dionysus.* Cambridge, 1948.

Wolfson

Harry A. Wolfson. *Philo: Foundations of Religious Philosophy in Judaism, Christianity, and Islam.* Cambridge, Mass., 1947.

PERIODICALS

A.J.P.   *American Journal of Philology*

C.P.   *Classical Philology*

C.Q.   *Classical Quarterly*

C.R.   *Classical Review*

C.W.   *Classical World* (successor to *Classical Weekly*)

H.S.C.P.   *Harvard Studies in Classical Philology*

H.T.R.   *Harvard Theological Review*

J.H.S.   *Journal of Hellenic Studies*

J.R.S.   *Journal of Roman Studies*

M.A.A.R.   *Memoirs of the American Academy in Rome*

Mus. Helv.   *Museum Helveticum*

Philol.   *Philologus*

Philol. Supp.   *Philologus Supplementband*

Proc. Br. Acad.   *Proceedings of the British Academy*

R.E.L.   *Revue des études latines*

Rev. d. Et. Anc.	*Revue des études anciennes*
Rev. Phil.	*Revue philologique*
Rhein. Mus.	*Rheinisches Museum für Philologie*
T.A.P.A.	*Transactions of the American Philological Association*
Y.C.S.	*Yale Classical Studies*

SOPHROSYNE

*Self-Knowledge and Self-Restraint
in Greek Literature*

I

The Heroic and the
Archaic Periods

DRAMATIC poets, orators, and philosophers of the fifth and fourth
centuries B.C. often drew upon epic poetry, especially the Trojan cycle,
for exemplars of the virtues and vices, as they were understood in the
classical period. When models of sophrosyne and its antitheses were
sought, a remarkable diversity appeared: Nestor, Menelaus, Diomedes,
and Odysseus are the epic exemplars of sophrosyne in Sophocles, Isocrates, and Plato, while Achilles and Ajax represent its opposite.[1] The
choice of models is instructive in several ways. It points to the differing
facets of masculine sophrosyne,[2] if such widely divergent heroes might
all be said to possess it; and it also points to an essential difference between the *Iliad* and the *Odyssey*, the pathetic and the ethical epic poems
(to use Aristotle's distinction),[3] if the hero of one is conspicuously devoid

---

[1] Nestor: Plato *Laws* 711E. Menelaus: Isocrates *Panath.* 72. Diomedes: Plato *Rep.* 389E.
Odysseus: Sophocles *Ajax, passim;* Plato *Rep.* 390D. Maximus of Tyre represents a much later
period in which the connotations of sophrosyne are so varied that almost any hero can
be regarded as *sôphrôn* in some respect. Odysseus is so described as a result of his endurance
(XXVI. 114A); Hector, Achilles, and Patroclus are *sôphrones* with respect to *erôs* (XXVI.
113A; XVIII. 86B). For the *sôphrôn erôs* of Achilles and Patroclus, see also Aeschines I. 141–
50. Achilles is excessively emotional (hence not *sôphrôn*) in Plato *Rep.* 388A–B. Ajax in
Sophocles' play is an exemplar of *hybris*, the antithesis of sophrosyne.

[2] Feminine sophrosyne (chastity, modesty, obedience, inconspicuous behavior) remains the
same throughout Greek history. The word is not used to describe the *aretê* of women in the
Homeric poems; but when it is so used (from the time of Semonides of Amorgos), the
behavior designated corresponds precisely to the *aretê* of Penelope and Andromache, who,
with Alcestis, become the classical exemplars of this excellence. The *exempla horribilia* of the
opposed vice, wantonness or, more generally, being a bad wife, are Helen and Clytemnestra.

[3] *Poetics* 1459b 14–16. In *Anth. Pal.* (9. 522) the *Odyssey* is called τὸ σῶφρον γράμμα.

of sophrosyne, while the hero of the other can become a type of the σώφρων ἀνήρ, the man of sophrosyne. Most important of all, the choice of exemplars makes it clear that sophrosyne is not a "heroic" virtue, since the two greatest fighting men of the Homeric epic, Achilles and Ajax, are the very ones who most notoriously lack this quality. It is no coincidence that these are the two whom Aristotle cites, along with Alcibiades, as exemplars of *megalopsychia* ("high-mindedness"),[4] an excellence that, although by no means identical with the heroic ideal of Homer, nevertheless shares certain characteristics of that earliest form of *aretê*. Certainly, by virtue of their passion for honor, the Homeric Achilles and Ajax may be said to possess a kind of *megalopsychia*.

The contrast between the *megalopsychos* and the *sôphrôn*, the high-minded man and the man of restraint, which significantly enough proves to be a contrast between the *hybristês* and the *sôphrôn* as well, is sharply drawn in the *Ajax* of Sophocles. From the very beginning of the tragedy we see how incompatible are the qualities of its two great men: the superb courage, the sense of honor, and the refusal to accept an affront, which dominate the *êthos* of Ajax; and the altogether more civilized, almost Periclean *aretê* of the humane, reasonable, well-balanced Odysseus.[5] Sophocles, like Aristotle, of course arrived at a conception of *aretê* very different from that of Homer, yet there is enough of the Homeric hero in his Ajax to make the contrast with his Odysseus significant for our study—to show, that is, the tension between the "heroic" and the "moderate," the "spirited" and the "gentle," the *agathos* and the *sôphrôn*, which is one of the persistent themes of Greek literature.[6]

A study of the four references to sophrosyne in the *Iliad* and the *Odyssey* confirms the impression that this quality (at least under its classical name) is of minor importance to the heroic age. Only the early, uncontracted forms of the noun and adjective, *saophrosynê* and *saophrôn*, appear—always in passages that have been regarded as late additions to the poems;[7] and their meaning is extremely limited, although even

[4] *Anal. Post.* B. 13. 97b. 15–25. The development of the concept of the high-minded man is traced by Gauthier; see pp. 21 ff. for its relation to the Homeric hero. A. W. H. Adkins' study of the terms of value used in the Homeric poems shows that while the hero is expected to be *agathos* ("brave") and *esthlos* ("noble") and to excel in the "competitive" virtues, he need not be *sôphrôn* to maintain his status as a hero (*Merit and Responsibility* [Oxford, 1960], 61 ff.).

[5] For a discussion of this contrast, see Bernard M. W. Knox, *H.S.C.P.* 65 (1961), 21–22.

[6] The appearance of this tension in Sophocles is discussed in Chap. II, and in Thucydides in Chap. III. For various attempts to reconcile the opposites, see Chap. V (Plato) and Chap. IX (the Church Fathers).

[7] See, for example, Eduard Schwartz, *Ethik der Griechen* (Stuttgart, 1951), 54–56; Albrecht Kollmann, *Wiener Studien* 59 (1941), 12–34.

among these four passages slight but significant differences appear. Sophrosyne at this stage in its history is devoid of moral and religious implications; in three of the four passages it clearly denotes "prudence" or "shrewdness" in one's own interest—a meaning that it never entirely loses, in spite of the much more extensive range of connotations it subsequently acquired.[8] Although such shrewdness is an obvious advantage to its possessor, it is insignificant compared with courage, skill in arms, or cleverness in planning (the principal components of the heroic *aretê*), and so is held in little value by the hero himself and by the society that depends on the hero for its preservation. Since social, political, and economic conditions in the Greek world have a bearing on the development of sophrosyne at each stage of its history, it is not surprising that the first major expansion in meaning and the first signs of high value attached to the word sophrosyne are found only with the growth of the *polis,* whose survival (both economic and political) depended on the operation of this form of excellence.[9]

If *saophrosynê* [10] is basically "soundness of mind"—that is, the state of having one's intellect unimpaired—we come closest to its original significance in the response of Penelope to Eurycleia's announcement that Odysseus has returned (*Od.* 23. 11–13): "My dear Nurse, the gods have made you mad, the gods who can make foolish [ἄφρων] even one who is exceedingly sensible [ἐπίφρων] and who have brought the light-

---

[8] This connotation survives in the commonplace remark of the Attic orators: ἐὰν σωφρονῆτε ("if you are sensible, if you know what's good for you").

[9] See Adkins, *op. cit.,* 76 ff., on the need for the "coöperative virtues" in the city-state.

[10] The word sophrosyne is a compound derived from the ô-grade of the root of *-phrēn* ("mind") and the Homeric *saos*—Ionian-Attic *sóos, sôs* ("healthy, safe, sound")—plus the suffix *-synê,* which forms a feminine abstract noun from the earlier adjective *saophrōn.* The contracted form of the noun appears first in the time of Theognis (*fl.* 540 B.C.), and its first syllable may be traced either to a contraction of the form *saos* (<*tu̯ə - u̯o - s) or to the Ionian-Attic variant *sôs* (<*tu̯ô - u̯o - s). See Walde-Pokorny, *Vergleichendes Wörterbuch der Indogermanischen Sprachen* (Berlin and Leipzig, 1930), I. 706. The suffix *-synê* is used to form abstract substantives from many adjectives and nouns. Originally it was the feminine of the adjective suffix *-sunos* (<*tunos, *tu-no-;* cf. Sanskrit neuter abstracts in *-tvana-*). See Carl D. Buck, *Comparative Grammar of Greek and Latin* (Chicago, 1948), 323, and Karl Brugmann, *A Comparative Grammar of the Indo-Germanic Languages,* trans. R. Seymour Conway and W. H. D. Rouse (Strassburg, 1891), 2. 163. The suffix became general and could be used to form abstract nouns directly from other adjectives and nouns. Such compounds usually have an ethical connotation and first become common in gnomic poetry. A. W. Verrall showed that in Attic prose of the fifth century such forms are rare and unproductive, but tragedy, following Ionian usage, employs them in many passages that in some other way as well reflect Ionian color or connection (*J.H.S.* 1 [1880], 260–92 and 2 [1881], 179–216). In Attic prose writers of the fourth century—especially Plato, Xenophon, Isocrates, and the other orators—sophrosyne and related forms are well established and carry no Ionian overtones.

minded [χαλιφρονέων] to *saophrosynê.*" [11] It is evident from the use of ἐπίφρων as a parallel and of ἄφρων and χαλιφρονέων as antonyms that *saophrosynê* here is the *mens sana,* primarily intellectual rather than moral; although it is well to remember that throughout its history sophrosyne, however "intellectual" it may be, is normally applied to some kind of behavior. The knowledge involved is revealed in human action and generally has a moral outcome. It is perhaps significant, in the light of later religious associations, that *saophrosynê* is here regarded as a gift of the gods, but in fact it shares this distinction with every quality or advantage (good luck, noble birth) that is not in man's power to secure. Sophrosyne does not acquire religious significance until its meaning has expanded to include the fear of overstepping boundaries, since it is this offense, above all others, that calls down the anger of the gods.[12]

The noun *saophrosynê* makes another appearance in the same conversation between Penelope and Eurycleia, when (*Od.* 23. 30) the nurse ascribes Telemachus' concealment of his father's plans to his σαοφροσύνεσι ("acts of prudence"). The use of the substantive in the plural, almost unparalleled in later Greek, suggests that the noun has not yet become completely abstract. Here again the basic meaning, "prudence in one's own interest," is unencumbered by moral or religious accretions.

The other two Homeric allusions, however, are more suggestive of later semantic developments, and in addition their context reveals the source of Homeric sophrosyne. In the *Iliad* (21. 462–64), Apollo's reply to Poseidon's challenge to battle (the earliest connection in Greek literature between Apollo and sophrosyne) contains a hint of what is to be an important aspect of the virtue—self-knowledge, combined with a vivid appreciation of the boundary between god and man: "Earth-shaker,

---

[11] Gilbert Murray (*The Rise of the Greek Epic* [Oxford, 1924], 26) suggests that the Homeric antonym of *saophrôn* is *oloophrôn* ("with destructive thoughts"); but *aesiphrôn* ("damaged in mind, witless, silly") is a more likely antonym, since *saophrosynê* in its earliest stage is turned inward, not outward, and concerns the possessor rather than society. For *aesiphrôn* see *Il.* 20. 183; *Od.* 15. 470, 21. 302; Hesiod, *Erg.* 335.

[12] In the archaic age the religious connotation becomes important, and sophrosyne emerges as the characteristic virtue of the Apolline code. The statement of Athene in Sophocles (*Ajax* 132 f.) that the gods love the *sôphrones* and hate the *kakoi* (who in this context are clearly the *hybristai*) indicates the religious sanction of sophrosyne. In its later development, however, sophrosyne moves away from religion once more (on this point see Wilamowitz, 2. 123–24) and operates as a kind of "artistic flair" in the field of morality (Bruno Snell, *The Discovery of the Mind,* trans. T. G. Rosenmeyer [Oxford, 1953], 162). Yet in so far as sophrosyne is thought to assist in the process of purifying the soul from the passions, it may have religious implications, whether for the mystery cults, for Plato, or for the Church Fathers. In the Apolline religion sophrosyne results in moderation and self-knowledge; in the mystery cults, etc., in *katharsis.*

you would not consider me *saophrôn,* if I were to fight with you for the sake of wretched mortals." The prudential element is still present (there would be no advantage to Apollo in accepting the challenge); but the first traces of self-knowledge as a component of sophrosyne are here, and they are especially interesting since Greek literature rarely shows us this concept from the point of view of the gods. In the archaic period "Know thyself" is the advice of Apollo to mankind, and sophrosyne has as its consequence "thinking mortal thoughts." In the present passage, however, Apollo may be said to think immortal thoughts, and it is even possible to find here a forerunner of the later concept of the *theoprepes* ("what is suitable or proper for the Divine nature").[13]

Another kind of self-knowledge, this time purely human and resulting in modesty (or even bashfulness), is implied by the adjective *saophrôn* in the *Telemachia.* Here it is Telemachus who comprehends his own position with respect to that of the great hero Menelaus, his host in Sparta, and remains silent from fear of presumption. His companion Peisistratus explains (*Od.* 4. 158–60): "He is *saophrôn* and feels shame in his heart . . . at embarking on hasty speech in your presence." In certain respects this is the most revealing use of *saophrôn* in Homer, because it shows the connection of sophrosyne with the young—an association rooted deep in Greek social organization and full of consequences for morality[14]—and because it is the first clear recognition of sophrosyne as a form of repression or control. Telemachus, unlike Eurycleia or Apollo, is called *saophrôn* because he checks some natural impulse (in this case, the impulse to speak out). Sophrosyne here is very close to *aidôs,* which has a similar outcome in another situation involving Telemachus (*Od.* 3. 24).[15]

In each of the two passages just described, Homer associates with *saophrôn* another word, more familiar and much more weighty in the heroic vocabulary, which serves to define the province of sophrosyne. Of

[13] The development of this concept, especially as seen in Xenophanes, is studied by Werner Jaeger, *The Theology of the Early Greek Philosophers* (Oxford, 1947), 38–54. It is hard to decide how characteristic of Apollo the sophrosyne of *Il.* 21. 462–64 actually is: another god in the same situation might say something of the kind, but other gods do engage in combat in behalf of mortal men and say nothing of the kind. Two exceptions to the rule that sophrosyne (in classical Greek usage) is a human, rather than a Divine, excellence may be found in Aeschylean tragedy: in the *Oresteia* and the *Prometheia* it seems clear that Zeus himself ultimately learns sophrosyne.

[14] An epigram by Christodorus of Thebes on a statue of Homer describes him as being crowned with sophrosyne *kourotrophos,* the "nurse of youth" (*Anth. Pal.* 2. 331–32).

[15] Telemachus tells Mentor that it is shameful (*aidôs*) for a young man to address an elder; here *aidôs* is more closely identified with *nemesis* than usual. Cf. also *Il.* 10. 238, where Agamemnon warns Diomedes against excessive compunction.

Apollo in the *Iliad* the poet says (21. 468–69), "For he felt ashamed [αἴδετο] to mix in combat with his uncle"; while of Telemachus in the *Odyssey* his friend says (4. 158), "He feels shame [νεμεσσᾶται] in his heart." The two verbs αἰδέομαι and νεμεσάομαι both mean "I feel ashamed"—that is, to do something which the heroic *aretê* rejects as unworthy. *Aidôs* and *nemesis,* the sense of shame and the feeling of righteous indignation, are the twin sanctions of the heroic age, and both have religious and social implications.[16] They derive their strength from the hero's respect for the power of the gods and for the opinion of his peers. *Aidôs* normally implies a sense of compunction based on respect for the rights of another; *nemesis* describes the reaction of others, human or divine, to a violation of *aidôs*. The roots of sophrosyne reach into the very depths of the Hellenic nature, if they are fed by *aidôs* and *nemesis.*

It is not surprising that *saophrôn* conduct is explained in terms of the sense of shame or compunction, for later Greek thought regularly acknowledges a close (often a causal) connection between *aidôs* and sophrosyne. A fourth-century Attic inscription,[17] for example, salutes Queenly (Πότνια) Sophrosyne as the daughter of *megalophrôn Aidôs*— a singularly felicitous affiliation, since the true complement to the *megalophrosynê* ("greatness of soul") that dominates Homeric *aretê* is *aidôs,* the sense of compunction which is capable at times of restraining the *thymos* of the warrior; and it is *aidôs* that acts as a forerunner to sophrosyne in epic poetry.[18] What the classical sophrosyne shares with the Homeric *aidôs* is chiefly a fear of overstepping boundaries.[19] It is for this reason that both can restrain *hybris,* the arrogant violation of limits set by the gods or by human society.

That the poet of the *Iliad* was himself keenly sensitive to the need for such restraint, both to avert disaster in the life of the individual and to prevent a society made up of self-assertive heroes from destroying itself, is evident from the content of many individual episodes and from the very pattern of the poem, determined as it is by the sequence of cause

---

[16] Carl von Erffa (*Philol. Supp.* 30 [1937], 30–36) discusses the relation between *aidôs* and *nemesis* in Homer. See also M. I. Finley, *The World of Odysseus* (New York, 1954), 114–54, and W. C. Greene, *Moira* (Cambridge, Mass., 1948), 18–19. On *aidôs* in Homer, consult also W. J. Verdenius, *Mnemosyne* 12 (1944), 47–60, and Adkins, *op. cit.,* 45–46.

[17] George Kaibel, *Epigrammata Graeca ex lapidibus conlecta* (Berlin, 1878), No. 34. *Eupolemos Aretê* ("Courage, victorious in war") is paired with Sophrosyne in this epitaph.

[18] *Aidôs* is invoked, for example, by Priam (*Il.* 24. 503): αἰδεῖο θεούς. There are many illustrations in literature, from the sixth to the fourth centuries, of the way in which *aidôs* is supplanted by sophrosyne: e.g., Theognis 1135–50 compared with Hesiod *Erg.* 190–200; Democritus, Frag. 208 DK compared with Theognis 409 f.; and the exegesis of the myth in Plato's *Protagoras* compared with the myth itself (322C–323A).

[19] See Greene, *op. cit.,* 10.

and effect, beginning with the *hybris* of Agamemnon and the unbounded wrath of Achilles, and culminating in the scene where Achilles achieves a kind of tragic self-knowledge in response to Priam's appeal to his *aidôs* (*Il.* 24. 503).[20] It is irrelevant that this saving power of restraint or compunction is never, in the epic, linked with the word sophrosyne. The feeling is older than the word, and situations that in the *Iliad* are accounted for by the presence or absence of *aidôs* (such as the conduct of Diomedes when insulted by Agamemnon) are interpreted in the fourth century in terms of sophrosyne.[21] The two qualities are by no means identical in nature or function (*aidôs,* for example, is more an objective condition, sophrosyne more a personal attitude; *aidôs* is felt in situations involving respect for and responsibility towards others, sophrosyne is more likely to be concerned with a conflict within the soul), but in so far as both tend to inhibit free indulgence in passion of any kind, they are undeniably akin.

Homeric society in general (especially its weaker members) places a high value on *aidôs,* but the hero himself, *qua* hero, is not obliged to respect it.[22] Violations of *aidôs* are frequent in the *Iliad,* whose great men aim at glory, resent affronts, are carried away by pride and anger (all characteristics of the *megalopsychos* according to Aristotle), and thus at crucial moments tend to ignore all restraint.[23] Such failure is a source of tragic experience, just as in the drama of the fifth century. Like sophrosyne in the plays of Aeschylus and Sophocles, *aidôs* is born of time and suffering. Hence *Pathei mathos,* ("From suffering comes wisdom") has much the same meaning for Achilles as for the House of Atreus in the *Oresteia.* Those heroes who from the first are capable of practicing restraint—(whose *thymos,* or "passion," does not drive them to extremes) —are thereby equipped to avoid tragic experience. A secondary hero, such as Diomedes, the nontragic counterpart of Achilles, is an example; he lacks the passion that leads Achilles to violate *aidôs* but that also gives him towering stature.[24]

---

[20] Cf. Cedric Whitman, *Homer and the Heroic Tradition* (Cambridge, Mass., 1958), 218, on Achilles' attainment of "the truly classical idea . . . that mysterious union of detachment and immediacy, of passion and order."

[21] *Il.* 4. 402; Plato *Rep.* 389E.

[22] See Adkins, *op. cit.,* 46 ff.

[23] E.g., Agamemnon's treatment of Chryses (1. 23–24); Achilles' treatment of Hector's body (24. 44–46).

[24] In addition to accepting Agamemnon's unjust rebuke in a *sôphrôn* manner, Diomedes receives from Apollo a warning about the need to respect the boundary between gods and men, which becomes part of the concept of sophrosyne in the classical period, although the word is not mentioned in the Homeric passage (*Il.* 5. 440–42).

The *Odyssey,* a story of romance and adventure rather than of warfare and tragic enlightenment, reflects a concept of *aretê* comprising a different balance of qualities, and demands of its hero, not the success in battle which is necessary for Achilles, but a combination of shrewdness and endurance with special emphasis on the latter. The expression of this new *aretê* is Odysseus' famous address to his soul (*Od.* 20. 18), which Plato approved as an utterance of sophrosyne (*Rep.* 390D): [25] "Endure, my soul, far worse have you endured." The key word here is "endure" (τέτλαθι, from τλάειν), and it was *tlêmosynê* ("endurance"), rather than *aidôs,* that won for Odysseus his status as an exemplar of sophrosyne in later times. If *aidôs,* as we have suggested, coincides with one aspect of the classical sophrosyne (restraint of *hybris*), *tlêmosynê* approximates another, the power of enduring physical and spiritual hardship. This capacity, also called *karteria,* is regarded as part of the sophrosyne of Socrates in Xenophon's *Memorabilia,*[26] but in the *Odyssey* the endurance shown by Odysseus is commended by the word πολύτλας, and his shrewdness by πολύμητις, πεπνύμενος, or πολύτροπος.[27] He is never called *saophrôn* in any sense of the word, nor does Homer refer to *saophrosynê* in the episode that above all others seemed to poets of the English Renaissance to prove the hero's sophrosyne or *temperantia*—the encounter with Circe, in which the herb moly became a symbol of chastity.[28] If, as is sometimes suggested, the *Odyssey* adds sophrosyne to the twofold *aretê* of the *Iliad* (*andreia* and *sophia,* to use the terminology of the fourth century), it is only in connection with Telemachus that this innovation is made explicit.[29]

When we turn from the *Iliad* and the *Odyssey* to the *Hymn to Dionysus* (the only Homeric Hymn to use the word *saophrôn*), we find a perceptible change. *Saophrôn* and *saophrosynê* in the two epic poems are predominantly intellectual (or prudential), with a hint in the *Iliad* and the *Telemachia* that the original "soundness of mind" is beginning to impinge on the sphere of morality: the *saophrôn* knows himself and avoids unsuitable conduct. The *Hymn to Dionysus,* which recounts the capture of the

[25] Plato quotes the line as an expression of *karteria* ("patient endurance") which in this context is equivalent to sophrosyne.

[26] *Mem.* 1. 6. 1–6.

[27] πολύτλας (5. 171); πολύμητις (2. 173); πεπνύμενος (8. 388); πολύτροπος (1. 1). The sophrosyne of Odysseus in later literature includes several aspects of the virtue which in the Homeric poem are not linked with the word itself: fidelity in marriage (Iamblichus *Vit. Pyth.* 11), endurance of misfortune (Maximus of Tyre *Orat.* XXVI. 114A), military discipline because of his rebuke to Thersites (Clement of Alexandria *Paid.* II. 7. 59, 2).

[28] Consult Douglas Bush, *Mythology and the Renaissance Tradition in English Poetry* (New York, 1957), 264–68.

[29] Telemachus has little importance as an exemplar of sophrosyne in later literature.

god by Etruscan pirates and his metamorphosis into a lion, describes the pilot of the ship as having a *saophrôn thymos* (7. 49). Although *saophrôn* still has a basically intellectual connotation (the pilot alone possessed sufficient insight to recognize that the prisoner was a god), it also suggests the calmness or self-control of the one member of the crew who remains at his post when the others huddle around him in panic. If this Hymn is a product of the seventh century, or possibly even of the sixth,[30] the blending of the intellectual with the moral is consistent with the interpretation of sophrosyne in elegiac poetry of the archaic period. The phrase *sôphrôn thymos* itself occurs in Theognis 754, where the moral connotation is emphasized by its antithesis: *atasthalia* ("arrogance," *hybris*).

The poems of Hesiod, the product of a nonheroic, peasant culture, set up a new standard of *aretê*, in which the value of measure, restraint, and self-control is enormously enhanced. Although Hesiod nowhere uses the word *sôphrôn*, which may not yet be current in mainland Greece, his view of life and of the relations between god and man is thoroughly imbued with sophrosyne in one of its later aspects: as the spirit of *Mêden agan* ("Nothing in excess"). Key words in the *Works and Days* are *metrios*, *mesos*, and *kairos* ("moderate, in the middle, due measure").[31] The life of the peasant is supportable only by the exercise of the cautious and prudent virtues, just as the life of the little Boeotian community is tolerable only when justice and *eunomia* ("good order") exist. If *hybris* triumphs, as in the myth of the Iron Age, *Aidôs* and *Nemesis* will depart from the earth (*Erga.* 190–200), but if justice prevails, peace and *eunomia* will result. *Eunomia*, which was already opposed to *hybris* in the *Odyssey* (17. 487), first becomes important for the *polis* in the *Theogony* and the *Works and Days*. Like *aidôs* it is a forerunner of sophrosyne, but on the social, rather than the individual, plane. Its close kinship with *Dikê*—they are both daughters of Zeus and Themis (*Theog.* 901–2)—prefigures the closeness of sophrosyne and justice in later Greek thought.[32] It was inevitable that sophrosyne and *eunomia* should be brought together, and this is done at first in the phrase *saophrôn eunomia* ("sound and orderly government"), which we find in Pindar and Bacchylides.[33] Still later, *eunomia* is partly replaced, as a civic virtue, by sophrosyne, a process that

[30] T. W. Allen, W. R. Halliday, and E. E. Sikes, *The Homeric Hymns* (Oxford, 1936), 379.

[31] See., e.g., *Erg.* 40, 306–7, 694.

[32] For many examples of this close relation, see Rudolf Hirzel, *Themis, Dikê und Verwandtes* (Leipzig, 1907), 180 ff. The departure of *Aidôs* and *Nemesis* became something of a commonplace in descriptions of the loss of innocence; see below, p. 18, for Theognis' substitution of Sophrosyne for *Aidôs*. In Juvenal 6. 1–20 the goddesses are *Pudicitia* and *Astraea*.

[33] Pindar *Paean* 1. 10; Bacchylides 13. 183–89.

is already beginning in Aeschylus and can be seen near completion in Thucydides and the Attic orators. But *eunomia*, like *aidôs*, differs from sophrosyne in being an objective condition rather than a personal, individual attitude. It is noticeable that Hesiod nowhere personifies any of the qualities that were later considered virtues of the individual.[34] The growing importance of sophrosyne in Greek literature of the fifth and fourth centuries coincides with the increase in self-consciousness and introspection on the part of the Greeks themselves.

Hesiod's view of human life and his cautious aspirations for the individual and society, while poles apart from the heroic *aretê* of the *Iliad* and even from the more realistic system of values reflected in the *Odyssey*, have much in common with Greek folk wisdom, especially as it is expressed in the sayings attributed to the seven Wise Men, statesmen who flourished in the early sixth century and whose reputation for wisdom seems to have been established during the next hundred-odd years.[35] With few exceptions the proverbs of the Seven advise the practice of self-control, particularly the conquest of pleasure (*hêdonê*) and passion (*thymos*) [36] or the recognition of limits in some form.[37] Pittacus, the tyrant of Mytilene early in the sixth century, is the only Wise Man to whom is ascribed an actual reference to sophrosyne—Θεράπευε σωφροσύνην ("cultivate [or 'honor'] sophrosyne")[38]—but this is unquestionably the ideal that inspires most of the maxims. The best-known of the sayings, *Gnôthi sauton* ("Know thyself") and *Mêden agan*, were inscribed in the late sixth century over the entrance to the Alcmaeonid temple of Apollo, who in the archaic age fulfills the hint of the *Iliad*

---

[34] See Herbert Abel, *T.A.P.A.* 74 (1943), 92–101.

[35] The earliest extant list of the Seven occurs in Plato *Prot.* 343A, but the legend that brought them together was doubtless much older. The names of the Seven vary from one ancient source to another. See P. W., "Sieben Weise" (Barkowski).

[36] "Flee from *hêdonê*" (Solon, DK 10. 3). "Be not passionate" (Solon, DK 10. 13). "Control *thymos*" (Chilon of Sparta, DK 10. 15).

[37] "*Metron* is best" (Cleobulus, DK 10. 1). "Understand *kairos*" (Pittacus, DK 10. 1). Critias (Frag. 7 DK) ascribes *Mêden agan* to Chilon. H. J. Mette, *Mêden agan* (Munich, 1933), discusses the varied traditions about the origin of the proverbs concerned with the Mean or due measure. For Aristotle's speculation (in the lost dialogue *On Philosophy*) about the place of the Seven in the history of philosophy and for his effort to determine the date and authorship of *Gnôthi sauton*, the "most divine" of the precepts, see Jaeger, *Aristotle*, 130.

[38] DK 10. 13. Cf. Diogenes Laertius 1. 78. Pittacus made the first recorded legal enactment designed to instil sophrosyne, the famous law that doubled the penalty for any offense committed in a state of intoxication (Aristotle *Pol.* 1274b 13). For Pittacus as a possible source of the gnomic warning against marriage above one's station, see A. E. Raubitschek, *Wiener Studien* 71 (1958), 170–72. Antipater of Colophon describes all Seven as guardians of sophrosyne (*Anth. Pal.* 7. 81).

that he will become the god of sophrosyne.[39] The great development of the influence of the Delphic oracle belongs to this same period—a time during which the priests of Apollo preached measure and restraint in public and private life and encouraged decency and civilized behavior in religious rites.[40] It was at this time that sophrosyne acquired a strongly religious flavor.

It would be useful to know why it was that the seventh and sixth centuries saw so great an increase in popular esteem for moderation, the rule of no excess. So striking and widespread a phenomenon can scarcely be traced to a single cause; not only religious but social, economic, and political elements are involved. E. R. Dodds has identified some of them, and he says, in part:

Without Delphi, Greek society could scarcely have endured the tensions to which it was subjected in the Archaic Age. The crushing sense of human ignorance and human insecurity, the dread of divine *phthonos,* the dread of *miasma*—the accumulated burden of these things would have been unendurable without the assurance which such an omniscient divine counsellor could give.[41]

This explanation, together with further analyses of the economic crisis of the seventh century and its effect on Greek attitudes, helps to account for the influence of Apollo, but not entirely for the direction this influence took; and we still need to explain the profound and widespread feeling for sophrosyne which we find in the sayings of the Wise Men, the Delphic Maxims, and early elegiac poetry, often based on gnomic traditions.

[39] See H. W. Parke and D. E. W. Wormell, *The Delphic Oracle* (Oxford, 1956) 1. 386 ff., for a discussion of the proverbs inscribed on the Alcmaeonid temple, which may have adorned its predecessor as well; and see *ibid.,* p. 392, n. 24, for ancient sources that refer to the proverbs. For the relation of the Seven Wise Men to Apollo and his Delphic shrine, see *ibid.,* 1. 388, and consult A. W. Burn, *The Lyric Age of Greece* (New York, 1960), 207-9.

[40] The earliest recorded response is a rebuke to the complacency of the people of Aegium (Parke and Wormell, *op. cit.,* 2, No. 1). Cf. also the carefully fostered tradition that the oracle was opposed to tyrants and gave them abusive responses (*ibid.,* 1. 124). A number of oracles stress the worthlessness of human life, the preference of the god for humble offerings rather than the hecatombs of the rich and ostentatious, and the paradoxical choice of some obscure person as the happiest or wisest of men.

[41] Dodds, 75. Dodds connects the tendency to look upon Zeus as "the awful judge, just but stern, who punishes inexorably the capital sin of self-assertion, the sin of *hubris*" (48) with the growing claim of the individual in the archaic age to personal rights and responsibility, which dissolved the old solidarity of the family, undermined the authority of the father, and caused tensions that led to feelings of guilt. These feelings were projected upon the heavenly father. If we accept this explanation, which Dodds concedes is incapable of proof, we have a reason for the intense interest in *hybris* during the archaic age and for the corresponding development of sophrosyne as the strongest safeguard against it.

It seems inescapable that the very conditions of Greek life in the seventh century—the continual struggle for wealth and power, in which the brilliant success of some city or of some great individual leader was quickly followed by an equally striking disaster, so that no good fortune could ever seem permanent—provided a background against which every prudent person must have concluded that excess leads to catastrophe, and that moderate hopes and ambitions are safest. Historical traditions, especially in Herodotus, and the kind of anecdote in which choral lyric abounds afford innumerable examples of such bewilderingly swift changes of fortune, to which the natural response would seem to be Alcman's famous warning (1. 16–18 Page): "Let no man soar to the heavens nor try to wed Aphrodite, the Queen of Paphos," or Phocylides' characteristic comment on conditions in the *polis* (Frag. 12 Diehl [3]): "I wish to be midway in the state [*mesos en polei*]."

There is special relevance in Phocylides' remark (which finds a parallel in Solon's passion for the Mean), because it is in the growth of the *polis* that we see conditions especially favorable to the development of sophrosyne. The *polis* by its very nature required a much greater exercise of restraint (*aidôs*, sophrosyne) than had the loosely organized Homeric society. It has often been observed that the self-assertion of the heroic individual was curbed when it encountered the restrictions imposed by the nascent *polis*.[42] In Finley's words, only by taming the hero could the community grow; and as we know from the harsh comments of Callicles in Plato's *Gorgias*, sophrosyne is one name for the force that tames the hero, that, in fact, makes him a citizen (492A–B).[43] The consequences of this painful adjustment for the individual are to be seen in tragedy (especially Sophoclean tragedy), whose most characteristic plot concerns the hero in conflict with society, a hero who carries his individualism to some extreme incompatible with the apparent welfare of the community.[44] The relation of this typical myth to the development of the concept of sophrosyne will be considered in Chapter II.

In addition to the pressure of the *polis* on the individual, there was also the pressure of class against class, of the new middle class against the hereditary aristocracy, and of the poor and landless against both. From this conflict emerged the conception of sophrosyne as an *aretê politikê*, appropriated at first by the aristocratic or oligarchic faction in the

[42] See, e.g. Wolfgang Schadewaldt, *Neue Wege zur Antike* 8 (1929), 103–4.

[43] Finley, *op. cit.,* 129.

[44] Helmut Kuhn, *H.S.C.P.* 52 (1941), 1–40, and 53 (1942), 37–88; see especially 53 (1942), 52 ff.

Greek city-states and later by the democrats, at least in Athens. In the sixth and fifth centuries, sophrosyne, for all its Ionian origins, became part of what may, with some reservations, be called the aristocratic Dorian ethical tradition,[45] seen in Theognis, Pindar, and (sometimes) Bacchylides. In all three poets, but most consistently in Theognis, sophrosyne is a "class" virtue, whose essential meaning resides in the knowledge of limitations, from which in Pindar it derives its strong religious affinity with Apollo, and because of which it tends to be linked with *hasychia* ("quietness") and *eunomia* ("good order").[46] Yet the potentialities of sophrosyne were so great that it did not remain frozen in the Dorian ethical system but continued to develop, even as Greek political forms developed, and always kept in close touch with the evolution of the Athenian *polis*.

Significantly, not only elegiac poetry of the sixth century and lyric poetry of the fifth, but also sepulchral inscriptions of the same period, furnish evidence of the close association of sophrosyne and the city-state. Epitaphs of this early age testify to the emergence of a new kind of *aretê* to take the place of the heroic ideal, a new balance of the physical and the intellectual, a blending of the heroism of the soldier (exercised now, not in search of personal glory, but on behalf of the city) and the excellence of the patriotic citizen in time of peace. The phrases chosen to describe this new form of excellence exhibit a high degree of similarity: *aretê kai sôphrosynê, agathos kai sôphrôn.*[47] Nearly all the early inscriptions of this type are Athenian, but it is difficult to estimate the true significance of this striking fact in the absence of an equal number of contemporary epitaphs from other states. Yet even though the bulk of our evidence for

[45] Sophrosyne and related qualities (such as *eunomia* and *hêsychia*) can be linked with the Dorian tradition only tentatively, so far as the seventh and sixth centuries are concerned, because not until after the Persian wars did the Greeks themselves show much awareness of this element in the contrast between Dorian and Ionian. It must be remembered that *eunomia* and *hêsychia* are vital to Solon's political program. In the sixth century the position of sophrosyne as an excellence valued by Dorian aristocrats rests mainly on the evidence of Theognis of Megara.

[46] See below, pp. 23 ff.

[47] See Paul Friedländer, *Epigrammata* (Berkeley, 1948), Nos. 71, 6, 31, 85; and cf. Simonides 128 Diehl (*aretê* and sophrosyne). In Friedländer, No. 88, the virtues are called *noos* and *anorea;* cf. the epitaph by Ion of Chios for Pherecydes, which mentions *anorea* and *aidôs* (5. 1 Diehl³). Pindar *Paean* 9. 46 praises the *saophrôn anorea* of the Theban seer Teneros. The adjective *sôphrôn* has a different meaning ("chaste, modest") in epitaphs for women. See Kaibel, Nos. 51 (*agathê kai sôphrôn*) and 53 (*esthlê kai sôphrôn*). Friedländer, No. 89, exemplifies a type of inscription that lists the virtues of the dead and includes a variety of predominantly intellectual qualities: *sôphrôn, euxynetos* ("clever"), *pinytos* ("shrewd"), *ta kala eidôs* ("understanding what is fair"). The first and last terms have moral implications as well.

Attic sophrosyne belongs to the period after the Persian wars, the epitaphs of the type mentioned above suggest that in the archaic age sophrosyne had already begun to be, not just the most Hellenic virtue, as has always been recognized,[48] but the most Athenian as well.

Here again it would be useful to know the reason, and again we find a complex situation with several possible explanations. One theory suggests an economic origin for Attic sophrosyne and connects it with the rise of a mercantile middle class.[49] The same spirit as animates the reforms of Solon (the insistence on measure, the balancing of one party against the others, the instinct for moderation as a shield against *hybris* and *stasis*) leads to the adoption by the emerging middle class of the virtue that symbolizes their innermost aspirations. It is also possible to find more purely political motives. As *hybris* comes to be considered the characteristic vice of tyrants (an association of ideas firmly established by the early fifth century),[50] its opposite, sophrosyne, becomes the virtue of the constitutional form of government which overthrows or wards off tyranny. Still a third hypothesis relates Attic sophrosyne to the historic blending of Dorian and Ionian elements in Athenian life. It is a commonplace that, in the poetry of the archaic age, Solon steers a middle course between those poles of the Hellenic world, Tyrtaeus with his Spartan austerity and Mimnermus with his Ionian hedonism. Jaeger, for example, points out that Athens "was the first to strike a balance between the outward-striving energy of the individual and the unifying power of the state." [51] Aristotle, in the *Politics,* seems to have interpreted the Greek character as a mean between the contrasting Hippocratic types, the violent, warlike Europeans and the tame, passive Asiatics.[52] In much the same way Athens blends in herself the contrasting qualities of the eastern and western Greeks. This *krasis,* as the Hippocratics might call it, was completed in the archaic age, and one of its results is Attic sophrosyne.

Solon himself does not, in the extant Fragments, employ any form of this word,[53] but his adoption of the principle of the Mean in political

---

[48] Wilamowitz, 2. 123–24; J. A. K. Thomson, *Greeks and Barbarians* (London, 1921), 118.

[49] George Thomson, *Aeschylus and Athens* (London, 1941), 283, 350; Gregory Vlastos, *C.P.* 41 (1946), 65–83.

[50] Aeschylus regularly associates *hybris* with the tyrant. The antithesis beween freedom and tyranny and between sophrosyne and *hybris* in his tragedies is studied by Bruno Snell, *Philol. Supp.* 20 (1928), 1–164. On *hybris* in a political context in early Greek poetry, see Del Grande, 45–53.

[51] *Paideia,* 1. 137.

[52] Jaeger, *Scripta Minora* (Rome, 1960), 313–14.

[53] Perhaps a mere accident of survival. Like all the gnomic poets, Solon makes free use of abstractions in -*synê* (*euphrosynê, doulosynê, aphrosyne, gnômosynê*). There is nothing to suggest,

life marks him as the first spokesman for Athenian sophrosyne; as such
he was remembered by the Attic orators of the fourth century and by
Aristotle.[54] In his efforts to secure economic justice Solon seems especially
conscious of taking a position "in the middle," between the rich and the
poor (25. 8–9 Diehl [3]), and of restraining excess; [55] but the Mean
underlies his conception of political justice also, as is shown by the close
causal connection that he establishes between the upsetting of the measure of power or liberty proper to the various classes, and the outbreak of
civil war (for instance, 3 and 5 Diehl [3]). Solon's political vocabulary includes several terms that later writers link closely with sophrosyne:
hêsychiê ("quietness" [3. 10 Diehl [3]; cf. 4. 5]); *eunomiê* ("orderly behavior,"
the antithesis to *hybris* and *koros* [3. 32–34]); *kosmos* ("order" [1. 11]); and
of course *dikê* (3. 14). The first two, as we have observed, denote the key
values of Dorian aristocracy later in the sixth century and throughout
the fifth. In Solon they have as yet no "class" meaning. *Hêsychiê* is
essentially a medical metaphor, opposed to "disturbance" and suggesting that balance of powers which in the body results in health and in the
polis leads to justice and peace.[56] *Eunomiê*, one of the ethical concepts
that Solon found in Hesiod and transplanted to Attic soil, implies moderation and restraint on the part of all groups in the *polis*.[57] The great political elegy that praises *eunomiê* for bringing order to the State and blotting
out *hybris* (3. 32, 34) contains the seeds of many later Greek utterances
on the need for restraint and moderation in the mutual relations of the
citizens. Not long after Solon's day it inspired some of Theognis' comments on the danger of class conflict, but Theognis characteristically
substitutes sophrosyne for *eunomiê* as the antithesis to *hybris* (39–42).

No one reading the Fragments of Solon's political poems, brief though
they are, can doubt that for him the middle way amounted to a passion.
He finds a variety of terms to express the concept of the Mean or of
measure, including μήτε λίαν ("not too much" [5. 8]); ἐν μεταιχμίῳ
(25. 8) to describe the position of the boundary mark which he established

---

however, that sophrosyne at this time implied moderation in political affairs; the word
for this is *mesos* (as in Phocylides, Frag. 12) or *metrios* (Solon 4. 7 Diehl [3]).

[54] Demosthenes 19. 251; Aeschines 1. 6, 7. Aristotle *Eth. Nic.* 1179a 10 ff., ascribes to Solon
the belief that those men are happy who, being moderately (μετρίως) equipped with external
goods, have performed the noblest deeds and lived σωφρόνως. This view may echo Herodotus'
account of Solon's response to Croesus (1. 30–32), although Herodotus does not use the word
sôphrôn in this connection. Plutarch *Solon* 14 records the advice of the Delphic oracle to
Solon: "Sit in the middle of the boat." Cf. Kollmann, *loc. cit.*, 16, on Solon as *"der erste Mann
der Sophrosyne."*

[55] Cf. Vlastos, *loc. cit.*, 81–82.   [56] *Ibid.*, 68–69.   [57] See Solmsen, *Hesiod*, 116.

between the rich and the poor; ἐν μέτροισι [58] (4. 7) when he bids the rich to quiet their hearts and put their proud minds "within the measures" (or "within boundaries"); and μέτρον γνωμοσύνης ("the measure of judgment," which knows the limits of everything [16. 1–2]). Solon speaks several times of the need to restrain (usually κατέχειν) either certain groups within the *polis* (as in 10. 5, 25. 6) or the excess (*koros*) to which they tend. The proverbial genealogy of *olbos* ("prosperity")—*koros*—*hybris* appears in his poetry with the qualification that *koros* brings forth *hybris* when great prosperity comes to men who do not possess a sound mind; *noos artios* (5. 10) here comes close to sophrosyne in its Homeric sense.

The words *sôphrôn* and sophrosyne begin to appear with some frequency in poetry of the sixth and early fifth centuries, showing for the first time definite moral and religious connotations. During this period it is always possible for *sôphrôn* to maintain its original significance of "sound-minded" or "prudent," and often it keeps the uncontracted form of the adjective. Thus Phocylides says (Frag. 11 Diehl[3]): "Many who are thoughtless [ἐλαφρόνοοι] seem to be *saophrones* because they move in orderly fashion." Ἐλαφρόνοος is to *saophrôn* as χαλιφρονέων is to *saophrosynê* in the *Odyssey*. The same meaning obtains in a line from Hipponax, which says that the best marriage for a *sôphrôn* man is to take a woman of serviceable habits, for this is the only dowry that will save the household (81. 1 Diehl [3]).[59] But important innovations are at hand, many of them in the collection that goes under the name of Theognis.[60] One of the major accomplishments of Greek poetry in the archaic period is the formulation of the "civic" *aretae* which were ultimately canonized as the Platonic or cardinal virtues. What Tyrtaeus did for *andreia*, Solon for justice, and Xenophanes for *sophia*, Theognis and his imitators did for sophrosyne.[61]

Undoubtedly their most far-reaching innovation is the use of sophrosyne as an antonym of *hybris* in both public and private life, a usage that reflects the encroachment of sophrosyne on the preserves of *eunomia* and

[58] The emendation of Kaibel and Wilamowitz for the papyrus μετρίοισι.

[59] A fragment of dubious authenticity. Later variants of this commonplace apply the word *sôphrôn* to the wife, with the meaning "chaste." E.g. Epicharmus 286 Kaibel, *Com.*

[60] Although the authorship and date of many verses in this collection are uncertain, it is generally agreed that most of them belong to the sixth and fifth centuries and may therefore be used as evidence for ethical developments during this period. See Jaeger, *Paideia*, 1. 187–93; Josef Kroll, *Philol. Supp.* 29 (1936), 1–284; Jean Carrière, *Théognis de Mégare* (Paris, 1948), 38–136; Burn, *op. cit.*, 258–64.

[61] The innovations of Tyrtaeus are discussed by Werner Jaeger, *Scripta Minora* 2. 75–114. On Solonian justice, see Vlastos, *loc. cit.*, and Solmsen, *Hesiod*, 107–23. Xenophanes (Frag. 2 Diehl [3]) substitutes *sophia* for athletic prowess as a civic ideal.

aidôs and sets the stage for its role in tragedy. Theognis is the first to provide sophrosyne with a political context. There is an obvious connection between this development and the civil strife that accompanied the transition from aristocracy or oligarchy to some form of democracy, often by way of tyranny, in many Greek cities during the seventh and sixth centuries. Theognis himself, a spokesman for the conservative Dorian nobility in Megara around the middle of the sixth century, expresses the feelings of his class in the face of the growing power of the lower orders, which first attained influence either with or soon after the rule of the tyrant Theagenes (traditionally dated *ca.* 640 B.C.). It is natural to consider "sound-minded" those who acquiesce in a traditional arrangement, and this is the doorway through which sophrosyne first enters the Greek political vocabulary. Theognis warns his young friend of the approaching upheaval (39–42): "Cyrnus, this city is in labor and I fear that it will bring forth a chastiser of our wicked *hybris*. The townspeople are still *saophrones*, but the leaders are inclined to fall into great trouble."

The situation here—especially the identity of the "leaders" [62]—is obscure, and while it is clear from the political orientation of the *Theognidea* that the townspeople are called *saophrones* ("right-minded") because they still subordinate themselves to the nobles, the antithesis between sophrosyne and *hybris* is implied rather than explicit. An imitator, perhaps dissatisfied with this lack of clarity, alters the second line to read (1081–82): "I fear that it [the city] will bring forth a man wantonly insolent [*hybristês*], the leader of harsh civil war." The revision changes the meaning of the passage and involves an awkward use of the word *hêgemôn* ("leader") in two different senses in as many lines (1082–1082a), but the antithesis between *hybris* and sophrosyne is now sharply defined.

Elsewhere in Theognis, sophrosyne and *hybris*, while contrasted, are not politically oriented. The famous reproach to Zeus for allowing the just to suffer and the wicked to prosper contains as its kernel the following lines (377–80): "How, then, son of Cronus, can your mind bear to hold the wicked and the just in the same respect, whether the minds of men are turned to sophrosyne or to *hybris?*" The alliance of sophrosyne

---

[62] Jean Carrière (*Théognis, poèmes élégiaques* [Paris, 1948], 97–98) suggests that the *hêgemones* (Theognis 41) are the new leaders of the middle class, while Kroll (*loc. cit.,* 121–26) identifies them with the aristocrats. Plutarch (*Mor.* 295D) says that the Megarians ἐσωφρόνησαν κατὰ τὴν πολιτείαν after the expulsion of the despot Theagenes, referring to a brief period of stability before the demagogues corrupted the masses with draughts of unmixed freedom. Kroll (*loc. cit.,* 115) traces the debt of Theognis in this passage to Solon 3. 5 and 36. See also F. S. Hasler, *Untersuchungen zu Theognis* (Winterthur, 1959), 34 ff. and 128.

with justice in this passage marks an important stage in its moral growth, while the opposition of both qualities to *hybris* prepares us for the use of this theme by Aeschylus. In the three passages of the *Theognidea* mentioned so far, sophrosyne has gone beyond the simple Ionian "soundness of mind" or "shrewdness in one's own interest" and has begun to imply something like "resistance to unjust ambition" or "refusal to seek wealth or power beyond one's due." For the first time it may perhaps be translated as "moderation" or even "self-control," with the reservation that it does not yet imply restraint of the physical appetites, only restraint of ambition or avarice. It has often and truly been observed that the value of the Mean is the central idea in the ethics of Theognis,[63] but it is untrue to say that the quality that embodied the Mean was sophrosyne.[64] Theognis associates sophrosyne with the idea of moderation only in the three passages mentioned above and in one other (753–54), which bids Cyrnus acquire possessions justly and keep a *sôphrôn thymos*, free from insolence—here *atasthalia*, a Homeric equivalent of *hybris*. Usually *sôphrôn* remains close to its Homeric connotation, as is shown by the frequency with which it is opposed to *aphrôn* or *nêpios* ("foolish, of unsound mind" [431, 454, 497, 665, 483]). A typical passage is one in which the poet observes that it is easier to beget and rear a man than to instil in him intelligence (430–31, 433–35): "No one has yet found a way to make a fool [*aphrôn*] wise [*sôphrôn*] or a bad man good.... If it were possible to make intelligence and put it into a man, the son of a good father would never become bad, but would be persuaded by wise counsels [*mythoi saophrones*]."

One other passage in Theognis shows a definite development in the meaning of sophrosyne and moreover connects it with social, rather than individual, ethics. These verses are especially striking because they contain the first personification of sophrosyne, in an adaptation of Hesiod's famous prediction about the departure from the earth of *Aidôs* and *Nemesis*, after the triumph of *hybris* and injustice in the Iron Age. In the *Theognidea*, Sophrosyne, appropriately enough, supplants *Aidôs;* she, together with *Pistis* (Good Faith) and the *Charites* (Graces) has returned to Olympus, leaving only *Elpis* (Hope) among mankind. Thereafter (1135–42): "No longer are just oaths kept faithfully [*pistoi*] among men, nor does anyone worship the immortal gods, but the race of reverent men has perished, nor do they any longer recognize law and

---

[63] E.g., Jean Carrière, *Théognis de Mégare*, 232.
[64] As does C. M. Bowra, *Early Greek Elegists* (New York, 1960), 154.

order." [65] Since the function of *Pistis* is clearly to guarantee the observance of just oaths, and no specific responsibility is assigned to the *Charites*, it seems that Sophrosyne is concerned with reverence for the gods and the preservation of law and order. She is therefore close to *Eusebeia* (Piety) and *Eunomia*. Whoever wrote this particular verse may well have been a contemporary of Pindar and Bacchylides, both of whom refer to *saophrōn eunomia*. The other early personification of Sophrosyne reflects much the same context of Dorian ideas: the Fragment of Epicharmus which describes Sophrosyne as a neighbor of *Hasychia* (Quietness [Frag. 101 Kaibel]). Later in the fifth century Critias makes her a neighbor of *Eusebeia* in his elegiac poem on the Spartan constitution (Frag. 6 DK).

The *Theognidea* also contain the earliest recorded exemplar of sophrosyne. In a bitter attack on the worship of wealth, the poet says that nothing else is accounted valuable, though you possess the sophrosyne of Rhadamanthys, the knowledge of Sisyphus, or the eloquence of Nestor (699–718). The association of Rhadamanthys with Sisyphus and Nestor, both noted for some kind of intelligence, and the appearance of Rhadamanthys elsewhere as a model of wisdom and good judgment suggest that sophrosyne here has an intellectual connotation—presumably distinct from the tricky cleverness for which Sisyphus was noted. Rhadamanthys seldom appears in later literature as an exemplar of sophrosyne, possibly because the intellectual aspect of the virtue is overtaken and surpassed by the moral (which Peleus and other models of self-control represent) and the political (typified by Solon and Pericles).[66]

[65] Reading εὐνομίας (Herwerden). The *Charites* (Euphrosyne, Thalia, and Aglaia) symbolize the elements of joy and festivity in human life and are naturally supposed to be present when a city is well governed and at peace. For the association of some of these qualities in an ode of Bacchylides, see p. 23. In the passage from Hesiod on which Theognis has modeled these lines (*Erg.* 190–200), *charis,* though present, is not personified. Hesiod says that when *Aidōs* and *Nemesis* depart, the *charis* belonging to the man who is *euorkos* ("faithful to his oath"), just, and *agathos,* will disappear, as will reverence for parents and fear of the gods (two nuances of *eusebeia*).

[66] Peleus: Aristophanes *Clouds* 1063. Solon: see n. 54 above. Pericles: Isocrates XV. 111, XVI, 28. Rhadamanthys is a type of self-restraint in Pseudo-Demosthenes *Eroticus* 30. The keen interest in assigning supremacy in wisdom, happiness, and other desirable qualities that inspired so many inquiries at Delphi caused Myson, one of the Seven Wise Men, to be pronounced *sōphronestatos* (Hipponax, Frag. 61 Diehl [3]). Another version of the story describes Myson as *sophōteros* (Diogenes Laertius 1. 106), and it is probable that even if *sōphronestatos* is the word the oracle actually used, it has an intellectual significance. *Sophos* and *sōphrōn,* while not identical (*sophos* implies being clever at something; *sōphrōn,* being prudent, often with moral consequences), are sometimes hard to distinguish in fifth-century literature. See Herodotus 4. 77, and cf. Fritz Wehrli, *Lathe Biōsas* (Leipzig, 1931), 42. Xenophon (*Mem.* 3. 9. 4) says that Socrates made no distinction between *sophia* and sophrosyne.

Still another far-reaching innovation in the *Theognidea* is the earliest specific linking of sophrosyne with maturity, as distinguished from youth. In the *Odyssey* there is no suggestion that sophrosyne belongs to any one time of life more than to another, although the young Telemachus is twice credited with the virtue. Later Greek thought is divided on the subject, appropriately enough, since sophrosyne has different aspects; and some of these belong to youth, others to age.[67] Theognis prays to Aphrodite for an end to labor and care (1325–26): "When I have finished the measure of youth with a cheerful heart, grant me the *ergmata sôphrosynês.*" These *ergmata* are probably "the works of wisdom," rather than self-restraint, since sophrosyne is not clearly connected with masculine chastity until the age of Euripides. Even so, it is unusual for Aphrodite to be involved in a prayer for this particular gift.[68] The contrast between this prayer of Theognis and the famous complaint of Mimnermus is probably unintentional, but it is almost as striking as Solon's deliberate rebuke to the Ionian poet.[69]

The extension of sophrosyne to mean "sobriety, avoidance of drunkenness," must have been in progress in the sixth century, but when Theognis uses *sôphrôn* in the context of the drinking party, it still means "sound of mind" and "intelligent" rather than "sober." One couplet says (497–98): "Wine makes light the head of fool [*aphrôn*] and wise man [*sôphrôn*] alike whenever they drink beyond measure." *Sôphrôn* is exactly like *sophos* in a similar verse on the same theme (499–502). The opposite is *aphrôn* or, in still another, similar verse, *nêpios* (483). There is as yet no suggestion that the *sôphrôn* man would avoid excessive drink, nor is there any hint of the theory developed in Plato's *Laws* I–II that the be-

---

[67] According to F. M. Cornford's theory of the origin of the cardinal virtues in a Pythagorean division of human life into periods, each of which has its appropriate virtue (*C.Q.* 6 [1912], 246–65), sophrosyne belongs to the young; and it is true that throughout its history there is a nuance of sophrosyne which is always recognized as proper to the young. See Plato *Laws* 710A on the temperamental sophrosyne natural to some children and young animals, and see Isocrates *Evagoras* 22 on sophrosyne ("obedience, discipline") as a virtue of childhood and adolescence. The sophrosyne of the old is the hard-won wisdom that comes with time and suffering (Sophocles, Frag. 718; Democritus, Frag. 294 DK; Plato *Laws* 665E) or, more often, is the control of the appetites. On the apparent sophrosyne of old men, in whom the passions of youth have abated, see Aristotle *Rhetoric* 2. 12–14.

[68] The reason is perhaps to be found in the nature of the poem; since the earlier part is a conventional prayer for satisfaction in love, inevitably addressed to Aphrodite, the same goddess is appealed to throughout. Solon's wish that in old age the *ergmata Kyprogenous* may be dear to him (20 Diehl [3]) may have been in Theognis' mind.

[69] Mimnermus, Frag. 1 Diehl [3]. Plutarch (*De virt. mor.* 445F) describes Mimnermus as wanton (*akolastos*) on the strength of this lament. Solon's response (22 Diehl [3]) is characteristic of his sophrosyne.

havior of a man at a drinking party will reveal whether or not he is truly *sôphrôn.*

Sophrosyne was indeed beginning to be connected with sobriety, as we learn from one of the Attic *skolia* (dating perhaps from the late sixth century), which also contains the earliest recorded antithesis between sophrosyne and *mania* (902 Page): "Drink with me, feast with me, love with me, be wreathed with me. When I am mad, be mad with me, when I am sane, be sane with me [σὺν σώφρονι σωφρόνει]." Although the verbal contrast is between sophrosyne and *mania,* the madness is obviously that of drink. The relation between these two types of irrationality and their common opposition to sophrosyne form a continuing theme in Greek literature.[70]

By the end of the sixth century a link was established between sophrosyne and the general idea of restraint or even abstinence, as is clear not only from its connection with sobriety, demonstrated above, but also from the even earlier use of sophrosyne to designate feminine *aretê.* The qualities expected of women in Homeric society (beauty, domestic skills, and chastity) continue to comprise feminine *aretê* throughout antiquity; and although Homer never uses the word sophrosyne in this connection, it is regularly so used in the classical period, when Penelope by reason of her faithfulness becomes the most prominent exemplar of the virtue. Semonides of Amorgos makes the first recorded allusion to sophrosyne in this sense. In his diatribe against women he reserves for the last and weightiest charge the accusation that whatever woman seems especially *sôphronein* is actually behaving most outrageously (7. 108–10 Diehl[3]). The infinitive *sôphronein* (occurring here for the first time) may mean "to be chaste" or may have a broader significance, "to be a good wife." Either nuance is possible also in a fragment from Epicharmus which says that the virtue of a *sôphrôn* woman is not to wrong her husband (286 Kaibel, *Com.*). Sophrosyne, once this usage becomes current, is the special virtue of women whether married or unmarried, and for women of both categories it is the most common of all tributes inscribed on memorial reliefs and tombstones.[71]

---

[70] Cf. *Anacreontea* 2. 6 Bergk, which speaks of singing a drinking song in a decent frenzy (*sôphrôn lyssê*). See also Anacreon 43. 3 Diehl, where ἀνυβρίστως is equivalent to *sôphronôs.* (The text preferred by D. L. Page [356] ἂν †ὑβριστιῶς† destroys the parallel). Horace *Odes* 1. 27, *verecundum Bacchum,* is in the same tradition. For various expressions embodying the idea of a *sôphrôn mania* or *sobria ebrietas* and for the transformations of this concept, see Hans Lewy, *Sobria Ebrietas* (Giessen, 1929).

[71] E.g., Kaibel, Nos. 78, 53; Johannes Geffcken, *Griechische Epigramme* (Heidelberg, 1916), Nos. 132, 140. The Latin equivalents are *casta* and *pudens,* which are ubiquitous on Roman

Lyric poetry, in common with the epic, makes frequent use of the themes of sophrosyne without employing the word itself. Wilamowitz in fact maintained that Archilochus, Alcaeus, Mimnermus, and Anacreon knew nothing of sophrosyne.[72] Yet Archilochus' address to his *thymos* on the proper reaction to good and bad fortune (67a Diehl[3]) and his praise of *tlêmosynê* (7. 6 Diehl[3]); and Alcaeus' advice to his friend Melanippus not to set his heart on things too great, since even Sisyphus could not escape death for ever, and man must bear with courage what cannot be avoided (B 6 Lobel and Page)—all these are valid expressions of the *sôphrôn* spirit.[73] One of the perennial themes of Greek lyric poetry is the meditation on human mortality, which easily gives rise to warnings against excessive hope and ambition. An early instance of this feeling is Alcman's Maiden Song, which describes the ruin that befell certain heroes who exceeded mortal bounds. The fear of *hybris* is expressed in a characteristic warning (1. 16–18, Page): "Let no man soar to the heavens nor try to wed Aphrodite, the Queen of Paphos." This type of admonition became a cliché, especially favored in dirges and victory odes, both of which found use for commonplaces on thinking mortal thoughts,[74] and Alcman is the first of a long line of lyric and tragic poets to find in mythology examples of *hybris* punished and, by implication at least, sophrosyne instilled.

Yet Alcman does not mention sophrosyne; and in fact, this word, although it is overtly connected with the themes of *hybris,* human mortality, mortal thoughts, and the mutability of fortune more often in the

---

epitaphs. So far as men are concerned, sophrosyne does not have a well-attested meaning of "chastity" until the latter half of the fifth century. Euripides, Frag. 446 Nauck (from the first *Hippolytus*), is an early example. Chastity was not expected of the Homeric hero, and there were no religious sanctions to support masculine chastity in Greek paganism, except in so far as belief in pollution led under certain circumstances to the practice of chastity as a means of purification. The sanctions that enforced feminine chastity were originally social rather than religious.

[72] Wilamowitz, 2. 123.

[73] The phrase *sôphrosynâs oiaka* ("the helm of sophrosyne") which occurs in the Parian inscription of Archilochus (*Tetram.* Frag. 51 p. IV B 18 Diehl[3]) is probably the work of the dedicator, rather than of Archilochus himself. Rudolph Pfeiffer (*Philol.* 84 [1928], 137–52) discusses the *tlêmosynê* of Archilochus (as well as the *tolman* of Sappho 2. 17) as their response to the sense of helplessness (*amêchaniê*) felt by the early lyric poets. This helplessness in the face of Divine will or fortune leads in tragedy to the suggestion that through sophrosyne man may become moderate in grief and learn to accept reversals calmly.

[74] J. T. Sheppard (*Oedipus Tyrannus* [Cambridge, 1920], lix ff.) discusses this commonplace and its relation to sophrosyne. Cf. Pindar *Pyth.* 2. 27–34, where Ixion's desire for Hera, the wife of Zeus, exemplifies *hybris* and the failure to respect the *metron.* Euripides (*I.A.* 543–45 and Frag. 503) refers to sophrosyne in connection with this *topos.* Callimachus (1. 20 Pfeiffer) cites a related commonplace, without using the word *sôphrôn.*

fifth century than in the seventh and sixth, is even in the later period rarely used by lyric poets. When it does occur, it refers to "civic" virtue more frequently than to the ethics of the individual in his private life. In the early fifth century, for example, Simonides, deeply concerned with the themes of mortality and the helplessness of man, often expresses the classical feeling for sophrosyne, as when he says (521 Page): "If you are a man, never say what tomorrow will be, nor, when you see a man happy, say how long he will be so, for swift is change, more swift than the turn of a long-winged fly." Yet his only extant reference to sophrosyne belongs, not to any of the lyric odes, but to another type of verse, the epitaph; and here he confirms the testimony of the Attic gravestones about the establishment of sophrosyne as one member of a pair of qualities that in the fifth century comprise the Hellenic ideal. His epitaph for Protomachus reads in part (128 Diehl): "O son of Timenor, never in the world will you cease to long for your dear son's *aretê* and *saophrosynê*." Another epitaph ascribed to Simonides (85 Diehl), which lacks the word sophrosyne but speaks eloquently of its spirit, records the modesty of Archedice, the daughter of Hippias, and says that she, although the daughter, sister, wife, and mother of tyrants, was never guilty of arrogance (*atasthalia*).[75]

Bacchylides casts further light on the progress of sophrosyne as a virtue of the *polis*. In an ode honoring Pytheas of Aegina for a victory at Nemea sometime before 480 B.C., he says that the renowned island of Aeacus is guided by *Areta*, with *Eukleia* (Fair Fame), the lover of wreaths, and *saophrôn Eunomia*, to whom belong feasts and who guards in peace the cities of pious men (13. 183–89 Snell).[76] Bacchylides here recalls the passages in Theognis that regard sophrosyne as the opposite of *hybris* in the *polis* and associate the personified Sophrosyne with law-abiding conduct and the Charites. The complex of ideas involving *eunomia,* peace, piety, and feasting also recalls Hesiod, whom Bacchylides still further resembles in the dithyramb on the "Demand for Helen." Here Menelaus reminds the Trojans that woe does not come to men through the fault of Zeus, since every man has the power to win *Dikê,* the servant of pure *Eunomia* and wise *Themis*—but through the fault of *Hybris,* who rejoices in furtive gains and acts of lawless folly (*aphrosynê* [15 Snell]).[77] *Eunomia*

---

[75] Simonides himself was linked in the popular mind with the idea of sophrosyne, as many anecdotes attest. Among these are the story of his warning to Pausanias (Plutarch *Cons. Apoll.* 6) and the testimony of Athenaeus about his renown for *kosmiotês* and sophrosyne (14. 656).

[76] Pindar, too, uses the word *eunomia* to describe the aristocratic constitution of Aegina (*Isth.* 5. 22).

[77] Cf. Homer *Od.* 1. 32–43, and Hesiod *Theog.* 901–3.

is now described as *hagna* rather than as *saophrôn,* but *hybris* is associated with one of the oldest antonyms of sophrosyne. In this ode the group of concepts often connected with the life of the *polis* is applied to man's conduct of his personal affairs, but the consequences affect the whole community.

Pindar weaves into his poetry many themes of sophrosyne (the praise of measure, gnomic reminders of mortal limitations, and warnings against *hybris,* supported by mythical *exempla*) [78] and gives them religious content by stressing the gulf between man and the gods; [79] he nevertheless uses the adjective *sôphrôn* only five times and entirely neglects the noun sophrosyne. Four of his five allusions occur in a context somehow connected with the State or with political conditions in Greece. The first Paean, of uncertain date, employs the very phrase *saophrôn eunomia* which occurs in Bacchylides' ode for Pytheas of Aegina. Beginning with an appeal for man to be content with due measure (*epi metra*), the Paean concludes with a prayer to Apollo to crown the children of Thebes with the blossoms of *saophrôn eunomia* (1. 10). The aristocratic bias of Pindar—or of his patron—leads him to associate sophrosyne with the sound and orderly rule of the conservative nobility. What is particularly memorable about this passage is the reference to Apollo: this is the first recorded prayer to the god of Delphi for the gift of sophrosyne.

The ninth Paean—which can be dated by its reference to the eclipse of the sun on April 30, 463 B.C.—again connects sophrosyne with the government of Thebes, when Pindar asserts that the local hero, Tenerus, was entrusted with the rule of the city by reason of his *saophrôn anorea,* his sober-minded courage (9. 46). Here, too, the god of Delphi is somewhere in the background, for Tenerus is not only a seer but also Apollo's son. Wilamowitz suggests that the eclipse is a symbol of evil, representing the dangers that threaten Boeotia and her allies as a result of the victory of Pericles and Ephialtes in Athens.[80] Still a third papyrus fragment, this time from a Parthenion, has also been thought to reflect Pindar's support of the anti-Athenian faction in Thebes.[81] The poet celebrates the family of Aeoladas, three generations of whom are taking

---

[78] See, e.g., *Ol.* 13. 47; *Pyth.* 1. 56–57, 2. 34, 4. 286, 9. 78; *Nem.* 11. 47; *Ol.* 5. 21–24, 13. 64; *Isth.* 5. 14, 7. 39; *Pyth.* 4. 90–93, 8. 1–14. Eduard Fraenkel (*Horace* [Oxford, 1957], 273–85), commenting on Horace *Odes* 3. 4, draws a parallel with Pindar *Pyth.* 1 and 8 which brings out the sophrosyne implicit in these two odes.

[79] See especially *Nem.* 6. 1–7 and *Pyth.* 10. 21–30.

[80] Wilamowitz, *Pindaros* (Berlin, 1922), 396.

[81] C. M. Bowra, in J. U. Powell, *New Chapters in the History of Greek Literature* (Oxford, 1933), Vol. III, 52 ff.

part in a procession at the Daphnephoria, and refers as follows (2. 66) to hostility shown them (by the pro-Athenian party?): "And then malevolent anger at the *sôphrones* ambitions of these men caused hateful strife, unrelenting, but they loved all the paths of justice." Both the word *sôphrones* and the allusion to *dikê* imply that the ambitions of this family constitute no danger to the State. It is evident that for Pindar, as for Theognis and Bacchylides, sophrosyne in the *polis* is allied with the other excellences—*aretê* or *anorea*, *eunomia*, and *dikê*—which by now have a well-established "class" meaning in the old-fashioned Dorian world.[82]

One of the two allusions to sophrosyne in the *Odes* deserves special notice because it forms part of the earliest recorded reference to a canon of cardinal virtues. The eighth Isthmian, which honors Cleander of Aegina for his victory in the boys' *pankration* in 478 B.C., introduces, according to the familiar epinician pattern, the myth of the legendary founders of Aegina, the Aeacids, and praises them for their possession of four virtues (24–28). Aeacus, the most virtuous (κεδνότατος) of mortals, gave judgments to the gods themselves, while his children excelled in courage (*anorea*) and were *sôphrones* and wise (πινυτοί τε θυμόν). Here are all four of the virtues later canonized by Plato and the Stoa, although only sophrosyne goes by its proper name. Justice is implied in the giving of judgments. *Anorea* is an epic term for courage, equivalent to the later *andreia*, and πινυτός is one of Homer's favorite epithets for the prudent Penelope or Telemachus.[83] *Eusebeia* ("piety"), which was often included among the civic virtues in the fifth and fourth centuries and was eliminated from the canon only when Plato's theory of the soul led him to adopt a set of four excellences in *Republic* IV, appears in the eighth Isthmian immediately after this passage, where it is cited as the special virtue of Peleus (29).

Amid the predominantly heroic ethical terminology of the ode, the precise meaning of *sôphrôn* is debatable. Is it the Homeric "soundness of mind," or does it have the moral implications found in Pindar's contemporary Aeschylus, or the political nuance that Pindar himself often favors? If, as I have suggested elsewhere,[84] the ode is intended to honor, not alone the hero Cleander, but also the entire city of Aegina, which

---

82 *Pyth.* 11, in honor of a Theban victor, also contains a political allusion praising moderation, this time in contrast to tyranny. Pindar says that of those in the *polis*, the midmost (τὰ μέσα) have the most enduring prosperity; he condemns tyranny, saying (54): "I am passionately attached to the common virtues [ξυναῖσι . . . ἀρεταῖς]." He then brings this statement into line with the conventions of the victory ode by remarking that envious evil is warded off if one who has secured the highest place and lives quietly flees from *hybris* (54–55).

83 E.g., *Od.* 1. 229, 4. 211, 10. 445.   84 *A.J.P.* 69 (1948), 304–8.

just two years previously had distinguished itself against the Persians (in contrast to the medizing of Thebes, its sister city), Pindar may be deliberately stressing a canon of civic virtues that were gaining recognition at this very time; and *sôphrôn* may be thought of as suggesting political moderation, the avoidance of *hybris,* as it undoubtedly does in the three Pindaric Fragments mentioned above.

The one remaining use of *sôphrôn* in the *Odes* is more traditional. In the third Pythian, which touches on many commonplaces of sophrosyne and uses the myth of Asclepius to illustrate the danger of forgetting the limits of mortality, Pindar applies the epithet *sôphrôn* to Chiron, the teacher of Asclepius (63). In all likelihood, and in spite of the context of warnings against *hybris,* it bears a predominantly intellectual rather than a moral significance, since Chiron is here spoken of in his capacity as the teacher of heroes. Elsewhere Pindar describes him, in a similar connection, as βαθύμητις ("deep-thinking" [*Nem.* 3. 53]). In such a context, however, it is especially difficult to distinguish moral from intellectual nuances.

Two more writers may be considered here. Both of them are eastern Greeks by origin, and both retain the Ionian intellectual concept of sophrosyne, although in one, Heraclitus, the concept is deepened by association with a systematic cosmology, while in the other, Herodotus, the word merely echoes the usage of everyday speech. Heraclitus is the first of the pre-Socratic philosophers to base an ethical system on a theory of physics and the only one before Democritus who refers to sophrosyne.[85] He is also the first writer to make explicit the link that Homer implied between sophrosyne and self-knowledge. In Fragment 116 (DK) he says: "It is possible for all men to know themselves and *sôphronein,*" and in Fragment 112 he goes so far as to say: "*Sôphronein* is the greatest *aretê,* and wisdom (*sophia*) consists in speaking the truth and acting in accordance with nature, paying heed to it." [86] The association of *sôphronein* with words indicating intellectual activity provides a clue to the meaning of this concept for Heraclitus. In spite of the emphasis elsewhere in his writings on the need to be moderate and suppress passion (Frags. 85, 110, 43), it is doubtful that *sôphronein* in these two

---

[85] Although the concepts of order, balance, and limit that are to be found in other pre-Socratic philosophers have an obvious relation to certain aspects of sophrosyne, the philosophers themselves apparently did not make the connection, nor did the Milesians apply their physical theories to the subject of ethics. The bearing that certain Pythagorean beliefs may have had on sophrosyne is suggested below, pp. 29–30.

[86] The MS reading *sôphronein* in these two fragments is restored by Kranz after being emended to *phronein* by Diels. For a vigorous defense of *sôphronein,* see Wilamowitz, 2. 123–24.

passages can mean "to be self-controlled, moderate," as is often assumed.[87] Rather it should be related to the contemplation of the human soul which is the source of understanding. Heraclitus repeatedly asserts that wisdom is one, and that it is *sophia* which enables man to share in the divine *logos* (Frags. 41, 32, 50). In Fragment 112, *sôphronein* (which in Fragment 116 stands side by side with self-knowledge as a possibility open to all men) appears in company with *sophia,* suggesting an affinity among all three concepts. *Sophia* is now defined as "to speak the truth and to act in accordance with nature, paying heed to it." Nature (*physis*) is to be connected with that universal *logos* which Heraclitus found by looking into his own soul (Frag. 101), and which must, he says, guide man in speech and action (Frags. 72, 73). The *physis* of Heraclitus is less like that of the Sophists than like that of the Stoics or indeed of Plato, when in *Laws* X he substitutes for the materialistic *physis* of his opponents a changed and spiritualized Nature in which the kindred of Mind (including *sophia*) are supreme. For Heraclitus *physis, logos,* and the *theios nomos* ("Divine law") of Fragment 114 are all related concepts, and the *sophia* that comprehends them and translates their precepts into speech and action must depend ultimately upon a profound and philosophical self-knowledge.

By self-knowledge Heraclitus seems to mean a searching examination into the soul to discover the universal law common to man and the cosmos. If he connects sophrosyne with this deep and essential self-knowledge, there should be nothing startling about the statement that *sôphronein* is the greatest *aretê.* It is another name for the faculty by which man may attain that wisdom whose object is the universal *logos.* Through this process man comes to know the law that governs his own soul and the rest of the universe. Clearly then, the concept of sophrosyne still has the Ionian intellectualism, but its meaning has become much more profound than the simple "good sense" of *Odyssey* 23. It has in fact developed the early hint of self-knowledge (which we saw in *Iliad* 21 and in the *Telemachia*) in such a way as to suggest the riches that await a further unfolding of these ideas in the tragic poets and especially in Plato.

Herodotus, despite his connection with Athens in the age of Pericles, may well be considered in the context of the archaic age, for his use of the word *sôphrôn* is predominantly Homeric, while in his moral and religious ideas he has more in common with the lyric and elegiac poetry of the sixth and early fifth centuries and with the more traditional elements in Aeschylean thought than with the prose writers of the later fifth

[87] As it is by Kathleen Freeman, *Ancilla to the Pre-Socratic Philosophers* (Oxford, 1948), 32.

century. Herodotus develops at length several ideas familiar in the gnomic writers and also in Simonides, Bacchylides, and Pindar: ideas having to do with the nothingness of man, the mutability of human affairs, the jealousy of the gods, and the dangerous folly of encroaching on boundaries set by Nature or by the Divine. The ruin brought about by *hybris* and the contrasting value of modesty provide Herodotus with the dominant moral theme of his work, a theme connected, as in Aeschylus, with the corresponding motives of tyranny versus freedom and of barbarism versus Hellenism. Many of the most memorable episodes of the *History* illustrate the downfall of a king or a state after flagrant acts of *hybris:* the story of Croesus, which stands as a prologue to the story of the rise and fall of the Persian Empire; the stories of Periander of Corinth and Polycrates of Samos; and the career of Xerxes—all illustrate this fundamental text of sophrosyne. But although Herodotus is the most fertile source in Greek prose of stories illustrating traditional ideas of sophrosyne,[88] he applies the word to none of the typical situations, and indeed he never uses the noun. For example, in his account of the debate among the Persian nobles over the rival forms of government, the danger of *hybris* is the chief argument advanced against both monarchy and democracy (3. 80–81), but the words *sôphrôn* and sophrosyne, which would almost certainly have appeared in any such discussion by Attic writers from Thucydides on, do not occur.[89] In the *History* we meet *sôphrôn, sôphronein,* and the adverb *sôphronôs,* always with some implication of soundness of mind, good sense, or occasionally sanity.

The fundamental meaning of *sôphrôn* for Herodotus becomes evident in a passage close to the beginning of Book I, which gives the traditional reason for enmity between Europe and Asia, the kidnaping of women. The Persians blame the Greeks for going to war for the sake of Helen, because although it is the act of unjust men to steal women, it is the part of fools (ἀνοήτων) to desire vengeance and of wise men (σωφρόνων) to pay no heed, since clearly women would not be carried off without their consent (1. 4). The antithesis between ἀνόητος ("fool") and *sôphrôn* shows that the latter has not developed beyond its Homeric connotation. Furthermore, the *sôphrôn* man referred to in a conversation between Xerxes and Demaratus (7. 104) is one with sense enough to value help and friendship. Xerxes uses the verb in a related "prudential" sense, when he apologizes to Artabanus for rejecting his good advice and says

---

[88] See, e.g., J. A. K. Thomson, *op. cit.,* 118; J. T. Sheppard, *op. cit.,* lxiv; W. C. Greene, *op. cit.,* 86.

[89] See Gregory Vlastos, *A.J.P.* 74 (1953), 337–66.

(7. 15): οὐκ ἐσωφρόνεον ("I was not using good judgment"). The adverb *sôphronôs* has a like meaning in the story of Anacharsis' report to the Scythian king, in which he says that among all the Greeks it is possible to conduct a conversation sensibly (*sôphronôs*) only with the Spartans (4. 77). The intellectual meaning is extended to include sanity in Book III, where *sôphronein* is the antithesis of madness in the story of Cambyses and Prexaspes' son (3. 35); and the verb means "to come to one's senses" in the episode of Cambyses' death at Ecbatana, after he awoke from his delusion about the prophecy involving a town by that name (3. 64). Only once, and then on a very small scale, does *sôphrôn* approach the meaning "moderate" in Herodotus. Otanes warns Darius not to take hasty action against the Magian usurper, but to behave with greater caution or moderation (ἐπὶ τὸ σωφρονέστερον [3. 71]). The relation between prudence and moderation is very close here.

One further phenomenon of the archaic age, the spread of the mystery religions, demands notice, since Pythagorean and Orphic beliefs were later held to have a bearing on sophrosyne. Our information about these cults is so fragmentary and elusive that it is impossible to do more than guess at the nature of their relation to sophrosyne. In Pythagorean writings of later times (such as the accounts of Pythagoras' life and teaching by Iamblichus and Porphyry) great importance is attached to sophrosyne in the sense of "self-restraint" or "abstinence" (the *sôphrôn* association of the sexes, the education of the young in a spirit of sophrosyne or good discipline), but nothing of this can be convincingly ascribed to Pythagoras himself or to his earliest followers. In the sixth century the important Pythagorean notions involved order, harmony, limit, and purification; [90] each of these was closely linked with sophrosyne by later philosophers, by Plato above all.

The first three of these ideas are expressions in physical terms of the point of view that in morality gave rise to sophrosyne. How important the concepts of order and harmony were in transforming the Socratic concept of sophrosyne (as seen, for example, in the *Apology* and the *Charmides*) into the Platonic, we may conjecture on the basis of the *Gorgias,* where sophrosyne is identified with the principle of order (*kosmos*) which holds together earth and heaven, gods and men (506D–508C), and of the *Republic,* in which sophrosyne in the soul and the State

[90] See G. S. Kirk and J. E. Raven, *The Presocratic Philosophers* (Cambridge, 1957), 217–64, for a sober assessment of the doctrines that may be ascribed to the Pythagorean school before Parmenides; and consult W. K. C. Guthrie, *A History of Greek Philosophy* (Cambridge, 1962), 1. 146–340.

is compared to a harmony "sounding the same note in perfect unison throughout the whole" and to a *symphônia* of the naturally inferior and the naturally superior on the question of which should rule (432A). The notion of limit was also a fruitful one for sophrosyne. The Pythagorean table of opposites begins (Aristotle *Metaphysics* A5 986a 24) with *peras* ("limit") and *apeiron* (the "unlimited"): the first is identified with Good; the second with Evil. When applied to morality, this doctrine, physical in origin, gives scientific support to the Apolline rule of moderation, and Plato makes use of it for just this purpose in the *Philebus,* when, as Jaeger says, he tries "to make ethics an exact science on the mathematical pattern." [91] Lyric and elegiac poetry show that the Greeks of the archaic and early classical periods were strongly inclined to identify what is limited or measurable with health of soul and safety, and what is unlimited and immeasurable with turbulence and danger. Aeschylus, from whose plays has been constructed a table of opposites not unlike the Pythagorean, consistently ranges sophrosyne and what is limited, measured, or restrained on the side of the Good.[92]

The idea of *katharsis* ("purification") also held great possibilities for sophrosyne, although in its origin this virtue had nothing to do with either purity or its opposite, pollution.[93] Only when the concept of purification was extended beyond mere ritual taboo and came to include the *katharsis* of the soul through some form of abstinence, usually the restraint of passion, did the notions of purification and sophrosyne coincide. This coincidence had occurred in all probability by the early fifth century, at which time purity (*hagnotês*) had acquired a moral connotation, and sophrosyne had begun to include some forms of self-restraint.[94]

Katharsis was sought by the Orphics, too, since they shared the Pythagorean dualism; and several aspects of Orphic belief, as it was popularly understood in the fifth and fourth centuries, made it natural to connect Orphism with the practice of sophrosyne. The supposed personality of Orpheus himself, whose music had a calming influence (and who, moreover, was associated with sexual purity), the importance of Apollo

[91] *Aristotle,* 87.

[92] See Chapter II, p. 33. The idea of proportion, which later has a close affinity with sophrosyne, is best exemplified in the archaic age by Alcmaeon's definition of health as a proportionate blending (*krasis symmetros*) of opposing powers; their excess is a cause of illness (Frag. 4 DK). Cf. the *sôphrôn krasis* referred to by the physician Eryximachus in Plato *Symp.* 188A.

[93] The concept of pollution is discussed by Dodds, 35–37; and at greater length by Louis Moulinier, *Le Pur et l'impur dans la pensée des Grecs* (Paris, 1952).

[94] The relation of purity and abstinence to morality is discussed by Adkins, *op. cit.,* 140–48.

in the cult, and the practice of various forms of abstinence by the members—all make it easy to understand why Theseus, however mistakenly,
could have ascribed Orphism to the *sôphrôn* Hippolytus.[95] Once again it
is Plato who makes the greatest use of "Orphic" elements to enrich his
doctrine of sophrosyne.[96] Moreover, Plato's development of the doctrine
of *katharsis* in relation to the soul—whether achieved through music, as
the Pythagoreans believed,[97] or through some form of abstinence—and
his tendency to link this *katharsis* with sophrosyne led the Neoplatonists
and the Church Fathers to assign a high place to the virtue. Plotinus and
his followers value sophrosyne as a means of purifying the soul from what
is material and of elevating it, step by step, towards the goal of union
with the One. Gregory of Nyssa and Gregory of Nazianzus ally sophrosyne, respectively, with *katharotês* ("purity") and *hagneia* ("holiness"),
which are key values in the ascetic life and lead the soul to God.[98] Such
an outcome—one that could not have been predicted on the basis of what
Homer and the writers of the archaic age meant by sophrosyne—is an
example of the adaptability of this concept, which nevertheless always
changes in ways consistent with its own essential nature, responding with
infinite sensitivity to the diverse stimuli of Greek life and thought.

[95] Euripides *Hipp.* 953. The evidence for Orphic rites and for the existence of a cult
is examined by W. K. C. Guthrie, *Orpheus and Greek Religion* (2nd ed.; London, 1952),
and Ivan Linforth, *The Arts of Orpheus* (Berkeley, 1941).

[96] See Ivan Linforth, *University of California Publications in Classical Philology* 12 (1944), 295–
314, for the suggestion that the imagery of the sieve in *Gorg.* 492D 1 ff. is Orphic. For an opposing view, see E. R. Dodds, *Plato, Gorgias* (Oxford, 1959), *ad loc.*

[97] See Kirk and Raven, *op. cit.,* 229.

[98] See chaps. VI (on the Neoplatonists) and IX (on the Church Fathers).

II

Tragedy

SOPHROSYNE, as we learn from Theognis, owes its first notable development beyond its Homeric beginnings to the stimulus afforded by conditions in the *polis*. Tragedy, too, is at least in part a product of these conditions, and it is no accident that the first great flowering of sophrosyne in Greek literature occurs in the work of the tragic poets. Many studies have demonstrated what tragedy owes to the conflict that occurred when the heroic individual encountered the restrictions imposed by the world order—whether manifested in religion or in the framework of the *polis*.[1] The characteristic expression of these religious and social restrictions is sophrosyne, the sense of measure, the reluctance to overstep boundaries. The prominence in Aeschylean tragedy of the conflict between *hybris* (one result of heroic *aretê* unrestrained by any Divine or human sanction) and sophrosyne accurately reflects the conditions that launched Attic tragedy on its course.

Sophrosyne is so fundamental to all three tragic poets that each one in his treatment of the concept reveals his basic beliefs about human life, and each interprets it in a characteristically different fashion. To Aeschylus sophrosyne is a masculine virtue, which he links with all the most favored elements in his *kosmos*. It is essentially religious. Its kernel is respect for the limitations imposed on man by the gods and only secondarily by human society. It has strong ties with the Mean and is more clearly political in its effects than it is in either of the other two poets. To Sophocles sophrosyne is no longer a specifically masculine virtue but is in fact generally opposed to the heroic, the *eugenês*, the *megalopsychos*, especially when heroic self-assertion is carried to an extreme.

[1] See, e.g., Wolfgang Schadewaldt, *Neue Wege zur Antike* 8 (1929), 103-4.

Sophocles interprets sophrosyne chiefly as the power to recognize reality and identifies it closely with self-knowledge. In his drama the tension between sophrosyne and the heroic principle, implicit in Homer, becomes explicit. To Euripides sophrosyne is one aspect of the rational element, eternally in conflict with the irrational. As such it has wide scope but appears chiefly as the control of the emotions and appetites, and now becomes predominantly moral rather than intellectual. Only for Euripides, among the tragic poets, does sophrosyne normally mean "self-control."

AESCHYLUS

Aeschylus associates sophrosyne with a set of key ideas—freedom, justice, defense against aggression, masculinity, Hellenism—to which he opposes a set of antitheses—tyranny, injustice, aggression, femininity, barbarism, and above all *hybris*.[2] The relation of these ideas to sophrosyne, while so regular as to constitute a major theme in Aeschylean tragedy, is far from static. It is possible to trace a steady increase in complexity from the comparatively clear-cut antitheses of the *Persians* to the realignment and reconciliation of motives in the *Eumenides*.

The *Persians* presents in a state of relative simplicity the opposition between *hybris* and sophrosyne which lies at the heart of Aeschylean tragedy. In other plays this theme and related themes are used in a more complicated (sometimes even a rather ambiguous) way, but here Aeschylus draws in Xerxes a paradigm of *hybris* and makes an unequivocal contrast between the barbarians whom he represents and the Greeks whose triumph at Salamis and Plataea is due to their possession of the virtues that their enemies lack. Finley has pointed out the persistent contrast between Persia and Greece (gold versus silver, pomp versus piety, conquest versus self-defense, tyranny versus freedom, Xerxes' motives in making war versus the battle cry at Salamis).[3] The alliance of sophrosyne and freedom is more prominent in the *Persians* than in any other play of Aeschylus; and there can be little doubt that the poet faithfully reflects contemporary Athenian opinion when he interprets the war

[2] Several of these antitheses have been traced through Aeschylean tragedy by Snell, "Aischylos," in connection with his study of *phobos*. Helen H. Bacon (*Barbarians in Greek Tragedy* [New Haven, 1961], 36 ff.) denies that Aeschylus polarizes Good and Evil around Greek and non-Greek, but in the case of the *Persians* at least this polarity seems inescapable. Although the noun sophrosyne does not appear in the extant tragedies, related forms occur twenty-two times: *sôphronein* eight times, *sôphrôn* eleven, *sôphronizein* once, *sôphronisma* once, and see *Supp.* 198 for a disputed compound noun with *sôphrôn*. Consult Gabriel Italie, *Index Aeschyleus* (Leiden, 1955).

[3] Finley, 210.

as an encounter between the forces of freedom and sophrosyne on the one hand and those of despotism and *hybris* on the other. An Attic *skolion* dated soon after the victory at Salamis expresses this view and unites the two concepts of sophrosyne and *eleutheria* in verses modeled on the antityrannical *skolia* in honor of Harmodius and Aristogiton. The couplet, as restored by Werner Peek, reads as follows:

Σοφροσσύνεν ἐνὶ κλά[δοις σ]μῖλα[κος ἡειμένος]
[Στρόμβιχε, ἐλε]υθερίας καλὸν ἐχειστέφανον.⁴

The meaning is something like: "Garbed in sophrosyne, Strombichus, amid the boughs of smilax, you wear a fair crown of freedom."

Among the antitheses of the *Persians* the fundamental contrast, and the one that includes all the others, is that between *hybris* and sophrosyne. This contrast becomes explicit at the climax of Darius' prophecy of the final disaster at Plataea. Everything in this speech calls attention to the impiety of the Persian host. The defeat at Plataea is to be a punishment for their *hybris* and godless thoughts (808), for they have ravaged the temples of Greece, and their fate will be a warning, even to the third generation, that mortal man must not direct his thoughts too high (οὐχ ὑπέρφευ ... φρονεῖν [820]). When *hybris* has blossomed forth, it bears a fruit consisting of *atê*, and from *atê* comes a harvest of tears (822–23).⁵ Zeus punishes excessive desires (827). Now that Xerxes has been divinely warned to respect limitations (σωφρονεῖν κεχρημένον [829]),⁶ Darius urges the Chorus to teach him with its reasonable coun-

---

⁴ *Hermes* 68 (1933), 118–21. Lionel Pearson (*C.P.* 52 (1957), 228–44) examines the evidence for a popular tendency to see the Persian war in terms of *hybris* and *nemesis*.

⁵ Recurrent patterns of imagery, of which recent studies have found a great number in Aeschylus (e.g., W. B. Stanford, *Greek Metaphor* [Oxford, 1936], and *Aeschylus in His Style* [Dublin, 1942], 96–100; Robert Goheen, *A.J.P.* 76 [1955], 113–37; R. D. Murray, Jr., *The Motif of Io in Aeschylus' Suppliants* [Princeton, 1958]; Otto Hiltbrunner, *Wiederholungs- und Motivtechnik bei Aischylos* [Bern, 1950]; B. H. Fowler, *A.J.P.* 78 [1957], 173–84), are connected, not with sophrosyne itself, but with its more dramatic antitheses. *Hybris*, for example, may be symbolized by blossom, fruit, and harvest (*Sept.* 601; *Supp.* 106) or by the medical imagery drawn from physical illness (*P.V.* 224–25, 977–78). Sophrosyne itself is occasionally suggested by metaphors involving restraint of some kind, such as the bit, the bridle, or the yoke (*P.V.* 1009–10), an anticipation of mediaeval and Renaissance iconography (as in Giotto's bridled *Temperantia* in the Arena Chapel in Padua, Raphael's *Moderatio* in the Stanza della Segnatura in the Vatican, and innumerable examples of sepulchral statuary in the baroque period). See Appendix for a summary of types of imagery connected with the theme of sophrosyne.

⁶ Rose, *ad loc.*, taking κεχρημένον as a participle of χρῆσθαι ("to be in need of"), translates: "Therefore give him wisdom with reasonable admonitions, for sorely he needs sobriety." H. D. Broadhead (*The Persae of Aeschylus* [Cambridge, 1960]) regards κεχρημένον (or κεχρησμένον) as a participle of χρᾶν ("to pronounce an oracle") and translates: "It having been declared [by the gods] that moderation must be observed."

sels to refrain from drawing upon himself the punishment of God by his overweening boldness (ὑπερκόμπῳ θράσει [831]). It is evident that verse 831 defines the content of *sôphronein* in verse 829; and nowhere do we find a more explicit statement of the intensely religious implications of this concept in the mind of Aeschylus. The god who is offended by the Persian *hybris* is Zeus *Kolastês* ("the Corrector"); and it is the impiety of the Persians, their failure to "think mortal thoughts," and their immoderate desires which constitute *hybris*.

The observance of limits is the essence of Aeschylean sophrosyne. In terms of the Apolline proverbs, *Mêden agan* is of primary importance to Aeschylus, as is *Gnôthi sauton* to Sophocles. The limits may be set by man, but often they are Divine, and the cardinal sin of the violator of sophrosyne is that, although mortal, he does not "think mortal thoughts." In the *Persians* the recurrence of words and phrases employing the root of *phronein* or some synonym is significant. Xerxes led his forces to disaster imprudently (δυσφρόνως [552]); he thought the thoughts of youth (νέα φρονεῖ [782]), unlike his ancestor Cyrus, whom the gods did not hate since the latter was prudent by nature (εὔφρων [772]); Xerxes, by his foolish notion (οὐκ εὐβουλίᾳ [749]) that he could master all the gods, even Poseidon, although he was but a mortal, showed that an illness of the mind (νόσος φρενῶν [750]) had taken hold of him. In this context *sôphronein* (829) seems to come at the climax of a long series of related words, which derive added meaning from their repetition, and it pronounces final judgment on the moral significance of Salamis and Plataea. To the excessive ambition and arrogance of Xerxes himself is added unrestrained emotionalism, a barbarian trait apparent in the lamentations of the Chorus.[7] Both kinds of excess are offenses against sophrosyne, and it is characteristic of the simple, antithetical pattern used in the *Persians* that both are committed by the same barbarian group. In the *Suppliants* and the *Septem* Aeschylus separates the two types of offense, assigns each to a different group and sets between them a figure who in some fashion represents a sophrosyne opposed to both extremes.[8]

The *Suppliants*, in fact, requires us to consider at least two kinds of sophrosyne, instead of the simple *Mêden agan* of the *Persians*. Here, as usual in Aeschylus and Sophocles, the situation that existed in the archaic

[7] Snell, 67 ff. The lamentations of the Chorus are particularly "oriental" from verse 935 on. Note the reference to the Mariandyan "howl." From verse 1102 on, the Chorus and Xerxes lament antiphonally in an equally abandoned way.

[8] It is questionable whether we should see in this development a confirmation of the later date of the *Suppliants*. See Albin Lesky, *Hermes* 82 (1954), 1–13, for a discussion of the papyrus fragment Oxy. xx. No. 2256. 3. Lesky dates the *Suppliants* after the *Septem*.

period still obtains: comparatively few references to sophrosyne occur, yet the concept is of major importance to the plot and the characterization. A clue to this importance lies in the frequent allusions to the *hybris* of the Egyptians. The chief connotation of *hybris* here is not that found in the *Persians,* but "lustfulness" with the accessory implication of "violence." In opposition to this flagrant *hybris,* and equally explicit, is the claim that the Suppliants are, and must take care to remain, *sôphrones.* But as the *hybris* of the Egyptians is different from that of the Persians, so, too, *sôphronein* has now altered in meaning. Quite evidently an important aspect of the Danaids' personality is their chastity, but only once does *sôphronein* have so limited a significance. Its usual meaning in this play is "to be modest, calm, self-controlled"—as in verses 198, 724, and 992. Danaus is the only spokesman for sophrosyne. His speeches to his daughters concentrate on this theme, possibly because, as critics often suggest,[9] it suits his role as father and gives him something to say in a part of the trilogy where he is dramatically superfluous. Possibly, however, Aeschylus gives him so much to say about sophrosyne for another reason: the tragedy has to do with two different offenses against this virtue—the violence of the suitors and the excessive emotionalism, combined with a distorted view of life, which the Danaids exhibit. The girls are, from the beginning, *sôphrones* in the sense of "chaste;" Danaus exhorts them to be *sôphrones* in the sense of "self-controlled;" and at the end of the play a hint begins to emerge that they must also learn yet another aspect of sophrosyne: moderation in their demands on life and a balanced view of their own role. The true nature of sophrosyne is revealed only gradually; there is even a kind of irony in the injunctions that Danaus constantly directs at his daughters, because not only their own natural sophrosyne (chastity), but also the kind that he enjoins (self-control), proves to be superficial and one-sided. The very fierceness with which they assert their devotion to their concept of sophrosyne constitutes a denial of the genuine and complete sophrosyne (moderation, balance) which alone could have prevented the tragic consequences of their demands on Argos. The speeches of Danaus show that he himself is unaware of the full meaning of sophrosyne. The richness and complexity of the concept, even at this comparatively early stage of its development, are suggested by the ironic use that Aeschylus makes of it here.

[9] Kitto, 6, 14; Rose, *ad* 991–95. E. T. Owen (*The Harmony of Aeschylus* [Toronto, 1952], 17) suggests a dramatic purpose for Danaus' preaching: it is a method of suggesting the continuing theme of trouble to come. Cf. Richmond Lattimore (*The Poetry of Greek Tragedy* [Baltimore, 1958], 14) on the inconsistent characterization of Danaus in the first and second plays of the trilogy.

From their first appearance in the parodos, the Danaids show themselves to be passionate, determined, and excitable—as emotional, in fact, as the Chorus of the *Persians*. Danaus' first speech is wholly concerned with the modesty, propriety, and humility befitting strangers and suppliants. Their words must be modest (αἰδοῖα [194]); audacity (τὸ θρασύ) must not attend their speech (197); nothing vain must proceed from their modest countenances (ἐκ μετωποσωφρόνων [198]),[10] and they are to remember that bold speech does not befit the weak (203). The keynote is struck in the first line (176): "Children, you must be prudent [φρονεῖν]. With your prudent [φρονοῦντι] father you have come." It is echoed with deceptive meekness by the girls' response (204): "Father, prudently [φρονούντως] and to the prudent [φρονοῦντας] do you speak." *Phronein* and *sôphronein* are identical in meaning, here as in the *Agamemnon* (176–81). Later Danaus sums up the content of his advice to his daughters when he bids them receive his current admonition and add it to the many other *sôphronismata* ("prudent counsels") of their father (992). *Sôphronein* has the precise significance of "preserve chastity or modesty" only once —at the end of Danaus' speech when he returns to his daughters with the promise of asylum in Argos. In twenty lines of exhortation he reminds them that their beauty is a temptation to men, and that they must not be a source of shame to themselves and him and of gratification to their enemies. "Only," he concludes (1012–13), "pay attention to these commands of your father, honoring chastity [*sôphronein*] more than life." *Sôphronein* is here for the first time used to describe the behavior proper to unmarried women.

The remaining allusions to sophrosyne also occur in a speech of Danaus, which looks backward to the prayer of the girls for Argos and forward to the approach of the Egyptians. Danaus commends the prayer in these words (710): "I praise these *sôphrones* prayers of yours." His use of *sôphrones,* however, underlines the irony of the situation because, while the theme of the benediction is fertility and peace, the Danaids, as Murray observes, not only "destroy peace by their slaughter of the Egyptians, but in refusing motherhood . . . renounce fertility in favor of sterility." [11] In the following lines Danaus orders the girls to face the Egyptian threat calmly and with self-control (ἡσύχως . . . σεσωφρονισμένως), not unmindful of the gods (724–25). The association of sophrosyne with the gods is again typical of the Aeschylean concep-

---

[10] See Rose, *ad loc.,* reading ἐν μέτρῳ 'πὸ σωφρόνων (Gilbert Murray) instead of Porsen's conjecture μετωποσωφρόνων for the MS μετώ πω σωφρονῶν.

[11] R. D. Murray, Jr., *op. cit.,* 81.

tion of the virtue. Zeus and Artemis—pure (ἀγνά) daughter of Zeus (144–45)—are the gods invoked by the Danaids themselves: Zeus in several capacities (as their ancestor, as the god of suppliants, as the protector of justice) and Artemis, significantly, as the guardian of virgins (1030–32).

Hazardous though it is to reconstruct the outcome of the trilogy, it is an attractive conjecture that the love of Hypermnestra for Lynceus brings harmony and fertility out of the hatred and repugnance of the Danaids for the Egyptians. The Danaids' attitude in this first play, while easy to understand (especially after the entrance of the herald), is essentially unbalanced in its hatred of marriage, and throughout the play it is clear that the violence is not all on one side.[12] The clue to the development of the trilogy comes at the end of the first play in speeches assigned variously by different editors. Whether they represent an exchange between two groups of Danaids or between the Danaids as a unit and a group of maidservants is immaterial to our argument. What matters is that several traditional allusions to the danger of excess are worked into the dialogue. The warning (1059), "Utter a prayer that is moderate [μέτριον] now," is followed by the question (1060), "What limit [καιρόν] do you teach me?" And the response comes back (1061), "No excess [μηδὲν ἀγάζειν] in what concerns the gods." This interchange —coming close upon a song that praises Aphrodite and Hera, in pointed contrast to earlier prayers to Artemis—forecasts the direction to be taken by the remainder of the trilogy.

The position of Danaus between the *hybris* of the Egyptians and the more subtle denial of sophrosyne by his daughters illustrates the pattern that Aeschylus also uses in the *Septem,* where Eteocles at first is a Mean between the various kinds of immoderate behavior on the part of the chorus of Theban women and the attacking Argives. The impact of the situation is less concentrated in the *Suppliants* than in the *Septem,* however, because the sophrosyne of Danaus himself is never an issue, nor is his own fate a matter of concern in the first part of the trilogy. The tragic figure caught between the two extremes is actually Pelasgos; and although he may be considered a spokesman for Hellenic restraint—as in his remark that his city likes brevity of speech (272)—it makes little difference to his fate whether he is *sôphrôn* or not, since his tragedy is one of situa-

---

[12] The Danaids are violent in their threat to defile the sanctuary (465), and they will ultimately commit the supreme act of violence by murdering their husbands. Hence the irony noted by R. D. Murray, Jr., in Danaus' speech (498–99): *thrasos* is indeed destined to bring forth *phobos,* and the Danaids will each kill someone *philos* in their ignorance of their true destiny.

tion rather than of character. In the *Septem,* however, the character of Eteocles and his possession—or lack—of sophrosyne are of first importance.

Several of the themes related to sophrosyne which appear in the *Persians* and the *Suppliants* recur in the *Septem* and are handled with increasing subtlety and effectiveness. Like the *Persians,* the play involves a contrast between a *sôphrôn,* pious community engaged in self-defense and an attacking force that is exactly the opposite—hybristic, impious, and aggressive. So far the Thebans and the Argives correspond to the Greeks and the Persians, but this time justice is not all on one side, as the device on Polyneices' shield (645 ff.) reminds us. This time, too, the positive merits of the defenders are set forth more explicitly, and the *hybris* of the attackers shows certain new features.

The second familiar theme, this time linking the *Septem* with the *Suppliants* rather than with the *Persians,* is that of male versus female: the male represents not only courage and resolution but also sophrosyne, while the female represents excessive emotion, in this instance fear. When Eteocles rebukes the Chorus, whose terror fills the early part of the play with the wildest emotion, we are reminded of Danaus' speeches to his daughters. Just as Danaus' major concern was to enjoin sophrosyne upon them, so Eteocles tells the Theban girls that they are hateful to *sôphrôn* folk (186). Yet there is a difference. By *sôphrôn* Danaus meant "modest, discreet" as well as "calm, well-behaved," but Eteocles constantly exhorts the Chorus to control itself and restrain its terror. The Theban girls are even more excited than the Danaids (as their use of dochmiacs for the parodos indicates), and Eteocles is much stronger in his condemnation, which he extends to the entire feminine sex (188). Woman, whether in a position of power ($\kappa\rho\alpha\tau o\hat{v}\sigma\alpha$) or in a state of terror ($\delta\epsilon i\sigma\alpha\sigma\alpha$), is *kakon* (190).

As has been pointed out, the offenses against sophrosyne—*hybris* and unrestrained emotionalism—which in the *Persians* were both displayed by the barbarians, are in the *Septem* divided between the attacking Argives, who are *hybris* personified, and the frantic women. Eteocles, who must seek to control both types of excess, is a Mean between the extremes; and Aeschylus makes him the true center of interest, not only in the larger issues of the drama, but even in the contrast between sophrosyne and *hybris*. Instead of being, like the Danaids, superficially *sôphrôn,* in one sense of the word, and at the same time violent and unbalanced, he is at first completely *sôphrôn* and then suddenly, when the Erinys strikes, completely the reverse. Up to verse 653 Eteocles is entirely rational, self-controlled, and—like the ideal king of the fourth-century philosophers—a source of self-control for his subjects. After he learns that Polyneices is to attack the seventh gate, he leaps to the conclusion that he must meet his brother there, and he loses control of himself. Now he is in turn exhorted to sophrosyne by the Chorus. It urges him not to be like Polyneices in anger (ὀργήν [678]) but to resist infatuation (ἄτα [687]), and it speaks of his evil desire (κακοῦ ἔρωτος [687–88]) and fiercely gnawing passion (ὠμοδακής . . . ἵμερος [692]). The Coryphaeus even alludes to the theme of male versus female, bidding Eteocles (712): "Obey the women, though it goes against the grain"—an oblique indication that the roles are now reversed. From this point on, the Chorus will be the spokesman for sophrosyne.[13]

The fate of Eteocles is not identical with that of Thebes, for he is destroyed while the city is saved. The reason for this contrast is not, as we are sometimes told,[14] that Eteocles sacrifices himself for the city, but rather that the city continues to act with sophrosyne, whereas Eteocles before our very eyes rejects this virtue. His transition from sophrosyne to *mania* and *kakos erôs* is the first manifestation of his helplessness before the power of the Erinys. Thebes, on the other hand, is saved because its cause is just and its champions are as *sôphrones* as the attackers are hybristic.[15] The contrast is emphasized through the arresting device used in the great central scene between Eteocles and the scout, in which the individual attackers are named and described, and their opponents selected, in accordance with *dikê* and *prepon*. The aspect of Argive *hybris* which Aeschylus chooses to stress is the boastfulness of all save Amphiaraus. Some form of the root of *kompein* ("to boast") is used with reference to each of the other attackers. Tydeus raves with his boastful (ὑπερκόμποις) trappings (391). Capaneus—ὁ κόμπος—does not think mortal thoughts (425). The very chariot mares of Eteoclus make barbarous noises, filling their muzzle gear with the breath from their proud nostrils (μυκτεροκόμποις [464]). In the person of Hippomedon, Phobos vaunts himself (κομπάζεται) at the gate (500). Not without a boast (ἀκόμπαστος) does Parthenius take his stand (538). Polyneices himself shouts threats (639–42). In the case of the defenders the reverse is true: Melanippus hates boastful words (410); Megareus lets his two hands do his bragging (473); Actor is not

[13] See Friedrich Solmsen, *T.A.P.A.* 68 (1937), 199 ff.

[14] E.g., Finley, 244 ff.; Snell, 87. For a summary of the arguments bearing on this question, see H. Lloyd-Jones, *C.Q.,* N.S. 9 (1959), 88–92.

[15] This is the answer to the question asked by Lloyd-Jones (*loc. cit.,* 89) about why Thebes escapes the curse.

boastful (ἄκομπος [554]). Why does Aeschylus stress this aspect of *hybris* and virtually ignore the other facets that are prominent in the *Persians?* The answer may perhaps lie in the emphasis placed throughout the trilogy on the power of words. The words of Apollo to Laius, the curse of Oedipus on his sons, the statement of Eteocles in the first line of the *Septem* that it is the duty of the king to say what the moment demands (λέγειν τὰ καίρια), the cries and lamentations of the Chorus which Eteocles points out will endanger the city (191–95), and now the boasts of the attackers—all are part of the same pervading pattern.[16]

By a bold stroke of the imagination Aeschylus mirrors the *hybris* of the attackers in their shields. It is as though the boasts that portend the destruction of the Argives were made tangible by being translated into blazons.[17] All the devices are highly symbolic. Tydeus has the heavens ablaze with stars and in the center the moon, which the scout calls an insolent device (387); Capaneus has a man brandishing a torch and promising to burn the town (432–34); Eteoclus, a man in armor climbing a scaling ladder and defying Ares to hurl him down (466–69); Hippomedon, the fire-breathing Typhon (493); Parthenopaeus, the Sphinx, a special taunt to Thebes (541); and, crowning irony, Polyneices has a figure of Dikê, advancing σωφρόνως ("modestly") and leading a warrior (645 ff.). Only Amphiaraus carries a shield without a blazon, a symbol of his desire, not to seem, but to be *aristos* (591–92).

The seer, who is posted at the sixth gate and is therefore mentioned just before Polyneices, is a figure of special significance, morally and dramatically both a parallel and a contrast to Eteocles. As a parallel he shares Eteocles' piety and sophrosyne; he stands to the *hybristic* attackers as Eteocles does to Polyneices. But he contrasts with Eteocles also, for in the face of certain knowledge that he is doomed to die, he maintains his self-control and always speaks and acts as a rational being. Eteocles recognizes an omen in the presence of this *dikaios anêr* among the impious (598) and thus implies that he feels akin to the seer. Like Eteocles in his rebuke to the excited women, Amphiaraus reproaches Tydeus and Polyneices for their acts of *hybris* (571 ff.). The scout specifically describes him as an ἄνδρα σωφρονέστατον (568), and Eteocles praises him as a σώφρων, δίκαιος, ἀγαθός, εὐσεβὴς ἀνήρ (610).[18] *Sôphrôn* in both passages

---

[16] Owen (*op. cit.* 41 ff.) discusses the tragedy in terms of the efficacy of words.

[17] The audience sees them only in the mind's eye. Presumably the shields of the champions are visible; Aeschylus does not describe them, except in the case of Hyperbius (512–14). The devices on the shields of the Seven described by Euripides in the *Phoenissae* are quite different and are not so much hybristic as designed to terrify.

[18] This is the second recorded allusion to a canon of four cardinal virtues. *Eusebeia* ("piety")

has the primary meaning of "modest" (opposed to *hybris*), for here lies
the contrast between the seer and his companions; but the intellectual
aspect of the word is still operative. The opponents whom Eteocles
is bidden to find are to be intelligent and honorable (σοφούς τε κἀγαθούς
[595]), and the one actually chosen is Lasthenes, whom Eteocles describes as mature in mind (γέροντα τὸν νοῦν [622]). Eteocles underscores
the likeness between Amphiaraus and himself by saying that the seer is
wont to be silent or to say what the moment demands (λέγειν τὰ καίρια
[619]),[19] the very phrase that he has already used to describe his own
function as king. At this point Eteocles is still *sôphrôn* (both self-controlled
and sound-minded)—as his meditation upon the difference between
Amphiaraus' character and his fortune reveals—but he does not realize
that his gnomic statement (601), "The harvest of *atê* is death," will
so quickly be proved true in his own case.[20]

   The emphasis laid upon the impious defiance of the gods by six of the
attackers and the contrasting reverence of Amphiaraus (as well as the
appeals of the Thebans to the gods) indicates that the chief significance
of the *hybris*-sophrosyne theme is still religious. The *hybris* of the Argives
resides mainly in their failure to "think mortal thoughts" and their confidence that the gods cannot stop them—not Ares nor even the thunderbolt of Zeus. The defenders, naturally, are models of *eusebeia*. Melanippus
honors *Aischynê* (Compunction) and is urged on by *Dikê*. Polyphontes is
a favorite of Artemis. Hyperbius has on his shield Zeus, who always defeats Typhon. Athene will ward off Hippomedon because she hates his
hybris (501–3). Amphiaraus seems especially dangerous precisely because
he alone of the attackers is *eusebês* (596): "Dangerous is he who fears the
gods." It is the Olympians, the rewarders of justice and sophrosyne,
who rescue Thebes, in spite of the king's death. The connection between

---

has as good a claim as *phronêsis* or *sophia* to a place in the original canon and is here more
appropriate than either, because Amphiaraus' one failure is in respect to prudence (βίᾳ
φρενῶν [612]). His reputation for sophrosyne is referred to by Euripides *Hyps.*, Frag. 12. 229–
31, 236 Page, and *Phoen.* 1112. For Amphiaraus as an exemplar of sophrosyne in Roman
imperial times, see Julian *Letter to a Priest* 303C. Cf. also Erwin Wolff, *Platos Apologie* (Berlin,
1929), 77 ff.

   [19] This phrase is sometimes applied to Apollo or even to Lasthenes, but the parallel with
Eteocles makes it likely that it belongs to Amphiaraus after all.

   [20] Finley (244) would take the parallel between Eteocles and the seer even further. He believes that the assertiveness of the heroic mind is checked, "against their will in Capaneus and
the other Argives, consciously and of their own choice in Eteocles and Amphiaraus. This return from the delusive freedom of heroic assertiveness to the bonds of earth, community, and
true freedom creates a final accord between Eteocles and the women." This interpretation
depends on the theory that Eteocles sacrifices himself and thereby saves the city; for this there
is no evidence in the play.

eusebeia and sophrosyne is strongly marked both in this play and in the *Oresteia*, where it again effects the salvation of a city.

In the *Prometheus Bound* the themes of freedom and sophrosyne, so closely allied in the *Persians* and the *Septem*, are for once divorced, and all who advocate sophrosyne are to some degree enslaved, while the champion of freedom rejects all counsels of moderation.[21] What Aeschylus intended to make of this situation remains mysterious, but the reconstruction of the trilogy which has won most favor in recent years [22] is that in which the brutal and tyrannical Zeus, newly enthroned and therefore harsh in the first play, will himself learn sophrosyne, just as Prometheus will be persuaded to restrain his bitterness and hate, and the two will ultimately be reconciled. In the surviving play the traditional antitheses to sophrosyne are about equally divided between Prometheus and Zeus,[23] but the sympathy of the audience is powerfully engaged on the side of the Titan. Whatever could be said in favor of Zeus later in the trilogy, almost everything in the first play speaks against him. The *hybris* ("violence, lust") which he displays towards Io inevitably recalls that of the Egyptians in their pursuit of the Danaids (except for the assurance of ultimate release and reward for Io—a pointer towards the solution). Zeus is ungrateful, suspicious, and violent, corresponding precisely to the familiar stereotype of the tyrant in the fifth century. But Prometheus, too, with his arrogant self-assertion, his steadily increasing contempt for all restraint, and his refusal to recognize the realities of the situation, clearly violates sophrosyne—as the Chorus, Oceanus, and Hermes in turn suggest, when they urge him to curb excess (178–80, 507) and learn to know himself (309) or to acquire *euboulia* ("good judgment" [1035]) and sophrosyne (983). The doctrine of *Pathei mathos* is implied for both Zeus (982) and Prometheus (1000),[24] and the use that Aeschylus

---

[21] Snell (145) suggests that Aeschylus in *P.V.* has reached the point where he values *to meson* more than *eleutheria*. Without certainty about the remainder of the trilogy, it is difficult to predict what will become of the theme of *eleutheria*, but the attitude of Athene towards the Mean in government in the *Eumenides* supports Snell's theory. The skolion referred to earlier (p. 34) reminds us that freedom and sophrosyne could be linked in the popular imagination as well as in the thought of Aeschylus.

[22] The list of those who accept a solution along these lines includes Wilamowitz, Nilsson, Festugière, Dodds, Kitto, and Solmsen. For a different view, see H. Lloyd-Jònes, *J.H.S.* 76 (1956), 55–67. Rose (9–10) denies the very existence of a Prometheus trilogy, suggesting instead that Aeschylus produced in Syracuse, where the requirements of the Attic festivals did not apply, a *Prometheia* consisting of the extant play and a *Prometheus Unbound*.

[23] *Authadia, thrasos, cholos, hybris,* and *chlidê* are especially prominent.

[24] On Zeus as tyrant, consult George Thomson, *Aeschylus and Athens* (London, 1950) 322. On the need for Zeus to learn sophrosyne, as well as the probable role of Athene in reconciling the rebel and the tyrant, see Thomson's reconstruction of the trilogy in the introduction to his edition of *Prometheus Bound* (Cambridge, 1932), 12–38.

makes of this solution to the problem of suffering in the *Oresteia* suggests
a comparable outcome here. The sophrosyne that must emerge before
Zeus and Prometheus can be reconciled will not, it may be supposed, be
the cautious prudence urged by Oceanus and Hermes (311, 983),[25] but
a self-knowledge and restraint worthy of the cosmic dignity of the Titan
and the king of the gods—something like the sophrosyne with justice
which Athene evokes in the name of Zeus at the conclusion of the *Oresteia.*

The treatment of sophrosyne in the *Oresteia* brings together all the
major themes that we have noted in the earlier plays: freedom versus
tyranny, male versus female, restraint versus *hybris.* The religious basis
of the virtue is still prominent, especially its connection with *eusebeia;* but
at the conclusion of the trilogy Aeschylus takes a long step forward and
relates sophrosyne to the life of the *polis,* doubtless because he perceived
how much Athens herself depended on the sophrosyne of her citizens.
Allusions to sophrosyne in a political context are still extremely rare for
Athens; the *Oresteia* (458 B.C.) is in fact our major source for the middle
of the fifth century. It may be that in spite of the connection established
between sophrosyne and freedom at the time of the Persian wars, this
virtue still carried predominantly aristocratic overtones for Athenians.
Perhaps after the reforms of Ephialtes, which introduced sharp and
continuing political conflict (Plutarch *Pericles* 7. 8), *sôphrôn* became
something of a "dirty word" for self-conscious democrats (rather like our
"sound," which is noncommittal in general use but politically implies
"conservative"). Only after the revolutions towards the close of the fifth
century exposed oligarchic pretensions to sophrosyne as false did the word
sôphrôn become available to the democrats (who regularly claim it as their
characteristic excellence in fourth-century oratory). An epigraphic allusion to sophrosyne in the mid-fifth century (in the Miletus decree of *ca.*
450–449) is difficult to interpret because the immediate context is lost,
but the words ἐὰν δὲ σοφρονῶ⟨σι (line 82) may be a warning to the
oligarchs in Miletus that they will receive Athenian support so long as
they display what they claim as the characteristic virtue of oligarchy—
sophrosyne.[26]

---

[25] Oceanus is the earliest example in tragedy of an ignoble sophrosyne. Lloyd-Jones
(*J.H.S.* 76 [1956], 66) is unique among recent critics in finding a kind word to say for him.
Snell considers his speech at verse 385 the "bankruptcy" of classical sophrosyne.

[26] The Miletus decree (*I.G.* 1 2 22 = *A.T.L.* II D 11) has been brought to my attention by
Russell Meiggs, who tentatively suggests that Miletus was at this time (450–449 B.C.) under
an oligarchy. He points out that the quota lists suggest a revolt from Athens in the mid-fifties
and the recovery of Miletus in 453, and he links this episode with the statement of the Old
Oligarch (*Ath. Pol.* 3. 11) that Athens once supported an oligarchy in Miletus. Since the de-

In the absence of other evidence for sophrosyne as an Athenian *aretê politikê* at this period, the *Oresteia* is doubly precious. At the conclusion of the trilogy sophrosyne ("moderation") emerges as the force that will save the *polis* from the two extremes of anarchy and despotism, and it is specifically designated as the characteristic virtue of Athens. This sophrosyne is not a "class" virtue but obviously owes much to Solon's middle way, and, as in Solon's political elegy, moderation and justice go hand in hand. In the *Agamemnon* the kinship of sophrosyne and justice (implied in the *Suppliants* and the *Septem*) is firmly established by the interweaving of the two virtues in the choral odes on which depends the moral atmosphere of the entire trilogy. Furthermore, the connection of sophrosyne with the doctrine of *Pathei mathos* becomes explicit in these same odes, which give out a theme to be echoed in the *Eumenides*. The key passage (176–81) first praises Zeus for setting mankind on the road to wisdom (φρονεῖν) and establishing the validity of the principle "Learn by suffering," and then immediately adds that σωφρονεῖν comes to men against their will (παρ' ἄκοντας).[27] The second part of the statement explicates the first.

---

cree is two years later than the "liberation," Meiggs infers that the first settlement has not been satisfactory and that Athens now needs to take stronger action, including the installation of a garrison and a political resident. He thinks that Miletus is still being governed by oligarchs, and sees in the words quoted a warning that Athens will be generous towards Miletus only if the oligarchs display sophrosyne (moderation or good sense?). Meiggs emphasizes, however, that there is no evidence that the decree represents a second stage of Athenian interference, or that the language of the decree necessarily indicates a Milesian oligarchy. A later date (426–425) for the decree, suggested by H. B. Mattingly (*Historia* 10 [1961], 174–81) is convincingly refuted by Meiggs (*H.S.C.P.* 67 [1963], 24–25).

[27] This passage—especially the doctrine of *Pathei mathos* and sophrosyne—has recently been attacked from two directions. Lloyd-Jones (*C.Q.* 6 [1956], 62 ff.) maintains that it embodies only a primitive conception of Zeus, entirely within the framework of the theology of Hesiod, and complains that the victims of the "law" in the *Oresteia* are not purified or ennobled but are merely killed, and that others learn from their death nothing but the uselessness of defying Zeus' law. See also, along these lines, J. D. Denniston and Denys Page, *Aeschylus, Agamemnon* (Oxford, 1957), xv, xxiii–xxix, 85–86. T. G. Rosenmeyer (*A.J.P.* 76 [1955], 225–60) makes the more radical suggestion that for Aeschylus the gods are no more than a *mise en scène*, an instrument of the poet's *apatê*, and therefore whatever Aeschylus says about Zeus in this ode has only a dramatic, not a religious, importance (256): "The recapitulation of the developments at Aulis is momentarily interrupted, at the point of Agamemnon's hopeless decision, to evoke a false picture of security in Zeus, and to underscore the enigma of the universal order, while at the same time holding out such make-believe panaceas as sophrosyne and the like." Rosenmeyer, too, complains that the victim never has a real choice (255): "Pathei mathos and know thyself are useless if the human agent is placed in a dilemma which leaves him no scope for restraint." But it is wrong to assume that Agamemnon had no choice, and it is unfair to Aeschylus to charge him with evoking "a false picture of security in Zeus" at this point in the tragedy. As Kitto observes ("Idea of God," 183 ff.),

In this passage *phronein* and *sôphronein* have substantially the same meaning: "understanding, wisdom, soundness of mind"—paraphrased by ὑγίεια φρενῶν ("health of mind") in the *Eumenides* (535–36). The source of this wisdom that comes to men even against their will (παρ' ἄκοντας being equivalent to *pathei*) is Zeus, or his daughter Dikê (Δίκα δὲ τοῖς μὲν παθοῦσιν μαθεῖν ἐπιρρέπει—" Justice allots wisdom to those who have suffered" [*Ag.* 250]), or in the final dispensation his ministers, the Eumenides (ξυμφέρει σωφρονεῖν ὑπὸ στένει—"It is advantageous to learn wisdom under stress" [*Eum.* 520–21]). The wisdom thus divinely instilled is the wisdom that controls *hybris* (or θρασύτης, often its equivalent in the *Agamemnon*[28]) and teaches man to observe the limits imposed by his own nature, the gods, or the *polis*. Connected with the theme of learning through suffering is that of late learning. When this appears in the *Agamemnon*—in the threats of Clytemnestra and Aegisthus to the Chorus (1425, 1620)—it contains no deeper significance than is customary in the gnomic tradition, and *sôphronein* means no more than "prudence"; but the σωφρονοῦντες ἐν χρόνῳ of the *Eumenides* 1000 is freighted with the *Pathei mathos* doctrine and with prophecies of Athenian destiny.[29]

The opposition between sophrosyne and *hybris* is prominent in the *Agamemnon*, where the *hybris* is chiefly that of Agamemnon himself and is symbolized by the blood-red carpet.[30] He realizes that to tread on the carpet is to tread sophrosyne underfoot, for he says (927–28): "Not to be unsound of mind [τὸ μὴ κακῶς φρονεῖν] is the best gift of God." But after his death our attention switches to the *hybris*, violence, and adultery of Clytemnestra and Aegisthus. That they have established conditions under which sophrosyne cannot exist is evident from the prayer of the Chorus in the second play (786), "that things may work out for those who wish

---

Aeschylus does not say in this ode that Zeus is all-wise, for at the moment he is not. What he does say is that Zeus has made wisdom possible: "Out of your suffering wisdom may come." It seems inescapable that society, as represented by Orestes and the Athenians, has actually achieved a higher degree of wisdom at the end of the trilogy than Agamemnon and Clytemnestra possessed at the beginning; this result justifies the doctrine of *Pathei mathos*. The gods also learn wisdom ἐν χρόνῳ, and not only the Erinyes but Zeus himself advances in morality in the course of the trilogy. See Eduard Fraenkel, *Aeschylus, Agamemnon* (Oxford, 1950), ad 176, for the "much higher plane of ideas" arrived at by Aeschylus than that found in the gnomic tradition. The implications of the *Pathei mathos* doctrine for this passage and for *P.V.* have been studied by Heinrich Dörrie, *Leid und Erfahrung* (Mainz, 1956), 324–30.

[28] E.g., 168, 222, 769 (*Thrasos*, the child of *Hybris*), 1399, 1437, 1671.

[29] That cities as well as individuals learn by suffering is evident from verses 709–11.

[30] See Goheen, *loc. cit.*, 128 ff., for a discussion of the imagery in this scene and its relation to the past *hybris* of Agamemnon and the fresh *hybris* of Clytemnestra.

to see τὰ σώφρονα." In the latter part of the *Agamemnon* the subsidiary theme of sophrosyne versus tyranny (already seen in the *Persians*) reappears. A tyranny has been set up in Argos, and the threats of Clytemnestra and Aegisthus reveal their tyrannical nature. Hence a prominent theme of the *Choephoroi* is freeing the city from the tyrants and establishing freedom, justice, and sophrosyne; this theme in turn leads to the political solution in the *Eumenides*. A link between the *Oresteia* and the *Prometheus* is the tendency of both to conclude that sophrosyne, while incompatible with tyranny, is also incompatible with unrestrained self-assertion on the part of those who are ruled. In the *Prometheus* neither Zeus the tyrant nor Prometheus the defiant rebel is *sôphrôn*, while in the *Oresteia* we learn that both despotism and anarchy are hateful to the spirit of the Mean.

The motive of masculine versus feminine appears in the *Oresteia* in a form less simple than in earlier tragedies. The feminine element is represented no longer by a chorus of terrified women, but rather by the towering figure of Clytemnestra, who violates sophrosyne in a new way. Aeschylus has now turned from the δείσασα to the κρατοῦσα woman (*Septem* 189–90). Clytemnestra's offense against sophrosyne takes the obvious form of adultery and the less obvious form of upsetting the proper order of society by her murder of her husband, which subjects Argos to the rule of a woman—or rather, of two women (*Choeph.* 304–5). References to feminine characteristics in the *Agamemnon* are uniformly derogatory: women are credulous, led by their emotions to believe what they wish to believe (483, 592), and they are luxurious (ἄβρυνε [918], connected with *hybris* [1205]).[31] The Chorus devotes a long ode to the evil deeds of women (1455 ff.), and finally Aegisthus, the adulterer and usurper, is addressed by the Chorus as γύναι (1625).[32] That sophrosyne is a masculine trait is implied when the Chorus says to Clytemnestra (351): "Woman, you speak prudently like a man of sense [κατ' ἄνδρα σώφρονα]." The *Choephoroi* adds something to our knowledge of sophrosyne in this context. Again, the Chorus sings a significant ode about the behavior of women in the grip of passion (585–651). Althaea, Scylla, and the women of Lemnos are mentioned, but the Chorus clearly has Clytemnestra in mind. Hence the earlier prayer of Electra is enlightening: she asks that she may be σωφρονεστέρα and εὐσεβεστέρα ("more

---

31 On ἀβρότης and χλιδή in Aeschylus and Pindar, see Snell, 81.

32 For the view that γύναι ("woman") is addressed to Aegisthus, see Fraenkel, *op. cit.*, and Denniston and Page, *op. cit.* The effeminacy of Aegisthus is indicated in *Choeph.* 305; his cowardice in *Ag.* 1224.

pure and pious") than her mother (140–41). The plea for purity indicates the difference in motive and therefore in moral status between the acts of Electra and Clytemnestra and marks an important step in the development of the religious ideas expressed in the trilogy.

The *Eumenides* brings the conflict of male versus female to a surprising climax in the debate before the Areopagus about the true parentage of the child. This debate has no explicit connection with sophrosyne but leads towards the solution of the moral chaos in the earlier plays of the trilogy. The acceptance of the masculine principle advocated by Apollo and approved by Athene (however illogical the grounds) reasserts the order that was upset when Clytemnestra murdered Agamemnon and gave Argos a tyrant in his stead—reasserts it, however, on a higher plane where justice and sophrosyne are both at work.[33]

The final scene before the Areopagus demonstrates the need for sophrosyne in human society and does so by recourse to the theme of fear, restated in terms of awe and reverence (*sebas, deinon, deos*), which awaken echoes of the "*phobos*-motive" prominent in the *Agamemnon*. In that play an atmosphere of dread and foreboding was established by the watchman in the prologue when he said that *phobos* ("fear") stood beside him, in place of sleep (14). The Chorus deepened the note of fear with its ominous hints of evil and danger (as in 100, 121, 253, 459–60), until Cassandra made all but tangible the terror that hung over the house of Atreus. There is a close link between sophrosyne and the theme of *phobos* in other plays of Aeschylus,[34] but the relation is usually one of opposition: terrified women (the Danaids, the Thebans) are urged by Danaus or Eteocles to be *sôphrones*, that is, to control their terror. In the *Prometheus* the relation is equivocal: fear of the unjust and violent Zeus gives rise to an unheroic sophrosyne in Oceanus and Hermes. In the *Choephoroi* fear is again personified at the very end, when Orestes, surrounded by the Furies, cries out (1024–25): "At my heart *Phobos* is ready to sing and dance with wrath," and the Chorus bids him not give way to fear (1052), an injunction echoed by Apollo near the beginning of the *Eumenides* (88). Obviously the Furies are linked with *phobos*, and Apollo represents deliverance from fear.

In the *Eumenides* the Furies make their case for maintaining fear as guardian of the heart (517 ff.). It is advantageous to learn wisdom under stress: ξυμφέρει σωφρονεῖν ὑπὸ στένει (520–21), an echo of *Ag.*

---

[33] See Kitto, "Idea of God," 186.

[34] Consult Snell for the development of this theme and the relation of *phobos* to sophrosyne in the *Eumenides*.

180–81. Neither anarchy nor despotism should be praised, for God has assigned power to the Mean in every way (526–30). *Hybris* is the child of impiety, from ὑγίεια φρενῶν comes happiness, and reverence leads to justice, as piety and *aidôs* lead to prosperity (533 ff.). This speech brings fear (*deinon, deos*) within the range of *sebas* ("reverence") and *aidôs* (525, 533, 546 ff.) and thereby begins the rehabilitation of *phobos*, so that it, too, may find a place in the new dispensation. That the position of the Furies has some justification and is, indeed, essential for the welfare of Athens is confirmed when Athene quotes what they have said. On the Areopagus, she asserts, *Sebas* and its kinsman, *Phobos*, shall prevent the Athenians from doing wrong by night or day (690–92). The townsmen should revere (*sebein*) neither anarchy nor despotism, nor banish utterly what is terrifying (*deinon*). *Sebas* is a bulwark for the country and the city such as neither the Scythians nor the Peloponnesians possess. The Scythians evidently represent anarchy, the Spartans despotism; by implication, the Athenians typify the Mean.[35]

When the Furies have consented to renounce their bitter resentment and become kindly goddesses, their benediction to the Athenians (comparable to the *sôphrones* prayers of the Danaids for Argos) visualizes the citizens seated beside Zeus, beloved by Athene, learning wisdom in time (σωφρονοῦντες ἐν χρόνῳ [1000]). Here is the true outcome of the doctrine of *Pathei mathos:* the establishment of sophrosyne with justice as the foundation stones of the Athenian *polis,* and the union of sophrosyne with reverence to achieve the Mean in government. *Phobos* has been made acceptable, just as *Peithô* (Persuasion), who was entirely evil and deceitful in the *Agamemnon,* becomes in the *Eumenides* a beneficent and wholesome power wielded by Athene, appropriately enough, in the first Athenian law court.[36] She even connects the two, when she bids the Furies hold sacred the *Peithous sebas* ("reverence for Persuasion" [885]) and give up their wrath. The gods themselves, we note—not just mankind—have learned sophrosyne ἐν χρόνῳ. Apollo, the first spokesman for Zeus, was the instigator of murder in the *Agamemnon* and the *Choephoroi* and was intemperate and abusive towards the older powers in the

---

35 Solmsen (*Hesiod,* 121, n. 70, and p. 209) finds the beginning of this contrast between governmental extremes in Solon 5. 7 ff. He compares Plato *Laws* III (693E ff., 697C, 698A ff., 701E), where, however, Persia represents the extreme of despotism; Athens, excessive freedom; and Sparta and Crete, *ta metria.*

36 On the conversion of *Peithô,* see Solmsen, *Hesiod,* 136, 200; Thomson, *Aeschylus and Athens,* 293–94; Owen, *op. cit.,* 129; and Goheen, *loc. cit.,* 130. F. M. Cornford (*Plato's Cosmology* [London, 1937], 361–64) finds analogies between the *Eumenides* and the *Timaeus,* including the role of *Peithô* in both.

Eumenides. The Furies themselves were foul daemons who delighted in human blood. But Athene, who persuades the old to join hands with the new and speaks for Zeus at the end of the process of reconciliation, is gracious to the older goddesses (881–84), a loving guardian over her people (927–28), and herself the perfect exemplar of *sebas, peithô,* and sophrosyne. The theme of reconciliation originates with Hesiod, but it is Aeschylus who first gives to sophrosyne a role in this process.

SOPHOCLES

In Sophoclean tragedy the conflict between *hybris* and sophrosyne no longer occupies the center of the stage. As Jaeger and others have observed,[37] this Aeschylean subject has retreated to the periphery, along with the corresponding theme of suffering as the punishment for guilt. To Sophocles the object of primary interest is not the deed but the doer, and in his tragedies suffering is likely to be either disproportionate to its cause or totally undeserved. As a result of this shift of interest both *hybris* and sophrosyne present different aspects from those found in Aeschylus. *Hybris* is more often an offense against human standards than an affront to the gods. The remark in the *Trachiniae* (280) that the *daimones* also hate *hybris* is significant, for it implies that naturally and primarily *hybris* offends mortals.[38] Sophrosyne, too, is more remote from its religious bases than in Aeschylus; except in the *Ajax,* its motives spring from the relations between man and man, rather than between man and god. Furthermore, the poet's interest in character leads him to emphasize the relation of sophrosyne to the other elements in a complex soul, rather than to concentrate on a situation in which sophrosyne has been violated. There is a noticeable increase in the variety of meanings attached to the words *sôphron* and *sôphronein* in Sophocles[39]—a reflection, no doubt, of contemporary usage; but on the whole it may be said that sophrosyne now tends to be intellectual in its implications, although the moral aspect is prominent in the *Ajax* and never wholly disappears. In terms of the Delphic proverbs, Sophoclean sophrosyne leans towards *Gnôthi sauton* rather than *Mêden agan.*

For the *hybris*-sophrosyne conflict of Aeschylus, Sophocles substitutes

---

[37] *Paideia,* I. 282–83; Kitto, 142. See Del Grande, 131–48, on the different dramatic treatment of *hybris* in Aeschylus and Sophocles.

[38] Cf. Opstelten, *Sophocles and Greek Pessimism* (Amsterdam, 1952), 69.

[39] In Sophocles, as in Aeschylus, the noun sophrosyne is lacking. Only thirteen related words are used in the extant tragedies: the adjective *sôphron* appears four times; the adverb *sôphronôs* once; and the verb *sôphronein* eight times. Consult Friedrich Ellendt, *Lexicon Sophocleum* (Berlin, 1872). Fragments in which the word *sôphrôn* appears are discussed in n. 88 below.

the struggle between the demands of the heroic nature (the *eugenês*) and the limitations imposed even on the hero by the realities of human life.[40] In the typical Sophoclean situation the central figure, who towers above ordinary beings and cherishes a noble standard of conduct to which he will sacrifice everything else, encounters disaster through a weakness that is inextricably connected with his strength: the hero, that is, pushes beyond permissible limits that form of *aretê* in which he excels, and thus reveals his failure to know himself perfectly or to know the truth about his circumstances. Ajax, Electra, both Heracles and Deianeira, Creon in the *Antigone,* even Antigone herself, and Oedipus in *Oedipus Tyrannus* are examples of this kind of failure in sophrosyne, which Sophocles some-times links with the theme of the nothingness of man. In addition to ex-cess, the Sophoclean hero is commonly marked by a second species of failure in sophrosyne (and this is clearly a failure in self-knowledge) —namely, delusion. If the theme of excess represents the moral aspect of sophrosyne in Sophocles, the theme of delusion illustrates the intellectual.

Delusion takes many forms and may be more or less prominent.[41] In the *Ajax* the temporary madness of the hero, which leads him to mistake animals for men, is sent by Athene; but long before this event Ajax has deluded himself into believing that he can triumph without the help of the gods (764–69, 770–75), a delusion specifically described (779) as οὐ κατ' ἄνθρωπον φρονῶν ("not thinking mortal thoughts"). This is the delusion, the violation of sophrosyne, that earns him the enmity of the goddess. In the *Trachiniae* delusion is a net of *atê,* woven around Deianira by Moira and Cypris; while in the *Antigone* a total lack of self-knowledge deludes Creon in his relations with everyone else. Often the theme of delusion is connected with a misunderstood oracle or prophecy: Teucer in the *Ajax,* Heracles in the *Trachiniae,* and Oedipus in the *Tyrannus* are victims of such misunderstanding. Even the *Philoctetes* shows a vestige of this theme. When the meaning of the prophecy of Helenus is fully explained by Heracles, Philoctetes makes that reasonable accommoda-tion to reality which is the essence of sophrosyne in Sophoclean tragedy.

After reading Aeschylus, who expresses through characters and Chorus alike a profound respect for sophrosyne,[42] one is at first baffled by

[40] Wolfgang Schadewaldt (*op. cit.,* 103–4) discusses the effect on the *aretê* of the heroic in-dividual when it is confined within the boundaries of civic virtue, so that a conflict results between the principles of individualism and communal life.

[41] On this theme, consult Karl Reinhardt, *Sophokles* (Frankfurt, 1947), 57 ff., and Opstelten, *op. cit.,* 124, 187–90.

[42] Kitto (110) discusses the reasons why the Aeschylean Chorus is in a position to make such pronouncements, while the Chorus of Sophocles often is not.

Sophocles' treatment of the subject. No heroic figure in Sophoclean tragedy speaks of sophrosyne with unalloyed admiration.[43] Ajax indeed recommends it to Tecmessa as a virtue proper to women, but in his "speech of deception" he shows that while he understands what *sôphronein* means to the rest of the world ("acquiescence in limitation"), he cannot himself accept it. Electra is even more specific in her rejection: she tells the Chorus that in her plight there is no place for *sôphronein* or *eusebein*. To the word *eusebeia* (and to *aidôs*) she in fact gives a new connotation, and we will consider in due course the possibility that she does the same for sophrosyne.[44] Secondary figures who urge sophrosyne or interpret its demands are unheroic (Creon in the *Oedipus Tyrannus*) or even, by a favorite Sophoclean irony, guilty of *hybris* themselves (Menelaus and Agamemnon in the *Ajax*).

How then does Sophocles create the impression that his tragedies are much concerned with sophrosyne?[45] He does it in three ways: by the device of contrasting characters, by the use of traditional *topoi* of sophrosyne (even without the word itself) in key choral odes, and by the very form of his tragic poetry, which, in its strict but apparently effortless control of the most intense emotion, illustrates sophrosyne in its ultimate perfection. The first two methods, which are largely a matter of content, will be discussed here. A consideration of the effect of poetic style in conveying an impression of sophrosyne would require a separate book; meanwhile Jaeger's perceptive remarks on "the firm harmonious repose" of Sophocles' poetry and the power of its sounds and rhythms to restore a sense of balance and proportion suggest the direction such a study might take.[46]

The reliance of Sophocles on the device of contrast for both structure and characterization is widely recognized.[47] It is this device in particular that enables us to see the relation of sophrosyne to the tragic action and character, and this fact explains why the choruses and the secondary figures, whatever their differences otherwise, often insist on the

---

[43] Schadewaldt (*op. cit.*, 104, n. 1) has compiled a list of concepts that are regularly associated in Sophoclean tragedy: *kleos* ("glory"), *eukleia* ("good repute"), *gennaion* ("nobility"), and *kalon* ("the fair") are opposed to *nous, phronein, euboulia, eulabeia, sôphronein* (all indicate intellectual processes or prudence). Cf. also Schmid-Stählin, *Griechische Literatur-Geschichte,* 1. 2. 470, n. 16.

[44] See p. 65.

[45] A very general impression: see, e.g., T. B. L. Webster, *Introduction to Sophocles* (Oxford, 1936), 27, 37, 65; Jaeger, *Paideia,* 1. 277; Opstelten, *op. cit.,* 110.

[46] *Paideia,* 1. 277.

[47] See Kirkwood, 83, 100, and Webster, *op. cit.,* 85.

need for sophrosyne (or some familiar equivalent) or else behave in an almost ostentatiously *sôphrôn* manner.

The publication of Whitman's book on Sophocles with its concentration on the heroic humanism of the Sophoclean tragic character has proved a healthy corrective to the traditional view that found in Sophocles' plays only a rather tedious moral lesson about the value of sophrosyne. No one is now tempted to overlook the poet's emphasis on the overwhelming nobility of the heroic soul or to interpret Sophoclean tragedy in too Aeschylean a light. It would be unfortunate, however, if Whitman's persuasive attack on "classicism" and his defense of the heroic should lead to an oversimplification in the other direction—lead, that is, to an uncritical acceptance of the values of the heroic figure as they seem to the hero himself. It is easy to be swept away by the magnificence of Ajax or the superb disdain of Antigone; inevitably the contrast between the heroic figure and its foils emphasizes the isolated nobility of the tragic soul. But to regard this as the view of Sophocles himself is to do an injustice to the complexity that he found in the nature of man; and to justify Whitman's interpretation of Sophoclean tragedy it is occasionally necessary to ignore whole scenes in certain plays or to regard as mere conventional framework speeches that actually are rich in meaning. Many of these speeches have to do with sophrosyne. It is Whitman's view that Sophocles has abandoned this word to "the little people who wish to be safe." [48] His comments deserve to be quoted in full, since they pose a serious problem:

Sophocles' dramas may well teach sophrosyne, but it is in the character of the hero that this sophrosyne is to be found, and not in the commonplaces and clichés of the chorus and lesser characters. *It is the hero himself who has the real self-knowledge* [italics mine]: the others have only rules of behavior. And yet, because in the mid-fifth century these rules of behavior had already become identified with sophrosyne in common intercourse, it forever appears that the protagonist moves blindly and arbitrarily along his fated road, while the static chorus and all the secondary figures stand firmly on the bed-rock of a settled and utterly correct ethic, approved and protected by the sanction of the gods themselves. Not even the hero himself can say that he acts from sophrosyne, for the word has already been pinned down to a code of behavior closely resembling philistinism.[49]

It is true that to accept the speeches of the choruses and the secondary figures as the view of the poet is often—not always—a mistake, but

[48] Whitman, 9.

[49] *Ibid.*, 8–9. S. M. Adams (*Sophocles the Playwright* [Toronto, 1957], 18–19) also suggests that Sophocles believes that sophrosyne is to be sacrificed to *tolma* ("daring"), *thrasos* ("boldness"), or even *hybris*, if the unwritten laws, interpreted in the light of *aidôs* and *eusebeia*, so demand.

it is equally erroneous to equate the hero's point of view with that of
Sophocles. If "sophrosyne is not to be found in the commonplaces and
clichés of the chorus and lesser characters," neither is it to be found in
the character of the hero, and it is futile to deny that the chief figures
regularly precipitate their respective catastrophes by some excess or delusion of their own. The hero's self-knowledge is never perfect; there is
always a blindness to something essential in himself or his situation, and
tragedy arises out of the interplay between his circumstances and his
admirable but imperfect nature. That is the real reason the hero cannot
claim sophrosyne: it is foreign to his nature, and he (unlike some
Euripidean heroes) recognizes the fact. The poet himself—not any one
of his characters, major or minor—is the one who truly understands
sophrosyne, and it is the entire poem, not any one speech or choral ode,
that conveys its significance. Hence it is essential to appreciate that one
of the functions of the secondary figures and the choruses is to remind us
of the normal Greek standards of conduct, including the conviction that
self-knowledge and moderation equip a man to face reality.

It is not at all necessary to think that Sophocles meant us to find
admirable the secondary characters and their easily achieved sophrosyne.
With one exception they are unheroic, and without exception they are
untragic. Aeschylus in the *Prometheus Bound* had already represented in
a distinctly unheroic light that advocate of sophrosyne, Oceanus, and in
Sophocles both Ismene and Chrysothemis exhibit something of the same
quality. They possess only what Plato was to describe in the *Republic* as
sophrosyne ὡς πλήθει and in the *Phaedo* as sophrosyne δημοτική[50]—
a virtue that is habitual, rather than philosophical, and consists mainly
in obedience to rulers and control of appetites. Neither Plato nor
Sophocles would regard this as anything but a low level of the virtue.
Creon in the *Oedipus Tyrannus* possesses a kind of sophrosyne that owes
more to intellectual analysis and conscious choice than does the sophrosyne of Ismene and Chrysothemis; theirs amounts to no more than a timid
acquiescence in the conventions of feminine behavior. If we were to assign stages of the virtue to Sophoclean characters (like the Neoplatonic
bathmoi), we would place Creon on the second rung of the ladder. He
abides by all the rules: he is cautious in assertions (569); he thinks
mortal thoughts; he refuses to act without consulting the gods (1438–39);
he prefers to enjoy untroubled the power of a king rather than to have
at once the name and the manifold troubles of a king (he calls this

[50] *Rep.* 389D–E; *Phaedo* 82A.

preference *sôphrôn* [589]); and he refuses to gloat over the downfall of Oedipus, who has so brutally threatened him. In all this it is legitimate to see a character designed for the express purpose of contrasting with Oedipus as sharply as possible; it is undoubtedly significant that Sophocles chooses sophrosyne as the basis of this contrast. That Creon is unheroic, untragic, and, as Kirkwood points out, unattractive,[51] makes him all the more effective as a foil to Oedipus.

The third rung of the ladder of sophrosyne may be assigned to Odysseus in the *Ajax*. His sophrosyne, which appears most markedly in his recognition of the common humanity that he shares with his enemy (121ff.), is of an enlightened variety, and, unlike Creon, he is a thoroughly sympathetic character. Where Creon is self-regarding in his sophrosyne, Odysseus is generous and magnanimous. By contrast to Ajax, however, he is lacking in the quality of heroism, that consciousness of supreme nobility which lies behind both the violence and the genuine *megalopsychia* of the hero. Only one of all Sophocles' *sôphrones* foil characters may properly be called heroic: Theseus in the *Oedipus at Colonus*. Not only does he display magnanimity in welcoming the outcast Oedipus to Athens and assuring him of protection—expressing himself with a commonplace of sophrosyne (567), ἔξοιδ' ἀνὴρ ὤν ("I know that I am mortal"); but he is twice specifically described with the key word of Sophoclean nobility, *gennaios* (569, 1636). His power of restraining his *thymos*, even when justly aroused by Creon, gives him the right to urge self-restraint upon the choleric Oedipus (592, 1180). Theseus alone in Sophoclean tragedy demonstrates the possibility of being at once *gennaios* and *sôphrôn*. Is it by accident that he appears in the *Oedipus at Colonus* as the representative of Athens, whose greatest achievement was the combination of just these qualities?

Sophocles' use of the Chorus in the interests of sophrosyne is very similar to his use of secondary characters. The Chorus often has a strong contrasting value; and since each Chorus is equipped with a well-defined personality, the type of sophrosyne it represents may differ from one play to another. Thus the Chorus of Salaminians in the *Ajax* uses *sôphronein* in the sense of "be moderate, self-controlled" (1264), an Aeschylean connotation employed by both Ajax himself and Menelaus in the same play. The Chorus advises Ajax to avoid boastfulness (386), partly out of genuine concern for him but partly also out of fear for its own fate if he is destroyed.

[51] Kirkwood, 131–32.

The Chorus in the *Electra,* also personally involved with the chief figure, at first urges moderation upon the heroine and reproaches her for violating *ta metria* (140) and for going to extremes in hatred (176), but its adherence to sophrosyne is little more than conventional. Once it has been convinced that Electra's murderous intention is justified, it accepts her interpretation of nobility, piety, and allied values and abandons its earlier resistance. Its only use of the word *sôphronein* is in a highly conventional phrase (465), εἰ σωφρονήσεις ("if you will be sensible"), a cliché in comedy and oratory towards the close of the fifth century.

It should be noted that the two explicit references to the verb *sôphronein* by the choruses of the *Ajax* and the *Electra* come not in the odes but merely in choral iambics, whose dramatic and spiritual weight tends to be negligible.[52] The real feeling for sophrosyne emerges from the odes themselves and is conveyed, neither by explicit comments on the doctrine of sophrosyne nor by pointed criticism of the conduct of the chief figures, but, more lyrically and subtly, by reflections upon the themes of sophrosyne familiar in Homer, lyric and elegy, popular proverbs, earlier tragedy, and Herodotus: the nothingness of man, the mutability of all things, the danger of *hybris* or of overmastering passion of any kind, particularly *erôs,* and the need for acquiescence in the Divine will.[53] The most significant and effective of these odes are, as we might expect, those sung by the choruses of the *Antigone,* the *Oedipus Tyrannus,* and the *Oedipus at Colonus,* which are composed of elders unselfishly concerned with the welfare of the *polis* and with eternal moral principles. The views on the danger of *hybris* which are expressed in the second stasimon of the *Oedipus Tyrannus,* the reflections in the second stasimon of the *Antigone* on the impossibility of checking the power of Zeus by a ὑπερβασία ἀνδρῶν

[52] Cf. Kirkwood, 188.

[53] For an exhaustive list of Sophoclean reminiscences of epic, lyric, and elegiac poetry, see Schmid-Stählin, *op. cit.,* 1. 2. 311–12, n. 6. Opstelten (*op. cit.,* 166 ff.) collects many of these allusions in connection with particular themes, as does Sir John Sheppard in his edition of the *Oedipus Tyrannus* (Cambridge, 1920), lix–lxxix. See also Webster, *op. cit.,* 39 ff. Neither in the following passages from earlier poetry nor in the Sophoclean odes is there any overt reference to sophrosyne; the effect is achieved without use of the word: Nothingness of man: Homer *Od.* 18. 130–31; Pindar *Pyth.* 8. 95; Simonides 15 Page; Bacchylides 3. 78 Snell; Herodotus 1. 32; cf. Sophocles *O.T.* 1187 ff. Mutability: Homer *Il.* 6. 146–49; Archilochus 67a, 6–7 Diehl[3]; Mimnermus 2 Diehl[3]; Theognis 159–60, 567, 591 ff., 657–58; Simonides 16 Page; cf. Sophocles *Ajax* 127 ff., *Trach.* 130 ff., *Phil.* 179 ff. Danger of *hybris:* Pindar *Pyth.* 11. 27; Solon 1. 11 Diehl[3]; Herodotus 7. 108; cf. Sophocles *Ajax* 760 ff., *O.T.* 872 ff. Overmastering power of *erôs* or Aphrodite: Pindar, Frags. 123, 127; *Nem.* 8. 4 ff.; cf. Sophocles *Trach.* 441 ff., 497 ff., 860, *Ant.* 781 ff. Delusion, *atê,* deceptive hope: Homer *Il.* 9. 502 ff.; Hesiod *Erg.* 498; Simonides 1. 1–10 Diehl[3]; Pindar *Nem.* 11. 45 ff.; Bacchylides 9. 18; cf. Sophocles *Ant.* 582 ff.

("overstepping by mankind" [604–5]) and the μὴ φῦναι ode in *Oedipus at Colonus* are more than merely conventional. They express profound and justified convictions about fundamental problems, and they do so in a way that contributes both to the dramatic effect and to the moral background against which the chief figures act.

Space does not permit an analysis of all the relevant odes. Sheppard's discussion of the use of familiar *topoi* of sophrosyne in the odes of the *Oedipus Tyrannus* suggests the richness of the material that Sophocles exploited.[54] The second stasimon of the *Antigone* offers an especially enlightening example of the technique. Coming after the episode in which Antigone and Creon clash and Antigone and Ismene are both condemned to death, the ode first devotes itself to a lament for the family of Labdacus, accursed from ancient days, and then turns to more generalized reflections. It touches upon such traditional topics as the contrast between Divine power and human weakness, the *atê* that follows excess in human life, the fickleness of hope and her gifts, and the theme of delusion leading to *atê*.[55] The dramatic effectiveness of this stasimon has been demonstrated, and it is true that its ambiguity on the question of precisely who is offending Zeus maintains suspense at a point in the plot where an open accusation would be disastrous; but in addition to conveying a "feeling of impending calamity for wrongdoing,"[56] the ode specifically suggests a kind of wrongdoing that the Greeks associated with the violation of sophrosyne, and it does so by the use of the *topoi* listed above. This stasimon and certain odes in the two *Oedipus* plays show this technique in its perfection, but all Sophocles' plays, except the *Ajax*, have at least one choral ode of this general type. The *Trachiniae* has its parodos on mutability (122 ff.) and its ode on the overwhelming power of Cypris (497 ff.); the *Electra* its *kommos* on the might of Zeus and the folly of excess in grief and hatred (137 ff.); and the *Philoctetes*, its ode on the pitiable lot of man (169 ff.) and its *kommos* on the disastrous effects of stubbornness (1095 ff.).

At least six of Sophocles' tragic characters, diverse though they are in

---

[54] Sheppard, *op. cit.*, lix–lxxix. In spite of the criticism of Sheppard's interpretation of the odes by Bernard Knox (*Oedipus at Thebes* [New Haven, 1957], 100), the background material that Sheppard collected is useful and relevant as an example of Sophocles' method of calling forth the associations stored in the minds of his hearers.

[55] Cf. 620 ff. with Theognis 403 ff. and 133–42, and with Solon 1. 67 Diehl.[3] Kitto, 162, n. 1, calls attention to the play on the word *atê*. See Del Grande (135) on parallels between Sophocles' use of ὑπερβασία and Aeschylus' use of παρβασία (*Sept.* 734–49) as synonyms for *hybris*.

[56] See Kirkwood, 208.

all except fidelity to a private standard of heroic excellence, precipitate their catastrophes through some defect in sophrosyne. The arrogance of Ajax, the stubbornness of Antigone and the tyrannical *hybris* of Creon, the rashness and violent temper of Oedipus, Electra's contempt for moderation, even the excessive credulity of Deianeira violate this far-reaching virtue (especially in its primary significance of soundness of mind or self-knowledge). To recognize this is by no means to accuse them all of serious failings proportionate to their punishment; only in the case of Creon in the *Antigone* do we feel that the punishment is justified (and only in this play is there a strong suggestion of the Aeschylean *Pathei mathos*).[57] But to deny them any failing is to ignore the degree to which they are responsible for what they do and suffer, and thus to rob them of their stature as tragic figures.

The relation of sophrosyne to the tragedy of the *eugenês* ("noble, well-born") individual is most clearly defined in the *Ajax,* which is justly regarded as the most Aeschylean of the tragedies.[58] It is Aeschylean in the prominence given to the conflict between *hybris* and sophrosyne and in the essential meaning assigned to these concepts (*hybris:* failure to think mortal thoughts; sophrosyne: respecting limits, both Divine and human), but the treatment of the theme is already intensely Sophoclean. Instead of making the demonstration of *hybris* the climax of the drama, Sophocles presents it in the Prologue and then deliberately minimizes it, after he has impressed us with both the shocking arrogance and the heroic stature of Ajax.[59] The rest of the play has to do with the rehabilitation of Ajax (*pace* Kitto),[60] partly through our sight of him when the madness has passed, but mainly through the interplay of contrasting characters: the *sôphrôn* Odysseus, the *sôphrôn* Tecmessa, and the mean-spirited and vengeful Atridae. Our final impression is of the greatness of the heroic nature, not of its concomitant *hybris*.

The words *sôphronein* and *sôphrôn* occur more often in this tragedy than in any other by Sophocles and are given several shades of meaning by different characters. The basic contrast between Ajax and Odysseus is underscored by the appearance of the goddess of sophrosyne, Athene herself (most beloved by Odysseus and most offended by Ajax) in the Prologue, where her function is to guide the two heroes to a revelation

---

[57] In the case of Ajax and Deianeira also, there is some hint of *Pathei mathos,* but it is not so explicitly stated as in the final utterance of the Chorus in the *Antigone*.

[58] See, e.g., Opstelten, *op. cit.,* 51, and Kamerbeek, *The Plays of Sophocles* (Leiden, 1953), 1. 16.

[59] See Adams, *op. cit.,* 25, and Bernard Knox, *H.S.C.P.* 65 (1961), 1–37.

[60] Kitto, 119: "It is . . . idle to talk of the 'rehabilitation' of Ajax."

of their fundamental *êthos*. The Prologue stresses both the supreme daring of Ajax and his delusion; [61] it gives Odysseus an opportunity to reject Athene's invitation to gloat over his maddened enemy, even as that enemy is seen gloating over his fancied prospect of torturing Odysseus, and it sums up the sophrosyne of Odysseus in his famous speech about the universal condition of mankind (125–26): ὁρῶ γὰρ ἡμᾶς οὐδὲν ὄντας ἄλλο πλὴν εἴδωλ' ὅσοιπερ ζῶμεν ἢ κούφην σκιάν ("For I see that we—all of mankind—are no more than phantoms or empty shadow"). What it means to be a *sôphrôn anêr* becomes clear not only from this speech, with its obvious contrast between Odysseus and Ajax, but also from the latter half of the play, in which the contrast is between Odysseus and the Atridae.[62] Athene offers a reminder of the (Aeschylean) religious basis of sophrosyne in her warning about the danger of boastful speech against the gods and undue pride in strength or wealth. She reminds Odysseus of the mutability of all that is mortal and concludes the Prologue with the famous observation that the gods love the *sôphrones* and hate the proud (*kakous* [132–33]).

The picture of the *sôphrôn* man is balanced by one of the *sôphrôn* woman. To Ajax it may seem that the sophrosyne of women consists in silence—"Do not question, do not ask; *sôphronein* is good" (586)—but Tecmessa's conduct—especially her speech on the true nature of the *eugenês* (485–524)—suggests what the Hellenic view of feminine sophrosyne really included. It is not inconsistent with a positive personality and genuine intelligence, and it reveals itself especially in the will to face reality, which here amounts to making the best of a situation common in ancient warfare, never less than tragic. Tecmessa, so often compared to Andromache in *Iliad* VI,[63] is actually in a worse plight than Hector's beloved and honored wife. From being the daughter of a free and wealthy Phrygian father, she has become a slave (her address to Ajax as "Ajax,

---

[61] The two aspects of his behavior that are opposed to sophrosyne are indicated by the words δυσλόγιστόν ("irrational" [40]) and τολμαῖς ("acts of audacity" [46]) and φρενῶν θράσει ("boldness of spirit" [46]) as well as by the references to *mania* ("madness" [59]) and *nosos* ("illness" [68]).

[62] We should miss part of the richness of contrasting characterization if we failed to note that the *hybris* of Menelaus and Agamemnon (shown towards Ajax and his family) not only emphasizes the sophrosyne of Odysseus, but also makes the *hybris* of Ajax (directed towards the gods) less offensive, because less cowardly.

[63] E.g., Kamerbeek on *Ajax* 550, 557. The obvious modeling of the scene on the farewell of Hector and Andromache (*Il.* 6. 476–81) gives Sophocles the opportunity for a characteristically subtle effect. The prayer of Ajax for Eurysaces is essentially that of Hector for Astyanax but for one thing: where Hector prays that his son may be better than his father, Ajax prays that Eurysaces may be luckier than he, but in all else the same (550–51).

master" [485, cf. 368] and her outright statement, "Now I am a slave" [489], are reminders of her humiliation), but she accepts the bitter fact and responds to it with love and tenderness instead of with hatred. The importance of these two *sôphrones* characters, Odysseus and Tecmessa, must not be ignored. If the wholehearted admirer of Ajax can persuade us that it is a proof of the hero's nobility to resent even to the point of murder the award of the arms to Odysseus,[64] it is more difficult to make us accept as noble two consequences of the hero's resentment: his gleeful anticipation of the pleasure of torturing Odysseus and his selfish abandonment of his concubine and child to whatever may await them, so that he may indulge his sense of honor.[65] But we can accept these two peculiarly distasteful consequences of Ajax' *hybris* and see them in relation to his whole nature precisely because Odysseus and Tecmessa, the primary victims of this *hybris,* are able to understand him out of the fullness of their own sophrosyne.

In Ajax himself there are traces of sophrosyne which make his present enslavement by *atê* (123) the more tragic. While it is going too far to say that Ajax "was—and but for an act of gross injustice, still would be—a man of supreme sophrosyne," [66] it is true that we are given glimpses of the hero's capacity for sophrosyne in earlier days (recalled especially in the speech of Athene [118-20]). Much more effective, however, in evoking our response to his present situation is the enigmatic speech in which Ajax meditates upon the theme of mutability. The procession of the seasons and the yielding of night to day and of sleep to waking are illustrations of sophrosyne in the natural universe (a dim foreshadowing of the "cosmic" justification of sophrosyne in Plato's *Gorgias*), and with them Ajax equates obedience to the gods and to rulers in the life of man. "And we," he adds (677), "how shall we not be forced to learn restraint [πῶς οὐ γνωσόμεθα σωφρονεῖν]?" [67] The bitterness with which Ajax asks

---

[64] Whitman, 62 ff.

[65] The Chorus wrongly supposes that the sight of his dependents may induce in Ajax some trace of *aidôs* (345). Note the emphasis in this play on gloating over one's fallen enemy, a violation of both *aidôs* and sophrosyne. Cf. Odysseus' rebuke to Eurycleia (*Od.* 22. 411-12), in which such gloating is condemned as unholy (οὐχ ὁσίη).

[66] Adams, *op. cit.,* 25. It is in the presence of gross injustice that sophrosyne is tested and proves itself. Whitman (*Homer and the Heroic Tradition* [Cambridge, Mass., 1958], 171) says of Ajax in the *Iliad* that he is, "more than any other figure on the Greek side," the man of *aidôs*.

[67] See the remarks of Knox, *loc. cit.,* 20, on the soliloquy. Ajax interprets as a sign of sophrosyne the cynical recognition that friends become enemies and enemies friends. As Kirkwood shows (109), this view is answered at a distance by Odysseus in the second half of the play. Odysseus' conclusion—that a change from friendship to enmity should not alter the recognition of a man's true worth—is made a sign of the contrast between the two men.

the question indicates what the answer must be for him, yet it is important that he has shown a comprehension of what sophrosyne means. It is typical of the Sophoclean tragic figure that he grasps the normal standards, but that his heroic nature will not permit him to adhere to them.[68] The tragedy of Ajax becomes more poignant when we feel this tension between *gnômê* and *physis*.

Other speeches about sophrosyne in the *Ajax* reveal only partial comprehension. It is characteristic of Sophocles' verbal irony that Menelaus and Agamemnon, both of whom are guilty of *hybris*, arrogantly urge sophrosyne upon Teucer. To Menelaus it is merely obedience to authority, in the city or the army, and is the result of *phobos* and *aidôs* (1073 ff.). Agamemnon makes the word σωφρονήσεις (1259) precisely equivalent to νοῦν κατακτήσῃ in verse 1256: both mean "to get some sense." The Chorus uses *sôphrônein* (1264) conventionally with the Aeschylean meaning: "Behave with moderation, observe limits." Only Athene's words and the behavior of Odysseus and Tecmessa reveal a sophrosyne that is more than perfunctory.

The function of sophrosyne in the other plays may be treated more briefly. We shall usually find its meaning expressed by the contrast or interplay of characters rather than by an explicit discussion, for after the *Ajax*, references to *sôphronein* and *sôphrôn* are rare. But to conclude that the poet is concerned with sophrosyne only when it is mentioned explicitly would be to ignore his skilful manipulation of his audience and their response to the *topoi* that we have mentioned as being linked with the concept of sophrosyne. The *Trachiniae* is an example of the implicit importance of sophrosyne in a drama where the word *sôphrôn* occurs only once (435), and then in a trivial connection.[69] In this play, as in the *Ajax*, the device of contrast is employed, but with a difference. Here there is no secondary figure whose *sôphrôn* behavior casts into relief the violation of sophrosyne by the chief character. Rather, there are two chief characters, each dominating one half of the play, who contrast with each other in almost every respect, including their attitude towards sophrosyne. There is special irony in the condition of Deianeira, who specifically and emphatically renounces κακὰς . . . τόλμας ("acts of wicked daring" [582]) and describes *thymos* ("passion" [543])and *orgê* ("anger" [552]) as alien to a woman of sense (νοῦν ἔχουσαν [553] paraphrases σωφρονοῦσαν),

---

[68] The same situation occurs in the *Electra*. On the significance of this speech see Reinhardt, *op. cit.*, 32–34.

[69] Here *sôphrôn* ("sensible") is opposed to νοσεῖν ("to be mentally ill"), a vestige of the Homeric conception of sophrosyne (*Od.* 23. 11–13).

yet causes the ruin of her household because of her foolish reliance on the unproved remedy of Nessus. To call her, as one critic does, "the embodiment of sophrosyne" [70] is to interpret that quality in the narrowest way. It takes both courage and intelligence to achieve sophrosyne, and Deianeira, with the best intentions in the world, fails both tests. She is indeed *sôphrôn* in her acceptance of the traditional role of a good wife, in her recognition of the overwhelming power of *erôs*, before which man is helpless, and in her consequent readiness to excuse her husband (like the *sôphrôn* Andromache in Euripides), and she gives expression to this exclusively feminine sophrosyne in the speech beginning at verse 436.[71] But at the crucial moment when she makes the choice on which everything depends, Deianeira nullifies all her claims to be a woman of sense by relying on a remedy for whose efficacy she has only δόξα ("opinion"), not proof (588–91). The contrast between her effort to achieve sophrosyne in one meaning of the word and her tragic failure to attain it in another sense is one of the Euripidean elements in this drama.

Heracles fails in sophrosyne, too, but in a different and much more obvious way. He makes no pretense of sophrosyne, which he would not, any more than would Ajax, recognize as an *aretê* proper to a great hero. His excess, which is one manifestation of his tremendous heroic stature (vividly recalled in his own speeches on the subject of his labors, 1046 ff.), lies in his lust and his selfish satisfaction of his passions at the expense of anyone who gets in his way. Like Deianeira, moreover, Heracles is the victim of delusion: they are both out of touch with reality. Reinhardt [72] has drawn an enlightening parallel between Heracles, who belatedly understands the oracle about his death when the name of Nessus penetrates his consciousness, and Cambyses in Herodotus 3. 64. Cambyses had interpreted an oracle predicting his death in Ecbatana as a reference to the capital of Media. When he found himself in a little town called Ecbatana in Syria, where he accidentally stabbed himself with his own sword, he understood the true meaning of the oracle. As Herodotus puts it, ἐσωφρόνησε ("he came to his senses").

The *Antigone* exhibits the same method of contrasting two characters lacking in sophrosyne: one intensely sympathetic; the other distinctly the opposite, yet not without a certain moral grandeur. Antigone's fail-

---

[70] Adams, *op. cit.*, 109. Cf. Webster, *op. cit.*, 75, 98, on the sophrosyne of Deianeira.

[71] The speech picks up Lichas' antithesis between *nosos* and sophrosyne (435) and plays with the concepts of sickness and health, madness and sanity. For the "wifely" sophrosyne of Andromache, see p. 71.

[72] *Op. cit.*, 73.

ure in sophrosyne (especially evident in her reactions to Ismene and Creon) [73] is, dramatically speaking, static; but the *hybris* of Creon is a major theme, developed in a series of increasingly dramatic scenes with the watchman, with Haemon, and finally with Teiresias. Creon, like Zeus in the Prometheus trilogy, is a tyrant, and, what is more, he too is new in his *tyrannis*—and is thus in two ways opposed to sophrosyne; moreover, he is a victim of his own delusions. The signs of the king's moral blindness are rapidly multiplied. By the end of the fifth episode he has revealed in his own nature almost every crime of which he accuses others, and has divorced himself from all the virtues he has claimed.[74] The turning against him of the tide of public opinion and finally of religious sanctions is expressed in a series of warnings by Haemon, Teiresias, and the Chorus, which include exhortations to prudence and moderation. The speech of Teiresias (1064–90) is, in fact, a veritable σωφρονίζων λόγος, to use a later Cynic expression; after it Creon yields to the advice of the Chorus and attempts—too late, of course—to undo what he has done. The *euboulia* which Teiresias regards as the best of goods is equivalent to sophrosyne; its opposite is μὴ φρονεῖν (1050–51). Indeed, the key word in the Antigone is *phronein*, which the chief characters interpret in very different ways.[75] At the end of the tragedy the Chorus is far from uttering a mere cliché when it observes that *phronein* is much the greatest part of happiness—the wisdom that boastful men learn only after suffering, in old age (1347–53).[76]

The concept expressed by both *phronein* and *sôphronein* becomes increasingly identified with the very essence of tragedy in the *Oedipus Tyrannus*, where the search for knowledge, which proves to be self-knowledge in the most literal sense, forms the substance of the plot,[77] and the poetic imagery is concerned above all with physical and spiritual blindness and sight. Oedipus is the supreme example of the Sophoclean

[73] Antigone betrays a lack of sophrosyne by her passionate and hostile reaction, first, to Ismene's refusal to help with the burial and, later, to her attempt to share the blame (69–70, 86–87, 542 ff.), as well as by her anger at Creon's interference with what she conceives to be her duty (32–33). Cf. Ismene's warning to her against meddling or doing more than is proper (περίσσα πράσσειν [68]) and her own claim to δυσβουλία ("imprudence" [95]), like Prometheus' boasted hamartia (*P.V.* 266). Creon's charges against her (*hybris* and ὑπερβασία [449, 480–82]) reveal his own character more than hers, but there is no reason to undervalue the comments of the Chorus about her θράσος (853) and ὀργή (875).

[74] Cf. C. M. Bowra, *Sophoclean Tragedy* (Oxford, 1944), 114.

[75] See Kirkwood, 233–39.

[76] *Pathos* and *chronos* are linked as teachers of sophrosyne in the *Oresteia*, too.

[77] For the view that the *hamartia* of Oedipus as Aristotle understood it is ignorance of his identity, see Martin Ostwald, *Festschrift Ernst Kapp* (Hamburg, 1958), 93–108.

hero whose strength is inseparable from his weakness. The magnificent self-confidence which reveals itself as early as the Prologue gives rise, as we watch, to the *orgê* and *thymos* so often referred to in the scenes with Teiresias and Creon.[78] The noble resolution that commands our respect when Oedipus is confronted with Creon's report from Delphi has as its counterpart the haste and rashness that—before the events of the play —have made possible the fulfillment of the oracles.[79] There can be no question about Oedipus' lack of sophrosyne in the sense of self-control and ordinary prudence, nor does he ever acquire this form of excellence —even in the *Coloneus*. What he does achieve before the close of the *Tyrannus* is the most profound and shattering self-knowledge, the essence of Sophoclean sophrosyne. And it is this self-knowledge, healing as well as wounding, that enables Oedipus to face the reality that he has sought throughout his life.

The function of Creon as a foil whose characteristic virtue is bourgeois sophrosyne has been discussed, and we have noted the absence in him of any touch of the heroic.[80] Even in Aeschylus there was an implication in a speech of Eteocles that if he obeyed the injunction of the Chorus and controlled his frenzy, he would lose his honor (*Sept.* 683–85). Sophoclean tragedy makes us fully aware that sophrosyne, like the *eugenes* (the "noble") in the *Ajax* or *phronêsis* and *eusebeia* in the *Antigone*, means different things to different people and may to the heroic nature seem like weakness or even cowardice. The clearest statement of this belief is found in the *Electra* in a scene that is especially effective because in it Sophocles echoes a key speech from the *Choephoroi*.

It has been clear from our first glimpse of Electra that she exults in the excesses with which the Chorus and Chrysothemis charge her—excess of anger and hatred as well as grief. She rejects τὸ μέτρον (236) and sets

---

[78] E.g. 337, 344, 364, 405, 524 ,674.

[79] See again Sheppard, *op. cit.*, lix ff., and the interesting remarks of Knox, *Oedipus at Thebes*, 195, on the final episode of the play.

[80] If Creon were our sole criterion, we might agree with Bowra's theory that the Greek nature had two conflicting ideals, the heroic mentality and the doctrine of the Mean, and that they excluded each other (*The Greek Experience* [Cleveland, 1957], 34). But it is an error to suppose that sophrosyne and dynamism (as Bowra calls it) are incompatible, for the highest form of sophrosyne (that which Pericles achieved in political life, Sophocles in tragic poetry, and the sculptors of the pediments of the temple of Zeus at Olympia in plastic art) is that in which the most passionate nature is held in perfect check. Cf. the perceptive remark of Opstelten, *op. cit.*, 94: "Apolline *metron* and sophrosyne certainly do not mean a tranquil mediocrity; they stand for a loaded balance which does not escape from, but overcomes the temptation to excess." As for Creon, see W. C. Helmbold, *A.J.P.* 72 (1951), 293–300, for the observation that Creon is a neutral figure who alone is given no development and at the end has not been "blinded by knowledge."

up independent standards of behavior consistent with her ἀγαθὴ φύσις ("noble nature"). As a verbal expression of this trait, she takes familiar ethical terms and fills them with new meaning. "If blood be not shed for blood, *aidôs* and *eusebeia* would be lost" (245 ff.). In such a situation as hers, she tells the Chorus (307–8): οὔτε σωφρονεῖν . . . οὔτ᾿ εὐσεβεῖν πάρεστιν ("there is no room for sophrosyne or piety"). Here is the echo of the *Choephoroi*; Aeschylus' Electra had prayed that she might prove σωφρονεστέραν πολὺ . . . τ᾿εὐσεβεστέραν ("far more chaste and pious") than her mother (140–41). In that context *sôphrôn* clearly referred to sexual purity. Sophocles, however, imagines an Electra who rejects sophrosyne; he must therefore give to this word the meaning "moderation," for even the Sophoclean Electra can still be chaste. The echo enables the poet to use his favorite device of contrast in a peculiarly effective way: Electra's nature is revealed by an implied contrast with the corresponding character in an earlier play, which is well known to the present audience. The Aeschylean Electra, who was genuinely different from her mother, could pray sincerely for sophrosyne and piety; this Electra, although chaste where her mother is wanton, is like Clytemnestra in rejecting moderation, and both mother and daughter lack self-knowledge. Yet as with *aidôs* and *eusebeia*, Electra has her own private interpretation of sophrosyne, hinted at in her first scene with Chrysothemis. The sister, like Ismene, is an ordinary woman, not brave enough to resist her masters, yet willing to admit that Electra's attitude is just (338–39, 1041–42). Electra accuses her of χλιδή ("luxuriousness") [81] and says that she herself would not desire Chrysothemis' favored position in the household, nor would Chrysothemis, σώφρων γ᾿ οὖσα (365). This phrase, which is admirably adapted to Sophocles' verbal irony, illustrates the difficulty of translating *sôphrôn*, for the word is susceptible to several interpretations. It can mean "if you had any sense" in the common colloquial phrase, or "if you were modest, not given to χλιδή"; but it can also mean "if you were genuinely *sôphrôn*, if you really understood what that virtue is," which would be appropriate in a play so full of debate about the meaning of familiar ethical terms.[82]

The *Philoctetes* depicts an absorbing conflict between two opposing ways of life: that of the ἀγαθὴ φύσις, which is fully developed in Philoctetes; and that of the sophistic guile and ruthless self-will embodied

---

[81] In lyric poetry and Aeschylean tragedy, χλιδή regularly has a connotation opposed to sophrosyne.

[82] See Kirkwood, 137–38, on the contrast between the two sisters in their use of familiar words, such as *kalon* and *kakon*.

in Odysseus. The struggle between Philoctetes and Odysseus for the soul of the *eugenês* Neoptolemus is reminiscent in certain ways of the *agôn* between the *Dikaios* and the *Adikos Logoi* in the *Clouds* of Aristophanes, which had been presented some fifteen years previously and reflected the same distaste for sophistic standards of education and conduct. One might expect sophrosyne to belong to the conservative and aristocratic, rather than to the sophistic, side in this debate, as it does in the *Clouds* (see, for example, 1006, 1027)—and, indeed, sophrosyne is perhaps implied in the rejection of deceit and of the philosophy of profit and victory at any price—but Sophocles makes no explicit statement on the subject. The other important theme of this play, the choice of Philoctetes, is more evidently connected with sophrosyne. Both Neoptolemus and Heracles, as well as the Chorus, employ familiar *topoi*—the necessity of bearing misfortunes as best one can (ἀναγκαῖον [1316–17]), the immortality of *eusebeia* (1443)—in persuading Philoctetes to renounce his wrath. As we have already suggested, his ultimate acceptance of his fate, after Heracles has confirmed and explicated the prophecy of Helenus, is an example of that adjustment to reality which is the essence of Sophoclean sophrosyne. But in spite of the implicit connection of sophrosyne with these two themes in the play, the only significant use of the word *sôphronein* shows quite another facet of its meaning and reflects a contemporary development in semantics. When, after Neoptolemus has abandoned the intrigue, Odysseus threatens feebly to report him to the Greek army, Neoptolemus taunts him with cowardice, saying (1259–60): "You have come to your senses! [ἐσωφρόνησας!] If you are always so cautious, you will live in safety." This use of the word is a clear expression of the tendency that we have noted among Sophoclean heroes to regard sophrosyne as incompatible with courage; [83] it foreshadows the confusion of sophrosyne and cowardice which Thucydides records (3. 82), and it explains Plato's continued interest in the relation between the *sôphrôn* and *andrikos* temperaments (*Politicus* 306b ff.).[84] But Sophocles merely applies the honorable name of sophrosyne to something ignoble —a purely semantic change—while the essential quality is not disparaged. It remains for the Sophists and some of their pupils to question or to reject the virtue itself.

The most notable reflection of sophrosyne in the *Oedipus at Colonus* is the one we have already remarked: Theseus, the representative of Athens,

---

[83] And not only heroes. Agamemnon in *Ajax* 1362 fears that he will seem a coward if he yields to Odysseus.

[84] See Chap. V, pp. 171, 184.

who combines the *sôphron* and the *gennaion,* is a contrast at once to the undiminished *thymos* of Oedipus and to the self-acknowledged *hybris* of Creon (883). The *thymos* and *orgê* of the aged Oedipus have sometimes been ignored or minimized in an effort to prove that the irascible hero has learned sophrosyne through suffering; but this is neither true nor characteristic of Sophocles.[85] The anger of Oedipus is so basic to his personality that if it were gone he would no longer be Oedipus, and the tremendously effective reversal of the movement of the *Oedipus Tyrannus* (noted by Kitto)[86] would be irrelevant. Oedipus still manifests *thymos,* and there is an interesting reminder in a speech of Antigone that this passion is characteristic of the whole family of Laius. Imploring her father in the name of *charis* and *eusebeia* to listen to Polyneices, she bids him remember what he has suffered because of his own father and mother and to learn from this the evil consequences of *kakos thymos* (1195–98). The conclusion of her speech (on the propriety of yielding to those whose pleas are just) strongly recalls the conclusion of Tecmessa's speech to Ajax on the nature of the *eugenês,* although Antigone substitutes a play on πάσχειν ("to suffer") for the one on *charis* in the *Ajax.* Whereas Ajax is apparently unmoved by Tecmessa's plea—although later he describes himself as having been softened by it (650–53)—Oedipus yields reluctantly and allows Polyneices to approach, but the temper in which he listens to his son is subtly conveyed by a comparison of their two ideas about the ξύνεδρος (Councillor) of Zeus. Polyneices says that Zeus has *Aidôs* as the partner of his throne in all that he does, and she should therefore be enthroned with Oedipus as well (1267–69). But Oedipus rejects this traditional appeal of the suppliant and maintains that primeval Justice—ἡ παλαίφατος Δίκη—is the partner of Zeus according to ancient beliefs (1381–82).[87] And it is justice, without a trace of either *aidôs* or *charis,* that governs the response of Oedipus to Polyneices. At the conclusion of this episode Antigone directs towards Polyneices her campaign against *thymos,* begging him to abandon the attack on Thebes, since he knows that it is destined to fail. She asks him (1420): "Why is it necessary for you to give way to anger [θυμοῦσθαι]?" His reply (1422–23) unmasks his false notion of honor: "It is disgraceful to be in exile and be thus laughed at by my younger brother." The reminder that

---

[85] Suffering has little educative effect in Sophocles. *Pathei mathos* is not so important in his view of life as in that of Aeschylus, although late learning is a persistent theme (*Ant.* 1347 ff.). Suffering reveals character in Sophoclean tragedy; it rarely improves it. In Euripides, realism asserts itself: suffering debases character.

[86] Kitto, 401.

[87] Cf. Plato *Prot.* 322C.

thymos is the source of disaster in three generations of the family of Laius illustrates both Sophocles' insistence on human responsibility and his habit of finding the cause of tragedy in some violation of sophrosyne.[88]

EURIPIDES

However substantial the differences between Aeschylus and Sophocles may seem, their likenesses far outweigh their differences when they are compared with Euripides, who reflects with unparalleled directness the intellectual, moral, and political ferment of his times and provides our most extensive evidence for the implications of sophrosyne in Attic speech during the last quarter of the fifth century. Euripides outstrips the other tragic poets both in the frequency with which he alludes to sophrosyne and in the variety of meanings that he gives the word,[89] and his plays reveal many of the effects that contemporary social and political changes were having on the popular attitude towards this concept. What Euripides himself felt to be the relation of sophrosyne to tragedy is everywhere apparent, but especially in the *Hippolytus* and the *Bacchae*, which derive much of their effect from a tension between conflicting ideas of the virtue. It is impossible to determine how much Euripides' new and individual approach to sophrosyne owes to contemporary influences, how much to his own temperament, but whatever the operative causes,

[88] The word *sôphrôn* rarely appears in the Fragments, two of which relate the virtue to feminine conduct; two others relate it to the contrast between youth and maturity. In Frag. 61, from the *Acrisius*, Sophocles says that those whose thoughts are *sôphrona* regard brevity of speech as an ornament in young girls (cf. Aeschylus *Supp.* 197; Sophocles *Ajax* 293). Frag. 621 (from the *Phaedra*) is the commonplace about the *sôphrôn* wife, man's greatest treasure (cf. Epicharmus 286 Kaibel, *Com.*) Frag. 622 (also from the *Phaedra*) describes as insecure a city in which *ta dikaia* and *ta sôphrona* are trodden underfoot—an unusual reference to "civic" sophrosyne. Frag. 850 says that a city in which parents are ruled by their children is not a city of *sôphrones* men, while Frag. 718 contrasts *hybris* with sophrosyne and assigns the one to youth, the other to age: *hybris* never in the world comes to the age of sophrosyne (ἥβης εἰς τὸ σῶφρον) but blossoms and withers in the young.

[89] The noun sophrosyne makes its first appearance in tragedy in Euripides, who uses it in the extant plays and Fragments a total of six times (*Me.* 635; *Hipp.* 1365; *I.A.* 544; Frags. 446, 503, and 959). A. W. Verrall (*J.H.S.* 1 [1880], 289–90) suggests that the use of the noun in the two versions of the *Hippolytus* has its source in hymns sung at Troezen in honor of the hero. Other forms of the root are used nearly one hundred times, a vast increase over its use by Aeschylus and Sophocles. *Sôphrôn* appears fifty-four times, *sôphronein* thirty-two, *sôphronôs* five times, *sôphronizein* twice. *Sôphronizein,* which occurs once in Aeschylus (*Supp.* 724) first becomes common in literature of the sophistic age, with the meaning "to render *sôphrôn* (that is, calm, sensible, prudent)"; cf. Antiphon *Tetr.* 2. 3. 3; Thucydides 6. 78, 8. 1. Euripides *H.F.* 869 contains an unusual use of the verb, in a strictly physical application, when it is said that Heracles has no command over his breathing: ἀμπνοὰς δ'οὐ σωφρονίζει. See J. T. Allen and Gabriel Italie, *A Concordance to Euripides* (Berkeley and London, 1954), for Euripides' use of these words.

their results separate him sharply from Aeschylus and Sophocles and range him on the side of the Sophists, Thucydides, and the Platonic Socrates, not necessarily in his conception of the virtue, but certainly in his methods of analysis and definition.

In Euripides, as in the older tragic poets, the concept of sophrosyne is related to a fundamental conviction about the nature of tragedy. To Aeschylus, who found the source of tragedy in *hybris*, the arrogant transgression of Divine and human law, sophrosyne was essentially religious, an acceptance of mortal limitations. To Sophocles, whose tragic concept was rooted in the imperfection of the heroic nature, sophrosyne was the self-knowledge that enables man to come to grips with reality. To Euripides, who saw in the triumph of the irrational over the rational the primary source of tragedy for the individual and society, sophrosyne is one of several names for the rational element. It is that quality, intellectual in origin, but predominantly moral in its application and effect, which controls and moderates the passions, whether lust, anger, ambition, cruelty, or even something so trivial as gluttony or drunkenness. Euripides has been called the first psychologist,[90] and very likely it was his keen interest in probing the motives to action and exposing the death struggle between passion and reason in the human soul that led him to set so high a value on sophrosyne, which is called in the *Medea* the fairest gift of the gods (636) and in Fragment 959 the most venerable of all virtues, since it dwells for ever with the good. Because he identifies sophrosyne with the mastery of passion, Euripides often applies the term to chastity or to some other form of self-control, a significance rarely found in Aeschylus and Sophocles; this new emphasis is the single most arresting element in his interpretation of the virtue.

Euripides is also the first tragic poet to exploit fully and deliberately the dramatic possibilities inherent in the manifold connotations of sophrosyne. It is true that in several tragedies involving various nuances of the virtue no particular dramatic effect is achieved by their interplay, and none seems to be intended; in such instances we merely see the wide scope of the word in ordinary usage. The *Iphigeneia in Aulis* (perhaps not Euripidean in its entirety) includes at least five such nuances—moderation (379), sanity (407), chastity (543–44), modesty (824), and good sense (1024)—but the poet does not deliberately play off one meaning against another. In several plays, however, he makes dramatic capital out of the fact that sophrosyne can mean several different things. The alternation between the meanings "chastity" and "moderation" in the

[90] Jaeger, *Paideia*, 1. 353.

Andromache is a case in point, as are the plays on the meanings "wise" and "chaste" in the *Medea,* or "wise" and "temperate" in the *Cyclops.*[91] But the greatest importance is attached to the multiplicity of meanings in those tragedies that illustrate the danger of taking a one-sided view of the virtue. This concern, which is most evident in the *Hippolytus* and the *Bacchae,* is the second striking innovation in Euripides' treatment of sophrosyne.

Both innovations owe something to sophistic influence. While Euripides' conception of sophrosyne must have originated in his own intuition, heightened no doubt by his observation of the suffering caused by the war with Sparta, it must also have been shaped by his participation in contemporary modes of thought. Certain Sophists appear to have been among the first to develop systematically the concept of sophrosyne as the control of man's lower impulses and appetites. Antiphon the Sophist, as we shall see, defined it as the rule and conquest of self (Frag. 58 DK). Gorgias' pupil Callicles, in the Platonic dialogue, regarded it as the limitation of appetite (491E), and Critias in his elegiac poem on the Spartan constitution interprets it as temperance in drink (Frag. 6 DK). The common view of the late fifth century is expressed in Agathon's speech in Plato's *Symposium,* which defines sophrosyne as the control of pleasure and desire (196C ff.). Most of the hostility towards sophrosyne which appears at this time stems from an interpretation of the virtue as a kind of spoilsport which deprives life of all that makes it worth living.[92] Euripides' interpretation of sophrosyne as a form of self-control belongs in this tradition.

His persistent criticism of limited or imperfect sophrosyne also finds parallels and perhaps inspiration in the sophistic challenge to traditional values. One thinks of Antiphon's attack on conventional law (Frag. 44 DK), Critias' attack on conventional notions about the gods (Frag. 25 DK), and the attack on sophrosyne itself by the *Adikos Logos* in the *Clouds* and by Callicles in the *Gorgias.* This critical reappraisal is the

---

[91] In the *Andromache,* whenever sophrosyne is referred to by the anti-Spartan Andromache and Peleus, it means chastity and is part of the attack on the notorious wantonness of Spartan women and the failure of their husbands to control them (235, 345–46, 595–96). When the word is used by Menelaus or the Chorus, against Andromache and Peleus, it means moderation (365, 686, 741), since the Spartans can claim this nuance of the virtue more plausibly than chastity. As we learn from Thucydides, sophrosyne in the sense of political moderation or conservatism is felt at this time to be a Spartan slogan. When Andromache uses the word *sôphrôn,* it is the antithesis to words meaning "wanton"; when Menelaus and the Chorus use it, sophrosyne is opposed to *thymos* and *orgê.* Cf. *Me.* 1369; *I.A.* 1024; *Cyc.* 337.

[92] See my article on opposition to sophrosyne in Greek thought, *T.A.P.A.* 78 (1947), 1–17.

background against which the *Hippolytus* should be read, although being earlier than most records of sophistic teaching, it might better perhaps serve as background for the development of the sophistic ideas themselves.

While sophrosyne has many ramifications in Euripides' drama, it is most frequently associated with certain recurrent themes, entirely different from the set of antitheses that Aeschylus connected with it, but equally persistent. One of these is the study of feminine psychology. In the extensive gallery of wicked and passionate women who people Euripidean tragedy, there are few whose destructive effect on society cannot be traced to a failure in sophrosyne; and in the case of Medea, Phaedra, and Hermione this failure is explicitly stated. As a counterpoise to the wicked woman Euripides develops in unprecedented detail the stereotype of the *sôphrôn* woman. The speeches of Andromache in both the *Troades* and the *Andromache,* as well as the conduct of Alcestis and other noble heroines, fill out a type (already suggested by Sophocles' Tecmessa) that was thereafter to remain constant in drama and oratory. The sophrosyne of a married woman naturally includes chastity, but Euripides broadens the concept to include other aspects of a good wife's behavior. Quietness and tact are part of it, according to Andromache, who in the *Troades* describes by the one word *sôphrôn* all her life under Hector's roof. Knowing what blame attaches to women who roam abroad, she stayed within the house, and she did not share in the gossip of other women but kept her own counsel. To Hector she presented a quiet glance and a silent tongue, knowing in what things she should prevail over her husband, and in what yield (645–56). In the *Andromache* another note is added, the absence of jealousy, which is appropriate because Andromache is here contrasted to the jealous Hermione. Macaria and Antigone, in the *Heracleidae* and the *Phoenissae,* exemplify the sophrosyne of the unmarried woman. Macaria says that for a woman silence and modesty (σωφρονεῖν) and staying quietly in the house are best (476–77), while Antigone, when Oedipus is concerned lest it be unmaidenly for her to accompany him into exile, concludes that it would be noble (γενναία), provided that she is modest in her behavior (σωφρονούσῃ [1692]).[93] The contrast with Sophocles' Antigone, for whom nobility and sophrosyne are incompatible, is arresting.

Masculine sophrosyne has a special importance in the *Hippolytus* and the *Bacchae,* to which we shall presently return. Apart from these two

---

[93] See Arthur Adkins, *Merit and Responsibility* (Oxford, 1960), 184, on Antigone's response. Other allusions to the *sôphrôn* wife include *Alc.* 181–82, 615; *I.A.* 1159, Frags. 909. 3, 545. 1, 543. 5.

instances the theme is not a favorite with Euripides, and he presents no stereotype of the *sôphrôn anêr*.[94] Only when a man represents a state, and the state is Athens, does Euripides in the extant tragedies endow a male character with unambiguous sophrosyne. Demophon in the *Heracleidae* and Theseus in both the *Suppliants* and the *Heracles* display certain characteristics of the *sôphrôn* man and the *sôphrôn polis*—notably the kind treatment of suppliants and defeated enemies and loyalty to friends—which were important elements in the "image" of Athens disseminated by Athenian propaganda (such as *epitaphioi logoi*) now and in the fourth century.[95] Eurystheus says that Athens spared him σωφρονοῦσα, having regard for the Divine, rather than showing enmity towards himself (*Heracleidae* 1012), and Theseus in the *Heracles* exhibits the kind of steadfast loyalty towards his friend that, as J. T. Sheppard has demonstrated, is at this time considered proof of sophrosyne.[96] Although Euripides (in the extant plays, at least) pays less attention than Aeschylus to sophrosyne as a virtue of the *polis*, a long fragment from the satyr play *Autolycus* contains an important reference to this form of excellence. It is remarkable for being the only passage in Euripides in which all four of the cardinal virtues are mentioned, and is even more remarkable for adding as a fifth, not *eusebeia*, but eloquence. With a reminiscence of Xenophanes' preference for *sophia* over athletic ability as a benefit to the *polis*, Euripides says (Frag. 282. 23–28):

It is necessary to crown with garlands men who are intelligent and courageous [σοφούς τε κἀγαθούς], both whatever man provides the finest leadership for the *polis*, because he is a man of restraint and justice [σώφρων καὶ δίκαιος ἀνήρ] and whatever man by his speech [μύθοις] wards off evil deeds, preventing battles and civil strife, since such actions are fair both for the entire city and for all the Hellenes.

---

[94] As E. M. Blaiklock observes (*The Male Characters of Euripides* [Wellington, 1952], xv), Euripides treats his masculine characters realistically. The sophrosyne of Amphiaraus (*Hyps.* Frag. 12. 229–31, 236 Page), well known throughout Greece, is equated with self-control (κοσμεῖν σαυτόν). Bellerophon, a well-established type of masculine chastity, discusses the *sôphrôn erôs* in *Sthen.*, Frag. 16. 22–25 Page.

[95] On the themes common to *epitaphioi*, consult Hermann Strasburger, *Hermes* 86 (1958), 21–22; J. H. Finley, Jr., *H.S.C.P.* 64 (1946), 40–45; and Guenther Zuntz, *The Political Plays of Euripides* (Manchester, 1955), 16–20.

[96] *C.Q.* 10 (1916), 72–79. See *H.F.* 1425–26. Kitto (228) calls attention to the warning note struck amid the praise of Athenian sophrosyne in the *Suppliants*. This play ascribes the characteristics of sophrosyne to Capaneus, the greatest *hybristês* of Aeschylus, *Septem*. For the view that Euripides' Capaneus is intended as a portrait of the *sôphrôn* Nicias, see Peter Giles, *C.R.* 4 (1890), 95–98.

The addition of eloquence to the canon is peculiarly fitting for the spokesman of sophistic rhetoric,[97] but for us the greatest significance attaches to the choice of sophrosyne as a quality in the man who can best lead the *polis*.[98] What this politically oriented sophrosyne may be is not revealed, but it would be dangerous to assume that for Euripides political sophrosyne has the same connotation as for Theognis, Pindar, or Aeschylus. In the fourth century sophrosyne is sometimes linked with good administration of the household or the State,[99] and it is likely that this usage was already familiar to Euripides. In its original significance of "prudence" or "good sense" sophrosyne could advance the security and prosperity of the *polis*, perhaps especially a *polis* like Athens, which was engaged in commerce and hence depended on wise foresight and clever administration even more than would states whose prosperity was derived from agriculture. If, as was suggested previously, "moderation" or "self-control" constitutes one gateway through which sophrosyne could enter the *polis*, "good sense" (resulting in wise administration) is another. Yet these two facets of sophrosyne are not sharply distinguished, in the political any more than in the moral sphere. A speech of Orestes in the *Electra* of Euripides refers to good administration (εὖ οἰκεῖν) of cities and households and, surprisingly, cites (377 ff.) as the virtue by which a man proves himself *aristos* and capable of such administration, the self-control of the peasant who is married to Electra.[100] Euripides does not in this passage describe the peasant as *sôphrôn*, but elsewhere he does (261; cf. 53) and clearly means by it "self-controlled" rather than "shrewd" or "sensible."

Another recurrent theme is that of *sôphrôn erôs*, a natural development of Euripides' interest in the effects of overmastering passion. The *sôphrôn erôs* is love in moderation, without the extremes of passion that lead to jealousy and violence. It is a theme assigned to the Chorus in both the *Medea* and the *Hippolytus*. "May sophrosyne, the fairest gift of the gods, cherish me," sings the Chorus in the *Medea* (635–36), following the scene between Jason and Medea in which he attempts (with a show of reasonableness) to prove that he is *sophos*, *sôphrôn*, and *philos* to Medea

---

[97] Eloquence (εὐγλωσσία) is also inserted into the canon of civic virtues by the Anonymous Iamblichi (Frag. 89 DK).

[98] Adkins (*op. cit.*, 191–92) maintains—because of the grammatical subordination of sophrosyne and *dikaiosynê*—that Euripides does not regard them as part of the *aretê* of the man who is *agathos*. It seems, however, that the subordination of these two virtues, and of eloquence in a parallel structure, indicates that all three are manifestations of *aretê* in different situations.

[99] E.g., Plato *Meno* 73A 6 ff.; Xenophon *Oik.* 7–8.   [100] Cf. Adkins, *op. cit.*, 195 ff.

and their children, while she erupts with fury. The effect of the ode is double-barreled: in addition to commenting on the rage and jealousy to which excessive *erôs* has led Medea, it also calls attention to the cold calculation with which Jason acts. If she is without sophrosyne, he is without *erôs*. In the *Hippolytus* it is the Coryphaeus who comments, after Phaedra's speech about her fight to overcome passion for the sake of reputation, that what is *sôphron* is always *kalon* and wins good repute among men (431–32). This episode concludes with an ode to *Erôs* which prays that the overwhelming power of this god may not be ἄρρυθμος ("without measure" [529]). The same subject occupies an ode in the *Iphigeneia in Aulis*, where the Chorus calls blessed those who enjoy Aphrodite with sophrosyne, and prays for *metria charis* ("delight without excess" [543 ff.]). Of the numerous fragments concerned with the subject, the most explicit and detailed is Fragment 388 which speaks of the existence of "another" *erôs*, belonging to the soul that is *dikaia, sôphrôn,* and *agathê,* and recommends that men who are pious and *sôphrones* choose this principle and bid farewell to Cypris. The notion of a *sôphrôn erôs,* which was to linger as a commonplace of Hellenistic poetry, is one of several lines of thought in which Euripides anticipates Plato.[101] But whereas Plato believes that it is possible for at least some men to control *erôs* (and other forms of the irrational), Euripides invariably shows the failure of sophrosyne.

Still another subject often joined with sophrosyne is that of *physis* ("nature"). Euripides, like every other contemporary writer, reflects the great debate over the relation of *physis* to *nomos* ("convention"). Sophrosyne is involved in at least two aspects of this debate: the problem of the origin of virtue (whether it comes from nature or education) and the equally fundamental question of what human nature is really like when it is revealed by suffering or ill treatment. With regard to the origin of

[101] The concept of a twofold *erôs* is comparable to that of the twofold *aidôs* in *Hipp.* Cf. *Sthen.* Frag. 16. 22–25 Page, on the *diploi . . . erôtes,* one leading to Hades, the other to sophrosyne and *aretê*; and see Frag. 503 (*Melanippe*) for part of a conventional choral ode about *metria . . . lektra meta sôphrosynês* ("love in moderation, with self-restraint"). This Euripidean theme often appears in the tragedies of Seneca, even in those modeled on Sophoclean sources. See, e.g., Seneca *Oedipus* 882–910 , where the Sophoclean ode ἰὼ γενεαὶ βροτῶν is replaced by a typically Euripidean prayer for a moderate life devoid of excess. For the theme of *sôphrôn erôs* in Hellenistic poetry, see Cercidas, Frag. 2a Diehl[3], a parody and perversion of Euripides, *Sthen.* Frag. 16. 22–25 Page. The *sôphron erôs* is a theme of Plato's *Phaedrus* and occurs also in Xenophon *Mem.* I. 6. 13. Cf. the *dikaios erôs* of Democritus, Frag. 73 DK. Kaibel (811) records a Hadrianic inscription honoring *sôphrôn erôs* in connection with the emperor's success in killing a bear. For the theme of *sôphrôn mania,* important in mystical religion and in literary criticism, see Hans Lewy, *Sobria Ebrietas* (Giessen, 1929), and my article in *C.P.* 43 (1948), 1–17.

virtue, including sophrosyne, Euripides is firmly of opinion that *physis* plays the chief role. He sees little hope that heredity can be altered by environment. Although the words of Hippolytus to Artemis reflect an extremely unbalanced character, they nevertheless describe faithfully the usual situation in Euripidean tragedy: *Aidôs* brings forth flowers for those who possess *to sôphronein* ("chastity") not as a result of teaching but in their very nature (78–80).[102] Teiresias in the *Bacchae* reiterates this idea: Dionysus will not compel women to be chaste (σωφρονεῖν . . . εἰς τὴν Κύπριν), but *to sôphronein* is inherent in one's *physis*. Even in the revels, the *sôphrôn* woman will be safe from corruption (314–19). The conviction that *physis* is *megiston* ("most powerful" [Frag. 810]) is consonant with Euripides' belief in the "moral impotence of reason" when it comes into conflict with the powerful irrational forces of the soul and the universe.[103] Another way of inquiring into the source of sophrosyne is to examine its relation to the gods. In this form the question is complicated by the great variety of Euripidean approaches to the Divine, but it is noticeable that definitions of sophrosyne tend to involve piety, as either cause or result.[104] In so far as a god symbolizes a natural force—some aspect of *physis*—we may perhaps say that sophrosyne is related to the gods, as the chastity of Hippolytus manifests the power of Artemis, but the relationship is obviously not Aeschylean. The concept of a god who leads mankind to wisdom through suffering is foreign to Euripides.

As for the true nature that is revealed by suffering, the answer in such plays as the *Medea, Hippolytus, Electra,* and *Hecuba* is the realistic one: when we see *physis* as it actually is, we see passion triumphant and sophrosyne defeated. The contrast between Euripides and Sophocles is nowhere greater than in their treatment of this problem. The *physis* revealed by suffering or some other test in Sophoclean tragedy is seldom *sôphrôn,* but it is at least *agathê* ("noble"). For Euripides, suffering has the same effect as poverty, which Orestes in the *Electra* maintains is a teacher of evil (376).

In his treatment of these and other themes Euripides employs the word sophrosyne with a variety of nuances. As we have observed, the most common meaning of all is "control of passion, appetite, or emotion." For

---

[102] In *Hippolytus,* as Pohlenz observes (1. 271), the sophrosyne of Hippolytus, which is his by nature, is never lost; but Phaedra's, which she cannot maintain, is by her own admission the product of training and practice.

[103] See E. R. Dodds, *C.R.* 43 (1929), 97–104. For the priority of *physis* over *trophê,* see also Frags. 333, 1068; *Hipp.* 921–22; *Hec.* 592–600. The opposite view is presented in *Supp.* 911 ff. and *I.A.* 558–72.

[104] E.g., *Hipp.* 995–96; *Ba.* 1150; *Or.* 502–3; Frags. 446, 388.

the first time in Greek literature the normal significance of sophrosyne is "self-control." Since sexual passion is so overwhelming a motive in Euripidean tragedy, the meaning "chastity" occurs with great frequency in the plays and the Fragments, usually referring to women, but sometimes also to men.[105] Related to this usage is the meaning "modesty"— as when Hecuba tells Helen that she would be dressed in rags, if she had more sophrosyne than effrontery (*Troades* 1027); so, too, is the general connotation of behavior suitable to a good wife. Control of anger (*thymos, orgê*) and the practice of forbearance towards an enemy are sometimes described as sophrosyne by Euripides,[106] in whose tragedies the victory of passion in the form of anger is common. The dangers of yielding to *thymos* and *orgê* were recognized by earlier authors,[107] but Euripides is especially sensitive to the consequences resulting from the triumph of anger and vengefulness. In the *Medea, Hecuba,* and *Heracleidae* he shows the horrors of vengeance so graphically as to shift the sympathy of the audience from the original victim to the oppressor when he in turn becomes a victim. Fragment 799 relates control of anger to the old theme of mortality: "Since our bodies are mortal, it befits any man who understands how to control himself [*sôphronein*] not to cherish immortal wrath."

Sophrosyne only infrequently designates the control of the appetites for food and drink, probably because these appetites are not sufficiently dignified for tragedy.[108] A play on two meanings of *sôphrôn* enlivens a passage in the satyr play, *Cyclops,* where the giant boasts that his god is his belly, and adds that to eat and drink all day and have no cares at all is "god" to one who is truly *sôphrôn* (334–38). *Sôphrôn* here means "sensible, wise," but in this context the fact that the word can also mean "temperate" would not be lost on the audience.[109]

Sophrosyne may also indicate resistance to ambition (as in *Hipp.*

[105] See, in addition to passages already cited: *El.* 923, 1080, 1099; *Or.* 558, 1132; *Hel.* 47, 932, 1684; *Troad.* 1056; *I.A.* 1159; *Me.* 1369; *Hipp.* 413, 431, 667, 1034; Frag. 909. 3; *Ba.* 314, 316, 318. Masculine chastity: Frag. 446 (from the first *Hipp.*); *El.* 53, 261; *Hipp.* 949, 995, 1007, 1035, 1100, 1365, 1402; *Hyps.* 12. 229, 236 Page. While masculine and feminine chastity are both described with the word sophrosyne, they derive from different aspects of this virtue: the masculine from self-control, resistance to excess, the opposite of *hybris;* the feminine from obedience or dutifulness.

[106] E.g., *Herac.* 1107; *Or.* 502; *And.* 741; *Ba.* 641.

[107] Theognis 631 f.; Epicharmus, Frags. 281, 282 Kaibel, *Com.*; Heraclitus, Frag. 85 DK.

[108] See Frag. 893 on the *sôphrôn* table; cf. Frags. 892, 413. Democritus (Frag. 210 DK) contrasts the frugal table set by sophrosyne and the lavish one set by *tychê* ("fortune"). "Sober" is the meaning of *sôphrôn* once or twice in the *Bacchae* (686, 940), but the connotation is uncommon elsewhere.

[109] For a similar play on words, see *Alc.* 753, where οὔτι σωφρόνως means both "noisy and overbearing" and "drunken."

1013), but in this area it impinges upon another aspect of the virtue—that of self-knowledge and "thinking mortal thoughts"—which should probably be classified under our second category, the intellectual, although the moral consequences are obvious. The distinction can never be precise, since the basic concept of sophrosyne as control of the passions and appetites—that is, of the irrational—implies that the virtue itself is allied with reason, and its etymology always reminded the Greeks of this fact.[110] Sometimes its intellectual affinities are more prominent than its moral implications; then it finds itself allied with *nous* (as in *Andr.* 231, 235, 237) and *sophia* (as in *Ba.* 641) rather than with *aidôs* or *eusebeia*, and opposed to *anoia* ("folly") rather than to *anaideia* ("effrontery"). The intellectual meaning—"understanding, wise judgment"—is inextricably bound up with the moral when Phaedra says that she had meant to endure her *anoia* in silence and bear it with sophrosyne (*Hipp.* 399). A like combination of intellectual and moral implications underlies Dionysus' remark to the Theban royal family at the end of the *Bacchae* (1341): "If you had known how to achieve understanding [*sôphronein*] when you were unwilling to do so, you could have been happy and had the son of Zeus as your ally." *Sôphrôn* sometimes means "wise, intelligent" in a fairly emphatic sense (*Me.* 311; *Hipp.* 704); but much more often it conveys a weaker intellectualism, such as permeates the common phrase ἢν σωφρονῇς and its variants, where *sôphronein* means merely "to be sensible, have ordinary prudence, *être sage.*" Next to chastity, this *sens intellectuelle affaiblie,* as De Vries calls it, is the most common meaning of *sôphrôn* in Euripides,[111] but the least important dramatically. The intellectual meaning has greater force in a phrase from the *Helen, sôphrôn apistia* (1617), which Dodds well translates "enlightened skepticism."[112] An extension of the original Homeric soundness of mind is "sanity," contrasted with *mania* or *nosos phrenôn,* as in the *Orestes* when Electra says (254) to her brother, who is terrified at the approach of the Furies: "You are growing wild-eyed, you are becoming frenzied, who were just now in your right mind [σωφρονῶν]."[113] Similarly, in the *Troades* Hecuba says that Cassandra's misfortunes have brought her to her senses (ἐσωφρονήκασ᾽ [350]).

A third important nuance, "moderation," must be distinguished, although it is often hard to determine whether the chief implication is actually moderation or self-control in some form. "Moderation" seems

---

110 Unlike the Romans, who found in *temperantia* no specifically intellectual associations.
111 G. J. de Vries, *Mnem.* 11 (1943), 86. E.g., *Ba.* 329, 504; *Troad.* 350; *Or.* 1509; *Hel.* 1657; *I.A.* 1024, 1208; *Herac.* 263; *Me.* 549, 884, 913.
112 Dodds, *loc. cit.,* 100.   113 Cf. *I.A.* 407: συνσωφρονεῖν contrasted with συννοσεῖν.

preferable when sophrosyne is associated with a revival of *hybris* in the Aeschylean sense. This is a feature of Euripides' late tragedies, the *Phoenissae* and the *Bacchae*, and it is appropriate that the Aeschylean meaning of sophrosyne—"observance of limits," especially those established by the gods—should reappear. The *hybris* of Eteocles in the *Phoenissae* takes the form of unjust ambition for *tyrannis*, in pursuit of which he is willing to commit any *adikia* (523–25). Jocasta brands this ambition *philotimia* (532) and tells him that it will not bring happiness, since sufficiency is enough for the moderate (τοῖς γε σώφροσιν [554]).[114] In the *Bacchae* Pentheus and his mother are accused of *hybris* (555, 516, 1297, 1303, 1347); and instead of indicating violence against men, as is usual in Euripides,[115] *hybris* again means the refusal of honor due a god. Moderation is an important aspect of sophrosyne in all references to the *sôphrôn erôs* and also in those passages that bring sophrosyne close to *aidôs* and *ta metria*.[116] There is a clue to the basic meaning of sophrosyne for Euripides in the fact that whereas for Aeschylus and Sophocles its closest neighbor is *phronêsis*, in Euripides it has a deeper kinship with *aidôs*.

The tension between two or more conceptions of sophrosyne and the exposure of characters whose sophrosyne is either incomplete or illusory are important elements in the *Hippolytus* and the *Bacchae*. Even earlier, in the *Medea*, Euripides had depicted Jason as a complacent bourgeois, who boasted that he was *sôphrôn* and criticized Medea for her lack of this quality, while in fact he was selfish and calculating, an example of pseudo sophrosyne like the nonlover in Plato's *Phaedrus*. The poet demonstrates in this play the Greeks' dawning awareness that even a virtue can lose its balance, and that this particular virtue may degenerate from authentic self-control into heartless cruelty.[117] The opposition

---

[114] The contrast between the heroic Aeschylean Eteocles and his counterpart in Euripides reflects the spread of *philotimia* and *pleonexia* in the course of the Peloponnesian war (traced stage by stage in Thucydides' *History;* see below, Chapter III). Eteocles is the would-be *tyrannos* of that time, as his brother is the *phygas*, the political exile of the age. Jocasta's use of the *metra* in nature (541–48) as an argument for sophrosyne is remotely comparable to Ajax' reference to nature in his speech of deception. The *hybris* of the attackers in the *Phoen.* echoes the same theme in Aeschylus; once again Amphiaraus alone has no arrogant blazon, but σωφρόνως ("modestly") bears an unmarked shield (1111–12).

[115] *Me.* 1366; *Herac.* 18; *H.F.* 708. Cf. Del Grande, 148–210.

[116] *Aidôs: .Hipp.* 78–81, 995–99; *I.A.* 379, 821–24; Frag. 209. *Ta metria: Me.* 119–30; Frag. 893. Other passages in which the primary meaning of *sôphrôn* is "moderate" include: *Andr.* 365, 686; *Herac.* 272; *Ba.* 1150; Frag. 505.

[117] It was this realization that led Aristotle to formulate the doctrine of the Mean, which opposed true sophrosyne to the equally vicious extremes of profligacy and insensibility (*Eth. Nic.* 1118b 28–1119a 20).

to sophrosyne in Euripides' plays concentrates on this kind of weakness —the lack of generosity and self-knowledge—rather than on the confusion of sophrosyne with cowardice which we sometimes find in Sophocles and Thucydides.[118]

The criticism of sophrosyne is only a minor theme in the *Medea;* in the *Hippolytus* and the *Bacchae* it is fundamental. Both plays regard sophrosyne, basically, as the power that resists the irrational. In one the opposing force is called *erôs* and is represented in the Prologue by Aphrodite; while in the other it is called by various names implying irrationality (*mania* itself or a synonym), and Dionysus is the divine representative, but the struggle is always the same. Aphrodite, as the nurse observes (*Hipp.* 360, 447), is not a mythological or a religious entity, but an irresistible cosmic power, while Dionysus stands for all the forces of nature, beautiful or terrible or both, which have nothing to do with reason and morality. Aphrodite herself belongs to his sphere (*Ba.* 773–74). It is the task of sophrosyne to control these forces, and the essence of the tragedy in both plays is that the sophrosyne of the chief figures is too limited to succeed.

The similarity between the situations in the two plays has been the subject of repeated analysis,[119] but less attention has been paid to the differences, one of which is the extent to which the *Bacchae* goes beyond the *Hippolytus* in its treatment of sophrosyne.

In the *Hippolytus* Artemis is the divine symbol of the force that attracts the young hero; this force is manifested in him as a fanatical chastity, and whenever he boasts of his sophrosyne, as he so often does (995, 1007, 1034–35, 1100, 1364–65), it is chastity that he means.[120] In the first scene there is an undeniable beauty—the beauty of wild places and intimacy with nature—associated with Hippolytus and his chosen way of life, but it soon becomes clear that he is in a very dangerous spiritual condition.[121] His sophrosyne is genuine but pitifully limited. Chastity alone is not the total virtue: *Mêden agan* (praised by the nurse [250 ff.]) and *Gnôthi sauton* are inseparable from sophrosyne, but Hippolytus is

[118] The only example of this confusion in Euripides is the reference to Odysseus in *Troad.* 422–23 as a *sôphrôn* woman. Cf. Sophocles *Phil.* 1259–60.

[119] E.g., Dodds, *loc. cit.;* Kitto, 383; Winnington-Ingram, 17 ff., 27, 174.

[120] The one exception—when Hippolytus says that ambition is not characteristic of the *sôphrôn* (1013)—recalls Creon in *O.T.* 589. One is tempted to hear in such a novel use of the word an echo of the recently performed *Oedipus.* Hippolytus' analysis of his own sophrosyne (995 ff.) indicates that its sources are piety, *aidôs,* and sexual purity.

[121] The same beauty and the same danger—the rejection of normal life—are associated with Camilla in the *Aeneid.*

without moderation or self-knowledge. His devotion to Artemis excludes
even the objective recognition that Aphrodite also has legitimate claims,
and his rejection of this goddess arouses well-justified fears in the huntsman (114–20).[122] On the human level there is a parallel act of *hybris:*
Hippolytus' denunciation of women and his tirade against Phaedra,
which is fanatically cruel and intemperate, and which drives her first to
revenge, then to suicide.

When Artemis ultimately appears, she herself confirms the impression
that Hippolytus' sophrosyne has already left with us. Far from making
it possible for Hippolytus to die in the odor of sophrosyne,[123] she can
only promise to take vengeance on some favorite of Aphrodite (1420–22).
Clearly she herself is not a rational force, any more than is her rival. As
Dodds observes, she is merely the negative pole, "the principle of aloofness, of refusal, ultimately of death,"[124] and it is no wonder that she
proves unable to control the force symbolized by Aphrodite, the Venus
Genetrix. Even within the play the defects of Hippolytus' sophrosyne are
recognized, notably by Phaedra in her final speech when she says that
by her death she will teach Hippolytus not to exult over her woes.
He will share her νόσος ("disease") and σωφρονεῖν μαθήσεται ("learn to
behave with moderation" [730–31])—one of the most effective plays on
the meanings of sophrosyne in all Greek literature. The nurse in an
earlier speech (358–61) comments on the impotence of sophrosyne as she
sees it in practice: "Those who are *sôphrones* nevertheless have evil
desires, even against their will. Cypris is not after all a goddess, but something greater, which has destroyed Phaedra and me and the whole
household."[125] She is actually referring to the chastity that Phaedra has
vainly tried to achieve, but her observation applies in a sense to the
sophrosyne of Hippolytus, too, which is so limited in scope as to be
helpless when confronted with the irrational.

In the futile effort of Phaedra to overcome her passion by self-control
(*sôphronein* [398–99]), Euripides sees yet another failure of the rational.
Unlike Hippolytus, Phaedra cannot claim to be *sôphrôn* by her very
nature. Her sophrosyne is an acquired virtue, which proves just as
inadequate as the "natural" virtue of Hippolytus (400–401), but in

---

[122] Cf. the unbalanced devotion of the Danaids to Artemis and the hint at the close
of Aeschylus' *Suppliants* that Aphrodite and Hera too must be honored.

[123] As S. M. Adams suggests, *C.R.* 49 (1935), 119.

[124] *C.R.* 43 (1929), 102.

[125] Aristotle rejects the possibility that the *sôphrôn* can have evil desires. According to
his system, Phaedra would be *akratês* (*Eth. Nic.* 1104b 5–7). On the sophrosyne of Hippolytus
and Phaedra, see Gilbert Norwood, *Essays on Euripidean Drama* (Berkeley, 1954), 84–89.

a different way. Phaedra confesses that, in common with the rest of humanity, she knows what is right but cannot put it into practice (380–81).[126] Ironically, it is in part because of her *aidôs* that she fails. The "good" *aidôs*, a sense of shame and concern for her reputation—especially as it affects her children (405–30)—prompts her to try to conquer Cypris by sophrosyne, but the "bad" *aidôs*, the compunction that leads her, against her judgment, to reveal to the nurse the nature of her illness (335), opens the floodgates of disaster.[127] The nurse, expressing herself in sophistic terms, maintains that by fighting so strong a power as *erôs* (against which the gods themselves are helpless) Phaedra is guilty of *hybris* (446, 474). According to this perverted view, it would actually be a kind of sophrosyne to give in and accept the common lot of gods and men. The nurse does not, however, go so far as to draw this conclusion. Her reversal of values is not complete, and at the climax of her speech she says (494) that Phaedra must give way to passion precisely because she is not *sôphrôn*—"chaste," the ordinary meaning of the word when applied to a woman.

Finally, in this wholesale condemnation of inadequate sophrosyne, Euripides does not overlook Theseus, who is here portrayed, not as the *sôphrôn* representative of Athens, but merely as an impetuous and blinded husband and father. While denouncing the sophrosyne of his son as mere hypocrisy (949–57), he betrays his own violation of sophrosyne by his indulgence in anger and rash judgment. His son concludes his defense with a statement (1034–35) that draws attention to the baffling nature of sophrosyne throughout the play: "Phaedra behaved with self-control [ἐσωφρόνησεν] although she had not the power to be chaste [σωφρονεῖν], while I, who have the power, have not used it well." The play on two slightly different nuances of *sôphronein*—"to control oneself" and "to be naturally chaste"—is impossible to render in English.[128]

The tragic inadequacy of partial sophrosyne is the theme to which Euripides returns in the *Bacchae* (this play, like the *Hippolytus*, could be subtitled "The Sôphrôn Hybristês"), but here his treatment is more complex and ironic. The pattern of the *Hippolytus* is after all relatively

126 Cf. *Me.* 1079. An illuminating study of Phaedra's environment as it affects her behavior is provided by R. P. Winnington-Ingram in *Euripide*, ed. J. C. Kamerbeek (Vandoeuvres-Genève, 1960), 169–91.

127 See E. R. Dodds, *C.R.* 39 (1925), 102–4.

128 A. E. Housman used this passage to support his theory that a noun σωφρόνη existed in tragedy; he maintained that "the line *she was virtuous though unable to be so* is a contradiction in terms" (*C.R.* 2 [1888], 242–45). It seems less contradictory if we recognize the typically Euripidean play on the multiple nuances of sophrosyne.

simple: on the mythological level the embodiment of passion is opposed
to the embodiment of chastity, and on the human level, passion destroys
those who try to suppress it, along with the innocent bystanders (but no
one is wholly innocent), since it is the nature of passion to be indiscriminate. In the *Bacchae* the irrational is once again opposed by human
reason, which proves unable to cope with the terrible forces of Nature,
seen this time in the form of orgiastic religious emotion. Again we discover the narrowness and imperfection of the sophrosyne which the
champion of reason claims to possess: he has chastity and sobriety
indeed, but without self-knowledge, imagination, or genuine understanding of reality. Yet Pentheus is more complex than Hippolytus.
Even his chastity and sobriety are superficial and insecure and give way
before the first serious temptation. He lacks poise and self-control in the
face of opposition, and he shows several of the traditional marks of the
tyrant.[129] Moreover, Dionysus, instead of being merely a symbol of the
irrational, as Aphrodite was, makes a startling claim to possess sophrosyne himself. It is the contrast between the two kinds of sophrosyne, that
of Pentheus and that of the Dionysiac god and his Asian Bacchae,
which lies at the heart of the tragedy.

What is the sophrosyne of Dionysus? Throughout the play he calls
himself *sôphrôn* and *sophos* and, in the face of Pentheus' emotional out-
bursts, displays an unearthly, if ultimately a sinister, calm.[130] This
is sophrosyne in a more or less conventional sense. But the chorus of
Asian Bacchae meanwhile lays claim to another kind of sophrosyne, and
this, too, is Dionysiac. At first this sophrosyne allies itself with the old
Hellenic doctrines of "Think mortal thoughts" and "Nothing in excess"
(395–401), but presently it is equated with a strange kind of wisdom
which accepts the most brutal, along with the most joyous, manifestations
of unrestrained emotion.[131] The beauty and freedom of the wild and the
ghastly rites of *sparagmos* and *omophagia* are equally a part of this wisdom.
Dionysus, as he himself says, is most terrible to men but also most
tender ($\delta\epsilon\iota\nu\acute{o}\tau\alpha\tau\sigma\varsigma \ldots \mathring{\eta}\pi\iota\acute{\omega}\tau\alpha\tau\sigma\varsigma$ [861]). The cruelty with which he
makes Pentheus ridiculous in his woman's disguise and sends him to his

---

[129] See Winnington-Ingram, 45 ff.; G. M. A. Grube, *T.A.P.A.* 66 (1935), 40; and
E. R. Dodds, *C.R.* 43 (1929), 97–104; *H.T.R.* 33 (1940), 155 ff.; and his edition of the
Bacchae (Oxford, 1960), xliii, 97, etc., for various post-Freudian analyses of Pentheus. Dodds
regards Hippolytus, too, as a victim of suppressed desires.

[130] Dionysus as *sôphrôn:* 504, 641. Another key word is *hêsychia;* the calmness of Dionysus
contrasts with the *thymos* and *orgê* of Pentheus (389, 636, 647, 997).

[131] Winnington-Ingram analyzes the mixture of joy and terror in the odes; see especially
pp. 38–39, 59 ff., 107.

death, the vengefulness of the Chorus, and the unbearable *anagnorisis* (recognition) to which Agave is subjected, all combine to make the sophrosyne of Dionysus a baffling quality. Is not Euripides attacking Dionysus and his sophrosyne, just as surely as he is exposing Pentheus and his? The reproach of Cadmus (1348), "It is not fitting for gods to imitate men (ὁμοιοῦσθαι βροτοῖς) in wrath," comes too close to the prayer of the old servant in the *Hippolytus* (114–20) to be ignored.[132]

But the analogy with the earlier play suggests the answer. The reproach is genuine and is directed against the anthropomorphic conception of the god; yet the revelation of the power that Dionysus represents is also genuine. Moreover, the hint that there is a kind of sophrosyne which can honor Dionysus without shaming Apollo (328–29) constitutes a significant advance over the *Hippolytus*. There the poet contented himself with exposing the failure of sophrosyne, on every level, to control passion. In the *Bacchae* he postulates the existence of another sophrosyne which can embrace *mania*—can, that is, understand the place of the irrational in the human soul and somehow come to terms with it. In effect, Euripides here calls attention to the paradox that had always been implicit in Greek drama (whether tragedy, comedy, or satyr play), the paradox expressed centuries later by a poet of the *Greek Anthology,* who observed that when Bacchus established the satyr drama at Sicyon, he taught sophrosyne to the townsman though he was himself a drunkard (ὁ μεθύων ἄστον ἐσωφρόνισεν [11. 32]).

It is no part of the dramatist's purpose to analyze this sophrosyne (that is a task for a philosopher, and Plato did not reject the challenge); nor can it be denied that some of its manifestations are appalling. But the response of Dionysus (1349) to Cadmus' reproach—"Long ago this was ordained by Zeus, my father"—is a guarantee that, dreadful and mysterious as these events are, they must be accepted.[133] Euripides does not pretend, any more than Aeschylus or Sophocles pretend, that reality is pleasant to contemplate; but he seems to suggest, as indeed each of them in his own way suggests, that there is a sophrosyne that enables man to face reality in all its manifestations. The total effect of the *Bacchae* is pessimistic in a characteristically Euripidean fashion—the failure of human reason, the shallowness of human pretensions to virtue, the malignity of the gods, and the indiscriminate operation of natural

---

[132] Both speeches reveal Euripides' intense concern for what may perhaps be called ὁμοίωσις βροτῷ ("the imitation of man") in his demands upon the gods.

[133] Cf. the closing words of Sophocles *Trach.* 1278, which ascribe to Zeus the responsibility for an equally terrible situation.

forces—but there is one gleam of hope: *eudaimonia* could somehow result from a sophrosyne that could understand the Dionysiac and avoid the denial of its demands which in the *Bacchae* is constantly equated with *hybris*.[134] "If you had known how to achieve understanding [*sôphronein*], when you would not do so," says Dionysus to Cadmus and Agave (1341–43), "you would be happy and have the son of Zeus as your champion." [135]

---

[134] E.g., 555, 516, 1297, 1347.

[135] Cf. the promise of a life without care to those who possess the γνώμαν σώφρονα ("modest frame of mind" [1002–4]). But Murray would read γνωμᾶν σωφρόνα with Housman's hypothetical noun σωφρόνη (*castigatrix*), while Dodds would emend to γνωμᾶν σωφρόν<ισμ>α θάνατος and translate "death is a corrective of his purposes." Euripides' treatment of sophrosyne in the *Bacchae* in certain respects anticipates the ideas expressed by Plato in the *Laws,* where he attempts to render Dionysus socially useful. Despite a fundamental difference in approach (Plato always assumes the supremacy of reason), there are two points of resemblance. One is the insistence that all must share in the worship of Dionysus. In the *Bacchae* Teiresias forestalls possible criticism of his and Cadmus' behavior by saying that the god makes no distinction between young and old but demands honor from all (206–9). Plato insists that just as the children and young men gather in choruses to honor the Muses and Apollo, the older men must form a chorus in honor of Dionysus. It is typical of the difference between the two approaches to Dionysus that whereas Euripides would have the old men serve the god and yield to his mysterious power, Plato turns the god to the service of education and the state, so that the drinking party, strictly controlled by law, may help old men renew their youth and preserve the effects of *paideia* (664C–667B 5). A more fundamental similarity lies in the view held by both Euripides and Plato that, under the influence of Dionysus, character is revealed. How ancient and widespread this belief was we learn from the lyric poets and the Attic *skolia,* which show that the Greeks felt it imperative yet profoundly difficult to discover a means of testing character; see A. Körte, *Hermes* 64 (1929), 69–86. In Euripides, to whom this theme is very important, the test is often time (*Hipp.* 428–30; Frag. 60), but in the *Bacchae* he indicates that such is also the power of wine (e.g., 314–18, 918–70, where the *physis* of Pentheus is laid bare). Plato takes over the search for a touchstone, and he, too, finds a test in wine but, unlike Euripides, strives to use the test for social and political ends. The symposium described in *Laws* I is designed to reveal the character of young men for the benefit of the State, and the particular quality tested by the device of *methê* is sophrosyne. In the *Laws* the effect of *methê* is good, and in the *Phaedrus,* where Divine madness is praised above human sophrosyne, the effects of *mania* are also good. This conclusion is not drawn in the *Bacchae.*

III

The Age of the Sophists

RATIONAL criticism of traditional values and unfettered speculation about ethics, politics, and religion were conspicuous activities of the first generation of Sophists, whose influence in Athenian intellectual life had already been manifest for at least a decade before the outbreak of the Peloponnesian war.[1] Their modes of thought had a powerful—often a disintegrating—impact on such concepts as justice, piety, and sophrosyne, which up to now had based their claims for the most part on religious or social sanctions or on uncritically accepted rules of conduct. Sophrosyne entered upon a new stage of its development under the rigorous scrutiny of the Sophists and those who adopted their methods of inquiry. Three of these methods were particularly effective:

1. The search for precise distinctions of words and ideas, which included the effort to define with greater exactitude the ethical concepts familiar in a vague and popular sense for generations.[2]

2. The application to ethics and politics of certain forms of argumentation which had been developed in the early stages of sophistic rhetoric, notably the arguments from probability, advantage, and nature. The third of these was itself only a special form of the debate over the relation of *physis* ("nature") to *nomos* ("convention"),[3] which gave rise in education and politics to such questions as "What is the source of *aretê* —nature or training?" and "How, if at all, can *aretê* be imparted?"

---

[1] For the view that the *Antilogies* of Protagoras are reflected in the *Ajax* and *Antigone* of Sophocles and that the treatise *On Concord* by Antiphon the Sophist influenced the *Alcestis* and *Medea* of Euripides, see John H. Finley Jr., *H.S.C.P.* 50 (1939), 35–84.

[2] The Sophists chiefly associated with this search for precision and clarity are Protagoras and Prodicus. See Heinrich Gomperz, *Sophistik und Rhetorik* (Leipzig, 1912), 198, 96–97.

[3] For a detailed study of this subject, see Felix Heinemann, *Nomos und Physis* (Basel, 1945).

3. The special study of human nature in connection with the State
and with rhetoric, the avenue to power in a democracy. This study was
concerned with motives for action—particularly appetites and passions
—and goals, both immediate and ultimate—chiefly power and pleasure.[4]
It often resulted in the "realistic" view of human nature which we have
already observed in Euripides and in the development of a hedonistic
calculus such as frequently underlay the ethical teachings of the great
Sophists. This study not only proved useful to oratory, for which it was
principally designed, but also influenced the writers of drama and history.

In regard to all three of these sophistic lines of thought, our best
witnesses are not the Sophists themselves, but Euripides and Thucydides,
who testify to the entire period between ca. 440 B.C. and the last years
of the fifth century, and who reflect the moral and intellectual as well
as the political developments of the period.

The fragmentary nature of our sources and the difficulty of dating such
Fragments as we possess make it hazardous to ascribe to any of the
Sophists a systematic study of sophrosyne; it is even more difficult
to determine their relative chronology and possible influence. Yet it
seems that two Sophists of the earliest group—those who taught in
Athens before the first visit of Gorgias in 427 B.C.—traced a connection
between sophrosyne and the overriding moral issues of the period, and
in so doing employed some of the sophistic approaches that we have described. These two Sophists are Protagoras and Antiphon. The contribution of Protagoras (if we may assume that Plato's *Protagoras* is true in
essentials to the known views of the Sophist) was to analyze the by now
familiar conception of sophrosyne as a virtue of the State and to fit it
into a coherent theory of the growth of civilization. Antiphon offered the
first formal definition of sophrosyne, one that recognized as its primary
function the control of passion.

The connection of sophrosyne with the welfare of the *polis* was a
commonplace in the Dorian world of Theognis and Pindar, and the
concept of moderation, whatever it might be named, had been part of
the Athenian political orientation ever since Solon; but it remained for
the age of the Sophists to ask what sophrosyne actually contributed to
the State, how it was related to other forms of *politikê aretê*, especially
justice, and how it originated. The precise formulation of all these
questions may have been the work of Socrates, but there is evidence that
the Sophists, too, were interested in the general problem. No surviving

---

[4] On the relation between the study of this kind of *physis* and Greek medicine in the fifth
century, see Jaeger, *Paideia,* I. 306 ff., and Max Pohlenz, *Hermes* 81 (1953), 418–35.

fragment of Protagoras' works refers explicitly to sophrosyne, nor is there general agreement that we may accept the testimony of Plato,[5] but the famous myth about the origin of human society undoubtedly reflects an authentic insight of the period depicted (the dramatic date is shortly before the outbreak of the war), and it is hard to believe that Plato devised so elaborate an imitation of Protagoras' style without also reproducing his thought.

In his speech before the gathering in the house of Callias, Protagoras treats sophrosyne as a part of what he calls *politikê technê* (or *aretê*), the teaching of which is his own specific skill (*Protagoras* 319A). His discourse is divided into two parts, myth and *logos*. According to the myth, after Prometheus had endowed mankind with the two gifts of fire and technical competence, which he had stolen from Hephaestus and Athene (321C–D), human beings were in danger of extinction because they still lacked civic ability (*politikê sophia*) and could not live together in cities without wronging one another (322B–C). Zeus therefore sent Hermes to give men *aidôs* and *dikê*, which were to be a source of order (*kosmos*) and friendship; and he specifically instructed Hermes that these gifts should not be distributed just to a few, as the various crafts had been, but that all men should have a share in them (322C–D), for otherwise cities could not exist. He added that whoever could not share in *aidôs* and *dikê* must be put to death as a threat to the city's health.[6] This is why, Protagoras explains, men consult a few specialists on a question of competence in some art or craft, but when they confer about *politikê aretê*, which requires *dikaiosynê* and sophrosyne, they ask the opinion of all men (323A). As further proof of the general belief that all men share *politikê aretê*, he points out that anyone who admits that he does not possess a knowledge of justice is considered mad and is punished (324A) "obviously because *politikê aretê* is thought to be acquired through practice [*epimeleia*] and learning [*mathêsis*]." From the discussion up to the point at which Protagoras clearly marks off *mythos* from *logos* (324D), several facts emerge: sophrosyne is an aspect of *politikê aretê;* it is synonymous with *aidôs*, and therefore its function must be to provide *kosmos* and *philia* in the community; and it is not a gift of nature but is acquired and therefore accessible to all.

The part of Protagoras' speech that is concerned with *logos* elaborates

---

[5] Antonio Capizzi (*Protagora* [Firenze, 1955], 259) and Eric Havelock (*The Liberal Temper in Greek Politics* [London, 1957], 87–94, 168–69) deny that the content of the myth is Protagorean. For a different view, see Jaeger, *Paideia*, 1. 299; Mario Untersteiner, *The Sophists* (Oxford, 1954), 72–73; and W. K. C. Guthrie, *In the Beginning* (London, 1957), 90–91, 140.

[6] Cf. Democritus, Frags. 257, 258 DK.

the last point—that *politikê aretê* is acquired—and explains that it is taught, not by any special teacher, but by the very institutions of each city and by all persons with whom the child comes in contact (325C–326E). In his effort to explain why the sons of good fathers often turn out poorly, Protagoras pays more attention than he does in the myth to the element of natural endowment, without which no kind of excellence can be developed. This admission accords with a Fragment of his *Megas Logos* (Frag. 3 DK) which says that teaching has need of both *physis* and *askêsis* ("practice, effort"). One other important element in Protagoras' doctrine about *aretê* may be inferred from Plato's dialogue: he denies the unity of virtue, holding that one may be brave but unjust, or just but unwise (329E). Even after a prolonged discussion with Socrates about the resemblances among the virtues, Protagoras will not class courage with the others but maintains that it is possible to be unjust, unholy, profligate, and ignorant, and yet supremely brave (349D).[7]

Antiphon the Sophist is known from substantial Fragments of two treatises: *On Concord (Peri Homonoias)*, dated *ca.* 439 B.C.; and *Truth (Alêtheia)*, dated towards the end of the same decade.[8] He defines sophrosyne in the first of these. Despite the common application of the word *homonoia* ("concord") to the affairs of the *polis*,[9] Antiphon links it rather with the ethics of the individual in his relation both to others and to himself. He dwells on the wretchedness of human life (Frag. 51 DK), especially in the long Fragment 49 on the problems of marriage.[10] The responsibility of having a wife is likened to being burdened with a second body, which doubles all the cares involved in supporting the first. These cares include concern for health, livelihood, and reputation, for the last of which Antiphon uses four synonyms: *doxa, sôphrosynê, eukleia,* and τὸ εὐ ἀκούειν. Each of the synonyms describes a slightly different aspect of good repute, but they are basically very similar. Sophrosyne, as the word is used twice in this Fragment, can mean only "outward reputation, won by good moral conduct." This connotation recalls the external type of sophrosyne depicted by the *Dikaios Logos* in the *Clouds*

---

[7] The canon of cardinal virtues still has room for five *aretae;* they are reduced to four only in Plato *Rep.* IV.

[8] See Wolf Aly, *Philol. Supp.* 21 (1929), 153; Finley, *loc. cit.,* 63 ff.

[9] E.g., Democritus, Frag. 250 DK; Thucydides 8. 93; Xenophon *Mem.* 4. 4. 16; Thrasymachus, Frag. 1 DK; Plato *Rep.* IV. 432A. Consult Alexander Fuks, *The Ancestral Constitution* (London, 1953), 102–6. *Homonoia* in the ethics of the individual is discussed in P.W. *Supp.* IV, *s.v.* Antiphon (Stenzel). See also Ragnar Höistad, *Cynic Hero and Cynic King* (Uppsala, 1948), 108–10, where the relevance of this kind of *homonoia* to Antisthenes is considered.

[10] The close parallels in thought and language between this Fragment and Euripides *Alc.* 882–84, *Hipp.* 258–59, and *Me.* 1090–1115, 235–36, are chiefly responsible for attempts to assign an early date to *On Concord.*

of Aristophanes and the superficial definitions of the virtue offered in the early part of Plato's *Charmides*.[11]

A greater degree of inwardness is achieved in another section of Antiphon's treatise, which deals, not with concord in the family, but with *homonoia* in the soul. Fragment 58 applies a kind of calculus to the choice between doing an injury to one's neighbor and refraining from such an act, and terms *sôphrôn* the man who chooses to avoid both the act and its unpleasant consequences. Whoever fears to harm his neighbor lest he suffer harm himself is more prudent (*sôphronesteros*). Whoever thinks he can do ill to his neighbor and not suffer is unwise (οὐ σωφρονεῖ), for such hopes have a way of recoiling. Immediately after these observations, in which *sôphrôn* and σωφρονεῖ clearly refer to self-regarding prudence, Antiphon uses sophrosyne with still a third nuance.[12] No one, he maintains, could judge more properly the sophrosyne of another man than one who blocks the immediate pleasures [13] of his own *thymos* and has proved able to rule and conquer himself; but he who chooses to indulge his immediate passions chooses the worse instead of the better. This interpretation of sophrosyne as "self-control" is confirmed and expanded by Fragment 59: "Whoever has neither desired nor touched what is disgraceful or bad is not *sôphrôn*, for there is nothing over which he has gained mastery and thus proved himself *kosmios* ("orderly")." Fragments 58 and 59 possess great importance because they clearly define sophrosyne as self-control, and because they emphasize the element of struggle and conflict in attaining it. This is the sophrosyne that is dramatized repeatedly by Euripides and constitutes one of the major themes in his tragedy. There is no anticipation in either Antiphon or Euripides of Aristotle's view that sophrosyne is a habitual state requiring no effort.[14] In their opinion the warfare between reason and passion is the ground from which this virtue springs; and it is characteristic of the antithetical thinking of the early Sophists that sophrosyne should be defined in terms of its opposite.[15]

None of these Fragments from the treatise *On Concord* betrays a sign of ethical radicalism. Their interest lies in their rational approach to sophrosyne, not in any sophistic "transvaluation." [16] But it is signifi-

---

[11] *Clouds* 1002–8; *Charm.* 159B, 160E.

[12] A development from one meaning to the other can be traced, but the two are not identical, in spite of Diels' translation *besonnen* or *Besonnenheit* in either case.

[13] For the phrase αἱ παραχρῆμα ἡδοναί, cf. Plato *Prot.* 356A and Xenophon *Mem.* 2. 1. 20.

[14] *Eth. Nic.* 1099a 15–20.

[15] Antiphon says that the *sôphrôn* person avoids τὰ αἰσχρά ("what is disgraceful"), a reminder of the closeness of sophrosyne to *aidôs* in Euripides.

[16] Equally traditional is the sentiment expressed in Frag. 61, on the danger of anarchy and the desirability of obedience in children.

cant that in Fragment 49 (on marriage) Antiphon uses a calculus of
pleasures or advantages, and that the same standard, one of personal
advantage, is again used in Fragment 58 to judge whether or not one
should harm one's neighbor. A similar recourse to the criterion of utility appears in the Fragments of *Truth:* this treatise lays a foundation for
ethical relativism by asserting that *physis* is superior in authority to
nomos, and equates pleasure with "natural" interest or advantage.[17] It
must be noted, however, that the conclusions drawn from the superiority of *physis* to *nomos* in the *Gorgias* and the Melian Dialogue are not
drawn by Antiphon; hence the treatise has been dated in the decade
between 440 and 430 B.C., before this sophistic commonplace had
become a justification for unrestrained individualism.[18]

Although Antiphon the Orator is to be distinguished from his name-
sake the Sophist, and there is good reason to regard as spurious the
Tetralogies that in antiquity were ascribed to the Orator, the references
to sophrosyne in these model speeches may be considered here because
the *Tetralogies* seem to date from the age of Pericles or the early years of
the war,[19] and they contain several allusions to sophrosyne as "self-
control," the concept that appears in the treatise *On Concord.* An exception is the appearance of the verb *sôphronein* as an antithesis to "madness" in the second speech of the *First Tetralogy* (1. 2. 5), which concerns
the murder of a man returning at night from a party. If he was slain by
robbers who failed to remove his clothing because they were frightened
off by passers-by, they were in their right minds (ἐσωφρόνουν) and were
not mad, in preferring safety to gain. All other allusions to *sôphrôn,*
sôphronein, and *sôphronizein* in the *Tetralogies* imply the control of appetites
and passions. In the third speech of the *First Tetralogy,* for example, it is
suggested that those enemies of the murdered man who were not in great
danger from him would have controlled themselves, because the danger
and disgrace involved in attacking him would have been sufficient to
check (σωφρονίσαι) their passion (1. 3. 3). The *Third Tetralogy* demonstrates the use of the argument from probability in the case of an old
man who has been killed by a younger one; and the assignment of responsibility for the first blow depends on whether it is more probable that the
old or the young will be *sôphrôn.* In the third speech it is asserted that
the young are more likely than the old to behave badly when drunk

[17] Frag. 44.

[18] Aly, *loc. cit.,* 117–33. See Finley, *loc. cit.,* 70 ff., for parallels between *Truth* and early plays
of Sophocles and Euripides, and for stylistic evidence tending to date the treatise to the beginning of the sophistic period.

[19] See Wilhelm Dittenberger, *Hermes* 32 (1897), 40; Wilamowitz, *Hermes* 22 (1887), 198;
K. J. Dover, *C.Q.* 44 (1950), 44–60; and Peter Von der Mühll, *Mus. Helv.* 5 (1948), 1 ff.

because their pride of family, their strength, and their inexperience with drink cause them to give way to their passions,[20] while the opposite conditions combine to restrain (*sôphronizein*) the old (3. 3. 2). The fourth speech in this *Tetralogy* counters this argument by maintaining that young men often exhibit sophrosyne while the old become violent in drink (3. 4. 2). The antitheses to sophrosyne here are *akolasia* and *hybris*, the latter in no Aeschylean sense. Instead of being the ultimate offense against god and man, *hybris* now refers to brutal violence in general or specifically indicates the crime of malicious assault, its normal meaning in Attic law.[21] Yet such is the elasticity of the word sophrosyne that it continues to serve as the opposite of *hybris* in the language of the courtroom. *Akolasia*, which begins to appear as an antithesis to sophrosyne in the middle of the fifth century,[22] is less technical and therefore broader in its applications. In the *Third Tetralogy* it refers both to lack of control over the temper and to excess in drink. [23] The use of sophrosyne in the *Tetralogies* is entirely consistent with its meaning in the Fragments of Antiphon the Sophist but provides no basis for identifying the two authors. The conception of the virtue as control of passion, akin to *kosmiotês*, evidently began to be common in Attic usage in the decade before the outbreak of the war. The testimony of the *Tetralogies* is particularly valuable because they provide the first evidence for references to sophrosyne in oratory. Moreover, since the speaker, even in model orations, would naturally employ terms familiar to the average jury, we may feel certain that this nuance of sophrosyne is already well established in popular speech and is not just a sophistic innovation.

The other prominent Sophists of the earliest group tell us nothing about sophrosyne, although if we possessed the works of Prodicus we might find that he applied his interest in precise distinctions to this concept, as he did to *andreia*.[24] It has been suggested indeed that the distinction between *aidôs* and sophrosyne that Xenophon ascribes to

---

[20] τῷ θυμῷ χαρίζεσθαι. Cf. Antiphon the Sophist, Frag. 58—χαρίσασθαι τῷ θυμῷ—where the phrase is also opposed to the concept of sophrosyne. The contrast between generations is a commonplace of the sophistic period (see, e.g., Thucydides 6. 13, Aristophanes *Clouds*), and sophrosyne is normally regarded as a trait natural to the older generation but desirable in the young.

[21] See Del Grande, 283–91, for this aspect of the concept of *hybris*.

[22] For *akolasia* and *akolastos* in the fifth century, see, e.g., Herodotus 3. 81; Euripides *Hec.* 607; the Old Oligarch *Ath. Pol.* 1. 5; Thucydides 3. 37. In the fourth century *akolasia* largely replaces *hybris* as the principal antithesis to sophrosyne, especially in Peripatetic writings.

[23] In a Fragment of the *Abuse of Alcibiades*, attributed to Antiphon the Orator, *akolasia* refers to sexual excess (Frag. 22. 67 Blass); this connotation tends to predominate in Hellenistic and later Greek.

[24] See Plato *Laches* 197B, D.

Cyrus actually goes back to Prodicus.[25] Cyrus points out that those who possess *aidôs* refrain from what is disgraceful in public, while those who possess sophrosyne restrain themselves even in secret—a distinction that recalls sophistic discussions of offenses committed with and without witnesses.[26] Ancient tradition made Xenophon a pupil of Prodicus,[27] but the version of the Choice of Heracles which he relates in the *Memorabilia* is said to come by way of Socrates, rather than directly from Prodicus, and we are specifically warned that the actual wording is not that of the Sophist (2. 1. 21). In the apologue *Aretê* and *Kakia* are distinguished partly by the fact that the first possesses, while the second lacks, *aidôs* and sophrosyne. A purely external value is given both qualities (2. 1. 22): *aidôs* is manifested by the face (τὰ ὄμματα) of *Aretê* and sophrosyne by her form (τὸ σχῆμα).

The next stage of sophistic influence on Athenian thought coincides with the Peloponnesian war. The greatest name is that of Gorgias, who resembles Protagoras in certain respects—particularly in the relativism of his morality, his hedonism, and his opportunism. Gorgias, unique among the Sophists, denied that *aretê* could be taught.[28] He held that *aretê* depends on *physis;* and although the teacher can awaken enthusiasm for *aretê*, he cannot impart it.[29] Furthermore, Gorgias is reported by both Plato and Aristotle to have denied that *aretê* is a generic concept. "Sophrosyne is not the same for a woman and a man, nor is *andreia* or *dikaiosynê*," says Aristotle in the *Politics* (1260a 27), "but much more correct are those who enumerate the virtues, as Gorgias does."[30] Each person possesses *aretê* in accordance with his activity and his age (*Meno* 72A). Hence the element of *kairos* (the "opportune time"), which Gorgias applied to rhetoric and poetry,[31] is equally important where virtue is concerned, and opportunism is fundamental to his ethics.

Gorgias' conception of *aretê* is elicited from Meno by Socrates in a series of questions designed to show that, for a man, *aretê* consists of the ability to rule in the city and to help his friends and harm his enemies (71E).[32] Later this *aretê* is more specifically defined as the ability to

---

[25] See Ludwig Radermacher, *Artium Scriptores* (Vienna, 1951), 68, on Prodicus, Frag. 10.

[26] *Cyr.* 8. 1. 31. Cf. Antiphon *Truth,* Frag. 44 DK; Critias *Sisyphus,* Frag. 25. 5–15 DK; and see also Euripides *Hipp.* 403–4, and the story of Gyges, Plato *Rep.* 359D ff.

[27] Philostratus *Vit. Soph.* 12. For the wide influence of Prodicus' parable of the choice of lives, see Untersteiner, *op. cit.,* 221.

[28] Plato *Meno* 95C.

[29] Plato *Gorg.* 460A.

[30] Cf. Plato *Meno* 71E.

[31] See Wilhelm Vollgraff, *L'Oraison funèbre de Gorgias* (Leiden, 1952), 21 ff.

[32] The virtue of a woman (71E), although no name is assigned to it, corresponds to the conventional conception of feminine sophrosyne.

achieve the fine things (καλά) that one desires (77B), these *kala* being enumerated as money, offices in the city, and, again, the ruling power (ἀρχή [78C]). This definition of *aretê* resembles that expressed by Callicles in the *Gorgias* of Plato, but we need not depend on Plato for an exposition of Gorgias' moral teaching. We have, in addition to the *Palamedes* and the *Helen*, an extremely informative Fragment of an *Epitaphios* which, since it deals with the virtues of the dead, stands as a major witness to Gorgias' use of the topic of *aretê* in epideictic oratory.

The *Palamedes* is the most conventional of the surviving works. Palamedes denies, for example, that he is a slave to pleasure (Frag. 11a. 15 DK), and maintains that he values *aretê* above wealth and is obedient to authority (32). Such conformity to tradition is probably more essential in a juridical speech—even a model speech—than in epideictic. The *Encomium* of Helen takes a more "sophistic" line. Its total effect is to deny human responsibility and to deprive man of the power of controlling his passions. The force of *erôs* is made to seem irresistible (Frag. 11. 19 DK), much as in the apology for adultery in the *Clouds* (1079–82) or the speech of the nurse in the *Hippolytus* (433–81).

The *Epitaphios*, brief though the extant fragment is, confirms the impression that Plato gives us of the implicit relativism and amorality of Gorgias' teaching.[33] One of the characteristics praised in the dead men is their opportunism,[34] the form that Gorgias' favorite principle of *kairos* takes in ethics. Vollgraff has pointed out the significance of the qualities selected for mention at the beginning of the epilogue.[35] Instead of the usual combination of military and civic virtues (the *aretê* and sophrosyne of the Attic tombstones), Gorgias praises the dead for preferring gentle equity to justice, and correctness of reasoning to the letter of the law (6. 15 ff.); these are preferences that the sophistic rhetorician customarily urged upon jurymen and the comic poets branded as signs of the new education. The word sophrosyne does not appear in the extant portions of the *Epitaphios*, but Gorgias employs three other terms that describe certain aspects of this quality and are in fact equated with it at various periods in ancient thought: *praon epieikes* ("gentle equity") *prepon* ("the fitting"), and *kosmiotês* ("orderliness").

It has been suggested that when Gorgias speaks of *entheos aretê* ("immortal courage"), *praon epieikes, authades dikaion* ("rigorous justice"), and

---

[33] Cf. Vollgraff, *op. cit.,* 171.

[34] τὸ δέον ἐν τῷ δέοντι καὶ λέγειν καὶ σιγᾶν καὶ ποιεῖν ⟨καὶ ἐᾶν⟩ ("to speak and be silent, to do and leave undone what is necessary at the necessary time" [Frag. 6 DK]). For a favorable interpretation of Gorgias' *kairos* as Divine law, see Untersteiner, *op. cit.,* 178.

[35] *Op. cit.,* 11 ff.

eusebeia ("piety"), he has in mind the four cardinal virtues; and in this group the second clearly has most in common with sophrosyne.[36] But these four excellences are not, in fact, listed as a group. *Aretê* forms part of a contrast between immortal courage and human mortality. *Praon epieikes* and *authades dikaion* are part of a different set of contrasting qualities; they are ranged against each other, as if they were mutually exclusive, and in the same construction correctness of reasoning is contrasted with the letter of the law. Finally, piety finds mention only some fourteen lines after the reference to justice and equity, while another code of excellence is described in the intervening lines.

It is in this code that a reference to the canon of cardinal virtues may more plausibly be seen, since the categories praised by Gorgias would not easily have taken just this form without the existence of such a group as we have already found in Pindar and Aeschylus. Gorgias tells us that the heroes were helpful towards those who suffered misfortune unjustly, but chastised those who prospered unjustly, being rigorous in the pursuit of advantage, well-disposed towards what is fitting (*prepon*). They checked folly by their own wisdom, were insolent towards the insolent but moderate (*kosmioi*) towards the moderate, fearless towards the fearless and terrifying among the terrifying. Finally—making a transition from the virtue of courage, by way of a reference to the heroes' acquaintance with both war and peace—Gorgias praises their piety under four subheads: reverence towards the gods, scrupulous care of parents, justice towards fellow townsmen, and faithful devotion towards friends.

The qualities thus approved and practiced by the dead heroes are evidently justice, wisdom, moderation, courage, and piety. In the first category it is clearly the presence or absence of justice in the dispensations of fortune that determines the reaction of the heroes. *Prepon*, which becomes a synonym for sophrosyne in the philosophy of Panaetius, is in this context closer to justice.[37] *Kosmiotês* is frequently associated with sophrosyne by the writers of the late fifth century, and the contrast between *kosmiotês* and *hybris* in this passage of the *Epitaphios* indicates that it takes the place of sophrosyne here. *Kosmios*, like *taxis* ("order"), seems in fact to have been a favorite word with the pupils of Gorgias,[38]

---

[36] The suggestion is made by Hieronymus Markowski, *Eos* 37 (1936), 111.

[37] The relation of *prepon* or *decorum* to sophrosyne in Stoic thought is discussed in Chap. VI, pp. 221 ff. Several possible interpretations of the puzzling phrase αὐθάδεις πρὸς τὸ συμφέρον are considered by Vollgraff, *op. cit.,* 32 ff.

[38] See Wilhelm Süss, *Ethos* (Leipzig, 1910), 104 f. The close link between sophrosyne and *kosmiotês* is apparent in e.g., Phocylides, Frag. 11 Diehl³; Aristophanes *Plutus* 563–64; Thucydides 1. 84. 3.

and it may be that *kosmios* replaced *sôphrôn* in the vocabulary of the great Sophist himself. If so, the importance assigned to the conception of *kosmos* and the heightened meaning of the word in Plato's *Gorgias* assume a new significance.

It is natural to turn from the great Sophists to their pupils, among whom Critias and the Platonic Callicles have noteworthy views on sophrosyne. Critias, whom Xenophon calls the most violent of the oligarchs, because of his ruthlessness as a leader of the Thirty Tyrants in 404 B.C.,[39] exemplifies the able and ambitious men who carried out in public life the implications of what they had learned from Gorgias, Protagoras, and other Sophists. The best known of Critias' works is the fragment of his satyr play, *Sisyphus,* which improves upon the sophistic argument that law is mere convention by suggesting that after law had been invented to keep mankind from offenses in public, the notion of the gods was devised to prevent wrongdoing in private.[40] In spite of the radical point of view underlying this theory, and in spite of Critias' record as a *hybristês* when the Thirty were in power, the treatment of sophrosyne in his elegiac poem on the Spartan Constitution is entirely conventional. Sophrosyne remains within the tradition of Dorian ethical ideals familiar as early as the elegies of Tyrtaeus and Theognis, and is particularly close to the concept of measure. Fragment 6 (DK) praises Spartan moderation in drink, in contrast to the excess practiced by other Greeks, and describes this moderation as being in harmony with the works of Aphrodite, sleep, Health, and Sophrosyne, the neighbor of Piety. There is no reason to suppose that the personification of Sophrosyne is a Dorian literary device, but it is a fact that we meet it first in Theognis and Epicharmus, both of whom make Sophrosyne a companion of other personified values honored in the Dorian *êthos: Eusebeia* and *Eunomia* in Theognis (1135–50), *Hasychia* in Epicharmus (101 Kaibel, *Com.*). *Hygieia,* health of body, is naturally and inevitably coupled with sophrosyne, health of soul. It supplies one of the most common metaphors for virtue in general in Plato's dialogues, and in the Roman period Sophrosyne and *Hygieia* are honored together on Pergamene inscriptions.[41]

The concluding lines of Critias' elegiac fragment contrast the momentary pleasures of drink with the lasting pains, recalling the hedonistic calculus of Antiphon the Sophist. Less sophistic, indeed completely conventional, is Critias' praise of measure (*metron*), to which he refers

[39] *Mem.* 1. 2. 12.

[40] Frag. 25. 5–15 DK.

[41] For Plato, see, e.g., *Gorg.* 526D; and cf. Pierre Louis, *Les Metaphores de Platon* (Paris, 1945). For *Hygieia* and Sophrosyne on an inscription in Phrygia, see Chapter VII below.

four times in this fragmentary poem.[42] Another elegiac verse (Frag. 7 DK) plausibly attached to the same poem credits the Spartan Chilon with the proverb *Mêden agan* and adds that all fair things are connected with the proper season (*kairos*). The chief value of this elegy is that it reflects the philo-Laconianism of the Athenian oligarchic faction and, by showing what aspects of sophrosyne were commended by this group, provides a kind of control for Thucydides' account of oligarchic and pro-Spartan values. It may be added that in Plato's *Charmides* the definition of sophrosyne as doing one's own work (τὸ τὰ αὑτοῦ πράττειν) is tentatively ascribed to Critias (161B). This idea, too, belongs to the Dorian tradition in so far as doing one's own work is opposed to meddling (πολλὰ πράττειν, *polypragmosynê*) and is thus equivalent to the aristocratic excellence, *apragmosynê*.[43]

The main tendency of the sophistic Fragments so far considered is to regard sophrosyne as the control of appetite for the ultimate advantage of the individual involved; this advantage is determined by a comparison of pleasures and pains. The profit motive is the standard of human behavior. Given this moral relativism, the next step is predictable: when it seems that yielding to the appetites produces greater pleasure than suppressing or limiting them, the hedonistic calculus will require that sophrosyne be rejected. This step is mirrored in the *Gorgias* of Plato and the *Clouds* of Aristophanes.

The *Gorgias* shows the defense of hedonism and *pleonexia* ("overreaching") by a man capable of using for his own purposes not only the rhetorical techniques imparted by Gorgias, but also his basic ideas about human society and its origins: Callicles' entire argument grows out of the sophistic opposition between *physis* and *nomos*. He maintains (483B–C) that *nomos* ("convention, law") is the device invented by the weak to restrain the strong from overreaching (*pleonexia*), and insists that according to the law of nature (κατὰ νόμον γε τὸν τῆς φύσεως [483E]; cf. τὸ τῆς φύσεως δίκαιον [484B]) manifested among animals and men alike, genuine justice requires that the strong have "more" (*pleon* [483D]) than the weak and inferior. By "stronger" (δυνατώτεροι, ἰσχυρότεροι), "superior" (κρείττονες), and "better" (ἀμείνονες, βελτίονες) Callicles means those who are wise and courageous with respect to public affairs and the proper way of conducting them (491B–C). Such men deserve to rule, and justice means that they should have "more"

---

[42] Frag. 6 DK: μέτριον γέλωτα (17), ὑπὲρ τὸ μέτρον (23), σύμμετρα (26), ἀμέτροισι πότοις (28).

[43] See pp. 98, 101 ff., and n. 58.

than those whom they rule. True happiness and *aretê* consist in having the strongest possible desires and in being able to satisfy them completely (492A,C; 494C).[44] The ability to satisfy these desires depends on the possession of *andreia* and *phronêsis*, two excellences that are never underrated in the sophistic age; indeed, they are both enlisted in the service of appetite, a curious anticipation of the Epicurean picture so repugnant to Cicero and Seneca: Pleasure surrounded by her handmaidens, the Virtues.[45] Gorgias' pupils regard as happiest of men the tyrant, who is subject to no restraint whatsoever; and Callicles therefore condemns sophrosyne, together with law and conventional justice, as the invention of the weak, who, unable to satisfy their own desires, try to impose an unnatural restraint upon the strong.[46] But for the strong nothing can be more disgraceful than sophrosyne and justice, which make slaves of those who would otherwise be free.[47] License and complete unrestraint, if supported by force, constitute true *aretê* and happiness. Hence Callicles labels the *sôphrôn* a fool (491E)[48] and maintains that the weak give praise to both sophrosyne and justice because of their own unmanliness (*anandria* [492B]). This is the strongest statement in Greek literature of the antithesis between sophrosyne and the "manly" virtues—whether designated as *andreia, megalopsychia*, or *to eugenes*—but the background of Callicles' attitude may be seen as early as the *Prometheus Bound*, and the antithesis is especially evident in the rejection of sophrosyne by Sophocles' self-consciously heroic Ajax, Antigone, and Electra.

The *agôn* between the Just and the Unjust Arguments in the *Clouds* of Aristophanes complements the speech of Callicles, reproducing with comic exaggeration the belligerent apologia of a representative of the same general type of *paideia*. In this case the attack on sophrosyne is not justified by a might-makes-right philosophy but is expressed in the simple terms of an elementary hedonism, based on a crude demand for immediate gratification of appetite. The Unjust Argument interprets sophrosyne narrowly, as restraint of appetite, particularly as chastity; as such he subjects it to prolonged ridicule, summing up his attack with the sweeping allegation that *to sôphronein* deprives a man of all the

[44] A speech in Euripides' *Cyclops* (336–38) reads like a satire on the cult of *physis* and the right of the strong: Polyphemus says that to satisfy one's appetites is "god" for the *sôphrôn* person, i.e., the man of sense.

[45] Cicero *De Fin.* 2. 21. 69, 2. 12. 37; Seneca *De Benef.* 4. 2. 1.

[46] Cf. Critias' theory of the origin of law (Frag. 25. 5–15 DK).

[47] Cf. the coupling of *akolasia* and *eleutheria* in *Gorg.* 492C and *Rep.* 557B.

[48] Cf. *Rep.* 348D, where Thrasymachus says that justice is mere folly (εὐήθεια).

delights of love, gaming, drinking, and feasting—in short, of all that makes life worth living (1071-74). The picture of the traditional education, defended by the Just Argument, is fragrant with the breath of the past, the honest, oldfashioned perfume of sophrosyne and *aidôs* (962, 1006, 1029). Yet it is noticeable that the details of the portrait of the *sôphrôn* youth (physical hardiness, devotion to athletics, propriety in conduct) are purely external. They are comparable to the sophrosyne of the young Charmides in Plato's dialogue, an entirely conventional and nonrational *aretê*, which cannot defend itself against attack and is therefore helpless against the destructive rationalism of the new *paideia*. The defeat of the Just Argument by the Unjust in the *Clouds* is paralleled by the helplessness of Charmides in his conversation with Socrates; and the difference between the two debates (those of the *Clouds* and the *Charmides*) in spirit and outcome is one measure of Plato's reaction to the challenge of sophistic immorality.[49]

One of the qualities with which Aristophanes links sophrosyne in the *agôn* of the *Clouds* is *apragmosynê* (1006), the gentlemanly aloofness and detachment so highly prized by Greek conservatives. Like sophrosyne itself, this excellence often has political implications, as it does in the *Birds* when the two Athenians leave the city in disgust and set out to find a place that will be *apragmôn* (44). There is no sharp dividing line between the moral and the political aspects of sophrosyne and *apragmosynê* in Aristophanes, because the qualities that distinguish a citizen as well bred, well behaved, and decent in private life are the same qualities as the poet ascribed to the oldfashioned moderate in politics. Certain keywords apply to both spheres: in addition to *sôphrôn* and *apragmôn*, the most common are *kosmios* ("orderly"), *metrios* ("moderate"), and *chrêstos* ("useful").[50] Aristophanes' point of view—not to be identified with that of any political party, but rather with a tenacious ideal of an incorruptible Athens—remains constant from first to last in his comedies, from the Fragments of the *Banqueters* to the *Plutus*.[51] The *locus classicus*

---

[49] The *agôn* in the *Clouds* illustrates the opposition to sophrosyne as self-control. The only trace in Aristophanes of the equation of sophrosyne with unmanliness is found in *Peace* 1297, where the son of Cleonymus, who threw away his shield, is said to come of a *sôphrôn* father. Here, too, a political nuance is likely, if sophrosyne is linked with the "peace party."

[50] *Kosmios: Thes.* 573; *Pl.* 89, 565; etc. Frag. 84 Kock describes as *sôphrôn kosmos* the controlled movement of a ship as it is rowed over the waves. *Metrios: Clouds* 1137, 1510; *Thes.* 1227; *Pl.* 245; etc. *Chrêstos: Clouds* 8; *Birds* 1449; *Frogs* 686, 735; *Pl.* 239, 901, 909, etc.

[51] The *Banqueters*, like the *Clouds*, dealt with the contrast between the old *paideia*, which produced sophrosyne, and the new, which made its pupils wanton (*Clouds* 529). The *Plutus* personifies Sophrosyne and *Kosmiotês* and links both with Poverty, while Wealth is linked with *hybris* (563-64). For a possible connection between the praise of poverty here and the teachings of Prodicus, see Wilhelm Nestle, *Vom Mythos zum Logos* (Stuttgart, 1942), 358.

for the combination of political and moral virtues in the idealized portrait of a gentlemanly product of the oldfashioned *paideia*, who takes a
conservative line in politics, is found in the *Frogs*, when the Chorus
advises Athens neither to substitute base metal for gold and silver coinage, nor to honor strangers of dubious parentage instead of the citizens
known to be well bred and *sôphrones*, just, noble, and gentlemanly,
brought up in the gymnasium, the choruses, and the schools of music
(721–30). Sophrosyne is still what it was in the *Clouds:* oldfashioned,
nonintellectual, essentially aristocratic.[52] It is associated, by implication,
with the oligarchic faction in a speech of Prometheus in the *Birds*, which
lists among Zeus's possessions sophrosyne ("soundness"), *euboulia*
("political prudence"), and *eunomia* ("lawabiding conduct"), and in the
next line names the standard equipment of the demagogues as the
thunderbolt, the dockyards, and insulting language (1540).

Occasionally sophrosyne carries a strictly moral connotation, without
a trace of political implications; then its meaning is almost invariably
"chastity" or "purity." It is a virtue of men and women alike [53] (whereas
sophrosyne the *aretê politikê* belongs only to men). The model of masculine chastity is Peleus, whose sophrosyne is praised by the Just Argument
in the *Clouds* and is derided by the Unjust.[54] The feminine exemplar is
Penelope, who is contrasted with the wanton Phaedra and Medea in
the women's reproach to Euripides in the *Thesmophoriazusae* (548). It is
this purely moral nuance that Aristophanes employs in the *Clouds* when
he describes that play as clean (*sôphrôn*), because it is free from the
conventional phallic symbols of Old Comedy (537). A tentative step
towards the development of sophrosyne as a term in literary criticism
is taken when the Chorus of the *Knights* applies the related adverb
sôphronikôs to the conduct of Aristophanes himself. When he presented
his earlier plays under the name of Callestratus, he refrained *sôphronikôs*
("modestly, bashfully") from rushing before the people to talk nonsense
(545). In almost all its applications to literary criticism before the
Hellenistic age, sophrosyne is predominantly moral and is predicated
of the writer rather than of his work.[55]

In one other meaning of sophrosyne Aristophanes resembles Euripides,
the Orators, and Thucydides, all of whom reflect the contemporary
Athenian habit of using *sôphrôn* as "prudent, sensible." The significance

---

[52] A like association of sophrosyne with the oldfashioned *paideia*, incompatible with the
demagogic principles of the popular leaders, occurs in *Knights* 334.

[53] Aristophanes *Lys.* 473 (feminine sophrosyne), 795–96 (masculine).

[54] Aristophanes *Clouds* 1063, 1067. Cf. Pindar *Isth.* 8. 40, *Nem.* 4. 95; Plato *Rep.* 391C 1–2.

[55] See my paper, *C.P.* 43 (1948), 1–18.

is especially clear in the *Wasps,* where the verb *sôphronein* has precisely the same meaning as the phrase νοῦν ἔχειν (1405, 1440). Like the Orators, characters in Aristophanes use the warning εἰ σωφρονεῖς ("if you have any sense").[56] Only in this fashion does any trace of the intellectual quality in sophrosyne survive. Everywhere else moral connotations prevail, and the combination of the moral and the political is the aspect of sophrosyne most typical of Aristophanes.

It is also most typical of Thucydides, who, however, presents a picture of far greater complexity. Although the historian often uses *sôphrôn* with the meaning "prudent, sensible," and the common phrase εἰ σωφρονεῖτε ("if you use good judgment") recurs frequently in the speeches he records, it is his tendency to connect sophrosyne with the chief moral issues of the *History* that is most instructive. There are two great themes in Thucydides: the contrast between Athens and Sparta; and the prolonged deterioration of Greece (seen especially in connection with Athens), because of the triumph of ambition and greed in the statesmen who succeeded Pericles in Athens and Archidamus and Brasidas in Sparta. Sophrosyne is involved in both issues, as well as in several subsidiary themes: the contrast between generations, the role of *anthrôpeia physis* ("human nature") in political action, and the various attitudes towards fortune (*tychê*) which Thucydides observed in political leaders and the Greeks in general.

The contrast between the simplicity of Herodotus' concept of sophrosyne and the complexity of Thucydides' suggests something of the effect that tragedy and sophistic, as well as political events, had on the development of the virtue. Thucydides resembles, in different ways, each of the tragic poets as they dealt with sophrosyne—Euripides more than the others, but Sophocles and even Aeschylus as well. He shares with Euripides a deep interest in the struggle between the rational and the irrational in human affairs. Among the irrational elements with which statesmen and generals must cope, the most dangerous are human emotions and fortune. Thucydides goes so far as to treat success or failure in this area as the supreme test of statesmanship, and like Euripides he regards sophrosyne as one of the manifestations of the rational (others are *pronoia,* "foresight," *gnômê,* "intelligence," and *euboulia,* "prudence"). The historian and Sophocles have in common their realization of the gulf between the bold and the restrained temperaments—what Plato later calls the *andrikos* and the *sôphronikos.* Sophocles

---

[56] *Lys.* 1093; *Frogs* 853. Aristophanes occasionally exploits the multiple meanings of sophrosyne, as in *Ecc.* 767, where *sôphrôn* implies both "law-abiding" and "prudent."

portrays this dangerous incompatibility as it affects the individual soul; for Thucydides it is one of the great destructive forces in Athens—where it leads to the conflict between the reckless Cleon and Alcibiades and the cautious Nicias—and, on an even larger scale, in the Greek world —where it underlies the hostility between confident, aggressive Athens and slow-moving, conservative Sparta. The resemblance of Thucydides to Aeschylus is slighter, but the two are alike in their conception of sophrosyne as an *aretê politikê*. The *sôphrôn polis* forecast at the close of the *Oresteia* would probably have won from Thucydides something like the praise he assigns to the constitution of the Five Thousand in 411 B.C.: the best government that the Athenians had enjoyed in his time (8. 97. 2).

Among the similarities between Thucydides and the Sophists, the one that most profoundly affects his treatment of sophrosyne is the practice of analyzing ethical and political terms and playing with several possible meanings of the same word in different contexts; this practice is largely responsible for the impression that we receive of sophrosyne as a term of manifold significance in Thucydides.[57] He resembles the Sophists also in divorcing sophrosyne from the religious implications that it had acquired during the archaic period and still possessed in tragedy, where Aeschylus and Sophocles commonly associate the virtue in some way with the Divine, and Euripides frequently criticizes the gods for their lack of sophrosyne. Again like the Sophists, Thucydides employs the arguments from probability, nature, and advantage, the last two of which he connects with sophrosyne as it is interpreted by the Athenians in the course of the Melian Dialogue.

While the contrast between Athens and Sparta is worked out in great detail and depends on many elements, it is to some extent a contrast between rival conceptions of sophrosyne. Both are presented through the device of speeches; first the speeches of the Corinthians and the Athenians at the council in Sparta before the war; then the speeches of Archidamus and Pericles, each of whom is a representative of his own tradition at its best and advocates a policy in harmony with that tradition. Throughout these speeches Thucydides employs a specialized vocabulary familiar from other sources of the period. Certain words are appropriated by Athens, others by Sparta, and still a third group contains terms and slogans that are used by both states, or by rival factions within them. *Apragmosynê* and *hêsychia* are distinctive Spartan and oligarchic qualities. *Prothymia* ("enthusiasm"), *synesis* ("intelligence"), *to drastêrion* ("activity"),

---

[57] On this trait in Thucydides, see A. W. Gomme, *A Historical Commentary on Thucydides* (Oxford, 1945–1956), 2. 301.

tolmê ("audacity," in a good sense), and *polypragmosynê* (also, and more surprisingly, in a good sense) belong to the Athenians.[58] One of the controversial qualities, belonging in some sense to both sides, is sophrosyne, but the word itself, as distinguished from the quality, is usually treated as Spartan and oligarchic. Nothing in Thucydides' allusions to sophrosyne is more significant than this fact, which beyond doubt reflects contemporary opinion. We have conjectured that from the reforms of Ephialtes to the Revolution of the Thirty the word *sôphrôn* was politically weighted in Athens (see p. 44). It would normally mean "sound, conservative, aristocratic, oligarchic" and would therefore be avoided by democrats. Thucydides' usage shows that the same was probably true on the international scene. His avoidance of the term sophrosyne in his descriptions of Athenian moderation recalls the practice of Sophocles. Since the "heroic" characters reject sophrosyne for themselves, the poet, when he wishes to commend the virtue, must do so by indirection. Thucydides, having accepted the claim of the Spartans and the oligarchs that sophrosyne is peculiarly their own, must find a different term to describe Athenian sophrosyne. The word he chooses is the one that Solon chose—*metrios,* traditionally a synonym for *sôphrôn* in a political context.[59]

The prevailing connotations of sophrosyne in the contrast between Athens and Sparta first come to our attention in the speeches delivered at Sparta before the outbreak of the war. The Corinthians draw a vivid sketch of the psychology of their Spartan allies and their Athenian enemies, presenting a contrast that greatly favors the Athenians. The first quality on which they comment is Spartan sophrosyne. The trustful spirit that characterizes Spartan domestic affairs produces sophrosyne ("stability"), they concede, but leads to ignorance (*amathia*) and lethargy (*hêsychia*) in external affairs (1. 68–69). The Athenians by contrast are described in terms of activity, boldness, and enterprise (1. 70). The speech is full of sharp antitheses, which are climaxed by the assertion that the Athenians consider *apragmôn hêsychia* ("leisurely aloofness") no

---

[58] For a detailed study of *apragmosynê,* see Wilhelm Nestle, *Philol.* 81 (1925), 129–40; and cf. T. H. Wade-Gery, *J.H.S.* 52 (1932), 224–25. On *polypragmosynê,* consult Victor Ehrenberg, *J.H.S.* 67 (1947), 46–67, and A. W. Gomme, *op. cit.,* on Thucydides 1. 32–34. Gustav Grossmann (*Politische Schlagwörter aus der Zeit des peloponnesischen Krieges* [Zurich, 1950]) discusses the relation of sophrosyne to *eunomia* as a political excellence (70–89) and brings together much of the evidence connecting sophrosyne with *apragmosynê* as individual and political virtues (126–37).

[59] See, e.g., Solon 4. 7, 16. 1–2 Diehl[3]; and cf. Thucydides 1. 76. 4, 1. 77. 2, 2. 65. 5.

more desirable than laborious lack of leisure (1. 70. 8). The association of sophrosyne with *apragmosynê* and *hêsychia* firmly establishes it as part of the conservative Dorian tradition, with which both words are often linked.[60] The noblest exemplar of this tradition is the old king Archidamus, whom Thucydides describes as wise and *sôphrôn* (1. 79. 2). His speech to the conference at Sparta, marked by just these qualities of intellectual and moral stability, analyzes the roots of Spartan sophrosyne and its outcome in political behavior in a more favorable light than the Corinthian estimate had shed.

Beginning with a reasoned discussion of the powers involved in the coming struggle and a warning against unrealistic hope (*elpis* [1. 81. 6]; cf. 1. 84. 4 on *tychê*, "fortune"), Archidamus advises his listeners not to regard the conduct he advocates as unmanliness (*anandria*) nor to be ashamed of a policy of slowness and caution (1. 83–84). The very freedom and good repute of Sparta are the result of this policy, which embodies in the truest sense intelligent moderation (sophrosyne *emphrôn* [1. 84. 1]) and has enabled Sparta alone among Greek cities to avoid *hybris* in prosperity and despair in adversity (1. 84. 2). Archidamus then proceeds to demonstrate that sophrosyne is the basis of the two most valued aspects of Spartan *aretê*. He sums up the national character in these words (1. 84. 3):

We are warlike and wise in counsel because of our orderly nature [*to eukosmon*], the one because a sense of honor [*aidôs*] springs chiefly from sophrosyne, and courage from the sense of honor, the other because we are brought up with too much *amathia* to scorn the laws and too much severity of discipline [σὺν χαλεπότητι σωφρονέστερον] to disobey them.[61]

The emphasis on *amathia* as a Spartan trait (already mentioned in the speech of the Corinthians, 1. 68. 1), contrasts with Athenian intellectualism, as does Spartan authoritarianism with Athenian love of freedom. Pericles, too, alludes to this contrast when he says in the

---

[60] For *apragmosynê*, see n. 58 above. *Apragmosynê* in a conservative political sense occurs in Aristophanes *Birds* 44, *Knights* 261; Antiphon the Orator 3. 2. 1; Plato *Rep.* 565A. Nestle (*loc. cit.,* 132) sees some hint—in Euripides *Me.* 298 f. and *Antiope*, Frags. 184, 193, and Aristophanes *Knights* 191—that the view of the *apragmôn* as unpatriotic was familiar in the last third of the fifth century. See also Gomme, *op. cit.,* on Thucydides 2. 40. 2. For *hêsychia*, cf. Pindar *Pyth.* 8. 1–2, where the word refers to international affairs. Internal *hêsychia* is mentioned in Pindar *Ol.* 4. 16. See also Epicharmus, Frag. 101 Kaibel, *Com.*; and Aristophanes *Birds* 1320–22.

[61] Cf. Sophocles *Ajax* 1073–80, where Menelaus insists that *phobos* and *aidôs* are essential to sophrosyne in the army.

Funeral Oration that the Athenians alone combine daring with reflection, whereas in all other people boldness (*thrasos*) depends on *amathia*, and with consideration comes hesitancy (2. 40. 3). One of the earliest signs of Athenian decay is Cleon's praise of *amathia* combined with what he calls sophrosyne ("discipline, obedience") in the Mytilene Debate (3. 37. 3–5).[62]

Spartan sophrosyne then, as analyzed in the speeches of both the Corinthians and Archidamus, has two principal facets: the tendency to maintain the status quo in external affairs and, internally, the repressive discipline and restraint essential to a militaristic regime. According to both views, sophrosyne is a cause of slowness to act—*hêsychia* (1. 69. 4, 1. 83. 3) or *bradytês* (1. 71. 4, 1. 84. 1)—which is interpreted by the Corinthians as intolerable sluggishness (1. 70. 4), by Archidamus as prudent deliberation (1. 84). In addition Archidamus links sophrosyne with the refusal to give way to delusive hopes about fortune and with Sparta's consequent immunity to overconfidence and despair—an important and original aspect of political sophrosyne in the *History*.[63]

That Athens, too, lays claim to a certain kind of moderation we learn from the speech of the Athenian ambassadors who address the conference at Sparta, and from Pericles himself in all three of the speeches reported by Thucydides. It is in these four speeches particularly that we observe a reluctance to use the word sophrosyne in connection with Athens, although situations are not lacking where the word would be entirely appropriate. The ambassadors at Sparta, in reply to the Corinthian attack on Athenian influence in Greece, first recall the heroism of their ancestors in the Persian wars (1. 73-75), using a series of words that describe Athenian conduct throughout the *History*—*prothymia* ("enthusiasm"), *tolmê* ("daring"), and *synesis* ("intelligence")—and then predict that if any other state should seize power from Athens, it would show that the Athenians by contrast had behaved with a certain moderation (τι μετριάζομεν [1. 76. 4]).[64] They conclude with a warning about the unpredictability of *tychê* in a long war and with a recommendation that Sparta employ *euboulia* while there is yet time (1. 78). Just as they prefer *metriotês* to sophrosyne in describing Athenian moderation towards the allies, so they choose to call by the name

---

[62] Cf. Euripides *Andr.* 479–85.

[63] Cf. 4. 18. 4, where the Spartan envoys after Sphacteria range sophrosyne against *tychê*. The Athenians at Sparta oppose *euboulia* ("good judgment") to *tychê* (1. 78. 1–4). For further observations on the deluding power of hope, desire, and fortune, see the speech of Diodotus, 3. 45. 5.

[64] Cf. Thucydides 1. 77. 2: other rulers are less *metrioi* than the Athenians.

euboulia what Archidamus describes as sophrosyne in his remarks about the danger of relying on *tychê* and *elpis*.[65]

The first oration of Pericles demonstrates his keen awareness of this danger. Although the main purpose of the speech is to encourage the Athenians to undertake the war by setting forth the resources on which they may rely (we note that Pericles is careful to give many sound reasons for his own *elpis*), it includes a warning that success will come only if the Athenians agree neither to attempt further expansion of the empire nor to expose themselves to needless risks while they are at war (1. 144. 1). The *pronoia* ("foresight") and sophrosyne which later generations considered typical of Pericles [66] inspire this characteristic attempt to check Athenian exuberance. The same statesmanlike gifts are applied in reverse in the third speech: now Pericles uses his *gnômê* ("intelligence") to counteract, not the *hybris* of the masses, but their unwarranted despair after the devastation wrought by the plague and the second Spartan invasion of Attica.[67] To bring them out of their *tapeinotês* ("dejection" [2. 61. 2]), he reminds them that their control of the sea opens up unlimited possibilities for future conquest, and he remarks significantly that he has never previously discussed this subject in his speeches (because it would seem too boastful), and he would not do so now if he did not see that they were unreasonably depressed (2. 62. 1–2). He urges them to base their attitude towards the enemy not on hope (*elpis*) but on reason (*gnômê*), from which springs genuine *pronoia* (2. 62. 5). The speech concludes with Pericles' famous observations on the nature of *tyrannis* and the deficiencies of *apragmosynê* when compared with the active principle (*to drastêrion* [63. 3; cf. 64. 4]). Everything in the speech, including the final appeal to Athenian pride in the verdict of history, is shrewdly calculated to revive courage and allay resentment against Pericles himself; it demonstrates the statesmanlike sophrosyne of the great leader and accounts for his success in dealing with his distracted people.

Immediately after reporting the speech and describing its consequences, Thucydides gives his estimate of the essential Periclean qualities: moderation in time of peace, foresight in time of war (2. 65. 5), and the ability

[65] Cf. the phrase σωφρόνως ἐκλογίζοιτο ("consider prudently") in the speech of Archidamus (1. 80. 2).

[66] On Pericles' foresight (also called *eulabeia*, "caution") see Plutarch *Pericles* 18. On his moderation (*metriotês*), see *ibid.*, 39. On his sophrosyne, see Isocrates *Antidosis* 190. Pericles appears as a type of *temperantia* in Perugino's painting of the cardinal virtues in the Collegio del Cambio in Perugia; the other exemplars of this virtue are the Roman statesmen Scipio and Cincinnatus.

[67] Cf. 2. 21. After the first invasion Pericles refuses to convene the Assembly lest the people act under the instigation of *orgê* ("emotion") rather than of reason (*gnômê*).

to control the emotions of the people—once again defined as *hybris* in prosperity and unreasonable dejection in misfortune (2. 65. 8–9). By contrast, Thucydides says, the successors of Pericles brought the state to disaster by their ambition (*philotimia*) and greed (2. 65. 7). Later he adds *pleonexia*, the form taken by *hybris* in public affairs (3. 82. 8).[68]

Although the power to cope with the irrational is described as sophrosyne by the Spartan king Archidamus and later (after the Sphacteria campaign) by the Spartan envoys to Athens (4. 18. 4), Thucydides avoids the word in his estimate of Pericles; and when he commends his restraint, he says (2. 65. 5): μετρίως ἐξηγεῖτο ("he governed the state with moderation"). The word sophrosyne is missing from the Funeral Oration also. It is surely remarkable that a speech celebrating the spiritual, political, and aesthetic values of Athens in the age of Pericles should contain no reference to this word, which more than any other sums up the inimitable balance of dynamism with restraint underlying the greatest achievements of that age. This balance is in fact the keynote of the Funeral Oration. Pericles captures the essential *aretê* of Athens in the famous observation (2. 40. 1), "We love beauty without extravagance and wisdom without softness,"[69] which is to this oration what Archidamus' analysis of Spartan sophrosyne is to his speech in Book I—a revelation of the very core of the national *êthos*. Each oration calls attention to a quality that could legitimately be termed sophrosyne,[70] but the two forms of *aretê* are sharply distinguished, and in accordance with the normal political vocabulary of the day, the word sophrosyne is applied to the cautious conservatism of Sparta rather than to the "measured grace" of Athens.

The Funeral Oration restates many of the views about Athens set forth in the speeches delivered at Sparta before the war, including the anti-thesis between Spartan *apragmosynê* and Athenian energy and aggressive-

[68] See A. W. Gomme, *J.H.S.* 71 (1951), 70–72, for objections to Thucydides' analysis of the reasons for Athens' defeat.

[69] A. E. Wardman, *C.Q.* 9 (1959), 38–42 proposes to translate as follows: "Our love of good things is compatible with economy and our love of discussion does not involve cowardice." A. W. Gomme, *Commentary, ad loc.*, criticizes Thucydides' use of the word *euteleia* on the ground that it implies cheapness. See J. T. Kakridis, *Der thukydideische Epitaphios* (Munich, 1961), 47–48, for criticism of Wardman's translation and defense of the word *euteleia* in this connection. In the fourth and third centuries *euteleia* ("frugality, austerity") is closely connected with sophrosyne by the Cynics; see Crates, Frag. 2 Diehl[3]: *Euteleia*, child of glorious Sophrosyne. For Cicero's suggestion that *frugalitas* is the appropriate Latin rendering of sophrosyne, see *Tusc. Disp.* 3. 8.

[70] Gomme (*Commentary, ad. loc.*) compares the Funeral Oration, especially 41. 1, to the Parthenon frieze and the close of Aeschylus' *Eumenides*. Felix Wasserman (*T.A.P.A.* 85 [1954], 46–54) discusses the idealized picture of the *mesoi* ("moderates") in the oration.

ness. Pericles echoes the Corinthians when he says that the Athenians alone regard the man who takes no part in public affairs, not as *apragmôn* ("minding his own business"), but as good for nothing (2. 40. 2). The ideal Athenian citizen is not called *polypragmôn* because of its invidious implications; but by rejecting *apragmosynê*, Pericles makes the contrast with Sparta unmistakable. Moreover, by alluding to the benefits conferred on other Greek cities by Athenian intervention (δρῶντες, ὁ δράσας [2. 40. 4]), he contrives to praise implicitly the quality of *polypragmosynê* on the international scene.

Only once in the *History* is *polypragmosynê* frankly used as a term of commendation. The Athenian Euphemus at Camarina tells the Sicilians that necessity has compelled the Athenians to do many things (πολλὰ πράσσειν [6. 87. 2]) and that their *polypragmosynê* benefits most of the Greeks. The realization that Athens will not hesitate to intervene compels the wrongdoer to control himself even against his will (ὁ μὲν ἄκων . . . σωφρονεῖν, a phrase that has Aeschylean overtones, ironical in this context), and the one wronged is thereby saved with no effort on his own part (*apragmonôs* [6. 87. 3–4]). *Polypragmosynê* thus becomes a word of praise, but only in a limited context; in civic life it remains an invidious term and is so used by most writers of the fourth century.[71]

The second great theme of the *History*—the triumph of *pleonexia* and *philotimia* over sophrosyne and *euboulia*—is traced in several stages. The process affects all of Greece, but Thucydides illustrates it with the most abundant detail in the case of Athens.[72] The first stage coincides with the plague, whose effects lead to unrestrained indulgence in *hêdonê* and to a condition of *anomia* ("lawlessness") which Thucydides holds responsible for permanent damage to Athenian morale.[73] The second stage is marked by the Mytilene Debate of the year 427, in which Cleon advocates a policy of ruthless brutality and pours scorn upon the intellect, the emotion of pity, and the reliance on discussion to determine policy—all Athenian traits of long standing. *Amathia* ("anti-intellectualism") is linked in his mind with sophrosyne ("authoritarian discipline"), and he echoes what Archidamus had said about the two qualities, even to the

---

[71] See Chapter IV, pp. 138 ff.

[72] The decline from Pericles to Alcibiades and Nicias is matched by the falling off in Spartan leadership from the sophrosyne of Archidamus (1. 84) and the *metriotês* of Brasidas (4. 81. 3, 108. 2–6) to the ruthlessness and cruelty of later generals. Thucydides did not complete the history of the war and thus could not show the final degradation of Spartan leadership in Lysander. Plato's description of the decline of the ideal state and the virtuous soul (*Rep.* VIII) has several features in common with Thucydides.

[73] Gomme, *Commentary, ad. loc.,* expresses doubts about the permanence of the damage.

point of preferring bad laws that are obeyed, over better ones that are ignored. His opponent, Diodotus, possesses an almost Periclean sophrosyne and *euboulia,* evinced in his remarks on the danger of haste, passion, and reliance on *tychê*.[74] His success in persuading the Assembly to revoke the cruel decree against Mytilene shows that the moral decay of Athens is still in its early stages.

Parallel to the Mytilene Debate is the equally vivid description of the fall of Plataea, culminating in speeches about the disposition of the prisoners which show the Spartans to be equal to the Athenians in cruelty and far more advanced in hypocrisy. The Plataeans ask in vain for *sôphrôn oiktos* ("pity" [3. 59. 1]) and *sôphrôn charis* ("grace" [3. 58. 1]). In each case the adjective, while no doubt chosen for its presumed appeal to Spartan tradition, recalls the use of *sôphrôn* with the implication "merciful" in Euripides' war tragedies.[75]

A third stage in the deterioration of Hellas is marked by the account of the revolution in Corcyra (3. 82), the classical example of *stasis* ("civil war"), which gave the Greek world a hint of the horrors that were to come in the next two decades. Here Thucydides reveals the effect wrought by warfare (the "violent teacher," as he calls it) on morals— precisely as Euripides traces the deterioration of individual morality under ill-treatment. External strife provoked civil war and made it more deadly. The transvaluation of ethical terms is an early and devastating result of civil conflict. *Andreia* is replaced by senseless rashness (*tolmê alogistos*), and sophrosyne is considered a cloak for cowardice (*anandria*). No one who remembers the signs in Attic drama of a tendency to confuse sophrosyne and cowardice will be surprised by this development, especially since one of the conclusions to which Thucydides comes in his account of the war years is that the antagonism between reason and emotion is now heightened, and reason is quenched by ambition, greed, hope, and fear. The noble daring of Periclean Athens (equivalent to *andreia,* because governed by reason) becomes something quite different in Cleon and Alcibiades, something closer to *thrasos* (in Platonic terms); and as it becomes wilder and more immoderate, it becomes more and more contemptuous of sophrosyne. Any conflict between the bold and the peaceful temperaments is potentially dangerous to the State, as Plato points out in the *Republic* and the *Politicus.* Their polarity is already

---

[74] A warning against reliance on *tychê* is joined with advice to practice sophrosyne in the speech of the Spartan legates (4. 18). Athens rejects their offer of peace because of her greed for "more" and because of the dominance of Cleon.

[75] See especially *Herac.,* whose central idea is that of *charis* (220, 241, 320, 438, 548, 767, etc.), implying pity or compassion.

hinted at in the statement of the Corinthians at Sparta (1. 120. 3) that it is the part of *sôphrones* men, if they are not wronged, to remain at peace, but of brave men (*agathoi*) to go to war if they meet injustice. It would be going too far to say that *agathos* is the antithesis of *sôphrôn* in this sentence, but a contrast is felt, as it is felt by Sophocles. Thucydides brings the contrast out into the open at Corcyra.

The Melian Dialogue shows in action the principles described in connection with Corcyra. Without a trace of embarrassment the Athenian representatives assert the right of the strong and reject every appeal to such traditional ideals as justice, religion, and *aidôs*. In their usage at this point in the *History,* sophrosyne means recognizing the realities of political life, acquiescence in the laws of nature that require the weak to obey the strong.[76] When the Melians describe the situation as one in which they must defend their freedom or incur the guilt of cowardice, the Athenians reply that such is not the case, ἤν γε σωφρόνως βουλεύησθε ("if you take thought for your own advantage"), for this is not an equal contest, concerned with honor, but a decision having to do with survival, and the Melians are greatly outnumbered (5. 101). Later in the dialogue the Athenians equate sophrosyne with realistic calculation and resistance to the irrational, when they comment on the lack of *euboulia* in the deliberations of the Melians and advise them to arrive at some more intelligent (σωφρονέστεραν) conclusion, instead of putting their faith in fortune and hope [77] or in the dubious loyalty of the Spartans.

The speeches delivered in Athens before the Sicilian expedition expose the decline in Athenian statesmanship and show how two remnants of Pericles' political legacy have been divided and turned against each other. Alcibiades, like Cleon before him, has inherited the aggressive thrust in Periclean policy and is in the process of driving the principles of *tolmê* and *drastêrion* to the extreme of *pleonexia*. Nicias, who has inherited the moderation that governed Pericles' foreign policy after 445 B.C., drives this principle to the opposite extreme of *apragmosynê*.[78]

---

[76] Cf. the speech of Hermocrates of Syracuse at Gela (6. 79) in which sophrosyne is equivalent to putting the claims of *physis* before those of *dikaion*. This is the sophrosyne of Oceanus in Aeschylus' *P.V.* and of Chrysothemis in Sophocles' *Electra*.

[77] The different attitudes towards *tychê* evinced by Athens and Melos are signs of the conflict between two opposing political philosophies; see Felix Wassermann, *T.A.P.A.* 78 (1947), 29–30. Thucydides' technique in revealing a fundamental contrast through the differing connotations of one and the same word is comparable to the device used by Sophocles to reveal contrasting characters; see Chap. II, pp. 65 ff. Richmond Lattimore, *A.J.P.* 68 (1947), 161–79 discusses the theme of the folly of *elpis* in Greek literature from Solon on.

[78] See Gomme, *loc. cit.,* 74–80, for Cleon and Alcibiades; and Allen B. West, *C.P.* 19 (1924), 120 ff., for Nicias. Consult also Jacqueline de Romilly, *Thucydide et l'impérialisme*

The contrast between the two leaders is stated in terms of the opposition between generations—the headstrong young men and the inactive elders (6. 13), a theme popular in tragedy and comedy at this time. The dominant trait of the young, of Alcibiades, and of the Athenian masses (both young and old, as it turns out) is *epithymia*—uncontrolled greed (6. 13. 1, 15. 2, 24. 4). Nicias, like Archidamus at Sparta, begs the older men not to be afraid of seeming cowardly if they vote against the expedition, and reminds them that *pronoia* (one of the great Periclean virtues) wins more victories than does *epithymia* (6. 13. 1). If we look to our own advantage (εἰ σωφρονοῦμεν), he says, we Athenians will realize that our proper concern is not with Sicily but with Sparta (6. 11. 7)—a restatement of Pericles' warning against embarking on further conquest or undertaking unnecessary risks (1. 144. 1). Alcibiades, of course, wins over the Assembly, partly by his observation that Athens cannot now afford to become *apragmôn*—another echo of Pericles (2. 63. 3)—but mostly because his audience shares his hopes and ambitions.[79]

In addition to these, another irrational element had its effect, which Thucydides mentions only in describing how the Athenians received news of the defeat when all was over. Then the people blamed not only the orators who had urged them on but also the oracle mongers and soothsayers and all the others who had encouraged them by divination to hope that they could conquer Sicily (8. 1. 1). This, together with the record of Nicias' fatal dependence on his soothsayers (7. 50. 4), is a further indication of the failure of post-Periclean leaders to control the irrational factors in politics and war.[80]

It remains to sum up the chief meanings of sophrosyne in Thucydides. As the passages so far considered have shown, sophrosyne is a flexible term that may be predicated of internal or external affairs. It is in the area of foreign policy that the greatest variation occurs, often depending on whether the state involved is a first-class or a minor power. Corcyra, about whom the term is first used in Book I, confesses that her policy of sophrosyne, which she thought would bring safety, has proved a source of danger (1. 32. 4). In her case it means isolationism, the effort to avoid

athénien (Paris, 1947), 156–57. Nicias is said to be a moderate (σωφρονεῖν) in Frag. 41 of the comic poet Telecleides (Plutarch *Nicias* 4. 5); see Gomme, *Commentary,* on Thucydides 4. 28. 5.

[79] Thucydides holds Alcibiades' private *epithymiae* ("appetites") responsible in large measure for the fall of Athens. For a different reason Cicero considers the *cupiditates principum* dangerous to the State (*Legg.* 3. 13. 30).

[80] Cf. 2. 21. 3, where Thucydides records the refusal of Pericles to convene the Assembly when the Athenians had been aroused by oracle mongers after the Spartan invasion of Attica in the first year of the war.

foreign entanglements. But when Sparta, one of the two greatest powers in Greece, boasts of her sophrosyne and equates it with *apragmosynê*, it cannot mean a policy of isolationism, because it is admitted that Sparta interferes with the constitutions of her allies. Rather, it indicates a non-provocative policy—what Archidamus calls τὸ βραδὺ καὶ μέλλον and Pindar *hasychia* (*Pyth.* 8. 1)—a policy fostered by the Dorian states especially in their contacts with one another.

For Athens the normal foreign policy was the reverse—*polypragmosynê* instead of *apragmosynê*—but occasionally she was advised, either by her own leaders or by foreign powers, to practice sophrosyne, which then implies caution or at least the repression of Athens' typical overconfidence. At one point a *sôphrôn* policy involves rejecting Corcyra's request for an alliance, because it would be prudent or advantageous to lull the hostility aroused by the Megara affair (1. 42. 3). Elsewhere it means accepting the peace proposals of Sparta after Sphacteria, because sophrosyne teaches that good fortune is mutable (4. 18. 4). Still later, sophrosyne would dictate a refusal to intervene in Sicily (6. 11. 7). Only rarely is a policy of intervention called *sôphrôn*, but this exceptional usage occurs when the ambassadors from Egesta urge Athens to join the alliance against Syracuse (6. 6. 2). Here the word *sôphrôn* reverts to its primary significance, "shrewd in one's own interest," a meaning common in Greek oratory where it is used with reference to both internal and external affairs. Thus Hermocrates of Syracuse, in his address to the assembly at Gela, three times uses the stereotyped phrase εἰ σωφρονοῦμεν ("if we show good sense [or] consult our best interests")—each time to commend some aspect of the policy which he advocated (4. 60, 61, 64). Similarly Diodotus in the debate over Mytilene speaks of the *sôphrôn polis* without reference to factional disputes; he means a city wise enough to encourage her citizens to speak fearlessly, without the threat of punishment if their advice is not followed (3. 42. 5). And amid the debate over Pylos, Thucydides describes as *sôphrones* the opponents of Cleon (4. 28. 5). In spite of the party quarrels in which the demagogue was involved, *sôphrôn* here, as Gomme observes, need not refer exclusively to the oligarchic faction, but may refer more generally to the men of sense who hoped that by sending Cleon against the Spartans in Pylos, they would either defeat the enemy or get rid of Cleon himself.

Normally, however, sophrosyne in internal affairs was the shibboleth of the oligarchs, as Thucydides' account of the civil war in Corcyra makes abundantly clear. The cry of equal rights for the many was raised by the democrats, while their opponents used the catchword *sôphrôn aristokratia*

(3. 82. 8). *Sôphrôn* is the operative word denoting oligarchy, because it was a commonplace of political thought that a democracy was more inclined to be turbulent, an oligarchy to be better disciplined.[81] Hence the word is usually present—like *eunomia, eutaxia,* and *kosmos*—in discussions of the Spartan Constitution,[82] yet it might be used of any moderate form of government, especially one in which the power of the masses was in some way restricted. Book VIII, which deals with the period from 411 to 406—during which sophrosyne, like *homonoia* and the "ancestral constitution," was topical in Athenian debates about politics—always connects sophrosyne with oligarchy or modified democracy. When, for example, Peisander came from Samos in 411, he told the Athenians that they could not hope for assistance from the Great King unless they adopted a more *sôphrôn* constitution (εἰ μὴ πολιτεύσομέν τε σωφρονέστερον) and put the offices of the state into the hands of fewer men (8. 53. 3).

That sophrosyne was also thought to be incompatible with the rule of a very small number or with tyranny, we learn from a statement of the Thebans at Plataea. They respond to the charge that their ancestors medized in 481 by pointing out that their constitution at that time was neither an oligarchy with equal rights before the law nor a democracy, but a dynasty of a few men, which is the closest thing to tyranny and the farthest removed from laws and the ideal of moderate government (τῷ σωφρονεστάτῳ ἐναντιώτατον [3. 62. 3]).[83] The Thebans imply that oligarchy is *sôphrôn* when they explain that the oligarchic faction in Plataea opened the gates to them because this faction wished the better element in the city to be the *sôphronistae* ("correctors") of the opinions of the rest (3. 65. 3). The political use of the word *sôphronistês* occurs elsewhere in the *History,* not necessarily with oligarchic implications. When Alcibiades tries to persuade the Athenians to accept an oligarchic constitution in order to curry favor with the Great King, Phrynichus argues against it on the ground that it will not win over the king, and that the allies prefer a democracy at Athens, since they know that the oligarchs would put the allies to death without a trial, whereas the

---

[81] The same point of view is expressed by the Old Oligarch, who credits the aristocrats with the least *akolasia* and *adikia* and charges the democrats with *amathia* ("ignorance"), *ataxia* ("disorder"), and *ponêria* ("knavery"), in *Ath. Pol.* 1. 5. This treatise is dated shortly before the outbreak of the war by Hartvig Frisch (*The Constitution of the Athenians* [Copenhagen, 1942], 47–62) but somewhat later by Wilhelm Nestle (*Vom Mythos zum Logos,* 407–8).

[82] Gomme, *Commentary,* on 1. 32. 4 and 1. 18. 1; cf. Grossmann, *op. cit.* 70 ff.

[83] The two superlatives are unusual. For a suggested emendation (τῷ σώφρονι πάντων ἀναντιώτατον, Herwerden), see Gomme, *Commentary, ad loc.*

democracy would be a refuge for the allies and a *sôphronistês* for the oligarchs (8. 48. 6–7).[84]

Almost all the references to sophrosyne or its cognates in Thucydides occur in reports of speeches—either direct or, as in Book VIII, indirect. Yet here and there Thucydides betrays his own point of view. Two passages are especially instructive. One is his estimate of Chian policy, which he emphatically approves. "Next to the Spartans," he says (8. 24. 4–5), "only the Chians of the people I have known were at the same time fortunate and moderate (ηὐδαιμόνησάν τε ἅμα καὶ ἐσωφρόνησαν), and the more their city grew, the more securely they regulated it (ἐκοσμοῦντο ἐχυρώτερον)." The comparison with Sparta, as well as the use of *kosmein* to explicate *sôphronein*, shows that what Thucydides commends in Chios is a conservative form of government in which the expansive and democratic tendencies natural to success and prosperity are checked. Thucydides' own views are apparent elsewhere in Book VIII, when he comments on the fate of the allied cities in which Peisander and other reactionary Athenians established oligarchies, in place of the democracies previously in control. Once the democrats had been driven out, the exiled oligarchs of Thasos and the other cities returned, and many of these subject cities were lost to the Empire. Thucydides observes that these cities, having acquired sophrosyne (σωφροσύνην δὲ λαβοῦσαι) and freedom in carrying out their plans, aimed at absolute *eleutheria,* rejecting the pretense of *eunomia* which the Athenians offered (8. 64. 5). Here the restoration of oligarchy is described as "acquiring sophrosyne," and this condition is equated with genuine *eunomia,* in contrast to the counterfeit of this excellence under the democrats.

Finally, there is the historian's comment on the Constitution of the Five Thousand, established in Athens after the Four Hundred had been deposed. It was the best government that Athens had had in his time, for there was a moderate blending (*metria synkrasis*) of the few and the many. Again *sôphrôn* is replaced by *metria,*[85] its closest synonym in political terminology and the one that Thucydides always prefers when he describes Athens, but his own bias is perfectly clear. A limited democracy, in which there should be no payment for office and the

---

[84] *Sôphronistês* has no factional implications when Euphemus tells the Sicilians not to try to act in this capacity for the Athenians at this late date (6. 87. 3).

[85] Consult Glenn Morrow, *Plato's Cretan City* (Princeton, 1960), 525, for the meaning of the phrase *metria synkrasis* applied to Theramenes' constitution, the philosophical background of the idea of a mixed constitution, and the possibility that Thucydides' description reflects Theramenes' own ideas on the subject.

rights of citizenship would belong to those who could fight as hoplites, appears to Thucydides to be "moderate." The situation that obtained in Thasos is reversed in Athens: in the former the shift from democracy to oligarchy is considered a change to sophrosyne; in Athens it is the change from the oligarchy of the Four Hundred to a democracy like that of Cleisthenes (the "ancestral constitution") that Thucydides considers moderate.

Sophrosyne never occurs in the *History* with the meaning "chastity," which is otherwise common in literature of the later fifth century. Like Euripides, Thucydides regards sophrosyne as the control of the irrational; but whereas the tragic poet dramatizes the conflict in the individual soul between sophrosyne and such passions as *erôs, thymos,* and *orgê,* the historian concentrates his attention on man as *politikon zôon* so exclusively that he portrays this struggle only in the context of the State. The scope of sophrosyne as he understands it is demonstrated by its synonyms, which invariably have a political connotation—words such as *euboulia, to eukosmon,* or *metriotês* (rather than the individual virtues of *aidôs* and *enkrateia*)—and by its antitheses, which include not only the traditional *hybris, orgê,* and *epithymia* but the more specialized Thucydidean and Periclean words for the active principle—*to drastêrion* and the like. There is also a tendency to oppose sophrosyne to *tychê.* Although much has been written about varying attitudes towards *tychê* in Thucydides and his contemporaries,[86] it may still be useful to point out in the *History* signs of a new development in the relation of sophrosyne to fortune. When the theme of fortune and its mutability appears in lyric and tragic poetry and in Herodotus, it usually teaches the doctrine of sophrosyne as it was understood in the archaic age: man must endure what is beyond his power to control. The age of the Sophists, however, felt a new confidence in the power of man to manipulate circumstances and to some extent control his fortune by *technê* and *gnômê.* While the older point of view is often expressed in the *History,* even by Pericles,[87] like an echo of Herodotus in Thucydides, the newer philosophy is more truly characteristic of Pericles and of the historian himself. We have found

[86] See, for example, Felix Wassermann, *T.A.P.A.* 78 (1947), 29–30; Friedrich Solmsen, *Hermes* 69 (1934), 400 ff.; Wolfgang Schadewaldt, *Neue Wege zur Antike* 8 (1926), 255 f.; John H. Finley, Jr., *H.S.C.P.* 49 (1938), 61 ff.

[87] E.g., 2. 64. 2: φέρειν δὲ χρὴ τά τε δαιμόνια ἀναγκαίως, τά τε ἀπὸ τῶν πολεμίων ἀνδρείως ("one must bear divine visitations as best one can, and the afflictions of the enemy with courage"), where τὰ δαιμόνια is equivalent to *tychê,* and ἀναγκαίως to σωφρόνως. Cf. Sophocles *Phil.* 1316–17. The appearance of proverbial wisdom in Thucydides is discussed by Claus Meister, *Die Gnomik im Geschichtswerk des Thukydides* (Winterthur, 1955).

that for Thucydides the word sophrosyne generally designates "moderation or stability in government" yet sometimes implies that provision against irrational elements (notably *tychê*) which is part of the new philosophy of self-reliance and foresight. Hence sophrosyne and *tychê* are no longer confined to the archaic pattern but hereafter find a variety of relationships, ranging from their absolute opposition in the individual ethics of Democritus to their realignment in the political thought of Plato.[88]

Thucydides' discussion in Book VIII of the constitutional crisis at Athens in 411 provides historical background for the brief Fragment of Thrasymachus' speech *On the Constitution*. Although in Plato's *Republic* the rhetorician Thrasymachus is made to take a radical view of the nature of justice and to praise tyranny as the height of felicity because it is subject to no restraint, his interpretation of sophrosyne in this Fragment is utterly conventional. Internal evidence suggests that the oration was composed either as a model speech or as a discourse to be delivered before the Assembly at a time when the ancestral constitution was a subject of discussion, the word *homonoia* was used to describe the reconciliation of rival factions, and Athens was still at war—probably 411 B.C.[89] Thrasymachus (who as a citizen of Chalcedon would have been barred from speaking before the Assembly himself, but might have composed the speech for someone else) maintains (Frag. 1 DK) that good fortune usually makes people wanton and quarrelsome (ὑβρίζειν τε ποιεῖν καὶ στασιάζειν), while adversity is wont to sober them (*sôphronizein*). His audience, however, has reversed the normal process: "We were wont to be sober [ἐσωφρονοῦμεν] in prosperity, but to lose our head in time of trouble [ἐμάνημεν ἐν δὲ τοῖς κακοῖς]." The sentiment recalls the words of Thucydides about Chios (8. 24. 4–5), when he implies that sophrosyne is almost unheard of in times of good fortune. In opposing *hybris* and *stasis* to sophrosyne, Thrasymachus uses the accepted political vocabulary of the day; *mania* is not one of the Thucydidean antitheses, but it is common elsewhere,[90] and the application to politics is readily understandable. Thrasymachus does not seem to have in mind any one faction when he speaks of the previous sophrosyne of the Athenians;

---

[88] Democritus, Frag. 210 DK. Plato (*Laws* 709D–710A), after discussing *technê* and *tychê* as they affect the ruler, maintains that the best *tychê* for a new state would be to have a ruler endowed with sophrosyne (here approximating *enkrateia* rather than *phronêsis*).

[89] See the analysis by Fuks, *op. cit.*, 102–6.

[90] E.g., Antiphon the Orator *Tetr.* 1. 2. 5; *Dissoi Logoi* 5. 1, 7 DK (see also n. 93). It appears often in the fourth century, especially in Plato (e.g., *Phaedrus* 241A) and Xenophon (*Mem.* 1. 1. 16).

sophrosyne means "stability," and *mania* is equivalent to *hybris* and *stasis*.

The concepts of *homonoia* and sophrosyne are joined in one of the orations of Andocides, who had returned from exile after the amnesty of 403 but was prosecuted in 399 on a charge of impiety. His address *On the Mysteries* treats sophrosyne as a political virtue but avoids both the tendency of Thucydides and Aristophanes to use the word as a party slogan of the oligarchs and the practice of fourth-century orators of making a stereotype of the *sôphrôn politês*. Andocides' usage, in fact, illustrates the political meaning of sophrosyne in the transitional stage at the close of the fifth century, when oligarchic pretensions to this virtue had been discredited, and democratic claims had not yet been established. Sophrosyne now means "moderation" *simpliciter* and suggests "reconciliation of enemies," a revival of an Aeschylean nuance, under circumstances not unlike those that presumably led to Aeschylus' own usage.[91] Reminding the jury of the occasions on which their ancestors had recalled the exiles and rallied to defeat foreign enemies, Andocides maintains that greatness will again be theirs if the citizens will practice moderation (*sôphronein*) and live in peace (*homonoein*) with one another (1. 109). Towards the end of the oration he says that to reconcile the citizens and put concord before vengeance is the work of men who are good and moderate (*sôphrones* [1. 140]). The more common interpretation of sophrosyne as a kind of moralized wisdom also appears in this oration, when Andocides describes as sophrosyne that wisdom which is learned from experience, particularly from mistakes of the past (1. 145).

This interpretation, a development of the ancient doctrine of *Pathei mathos,* seems to be a fundamental part of Andocides' outlook, for it reappears in his two other genuine orations, *On His Return* and *On the Peace with Sparta*. In the first of these, delivered *ca.* 409–408, the application is personal. Admitting his part in the mutilation of the Hermae in 415, but blaming it on youthful folly or bad company (2. 7), Andocides seeks to associate his errors with the misfortunes common to mankind. They are happiest, he says, who make the fewest mistakes, and wisest (*sôphronestatoi*) who repent most readily (2. 6). In the second speech (391 B.C.) sophrosyne is once again a political virtue, to be applied in this instance to Athenian foreign policy; here, too, it is the ability to profit by past mistakes.[92]

[91] The notion of reconciling opposite factions or moderating extremes is implicit in the sophrosyne of the *Eumenides,* which was produced amid the tense circumstances surrounding the reforms of Ephialtes.

[92] Andocides reminds the Assembly of the mistakes Athens has made in the past by ally-

In the *Invective against Alcibiades* by Pseudo-Andocides,[93] sophrosyne also has a political significance but an entirely different one. After the violence of the Thirty Tyrants had discredited the cause of oligarchy, most of the fourth-century Attic orators from Lysias to Demosthenes rejected the fifth-century conception of this party as notably *sôphrôn*. From now on, the *sôphrôn kai metrios politês* is invariably a democrat; the oligarch, if mentioned at all, is charged with *hybris*. The *Invective* shows many signs of this point of view. The fourth-century atmosphere is already palpable in the description of the *sôphrôn* citizen as one who takes precautions against tyranny (4. 24), and in the coupling of justice and sophrosyne as antitheses to the lawlessness of Alcibiades and his ancestors (4. 34, 40). Among the Attic orators, Antiphon and Andocides constitute a small minority, allied with the Sophists, Aristophanes, Euripides, and Thucydides in their manner of interpreting sophrosyne. The remaining orators, even Lysias, have much stronger affinities with Xenophon than with Thucydides and uniformly reflect the conditions of the fourth century.

Important, though entirely disparate, contributions to the development of sophrosyne were made during the age of the Sophists by the two philosophers, Socrates and Democritus. It is admittedly difficult to disentangle Socrates from Plato, but the value of seeing him against the background of his contemporaries would seem to justify the attempt. Only a small body of doctrine is widely accepted as genuinely Socratic. This nucleus of ideas includes the following: that *aretê* is *epistêmê* ("knowledge"), that the care of the soul is the true purpose of life, that the virtues are inseparable, and that self-control is the foundation of

---

ing herself with Argos and becoming involved in war with Sparta. "The examples furnished by our past mistakes are sufficient to prevent the *sôphrones* from erring again." Another facet of sophrosyne, "good repute," appears in the speech *On the Mysteries* (131). Cf. Antiphon the Sophist, Frag. 49.

[93] Friedrich Blass (*Die attische Beredsamkeit* [2] [Leipzig, 1887], 1. 338) assigns the speech to the early fourth century on grounds of style; and K. J. Maidment (*Minor Attic Orators* [London, 1941] 1. 538–59) agrees, chiefly on grounds of content. Antony Raubitschek (*T.A.P.A.* 79 [1948], 205) argues that it may be genuine. The early fourth century is the date commonly assigned to another work dependent on sophistic doctrine, the *Dissoi Logoi*, a series of antilogies in the manner of Protagoras. One pair of arguments deals with the proposition that madmen and sane, wise men and fools (1) say and do the same things and (2) do not say and do the same things. Throughout this argument sophrosyne and *mania* are used antithetically (5. 1, 7 DK). The word sophrosyne does not appear in the treatise of the Anonymous Iamblichi on *aretê*, which attempts to prove that the rule of *nomos* benefits even the strong, but its place is taken by *enkrateia* (4. 1 DK). In refuting the view that obedience to law is cowardice and that *pleonexia* is true *aretê*, the author attempts to show that *nomos* is actually based on *physis*. A. T. Cole (*H.S.C.P.* 65 [1961], 127–63) suggests that the treatise is influenced by the philosophy of Democritus.

moral conduct.[94] All these views have a bearing on sophrosyne. In particular, the emphasis on man's primary duty of tending his soul leads to a process of endless questioning, both of self and of others, which aims at self-knowledge. Hence Socrates is always portrayed in the dialogues written by his admirers as the embodiment of the Delphic *Gnôthi sauton.* The other aspect of his personality which left an imperishable impression is his self-control. This quality appears in Xenophon's portrait of Socrates as *enkrateia,* in the works of Antisthenes and Aristippus as *autarkeia,* and in Plato's reflection of the Socratic personality as sophrosyne. The erotic nature of Socrates is still another common theme in the dialogues inspired by his life and personality; this, too, has a bearing on sophrosyne, because it was a *sôphrôn erôs* that governed his relation to his pupils.

The connection between Socrates and the great Sophists is evident chiefly in the tendency of his questioning. Nothing is more striking in the dialogues of Plato and Xenophon that profess to reproduce the conversations of Socrates than his persistent refutation of conventional ideas accepted by the average man without examination. The question "What is X?" which sets off so many Platonic dialogues is surely a reflection of the Socratic practice. The result of these dialogues is invariably negative, at most a kind of purgation of false ideas (as the *Sophist* suggests [230B]), which leaves the soul ready for the pursuit of knowledge; and we have no reason to believe that Socrates ever answered the questions that he asked, except implicitly by the life he lived. It is significant, however, not only that he was interested in many of the same ethical problems as engaged Protagoras and other Sophists—the source of moral obligations, the relation of appetite and passion to ethical and political conduct, the role of education in imparting *aretê*—and often surpassed them in the unconventionality with which he approached these problems, but that he reacted strongly against their relativism and hedonism.

Although Democritus was by birth a colonial and his approach to sophrosyne was the personal and individualistic one of an Ionian thinker who escaped those influences—Attic tragedy and the Athenian *polis*—that molded sophrosyne in the fifth century,[95] he, too, was interested in many of the same problems as were Socrates and the Sophists. His contribution to the doctrine of sophrosyne consists of his *sôphrôn* hedonism. Pleasure occupies a central position in the ethics of

[94] Aristotle ascribes to Socrates inductive argumentation and universal definition (*Metaph.* M4. 1078b 27).

[95] Witness his famous complaint (Frag. 116 DK): "I came to Athens and no one knew me."

Democritus, yet unlike Callicles and other pupils of the Sophists, he regards sophrosyne not as an obstacle but as a positive aid to the enjoyment of pleasure. Moderation, *metriotês* or sophrosyne, is the key to the sensible hedonism of Democritus; this note runs all through his ethical maxims, presenting the greatest possible contrast to contemporary sophistic arguments that happiness, pleasure, and the satisfaction of appetite are incompatible with self-restraint. Democritus is probably the first philosopher to justify systematically the already popular conception of sophrosyne as the control of appetite; he elevates and expands this notion to make it one of the chief sources of *euthymia* ("contentment"), his *summum bonum*. Most of his references to sophrosyne occur in connection with *terpsis* ("enjoyment"), *hêdonê* ("pleasure"), and related terms. A typical observation maintains (Frag. 211 DK): "Sophrosyne increases delights and makes pleasures greater."[96]

Democritus distinguishes between good and bad pleasures and frequently shows that the best pleasures are somehow connected with intellectual and spiritual values, especially the *kalon* (as in Frags. 207, 189, 194). His conception of sophrosyne includes the element of *autarkeia* ("independence"), in whose company it is opposed to *tychê*.[97] According to Fragment 210, "*tychê* sets a costly table; sophrosyne one that is self-sufficient [*autarkês*]." In Fragment 176, Democritus describes *tychê* as munificent but undependable and says that nature is self-sufficient. Evidently then sophrosyne and nature have this in common: both enable man to attain self-sufficiency. Other qualities akin to sophrosyne are *sophia* and *phronêsis*,[98] which are also opposed to *tychê* (Frags. 197, 119). The *euthymos* and *autarkês* individual enjoys only the proper pleasures (ἡδοναὶ ἐφ᾽ οἷς δεῖ), not those that are bound up with *tychê*.

Several of these key ideas—fidelity to nature, distrust of fortune, and the need for moderation—appear in the introductory sentence of Democritus' *On Contentment*, which says that he who is to achieve this condition must not be overactive in public or private and, whatever he does, must not grasp what is beyond his own power and nature. If *tychê* leads him to excess, he must resist the temptation to seize more than his powers permit, for moderation is safer than superfluity (Frag. 3 DK).[99]

---

96 Cf. Frag. 232: "The pleasures that come least often give most enjoyment."

97 *Autarkeia* is a link with several Hellenistic philosophies. Zeph Stewart (*H.S.C.P.* 63 [1958], 179–91) discusses the influence of Democritus on the Cynics. For the debt of Epicurean ethics to Democritus, see Robert Philippson, *Hermes* 59 (1924), 414; for his influence on the Skeptics and on Plato, see Paul Natorp, *Die Ethika des Demokritos* (Marburg, 1893), 68.

98 See Hermann Langerbeck, Δόξις ἐπιρυσμίη (Berlin, 1935), 72.

99 Kurt von Fritz (*Philosophie und sprächlicher Ausdruck bei Demokrit, Plato und Aristoteles* [New York, 1938], 23) suggests that all Democritus' moral precepts are based on three prin-

These ideas have great importance in Hellenistic philosophy, for in many
ways Democritus foreshadows the concerns of the late fourth century:
in his defense of cosmopolitanism, for instance (Frags. 246, 247), and
his ideal of tranquillity. Like the Epicureans he values sophrosyne, not
at all for its usefulness to the *polis,* but for its help in the attainment of
personal happiness. That he sets a high value on it is evident from two
further Fragments, one of which (208) says that a father's sophrosyne
is for his children the greatest precept. The other (294) is an expression
of a traditional Hellenic belief: "Strength and beauty are the good
things of youth, but sophrosyne is the flower of age." [100]

---

ciples: χρὴ ἐόν ("necessity"), μέτριον ("moderation"), and μη πολλὰ πρήσσειν ("not
'meddling' "), the last two of which are synonyms for sophrosyne in the late fifth century.
For the relation of μὴ πολλὰ πρήσσειν to the Platonic τὸ τὰ αὑτοῦ πράττειν ("doing one's own
work"), see Philippson, *loc. cit.,* 386–89. Democritus' and Epicurus' concepts of nature
are compared by Langerbeck, *op. cit.,* 61.

[100] Sophrosyne is linked with the restraint of appetite in the interests of pleasure in all the
Fragments except 54 and 67, which are perhaps to be assigned to the Pythagorean Democrates.
In these Fragments alone, sophrosyne has the older, "intellectual" connotation and is the
antithesis of folly, rather than of licentiousness (Frag. 67: τὸ εὔηθες, "folly"; Frag. 54:
οἱ ἀξύνετοι, "the witless").

IV

Xenophon, the Minor Socratic Schools, and the Attic Orators of the Fourth Century

AT the close of the fifth century the concept of sophrosyne included a wide range of nuances, most of which had developed under the pressure of the great forces at work—especially in Athens—during that period of rapid change. These influences were the continued unfolding of Attic democracy, the conflict between oligarchic and democratic factions in the Greek states, the Peloponnesian war itself, the flowering of tragedy and comedy, and the sophistic movement, together with the reactions it provoked. In the fourth century, too, it is possible to identify certain influences—again chiefly Athenian—that shaped the further growth of the concept of sophrosyne, but they were now by no means so numerous. There were in fact only two great forces responsible in the main for the altered significance of the word sophrosyne in the fourth century: the Athenian *polis*, in its domestic and external affairs, and the memory of Socrates.[1]

The influence of the *polis* is most clearly seen in the speeches of the Attic orators, which delineate to perfection the *sôphrôn politês*— the law-

---

[1] The memory of Socrates had its most lasting effect on sophrosyne through the mediation of Plato, which is discussed in Chap. V. Another force that obviously influences sophrosyne is rhetoric, but this affects the form in which the concept is presented, more than the concept itself.

abiding citizen—whom the conditions of Athenian society in the fourth century converted into an ideal. There are slight variations in the picture drawn by the various orators (Isaeus, for example, omits one facet that Lysias and Demosthenes both emphasize), but three essentials are nearly always present: the *sôphrôn* citizen is a fervent democrat, who hates oligarchy; he is loyal and generous to his fellow citizens and therefore quick to perform "liturgies"; and in private life he is self-effacing, inoffensive, averse to litigation. Beyond the borders of Attica events were also taking place which affected the concept of sophrosyne: the rise and decline of Sparta and later of Thebes, the growth and collapse of the Athenian Second Maritime Confederacy, the revival of the danger from Persia, and finally the threat of Macedon. The concern felt by many Greeks over the futile, endless warfare between Hellenic states or leagues of states prompted some to extend the scope of sophrosyne so as to include moderation and restraint in international relations. Isocrates was the spokesman for this point of view. Another development, on the frontier between politics and philosophy, singled out sophrosyne as the characteristic virtue of Sparta, making it the basis of her envied stability, moral conservatism, and military discipline. This tendency, already strong in the fifth century, was intensified in the fourth, particularly in the semi-historical, semi-philosophical writing of which Xenophon's *Constitution of the Lacedemonians* affords a fair sample. It provoked a reaction in some quarters, particularly the school of Isocrates, and may be partly responsible for the patriotic fervor with which Isocrates propagated his commonplaces about the *archaia aretê* of Athens herself, in which he made sophrosyne a basic ingredient.

The multiplication of philosophical schools in the wake of Socrates had major consequences for sophrosyne. The automatic reflex of such schools or of their founders seems to have been inquiry into moral values, primarily those of Socrates himself. Among these values sophrosyne was inevitably emphasized, although it was variously interpreted by the divergent Socratic schools. Not only Plato but also Antisthenes, whom tradition represents as the precursor of Cynicism, and even the Cyrenaic Aristippus found the Socratic self-command peculiarly significant, whether it was called sophrosyne, *enkrateia*, or *autarkeia*. Some of Socrates' most ardent admirers founded no school but tried to recapture his personality and teaching in dialogue form; to this group belong Aeschines of Sphettus, who wrote seven Socratic dialogues, and Xenophon.

XENOPHON

In all his writings—Socratic, biographical, didactic, and historical—Xenophon demonstrates the wide scope assigned to sophrosyne in the ethical vocabulary of the fourth century. Moreover, he is on familiar terms with the canon of virtues—piety, wisdom, justice, courage, and sophrosyne (or *enkrateia*)—which was already known in the fifth century and was destined to take definitive shape in the fourth. Xenophon foreshadows the borrowing of the topic of the virtues (not necessarily or only these five) by prose writers of every kind, but especially historians, in the fourth century and thereafter. Although the study of *aretê* and its component parts formed one of the principal tasks of the philosophers—Socrates and Plato above all—the topic of the virtues and vices held vast possibilities for oratory as well; and we have already seen how Gorgias, for example, discussed the heroic qualities of the dead in his *Epitaphios,* and how Pericles in the Funeral Oration celebrated the virtues of Athens herself.[2] The Sophists had enriched the topic in several ways: by defining the virtues, by relating them to the life of the State as well as to private life, by finding exemplars in poetry and myth, and by adapting to prose certain devices, such as the personification of virtue, which had long been used by the poets. Now in the fourth century Isocrates made this topic his own, adding a wealth of commonplaces and exemplars which constituted his legacy to his pupils and ultimately became the property of every writer of rhetorical prose in the Graeco-Roman world. Xenophon was in a position to benefit from both ways of approaching the subject of the virtues—the philosophical and the rhetorical. Both the *Agesilaus* and the *Memorabilia* employ a canon of virtues as a framework for eulogy. The contents of the canon differ, as we shall see, even within the *Memorabilia,* but both treatises include piety in every list of virtues and place great emphasis on *enkrateia,* either as a subhead of sophrosyne or as a separate virtue in its own right.

Xenophon uses the word sophrosyne with remarkable frequency and diversity of meaning. No earlier writer—except perhaps Euripides—refers so often to this virtue, with such a variety of connotations. Xenophon was interested in several problems concerning sophrosyne: the method of acquiring it and the possibility of losing it; its value to the ruler and to the State; its relation to other virtues, such as *aidôs*; and its central position in the personality of Socrates. It is in his Socratic

[2] See Chap. III, pp. 93–94, 106–7.

writings and those that deal in some way with education or encomium that Xenophon discusses these problems; the *Hellenica* and the *Anabasis* merely reflect contemporary usage in their allusions to sophrosyne and related words, showing a strong preference for an intellectual—or, perhaps better, "prudential"—significance.[3] The moral connotations of the word are more prominent in the *Memorabilia*.

The literary type of the Socratic dialogue came into vogue within a decade after the death of Socrates. Xenophon's *Memorabilia*, which was composed of several different elements—apologia, memoirs, dialogue— put together over a period of many years,[4] reflects the author's acquaintance with at least some of the earlier representatives of the genre, especially the dialogues of Antisthenes, whose view of Socrates Xenophon is inclined to adopt. Since Socrates' most memorable occupation was discussing the nature of the virtues, the typical Socratic dialogue reproduces such a conversation. Early in the *Memorabilia* Xenophon lists the subjects that Socrates discussed—always "human," rather than "divine," topics. They consist of five moral virtues and their opposites and four questions connected with the State. The virtues are piety, the *kalon* ("the fair," as much moral as aesthetic), justice, sophrosyne, and courage (I. I. 16). The omission of wisdom (*phronêsis* or *sophia*) from this canon is noteworthy. Since the antithesis to sophrosyne is given as *mania* ("madness" or "irrationality"), sophrosyne here is more intellectual than moral and can take the place of *phronêsis*, without, however, entirely sacrificing its moral connotations. It is significant that when discussing the loss of sophrosyne by Alcibiades and Critias, once they had parted company with Socrates, Xenophon employs two antitheses for *sôphrôn: agnômôn* ("heedless") and *akratês* ("profligate"), thus calling attention to the twofold nature of sophrosyne.

Although he lists the subjects that Socrates was wont to discuss, Xenophon does not at this point launch a Socratic dialogue. In the first two chapters of Book I he defends Socrates against the indictment of

---

[3] *Anabasis* 6. 2. 11; 7. 3. 17; 7. 6. 41, 42 (all variations on the phrase ἦν σωφρονῆτε, "if you are sensible"); 6. 1. 28; 7. 7. 24 (*sôphronizein*, "to bring to one's senses"). *Hellenica* 2. 3. 24; 4. 3. 6; 6. 2. 39; 6. 3. 5; 7. 1. 24 (*sôphrôn*, with the general implication of "prudent, sensible"); 7. 3. 6 (*sôphrôn*, "virtuous," opposed to *ponêros*, "wicked").

[4] Beginning probably *ca.* 393, when Polycrates published his *Accusation,* and continuing for at least a decade. Xenophon's sources and the extent of his originality are disputed. For Antisthenes as a source, see Olof Gigon, *Kommentar zum ersten Buch von Xenophons Memorabilien* (Basel, 1953); for Plato, see Ernst Gebhardt, *Polykrates' Anklage gegen Sokrates und Xenophons Erwiderung* (Frankfurt, 1957). J.-H. Kühn (*Gnomon* 32 [1960], 97–107) defends the ability of Xenophon (as shown in the *Anabasis*) to create a picture of a personality, without depending on literary sources.

399 B.C., which charged him with two crimes: rejecting the gods of the state and introducing new gods, and corrupting the youth (1. 1. 1). Furthermore, he replies to the *Accusation* of Polycrates, which supplied a detailed explanation of the so-called corruption. These two charges determine the content of Xenophon's defense and account for the total concentration of Chapter I on the virtue of piety (*eusebeia*) and of Chapter II on sophrosyne and various forms of helpfulness (*ôphelia*)— to the State, to family, and to friends. Although he mentions the canon of virtues, Xenophon does not use it as the basis of an encomium here, as he does in Book IV (8. 11, for example). The justice of Socrates is very briefly described in Chapter I as an adjunct of piety (17–18), and his courage is entirely ignored.[5] Even the interpretation of sophrosyne, which was largely intellectual in 1. 1. 16, is affected by the terms of the indictment and becomes predominently moral in Chapter II, where its function is to refute the charge that Socrates corrupted the young.

There are three components of sophrosyne in Xenophon's portrait of Socrates at this stage of the *Memorabilia: enkrateia* ("control over the appetites and passions"), *karteria* ("endurance of cold, heat, and toil"), and *autarkeia* ("contentment with little, independence of external things"). The first two are subheads of sophrosyne in the *Agesilaus* (5. 1–7) as well, but *autarkeia* is uniquely Socratic—the true source of his tremendous appeal to the Cynics. Xenophon's conception of Socrates as the *sôphrôn anêr* is much closer to the Cynic tradition than to Plato's picture, which, while it does not ignore the ascetic element, includes many other nuances that Antisthenes and Xenophon normally omit. Since, however, the charge of corruption, as expanded by Polycrates, included teaching the young to despise the established laws, it is not enough to describe Socrates as self-controlled, enduring, and independent and to show that he taught the young to imitate him (1. 2. 18). Xenophon is obliged to expand the topic of sophrosyne still further, to include a defense of Socrates' influence on Athenian politics.

This part of the defense includes an assurance that Socrates' *phronêsis* had no bad effect on the *polis*—since it was combined with persuasion rather than violence (1. 2. 10–11)—and a detailed refutation of the well-known theory that Socrates was responsible for the evil inflicted on the state by Critias and Alcibiades. Because their vices were, in the first case, violence and greed and, in the second, licentiousness

---

[5] Gigon (*op. cit.*, 26) suggests that the omission of references to Socrates' courage may be explained by the fact that in all the famous episodes that proved his *andreia*, he was closely linked with Alcibiades, whom Xenophon wished to eliminate from the biography of Socrates.

and *hybris* (1. 2. 12), sophrosyne is the virtue that they both conspicuously lacked. Xenophon must therefore show that Socrates was not responsible for this deficiency. He does so by asserting that Socrates possessed both sophrosyne and a knowledge of dialectic, but that Critias and Alcibiades were interested only in the second and, indeed, would have preferred death to the kind of life Socrates led (1. 2. 14-16). To avert the charge that Socrates should not have taught his pupils about politics before teaching them sophrosyne (1. 2. 17), Xenophon next maintains, rather inconsistently, that while they associated with Socrates, the two actually did practice sophrosyne, believing at that time that such conduct was best (1. 2. 18).⁶ This statement in turn obliges Xenophon to explain how virtue, once learned, can be forgotten, and he embarks upon a refutation of Antisthenes' view—that virtue cannot be unlearned—by maintaining that everything good, especially sophrosyne, depends on training (*askêsis*) and can be forgotten when training stops (1. 2. 21-23).⁷ He adds that Socrates deserves praise for teaching Critias and Alcibiades sophrosyne in their youth, when they would naturally be most heedless and profligate (1. 2. 26), for persevering in sophrosyne himself (1. 2. 28), and for censuring Critias' licentiousness so severely that Critias thereafter bore a grudge against him (1. 2. 29-31).

The remainder of Chapter II refutes the other charges of Polycrates (49-61) and reiterates that Socrates, by his piety and his teaching of *aretê*, deserved well of the state (62-64). The pattern thus established— praise of Socrates' piety and of his morality, considered first under the rubric of sophrosyne or *enkrateia*, then under that of conduct towards the state, family, and friends—is repeated in 1. 4-7, so that 1. 5-6, on the restraint of appetite, corresponds closely to 1. 2. 1-5.⁸ In this further discussion of Socrates' self-restraint, the same three aspects are eulogized. Xenophon praises *enkrateia* as the foundation of all virtue (1. 5. 5) and ascribes to Socrates not only restraint of bodily pleasure but also *enkrateia* in regard to money,⁹ and in the following chapter reverts to the subject of *autarkeia* and *karteria* (1. 6. 1-8). He reports a conversation

⁶ See Gigon (*op. cit.*, 53) for a comparison with Plato's *Gorgias*, where rhetoric and sophrosyne correspond to dialectic and sophrosyne in the *Memorabilia*.

⁷ Cf. *Cyr.* 7. 5. 75, where the acquisition and loss of sophrosyne are discussed.

⁸ Before taking up this scheme in 1. 4, Xenophon inserts a single chapter (1. 3) which briefly treats the two crucial subjects: first, Socrates' piety, and then his *euteleia, autarkeia,* and *enkrateia.* For the threat to *enkrateia* resulting from a kiss, cf. *Ages.* 5. 4.

⁹ The same pattern (piety and morality) is followed in Xenophon's *Apology*; see especially 19, on sophrosyne and *enkrateia. Enkrateia* where money is concerned becomes a subhead of justice in *Ages.* 4. 3-4.

between Socrates and Antiphon the Sophist, which concludes with Socrates' statement that happiness consists not in luxury and extravagance, but in having as few wants as possible, since to have no wants at all is divine (1. 6. 10).[10] An aspect of *autarkeia* often encountered in the *Memorabilia* is the independence (*eleutheriotês*) of the teacher who refuses to accept fees and is therefore not bound to converse with anyone (1. 2. 6). This subject, too, arises in the conversation with Antiphon, who tries to interpret Socrates' rejection of payment as a sign that his knowledge is worthless. By likening the Sophist who demands a fee to a prostitute and comparing his own practice to that of a person who is *sôphrôn* in affairs of love, Socrates implies that *autarkeia* in this sense is a form of sophrosyne (1. 6. 13).

Book IV repeats the pattern of 1. 1–2 and 1. 4–7 on a larger scale, again attempting to prove that Socrates preferred to give moral training before training in speech and action (4. 3. 1; cf. 1. 2. 17: sophrosyne before τὰ πολιτικά). The importance of sophrosyne is, if anything, enhanced: it has now become the heading under which other virtues are discussed. After observing that Socrates believed facility in speech and action, without sophrosyne, to be only a source of injustice and wrong-doing, Xenophon proceeds to discuss the first division of sophrosyne, which is sophrosyne towards the gods, or piety (4. 3. 1–2).[11] The second moral virtue discussed is justice, which is not related to sophrosyne;[12] and the third is *enkrateia,* which is regarded as a necessary preliminary to efficiency in political and private affairs (4. 5. 1) and is also said to be essential for attaining wisdom (*sophia*), sophrosyne, and even pleasure (4. 5. 6, 7, 9). An attempt is made to link *enkrateia* with dialectic (the second subject that Socrates taught, after morality) through an untranslatable word play on the active and the passive voices of the verb *dialegein* ("to classify" and "to discuss"), which assigns to *enkrateia* the power to sort out the most important things and to choose the good and reject the bad (4. 5. 11). It is perhaps in such passages that the inspiration for the Stoic definition of sophrosyne (*phronêsis* in choosing, *SVF* 1. 200) should be sought.[13] The final eulogy of Socrates, at the close of

[10] This statement corresponds to the Cynic ideal and is also attributed to Diogenes of Sinope (D.L. 6. 104). In the attempts of later philosophers and theologians to imitate the Divine nature, asceticism usually plays some part.

[11] Cf. 4. 3. 17: "To please the gods is the greatest sign of sophrosyne."

[12] Xenophon inserts at this point a dialogue between Socrates and Hippias which deals with justice, but is not a development of the preceding remarks.

[13] See Chap. VI, n. 65, for other anticipations of the Stoic definition, including *Mem.* 4. 8. 11, 3. 9. 4.

Book IV, organizes his virtues into a canon consisting of piety, justice, wisdom (*phronêsis*), and *enkrateia*, which is again defined as never choosing the more pleasant in preference to the better course (4. 8. 11). *Enkrateia* corresponds to sophrosyne in the canon of Book I (1. 16 and 2. 15), and since the connotations of *enkrateia* are entirely moral, there is need for an unequivocally intellectual excellence—a need met by *phronêsis*.[14]

Although Xenophon habitually in the *Memorabilia* calls attention to the moral aspects of sophrosyne,[15] he is careful to state in Book III that Socrates made no distinction between *sophia* and sophrosyne (9. 4), since both consist in knowing what is good and fair and doing it, and in knowing what is disgraceful and avoiding it. Justice and "all virtue" are identified with *sophia*, through their common identification with the Fair and the Good. *Mania*, which in 1. 1. 16 is the antithesis to sophrosyne, here becomes the opposite of *sophia* (3. 9. 6).

An isolated use of *sôphronein* in a military context, equivalent to εὐτακτεῖν ("to be orderly") and to πειθαρχεῖν ("to be obedient"), occurs in a conversation between Socrates and the younger Pericles (3. 5. 21), who laments that these qualities, which are most essential in the army, are now the most neglected. In this passage Xenophon uses the topic of *degeneratio* in a way reminiscent of Isocrates. He, too, mourns for the *archaia aretê* of Athens, which flourished both in the legendary days of Cecrops and in the historical period of the Persian war (3. 5. 9–14), and, like Isocrates, locates this virtue only in the Council of the Areopagus in present-day Athens.[16] Unlike Isocrates, Xenophon believes that this type of *aretê* still exists in Sparta, where *aidôs*, obedience, and *homonoia* ("concord") offer a model that Athens would do well to imitate (3. 5. 15–16).[17]

The *Oikonomikos*, which opens with a discussion of enslavement to the

[14] The response of the oracle to Chaerephon as reported in *Apol.* 4. 15–17 contains a vestigial canon of virtues: freedom from passion (equivalent to *enkrateia*), justice, and sophrosyne, which in the later comments on the oracle is treated as a synonym of *sophia*, yet is also opposed to *hybris* (19). See Plato *Apol.* 20D 7 ff.–31C. for the canon of virtues interpreted with reference to the true statesman; for Xenophon the *aretae* of Socrates are not politically oriented. Erwin Wolff (*Platos Apologie* [Berlin, 1929], 96–99) compares the treatment of the canon of virtues in the two Apologies.

[15] In *Mem.* 2. 1. 21–34, the apologue of Heracles at the crossroads, sophrosyne is allied with *aidôs* and *katharotês* ("modesty" and "purity") in the description of *Aretê*. There is no way of determining how much of the language used here goes back to Prodicus, the inventor of the apologue.

[16] Cf. Isocrates *Areop.* 37–38.

[17] These virtues play an important role in Spartan education as described by Xenophon in the *Constitution of the Lacedemonians*.

appetites, contains much the same kind of conversation with Socrates as the fourth book of the *Memorabilia.* The special contribution of this little treatise to the subject of sophrosyne lies in its picture of the *vita rustica* as nurse of *aretê*—a topic much expanded by Cicero (who in his youth translated the *Oikonomikos*) [18]—and in its application of sophrosyne to the duties of both husband and wife. At first it appears that sophrosyne is confined to the woman's role, for the bride of Ischomachus protests that she can do nothing to help her husband manage the estate; her mother has told her that her task is to be a good wife (*sôphronein*). The verb sums up the whole duty of the married woman, including, of course, fidelity to her husband, but much more as well. Ischomachus responds that man and wife must both be *sôphrones*—must, that is, behave in such a way as to preserve and add to their property, when they can do so with justice (7. 14–15). Sophrosyne in his usage is practical wisdom, manifested particularly in the qualities of orderliness and systematic arrangement which Ischomachus teaches his wife to impose on the pots and pans and all their household goods (8). Although the qualities proper to men and women differ in many respects, *enkrateia* ("self-control"), like memory and the capacity for taking pains, is common to both (7. 26–27).

The *Agesilaus* and the *Cyropaedia* are the other two works of Xenophon that show a marked interest in sophrosyne, and both link the virtue with the concept of the ideal ruler. The *Agesilaus,* which was to be one of the fountainheads of eulogy in Graeco-Roman rhetoric and historiography,[19] juxtaposes two methods of celebrating the life of the Spartan general: praise of his birth, family, native land, and achievements in chronological order (1–2); and description of his virtues (3–8). The first method is the one already employed by Isocrates in the *Evagoras,*[20] which discusses the virtues of the king in connection with his achievements, instead of

---

[18] For Cicero's use of this *topos,* see Chap. VIII, p. 274. Xenophon believes that husbandry instils justice and cooperation (5. 12, 5. 14). Hunting is another occupation that he considers a source of virtue (13. 15), specifically of self-restraint (*enkrateia, Cyr.* 8. 1. 36). This belief persists as a topic in Roman poetry, where, e.g., Ovid links hunting and chastity in the case of Cephalus and Procris (*Metam.* VII. 694–861). The *Oikonomikos,* like the *Gorgias* of Plato, connects sophrosyne with genuine leadership (here kingship, rather than the art of the statesman) and links despotism with its opposite, which is compared to the condition of Tantalus in the afterlife (21. 11).

[19] Its influence is apparent in such Latin works as Cicero's *De Imp. Cn. Pompei,* Nepos' *Atticus* (where, however, the virtues of peacetime are distinguished from those suitable in time of war), Tacitus' *Agricola,* and Pliny's *Panegyric.*

[20] Assuming that the *Evagoras* was composed soon after the death of the king, who was assassinated in 374 B.C.

allotting to them a separate section. The canon of excellence in the *Agesilaus* consists of piety (not mentioned in the *Evagoras*), justice, sophrosyne, courage, wisdom (*sophia*), and, in addition, patriotism and something akin to affability (τὸ εὔχαρι [8. 1]). Sophrosyne here includes two of the same elements as in the *Memorabilia*—enkrateia and *karteria,* but not *autarkeia.* The requirements of a military career influence the interpretation given each of the virtues. Thus piety is shown by fidelity to oaths, which gained the trust even of the enemy (3. 2), while the value to a general of great powers of endurance is stressed in the praise of sophrosyne (5. 2-3). Agesilaus' affability, simplicity, and friendliness are admirable in so great a man and are contrasted with the pride and aloofness of the Persian king (8. 1-6, 9). In the summary of the virtues of Agesilaus this quality is called *praotês* (10. 1), and Xenophon even goes to the unusual length of treating the word *tapeinos* ("humble, lowly") as a term of praise, in commenting on Agesilaus' lack of arrogance (11. 11). *Praotês* and sophrosyne are synonymous in the parallel phrases εὐτυχῶν δὲ πρᾷος εἶναι ("to be gentle when things go well" [11. 2]) and σωφρονεῖν ἐν ταῖς εὐπραξίαις ("to be modest in good fortune" [10. 1]), where both words denote absence of arrogance.[21] Like Isocrates in the *Evagoras* and the *Nicocles,* Xenophon uses the commonplace that a king must be a *paradeigma* for his subjects. He asks who could become impious after imitating one who was pious, and continues with a canon that includes both sophrosyne and *enkrateia; hybris* is the antithesis to the first, *akrasia* to the second (10. 2).

The ruler as *paradeigma* is a theme frequently referred to in the *Cyropaedia.* We learn, for example, that Cyrus taught his people sophrosyne by refraining from *hybris,* although he had the power to commit it, and that he thought he could best instil *enkrateia* by showing that he was never carried away from the pursuit of the Good by the pleasures of the moment (8. 1. 30).[22] As in the passage from the *Agesilaus* just cited, sophrosyne and *enkrateia* are distinguished but remain closely related. Sophrosyne has a wider scope than *enkrateia,* which is usually restricted to the control of appetites and passions. Xenophon never explicitly distinguishes between the two, but in the same passage in the *Cyropaedia* he does distinguish between sophrosyne and *aidôs,* in terms reminiscent

---

[21] See Chap. VIII, pp. 301 ff. for the possible coalescence of *praotês* and sophrosyne to form the imperial virtue of *clementia.* Tapeinotês is a virtue also in the *Const. Lac.* 8. 2. For sophrosyne as a virtue hard to maintain in time of good fortune, see *Cyr.* 8. 4. 14, where the opposing vice (as usual in this commonplace) is *hybris.*

[22] Cf. the definition of *enkrateia* in the eulogy of Socrates, *Mem.* 4. 8. 11.

of Antiphon and Critias. *Aidôs* is that which causes us to avoid what is disgraceful in public; sophrosyne has the same effect even in private (8. 1. 30).[23]

The *Cyropaedia* is much concerned with the general problem of instilling virtue, which was one of the overriding issues of all fourth-century literature. Like Plato, Xenophon assumes that the important thing is to educate the ruling class, and he devotes some attention to the methods used in his idealized Persian state to instil the proper qualities in each age group of this class. From his discussion it appears that sophrosyne is the excellence peculiarly associated with youth. Young boys are sent to school to learn justice and sophrosyne: the first by actual practice in trying cases, the second by imitating the example of their elders (1. 2. 8). Obedience and *enkrateia* (again, the restraint of appetite) are also learned during this early period. The next age group, that of the ephebes, must spend a decade on sentry duty, both to guard the city and to learn sophrosyne, the quality that enables men to perform wearisome tasks (1. 2. 9). The sophrosyne of the younger boys is obedience and orderly behavior; that of the ephebes is close to *karteria*.[24]

A dialogue between Cyrus and Tigranes centers on the question whether sophrosyne can be acquired, and how. Tigranes, son of the King of Armenia, tries to persuade Cyrus to spare his father (who has led an unsuccessful revolt); he bases his plea on the assertion that the king will now be a more useful subject, since he has become *sôphrôn* through being caught in an act of injustice. Sophrosyne here is opposed to *aphrosynê* ("folly") and denotes knowledge of one's situation or adjustment to reality. Like Socrates in the *Memorabilia*, Tigranes holds that no other quality—whether strength, courage, wealth, or power—is useful without sophrosyne (3. 1. 16). Cyrus replies that if the king has indeed become *sôphrôn* in the space of a single day, Tigranes must assume that sophrosyne is not something learned (*mathêma*) but, like grief, is an emotion (*pathêma*) of the soul, for such an instantaneous conversion would be impossible if *phronêsis* ("reasonableness") were a necessary antecedent of sophrosyne (3. 1. 17). Tigranes' argument places great

---

[23] This distinction is sometimes ascribed to Prodicus; see Chap. III, p. 92, and cf. Antiphon, Frag. 44 DK, and Critias, Frag. 25 DK.

[24] Whatever else it may become, sophrosyne throughout Greek literature is always the virtue proper to the young, and of course to women—i.e., to all those members of society of whom obedience is required. In a comparable description of education by age groups, the *Const. Lac.* 2–4 assigns obedience, sophrosyne, and *aidôs* to the youngest boys; sophrosyne and *aidôs* to the next older group as well; and manly valor to the third.

emphasis on the power of punishment to bring a man to his senses (the basic meaning of *sôphronizein* [3. 1. 20, 22, 27]).[25] This discussion—like the remarks on *askêsis* as a source of sophrosyne in the *Memorabilia* (1. 2. 21–23)—doubtless echoes the debates in the philosophical schools over the difference between intellectual and moral virtues and the methods of instilling each type. Habituation or practice (*askêsis*) was always considered the source of moral virtue. Tigranes' argument perhaps contains also a reminiscence of the still popular theme of *Pathei mathos*.

The military aspects of sophrosyne (obedience, orderliness, discipline, and even knowledge of strategy) are prominent in the *Cyropaedia*,[26] as in the *Agesilaus*. In addition to these and to the familiar connotations of moderation, restraint of appetite, and prudence, sophrosyne occasionally means "chastity," as in the episode of Panthea, the beautiful captive, whom Cyrus promises to honor because of her sophrosyne and perfect virtue (7. 3. 12).[27]

THE MINOR SOCRATIC SCHOOLS

The self-control, hardiness, and self-sufficiency of Socrates, which in Xenophon's view formed the essence of his sophrosyne, made a deep impression on many other admirers as well, if we may trust the ancient accounts of the life and teachings of Aeschines of Sphettus, Antisthenes, and even Aristippus. Since, however, it seems highly probable that many elements in this tradition are products of the imagination,[28] they must be treated with reserve, particularly when they relate to the influence of Antisthenes on Diogenes and on Cynic morality. According to the ancient biographers, both Aeschines of Sphettus and Antisthenes emphasized practical morality, and this tendency determined their attitude towards sophrosyne. Aeschines wrote a Socratic dialogue named for Callias—who figures in many works of Plato and Xenophon as a type of the rich young man—and in it, according to the reconstruction by Dittmar,[29] he discussed the relation of happiness to *aretê*, showing that *aretê* consists chiefly in *enkrateia* and sophrosyne, of which the rich man, enslaved by pleasure, has no share. Another dialogue, *Miltiades*, which

---

[25] Cf. 2. 2. 14, where fathers teach their sons sophrosyne by making them weep, and 8. 4. 14, where bad fortune is said to render a man *sôphrôn*.

[26] See 3. 3. 58; 5. 3. 43; 5. 4. 44.

[27] Cyrus himself displays both sophrosyne and *hosiotês* ("scrupulous purity") in refusing to look upon Panthea (6. 1. 47).

[28] See D. R. Dudley, *A History of Cynicism* (London, 1937), 1–16, for a convincing attack on the traditions about Antisthenes and his relation to Diogenes and later Cynics.

[29] Heinrich Dittmar, *Aischines von Sphettos* (Berlin, 1912), 199.

has been described as a dialogue on sophrosyne,[30] contrasted modern education and its results to the older Attic culture, whose chief characteristics (as in *Mem.* 3. 5. 8–20) were modesty and propriety in behavior.

Antisthenes, too, seems to have taken a one-sided view of Socratic sophrosyne. Misunderstanding the motives with which Socrates practiced *enkrateia* and the other ascetic virtues,[31] he established as an end what was for Socrates no more than a means. The attitudes of the two men towards pleasure reveal their fundamental difference: in contrast to the genuine freedom of Socrates, Antisthenes is imprisoned within his own rigid conception of *autarkeia*. According to Diogenes Laertius, Antisthenes said that he would rather suffer madness than pleasure (6. 3); the only pleasure he considered good was that secured by toil (*ponos*). He was famous for his *enkrateia* (D. L. 6. 15) and was said to have learned from Socrates hardiness (τὸ καρτερικόν) and absence of feeling (τὸ ἀπαθές [D. L. 6. 2]). Since he believed virtue to consist in deeds, not words or learning (D. L. 6. 11), his sophrosyne had nothing to do with the intellect. He warned those who possessed this virtue to refrain from studying literature, lest they be perverted by alien influences (D. L. 6. 103).

Diogenes alleges that Antisthenes in turn was the source from which the Cynics, Diogenes of Sinope and Crates, learned, respectively, *apatheia* and *enkrateia,* and Zeno the Stoic, *karteria* (6. 15). Although it is precisely here that Diogenes inspires the least confidence,[32] there is no doubt that the ascetic ideal of the Cynics included an extremely narrow conception of sophrosyne, entirely divorced from the theoretical life.[33] Diogenes of Sinope, in defining *paideia* as sophrosyne for the young (D. L. 6. 68), obviously has in mind the disciplinary aspects of the virtue—those that Xenophon describes as being instilled in Spartan and Persian boys in the earliest stages of their education. Crates, in the famous elegy that personifies Sophrosyne as the mother of *Euteleia* (Frugality [Frag. 2 Diehl [3]]), locates her accurately among the Cynic cardinal virtues, at some distance from the more gracious qualities, such as *Hêsychia* and the *Charites,* which are elsewhere her close companions.[34] Even *aidôs,* the mother of sophrosyne in one Attic inscription, is cut off from the Cynic self-

[30] Rudolf Hirzel, *Der Dialog* (Leipzig, 1895), 1. 134.

[31] Heinrich Maier (*Sokrates* [Tübingen, 1913], 506 ff.) analyzes the proofs of Antisthenes' fanatical devotion to Socrates as the prophet of freedom and moral autonomy.

[32] See Dudley, *op. cit.,* 1–58.

[33] Audrey Rich (*Mnemosyne* 9 [1956], 23–29) draws attention to the paradox by which the only genuine *autarkeia* is to be found in the Aristotelian ideal of the contemplative life, which, being intellectual, was not acceptable to the Cynics.

[34] *Hêsychia:* Epicharmus, Frag. 101 Kaibel, *Com.;* the *Charites:* Theognis 1135–50.

sufficiency, which, supported by a radical endorsement of *physis* and a radical rejection of all *nomoi*, expressed itself in affronts to decency and in the renunciation of conventional restraints (D. L. 6. 46). Indeed, the filth and eccentricity, the deliberate lack of modesty, which became the hallmark of Cynicism in the later fourth and the third centuries (and in the revived Cynicism of the first century after Christ), might well serve as an appropriate symbol of the distortion of sophrosyne by this school.[35] The antithesis to sophrosyne in Cynic thought was neither *hybris* nor *akolasia* but *tryphê* ("extravagance"), as Crates' elegy suggests. This antithesis illustrates the sympathy felt by the Cynics for the ethical precepts of Democritus, who linked sophrosyne with frugality and self-sufficiency and opposed it to extravagance.[36]

It was the Cynics of the third century who, on the basis of Crates' *spoudaiogeloion* ("mixture of seriousness with jest"), developed the diatribe, often described as a *sôphronizôn logos*, which imparted some flavor of Cynic sophrosyne to a wide variety of literary types—the Stoic treatise on morality, the verse of Phoenix of Colophon and Cercidas of Megalopolis, Roman satire, the oratory of the Second Sophistic, and the homilies of certain Church Fathers.[37] The immense influence of the Cynic-Stoic diatribe helps to explain the wide diffusion in Graeco-Roman times of the ascetic concept of sophrosyne, which is summed up in Antipater's epitaph for Diogenes, where the famous wallet, cloak, and staff of the Cynic prototype are termed the weapons of *autarkês* sophrosyne (*Anth. Pal.* 7. 65).

Socratic self-mastery took a different form in the hedonistic philosophy of Aristippus, traditionally represented as the founder of the Cyrenaic school; he regarded pleasure as the end in life and considered bodily gratification superior to any other pleasure.[38] Unlikely though it may seem, there is a relationship between the Cyrenaics and the morality of Socrates, again by way of *autarkeia*. The essence of Cyrenaic hedonism lies in the belief that life offers most to the man who never denies himself a pleasure yet is always sufficiently master of himself to do without

[35] Cicero describes the Cynic lack of *verecundia* in *Off.* 1. 148.

[36] Zeph Stewart (*H.S.C.P.* 63 [1958], 179–91) discusses the development of a hedonistic Cynicism in the mid-third century B.C. For Julian's denunciation of the debased Cynicism current in his day, see Chap. VII, p. 250.

[37] See Chap. VI (the later Stoa), Chap. VII (Phoenix and Cercidas), Chap. VIII (Roman satire), and Chap. IX (Patristic writings).

[38] Consult G. C. Field (*Plato and His Contemporaries* [London, 1930], 159–60) for a discussion of the question whether it was the elder Aristippus or his grandson who actually founded the Cyrenaic school.

it if necessary (D. L. 2. 74). The common aim of all the Hellenistic philosophies, to render man secure against the blows of chance, is evident in this Cyrenaic attempt to attain steadfast composure under all circumstances. With the Cyrenaics the Socratic *autarkeia* took the form of subjecting appetite to the dictates of prudence in order to secure the greatest ultimate pleasure (a device subsequently adopted by the Epicureans). As in the *Odes* of Horace both Stoic and Epicurean principles sometimes issue in the same practical advice, even couched in the identical vocabulary of *modus* and *temperantia,* so the Cyrenaics had one area of identity with the Cynics, resulting from their common admiration for the self-mastery of Socrates. The point is made by Maximus of Tyre (*Orat.* I, 23B Hobein), who observes that Aristippus ἐσωφρόνει ("behaved with self-restraint") no less than did Diogenes.

THE ATTIC ORATORS

The development of sophrosyne as a civic virtue, which was well under way in the fifth century, continued in the fourth, where it is best observed on a practical level in the speeches of the Attic orators and on a theoretical level in Plato. The orators provide us with a rare opportunity (available otherwise only in comedy and, to some extent, inscriptions) of studying what sophrosyne meant in ordinary speech, without philosophical refinement or poetic embellishment. In Attic oratory we expect a concept of the virtue that will be readily understood and accepted by the average Athenian serving in the jury or the popular assembly. What we find is a democratic sophrosyne, in certain respects dramatically different from the civic virtue of the fifth century, and different in ways that are readily traceable to the changing conditions in the *polis.*

The identification of sophrosyne with the democratic spirit, rather than with the oligarchic or aristocratic—with which it was most often linked in the fifth century—is clearly a sign of Athenian revulsion from the tyranny of the Thirty, with its proscriptions and confiscations. The return of democracy after the expulsion of the Thirty is described in so many words as the restoration of a *sôphrôn politeia.*[39] So violent was the reaction against the oligarchs that even far down into the fourth century, at a time when the external threat to Athens from Philip was the paramount issue in public life, the antithesis between the *sôphrôn* democrat and the disloyal oligarch persists as a rhetorical topic in the speeches of Demosthenes and Aeschines. This democratic orientation is the principal novelty in the popular fourth-century view of sophrosyne, but the

[39] Aeschines *Orat.* 2. 176.

orators also place new emphasis on certain other characteristics of the *sôphrôn* citizen: his readiness to serve the State, especially by the performance of "liturgies," and his quiet, inoffensive behavior in private life. Neither of these facets is mentioned by the orators of the late fifth century, Antiphon and Andocides.[40] In fact, the stereotype of the *sôphrôn* citizen, with his well-defined traits, could only result from the peculiar conditions that prevailed in Athens after the disaster of the Peloponnesian war and the collapse of the high hopes that had been founded on the intellectual and spiritual, no less than the political, aggressiveness of the fifth century. To accept *apragmosynê* as the token of good citizenship was to say farewell to the Periclean spirit in Athenian life.[41]

This concept of sophrosyne is fresh and vigorous, not yet a stereotype, in Lysias, whose family suffered much at the hands of the Thirty Tyrants; but already it seems well established in the minds of those whom he hopes to influence by his speeches that the *sôphrôn* (or *metrios* or *kosmios*) citizen combines hatred of oligarchy with orderly, law-abiding, responsible conduct in public and private life. Since Lysias was often employed as a logographer by individuals hovering on the fringes of the Thirty, we sometimes find him spreading the cloak of sophrosyne around the questionable trappings of an ex-cavalryman like Mantitheus, who seeks to conceal his antidemocratic military service behind his exemplary decorum in private life. After maintaining that he has lived a life of decent moderation (*metrios* [16. 3]), Mantitheus analyzes its content: he has provided his sisters with liberal dowries, allowed his brother the larger share in their joint patrimony, behaved so circumspectly that no one has a grievance against him, won the contempt of all the young bloods by his decorum, avoided law suits, defended his country in arms, and has even chosen, he says, to serve in the infantry, the more dangerous branch of the service (16. 10 ff.). Mantitheus characterizes his conduct as both liberal and moderate (16. 18) and asks the jury not to condemn him for wearing his hair long, in the Spartan fashion, since many who dress in a more conservative way actually harm the state.

This is the most detailed definition of the *metrios* or *sôphrôn bios* in the

---

[40] In Antiphon sophrosyne usually means self-control, while in Andocides it is sometimes related to politics, but in a special way characteristic of the period of factional disputes in Athens at the close of the fifth century. See Chap. III, p. 116.

[41] *Apragmosynê* was part of the aristocratic, oligarchic, and "Dorian" *êthos* in the fifth century, and in foreign policy it signified a tendency to maintain the status quo. In private life, where it implied aloofness, avoidance of meddling, it was doubtless admired by all classes of society. It is clear from the constant emphasis fourth-century orators laid on this and related values that, for the time being at least, the "inactive" principle had triumphed over the "active" in Athenian life.

speeches of Lysias; but separate elements appear elsewhere, especially that of minding one's own business, for τὸ τὰ αὑτοῦ πράττειν, the watchword of the aristocrats, has now been absorbed into the Attic ideal of citizenship. *Hêsychia*, too, the Dorian political virtue praised by Pindar,[42] has maintained its connection with sophrosyne, now that the latter is claimed by the democrats. In the *Oration on the Scrutiny of Evandrus* Lysias warns that Evandrus will boast of his family's services to the state and say that he himself is *kosmios* and, unlike so many Athenians, minds his own business (26. 4). The jury, however, should reject these claims, for the state would have been better off without those public services, which led to the overthrow of the democracy; and "with reference to his quiet behavior (*hêsychiotês*), we should not examine his *sôphrôn* conduct now, when he has no chance to misbehave, but investigate his lawless conduct when he was free to act as he chose" (26. 5). *Kosmios, hêsychos, sôphrôn, apragmôn*—all the familiar aristocratic values have been thoroughly "democratized" in fourth-century Athens.[43]

The performance of "liturgies" (such as outfitting warships, subsidizing religious processions, or paying for the production of plays in the dramatic festivals) had always been a matter of civic pride to the Athenians. Now it became one of the commonplaces of sophrosyne to recall such liturgies, because they were regarded as proof that the citizen had expended his fortune on behalf of the state, while practicing admirable economy in private life.[44] Both Lysias and Isaeus employ a related commonplace: the most laborious liturgy is to be orderly and moderate (*kosmios* and *sôphrôn*), to resist the temptations offered by pleasure and profit, and to conduct oneself in such a way as to give no offense to any fellow citizen.[45]

Still another cliché of the courtroom is the appeal for the conviction of a defendant on the ground that his punishment will render *sôphrôn* (or *kosmios*) anyone else who might contemplate the same offense.[46] Exemplary punishment is a favorite *topos* in the orators, who often describe the function of legal enactments as *sôphronizein* ("to render law-abiding [or] well-behaved").[47]

---

[42] *Pyth.* 8. 1–2; *Ol.* 4. 16.

[43] *Kosmios* and *sôphrôn* continue to be synonymous in purely private, nonpolitical connections, although as a matter of fact Lysias rarely so uses the words. One example occurs in *Orat.* 19. 16.

[44] Lysias 12. 20; Demosthenes 38. 26; Isaeus 7. 39, 41.

[45] Lysias 21. 19; Isaeus, Frag. 35.

[46] E.g., Lysias 6. 54, 14. 12, 15. 19, 27. 7.

[47] For Lysias and Isocrates, the effect of exemplary punishment (*sôphronizein*) is usually to render the other citizens moderate, orderly, and responsible. For Demosthenes and

By far the most common meaning of sophrosyne in Lysias' *Orations* is the "civic" one: moderate and law-abiding conduct toward one's fellow citizens. This aspect of sophrosyne overrides all others; the intellectual nuance is rare (even the commonplace phrase ἐὰν σωφρονῆτε hardly occurs in Lysias), *sôphrôn* means "chaste" in just two passages (1. 10, 3. 4), and *sôphronein* has the connotation "to be of sound mind" only in the speech ascribed to Lysias in Plato's *Phaedrus* (231D).[48]

Isaeus terms the ideal citizen *metrios* or *kosmios* more often than *sôphrôn*, but his conception of this ideal closely resembles that of Lysias, with the notable exception that he ignores the strictly factional element. Since the speeches of Isaeus deal with private cases, mostly involving inheritance, they rarely allude to public affairs and never describe the *sôphrôn* or *metrios* citizen as a foe of oligarchy. Isaeus assigns great importance to minding one's own business. The speaker in his first oration says, for example, that he and his brothers were brought up in so respectable a fashion (*sôphronôs*) that they never entered a law court, even as listeners.[49] Isaeus' other favorite commonplace presents the payment of liturgies as proof of *metriotês* or sophrosyne. One of his speeches asks a rhetorical question: What must the *metrios politês* do? The answer is that he must refrain from taking by force the property of others and must preserve his own for the good of the state, contributing freely in time of need and concealing no part of his fortune (7. 39).[50]

Demosthenes shows little originality in his references to sophrosyne, but these are so extremely numerous as to suggest that the concept is an important one, even though taken entirely for granted, in the ethical vocabulary of his audiences. Two principal connotations, the intellectual and the civic, are evenly balanced in his speeches. Demosthenes appeals much more often than do Lysias and Isaeus to the judgment of the *sôphrôn anthrôpos* or the *sôphrôn dikastês*, the man of common sense, shrewdness, and practical experience (1. 27; 2. 22; 11. 15; 6. 19; 24. 101; 23. 193; 23. 197; 3. 25). The colloquial phrase ἐὰν σωφρονῆτε ("if you are

Aeschines, it is more likely to make them self-restrained, decent, and, in the case of women, chaste. See Lysias 1. 47, 6. 54, 14. 12, 15. 9, 22. 20, 27. 7, 30. 24; Isocrates *Areop.* 20 (ποιεῖν σωφρονεστέρους); Demosthenes 2. 18, 21. 227, 24. 101, 59. 86; Aeschines 1. 139.

[48] *Sôphronein* is opposed to *nosein* ("to be ill"), but the subsequent contrast between self-control and bad judgment (*kakôs phronein*) is a reminder that soundness of mind includes control of the appetites.

[49] Cf. 4. 28–30, where the plaintiffs describe themselves as *kosmioi*, not *philopragmones* ("busybodies").

[50] The citizen who contributes to the State may also be called *spoudaios* ("zealous" [7. 41]). Antitheses of sophrosyne and *kosmiotês* include *pleonexia* ("overreaching" [11. 36]), *tolmê* ("boldness"), and *ponêria* ("wickedness" [Frag. 12]), as well as the usual *hybris*.

sensible") comes often to his lips, as it does to those of Aeschines and Isocrates.[51]

In his allusions to the *sôphrôn* citizen, Demosthenes has more to say about social than about strictly political conduct; yet in one notable passage he maintains the fourth-century connection between sophrosyne and democracy and their joint opposition to *hybris* and oligarchy. His speech against Timocrates divides the citizens according to their prefer-ence for one faction or the other. Those who choose to be ruled by laws are moderate and useful (*sôphrones* and *chrêstoi*); those who desire an oligarchy are cowardly and servile (*anandroi kai douloi* [24. 75]). The usefulness of the *sôphrôn* citizen is a favorite commonplace with Demos-thenes, who links both *chrêstos* and *chrêsimos* with *sôphrôn* (25. 24, 97; 38. 26). *Chrêstos* as a term of approbation appears early in the Athenian political vocabulary, and it was partly through association with the concept of usefulness that sophrosyne won a place among the civic virtues.[52] Already in the *Plutus* of Aristophanes the *chrêstoi* and *sôphrones* are linked (387), and this alliance is confirmed in the course of the fourth century. Demosthenes also makes much of the relation between sophrosyne and law: obedience to the laws results in sophrosyne, respect for elders, and orderliness (*eutaxia*)—the solemn and beautiful qualities by which the city becomes well regulated and safe (25. 24).[53] The appeal to historical exemplars of sophrosyne plays a part in the speeches of Demosthenes, Aeschines, and Isocrates;[54] and Demosthenes combines the *topos* of the liturgy with that of the *mos maiorum* in a way that found imitators in Rome. He says in the *Third Olynthiac* that the ancestral heroes erected many superb public buildings but in private

[51] Demosthenes 58. 56, 6. 28, 15. 16. Aeschines 1. 123, 3. 117, 3. 242. Isocrates *Helen* 31, 38; *Paneg.* 165; *Areop.* 13; *Antid.* 242, 304.

[52] See A. W. Adkins (*Merit and Responsibility*, 197, 215, n. 6) on the connection between *chrêstos* and *agathos* in Greek society. *Spoudaios* has much the same implications as *chrêstos* in the orators. On the tendency to treat *sôphrôn* and *spoudaios* as synonyms in Peripatetic educational treatises, see Adolf Dryoff, *Die Ethik der alten Stoa* (Berlin, 1897), 261.

[53] Cf. 24. 210 and 59. 86. In the spurious oration, 26. 25, the fruits of lawlessness are given as *mania, akrasia,* and *pleonexia;* the results of obedience to law are *phronêsis,* sophrosyne, and *dikaiosynê.*

[54] Demosthenes uses exemplars least. Isocrates employs exemplars from mythology more than do the other orators, who usually cite historical models. Most of the great Athenian statesmen of the past—Solon, Dracon, Cleisthenes, Miltiades, and Pericles—serve the orators as models of sophrosyne, either in private life (where they are modest, chaste, and decorous; cf. Aeschines 1. 7, 20; 3. 257) or in public life (where their role is usually that of *sôphronistês* for their fellow citizens; cf. Isocrates, 15. 111, 16. 28). See Karl Jost, *Das Beispiel und Vorbild der Vorfahren* (Paderborn, 1936), and Gisela Schmitz-Kahlmann, *Das Beispiel der Geschichte im politischen Denken des Isokrates, Philol. Supp.* 31 (1939), 1–38.

were so modest (*sôphrones*) and true to the spirit of the Constitution that
the homes of Aristides, Miltiades, and their like were no more splendid
than the houses of ordinary men (25).[55]

Sophrosyne as self-control exercised in various circumstances—the
aspect that is on the whole most prominent in Xenophon but rarely appears in Lysias and Isaeus—makes a better showing in Demosthenes,
who will speak of a man as being *sôphrôn* with respect to gluttony,
drunkenness, or extravagance (38. 26), anger (*Proem.* 43. 1. 2), or sexual
appetites (2. 18; 18. 216; 19. 285; 45. 80). Sophrosyne regularly denotes
chastity when it refers to feminine virtue (19. 196; 59. 11).[56] A revealing sidelight on the popular misunderstanding of sophrosyne emerges
from the *Oration against Stephanus,* where Demosthenes warns the jury
against mistaking the gloomy expression of Stephanus for a proof
of sophrosyne; rather, it means that he is a misanthrope, for he assumes
this attitude, not because he is modest and high-minded, but because
he wishes to discourage beggars (45. 68). It is probably the same
tendency to associate sophrosyne with a certain austerity or at least un-
sociable behavior that leads Isocrates, in his letter to Antipater, to
recommend a combination of sophrosyne and *charis* ("graciousness,
charm" [4. 2]).[57]

The speeches of Aeschines contain a great many allusions to sophrosyne, of which a disproportionate number refer to chastity or some other
aspect of decent behavior, since *Oration* I is an accusation against
Timarchus for prostitution. The discourse not only gives us some idea
of the popular attitude towards pederasty, and the supposed distinctions
between a *sôphrôn erôs* and a dishonorable association, but tells us about
numerous laws that Aeschines interprets as injunctions to sophrosyne.
He maintains that the lawmakers as a matter of course made laws
designed to instil sophrosyne before making any other enactments, on
the theory that where good behavior (*eukosmia*) is greatest, the city is
best governed (1. 20–22). Specific laws are read aloud by the clerk, to
prove that Solon was interested in sophrosyne περὶ παιδῶν (1.7, 20), and
that it is a function of law to render lovers chaste (*sôphronizein* [1. 139]).
The punitive intention of the laws is also emphasized (1. 36, 192). In

[55] See Sallust *Cat.* 13–14 and Horace *Odes* 2. 15.

[56] "Chastity" is the regular meaning of sophrosyne in the spurious *Eroticus,* attributed by
Blass (*Attische Beredsamkeit* 3. 406–8) to a writer influenced by Isocrates; note that sophrosyne
has this significance in Isocrates *Nic.* 36–37.

[57] Erotic epigrams in the *Greek Anthology* regularly contrast sophrosyne with beauty and
charm (Rufinus 1. 149; Agathias Scholasticus 1. 29). The disgust felt by Theseus at Hippolytus' asceticism is probably a typical reaction to the puritanical sophrosyne.

addition to citing actual laws, Aeschines employs the *exemplum* to prove that the greatest Athenian statesmen were themselves models of sophrosyne (here "decency, honorable behavior") and made it their chief business to guide the *polis* towards this excellence. Solon, Pericles, Themistocles, and Aristides were all such models of decorum that when addressing the people they restrained their gestures and kept one arm inside the cloak (1. 25; cf. 3. 257).[58] Aeschines appeals to historical and poetic exemplars of the *sôphrôn* and lawful *erôs*—Harmodius and Aristogeiton, Achilles and Patroclus (1. 140)—and quotes Euripides on the love that leads to sophrosyne and *aretê* (Frag. 672 Nauck). His evident purpose in all these allusions is to create a link in the minds of his audience between the civic sophrosyne ("modesty, usefulness, inoffensiveness"), which was familiar in all the oratory of the fourth century, and individual morality, the erotic sophrosyne, which was equally familiar in the plays of Euripides, in Old and Middle Comedy, and in philosophical discussions such as the *Symposium* and *Memorabilia* of Xenophon, and the *Symposium* and *Phaedrus* of Plato. His emphasis on the importance to the State of laws that enforce sophrosyne is a good example of the effort to relate an individual virtue to the public welfare, which Aristotle recommends to orators in the *Rhetoric* (1366b 13–15).

The stereotype of the *sôphrôn politês* is analyzed in the speech *Against Ctesiphon*, where Aeschines examines the distinction between the natural qualities of the δημοτικὸς ἀνὴρ καὶ σώφρων ("the democratic and moderate citizen")[59] and his opposite, who is not even an *anêr* but an *anthrôpos* and is denounced as oligarchic and worthless (φαῦλος). The essential qualifications for the *sôphrôn* citizen are (3. 168): first, that he be of free birth on both sides; secondly, that he come of ancestors with a good record of public service (or at least with no enmity towards the State); thirdly, that he be *sôphrôn* and *metrios* in his daily life, so that he will never need to take bribes to finance his profligacy; fourthly, that he have good judgment and facility in speaking—the first is more essential than the second; and fifthly, that he be courageous (*andreios*). This passage forms a little epideictic oration within the speech as a whole, following the conventional topics of eulogy—birth, ancestry, and virtues: the virtues here are sophrosyne, first and foremost, then a kind of wisdom suited to public life, oratorical ability,[60] and, last of all, courage.

---

[58] The sophrosyne exemplified or instilled by the great Attic lawgivers is more often the virtue of private conduct than a genuine *aretê politikê*.

[59] Cf. Demosthenes *Ep.* 3. 18 for this phrase.

[60] See Euripides *Autolycus*, Frag. 282. 23–28 Nauck, and *Anon. Iamblichi* Frag. 89 DK.

Although it seems, at first glance, redundant to demand that the *sôphrôn* and democratic citizen be *sôphrôn*, Aeschines actually refers to two different aspects of the virtue. In the first instance, *sôphrôn* alludes to the civic virtue, moderation, while in the second, it indicates control of the physical appetites. These topics of epideictic are turned against Demosthenes, who, Aeschines maintains, shows all the characteristics of the oligarchic type: he is of foreign descent (Scythian, in fact); has a family tradition of hatred towards Athens; is eloquent indeed (Aeschines can hardly deny this) but cowardly and useless to the state; and in private life he is extravagant, licentious, and unable to save money and therefore depends for support on bribes from the king of the Persians (3. 173). In addition, he is a meddler (*periergos*, equivalent to the traditional epithet, *polypragmôn*). The way in which Aeschines amplifies the stereotype of the *sôphrôn* citizen shows that it is still considered effective, still worth an orator's serious attention, even in the last years of Athenian independence.

One final oratorical flourish, in the *Epitaphios* of Hypereides, also links sophrosyne with the Athenian *polis*.[61] Like the sun which shines on the whole world and provides birth and sustenance for the *sôphrôn* and *epieikês* ("the moderate and reasonable"), so Athens bestows her gifts on mankind, punishing the wicked, helping the just, guaranteeing equity in place of *pleonexia* (6. 5).[62] The parallel between the beneficiaries of the sun and of the *polis*—in the one case the *sôphrôn*, in the other the just who are preserved from *pleonexia*—is a final assertion of the two cardinal excellences that Aeschylus had long ago designated as the cornerstones of Athenian democracy—justice and sophrosyne.

ISOCRATES

Although as a group the Attic orators made effective use of the topic of the *sôphrôn* citizen and from time to time—especially in the oration of Aeschines against Timarchus—attempted to arouse *odium* and *indignatio* through emotional appeals based on an interpretation of sophrosyne as decency or chastity, they were only on the threshold of the great rhetorical development of the topic of sophrosyne which reached a peak in Ciceronian oratory and continued on into the Second Sophistic. Isocrates made important contributions to this development:

---

[61] Hypereides also alludes to the *sôphrôn* upbringing of the heroes in his *Epitaphios* (6. 8) and links with the *sôphrôn bios* many of Lycurgus' services to the state (Frag. 118).

[62] The restoration of the phrase *sôphrôn kai epieikês* seems convincing. Cf. Lysias 2. 57 for sophrosyne and *deos* ("reverence") as the gift of Athens to the Aegean world.

notably by using a canon of virtues in encomium, by paying special attention to the excellence of the ruler and his role as *paradeigma,* and by frequent recourse to the topic of the ancestral virtues, among which sophrosyne ranks high. In each of these categories Isocrates was a model for Cicero; he did not, however, provide a precedent for the treatment of sophrosyne as a topic of invective, in which Cicero has no peer and in which, for variety and subtlety, the Roman orator far surpasses even Aeschines.

The topic of sophrosyne as a political virtue is expanded by Isocrates, who shows conventional concern for the effect of individual morality on the internal affairs of the *polis* and uses the same vocabulary as Lysias and Demosthenes to describe the desirable type of citizen. His chief originality lies in his attempt to apply sophrosyne, as political moderation and restraint, to international affairs, but he does so with a superficiality and even a naïveté that contrast unfavorably with the realism of Thucydides in treating these same topics. Isocrates identifies individual, personal morality with the morality of the State and always insists that Athens must adopt the same standard of sophrosyne as the individual citizen. Nothing in his pronouncements on foreign policy suggests a rigorous consideration of what sophrosyne would actually mean in the context of Athenian power, commitments, and aims, whether immediate or long-range.

Isocrates is always severely critical of Athenian democracy in his own time and often suggests that the absence of sophrosyne is the cardinal evil. He reviews domestic affairs chiefly in the *Areopagiticus* and the *Panathenaicus,* and foreign policy in the *Panegyricus* and *On the Peace.* In all four addresses he appears as a *laudator temporis acti* and helps to construct that semi-mythical picture of Athens in her golden age of sophrosyne and justice which soon became a commonplace in history, biography, and rhetoric.[63] A typical expression of his attitude is the idealized portrait in the *Areopagiticus* of the well-disciplined, healthy state, which valued sophrosyne and *metriotês* (4, 13, 20) and entrusted control of education to the Areopagus, whose members all shared not merely noble birth but great *aretê* and sophrosyne (37). The conduct of the young in those days is described in terms reminiscent of the *Dikaios Logos* in the *Clouds*; Isocrates says that they did not frequent gambling dens or associate with flute girls, but even in the streets always behaved with great *aidôs* and sophrosyne (48).[64] In each of these passages, so-

---

[63] According to Isocrates, the architects of Athenian sophrosyne are Solon and Cleisthenes.
[64] Cf. Aristophanes *Clouds* 962, 1006.

phrosyne is the old aristocratic ideal of quietude, restraint, and *eukosmia*. It is significant that Isocrates often associates this kind of sophrosyne with good birth (*Panath.* 197; cf. *Ad Nic.* 43).

Many of the same topics reappear in the *Panathenaicus,* which was composed near the end of Isocrates' long life. Especially notable in this discourse are the comparison of Athenian and Spartan sophrosyne and the admission that there exists among the virtues a hierarchy, which depresses the value of *andreia* and exalts sophrosyne. Isocrates concedes that outsiders may contrast Athenian disorderliness with Spartan sophrosyne and discipline (Xenophon frequently did so), but he insists that the two conditions are the consequence of the two types of power, on sea and on land. Hegemony on land is won by sophrosyne, obedience, and good order, but sea power is won by the crafts concerned with shipbuilding and by penniless men.[65] Before she embarked on a thalassocracy, Athens was not inferior to Sparta; her kings trained their people in *aretê,* justice, and great sophrosyne (111–15, 138); and Isocrates maintains that the Athenians of former days were more admired for their endurance and sophrosyne than for their courage, since courage may belong to the base, while the other virtues are the product of good birth and education (197).[66]

The two addresses that deal with foreign policy are alike in advocating sophrosyne and condemning *hybris, akolasia,* and *polypragmosynê* in Athens' relations with other states, and in praising the ancestors for their ideal behavior. Otherwise there is a great difference between the two speeches, reflecting the change in Athenian power and hopes between 380, the year of the *Panegyricus,* and 355, after the collapse of the Second Maritime Confederacy. In the earlier address Isocrates hopes that Athens may again lead the Greeks against the barbarians; hence he lists the services of Athens to Greece and idealizes her past, when sophrosyne towards the allies was linked with *homonoia* ("concord" [3, 104, 173]). Sophrosyne in the *Panegyricus* means considerate treatment of allied states (81). In *On the Peace* it means renouncing the ambition to have allies. Isocrates now terms the recent, disastrous policy of Athens *polypragmosynê* ("meddling [30]), pronounces it inferior to sophrosyne ("isolationism" [58]), and demands that the Athenians transfer to their public life the virtues they praise as individuals (119). The topic of the golden age of Athenian sophrosyne and justice is used once more, but

---

[65] Cf. the Old Oligarch, *Ath. Pol.* I. 2, 5–6.

[66] The model of sophrosyne and justice is now Menelaus (72), who because of these virtues was deemed worthy to become the son-in-law of Zeus.

with a different purpose: to contrast both Athenian and Spartan success and fair reputation in the days when they practiced sophrosyne with
their later *hybris,* which led to the fall of both empires (93, 102, 104, 119).
Isocrates says in so many words (119): "Unrestraint [*akolasia*] and arrogance [*hybris*] have proved to be the cause of our woes, sophrosyne of our
blessings." He is so intent on identifying the virtues of public and private
life that he maintains that States, being immortal, cannot escape paying
the penalty for their sins, which men may evade by death. In calling attention to Athenian *polypragmosynê* and blaming it for her collapse,
Isocrates implicitly rejects the Periclean boast that Athens by her intervention brought many benefits to Greece. In Thucydidean terms,
Isocrates advises Athens to reconcile herself to being a second-class
power, whose safest course is a quiet, nonprovocative foreign policy.

The other area connected with sophrosyne in which Isocrates shows
a certain originality is in his theorizing about the virtues of the ruler
and the education of the prince. These topics are treated in a large
number of Isocrates' works, whether protreptical addresses and letters
or outright eulogies. The portrait of the ideal ruler appears in *Nicocles
or the Cyprians* and *Evagoras.* In each of these, sophrosyne, as a virtue of
the ruler, is neither intellectual nor civic but moral: self-control, resistance to the temptations offered by pleasure and power, or even virtue
simpliciter.[67] Both addresses also insist on the obligation of the ruler to
serve as a model of virtue, and both show a tendency to create a
hierarchy among the virtues.

The *Nicocles* proclaims sophrosyne and justice, which are continually
paired by Isocrates, to be the most valuable of the virtues, because of
the benefit they bestow on mankind (29–30). Sophrosyne proves to have
a limited connotation as practiced by Nicocles himself: since ascending
the throne he has never approached any woman save his wife (36–37).
The motives for his restraint are listed at considerable length: eight
reasons are given, four of which are peculiar to the position of a king,
while four apply to ordinary men (43 ff.). Among these reasons,
two seem especially characteristic of the thinking of the period: the king
must be *sôphrôn* as a model for his subjects, and he should cultivate sophrosyne and justice because they are found only in the noble, whereas

---

[67] As a political excellence sophrosyne is now entirely different from the democratic virtue
of the other fourth-century orators. It is the self-restraint of the king, which induces his subjects to practice self-restraint in their turn. The civic virtue of sophrosyne did not survive the
Athenian democracy which gave it birth, but the sophrosyne of the ruler was one of the
most persistent and influential aspects developed in the entire history of the concept, and
was especially fruitful in history and oratory.

courage and cleverness may belong also to the base. The king should be supreme in virtues that are worthy of the greatest praise (43–44). Isocrates, as we saw in connection with the *Panathenaicus,* is likely to distinguish *andreia* from the other virtues and to place it at the bottom of the canon. He sometimes advocates wisdom, justice, sophrosyne, and "all *aretê*," omitting even to mention *andreia.*[68]

The *Nicocles* contains two other ideas of some significance for the fourth-century development of sophrosyne: the need for a way to test *aretê* and the contrast between two or more "levels" of a given virtue. Isocrates says that we should not test all the virtues in the same circumstances, but justice in time of need, sophrosyne in time of power, and self-control (*enkrateia*) in the flower of youth (44). The contrast between sophrosyne and *enkrateia* shows that the former is not actually as limited as the earlier references in this speech suggest; it can still denote the antithesis to *hybris.* Unlike Plato, who in the *Laws* seriously discusses the need for a way of testing virtue—sophrosyne especially (649–50)— Isocrates makes no attempt to suggest a specific test, but is satisfied by past performance; and he does not emphasize the importance to the State of such a test. Another idea that occurs frequently in fourth-century discussions of *aretê* is the contrast between virtue based on nature and virtue that owes something to reason as well. Those who are orderly (*kosmioi*) by nature deserve praise, but still greater praise is due those who are such as a result of reasoning (μετὰ λογισμοῦ). Sophrosyne that comes by chance (*tychê*), rather than by good judgment (*gnômê*), may be lost, unlike the virtue that is grounded in both nature and reason (46).[69]

The panegyric of Nicocles' father, Evagoras, may well be the most influential of all the works of Isocrates, through its impact on epideictic oratory and historiography. In it Isocrates maintains that he is the first to eulogize *aretê* in prose (8); thus he proclaims both his intention of rivaling the poets who had previously dealt with this subject, and his preoccupation with the central theme of excellence. The method that he uses is to celebrate the achievements of Evagoras in chronological

[68] *On the Peace* 63. Other examples of hierarchies among the virtues: *Ad Dem.* 6, 19, 38; *Phil.* 125 ff.; *Ad Nic.* 30, 31; *Panath.* 72. Contrast Isocrates' preference for justice and sophrosyne with the choice customarily made by the Sophists of the fifth century, who preferred *sophia* and *andreia* (*physis* over *nomos*).

[69] *Ad Nic.,* a protreptic address loosely constructed of many familiar ethical maxims, includes a number having to do with sophrosyne, such as the admonition to the young prince to serve as a model of this virtue and make his subjects *sôphronesteroi* (29). Another collection of gnomic exhortations, addressed this time to a private citizen, comprises the *Ad Demonicum:* see especially 15, 21, and 46 for commonplaces relating to sophrosyne familiar from lyric and elegiac poetry.

order, mentioning the various *aretae* in connection with appropriate deeds, and beginning with the praise of Evagoras' ancestry and *physis*. Sophrosyne is assigned to the period of childhood and is grouped with the physical excellences of beauty and strength—an arrangement that was imitated by eulogists well into the Patristic age.[70] Sophrosyne of this kind is nothing more than obedience and orderly conduct. When Evagoras became a man, the excellences of childhood grew with him; and to them were added courage, wisdom, and justice (23). Sophrosyne now indicates restraint of appetite (45), as it does in the *Nicocles*. Among the virtues that the ruler's example instilled in his people, Isocrates mentions *praotês* ("gentleness") and *metriotês* ("moderation" [49; cf. 75, 76]), both of which are traditionally related to sophrosyne and in this passage probably have a political significance. As the sophrosyne of the ruler in Isocratean eulogy tends to be confined to self-restraint, the sophrosyne of his subjects is usually obedience or quiet behavior rather than more positive civic virtue.

The *Evagoras* affords one of the very rare examples in the fourth century of the rhetorical use of a canon confined to wisdom, justice, courage, and sophrosyne. The absence of piety from the list is noteworthy, because it contrasts with the practice of Xenophon[71] and of Isocrates himself elsewhere. When he first uses a canon of virtues in epideictic, Isocrates credits Theseus with courage, wisdom, piety, sophrosyne, and "the rest of *aretê*" (*Helen* 31), and in *On the Peace* he warns that Athens as a whole cannot win happiness without the same forms of excellence— piety, sophrosyne, justice, and "the rest of *aretê*" (63).[72] The sophrosyne of Theseus in the *Helen* offers a clue to the civic connotations of the term when applied to an Athenian leader, whether mythical or historical. Theseus is called *sôphrôn*, not because of his moderation or self-control, but because of his wise administration (*dioikein*) of the *polis*. None of the other three virtues as defined by Isocrates in this passage has a political function.[73]

It was in the *Evagoras*, the *Helen*, and other discourses with a strong epideictic flavor that Isocrates provided a model for later orators and

---

[70] For a somewhat similar grouping, see Xenophon *Const. Lac.* 2. 3 and *Symp.* 8. 8. The place of sophrosyne in Patristic eulogy is discussed in Chap. IX.

[71] Especially the *Agesilaus*. No eulogy of the Spartan king could omit piety, because he made a great display of religious observances. In the *Hellenica* much is made of his sacrifices to the gods.

[72] Cf. *Panath.* 204, 216.

[73] Theseus demonstrated *andreia* by the risks he took "on his own" (αὐτὸς καθ' αὑτόν), *epistêmê* by the battles he fought in common with the whole city, and piety by his response to the supplications of Adrastus and the children of Heracles.

also for historians trained to write rhetorical prose. Eulogy and vituperation are prominent in all the Hellenistic historians directly influenced by Isocrates and in those who carried on his tradition. Polybius' condemnation of historians who substitute eulogy for history (12. 25C; cf. 10. 21) shows how widespread this trend became, supported, to be sure, by philosophical as well as rhetorical forces;[74] and we shall learn from the Roman historians that one of the most enduring legacies of the rhetorical schools was this very device of converting the canon of cardinal virtues into a framework to support the biographical approach to history.

The educational views of Isocrates are necessarily in close touch with his political ideals, since political discourse was the primary subject of his *paideia*. The two works that deal specifically with his career as a teacher, the fragment of his programme, *Against the Sophists,* and the vindication of his entire career, the *Antidosis,* show Isocrates' lifelong concern for sophrosyne as an excellence that the teacher should stimulate in his pupils, and both reveal his conviction that political discourse is the best way of doing so.[75] His purely rhetorical doctrine also contains certain elements related to sophrosyne—in addition to his frequent use of the topic of the virtues in epideictic. One such element is the adaptation of the principles of the *prepon* ("what is fitting") and *kairos* ("what is opportune") in oratory.[76] Both concepts are akin to sophrosyne in its aesthetic aspect, and the *prepon,* especially as developed in Peripatetic theories of style, may be considered the chief rhetorical expression of sophrosyne.[77]

[74] Although Theopompus, for example, doubtless learned from his teacher Isocrates how to employ the topic of virtue and vice in historiography, he may also have been inspired by the Cynic philosophy to criticize individuals and states for moral weaknesses, including lack of sophrosyne. Throughout the *Philippica* he castigates Philip for profligacy, drunkenness, and inability to live σωφρόνως (Frags. 27, 224, 225, 236 Jacoby). The people of Illyria, Byzantium, and Chalcis are collectively stigmatized as deficient in sophrosyne (Frags. 39, 62); while Agesilaus and the Spartans are praised for their *enkrateia* (Frag. 22), and Lysander is commended for being σώφρων and able to master every pleasure (Frag. 20).

[75] In *Against the Sophists* Isocrates condemns the Sophists for professing to teach *aretê* and sophrosyne, yet failing to do so (6); he holds that the eristic philosophers do concern themselves with these excellences, whereas the Sophists inculcate only *polypragmosynê* and *pleonexia* (20). Isocrates denies that any art can instil justice and sophrosyne in those who are without a good *physis,* but thinks that political discourse is of the greatest assistance in stimulating these virtues (21). Cf. *Antid.* 84, where Isocrates invites comparison with the eristic philosophers who profess to turn men towards sophrosyne and justice.

[76] See, for example, *Against the Sophists* 13, where *kairos* and the *prepon* are mentioned in connection with the qualities that distinguish good oratory; and *Panath.* 85 on *kairos* and *metriotês* in speech.

[77] For the identification of sophrosyne and the *prepon* in the ethics of Panaetius, see Chap. VI, pp. 220–22.

In the *Antidosis* Isocrates observes that one of the natural qualifications of a good orator is audacity combined with restraint (*tolmê meta sôphrosynês* [190]). In its own way, and in a relatively limited area, this phrase reconciles the two principles in the Greek character whose opposition we have traced from Homer. Efforts to mingle and adjust the rival tendencies are most often found in discussions of political history or theory; Isocrates is the first to apply the commonplace to rhetoric.[78]

In this, as in several more important areas of his thought concerning sophrosyne—its value for the State, its dominant position in the "ancestral constitution," its place in the character of the ideal ruler, the need for the State to devise methods of instilling sophrosyne, the existence of levels or stages of *aretê*—Isocrates invites comparison with Plato, who in the same *polis* and at the same time was confronting the same problems. But if now and again the reader is inclined to suspect that within Isocrates there was a Plato struggling to get out, the impression is only fleeting. The differences are fundamental. In accepting the challenge to the principles and aims of rhetorical education flung down by Plato's *Gorgias* and *Protagoras,* Isocrates steadfastly rejects the most essential and characteristic elements in the whole Platonic system: the belief that *aretê* is unified, that it can be taught, and that it must be based on knowledge of absolute values rather than on opinion.[79] Given these differences, Plato was bound to arrive at solutions to the great fourth-century questions about *aretê*—its nature, its relation to the individual and society, how it can be instilled—that differed from Isocrates' solutions in almost every conceivable way. As I shall attempt to show in the following chapter, Plato surpassed Isocrates in clarity, precision, and depth of thought about these matters—in everything except the power to influence his contemporaries. For it was Isocrates—especially the Isocrates of the *Evagoras* and the *Nicocles*— who found the wider audience for his views on sophrosyne and transmitted them, via the orators and historians who emerged from his school, to the prose writers of succeeding generations in both Greece and Rome.

---

[78] Isocrates' references to sophrosyne in private life are for the most part conventional in content and phrasing. One point of interest is his tendency to link sophrosyne with culture (as Cicero later associates *temperantia* with *humanitas*). See, e.g., the description of the cultivated man in *Panath.* 31–32 (although the word sophrosyne does not occur, the conditions necessary for the existence of *paideia* include two traditional components of sophrosyne) and the observation in *Busiris* 21–22 that the culture of the Egyptian priests depends on their sophrosyne and leisure.

[79] Jaeger (*Paideia* 3. 46–70 and nn. 32a, 44) discusses the relation of Isocrates to Plato, especially the reaction to the *Gorgias* and *Protagoras* expressed in *Against the Sophists*.

V

Plato

IN spite of the more spectacular and extensive influence of Isocrates on his own generation, it does not need to be demonstrated that Plato's impact was ultimately both greater and more lasting. His place in the history of sophrosyne exemplifies his sovereign effect on Greek thought in general, for with him the development of this concept reaches a climax. Not only did he reconsider most of the earlier interpretations of the virtue which had emerged from the archaic and the classical worlds —now shattered for ever by the crises of the late fifth century—and re-integrate them into a new unity, but he so extended its scope that all subsequent interpretations were the result, in some fashion, of his achievement.

The first great expansion in the meaning of sophrosyne coincided, as we have seen, with the flowering of the Athenian *polis* and the birth of tragedy. These events are inseparable. By the middle of the sixth century, sophrosyne had been recognized as the characteristic excellence of the Athenian citizen in time of peace, celebrated in epitaphs together with *areté*, the corresponding virtue in time of war. Sophrosyne was a term that expressed the all-embracing order and the morality of restraint and limitation which the *polis* demanded. At this point the purely individual heroic ideal, always capable of being intensified to the point of *hybris*, came into conflict with the demands of an established order (cosmic and political), which limited the self-assertion of the hero and required him to obey its primary law of measure. From this conflict was born Attic tragedy, which throughout its brief century of life focused attention on the antithesis between *hybris* and sophrosyne. With the decline of the democratic Athenian *polis* at the close of the Peloponnesian war came inevitably the decline of tragedy.

Inevitably, too, sophrosyne had to undergo modification, since its principal arenas, the *polis* itself and the theater of Dionysus, were so radically altered. But instead of becoming fossilized (like *hybris*) or virtually disappearing (like *aidôs*), sophrosyne entered its second period of notable development in the fourth century—mainly as a result of philosophic interest in its relation to the ethics of the individual and the State.

Ironically, Plato's most far-reaching contribution to the history of sophrosyne was his arbitrary establishment of the canon of four cardinal virtues in the fourth book of the *Republic*. Although a tentative and shifting alignment of four or five primary virtues had been known at least as early as Pindar and Aeschylus, it was Plato who defined the canon for all time and is therefore responsible for the special development of sophrosyne in Hellenistic, Graeco-Roman, and Christian thought which resulted from its inclusion in the Platonic tetrad. Rejected by Aristotle, the canon was adopted by the Stoics, although it did not correspond to their theory of the soul, and thereafter it found its way to Rome, to the Church Fathers, and ultimately to the literature and art of the Middle Ages and the Renaissance. The appearance of a personified *Temperantia* pouring water into a vessel of wine among the cupola mosaics of St. Mark's in Venice, holding an hourglass in the fresco of Good Government in the Palazzo Pubblico in Siena, or sheathing a sword while she grasps a bridle between her teeth on the walls of the Arena Chapel in Padua; the vision of *Temperanza* accompanying the triumphal chariot of the Church in Canto XXIX of Dante's *Purgatorio;* and the character of Temperaunce in Book II of Spenser's *Faerie Queen*—all must ultimately be traced back to Book IV of the *Republic*.

Apart from this accidental result of his tremendous influence on Hellenistic philosophy, Plato contributed more generously to the development of sophrosyne than did any other writer of any period. So rich and complex is his thought on the subject that it is difficult to separate the theme of sophrosyne from the multitude of other subjects with which it is constantly interwoven: the soul and the State, love, pleasure, education, eschatology, the universe. Since, however, Plato's three great topics are ethics, politics, and cosmology, we shall attempt to show the relation of sophrosyne to each of them—considering in some detail the *Charmides, Gorgias, Republic, Phaedrus,* and *Laws* and noting significant passages in the *Phaedo, Symposium, Philebus, Timaeus,* and *Statesman.* That sophrosyne is intimately connected with ethics and politics is self-evident, but its place in Plato's cosmology often escapes notice because of his vocabulary. Here, just as in lyric poetry and Sophoclean tragedy, it is essential to identify the concept of sophrosyne when it appears under a variety of names—including *taxis* ("arrangement"), *kosmos* ("order"), *symphônia* ("agreement"), and perhaps even *systasis* ("compromise")—instead of limiting our study to the word sophrosyne itself.

Plato's treatment of sophrosyne is intensely dynamic. The earliest stage is naturally the most Socratic: it is dominated not only by Socrates' conception of virtue as knowledge but also by Socrates himself as the exemplar of sophrosyne. This stage is represented in the dialogues by the *Charmides*. A later stage finds Plato refining and deepening the popular interpretation of sophrosyne as the restraint of appetite. His own distinctive contribution is the theory that all virtue depends on orderly arrangement within the soul. This view is responsible for the treatment of sophrosyne in the *Gorgias* and is further developed in the *Republic*. A third stage is reached in the late dialogues: Plato's interest in movement and change causes him to give renewed attention to the appetites and passions and to accord them a higher status in the pattern of the soul's activity than he had been willing to concede in the *Republic*. To rehabilitate the appetitive element in the soul, it is necessary to impose order on this microcosm, as reason brings order out of chaos in the macrocosm of the universe. Hence the greatly increased importance of sophrosyne in the *Laws* parallels the emphasis on other terms denoting order, compromise, and arrangement in the *Timaeus* and the *Statesman*. As we shall see, Plato's strengthened concern for the "inferior" aspects of the human soul also has important consequences for sophrosyne in the *Phaedrus* and *Philebus*. Although it thus seems possible (with due regard for chronological uncertainty in the case of many dialogues) to trace a development in Plato's theory of sophrosyne, a topical treatment of the subject is inadvisable, because of the danger of abstracting any definition from its context. The dramatic structure of each dialogue and the character of the interlocutors who are to be refuted or convinced always determine how sophrosyne is to be regarded. It is necessary, therefore, even at the cost of some repetition, always to deal with this excellence within the framework of specific dialogues.

The earliest of the three stages just described derives its peculiar flavor from the character of Socrates. It would be possible to show that he is for Plato an exemplar of all four cardinal virtues; but there can be little doubt which virtue is most "Socratic," and the recognition of

Socrates as the σώφρων ἀνήρ is often vitally important to the total impact of a dialogue, notably the *Charmides, Symposium,* and *Phaedrus.* Socratic sophrosyne has three principal facets: self-knowledge, the *sôphrôn erôs,* and what Socrates' admirers called *enkrateia* ("self-control") or *autarkeia* ("self-sufficiency, independence"). The third aspect is more subtle than mere physical hardihood and indifference to comfort—with which the Cynics and the Cyrenaics often confused it. The genuine Socratic *autarkeia* is a unique self-mastery in any situation, which Plato portrays on the dramatic level in most of the Socratic dialogues. Whenever he conveys the impression that Socrates is truly the master of himself and of every situation, that he is never at a loss—whatever his ironic subterfuge; and that moreover he is honestly in search of the truth at all costs and welcomes correction if it brings him closer to his goal, he conveys the essential sophrosyne of his teacher. Sir Richard Livingstone, pointing out that the character of Socrates provides an example of what sophrosyne is, also observes that sophrosyne in style may be found in the concluding paragraphs of the *Phaedo.*[1] The combination of stylistic sophrosyne with a portrait of the *sôphrôn* Socrates is not uncommon in the dialogues.

THE *CHARMIDES*

A consideration of Plato's view of sophrosyne must begin with the *Charmides,* which introduces many themes that reappear in other dialogues: the identity of sophrosyne with some form of knowledge; the contrast between the external and the internal—body and soul, opinion and knowledge, seeming and being; the comparison of virtue to an art (*technê*), especially medicine; the parallel between sophrosyne ("health of soul") and physical health; and, most striking of all, the Socratic *erôs* in its physical and intellectual manifestations. The *Charmides* is also prophetic of the way in which the dramatic element is made to complement the dialectical in all the dialogues much concerned with sophrosyne (the *Gorgias, Symposium,* and *Phaedrus*). In this instance, both setting and characterization support and dramatize the search for a definition of the virtue. The setting is a palaestra, which evokes the image of physical exercise, suppleness, and health, to which correspond the mental gymnastics and intellectual subtlety of Socrates and the conception of sophrosyne as health of soul, the true source of physical health. The dramatic date is significant: it is the year 432, and Socrates has just

[1] Livingstone, *Portrait of Socrates* (Oxford, 1938), lvi.

returned from Potidaea, where, as we know from the *Symposium* (219E ff.), he has distinguished himself by his courage. Plato here makes effective use of the device that contributes ethical and pathetic persuasion to so many Socratic dialogues: his readers' knowledge of the destiny awaiting his characters and Athens herself in the future beyond the dramatic date of the dialogue. It is the same retrospective awareness that endows with special meaning Thucydides' version of the Funeral Oration of Pericles or certain speeches of Oedipus in the *Coloneus,* when it was produced after the death of Sophocles himself.[2] Plato uses this device most insistently in the *Gorgias,* where the references to the approaching trial and death of Socrates are scarcely veiled; but already in the *Charmides* he exploits both the personalities and the ultimate destinies of Charmides, Critias, and, of course, Socrates above all. There is deliberate irony in the emphasis, early in the dialogue, on the glorious ancestry of Charmides and Critias—the heroic past which carries with it the promise of an honorable future (157E ff.)—for Critias became the leader of the Thirty Tyrants, "the most violent of the oligarchs,"[3] and took into that brutal conspiracy his nephew Charmides, who died with him fighting against the democrats in the Peiraeus. In the course of his tyranny Critias even proposed a law aimed at suppressing the eternal questioning of Socrates himself—who in the cheerful and unshadowed palaestra of Plato's dialogue discusses with him the correct organization of the State and the usefulness of sophrosyne to the administrator.

In the *Charmides* Socrates demonstrates the true nature of sophrosyne more memorably—for most readers—through his *êthos* than through his dialectic. In a brief foreshadowing of the device that is much more developed in the *Symposium,* Plato calls attention to the *erôs* of Socrates at the very moment when Charmides enters the palaestra (155D); he uses this means to contrast the "outer" with the "inner" and to introduce the first reference to passion as a wild beast.[4] The fact that Socrates' *erôs* is actually directed towards the intellect of Charmides, rather than towards his physical beauty, is a constant reminder of sophrosyne in the popular sense of self-control. The reminder has special value because everything in the dialectic of the *Charmides* directs our attention to other nuances of the virtue, and even the portrait of Socrates himself gives greater prominence to intellectual than to moral sophrosyne.

The very arrangement of the cast of characters is significant:

[2] See Kitto, 389.

[3] Xenophon *Mem.* 1. 2. 12.   [4] Cf. *Rep.* 588C, *Tim.* 70D ff., *Phaedrus* 246A ff.

Charmides—the exemplar of temperamental sophrosyne (the *dêmôdês* quality of *Laws* 710A, which belongs to certain animals and children naturally restrained in their appetites), who cannot explain what sophrosyne is and therefore, by Platonic standards, does not truly possess it—is seated between Critias and Socrates. Critias, as befits a pupil of the Sophists, represents both their approach to ethical values and their habits of debate.[5] Socrates symbolizes genuine sophrosyne, the philosophical virtue, the inner reality in contrast to the mere semblance embodied in Charmides and the illusion of intellectual comprehension which Critias represents.[6] As the symbolic seating arrangement is established, setting and character at once make themselves felt. Charmides appears to be modest and ingenuous, and his uncle claims for him beauty (154A), wisdom (155A), and sophrosyne (157D). Socrates endorses only the first of these claims and even here is interested more in beauty of soul than of body (154D–E). The metaphor of health, which Plato so frequently associates with sophrosyne, provides the first approach to the virtue in the *Charmides*. Socrates undertakes to cure the boy's headache and, after stating the principle of the Whole in medicine— the head cannot be cured without the entire body—extends it still further by maintaining that the body cannot be healed without the soul. In fact, it is sophrosyne in the soul that guarantees health in the body (157A).

The serious search for a definition now begins, following a symmetrical pattern which moves from the outer to the inner and from a lower level of popular morality and instinctive response to a higher one of intellectual analysis.[7] Plato repeatedly calls attention to the purpose and the technique of the search, as when Socrates bids Charmides look within himself to find the answer (160D), or sets forth the purpose of the *elenchus*—to prevent himself from supposing that he knows what he in fact does not know (166D). These techniques of the Socratic investigation—bringing out the knowledge that lies unrecognized within and purging the soul of ignorance in preparation for learning—are both

---

[5] Critias is full of confidence in his capacity for debate, able to quote the classical poets to support his arguments, anxious to impress his audience (162C), loath to confess bewilderment (169C–D), quick to accuse Socrates of seeking victory, not truth (166C); and he thinks he knows what he does not know.

[6] See Paul Friedländer, *Platon*[2] (Berlin, 1957), 2. 61–74, for a discussion of this technique of characterization.

[7] The dialectical processes of the *Charmides* are analyzed by T. G. Tuckey, *Plato's Charmides* (Cambridge, 1951). Our interest lies in the pattern of the argument, rather than in the particular steps.

processes of sophrosyne; and it is well to realize that this virtue has a part in the dialectic of Socrates as well as in his *êthos*.[8]

The definitions of sophrosyne that are now proposed show that Plato is looking both backward and forward: back to some of the associations that had clustered around sophrosyne from earliest times, forward to the direction in which Socrates' teaching led. The four traditional definitions that in quick succession are produced, examined, and rejected are *hêsychia* ("quietness"), *aidôs* ("modesty"), doing one's own work, and self-knowledge. All are shrewdly chosen, not only to suggest the limited extent of popular understanding of the virtue (rooted in the Dorian system of ethics, supported by the Delphic code, on the whole unreflective and superficial), but also to initiate the characteristic movement of the dialogue from the external to the internal. Charmides' first suggestion is entirely external, as well as traditional in the aristocratic code of behavior: sophrosyne is a kind of quietness in walking, talking, and such activities (159B). Persuaded to give up this definition,[9] he next "looks within" and finds that sophrosyne is *aidôs* (160E). He has indeed moved inward, but he is still bound by the inflexible Dorian tradition. Again refuted,[10] he next offers a definition that he hints belongs to Critias: sophrosyne is attending to one's own affairs (161B). Anyone who has followed *apragmosynê* and *polypragmosynê* through the literature of the late fifth century will recognize the aristocratic bias behind this definition, and anyone who has read the *Republic* will be aware of the possibilities for development inherent in the phrase.[11] Here it is unsuccessfully defended as a definition of sophrosyne, first by Charmides and then by Critias, with whose entrance into the debate the argument becomes more sophisticated (in the original sense of the word), and the spirit rather less gentle.

The first allusion to the Good is made with apparent casualness when Critias alters "doing one's own work" to "doing good things" (163E)— a slight enough change, but one that allows Socrates to introduce the

---

[8] The connection of self-knowledge with sophrosyne is specifically stated in *Tim.* 72A; this topic is developed at great length by the author of *Alc.* I (see especially 131B). That the *elenchus* results in sophrosyne, we learn from *Soph.* 230D.

[9] On the ground that sophrosyne is *kalon* (again external), but quietness is sometimes the reverse of *kalon* (160B).

[10] For sophrosyne must be *agathon* (more inward than *kalon*), but Homer (*Od.* 17. 347) denies that *aidôs* is always *agathon* (161A).

[11] See Chap. III. In *Tim.* 72A, doing one's one work is again made an aspect of sophrosyne. A. E. Raubitschek (*Wiener Studien* 71 [1958], 170–72) traces the maxim back to Pittacus; in its earlier stages it has no reference to politics.

theme of utility (sophrosyne must somehow be beneficial), to compare the *sôphrôn* man to the craftsman, and finally to identify sophrosyne with knowledge. Critias makes possible the transition to *epistêmê* by asserting that sophrosyne is self-knowledge, that in fact the Delphic proverb is the greeting of the god to his worshipers and is equivalent to the command "Practice sophrosyne" (164D). This suggestion completes the preliminary series of traditional definitions and prepares for the next stage of the discussion by calling attention to the intellectual element implicit in sophrosyne. Picking up the clue in the word *gnôthi*, Socrates suggests that sophrosyne is indeed some form of knowledge (165C); the consideration of this hypothesis occupies the remainder of the dialogue. All subsequent definitions are variants of *epistêmê*: sophrosyne is knowledge of itself (supposedly a paraphrase of *gnôthi sauton*), knowledge of other sciences and of itself, knowledge that one knows and does not know, and finally knowledge of what one knows and does not know. The last stage is reached when Critias admits that the knowledge that makes us happy is not sophrosyne at all but the knowledge of Good and Evil (174B); and we realize that the actual subject of the dialogue has been the examination of the Socratic equation of virtue and knowledge, rather than the study of any one aspect of virtue.

In the long section devoted to the testing of Critias' definitions, the antitheses "outer" and "inner," "lower" and "higher," continue to be applied. The argument moves from doing one's own work to knowing oneself and from doing what is good to knowing the Good. The last pair of terms suggests the contrast between the active and the theoretical life which is developed at greater length in the *Gorgias,* still in connection with sophrosyne. Another foreshadowing of the *Gorgias* is the comparison of the *sôphrôn* man to the possessor of an art (*technê*). Since the craftsman (*dêmiourgos*) who applies a *technê* for the good of the whole is important for Plato's doctrine of sophrosyne—not only in the *Gorgias,* but even more in the *Republic* and the *Laws*—we should note the characteristics of a *technê* in the *Charmides*. The question of knowledge is raised—does the doctor or other craftsman *know* when he is likely to profit by his art? (164B)—but much more emphasis is laid on the usefulness of the art (164B, 165C, 167B, 172D, etc.). It is in connection with this theme of utility that the political implications of sophrosyne first enter the discussion. Sophrosyne would benefit the State if the *sôphrôn* man knew what he knew and what he did not know and could observe this condition in others, because every man would then do what he knew how to do, and the State ruled by the *sôphrôn* man would be ruled well (172A).[12] That the craftsman uses orderly arrangement to achieve his object is not stated. This is one of the principal attributes of the *dêmiourgos* from the *Gorgias* on, and it seems to be Plato's own contribution to the understanding of *aretê* as *technê*.

Since the result of the conversation with Critias is the paradox that sophrosyne is not beneficial (169B)—a conclusion that Socrates refuses to accept—the quest for a definition is suspended. But Charmides, however incapable of dialectic, is sensitive to the ethical mode of persuasion and insists that Socrates is not genuinely ignorant of sophrosyne (176B). The boy will therefore submit to his "incantations;" [13] and when to his own inclination is added the support of Critias' authority, Charmides is able, by a show of obedience to his guardian, to demonstrate his possession of sophrosyne in a limited but genuine sense—that of *aidôs*. Thus Plato concludes the dialogue at the point where it began, with the instinctive, nonphilosophical sophrosyne of Charmides.

If we assess the results of the dialogue, we find that, in addition to exposing as superficial the most widely accepted traditional definitions of sophrosyne and employing characterization in such a way as to leave an impression of the difference between false and true, superficial and profound sophrosyne, more lasting than the memory of any mere process of argumentation, Plato has also examined the equation of virtue and knowledge and the analogy between knowledge and various techniques. He has brought sophrosyne within the orbit of the two concepts most important for the Socratic approach to virtue: *epistêmê* and *technê*. What he has not done is to refer, even in passing, to the definition of sophrosyne that is most common in the late fifth century and indeed in Plato's own later dialogues: control of the appetites and passions. The reason is clearly that such a definition would not contribute to the purpose of the dialogue—the discussion of virtue as knowledge. In later dialogues, as Plato moves away from the Socratic position, he becomes increasingly interested in sophrosyne as the means of controlling the irrational in man, and in the last of his works, the *Laws*, this conception of sophrosyne is completely victorious.[14]

---

[12] The development of this idea is reserved for the *Republic*, where, however, it is linked with justice, rather than with sophrosyne.

[13] Cf. *Laws* 664B and 665C for the incantations that are to mold the soul to virtue.

[14] For the definition of sophrosyne in the latter part of the fifth century as the control of appetites and passions, see chaps. II and III on Antiphon the Sophist, Euripides, and Aristophanes. The omission of this nuance of sophrosyne from the *Charmides* illustrates the danger of abstracting any Platonic definition from its context.

THE *PROTAGORAS*

The definition of sophrosyne that we miss in the *Charmides* is prominent in both the *Protagoras* and the *Gorgias*. Even though, in the
Protagoras, Socrates insists on the unity of the virtues and equates
sophrosyne with wisdom (*sophia*), on the ground that both have as their
antithesis the same vice (folly, *aphrosynê*, [332B–333B]), Plato introduces
two other qualities as opposites of sophrosyne: wantonness (*akolasia*) and
the puzzling condition of "being inferior to oneself." The first of these
antitheses, which occurs in the speech of Protagoras, represents the current popular belief; the second hints at one of Plato's most characteristic methods of interpreting sophrosyne. In other dialogues, especially
the *Republic* and the *Laws,* the concept of being inferior or superior to
oneself leads to an analysis of the parts of the soul, or a recognition of
conflicting tendencies, and permits sophrosyne to be defined as the
harmony of these parts.[15] The *Protagoras* does not explore this approach
to sophrosyne, but its presence in the dialogue marks an advance over
the *Charmides*. Another subject destined for increasing emphasis is the
relation of pleasure to the Good. Socrates' apparent willingness to
equate the two in the *Protagoras*[16] enables Plato to demonstrate the need
for an art of measurement, a standard by which to choose among
available pleasures, so that once again *epistêmê* is essential, even for the
polloi. The pleasures associated with sophrosyne form an important topic
in the *Republic,* the *Philebus,* and the *Laws.*[17]

THE *GORGIAS*

Plato's systematic study of sophrosyne as the control of appetites and
desires begins with the *Gorgias,* where the virtue is defined, when first
mentioned, as the *polloi* define it—"the control of pleasures and appetites
in oneself" (491D); no other definition is ever suggested. Firmly rejecting the hedonism of the *Protagoras,* Plato constructs the *Gorgias* upon the
contrast between two ways of life: the Socratic, which aims at the Good,
and the Sophistic, which seeks power and pleasure. The Good is characterized by order, one of whose manifestations is sophrosyne; the life
of pleasure, which rejects order, embraces the opposite of sophrosyne,
wantonness (*akolasia*). There is a complete parallel, anticipating the

[15] E.g., *Rep.* 430E, *Laws* 689B.
[16] On the hedonism of Socrates in the *Protagoras,* real or apparent, see Jaeger, *Paideia,* 2.
142–43. The view that it is genuine is defended by Richard Hackforth, *C.Q.* 22 (1928), 39–
42; see also G. B. Kerford, *J.H.S.* 73 (1953), 42–45.
[17] See especially *Laws* 734A ff.

Republic, between the excellence of the soul and of the State. Once again Plato makes dramatic use of character, reinforcing the arguments of each speaker by his *êthos.* The first "act" of the dialogue, devoted to eliciting from Gorgias a consistent statement about the nature of rhetoric, is the least important of the three for sophrosyne; yet it introduces the important theme of the comparison between the physician and the orator, draws attention to the achievements of the great Athenian statesmen, and prepares us, by Gorgias' uncertainty about the moral responsibilities of the rhetorician, for the naked amorality of his two pupils.

In the debate with Polus, not only does the tone of the conversation at once become unusually acrimonious, but the fundamental issues of the dialogue begin to appear. Socrates proposes his famous equation between the four varieties of art (*technê*), all rational and aiming at the Good, and the four empirical knacks, which are branches of flattery and are irrational and hedonistic. This equation has a number of important results. Rhetoric takes an inferior place, since it is allied with cookery and cosmetic among the subdivisions of flattery; and pleasure is diametrically opposed to the Good. As a result, sophrosyne—explicitly defined as the control of pleasure—takes a lofty position on the Socratic scale of values. Moreover, the presence in the equation of both gymnastic and medicine among the arts and cookery and cosmetic among the flatteries guarantees that the parallel between sophrosyne ("health of soul") and physical health will be even more central than it was in the *Charmides.* The metaphor proves particularly dynamic in connection with the Socratic paradox often referred to in the conversations with Polus and Callicles—the desirability of being punished if one has done wrong.[18] Socrates prepares for it by establishing the parallels between body and soul: just as the sick man is less wretched if he undergoes medical treatment, however painful, so, too, the wrongdoer is less wretched if he is punished than if he escapes (479A ff.). The metaphor applies with equal validity to the State, in the comparison between politicians who have stuffed the city with harbors and arsenals without regard for sophrosyne and justice, and caterers who stuff men's bodies and cause an unwholesome swelling, instead of genuine health (518C–519A); it is pursued to the very end of the dialogue, where it culminates in the myth of the soul's judgment. When all bodily concealments are removed, and the naked soul is exposed with the scars of all its crimes,

[18] Cf. *Rep.* 591B ff., and note the relation to sophrosyne implied by calling the Reformatory of *Laws* 908E a *Sôphronistêrion.*

Socrates' one concern will be to present to the judges the healthiest soul possible (526D).

It is the third "act," the conversation with Callicles, that is crucial for sophrosyne. The intensity of the dialectical argument is matched by the tone of passionate indignation with which Plato records it. Socrates, whose trial and death at the hands of an irrational and immoral society are repeatedly foreshadowed, stands forth as the embodiment of the orderly life, intelligently organized to achieve the Good, in contrast to Callicles, who expresses with overwhelming assurance the case for a totally disordered life of *pleonexia* ("self-seeking"), aimed solely at the satisfaction of the appetites. His argument (summarized in Chapter III) is based on a conception of the law of nature—νόμος τῆς φύσεως (483E)—which dismisses as mere products of convention such traditional values as sophrosyne and justice.[19] His attack on sophrosyne is particularly comprehensive in that it unites the two chief lines of argument against this virtue current in the late fifth century: the profligate's hostility to that which interferes with the satisfaction of his appetites, and the "strong man's" contempt for what he regards as cowardice.[20] Socrates' defense of sophrosyne and justice is revolutionary in its implications, some of which are fulfilled only in the *Republic* and the *Laws*. It involves nothing less than a justification of these traditional values and all their kindred on the basis of a new concept of soul, together with a theory of nature totally opposed to that of Callicles and the sophistic materialists whom he echoes. The importance of these innovations, especially the second, can scarcely be exaggerated, because the conception of nature as order (*kosmos*) is essential to the psychology of the *Republic*, the political theory of the *Republic* and *Laws*, and the theology of the *Timaeus* and the *Laws*.

From the very beginning of the argument with Callicles, Socrates has stressed the need for internal harmony and agreement in the soul

[19] The coupling of these two virtues in Callicles' attack (which conversely shows great respect for the utility of *sophia* and *andreia*) is the first hint in this dialogue of their close relation. In the subsequent discussion of virtue in the soul, sophrosyne and justice are used interchangeably, and in the myth at the close of the dialogue, when sophrosyne has disappeared altogether, the word *dikaiosynê* conveys the same implications. See Curtis Larson, *A.J.P.* 72 (1951), 402–4.

[20] See Chap. III, pp. 96–97. An innovation in the *Gorgias* is the parallel attack on the life of the philosopher as *anandria* ("unmanliness"), which establishes the identity of the *sôphrôn* and the contemplative lives. In the *Republic*, too, the philosophic temperament is the *sôphrôn physis* (410E). For the continuation of some of these ideas in Patristic thought, where the contemplative life merges into the ascetic life (based on the practice of sophrosyne), see Chap. IX.

(482B–C). The question whether the tyrant—whom Callicles considers the happiest of men—must also rule himself introduces the word *sôphrôn* into the discussion; it is the definition of the *sôphrôn* man as "self-controlled and ruling the pleasures and appetites in himself" (491D) that provokes Callicles' outburst against the virtue. The climax of Socrates' response is a comparison of sophrosyne in the soul to *kosmos* or *taxis* ("order" or "arrangement") in the physical universe (506–508). The way has been prepared for this analogy by the resumption of two themes introduced, in a somewhat different connection, in the debate with Polus: the opposition of pleasure and the Good, and the two principal characteristics of art—that it is rational and that it aims at the good of the whole. Callicles unwarily concedes that there is a difference between good and bad pleasures (495A, 499B) and thus permits Socrates to return to the topic of the choice of lives: the rational life which aims at the Good and the irrational which embraces any pleasure, good or bad (501B–C). The search for the Good presupposes both an art and a craftsman (*technikos, dêmiourgos*) who organizes his material according to a pattern (504A). In any art, Socrates points out, the criterion of excellence is the order (*taxis*) and harmony of the parts (503E). This statement holds good in every context—bodily health, health of soul (which is sophrosyne and justice), the excellence of the State and of the physical universe (504A–505C). In fact, it is the principle of order that holds together (συνέχει) heaven and earth, gods and men: community (*koinônia*), friendship (*philia*), orderliness (*kosmiotês*), sophrosyne, and justice are all names for the same force. Hence the term applied to the universe is *kosmos,* rather than disorder (*akosmia*) or wantonness (*akolasia*) (506D–508C).[21]

Brief though it is, this passage is extremely suggestive. In the first place, while sophrosyne as "health of soul" was a familiar metaphor, no one had previously defined the virtue as "good order or arrangement within the soul."[22] Not only is sophrosyne for the first time related to the soul in a specific, nonmetaphorical, almost scientific way and identified with the condition of orderly arrangement therein, but the

---

[21] The identity of *kosmos* and sophrosyne is implied by the acceptance of their antitheses as synonyms. Here, as often in Plato, the multiple meanings of sophrosyne provide a convenient bridge from one argument to another. On the philosophical antecedents of this passage, see E. R. Dodds, *Plato, Gorgias* (Oxford, 1959), *ad loc.,* where a Pythagorean source for the idea of a common mathematical principle holding together the *kosmos* is accepted. The history of *philia* as a cosmic principle is traced by Werner Jaeger, *Nemesios von Emesa* (Berlin, 1914).

[22] Jaeger (*Paideia,* 2. 146) points out that it was an innovation to use the word *kosmos* to mean an orderly system within the soul, although the adjective *kosmios* had signified orderly behavior at least as early as Solon.

new definition implies a rejection of the unitary soul and at least a readiness to accept a theory of "parts"—even though there is in the *Gorgias* no specific discussion of the nature, or number, of these "parts." [23] These two innovations—the concept of the soul as composite and the definition of sophrosyne as its *kosmos* or *taxis*—mark Plato's first important advance over the earlier, Socratic conception of sophrosyne as a form of knowledge. Whether the inspiration for either or both is to be found in Pythagorean doctrines (of which there are other traces in the *Gorgias*) [24] is less important than the fact of Plato's originality in visualizing a *kosmios psychê*.

Furthermore, the passage in question supplies a fresh justification for the practice of the time-honored civic virtues—an essentially aesthetic justification, behind which lies still another, less aesthetic than ontological. The comparison between the cosmic order and the virtuous condition of the soul (which has already appeared in tragedy with specific reference to sophrosyne) [25] rests for Plato on the assumption that both are products of art: the orderly arrangement of parts according to a pattern by a craftsman. This analogy suggests that the function of the governing element in the soul is to arrange its parts in such a way as to secure the good of the whole. Sophrosyne and justice are thereby transformed from ordinary civic virtues into organizing principles akin to the principle of order in the universe. [26] The bearing that this analogy has on the State will become obvious in the *Republic*, which spells out several points at which the *Gorgias* merely hints. [27] For example, the precise meaning of *taxis* or *kosmos* in the soul is never explained in the *Gorgias*,

[23] Dodds (*op. cit.*) denies that tripartition appears in the *Gorgias* (see his comments on 493A 3–4); and indeed there is no reason to believe that Plato developed the theory before it was called forth by the special requirements of the *Republic,* but it seems impossible to deny that the concept of a *composite* soul underlies such a passage as 503C ff. See W. K. C. Guthrie, "Plato's Views on the Nature of the Soul," *Récherches sur la tradition platonicienne* (Vandoeuvres-Genève, 1955), 5–6.

[24] For the view that the tripartite soul is Pythagorean in origin, see A. E. Taylor, *A Commentary on Plato's Timaeus* (Oxford, 1928), on 69C. According to Dodds, Pythagorean elements in the *Gorgias* include—in addition to the doctrine of geometrical proportion (see n. 21 above)—the allegorical interpretation of the myth of the waterbearers (492D 1 ff.).

[25] See Sophocles *Ajax* 646–77 and Euripides *Phoen.* 543 ff., for the suggestion that the parallels between the cosmos and human life justify or demand the practice of sophrosyne.

[26] See Maguire, especially 160–63, 175, and cf. Cicero: *vitae modus atque constantia,* which imitate the *caelestium ordinem* (*De Sen.* 21. 77).

[27] See Maguire (167–68) on Plato's later substitution of the Forms for the principle of cosmic order as a model for the soul. Later still, these ideas bear fruit in the *Laws*. See the comment of Solmsen (*Theology,* 70) on *Gorg.* 506–508 as proof that Plato early believed in the fundamental unity of the issues involved in the interpretation of the universe with those confronting the moralist, the political thinker, and the statesman, and on the continued presence of this conviction in the *Laws*.

nor are we told how the orderly arrangement is to be secured. Moreover, as we have noted, the *Gorgias* merely implies the existence of parts in the soul (503C, 493B, 496E) without specifying what they are. The important point here again is that Plato for the first time recognizes something that will later be of great consequence to his theory of sophrosyne—its kinship to the common principle affecting everything in the universe. This innovation may with some confidence be linked with Plato's interest in Pythagorean doctrines.[28]

In addition to pioneering a new conception of sophrosyne and a new justification for moral virtue in general, the *Gorgias* makes still further contributions to the history of Platonic sophrosyne. It establishes once again the unity of the virtues (as in the *Protagoras*, but for different reasons)[29] and, still more important, finds a way to unite the Socratic concept of sophrosyne as an *epistêmê* (dominant, as we have seen, in the *Charmides*) with the popular definition of the virtue as the control of appetite (assumed in the *Protagoras* and explicitly stated in the *Gorgias*, the *Phaedo*, and the *Symposium*).[30] The bridge is the concept of *technê*, which always implies *epistêmê* on the part of the craftsman and which is here applied to the orderly arrangement of the parts of the soul so as to achieve self-rule, the domination of appetite by reason.

Still another innovation is the use of an eschatological myth to confirm in poetic terms the assertion that the virtuous man is happy.[31] The myth gathers into a final unity all the principal themes of the dialogue. The souls of those whom Polus and Callicles admire, such as the Great King or the tyrant Archelaus, may appear before the judges scarred by a lifetime of injustice and *hybris*, and will accordingly be sent to the place of punishment (524E–525D). It is almost always the case, Socrates observes, that power leads to wickedness. The private citizen is more apt to live a holy life, and it is especially likely that the philosopher,

---

[28] J. S. Morrison (*C.Q.* 8 [1958], 198–218) presents the evidence for Pythagorean influence on Plato's political thinking in the *Gorgias*, including his identification of sophrosyne with geometrical proportion. For Plato's later definition of sophrosyne (in unmistakably Pythagorean terms) as harmonic proportion (*Rep.* 431D ff.), see, in addition to Morrison, Guthrie, I. 317.

[29] In *Prot.* 333C and 351B, the unity of the virtues rests upon their identity with knowledge. In *Gorg.* 507A–C, it rests on the fact that the *sôphrôn* person does what is fitting in every situation and is therefore pious, just, and brave (for the development of this theory in the Middle Stoa, especially by Panaetius, see Chap. VI).

[30] *Gorg.* 491D, *Phaedo* 68C, *Symp*, 196C ff.

[31] An innovation, that is, if the *Gorgias* precedes the *Phaedo*. Eschatology, which regularly appears in mythical form to assure us of the triumph of virtue, ultimately emerges in the *Laws* on the plane of physics. See Solmsen, *Theology*, 158.

who has attended to his own affairs and avoided *polypragmosynê* in this world, will win the approval of the judges and be sent to the Islands of the Blessed (526C). Thus the contrast between the active life and the contemplative—the one in search of power and pleasure, and the other in pursuit of order, justice, and sophrosyne—is extended to the life after death; and the question of which life produces happiness is answered *sub specie aeternitatis*.

THE *PHAEDO*

The tendency towards asceticism so noticeable in the *Gorgias* is still more pronounced in the *Phaedo;* and nowhere is it stronger than in the assumption that sophrosyne is part of the philosopher's preparation for death, the *meletê thanatou* (64A, 67C, 114E). The atmosphere of the mystery religions and the total orientation of the dialogue towards death, instead of life, endow sophrosyne with a degree of hostility towards the senses and all sensual pleasures that is not typical of Greek thought in general or of Plato himself.[32] The concept of the unitary soul is clearly responsible for the extraordinary severity with which Plato regards the appetites and passions in the *Phaedo*. Immortality is possible only for the intellectual element in man; contact with the body results in contamination, which imprisons and weighs down the soul. If purity is to be achieved, the appetites must be suppressed—not merely regulated; and it is sophrosyne that accomplishes this suppression. Hence the purity and the freedom of the soul, its chance of happiness hereafter, depend directly on the practice of sophrosyne in life.

In connection with this doctrine of *meletê thanatou*, Plato touches on the distinction between various stages or levels of virtue which becomes fundamental for his political and educational theories, and which later inspires much Neoplatonic and Christian theorizing about various stages of *aretê* in the ladder of perfection. The distinction is one of motive. Only the philosopher is truly *sôphrôn*, because only he renounces *epithymia* for the love of wisdom (82C). The inferior motives for practicing self-restraint—love of money or honor— produce an inferior variety

[32] The normal Platonic interpretation of sophrosyne in relation to the appetites is suggested by the statement in *Rep.* 571E that the *epithymêtikon* (the "appetitive element") must be neither starved nor stuffed. Plato's unequivocal adoption in the *Republic* of the tripartite soul, which assigns the appetites and passions, not to the body alone, but to some aspect of the soul itself, produced a less ascetic conception of sophrosyne. For a discussion of the consequences of the unitary and the plural concepts of the soul in Plato, see Guthrie, *loc cit.* (n. 23 above), 5–6. The connection of sophrosyne in the *Phaedo* with the *meletê thanatou* had a disproportionate effect on the interpretation of this virtue in Patristic thought. See Chap. IX.

of virtue. In the *Republic* such practice of sophrosyne is one of the earliest signs of deterioration in the political constitution or in the soul: the oligarchic man practices sophrosyne for the sake of avarice, and although his conduct is not outwardly different from that of the citizen in the ideal state, inwardly there is a vast difference: corruption has begun. In the *Phaedo,* Plato describes the semblance of sophrosyne in the man who avoids certain pleasures so that he may obtain other pleasures (the hedonistic calculus of the *Protagoras*), as a foolish (εὐήθης) sophrosyne; those who practice it are actually self-restrained by reason of a kind of wantonness—ἀκολασίᾳ τινι σώφρονες (68C–E).³³ How far this type of *aretê* is from genuine sophrosyne, Plato reminds us in his discussion of the destiny of the souls who have achieved "bourgeois" virtue (*dêmotikê aretê*), called sophrosyne and justice, not through philosophy but through habit and practice. They are reincarnated as bees, wasps, ants, or some other social animal that enjoys an orderly existence without *epistêmê* (81E). The danger of such imperfect participation in *aretê* is demonstrated vividly in the *Republic,* when (in the myth of Er) the soul of one who had lived in a well-ordered state and possessed virtue by habit, not philosophy, unwarily chooses for his next life the lot of a tyrant (619C).³⁴

THE *SYMPOSIUM*

The degree to which Plato's treatment of sophrosyne depends on the context of the dialogue in which it occurs becomes evident when we turn from the otherworldly orientation of the *Phaedo* to the *Symposium.* Here the emphasis is on life and the proper direction of the "life-force" which can enable the soul to view Beauty itself by a process of ascent comparable to the intellectual ascent to the Forms suggested in the *Republic.* It

---

³³ *Sôphrosynê dia akolasian,* although treated with scant respect amid the austerity of the *Phaedo,* receives more favorable consideration in the *Republic* and the *Laws,* since this is the level of virtue with which all but the philosophers and the members of the Nocturnal Council must be content. The mass of the citizens will practice sophrosyne because they are persuaded by their rulers that this course will enable them to avoid greater disadvantages, and they will therefore be δι'ἀκολασίαν σεσωφρονισμένοι. See Gould, 121.

³⁴ Still another facet of Plato's treatment of the soul in the *Phaedo* has a certain relevance for sophrosyne, although its importance appears only in later dialogues. Soul—being intermediate between Being and Becoming, a link between the Forms and the physical world—rules the body and is the source of its activity (79E–80A, 94B, 105C–D); this concept represents the soul as movement. But since it is akin to the Forms, the soul is uniquely capable of imitating that order and harmony which the Forms possess, and of putting them into effect in the physical world. This concept makes the soul the ordering principle and is essential to the view of sophrosyne as accomplishing in human life what *kosmos* or *taxis* achieves in the universe.

is the peculiar attribute of sophrosyne, alone among the cardinal virtues, that it has a prominent place in the dialectic of Beauty as well as in the dialectic of Reason.

Both Beauty—the object of the soul's desire in the *Symposium*—and the Good—the goal of Reason in the *Republic*—are characterized by the orderly arrangement that the *Gorgias* associates with sophrosyne. To participate in either Beauty or the Good, the soul is obliged to achieve sophrosyne within its own microcosm. So far as participating in the Good is concerned, sophrosyne is not more prominent than the other three cardinal virtues, but in connection with Beauty it is uniquely important, because of the special responsibility of this *aretê* for the control of *Erôs*, which is awakened by Beauty. This importance is most evident in the *Phaedrus* (254B), but it is implicit also in the various accounts of the soul's commerce with *Erôs* in the *Symposium* and in the description of the effects of the *orthos Erôs* in the *Republic* (402E–403A). In the *Symposium* the varied approaches to the nature of *Erôs* involve sophrosyne in such different ways as to suggest something of the scope of the virtue in Plato's thought.

The speech of Eryximachus contains a passage strongly reminiscent of the "cosmological" section of the *Gorgias*. The physician maintains that when the heavenly *Erôs* prevails, the physical elements in the universe are brought into harmony, so that a *sôphrôn krasis* ("orderly mixture" [188A]) results, with consequent fertility and health for mankind and animals. This scientific approach to *Erôs*, which utilizes the distinction between heavenly and earthly *Erôs* made by Pausanias in the previous speech (180D ff.), contains echoes of Pythagorean physical theories— notably the reference to *homonoia* among opposites as a kind of *Erôs*, and the allusion to *harmonia*, another manifestation of love, in musical theory and social life. The heavenly *Erôs* is described as *kosmios* in its effect on physical qualities (the hot, cold, dry, and moist), while the other *Erôs*, which causes damage, is characterized as *hybris*. *Pleonexia* and *akosmia* are held responsible for the mutual encroachments of the elements (188A) —an instance of the description of physical processes in ethical terms that Plato took over from the pre-Socratic philosophers.[35] This is the clearest statement anywhere of Plato's belief in the operation of sophrosyne in the cosmos and in the complete parallelism that exists in every department of being. In the later dialogues, as has been pointed out, the role of sophrosyne in cosmology is obscured by Plato's habit of reserving this term for the description of order and harmony in the soul and the

---

[35] E.g., Anaximander, Frag. 1 DK; Heraclitus, Frag. 94 DK.

State, while its appearance in the universe is usually described in terms of *symmetria, taxis,* or *symphônia.*[36]

Other references to sophrosyne in connection with *Erôs* in the *Symposium* are in a more traditional vein and exploit its moral implications. The speech of Agathon, indeed, belongs to the history of sophrosyne in epideictic oratory, for it applies the conventional topics of the four cardinal virtues to the eulogy of *Erôs* and shows in what way the god possesses each of them. The treatment of sophrosyne provides an amusing example of sophistic word-play. Agathon takes the popular conception of sophrosyne as the mastery (τὸ κρατεῖν) of pleasures and appetites (196C ff.) and points out that no pleasure is greater (κρείττω) than *Erôs.* Hence the pleasures are inferior to *Erôs* and, if inferior, are subject to him. But if this is so, he must rule them; and by definition the rule or mastery of pleasure is sophrosyne. The play on the meanings of the verb κρατεῖν amounts to a parody of Plato's own customary approach to sophrosyne, for in his more serious discussions he often calls attention to the puzzling character of the phrase κρείττω αὐτου and relates it to the existence of opposing tendencies in the soul.[37]

Socrates' speech, like that of Eryximachus, makes use of the division of *Erôs* into two kinds and relates sophrosyne and justice to the good *Erôs,* but instead of the cosmic implications Socrates develops the political. His *Erôs* seeks intellectual, rather than physical, fulfillment and becomes "pregnant" with *phronêsis,* whose greatest and fairest aspect, according to Socrates, is that ordering of cities and households which is called sophrosyne and justice (209A–B). The extension of the concept of order to the State is part of the progression in the dialogue, which regularly utilizes material introduced in earlier speeches to perfect, in ladderlike stages, the structure of the whole. The ladder, indeed, is the dominant symbol of the dialogue; it is most vividly realized in the speech of Socrates but actually operates throughout the entire work.[38]

The culmination of all the speeches is that of Alcibiades, who eulogizes not *Erôs* but Socrates, and finds in his character whatever good qualities have hitherto been ascribed to the god. The contrast between "outer" and "inner"—appearance and reality—which marked the discussion of sophrosyne in the *Charmides,* reappears in the famous description of the

---

[36] E.g., *symmetria: Tim.* 87B 6 ff., *taxis: Tim.* 30A, *symphônia: Tim.* 47D. In *Laws* 906B–C, there is an isolated instance of the application of sophrosyne and *pleonexia* to cosmic as well as to political and medical conditions.

[37] E.g., *Rep.* 430–31; *Laws* 689B.

[38] The ascent of *Erôs* parallels the ascent of the mind in *Rep.* VI–VIII; and the degeneration of the soul in *Rep.* VIII–IX is actually the downfall of *Erôs.* See Cornford, 76–77.

outwardly erotic physiognomy of the Silenus-like Socrates and the inner sophrosyne that frustrates Alcibiades' attempt to seduce him (216D– 219D). The sophrosyne of Socrates in this context takes the form of chastity, which in the light of the preceding speeches we now understand as the application of the principle of order and restraint to the soul. Plato makes clear, in his references to Socrates' heroism at Potidaea and Delium, that he also possesses the virtues of courage and hardiness (*andreia* and *karteria*), so often held to be incompatible with sophrosyne. The virtues playfully ascribed to *Erôs* in Agathon's speech are seriously attributed to Socrates, and Alcibiades, who has not heard Socrates' own description of *Erôs,* yet shows that the concept of love as a medium of education—the *sôphrôn Erôs*—is the one that governs the life of Socrates himself.

THE *REPUBLIC*

In the *Republic,* where Plato's political and ethical thought reaches its first great climax, sophrosyne is conceived much as in the *Gorgias,* but the description of its nature and function includes more detail. Our study will limit itself to the following points: the two definitions of sophrosyne in books III and IV, with the corresponding discussions of education; the "cosmological" justification for the virtues in Book VI; and the relation of sophrosyne to the corrupt constitutions and psychologies in Book VIII.

Like the *Gorgias,* the *Republic* assumes that the purpose of the State is the realization of certain ethical values. The explicit assertion of this hypothesis and the arbitrary assumption of a complete parallel between the State and the soul are responsible for the isolation of the four primary virtues and the systematic analysis of their relation. Behind the plan of the first four books lies the concept of the tripartite soul, which determines the manner in which the appetites and the passions will be regarded. Since they are now connected with the soul itself, rather than merely with the body which contaminates the soul (as in the *Phaedo*), they have a higher status than in any psychological system based on a unitary concept of the soul. The consequences for sophrosyne are immediately evident: its duty will be to regulate and order, rather than to suppress the appetites. The first movement of the dialogue leads to the identification of the virtues and the definition of each in terms appropriate to the State and the individual. It is important to realize that the *aretê* thus readily isolated and defined is only "civic" virtue, whose shortcomings we know from the *Phaedo*; the definitions of Book IV are by no means Plato's last word on the subject.

The first need for a definition of sophrosyne arises from the discussion of the elementary training of the prospective guardians in books II and III. The decision to seek an understanding of justice in the soul by contemplating it in the macrocosm of the State has led to the establishment in Book II (369B–372D) of the "first city," the simplest possible political organism, in which each individual performs his proper task, and only the necessary appetites are satisfied. Justice and sophrosyne of a kind undoubtedly exist in this city,[39] but a society so simple and innocent (a city of pigs, Glaucon calls it) cannot endure, and its virtues are not defined. The inquiry passes to a second city, whose involvement in warfare dictates the addition of a warrior class to the farmers, craftsmen, and tradesmen of the first (373D ff.).

The ground is laid for a distinction between sophrosyne and *andreia* by the recognition of two opposing temperaments, the gentle and the spirited (πρᾶον καὶ μεγαλόθυμον), which must be combined in the guardians through their proper education in music and gymnastics.[40] Training in humane studies (*mousikê*) comes first; and since poetry is the chief form of *mousikê*, Plato illustrates the standards that should be applied, by reviewing passages from Homer and accepting or rejecting them according as they do or do not instil *andreia* or sophrosyne. Hence the need for a provisional definition of each virtue. Sophrosyne ὡς πλήθει ("as usually understood" or "for the majority") involves such things as these: to be obedient to those in authority and to rule the pleasures that have to do with the appetites for drink, sexual indulgence, and food (389D–E).[41] The phrase ὡς πλήθει indicates that sophrosyne is here interpreted on a popular level, and the Homeric passages next considered confirm this judgment, for they contain examples only of obedience and self-control and their opposites.[42] Since the form of poetry also has moral consequences, Plato next discusses the ethical value of the various poetic types and the musical modes and rhythms; he shows, in

---

[39] Presumably *sophia* and *andreia* do not exist there, since the classes to which they belong do not yet exist; as individual virtues, however, they may be present in the souls of citizens.

[40] Cf. *Lach.* 196E; *Charm.* 159B ff.; *Prot.* 331D, 347E; *Laws* 963E; *Statesman* 306C–311C; *Theaet.* 144A; as well as *Rep.* 410B ff. and 503C. The persistent coupling of sophrosyne and *andreia* in Plato is discussed by Édouard des Places, S. J., *Pindar et Platon* (Paris, 1949), 118–21.

[41] Aristotle confines his concept of sophrosyne to these two facets of the Platonic virtue: obedience (*Pol.* 1260a 20–24) and control of appetite (*Eth. Nic.* 1118a 23–26).

[42] The further criticism of mimetic poetry in Book X depends on the tripartite psychology not yet established in Book III. Plato there accuses the poets of stimulating the appetitive element—thus weakening the rational (606D–E)—and of enthroning pleasure and pain instead of law as rulers of the State (607A).

connection with the second of these subjects, a characteristic preference for simplicity (*haplotês*), which generally has favorable connotations in Greek thought.[43] Simplicity in music is a source of sophrosyne in the soul, while in gymnastics it produces health of body (404E); the parallel is important in the *Republic,* as in the *Gorgias.*

The aim of the early musical and gymnastic education is summed up near the close of Book III, where the excess or deficiency of each temperament is described once more, and the proper harmony of the two is said to result in the *sôphrôn* and brave soul (410E). Although it is the chief aim of this part of the dialogue to prove that both qualities are necessary in the guardian class, there is a strong hint of the differentiation of value which later becomes explicit in the *Laws,* when Plato describes as philosophical the nature that he has called gentle in Book II (375C). The perfection of this philosophical nature is sophrosyne, and to the extent that the philosophical life—the contemplative life of the *Gorgias*—is superior to the active life, sophrosyne is superior to *andreia.* In the long history of opposition between the two temperaments—which, as we have noted, is one of the enduring themes of Greek literature—Plato is the first to suggest that the *sôphrôn physis* is superior to the spirited. In the *Republic* this superiority is for the most part only implied,[44] but it becomes

---

[43] Simple rhythms express *andreia* and *kosmiotês* (399E, 401A ff.). *Poikilia* ("complexity, intricacy") is usually repugnant to Plato, as if somehow opposed to orderliness; we note that *poikilia* prevails in the corrupt democratic constitution of *Rep.* 557C, and that it is again condemned in music in *Laws* 812D–E. The influence of Damon's theory of musical *êthos* on Plato is assessed by Warren Anderson, *T.A.P.A.* 86 (1955), 88–102. See Damon, Frag. 4 DK on the power of music to reveal courage, sophrosyne, and justice in the soul; and consult Jaeger, *Paideia,* 2. 404, n. 110. A controversial conclusion in *Rep.* 399B is that the Phrygian mode is *sôphrôn* and *metrios;* Aristotle regards it rather as ecstatic (*Pol.* 1342b 4–13) and recommends only the Dorian mode for the education of younger pupils (1340a 34–1340b 5). It is likely that the traditional Greek approval of the Mean enters into the preference for these two modes, since both the Dorian and the Phrygian are midway between the high-pitched Mixolydian and Syntonolydian and the low-pitched Ionian. The lyric poet Pratinas recommended the Aeolian scale as midway between the high and the low pitch; see D. B. Monro, *The Modes in Ancient Greek Music* (Oxford, 1894), 8–9. Ptolemy explains the power of the Dorian mode to induce order and stability in the soul on the basis of its mean position; see Ingemar Düring, *Die Harmonielehre des Klaudios Ptolemaios* (Göteborg, 1930), 99. Plutarch, *On Music,* summarizes ancient theory on the moral effects of the different modes. Rhythm also had a part in musical *êthos,* if we may trust the anecdote about Pythagoras (or Damon) who quieted a riotous mob through the influence of spondaic measures (Quintilian 1. 10. 32); consult Hermann Abert, *Die Lehre vom Ethos in der griechischen Musik* (Leipzig, 1899), 54–55, 126–65. Plutarch terms *sôphrôn* the paean, the special verse form sacred to Apollo (*Mor.* 389B).

[44] The primary education described in books II and III is more concerned with sophrosyne than with *andreia,* and the chief standard applied to the materials and methods of education is the effect they have on the development of sophrosyne (e.g., 390A–C).

one of the basic premises of the *Laws*. Such a hierarchy among the virtues could be conceived of only at a level below the highest (where all the virtues are united). In the *Laws*, where Plato is for the most part concerned with an inferior kind of virtue, he repeatedly arranges the individual *aretae* in a hierarchy and always puts *andreia* at the bottom of the scale.

With the emergence of three classes in the State (for to the farmers and craftsmen of the first city have been added the guardians, who are now divided into rulers and auxiliaries), the second city is fully established; and it becomes possible to locate justice, since it is arbitrarily assumed that the city will be characterized by wisdom, courage, sophrosyne, and justice. If the first three are identified, what remains must be justice. Here is the canonization of the four virtues that left so deep and permanent an impression on later Greek thought, although in the scheme of the *Republic* it is provisional, and the definitions themselves are valid only on the comparatively low level of understanding required at this stage of the argument.[45] *Sophia* and *andreia* are easily located as the characteristic virtues of the two highest classes, and *andreia* is significantly described as *politikê*, being distinguished from the quality of courage found in animals and slaves because it is based on education and is therefore tenacious of right opinion (430C). As in the reference to τὸ πλῆθος ("the majority") when sophrosyne was under discussion in Book III (389D), Plato thus warns us that the *aretê* here described is inferior to that which derives from philosophical understanding; what he says of *andreia* applies equally to the other virtues, even to *sophia* or *phronêsis*.[46]

Sophrosyne is now defined anew: to the two elements of the earlier definition (obedience and self-restraint) is added a third and highly significant one, on which rests the true importance of this virtue to the State. Sophrosyne is first said to be like a kind of concord (*symphônia*) or harmony (430E) and then: "It is a kind of cosmos, somehow, and a control of certain pleasures and appetites, as they say when they call someone master of himself in some fashion." The extremely tentative nature of this definition and the subsequent detailed explanation of the mysterious phrase "master of oneself" suggest that sophrosyne is a more complex virtue than either *sophia* or *andreia*. Plato explicates each term

---

[45] The plurality of *aretae*, as noted above, is another indication that the definitions are not final. They employ the empirical terms required by consideration of the phenomena of the State and the soul, and are "dianoetic" rather than "noetic." See Gould (pp. 180–81) for an attempt to correlate the stages in the "plot" of the Republic (up to Book VII) with the segments in the Divided Line. Books II to IV correspond to the sphere of *dianoia*.

[46] *Phronêsis* is virtually equivalent to *euboulia*, "political [or] practical wisdom" (428B).

in the definition with a reference to the relation of the conflicting elements in the State, and concludes that if the rulers and the ruled hold the same opinion about which should rule, the city will possess sophrosyne in the sense of *harmonia.* Unlike *sophia* and *andreia,* which are virtues of certain parts of the State, sophrosyne is a virtue both of the whole and of each part. Hence it is properly compared to a harmony "sounding the same note in perfect unison throughout the whole," and to a *symphônia* of the naturally inferior and the naturally superior on the question which should rule (432A).[47] As the omission of every other element in the final definition shows, Plato regards concord or harmony as the essential sophrosyne—for the purposes of the *Republic.*

The parallel of the soul and the State requires that the same three elements be found in the microcosm as in the macrocosm; the soul is therefore said to be composed of three parts—the rational, the spirited, and the appetitive—which achieve their proper excellence through the practice of the same four virtues already located in the well-ordered city.[48] Again the essential nature of sophrosyne is found in *philia* and *symphônia,* which exist whenever the ruling part and the two that are ruled agree that the rational element should be in control and do not rebel against it (442C–D). Again sophrosyne must be practiced by all three parts of the soul; it is never, for Plato, as for many later Platonists, solely the virtue of the appetitive part.[49]

[47] The Pythagorean affinities of this passage have often been noted. Morrison (*loc. cit.,* 215) comments on the substitution of the harmonic *isotês* as the bond of union for the geometric proportion of the *Gorgias.* Consult Guthrie, I. 317. See *Laws* 688A–689B for an interpretation of *phronêsis,* rather than sophrosyne, as a *symphônia* in the soul and the State.

[48] The *thymoeides* and the *epithymêtikon* and the corresponding classes in the State owe something—as Jaeger has shown (*Scripta Minora* [Rome, 1960], 2. 309–18)—to the Hippocratic study of types of character. The description of the Asiatic nations in *On Airs, Waters, and Places* portrays them as tame and peaceful, easy to rule, passive because of the climate, engaged in crafts, fond of gain and sensual pleasures—all traits of the third class in the State or (*mutatis mutandis*) of the corresponding part of the soul, while the European nations have many characteristics that Plato assigns to the second class in the State and the *thymoeides* in the soul. Jaeger shows that Plato took the very word *thymoeides* from the Hippocratics.

[49] See Chap. VI, pp. 234 ff. *Rep.* 433A, which discovers *dikaiosynê* in the division of labor, has a bearing on sophrosyne, not only because Plato suggests that justice supplies the other virtues with the power of coming into existence and then keeps them safe (433B)—an indication that justice is the primary virtue among the "civic" *aretae,* although not necessarily in other categories—but also because the definition of justice borrows from the traditional concept of sophrosyne. We are familiar with the definition of sophrosyne as doing one's own work (*Charm.* 161B), and we have found *polypragmosynê* opposed to sophrosyne in Thucydides and the orators. That Plato now defines justice as doing one's own work and applies this definition to the virtue of the soul and of the State, each in its ideal condition, shows that he is widening the hitherto narrow and legalistic scope of *dikaiosynê* by endowing it with some of the attributes of sophrosyne. In this process we have one of the best examples of a most char-

Precisely as the first definitions of the virtues called forth the exposition of elementary moral training by music and gymnastics, so the second set of definitions leads to the discussion of the advanced intellectual training of those guardians capable of becoming philosophers. Books V to VII pursue this topic—supposedly a disgression, but actually the culmination of the picture of the ideal state and the perfectly virtuous soul. The education of the rulers requires them to advance beyond the *politikê aretê* described in Book IV and to substitute for the right opinion that sufficed at the lower level a metaphysical grasp of ethical values, derived from contemplation of the Form of each separate virtue and confirmed by an understanding of the Form of the Good. Book VI contains a description of the activity of the philosopher which amplifies and revises the "cosmological" passage in the *Gorgias*. The philosopher-statesman who gazes at the order and harmony of the eternal realities (the Forms) tries to imitate them and to liken himself to them as far as possible. Thus, by associating himself with what is Divine and orderly (*kosmios*), he assumes these qualities himself. If then he is constrained to practice impressing on the characters of men what he sees in the realm of the Forms and not just to shape himself, he will prove no mean craftsman of sophrosyne and justice and all *dêmotikê aretê* (500D). In the course of his task, he will often glance at the Forms of the virtues (τὸ φύσει δίκαιον, καλόν, σῶφρον, etc.) and then at that which he is reproducing in men (501B).

In this picture of the Demiurge, Plato's favorite type of intelligent activity according to a pattern, are depicted the two levels of comprehension of the virtues required in the State. The philosopher-ruler contemplates the values as they actually are (φύσει, "in their nature") in the Forms, and cannot resist trying to reproduce them in his own soul. Thus he becomes as well ordered (κόσμιος, a significant epithet) and godlike as a man can be (500D), and the irresistible causation exercised by the Forms is indicated. Then he turns, however reluctantly, to his duty as statesman and stamps these same characteristics on the citizens, who thus possess *dêmotikê aretê*—the result, not of *epistêmê* on their part, but merely of right opinion. This passage improves on the corresponding section of the *Gorgias* by substituting the Forms for the physical universe

acteristic tendency of Plato's thought—one that Aristotle decisively rejected. There is, of course, a vast difference between the meaning of τὸ τὰ αὑτοῦ πράττειν as Critias explains it in the *Charmides* and as Socrates uses it in the *Republic*. Cf. Joseph Moreau, *La Construction de l'idéalisme platonicien* (Paris, 1939), 239.

as the model imitated by the craftsman; the most decided advantage consists in the more direct connection between the Forms and the human soul.[50]

The study of the corrupt constitutions in Book VIII, with the analogous references to the degenerate types of soul, shows the crucial importance of sophrosyne for the health of each organism. There are two fundamental causes of corruption—one emphasized in connection with the State, the other with the soul—and both result from the absence of sophrosyne. Loss of *homonoia* is the first cause: *stasis* ("discord") arises with the loss of the agreement that existed in the ruling class (545D): that is, sophrosyne, the harmony and *philia* of the political organism, disappears, and the parts become unbalanced. Timocracy, the first stage in the corruption of the ideal state, represents the triumph of the *thymoeides* (the "spirited element" [547E]), which exaggerates the value of honor, prefers gymnastics to music (548C), and secretly lusts after wealth and pleasure (548B).[51] The second stage is oligarchy, in which wealth is the criterion (550C), *polypragmosynê* prevails (552A), and unity disappears, as the city splits into rich and poor (551D). Democracy develops from oligarchy when wealth is pursued to the point of wantonness—which is incompatible with sophrosyne (555C)—and the poor turn against the rich (557A). Tyranny in turn develops from democracy when the lust for liberty leads to anarchy and ultimately to the rise of a factional leader who becomes a despot (564A, 566A ff.).

The parallel corruptions in the soul result from a similar progressive abandonment of sophrosyne, an upsetting of the balance in which every element performed its function. The disintegration is marked in the individual by the increasing domination of pleasure over Reason—the second result of the loss of sophrosyne. The timocratic man indeed, like the corresponding State, covets chiefly honor (548C, 550B) and, while lacking in Reason (549B), is still not completely given over to the appetites (550B). It is in the oligarchic man that the *epithymêtikon* (the "appetitive part") first reaches the throne (553C), enslaving both Reason

---

[50] Cf. Maguire, 167–68. The *Republic* fills out several hints of the *Gorgias,* by defining the *aretê* of the soul as ruling and administering (353D) and by establishing the existence of parts of the soul, so that the notion of a *kosmos* therein becomes more intelligible. This passage in the *Republic* is one source of the great Hellenistic commonplace about the duty of the ruler to provide his subjects with a model of virtue; Isocrates is another, and probably more influential, source.

[51] Cf. *Phaedrus* 256C–D, where the yielding of the lovers to temptation is the result of their leading an unphilosophic, *philotimos* life.

and Spirit. In the oligarch, appetite is still controlled, but with unworthy motives; thus a kind of *akolasia* already prevails (554C–D). The democratic man emerges when the unnecessary desires get the upper hand (559A ff.), and the tyrannical man when the lawless desires, which most men indulge only in their dreams, are victorious (571B ff.).

The greater length of the description of the degenerate souls and its vivid detail suggest that Plato's primary interest in this section lies with the individual, rather than with the social, corruption. He often refers to the violation of sophrosyne on the downward way. In the oligarchic man the appetitive element, as we have noted, is supreme; he has only the appearance of *homonoia* (554E), and already the unity on which the health of the soul depends has vanished. The democratic man lacks even the semblance of unity, and in his indulgence of the unnecessary desires his soul is prevented from attaining sophrosyne and *phronêsis* (559B–C). A transvaluation of terms strikingly similar to that recorded by Thucydides in connection with the civil war in Corcyra occurs in the democratic soul: *aidôs* is called foolishness; sophrosyne, cowardice; moderation and orderliness, rusticity and illiberality; while the vices of *hybris,* anarchy, wantonness, and shamelessness are correspondingly exalted (560D). Worse yet, the lawless desires of the tyrant drive out any decent appetites and purge their victim of sophrosyne (573B). In its place comes madness (*mania*) whose forms—like the forms of the bad *mania* in the *Phaedrus*—include *erôs* and drunkenness. At the end of the process of corruption the two principal signs of sophrosyne—the control of appetite by reason and the harmonious agreement within the soul that this control should be exercised—have completely disappeared.

THE *PHAEDRUS*

Of the remaining dialogues the most important for sophrosyne are the *Phaedrus* and the *Laws:* the first because of its ambiguous attitude towards this excellence; the second because of the enormously increased emphasis put on sophrosyne as the goal of education. The *Phaedrus* superficially resembles the *Symposium* because of its concentration on *erôs* as a way of elevating the soul, a way parallel and not inferior to the dialectical method outlined in the *Republic;* but there are equally significant differences. One difference that affects sophrosyne is the appearance in the *Phaedrus* of the tripartite soul, a concept with which the *Symposium* has no concern. This innovation brings with it a much more detailed consideration of the role of desire (*epithymia*). In the *Republic* each part of the soul is actuated by some form of desire, the parts being distinguished according to the object of desire;[52] in the *Phaedrus*, too, where the tripartite soul is vividly described in the myth of the charioteer, it is evident that each part is moved by the force of *erôs*. Hence there is a new emphasis on sophrosyne, whose function of controlling desire is extended from the *epithymêtikon* properly so called to the spirited and rational parts of the soul as well.[53]

Just as the structure of the *Symposium* is governed by the symbol of the ladder that the soul of the lover ascends, so the structure of the *Phaedrus* is determined by the pattern of the diaeresis, reaching down from the Forms and coming ever closer to contact with the particular.[54] This favorite dialectical method of Plato's later dialogues is applied somewhat informally to Soul in the first speech of Socrates and to Madness in the second. Soul is divided into rational and irrational *eidê* or aspects: the first is able, as we know from the *Republic*, to reach the Forms independently through the instrument of the *logos;* the second requires the assistance of two other forces, *erôs* and rhetoric. The first half of the dialogue (notably the two speeches of Socrates) illustrates the erotic method of influencing and molding the irrational soul; the second, the rhetorical method. The goal of each is ultimately the same: training the soul—of the beloved, in the first section; of the hearer, in the second. Both sections pay close attention to the problem posed by the differentiation of souls into various kinds or types—a problem that does not affect the dialectical method but is crucial for *erôs* and rhetoric. Both sections expose a false or base conception—of *erôs* and rhetoric, respectively. And finally, both methods of education are intimately connected with the historical Socrates, whose teaching effected the union of *logos* and *erôs*. The differences between the erotic and the rhetorical sections of the dialogue are naturally very great. Certain elements of Plato's philosophy

[52] See especially *Rep.* 580D 7, where each *eidos* of the soul has its own *epithymia*. On the operation of *erôs* ("a single fund of energy") through three main channels in the soul, see Cornford, 71.

[53] The direction of the movement of the dialogue constitutes another difference between the *Phaedrus* and the *Symposium*. The emphasis is now on the downward movement, from the Forms to the individual soul, rather than the upward movement of the soul to the vision of Beauty itself (*Symp.* 211E), which provides the *Symposium* with its characteristic ladderlike structure. In the *Symposium* the lover has not seen Beauty itself before he begins his ascent; in the *Phaedrus* the Forms have been glimpsed before the incarnation of the soul, and it is the recollection of the Form of Beauty that awakens desire in the lover (250B–C). Thus reminiscence is for the first time connected with *erôs*. Still another innovation in the *Phaedrus* is the second method of rehabilitating the irrational soul, the method of rhetoric, which in Plato's earlier dialogues would not have been considered capable of conducting the soul to *aretê*.

[54] The *Phaedrus* is analyzed along these lines by Friedrich Solmsen, *Die Entwicklung der aristotelischen Logik und Rhetorik* (Berlin, 1929), 272–93.

are confined to the first, others to the second, as if the sharp division in the dialogue allowed Plato for once to separate features of his thought that were ordinarily combined. Sophrosyne, however, is involved in both approaches, erotic and rhetorical, and is in fact connected also with the purely dialectical method, which Plato merely indicates in his diaeresis of the soul (e.g., 237E) but does not pursue in the *Phaedrus.* The varied connotations conveyed by the word sophrosyne enable it to find a place in the scheme of education intended for both the rational and the irrational elements in the soul.

The first speech of Socrates finds in every person two motives for action, the innate appetite for pleasure and the acquired opinion which seeks the best (237D). If the first prevails, *hybris* results in the soul; if the second, sophrosyne. *Hybris* has many manifestations, corresponding to the various appetites: here Plato mentions gluttony, drunkenness, and *erôs.* In this informal diaeresis of the soul, sophrosyne is equivalent to rationality; and if Plato were to discuss the manner in which the soul in its rational or *sôphrôn* state could reach the Forms, he would need only to refer to the educational system of the *Republic,* designed to produce the philosopher-king. In the erotic terminology of the speech (which exposes the bad kind of *erôs*), *nous* and sophrosyne are opposed to *erôs* and *mania* (241A), and the conventional superiority of sanity is upheld.[55] In the second speech, while the antithesis is maintained and repeatedly stressed, the system of values is reversed. Socrates now eulogizes *erôs* as a form of Divine madness infinitely superior to mere human rationality. For once, anything connected with human reason, such as sophrosyne or *technê,* is disparaged—perhaps the most arresting difference between the first and the second sections of the dialogue.

If we integrate the analysis of madness in the second speech with the diaeresis of the soul in the first—as Socrates encourages us to do when he uses these two passages to illustrate the process of synthesis and division (265D–266A)—we find that, while the rational or *sôphrôn* side of the division remains unchanged, the irrational must now be further subdivided into *epithymia* (with all its base manifestations, including the bad *erôs*) and *mania,* the Divine madness, which has four forms: prophecy, orgiastic madness, poetry, and *erôs.* Each form of Divine madness is superior to the corresponding form of sophrosyne, mere human rationality (244B, 244D, 245A–B)—a situation somewhat reminiscent of the contrast between the rational and the irrational in religion which

---

[55] Sophrosyne in this connection is not, however, the noblest aspect of the virtue. It is comparable, as Hackforth points out (47), to the sophrosyne *dia akolasian* of *Phaedo* 68E.

underlies the *Bacchae* of Euripides.[56] The Divine *erôs* is equivalent to the philosophic *erôs* described by Diotima in the *Symposium,* and like that *erôs* depends for its effectiveness on the practice of sophrosyne: not the sophrosyne of the calculating nonlover in the speech of Lysias and the first speech of Socrates (which is *sôphrosynê dia akolasian*), but a sophrosyne that participates in the Form of the virtue and is therefore entirely different from mere human rationality.[57]

Two passages in the myth of the charioteer demonstrate the worth of the Divine sophrosyne. First, sophrosyne is one of the Forms residing in the region beyond the heavens, where it is glimpsed by the soul before incarnation, together with the Forms of the other moral values, of *Epistêmê,* and of Beauty (247D–E, 250B).[58] Although Sophrosyne, like Justice and *Phronêsis,* is unable to arouse recollection in the human soul, except dimly in some few cases—and therefore cannot by itself inspire a return to the Forms—its association with Beauty in the Plain of Truth has still some effect, and indeed a crucial one, when the soul beholds the beautiful on earth and is reminded of the Form that it resembles. The passion that causes the soul, under the figure of the charioteer and his two horses, to desire the beautiful object is restrained if the charioteer remembers the Form of Beauty that he beheld, together with Sophrosyne, on her sacred throne. The *hybris* of the unruly horse is checked, and the highest degree of virtue and happiness is attained (254B–E), provided the charioteer and the good horse always prevail over the suggestions of the bad horse.[59] Both lover and beloved are self-controlled and orderly in this life, and after death their souls gain wings and win the

[56] Except that in the *Phaedrus* Divine madness is always a cause of good, whereas in the *Bacchae* it has nothing to do with morality or goodness. In Euripides the irrational is superior to the rational in power alone. For the later development of the concept of Divine madness in poetry and its contamination with *sôphrôn mania,* see my article in *C.P.* 43 (1948), 13–16.

[57] It is comparable to the sophrosyne of Socrates described in the speech of Alcibiades in the *Symposium,* which illustrates the *sôphrôn erôs* of Diotima's theory.

[58] Since this sophrosyne is Divine, not mortal, it is not included in the disparagement of 244B ff.

[59] Although in most respects the symbol of the charioteer and his two horses, one good and one bad, corresponds to the tripartite psychology of the *Republic,* it differs in that the bad horse is bad intrinsically and not just when his *epithymia* is excessive. The harmony sought in the *Republic* is not possible for the human soul in the myth of the *Phaedrus.* The souls of the gods, however, which are also represented as tripartite, are perfectly harmonious; all three elements are "good and of good stock" (246A)—i.e., simple, of one nature. The myth of the charioteer becomes for later Platonists, pagan and Christian, the standard symbol for the operation of sophrosyne in the soul, and one that they treat with considerable freedom. See, for example, Plotinus' substitution of Sophrosyne by herself on her throne for Plato's Beauty with Sophrosyne in his allusion to *Phaedrus* 254B (*Enn.* 1. 6. 9). On the Church Fathers' habit of conflating the myth with various Biblical texts, see Chap. IX.

greatest good that either human sophrosyne or Divine madness can secure (256B).[60] That this achievement depends on sophrosyne and madness in combination, the one controlling the other, is made perfectly clear by Plato's description of the second-best condition: again the recollection of Beauty arouses desire for the beautiful, but the bad horse sometimes overpowers the charioteer and the good horse, and as a result the souls of the lover and the beloved are wingless, although gifted at least with the desire for wings (256D). The sole difference between this state and the first lies in the absence of sophrosyne and *aidôs*.[61] So that we may realize, however, the need for both elements— madness and sophrosyne—Plato immediately reminds us of the worthlessness of "human sophrosyne" by itself, for Socrates observes that even the second-best condition is superior to that which results from yielding to the nonlover, who is tinged with mortal sophrosyne (mere calculation) and can beget in the soul of the beloved only a false *aretê* (256E).[62]

The second part of the *Phaedrus*, devoted to rhetoric, has almost nothing to say of sophrosyne, but the total emphasis on reason and the deep interest in *technê* imply its presence. Plato's demand for order in a good speech (277C) recalls the *Gorgias*, where *technê*, in oratory as in every other activity, implies order and sophrosyne. The only explicit reference to sophrosyne relates it to the moral function of rhetoric, which is to please God; Socrates says that it is the *sôphrôn*, the man of judgment,[63] who labors to achieve this end (273E). The word appears once more with the familiar moral connotations in the prayer at the close of the dialogue. Socrates asks Pan and the other tutelary divinities of the place (whose help he has invoked earlier, before his second speech) to grant him harmony without and within (an important theme of the *Charmides*) and only so much wealth as the *sôphrôn* man can make off with (279B–C). The prayer links the various themes of the dialogue:

[60] This passage is one of those in which sophrosyne of style accompanies a portrayal of *sôphrôn* behavior. Hackforth (109) comments on the "strong but controlled eloquence" of 256A 7–B7.

[61] In the case of the first soul, the sense of awe inspired by the sight of Beauty is, as Hackforth points out (98), the positive aspect of sophrosyne: "not a passionate self-suppression, but a passionate self-surrender."

[62] Several passages in the description of the charioteer and his adventures recall the diaeresis of the soul in Socrates' earlier speech—particularly the statement that the good horse is a lover of honor with sophrosyne, *aidôs*, and true opinion (*doxa;* Hackforth's translation of this phrase as "genuine renown" dulls the echo of the earlier speech [237E]); and the description of the other horse as a companion of *hybris* and boasting (253D–E; cf. 237E, 238C).

[63] The phrase ὁ νοῦν ἔχων in the same passage is equivalent to *sôphrôn* and confirms its meaning in this context.

beauty, friendship, wisdom, external and internal goods, and the sophrosyne that is necessary for intelligent use of all the other goods. It is not without significance that this, one of the few prayers ascribed to Socrates in Plato's dialogues, is a prayer for sophrosyne, the quintessential Socratic *aretê*.

THE *TIMAEUS*

Aspects of sophrosyne traditionally linked with the Socrates of the early dialogues are also emphasized in three of the late ones—the *Timaeus*, the *Sophist*, and the *Statesman*—even though the figure of Socrates himself is now diminished in importance and in the *Laws* finally disappears. The *Timaeus*, which has almost nothing explicit to say about sophrosyne, nevertheless provides a background helpful to the understanding of Plato's view of the virtue throughout his final dialogues, as well as his treatment of the closely related concepts of measure (*metriotês*) and limit (*peiras*) in the *Philebus*, order (*taxis*) in the *Statesman*, and symmetry (*symmetria*) in the *Sophist*.[64] Special significance attaches to the ethical implications of two problems: the manner in which cosmos is produced out of chaos, and the relation of the mortal and immortal aspects of the human soul.

In dealing with the first of these questions Plato establishes those analogies between macrocosm and microcosm, the universe and the human soul, that were to be of increasing moral significance for later philosophers, pagan and Christian alike. In both the universe and the soul, cosmos can be brought out of chaos only through a compromise between Reason and Necessity; this compromise is effected in the universe by the Demiurge, using persuasion, and in the human soul by the partial triumph of the immortal element (Reason) over the mortal (Necessity), "built on" to the immortal part when the soul becomes incarnate (69C). The passions and appetites—which are dreadful but "necessary," as Plato repeatedly reminds us (69D), and are the source of disease in the soul (86B ff.)—are the responsibility of the body. Now for the first time, in fact, all three parts of the soul are given precise corporeal locations: *Nous* (the only immortal part) in the head (69D–E), *Thymos* in the chest (70A–D), and the *Epithymêtikon*, the seat of sensation and desire

---

[64] Gould (201) notes the importance of some of these ideas and terms in the late dialogues and attributes their presence to the mood of compromise he finds there. See also Gould, 198, n. 4, on the recurrence of *systasis*, to indicate the combination of different factors, in the *Timaeus* and the *Laws*.

(77B), greedy and clamorous, but again "necessary," below the midriff (70D–71D).

The fundamental cause of evil in the universe and the human soul alike is the lack of correct proportion between Reason and Necessity. Hence Plato emphasizes the need for proportion (*symmetria*) and order (*kosmos*) in macrocosm and microcosm. The relevance of sophrosyne seems as obvious here as in the "cosmological" section of the *Gorgias* or the speech of Eryximachus in the *Symposium,* but in the late dialogues Plato normally confines the word to ethical and political contexts. Yet Cornford's analogy between the *Timaeus* and the *Oresteia*—which compares the Furies to Necessity and Athene to Reason and emphasizes the role of persuasion in reconciling the two [65]—is suggestive in this connection. Without pressing too far the terms of the analogy, it is tempting to conclude that, just as the outcome of the *Oresteia* is the emergence of sophrosyne (with justice) in the *polis,* so, too, the orderly universe of the *Timaeus* is an expression of sophrosyne in the cosmos.

Against the new cosmological background, Plato sets some old ideas. The need for symmetry between body and soul—the most important kind of symmetry so far as health and *aretê* are concerned (87D)—leads to the familiar demand for a combination of musical and gymnastic education, so that soul and body may be equally healthy and evenly matched (88B). Since soul and body must be brought into harmony (88C), the best way for man to nourish the Divine element in himself is to learn the harmonies and revolutions of the universe, so as to make the part that thinks similar to the object of its thought (90D).[66] The "cosmological" passage of the *Gorgias* is thus recalled, but the concept of *kosmos* and the nature of the harmony that must be achieved are now based on a much more detailed theory of the universe.

The sole reference to sophrosyne in this section of the *Timaeus* has an oldfashioned, Socratic ring. Plato explains that the gods—in the effort to make the mortal kind as good as possible, and knowing that the appetitive part of the soul is without a share in *logos* and *phronêsis*—have made it the organ of divination (traditionally associated with the liver [71D–E]). No one in his right mind can prophesy truly; only someone deranged can do so. The interpretation of dreams and prophecies, however, is the task of the rational, according to the old saying that to do

---

[65] F. M. Cornford, *Plato's Cosmology* (London, 1937), 361–64.

[66] This passage, in combination with other Platonic references to the concept of ὁμοίωσις θεῷ ("imitation of God, assimilation to God"), had important consequences for sophrosyne in Patristic thought. See Chap. IX.

and to know one's own affairs and to know oneself belongs to the *sôphrôn* alone (72A). This reversion to one of the oldest interpretations of sophrosyne is typical of the late dialogues, which tend to revive the association of the virtue with *Gnôthi sauton* and *Mêden agan*; this is perhaps another manifestation of the respect for old age, the distant past, and traditions connected with the oldest layers of Greek thought, which is so marked a characteristic of the *Laws*.[67] In the context of the *Timaeus* itself, the most significant result of this remark is to establish the need for the co-operation of the irrational and the rational and to identify sophrosyne with the controlling, ordering aspects of reality.

THE *SOPHIST*

The *Sophist* offers another example of the tendency to revive the old Socratic nuances of sophrosyne, this time in connection with the problem of evil in the soul. There are two varieties of such evil: disease and ignorance. The first is a kind of disharmony (228A), the second a form of disproportion (228D), and they can be corrected, respectively, by punishment and instruction. That form of the soul's disease called discord (*stasis*), which results from the conflict of reason and opinion with desire, appetite, and pleasure (228A), naturally reminds us of the *Republic*, where the harmony of these elements is called sophrosyne, but Plato does not apply the term to this condition here. Instead, he reserves it for the state that exists when the other evil in the soul, ignorance in its worst form—thinking one knows what one does not know—has been expelled by the process of dialectical refutation (the *elenchus*). When the soul has been purged of false opinion, as the body is purged by medicine, it achieves what Plato describes as the best and most *sôphrôn* state (230D). Thus sophrosyne is again, as in the *Timaeus*, linked with Socratic self-knowledge and with health of soul, the most persistent Socratic metaphor.

THE *STATESMAN*

The *Statesman*, which applies the characteristic methods of Plato's later dialogues to the old Socratic subject of the statesman and his *technê*, employs some of the cosmological ideas of the *Timaeus* and makes their relevance to ethics explicit. The relation to the *Timaeus* is marked in the myth of the alternate cosmic cycles, in the first of which the

---

[67] Plato is fond of introducing these ancient commonplaces with some such phrase as: "A good old saying tells us." Cf. *Tim.* 72A with *Phil.* 45D; and see *Menex.* 247–48, where the archaic warning *Mêden agan* is again related to sophrosyne.

universe owes its movement to the Demiurge and enjoys order and harmony, while in the other it undergoes a reverse movement, caused by its own fate and "innate desire" (272E),[68] and suffers increasing disorder as a result of the material element always present in nature. In this myth, as in the *Timaeus,* Plato reiterates the parallel between human life and the life of the universe, referring to the relationship as a kind of imitation—*mimêsis* (273E–274A, 274D)—of the macrocosm by the microcosm and implying that the same conflicting elements of *kosmos* and *ataxia* are at work in both. Again the word sophrosyne is avoided in this connection; it is reserved for the strictly ethical discussion of the statesman's primary task, that of weaving into the fabric of the State the two opposing temperaments, the *sôphrôn* and the *andrikos.* To this subject, already extensively treated in the *Republic,* the *Statesman* adds a fresh discussion of several topics,[69] including an important analysis of the opposition between the two as a source of conflict in the State (307C ff.). The most arresting innovation is the hint that the very Forms of the *sôphrôn* and the *andrikos* are hostile to each other (307C). Hence their opposition is as deep-seated as can be; the actions and the individuals in whom these qualities are reflected will by their hostility endanger the State. Plato indeed shows some hesitation about suggesting incompatibility among the virtues (306A–D), especially at the level of the Forms; but most of his discussion is based on empirical observation of human types, rather than on a consideration of true *aretê.* The description of the inopportune and excessive indulgence of the *sôphrôn physis* which leads to an unwarlike disposition of the entire State and ends in slavery (307E) reads like a commentary on the remarks about the danger of *apragmosynê* and *hêsychia* attributed by Thucydides to Pericles and Alcibiades.[70] Plato, like Pericles, generally avoids using the noun sophrosyne to describe undesirable quietism, and substitutes the

[68] The same phrase (ἔμφυτος ἐπιθυμία) is used in *Phaedrus* 237D to describe the instinct that leads the soul to *hybris;* its antithesis there is *doxa* ("acquired opinion"), which leads to sophrosyne.

[69] E.g., qualities connected with *andreia*—quickness, vehemence, sharpness (306E)—and sophrosyne—quietness, slowness, gentleness (307A)—and a list of terms used to indicate excess or inappropriateness in each category (307B–C): *hybris* and *mania* in the one case, cowardice and sluggishness in the other. The need to harmonize these qualities, especially by the combination of musical and gymnastic education, is one of the most persistent topics in Plato's dialogues, and one to which he applies various points of view.

[70] See Chap. III above. Plato's awareness of the danger to the State if conflict arises between the two temperaments reaches its peak in the *Statesman.* While in the *Laws* he discusses at great length the need to harmonize the two, he nowhere expresses such intense concern as he does in this dialogue.

circumlocution *sôphrôn physis* or, more often, some form of *kosmios,* which is the most persistent synonym for *sôphrôn* in all its varied connotations throughout the dialogues (307E, 309B, 309E).

The metaphor of weaving, introduced much earlier in the dialogue as an illustration of the task of kingship (279B–283A, 287B), finds its true purpose in the description of the process of constructing a society from the opposing types. Those who tend towards *andreia* will form the warp, those who incline towards *kosmiotês* the woof (309B); and the two natures will be bound together by bonds that unite both the Divine and the animal parts of the soul. The Divine bond is true opinion,[71] imparted by the statesman, which renders the *andreia physis* more gentle and inclined towards justice and the *kosmia physis* truly *sôphrôn* and wise (309D–E), while the human bonds include intermarriage and adoption. The weaving together of opposites recalls the emphasis on compromise and persuasion in the *Timaeus* and anticipates the great importance of mixture in the *Philebus.* Another link with the *Philebus* is the appearance in the *Statesman* of the concept of the Mean (*to metrion*) as a device by which to measure excess and defect (283C) and thus to arrive at truth (284D).

THE *PHILEBUS*

The *Philebus* indeed reveals that Plato now sees in the concept of moderation the key to several important problems.[72] The principle of limit, which is involved in the classification of pleasures, the standard of the Mean, by which each factor in the good life is judged, the identification of symmetry with beauty, even the admission that mixture (of knowledge and pleasure) is essential for happiness—all indicate the trend of Plato's thinking. The hierarchy of goods established at the close of the *Philebus* is highly significant. In the first place stands measure (or the Mean); in the second, symmetry. As Hackforth suggests, these two are not so much ingredients of the good life as its conditions:[73] the first aims at the proper quantitative determination of each kind of knowledge or pleasure; the second looks at the good life as a whole and apprehends the relation of its parts. The ingredients themselves are

---

[71] See Gould (215) on this bond and its reappearance in the *Laws.*

[72] Like Plato, W. B. Yeats in his old age assigned increasing importance to measurement. Yeats's contrast between "Asiatic vague immensities" and the "intellect . . . calculation, number, measurement," which he considers the distinguishing genius of Europe ("The Statues," *Collected Poems of W. B. Yeats* [London, 1952], 375–76), has something in common with Plato's attitude in the *Philebus* and other late dialogues.

[73] Richard Hackforth, *Plato's Examination of Pleasure* (Cambridge, 1945), 138.

contained in the subsequent categories, ranging down from wisdom or mind to a vaguely described sixth class, which admits pleasures such as those allied with health and sophrosyne (63E).

Sophrosyne in the *Philebus* generally refers to self-restraint, its classical role where pleasure is concerned. In one of several anticipations of Aristotle, Plato says that the *sôphrôn* man takes pleasure in his sophrosyne (12D),[74] and elsewhere he describes the pleasures of the *sôphrôn bios* as moderate and subject to the principle of limit.[75] As in the *Timaeus* and the *Sophist*, he revives the connection of sophrosyne with a traditional theme when he has Protarchus say, not without irony, that it is splendid for the *sôphrôn* man to know everything, but the next best thing is for him to know himself (19C). Socrates alludes to the other Delphic proverb in his comparison of the pleasures of *hybris* and of sophrosyne, when he remarks that the *sôphrôn* man is restrained by the proverb *Mêden agan*, to which he gives obedience (45D).

One of the marked differences between Plato's discussion of pleasure in the *Philebus* and his earlier considerations of the subject, especially in the *Gorgias*, lies in his new basis for judgment. In earlier dialogues Plato condemned the pleasures of the body, when excessive, for moral reasons, but now he appeals to metaphysics or even cosmology. Pleasure is akin to the unlimited (31A); its intensity offends *phronêsis* and *Nous* (63E). The standards by which bodily pleasures are measured are the same standards as those applied to movements and changes in the universe. It is true that this point of view was already implicit in the "cosmological" passage of the *Gorgias*, but it was only a small factor in that dialogue. Now it has expanded to include almost everything in Plato's philosophy; its effects on the final stage of his thought are everywhere apparent in the *Laws*.

THE *LAWS*

The *Laws* by its very subject invites comparison with the *Republic*—a comparison that at every level reveals marked differences, not the least where sophrosyne is concerned. No longer is there a precise identification of ethics and politics, resulting from an explicit and repeatedly stressed parallel between the soul and the State.[76] Much of what Plato has to

---

[74] Cf. *Eth. Nic.* 1099a 15-20, 1104b 4-8.

[75] E.g., 45D ff.

[76] Traces of the parallel remain, such as the comparison of the part of the soul which feels pleasure and pain to the common people in the State (689B ff.). The theme of *symphônia*, which in the *Republic* applied equally to the soul and the State, is still important in the *Laws* but now refers to the agreement in the soul between *phronêsis* and the appetites; and although in the discussion of the reasons for corruption in the Athenians and Persians of old, the parallels

say about sophrosyne in the *Laws* has no relation to anything but the individual. He travels, in fact, a long way towards the personal, non-political ethics of the Hellenistic philosophers, as may be seen from the discussion in Book V of the pleasures connected with the *sôphrôn* life and the life of wantonness (733D ff.).[77] Yet even when no parallel with the virtues of the State can be adduced, sophrosyne, like the other forms of moral excellence, is always seen within the framework of the State, and we are often reminded that all legislation is designed to secure *aretê*. It is one of the great innovations of the *Laws* that sophrosyne to a considerable extent replaces justice as the aspect of virtue which the lawgiver is most intent upon securing.

The hierarchies of virtues, goods, and values which are so persistent a feature of the *Laws* repeatedly elevate sophrosyne to a position of greater importance than it enjoyed in the *Republic*. Although it is never the leader of the tetrad—a post invariably assigned to *phronêsis* (631C 6) or *Nous* (963A 8)—it is the quality without which the other goods are valueless (696B, 697B, 710A, 728E–729A) and is essential even in its ordinary, unphilosophical form (710A).[78] The chief reason for its special prominence is the orientation of the dialogue towards the education of the irrational soul, largely through a process of habituation which will guarantee the correct response to pleasure and pain. Education in the *Laws* begins even earlier than in the *Republic*[79] and is directed in a marked degree towards the appetitive principle which, if not controlled, threatens to overwhelm the element of reason. Since sophrosyne is the virtue proper to the *epithymêtikon*,[80] it is naturally of first importance in the system of education outlined in books I, II, IV, and VII. Plato's

---

between soul and State are clearly set forth (689C), usually the individual is paramount. In this passage the soul and the State are divided into only two parts—the rational and the irrational; such bipartition is typical of the *Laws*.

[77] This discussion strongly influenced the Epicurean view of pleasure, happiness, and the *summum bonum*. For Epicurean sophrosyne, see Chap. VI, pp. 211–13.

[78] But sophrosyne apart from the rest of *aretê* is not worthy of honor (696D) or not worth talking about (710A). It may be significant that in one hierarchy where sophrosyne is ranked ahead of justice, it is described as the μετὰ νοῦ σώφρων ψυχῆς ἕξις (631C 1 ff.); while in another, sophrosyne unaccompanied by *phronêsis* or *Nous* is rated lower than *dikaiosynê*—if the virtues are listed in ascending order (964B 5–6).

[79] Regulations designed to improve the physical health of the child begin with directions for the conduct of pregnant women (798E); and minute care is taken that mothers and children avoid excessive pleasure and unmixed pain, so that they may pursue a middle way which will make them cheerful—a condition described as being like God (791C–793A). The great emphasis on *paidia* ("play") as a mode of *paideia* ("education") results from the early beginning of the process of habituation.

[80] Although Plato has much to say about *epithymia*, the term *epithymêtikon* is not common in the *Laws*; nor is *thymoeides*.

concern for the irrational soul and its appetites is of course one of the
striking features of his later dialogues (revealed, for instance, in the attention to *erôs* and rhetoric as methods of molding the irrational soul in
the *Phaedrus*) and is connected with his interest in all the ways in which
movement and change appear in the universe. The appetites and passions are one aspect of movement; as such they now claim a place in
the world order and demand to be utilized in society.[81] Sophrosyne is
a principal means by which they are enabled to take their proper
place.

Since the texture of Plato's thought is so closely woven, it is not surprising to find that his interest in movement and change, the basis of
his physics, is related to another prominent theme of the late dialogues—
that of moderation, proportion, the Mean, symmetry, and harmony—
a theme linked to the problem of adjustment and compromise which
becomes crucial when movement is recognized as a valid aspect of
reality. As we have often observed, these concepts are analogues in one
realm or another of the concept of sophrosyne. There is no break with
Plato's earlier philosophy, for the importance of order (*kosmos, taxis*) in
the universe, the State, and the soul was clearly seen in the *Gorgias* and
the *Republic;* but Plato's later study of cosmology and physics gave new
support to his earlier position and resulted in a more lively awareness of
the far-reaching importance of moderation and proportion in all departments of being.

Sophrosyne, furthermore, shares with the other virtues the enhanced
importance given all qualities that are akin to soul by Plato's discovery
that soul (as movement, life) has priority over all soulless things.
Although not specifically mentioned, sophrosyne and justice are
certainly among the *êthê* ("moral characters") which Plato describes as
akin to soul, and are therefore prior in status to everything material and
mechanical (896D). The new basis for the primacy of soul is religious,
and a major difference between the *Laws* and the *Republic*—which
affects much in the later treatise, including the ethical values—is the

---

[81] See *Phaedrus* 237D, 255C ff., and 271B ff. for the integration of the irrational *eidê*
into the structure of the soul, and see *Tim.* 88–89 and *Laws* 898B for the recognition of irrationality as an aspect of movement. In the *Epinomis* the relation of movement to the irrational
elements in the human soul is made more explicit than in the genuine Platonic dialogues; see
especially 977B–978B, 979C–D. In the *Laws* the cosmology of Book X is on the whole kept
distinct from ethical psychology. On the relation of Plato's interest in movement to his view
of the lower parts of the soul as essential, see Solmsen, *Theology,* 144, 148, n. 39. Consult also
J. B. Skemp, *The Theory of Motion in Plato's Later Dialogues* (Cambridge, 1942), 113 ff., for the
fusion of ethics with cosmology. The various implications of *kinêsis* in the late dialogues are
discussed by Solmsen, *Aristotle's System of the Physical World* (Ithaca, 1960), 20–66.

extent to which the State is now founded on religion.[82] Religion had a place in the *Republic,* to be sure, but it was not the structural basis of society. In the later work Plato sets forth a new concept of law, as a product of mind, which is in turn an aspect of soul; and in connection with this new, divinely produced law, the virtues of justice and sophrosyne enjoy a position more exalted and more securely founded on an objective view of nature than in the *Republic.*

The shifting relation between sophrosyne and justice is one of the central problems of Platonic ethics. The great tendency of the *Republic* was to develop justice away from mere legalism by endowing it with some of the properties of sophrosyne; the functions of the two virtues in the soul and the State were complementary. In the *Laws,* although the two are often coupled, and justice is clearly an essential quality of the State, the greater emphasis on the ethics of the individual and on the training of the irrational soul leads to a more pronounced concern for sophrosyne. At the highest level sophrosyne and justice are of course identical, and in the discussion of "true law"—as opposed to class legislation—they are always named together. But sophrosyne in the *Laws* is almost always a less exalted quality than that which in the *Republic* (and again in *Laws* 964A 4 ff.) is identified with the other cardinal virtues. It is either the power of self-mastery (τὸ κρατεῖν αὑτοῦ, τὸ νικᾶν αὑτόν), instilled by education in conformity with the laws, or it is the ordinary, popular, "natural" virtue which Plato carefully distinguishes from the philosophic variety—identified with *phronêsis* (710A 5 ff.).[83] As in his treatment of *andreia* (where "natural" virtue and "civic" virtue replace the philosophical courage of the *Republic*),[84] so, too, with so-

---

[82] See Solmsen, *Theology,* 132.

[83] The specific statement of what he means by ordinary sophrosyne is part of Plato's description of the ideal ruler who can most easily put into effect the ideal constitution. He must be young, possessed of a good memory (important on the philosophical level in the myth of the *Phaedrus* and on the psychological level in the rhetorical section of that dialogue), facility in learning, courage, and a noble nature. If these qualities are to be of any value, he must also possess sophrosyne of the ordinary kind (δημώδης) which springs up in children and animals who are moderate in respect to pleasure (710A 5). Like the physical *andreia* of *Laws* 963E ff., such sophrosyne lacks *phronêsis.* The next higher grade of sophrosyne, which renders a person κρείττων αὑτοῦ, and the education by which it may be instilled are the subject of the detailed discussion in books I and II. The sophrosyne that is identical with the other three cardinal virtues is assigned as a subject of study to the guardians in Book XII (965C 9 ff.). The unity of the virtues is the aspect of the problem of the One and the Many which has the most immediate relevance to the State.

[84] For an analysis of the various levels of *andreia* in the *Laws* (physical *andreia*, civic *andreia,* instilled by the education prescribed by law, and that which is accompanied by *phronêsis*), see Herwig Görgemanns, *Beiträge zur Interpretation von Platons Nomoi* (Munich, 1960), 114–29.

phrosyne Plato now interests himself chiefly in those aspects that had received short shrift in the *Charmides* and even in the *Republic*.

In view of the great length of the *Laws* and the persistence of the themes of sophrosyne, we can do no more than indicate a few passages in which Plato's interpretation of this virtue shows some distinctive novelty or achieves special significance in the structure of the whole treatise. Books I and II suggest the importance of the cardinal virtues in general to Plato as he takes up once more the problem of the ideal state. Where the *Republic* began by attacking the sophistic theory of the right of the strong (to which Plato returns in Book IV of the *Laws*), the later dialogue begins with a study of various constitutions and the virtues at which they aim. (It is still assumed that *aretê* is the aim of all legislation [631B]). Since books I and II serve as a preface to the legislation that comprises the balance of the treatise, and embody an example of the proper method for the legislator to follow, Plato's reasons for choosing to discuss the education and the laws that will produce sophrosyne are of interest. One reason is evidently the parallel between *andreia,* the aim of the Dorian states, and sophrosyne; since both can be brought under one heading—self-mastery, resistance to pain (*andreia*) and to pleasure (sophrosyne)—the criticism of the Spartan and Cretan constitutions can be balanced neatly by positive suggestions for instilling the rival virtue. Furthermore, Plato had ready to hand an easy method of developing sophrosyne, which was again parallel to a well-known Spartan device for developing *andreia*. And, finally, a discussion of the symposium provided a direct introduction to the subject of musical education, which is, if anything, more fundamental in the *Laws* than in the *Republic*.

Plato's method in Book I is first to criticize the Dorian belief that war is the natural condition of society and that legislation should therefore aim to produce *andreia*; secondly, to set up an opposing ideal, which substitutes peace for war, and the peaceful virtues, especially sophrosyne, for *andreia;* and thirdly, to suggest an institution by which sophrosyne may be developed, comparable to the common meals (*syssitia*) of the Dorian communities. This device is the symposium, which was always an informal adjunct to the traditional Ionian-Attic *paideia*[85] but was condemned by Sparta as a source of drunkenness and excessive pleasure (637A). Plato's adaptation of this time-honored institution to the service of the State is exactly parallel to his use of *erôs* in the *Symposium* and the *Phaedrus* for the purpose of education. Like *Erôs,* Dionysus becomes civilized and socially useful through sophrosyne—a truly Greek solution,

[85] See Jaeger, *Paideia,* 2. 176–77.

reminiscent of the way the priests of Apollo had curbed and channeled the tumultuous energies of the Bacchae centuries earlier.

The Athenian stranger establishes the view of sophrosyne that is to obtain throughout the *Laws,* when he points out that no one can become *sôphrôn* without fighting against many pleasures and appetites, and conquering them by word, deed, and *technê,* in play and in earnest (647C).[86] The legislator must provide a test (*basanos*)[87] and a training ground (*meletê*) for sophrosyne. The drinking party, which offers the State a cheap, harmless, and quick method of discovering the nature and disposition of individual souls (650A–B), tests the capacity of the young for self-restraint when the inhibitions of sobriety are removed (649A–B) and (the most original of these ideas) safeguards *paideia* by enabling older men to renew their youth. The Chorus of Dionysus in the new state is to be composed of older men who, becoming more *sôphrones* as the years go by, stand in particular need of a medicine to relax the crabbedness of age and to remove the sense of shame that prevents them from singing in public (665B–D). The establishment of music—the hymns and chants that cast a spell on the soul and assert that the good life is the pleasant life (664B)—at the heart of the educational system of the *Laws* makes it essential for old as well as young to join the choruses and continue to enchant themselves throughout their lives. The organized drinking party accomplishes this end, and, for the purposes of the dialogue, the discussion of *methê* ("intoxication") introduces the first discussion of musical *paideia* and the standards by which it is to be judged.

In recognizing sophrosyne as the quality of older men, Plato strikes a note heard throughout the *Laws.* In Book III the Athenian stranger calls the discussion in which the three old men are engaged a *paidia presbytikê sôphrôn*—an "old man's sober game" (685A). Shortly thereafter he describes the dangers inherent in giving supreme power to the young as a neglect of due measure that leads to disorder, *hybris,* and injustice (691C); and he praises the Spartan lawgiver Lycurgus for blending with the bold force of the kings the *sôphrôn dynamis*—the sober power—of old age (the elders). The qualities of mixture and moderation (reminiscent of the *Philebus*) ensured the survival of the Spartan constitution when the contemporary governments of Argos and Messene failed because they had neglected the maxim of Hesiod, "The half is more than the whole" (690E). The prominence of Hesiodic and Aeschylean themes in the

---

[86] Cf. Antiphon the Sophist, Frag. 59 DK.

[87] On the history of the *basanos* in earlier Greek thought, see Wolfgang Schadewaldt, *Monolog und Selbstgespräch* (Berlin, 1926), 119 and nn. 1 and 2.

Laws is one of the striking proofs of Plato's increased respect for tradition
at this stage of his thinking, and it is even possible that the emphasis on
the wisdom of old age—the old age of the individual and of the culture
—helps to account for the importance given sophrosyne—the flower of
age, as Democritus calls it (Frag. 294 DK)—in this work of Plato's own
advancing years.

As the Athenian stranger explains the value of the duly regulated
symposium, he introduces most of the psychological principles on which
the *Laws* will be based: the description of pleasure and pain as the two
springs of human conduct (636D–E); the definition of *paideia* as proper
nurture, which leads the soul of the child to love that which he must
master perfectly in manhood—that is, *aretê* (643D); the picture of man
as a puppet in the hands of the gods, pulled by the golden strings
of reason and the steel cords of passion (645A, 804B);[88] the definition
of *aretê* itself as the complete agreement (*symphônia*) of reason and habit
with respect to pleasure and pain (653B); and the conception of man as
unique among living creatures in having a feeling for order which, in the
form of rhythm and harmony, is imposed on the instinctive movements
and noises of the young, so as to produce music and gymnastics (653D ff.,
664E ff.). Each of these principles provides a reason for Plato's emphasis
on sophrosyne—the virtue that controls pleasure and produces order
and harmony.

The discussion of the aim of legislation in Book I introduces a statement of far-reaching significance, which comes in connection with the first
of several classifications of goods. The stranger maintains that the purpose of the laws is to make those who use them happy by supplying two
categories of goods, Divine and human. The Divine goods are the
virtues, ranked in order as wisdom (*phronêsis*, not *sophia*, as in the canon
of *Rep.* 504A 4–6), sophrosyne joined with Mind (μετὰ νοῦ), justice, and
courage; while the human goods are health, beauty, strength, and
wealth (631B–C). Nature, which the legislator must follow, has ranked
the Divine goods before the human, and among the Divine goods the
leader is Mind (*Nous*, 631D, there equivalent to *phronêsis*). Mind must
join together all the laws enacted by the legislator and show that they
follow sophrosyne and justice (632C–D). The meaning of this brief pas-

---

[88] The picture of man as a mere puppet in the hands of the gods has contributed heavily
to the impression, recorded by many readers, of weariness and pessimism on the part
of Plato in the *Laws* (see, e.g., Gould, 79, 100), but its importance should not be exaggerated.
More characteristic of Plato in his last work is the reminder that man deserves honor because
his soul is in some fashion divine (e.g., 727A ff.).

sage unfolds only gradually, as we set beside it two other sections—one in Book IV, the other in Book IX. The first (714C), which takes up again the subject of *Republic* I—the false conception of justice as the interest of the stronger—criticizes all existing laws as class legislation, made in the interest of whatever party rules rather than for the good of the whole (715A–B). With a reminiscence of the myth of the *Statesman* (itself an echo of Hesiod),[89] Plato says that in the age of Cronus, God set daemons to rule the human race and provide mankind with peace, *aidôs, eunomia,* and justice. Such theocracy provides the best rule, and we should imitate it by obeying what is Divine in us, the law of Mind (714A). This passage marks the beginning of a new ideology, one that regards Law as an expression of Mind, which in turn is a manifestation of the Divine. This line of thought is not fulfilled until books IX and X, where Plato links Mind with Soul and thereby gives it a high status in accordance with his belief that Soul—with all its kin (892B; cf. 896D)— is prior to everything material and mechanical. But Law is a product of Mind, and individual laws are also νοῦ γεννήματα—"offspring of Mind." Hence the laws share in the divinity that belongs to both Mind and Soul.

Now we remember that in Book I the laws of Mind were to follow sophrosyne and justice, and in Book IV were to aim at the common good (*koinon*). Book IX reiterates that the *koinon* binds together the State (like the *koinônia* of the *Gorgias*), and that ordinary men need the law to guard them in putting the public interest before *pleonexia* and self-seeking (*idiopragia,* here antithetical to sophrosyne and justice [875A–D]). Hence we must conclude that sophrosyne and justice are the principles sought by Mind in its legislation (cf. 632C–D), which aims at the good of the whole; and these two principles are now themselves endowed with divinity and are based on the new concept of nature which Plato first hints at in Book I (631) and develops in Book X as the basis of his religion and cosmology.

Book X contains much else that bears on the same problem, notably the repeated association of sophrosyne with the Divine (e.g., 906A–B). In the constant battle between Good and Evil in the heavens, the gods and daemons are man's allies. We are damaged by injustice, *hybris,* and folly (*aphrosynê*), but we are saved by justice, sophrosyne, and wisdom,

---

[89] The children of Zeus and Themis are Peace, Justice, and Good Order—*Eirênê, Dikê,* and *Eunomia* (*Theog.* 901 ff.). *Aidôs* is another moral value important in archaic religious thought which Plato in the *Laws* does much to revive. See Jaeger, *Paideia,* 3. 122, and Friedrich Solmsen, "Hesiodic Motives in Plato," *Hésiode et son Influence* (Vandoeuvres-Genève, 1962), 191–93.

which dwell in the gods and to a small extent in us. Plato demonstrates the parallels among all levels of reality by saying that the evil of *pleonexia* ("overreaching") is called "disease" in physical bodies, "pestilence" in the seasons, and "injustice" in cities and constitutions.[90]

No passage concerned with sophrosyne in the *Laws* proved more influential in later philosophy than those that insisted on its likeness to the Divine. A memorable statement of the principle in the early books is contained in the exhortation to the immigrants who are to settle the new state—an exhortation that anticipates the style of a sermon and begins with the supposedly Orphic description of God as holding the beginning, the end, and the middle of all things (715E–716A). Justice (the Hesiodic *Dikê*) follows God, and in her train comes every man who wishes to be happy, behaving in a humble and orderly fashion. The approving reference to being humble (*tapeinos*), almost unique in classical thought, is followed by a denunciation of *hybris*, not only for its own sake, but because of the evil consequences it brings to the sinner, his house, and his country (an Aeschylean motive). Then comes the exhortation to sophrosyne (716C–D):

What conduct is dear to God and follows after Him? . . . God would be for us the measure of all things . . . and he who would be dear to Him must become like Him, so far as possible. According to the present reasoning, the *sôphrôn* among us is dear to God, for he is like Him, and the man who is not *sôphrôn* is not like Him, but different and unjust.[91]

This is the key text for the role of sophrosyne in the process of assimilation to God (ὁμοίωσις θεῷ), on which its value for the Platonists among the Church Fathers largely depends. Among all Platonic passages dealing with sophrosyne, it is second in influence only to the myth of the charioteer in the *Phaedrus*.

The type of education in music which is described chiefly in Book VII

---

[90] *Pleonexia* here is equivalent to *akolasia* in *Gorg.* 508A; cf. also *Symp.* 188A and *Rep.* 609A ff.

[91] This passage harks back to the discussion in the *Gorgias* of the relation of the *sôphrôn* person to the gods and to his fellow men (507B ff.): Without sophrosyne it is impossible to be dear to man or God, for *koinônia* ("fellowship, sharing") is essential to *philia*. The imitation of God, which is the aim of Plato's legislation, is actually a contradiction of those traditional warnings against likening oneself to God which were among the earliest themes of sophrosyne. The conflict between *hybris* and sophrosyne, which had provided tragedy with one of its most fruitful subjects, has now largely lost its meaning, but a different conception of sophrosyne has developed and is in the process of becoming an essential part of the Platonic notion of ὁμοίωσις θεῷ. This new conception results from the belief that God Himself is *sôphrôn*—an idea that scarcely occurs in tragedy. The problems inherent in this notion are among the favorite subjects of Hellenistic philosophy and the Church Fathers.

proceeds from the conviction that sophrosyne makes men like unto God. A new manifestation of Plato's lifelong concern with harmonizing the *sôphrôn* and the *andrikos* principles in the human soul appears in the identification of *sôphrôn* music with the feminine type, and of *andrikos* with the masculine (802D-E).[92] There is a corresponding treatment of sophrosyne and *andreia* in the dance (815D), culminating in the discussion of the drama, in which Plato insists on the complete identity of *eudaimonia* ("happiness") and *aretê* and maintains that the work of the legislator—that is, this very treatise—is the "truest tragedy," the only one that will be admitted to the ideal state (817B-D).[93]

A final proof that sophrosyne is the guardian of the State established in the *Laws* emerges when Plato bestows the name *Sôphronistêrion* (House of Correction) on the reformatory to which are to be condemned criminals guilty of impiety by reason of folly, without wickedness of character (908E). The institution is without precedent, and the name is apparently Plato's own invention; but it is impossible to say whether he was inspired by Aristophanes' famous *Phrontistêrion* or by the officer called *Sôphronistês* who supervised the morals of the Athenian ephebes.[94] The term implies that there is hope of a cure for these criminals, whom the members of the Nocturnal Council are to visit with the aim of bringing them to their senses (the literal meaning of *sôphronizein*); and the law provides that such a prisoner is to be released after a minimum of five years, ἐὰν δοκῇ σωφρονεῖν ("if he seems to be of sound mind"). The Nocturnal Council itself is charged with the safety of the constitution, and at the end of Book XII, Plato tells us that the supreme object

---

[92] The need for both *praotês* ("gentleness") and *orgê* ("passion") in the soul (another facet of the same question) is discussed in Book V, where Plato gives a different reason from the one offered in the *Republic* for fostering both instincts. There the guardian needed gentleness to deal with the citizens and passion or harshness to repulse enemies; here *praotês* is to be directed at wrong-doers within the State who are curable, while *orgê* is needed to cope with incurable sinners (731C-D). The discussion of music in Book VII employs an isolated forerunner to the later aesthetic use of the term *sôphrôn*. Plato speaks with approval of the σώφρων Μοῦσα καὶ τεταγμένη ("the sober and orderly Muse" [802C]) and opposes to this austere type of music the γλυκεῖα ("sentimental" or perhaps "vulgar") Muse. The moral implications of the word *sôphrôn* are still predominant, but later, purely aesthetic developments are foreshadowed.

[93] See Helmut Kuhn, *H.S.C.P.* 53 (1942), 37–88, especially 77.

[94] For epigraphical references to the *Sôphronistês* (the earliest of which is dated 334–333 B.C.), see Chap. VII, pp. 254–55. The first literary allusion occurs in Aristotle *Ath. Pol.* 42. The noun *sôphronistês* in the sense of "corrector, chastiser" becomes current in the late fifth century; but Wilamowitz (*Aristoteles und Athen* [Berlin, 1893], 1. 192) maintains that the office of *Sôphronistês* did not exist in the time of Plato and Isocrates and was instituted only under Lycurgus. Consult P. W., *"Sôphronistês"* (Oehler). Plato's originality in establishing the *Sôphronistêrion* is discussed by Glenn Morrow, *Plato's Cretan City* (Princeton, 1960), 491.

of their investigation is *aretê,* which they must understand in its plurality as four virtues and in its unity as one (963A–966B). This knowledge is specifically distinguished from the mastery of the popular virtues (*dêmosiae aretae* [968A]) and is, one may suppose, identical with the object of dialectic in the *Republic* (537B ff.). Thus the *Laws* ends, as it began, with a solemn assurance that the aim of legislation is to realize in the State the four cardinal virtues; and Plato's life work ends, as it began, with the affirmation that the well-being of the *polis* depends upon the guidance of the philosopher in whom *aretê* and *epistêmê* are united.[95]

---

[95] This conviction goes back, not just to the *Gorgias* and the *Republic,* but to the *Apology;* see, e.g., 29D ff.

VI

Philosophy after Plato

DURING the centuries after Plato, significant innovations in the concept of sophrosyne belong entirely to the philosophical schools. Neither literary nor popular usage in Hellenistic and Graeco-Roman times went beyond the connotations developed in the classical period; and although the whole range of these connotations was maintained here and there in literature, we note a greater emphasis on the motive of self-control, a corresponding decline in other meanings, and an especially marked change in the political implications of sophrosyne. Even among the philosophers, only a small number took a view of sophrosyne which was in any way original.[1] The Epicureans added almost nothing, while the Academy after Plato, the later Peripatetics, and the Neopythagoreans were of secondary importance. But Aristotle, the Stoics, and the Neoplatonists all developed nuances of sophrosyne that were in some way new and characteristic of their respective systems, and in so doing permanently affected the history of the concept. This chapter will concern itself chiefly with these three philosophical approaches and will deal only summarily with the other schools.

ARISTOTLE

Aristotle's principal contributions to the doctrine of sophrosyne are contained in the *Nicomachean Ethics* and result from three important trends in his thought: his distinction between intellectual and moral virtue, his introduction of the doctrine of the Mean into the discussion

[1] In philosophy, too, the meanings already developed in classical thought persisted. The originality we speak of consists, not in wholly new definitions, but in new analyses of the basis of moral virtue and in new perceptions about the relevance of sophrosyne to other philosophical concerns.

of moral virtue, and his tendency to limit and define as precisely as possible the scope of each individual virtue. His most obvious departure from Platonic precedent occurred when he abandoned the canon of four cardinal virtues, but the permanent importance of this step is diminished by Zeno's restoration of the tetrad as the basis of Stoic ethical theory.[2] The example of Plato and Zeno, rather than of Aristotle, prevailed among most philosophers and rhetoricians in the Hellenistic and the Roman periods.

Aristotle did not immediately repudiate the canon, for in the Fragments of his *Protrepticus* the four virtues still appear as a group. Iamblichus, quoting this early work, shows that all men prefer what is in agreement with their own character—the just man living justly, the *sôphrôn* in accordance with τὸ σωφρονεῖν, and so forth.[3] Furthermore, in a citation from Cicero's *Hortensius*, St. Augustine preserves Aristotle's praise of the divine bliss of pure contemplation and his description of the Isles of the Blessed, whose inhabitants, having no human desires, no longer need justice, courage, *temperantia*, or even prudence.[4] In Book X of the *Nicomachean Ethics*, where Aristotle pronounces the life of *theôria* superior to the active life, he again dismisses four moral virtues as unnecessary in the highest state of happiness. It is true that he now substitutes liberality (*eleutheriotês*) for prudence (which has in the meantime become an intellectual virtue) in order to fill out the tetrad, but the other three qualities of the active life remain the same as in Plato's canon: justice, courage, sophrosyne (1178b 10–18). The appearance of a group of four moral excellences in such a context seems to be a lingering reminiscence of the *Protrepticus*, since elsewhere in the *Ethics* Aristotle refuses to limit the virtues to so small a number.[5] He had several reasons for rejecting the Platonic canon: the most obvious was that he drew no such precise parallel between the soul and the State as that on which Plato had erected his ethical theory in the *Republic*; furthermore, he so narrowed the

---

[2] See especially *SVF* 1. 201.

[3] Frag. 52 Rose = Frag. 40 Düring. On the date of the *Protrepticus* and its place in Aristotle's work, see Düring, *Protrepticus,* 33–35, 281–86.

[4] Frg. 58 Rose (= C 43: 5 Düring) from Augustine *De Trin.* 14. 9. 12. See Düring, *Protrepticus,* 211–12, for a discussion of the source of this passage in Aristotle. Eloquence is added to the canon by Cicero, doubtless a concession to the orator Hortensius.

[5] In Book II he lists six virtues, to which are later added justice (Book V) and the two intellectual virtues, *phronêsis* and *sophia* (Book VI). Cf. *Rhet.* I. 9, where nine virtues are discussed. The four Platonic virtues also appear in *Pol.* 1323a 26–28, 1323b 33–36; while in 1334a 22 ff. Aristotle mentions *andreia, karteria, philosophia, sôphrosynê,* and *dikaiosynê,* and in 1259b 24–25, *sôphrosynê, andreia, dikaiosynê,* and "all the other dispositions of this kind." Cf. also *Top.* 107b 38–108a 2, and consult Jaeger, *Aristotle,* 84, 231.

scope of each virtue that to do justice to the whole range of human conduct he had to recognize a greater number of *aretae*. Moreover, Aristotle always tended to bring philosophical theory into greater proximity to ordinary Greek thought, and although the canon of cardinal virtues has deep roots in ethical and political tradition, popular thinking always recognized many other forms of *aretê* as well.

The abandonment of the canon is only the most striking of Aristotle's innovations in ethics where sophrosyne is concerned. Of greater permanent importance is the theory of the Mean. After the early period in which he agreed with Plato that moral action is based on knowledge of the Good and that an absolute measure could be found in God, Aristotle substituted for the absolute, mathematical mean of Plato's *Philebus* (and his own *Protrepticus* and *Eudemus*) a flexible mean, relative to the individual concerned. This doctrine comes into play in the *Ethics* when Aristotle treats the moral virtues, after first setting forth a theory of the soul which requires a distinction between intellectual and moral *aretae*. In the first book of the *Ethics* he distinguishes three faculties in the soul (1102b 13–25): the vegetative, the appetitive, and the rational; the appetitive is from one point of view irrational, from another rational. Moral (or ethical) virtue belongs to the second faculty and is acquired through habituation; intellectual (or dianoetic) virtue belongs to the rational soul and is instilled by teaching.[6] Aristotle names sophrosyne and liberality as examples of the category of moral virtue (1103a 6–7), which he defines as acting in the best way in relation to pleasures and pains (1104b 27–28),[7] and which he locates in a mean between excess and deficiency (1107a 2–6). No longer is there a connection between metaphysics and ethics—except at the very highest level. Practical morality can now exist apart from pure contemplation.

In Book II of the *Ethics* Aristotle explains the doctrine of the Mean in terms that reveal its growth out of medical parallels: for example, the application of physical analogies to the virtues, and the discussion of ex-

---

[6] Plato often distinguishes between different kinds of virtue; e.g., in *Phaedo* 69B he recognizes civic and philosophic virtue. But both categories include all four cardinal virtues—thus anticipating the Neoplatonic theory of *bathmoi*, stages or grades of excellence. In the *Republic* the recognition that *phronêsis* is the perfection of the element of *Nous* in the soul, while *andreia* and sophrosyne belong to the irrational faculties, is a step towards the distinction between dianoetic and moral virtue; but sophrosyne, like justice, is also a virtue of the entire soul, rational as well as irrational. D. A. Rees (*J.H.S.* 77 [1957], 112–18) cites tendencies in Plato to accept a bipartite soul. See also Werner Jaeger, *Scripta Minora* (Rome, 1960), 2. 491–509, and Rees, in Düring, *Aristotle and Plato*, 191–200.

[7] Cf. *Laws* 653B–C, where true *paideia* is said to consist in being educated from childhood to like and to dislike aright.

cess and defect in moral qualities.[8] The more remote background of the theory must not, however, be forgotten, even though the precise formulation found in the *Ethics* owes much to medical precedent. The traditional Greek feeling for moderation, which gave rise to the Delphic maxims, to the pre-Socratic search for proportion and balance in the physical world, to the myths of *hybris* in tragedy, to the ethical doctrines of Democritus, and finally to Plato's effort to apply to moral decisions an absolute *metron*—this feeling finds its most comprehensive expression in Aristotle's theory of the Mean. The fact that Aristotle uses the Mean to arrive at his own definition of sophrosyne should not blind us to the presence of sophrosyne, in a larger sense, as the very foundation of the Mean.[9]

The combination of these two theories—the theory of the soul in Book I, with the resulting distinction between intellectual and moral virtue, and the doctrine of the Mean in Book II—is responsible for most of what is new in the definitions of the virtues in books III and IV. The third major innovation in Aristotle's concept of sophrosyne—his drastic reduction of the scope of the virtue—is the result partly of the biologist's habit of separating each species from its neighbors and partly of the logician's desire to make his distinctions absolutely precise. There may also be a reaction against Plato's way of looking at these matters, his fondness for extending the scope of the cardinal virtues, breaking down the barriers, making the many into one. Aristotle's instinct was precisely the opposite, and in limiting sophrosyne to a more restricted field, he returned to the view current in Greek popular morality.

In the *Ethics* all the moral virtues are related to pleasure and pain,[10]

---

[8] See Jaeger, *op. cit.* (above, n. 6), 500 ff.

[9] Aristotle's theory of the Mean may have resulted from his effort to improve upon Plato's method of adjusting the appetites and desires according to the dictates of *phronêsis*. In the *Republic* each part of the soul has its own specific kind of desire, and it is the function of the rational part to determine to what extent each desire should be gratified. Sophrosyne causes all three parts to acquiesce in the judgments of *phronêsis*, courage sustains these judgments, and the resulting condition is justice. Aristotle evidently sought a more precise method of determining the extent to which appetites and passions should be satisfied. His method was to measure them against a qualitative mean; this method was suggested by Plato himself in the *Philebus*, when he, too, sought to improve upon the *Republic* and find a more reliable, because mathematically more exact, process of measuring moral phenomena. Aristotle's innovation consisted in rejecting the universal, unvarying, cosmic norm of the *Philebus* in favor of an adjustable standard, which he defends in the *Ethics* by reminding us that it is impossible to achieve absolute precision in morality. Cf. H. W. B. Joseph, *Philosophy* 9 (1934), 168–81.

[10] As in Plato's later ethics. The importance of pleasure and pain in moral virtue is another reason why Aristotle makes sophrosyne, the traditional mistress of the appetites, the basis of his ethical system.

but sophrosyne is particularly important where pleasure is concerned, for its specific function is to find the Mean with respect to *hêdonae* (1107b 4–6, 1117b 23–6). It is less closely concerned with pain, and only with the pain caused by the absence of excessive pleasure (1118b 28–33), not the pain that it is the function of courage to endure.[11] As the narrowing process continues, we find that sophrosyne is concerned only with the pleasures of the body, and only with those that man shares with the lower animals, namely taste and touch. But even taste plays a minor role; it is really the sense of touch that gives pleasure in eating and drinking.[12] As a result, sophrosyne is defined as a *mesotês* (a "mean state") concerned with three kinds of bodily pleasure: eating, drinking, and sexual intercourse (1118a 23–26). The vice of excess is wantonness (*akolasia*) with respect to the same pleasures, and the vice of defect is insufficient enjoyment of pleasures (*anaisthêsia*), a condition that Aristotle admits is very rare (1107b 6–7, 1119a 5–7).[13] He is careful to correct the current view that sophrosyne itself is abstinence from pleasure.[14] The *sôphrôn* person enjoys pleasure in moderation; he merely avoids the wrong pleasures and any pleasure in excess (1119a 11–20, 1153a 27–35). Book III concludes with a reminder that sophrosyne renders the appetitive element

[11] Thus sophrosyne is prevented from overlapping *andreia*.

[12] Aristotle mentions a glutton who wished for a throat longer than a crane's so as to prolong the sensation of touch as he ate (*Eth. Nic.* 1118a 32–1118b 1; cf. *Eth. Eud.* 1231a 16–17, where the name is given: Philoxenos, son of Eryxis). The famous climax of Catullus 13. 13–14 is a variation on the jokes made by comic poets about Philoxenus.

[13] Doubtless it was merely the pattern of the Mean which induced Aristotle to supply the unfamiliar vice of *anaisthêsia* to balance *akolasia*. *Anaisthêsia* is not to be confused with asceticism, which regards the pleasures of the body as good, but sacrifices them to secure a still higher good; nor with the Stoic ideal of *apatheia*, which would eliminate, rather than moderate, passion (not pleasure). When the pattern of the Mean was abandoned by later Peripatetics, *akolasia* alone survived as the normal antithesis to sophrosyne; see *Virtues and Vices* (1250a 21–23). Yet the vast prestige of Aristotle led from time to time to a revival of the *mesotês* pattern, with considerable variation in the extremes between which sophrosyne constituted the Mean. For example, in Philo Judaeus *Quod Deus* 34. 164, the extremes are extravagance and meanness; in Gregory of Nyssa *De Virg.* 283. 17 ff., excessive yielding to pleasure and utter hatred for marriage, or *De Paup. Amand. PG* 46. 457C, gluttony on the part of one's self and starvation of one's brother; in Philostratus *Vit. Apoll.* 29, arrogance and undue humility in a ruler; in Martin of Bracara *Formula* 8, p. 249 Barlow, *prodigalitas* and *sorditas*.

[14] This is but one of several proofs that even in the classical period a distorted view of sophrosyne was current (cf. Theseus' remark to his son in Euripides *Hipp.* 949–57). Aristotle's conception of sophrosyne is entirely humanistic; the *sôphrôn* man enjoys normal human pleasures and is not to be confused with the *hagnos*, who in his purity resembles God. On this distinction, consult R. A. Gauthier, O.P., and Jean Yves Jolif, O.P., *Aristote, L'Éthique à Nicomaque* (Paris, 1958), 2. 238 ff. We shall find that Patristic writers tend to identify sophrosyne with *hagneia* and thus produce a concept of sophrosyne that would have seemed inhuman to Aristotle.

obedient to reason and describes the *sôphrôn* man as having an appetite for what he may rightly desire, in the right way, and at the right time (ὧν δεῖ καὶ ὡς δεῖ καὶ ὅτε [1119b 17]).

Although the difference between the Mean and the two extremes is usually stated in quantitative terms, it is qualitative as well. Aristotle specifically observes that there can be no excess or deficiency in sophrosyne or courage considered in themselves—that is, rather than as mean points on a scale—because the excellence that in one sense is a mean is in another a *summum* (1107a 17–18, 20–27). Thus he refuted in advance, but did not succeed in forestalling, what was to be a major objection to Peripatetic ethical theory. The charge that Aristotelian moderation permitted a certain amount of indulgence in vice, while it set limits to the pursuit of virtue, proved a serious obstacle to understanding between Peripatetics and Stoics in Hellenistic and Roman times.[15]

The theory that moral virtue is a habit of choice (1106b 36) leads not only to a new emphasis on the agent's state of mind—as determining the moral quality of his act (1105a 28–33)—but also to the prominence of pleasure and pain as an index to the possession of virtue. As Plato in the *Laws* held that good moral character depends on the development of the correct habitual response to these two stimuli—the twin fountains of morality—so Aristotle maintains that the pleasure or pain attending a given action will reveal the moral character of the agent. A man is *sôphrôn*, for example, not because he abstains from excessive bodily pleasure, but because he enjoys abstaining (1104b 5–6).[16] He who does not enjoy such abstinence but is obliged to overcome base desires in order to obey the commands of reason is *enkratês* ("continent, self-controlled"). In Aristotelian terms, the charioteer of the *Phaedrus* who defeats the promptings of the bad horse after a sharp struggle is not *sôphrôn* but *enkratês*. Sophrosyne is the effortless, because habitual, harmony of

---

15 See Cicero *T.D.* 4. 17. 38 ff. for the Stoic view. Opposition to the Aristotelian *mesotês* is one manifestation of the perennial hostility to, and radical misunderstanding of, the whole concept of moderation, which ranges from the Aeschylean Prometheus' rejection of any limit to his wrath all the way to Auden's description of the Star of Bethlehem as most dreaded by the wise because it pronounces "the doom of orthodox sophrosyne" ("For the Time Being: A Christmas Oratorio," *The Collected Poetry of W. H. Auden* [New York, 1945], 428–29).

16 This statement has its origin in *Phil.* 12D, where Plato says that the *sôphrôn* man enjoys his sophrosyne. For a survey of the differences between Aristotle's and Plato's views of sophrosyne and a summary of what they have in common, see Franz Dirlmeier, *Aristoteles, Nikomachische Ethik* (Darmstadt, 1956), 348–50. Notable omissions by Aristotle include the absence of a close link between sophrosyne and *andreia, dikaiosynê, kosmiotês*, or *homonoia*. In common with Plato, Aristotle maintained the relation between sophrosyne and pleasure already established in the fifth century and the traditional hostility to wantonness. Dirlmeier calls attention to the likeness of Aristotelian sophrosyne to Plato's civic virtue, based on right opinion.

appetite and reason, the perfection of the healthy soul that needs no physician.

Book VII, which is entirely given over to a consideration of the problems of moral strength and weakness, degrees of volition, and the nature of pleasure, makes the first rigorous distinction in Greek thought between sophrosyne and *enkrateia*.[17] It begins with the observation that three kinds of moral character are to be avoided: vice (*kakia*), incontinence (*akrasia*), and brutishness (*thêriotês*).[18] This statement in itself reveals that *enkrateia* cannot be a virtue, since its antithesis, *akrasia*, is not identical with vice. *Akrasia* is that condition in which the appetite for excessive bodily pleasure overcomes the dictates of reason. Aristotle's discussion of it constitutes an attack on the Socratic paradox that no one does wrong knowingly, and lends support to the view expressed by Euripides in the *Medea* and the *Hippolytus* that the *logos* by itself is unable to guarantee right conduct.[19] Aristotle thus readmits to philosophical consideration the phenomenon of the *video meliora proboque, deteriora sequor*[20] and focuses attention upon the element of volition together with the forces that can overwhelm it. Both the *sôphrôn* and the wanton (*akolastos*) act deliberately, from choice, without a struggle; the *enkratês* and the *akratês* both struggle against their desires, victoriously in the first case, unsuccessfully in the second. The conduct of the first pair has become habitual; not so that of the second. If the relation among the four were reduced to a diagram, we should have a vertical line with the *sôphrôn*, the man of principle, at the top, and the *akolastos*, who has lost all principle, at the bottom. Above the *akolastos* is the *akratês* ("incontinent, morally weak"), who is mastered by passion to the point of abandoning principle, but not to the point of forgetting it. Above him, but below the *sôphrôn*, is the *enkratês*, who knows that the appetites are evil and so refuses to follow them; when his obedience to reason becomes habitual, so that he no longer needs to struggle, the *enkratês* will become *sôphrôn*.[21]

The analysis of these four qualities is the most detailed and pains-

---

[17] Plato had defined sophrosyne as ἐγκράτεια ἡδονῶν (*Rep.* 430E). Doubtless there was much discussion in the Academy and later in the Lyceum about the relation of sophrosyne to *enkrateia* as well as to *karteria* ("endurance"). One current opinion refuted by Aristotle held that the *sôphrôn* is always *enkratês* and *karterikos,* and that the converse also held true (*Eth. Nic.* 1145b 14–17).

[18] 1145a 15–17.

[19] *Me.* 1078–79, *Hipp.* 375 ff. In contrast to the belief of Socrates and Plato that *aretê* is *epistêmê,* Aristotle explicitly denies that the virtues are forms of *phronêsis*; he adds, however, that they are not without *phronêsis* (1144b 19–21).

[20] Cf. Ovid *Metam.* 7. 20–21.

[21] The relation between the *enkratês* and the *sôphrôn* was still a subject of controversy in later Peripatetic treatises; see *Magna Moralia* 1201a 10 ff. and 1203b 13 ff.

taking in the *Ethics*,[22] but elsewhere in the treatise Aristotle also distinguishes sophrosyne with great precision from such old companions as *aidôs*,[23] *andreia*,[24] *karteria*,[25] *dikaiosynê*,[26] and *phronêsis*.[27] Yet another virtue, which owes its prominence to Aristotle, is contrasted with sophrosyne in a passage of peculiar interest. *Megalopsychia* ("greatness of soul") is the virtue of the man who considers himself worthy of great things and who is worthy of them. He is contrasted with the man who is worthy of little and who admits it (1123b 5). The latter is *sôphrôn*. In this passage (as in 1125b 12–13, where it is said that the unambitious man may sometimes be praised as *metrios kai sôphrôn*), *sôphrôn* is clearly used in a much less technical sense than the one that Aristotle established in Book II. It now means "modest, unassuming" and recalls the traditional association of sophrosyne with self-knowledge—although in this case the great-souled man also knows himself. The distinction between the two

---

[22] Except for the distinction between *sophia* and *phronêsis* in Book VI.

[23] Not a virtue, but a *pathos* (1108a 30 ff.), a fear of disrepute, suitable only to the young (1128b 10–21).

[24] Another virtue of the irrational soul, but one that has to do with pains rather than pleasures (1115a 5 ff.).

[25] The endurance of pain, related to *andreia* as *enkrateia* is related to sophrosyne. Its opposite is softness (*malakia*), sometimes confused with *akolasia*, as in the case of persons too fond of amusement; but the *malakos* does not pursue pleasure to excess: he merely desires inactivity too much. See 1150a 31 ff.

[26] Aristotle illustrates the difference between sophrosyne and justice by considering two cases of adultery, one committed for profit, the other for pleasure. The first is unjust but not wanton; the second is wanton but not unjust (1130a 24–27).

[27] Sophrosyne is the preserver of *phronêsis* (1140b 11–12), a definition based on etymology (cf. Plato *Crat.* 411E); but *phronêsis* is essential to the very existence of sophrosyne, for only in conjunction with *phronêsis* can a natural disposition towards sophrosyne be developed into genuine moral virtue (1144b 1 ff.). One of the main differences between the earlier *Eudemian Ethics* and the *Nicomachean Ethics* (a difference that affects the view of sophrosyne in each treatise) is that in *Eth. Nic.* 1107a 1–2, where moral virtue is defined, the principle by which the Mean is determined is the standard of the *phronimos*, the possessor of *phronêsis* ("practical wisdom"). In *Eth. Eud.* 1227b 5–11 the definition of moral virtue omits any reference to *phronêsis*, which at this stage of Aristotle's development is still close to the Platonic contemplative wisdom (see Jaeger, *Aristotle*, 239 ff.). The treatment of sophrosyne in *Eth. Eud.*, although briefer than in *Eth. Nic.*, is in most respects similar. It is described as a state of character, *hexis* (1220b 18–20), as a *mesotês* between wantonness and insensibility (1221a 13–15), is shown in relation to bodily pleasures, and is not identical with *enkrateia* (1231b 2–4). *Eth. Eud.* includes an analysis of *akolasia* into its subdivisions comparable to the diaeresis of *hybris* in *Phaedr.* 238A–B (1231a 17–21). The diminished range of *hybris* in the fourth century is suggested by the substitution of *akolasia* as the normal antithesis of sophrosyne. Among the most important additions to the treatment of sophrosyne in *Eth. Nic.* are: the distinction between the goods of the body and of the soul, and between common and peculiar desires, the amplified description of the pleasures of lower animals, the more detailed description of the *sôphrôn* and the *akolastos*, the elaborate comparison of wantonness and cowardice, and the more detailed account of *akolasia* in children.

types is Aristotle's contribution to the recurrent theme of the opposing strains in the Greek character—a typically dry and unemotional comment, in contrast to Plato's elaborate expositions of the danger to the State when the two conflict.[28] Thomas Aquinas, in his commentary on the *Ethics,* seeks in Aristotle some recognition of the virtue of humility and, in default of anything more explicit, maintains that in this passage *sôphrôn* is equivalent to *humilis.*[29] In Christian morality, sophrosyne of this kind is a highly desirable form of excellence. To Aristotle, contrasting it with *megalopsychia,* such sophrosyne is no more admirable than *tapeinotês* ("lowliness") itself.

If Aristotle can use *sôphrôn* in a purely popular sense even in the *Ethics,* it is not surprising that in the *Politics* and the *Rhetoric* the word often carries traditional connotations. In the *Politics* sophrosyne may mean the opposite of *hybris* in the *êthos* of a State (1334a 25–28) and must therefore be equated with *kosmiotês* or *metriotês* in the language of contemporary oratory; but more often than not, it implies self-restraint of some kind (for example, 1335a 22, 1263b 9 ff., 1267a 10), and this brand of sophrosyne is predicated of the State as well as of the individual, for Aristotle points out that courage, justice, *phronêsis,* and sophrosyne have the same meaning in both contexts (1323b 33–36).

One of the questions considered in the *Politics* is whether virtue is the same for the ruler and the ruled. This problem is part of the larger question of who can possess moral virtue. In the *Ethics* Aristotle excludes the lower animals, to whom sophrosyne can be ascribed only metaphorically (1149b 30–34), and also the gods—how absurd to praise them for not having evil desires (1178b 15–16)—leaving moral virtue the prerogative of human kind.[30] It remained to consider whether certain types of human beings—slaves, women, and children—who belong to the category of the ruled could possess sophrosyne and, if so, whether their virtue was identical with the sophrosyne of the ruler. In the *Politics* the problem is solved, quite Platonically, by a reference to the nature of the soul, which, like the State, contains a ruling and a subject element,

---

[28] Cf. *An. Post.* 97b 15, where the three exemplars of *megalopsychia* are Alcibiades, Achilles, and Ajax, all noted for their lack of sophrosyne.

[29] See Gauthier, 456. The passage in the Commentary of St. Thomas Aquinas is II. 2.

[30] Cf. *De Gen. Anim.* 717b 27, on sophrosyne in animals, and see *Eth. Nic.* 1145a 15–17, for the contrast between *aretê* and *thêriotês.* The moral virtues or their approximations in animals became a topic of some interest in later antiquity (see Plutarch *Mor.* 988 f. on sophrosyne in animals). Through the *Physiologus* the subject achieved wide currency in the Middle Ages. The association of the elephant, the camel, the dove, the ermine, the tortoise, and the unicorn with various aspects of sophrosyne or *temperantia* is important for the iconography of this virtue in the Middle Ages and the Renaissance.

each with its proper virtue. The various parts of the soul are present to different individuals in various ways. The ruler must possess intellectual and moral virtue completely; the others should have whatever is appropriate to their respective natural conditions. Hence sophrosyne is not identical for men and for women, or for master and slave. The slave needs just enough of the virtue to prevent him from doing his work badly because of wantonness (*akolasia* [1260a 36]). In this context sophrosyne obviously refers to control of the appetites. In connection with women its meaning is a little more comprehensive. For the ruler—and for a man —sophrosyne is conducive to command. For one who is ruled—and for a woman—it is conducive to obedience (1260a 20–24; 1277b 17 ff.). This view of feminine *aretê* aligns Aristotle with most of the Greeks (except Socrates and Plato) and recalls especially the attitude of Sophocles' Ajax toward Tecmessa.[31]

A second question concerned with sophrosyne in the *Politics* is the effect of good fortune on the individual and the State. Aristotle holds that men have the same *telos* individually and collectively; therefore the State needs the same virtues as the individual. Courage and hardiness are necessary for the active life; love of wisdom is necessary for times of leisure; and sophrosyne and justice are needed in both seasons, but especially in time of peace (1334a 22–25). It is disgraceful for a State to be brave and successful in time of war and yet behave slavishly in peacetime.[32] They have great need of sophrosyne and justice who are considered prosperous and enjoy all the blessings. Since the sophrosyne of the *Ethics* could not be applied literally to the State, its meaning in this passage is broader and more traditional: "modesty." Aristotle also tends to maintain the broader significance of the word in his discussions of Plato's political theories, as when he objects to the statement in the *Laws* that the amount of property belonging to the State should be large enough for the citizens

---

[31] In *Eth. Nic.* 1117b 31–32 Aristotle denies that *akolasia* is a term applicable to those who gossip too much, but in the context of the *Politics* he reverts to the tradition that feminine sophrosyne includes silence; cf. 1277b 17–24. Plutarch (*Concerning Talkativeness* 11) refers to gossip as *akrasia* or *akolasia* and says that a woman lacks sophrosyne in so far as she fails to hold her tongue. In his vocabulary, talkativeness is *polypragmosynê*, now reduced to a narrow scope.

[32] That war usually compels men to be moderate and just, while good fortune and leisure breed *hybris*, is a commonplace familiar in rhetoric and oratory from the time of Thrasymachus and is rooted deep in Hellenic thought. Cf. Hesiod *Erg.* 314–16 on *aidôs* and *tharsos*; Aeschylus and Herodotus on *koros, hybris,* and *atê*; Lysias *On the Cripple* 18; Isocrates *Areop.* 1–5. Both Andocides and Isocrates apply this commonplace to the State, as do the Roman historians (e.g., Sallust *Jugurtha* 41. 1). The opposite view—held by realists like Euripides and Thucydides—is less often encountered.

to live in a *sôphrôn* manner. Aristotle prefers "a *sôphrôn* and liberal manner," for without liberality, sophrosyne may degenerate into hardship (1265a 33–34); this formula (ἐλευθερίως ἅμα καὶ σωφρόνως) is the one he actually uses in his own ideal constitution when he discusses the amount of territory that should be included in the State (1326b 31–32).[33] *Sôphronôs* in this context means "moderately," "modestly," or even "frugally."

Nowhere in Aristotle's discussion of the constitutional government that he thinks closest to the ideal is there a mention of sophrosyne, although the very essence of this constitution is moderation in every aspect of its existence.[34] Recalling that *aretê* is a *mesotês*, Aristotle praises the *mesos bios* as best for the State and the individual (1295a 39 ff.); he describes the middle class (the *mesoi*) as most ready to obey reason, least inclined to seek or shun office, and best in achieving friendliness and a sense of common purpose (1295b 23); and he concludes his eulogy of the middle way by quoting Phocylides' wish to be midmost in the State (Frag. 12 Diehl [3]). Yet, like Solon and Thucydides, he entirely omits the word sophrosyne from his vocabulary of moderation. He does indeed remark that sophrosyne is not characteristic of tyranny or of the worst form of democracy (1319 b 27 ff.), but he means only that licentiousness (*anarchia*) prevails in both these constitutions because they allow slaves, women, and children—the classes that should be ruled—to live as they please.[35] For Aristotle sophrosyne never means "moderation in government" nor does it ever have an organic relation to the State.[36] As the *Rhetoric* reveals, it is hard for Aristotle to conceive of sophrosyne as a social virtue. In the *Ethics,* to be sure, when he argues that contemplation is the highest activity because it is self-sufficient, he points out that the just, *sôphrôn,* and brave man requires others towards whom, or with

[33] See the comment of Glenn Morrow (in Düring, *Aristotle and Plato,* 154–55) that Aristotle's fondness for the virtue of *eleutheriotês* ("liberality"), which does not appear in Plato's table, constitutes a real difference between the two men. It might be added that Plato's enthusiasm for sophrosyne and Aristotle's comparative lack of interest represent another difference. Cf. also *Pol.* 1333a 30–36, 1338b 9–38. In his criticism of the community of wives (*Pol.* 1263b 8–14) Aristotle gives sophrosyne the same meaning as in *Eth. Nic.* See also *Pol.* 1236b 7–14.

[34] Ross, 259, suggests that Aristotle has in mind the Constitution of the Five Thousand, which Thucydides also admired.

[35] The tyrant himself and his supporters are advised to practice sophrosyne in bodily enjoyment (1314b 23–24), so as to avoid arousing public resentment.

[36] An application of the idea of sophrosyne, without the word, occurs when Aristotle describes the Greeks as a mean between the northern barbarians and the Asiatics, combining the spiritedness of the first with the intellect of the second (*Pol.* 1295a 34 ff., 1327b 16 ff.).

whom, he can practice these virtues (1178a 9 ff.); but this statement is inspired by the need to distinguish *theôria* from the moral virtues. The *Magna Moralia,* representing a later generation in the Peripatos, reflects Aristotle's usual view accurately enough in the observation that the *sôphrôn* man is such αὐτὸς καθ᾽ ἑαυτόν—"in and by himself" (1193b 14–15).

Both the *Ethics* and the *Politics* are deeply concerned with the problem of moral education, which was in the Greek tradition always the responsibility of the lawmaker. In both works Aristotle relies on the traditional triad of nature, habituation, and teaching (*physis, ethos,* and *logos,* in *Pol.* 1332a 39–40; *physis, ethos,* and *didachê* in *Eth. Nic.* 1179b 20–21). The contrast between natural capacity for a virtue and its fulfillment, through habituation and the addition of *phronêsis,* is illustrated by Aristotle's distinction between the adjectives *sôphronikos* and *sôphrôn* (*Eth. Nic.* 1144b 1 ff.): the former indicates potentiality; the latter, fulfillment. The special importance of sophrosyne in the process of education becomes clear with the assertion that unruly passion is the chief obstacle to learning—because it deafens us to the appeal of reason (*Eth. Nic.* 1179b 13 ff. and 26 ff.). Hence the control of passion—sophrosyne—is the necessary basis for all training in moral virtue. Since the young find it unpleasant to live in a *sôphrôn* and hardy fashion, Aristotle believes that their upbringing should be regulated by law; for once sophrosyne and *karteria* have become habitual, they will cease to be painful (*Eth. Nic.* 1179b 34).[37]

The discussions of sophrosyne in the *Rhetoric* are geared to a special purpose and are less technical, philosophically speaking, than those in the *Ethics* and *Politics;* although in another sense, of course, they are highly technical. They comprise the earliest extant consideration of the role of sophrosyne in rhetoric,[38] and they recognize the usefulness of this quality to epideictic oratory and ethical persuasion. In the *Rhetoric,* as in the *Ethics,* Aristotle refuses to limit the *aretae* to the Platonic canon and lists no fewer than nine virtues in all. The very definition of *aretê* in the *Rhetoric* (1366a 36–39) is noticeably less precise than that in the *Ethics:* virtue is a faculty, *dynamis* (specifically denied in the *Ethics*

---

[37] See 1180a 4 ff. for the need to regulate adult conduct by law. Other suggestions about education to instil sophrosyne include exploiting the moral effects of music (*Pol.* 1338b 4–8, 1340a 18–b 19, 1341b 32–1342a 4, 1342b 12–33). See Chap. V, n. 43, for Aristotle's disagreement with Plato on what constitutes *sôphrôn* music.

[38] The *Rhetorica ad Alexandrum* does not mention sophrosyne, although the spurious final chapter includes it with the other three cardinal virtues among the goods of the soul (1. 2, p. 104 Spengel-Hammer).

1106a 6–10); the element of choice is ignored, as is the standard of the Mean. In fact, the only aspect of virtue significant for the orator is its usefulness to society. *Aretê* is therefore defined as a faculty of conferring benefits, and the greatest virtues are those that are most useful to others. Plato had regarded sophrosyne as no less a social virtue than justice itself, and even when he was most inclined to treat it as a virtue of the individual (as in some parts of the *Laws*), he still regarded it as affecting the State in various ways; to Aristotle, however, sophrosyne is the most personal of the virtues and therefore the most difficult to praise in terms of social utility. His solution is to define it as the virtue that disposes men in regard to the pleasures of the body as the law commands (1366b 13–15), but even so he rates it below justice, courage, and liberality. In the *Topics*, however, where he is not bound to consider the effect on an audience, he values sophrosyne above courage, as being always useful, while courage is only occasionally needed (117a 36).

The second discussion of sophrosyne in the *Rhetoric* arises from the analysis of character according to several categories, including age and fortune (1388b 31 ff.). The young lack self-control in regard to sensual pleasures: all their mistakes result from excess and from neglecting the maxim of Chilon, *Mêden agan* (1389b 2–7).[39] The character of the old is just the opposite: their appetites are weak, and they appear *sôphronikoi* (1390a 14–15),[40] but in truth their desires have slackened and they are mastered by love of gain. Aristotle concludes that whereas the young are brave but lack sophrosyne, the old are *sôphrones* but cowardly. Men in their prime enjoy a mean state of character, combining courage with sophrosyne (1390b 3–4).[41] The discussion of the effect of good birth, wealth, and power on human conduct agrees with the corresponding passage in the *Politics* and finds that the rich tend towards *hybris,* and the poor, weak, and unfortunate towards the opposite condition (1390b 32–1391a 19). Both topics—the characteristics of the various times of life and the effects of good and bad fortune—were used in connection with sophrosyne in Attic oratory as early as the fifth century; Aristotle merely reduces a well-established tradition to a system. The

---

[39] Cf. Frag. 3 Rose, from the dialogue *On Philosophy*, which discusses other proverbs of the Seven, including *Gnôthi sauton.*

[40] Note the distinction between *sôphronikos* and *sôphrôn*, and cf. *Eth. Nic.* 1179b 32–34 and *Top.* 117a 32, where Aristotle says that the young have the greatest need, but the smallest inclination, for sophrosyne.

[41] Theophrastus did not include the *sôphrôn* man among his *Characters,* but Aristotle's description of him in the *Rhetoric* gives a fair idea of what such a character sketch might have included.

first of these topics remained static, but the second was destined for further development in the Hellenistic era, when everything connected with *tychê* ("fortune") received the most serious attention. In the classical period it had generally been agreed that *eutychia* leads to *hybris,* bad fortune to sophrosyne. In the succeeding era there was a shift of emphasis. Bad fortune was ever in man's thoughts, and the aim of all the philosophical schools was to provide an armor against it. We shall find again and again that sophrosyne came to be looked upon as a part of this defensive equipment—the *aequus animus* of Horace. The philosophical development of this *topos* belongs not to Aristotle but to the Hellenistic philosophers, especially Epicurus.[42]

Both early and late in his career—in the *Metaphysics* and the *Ethics*— Aristotle shows keen interest in the Platonic goal of assimilation to God, although he does not use the actual phrase ὁμοίωσις θεῷ. For Plato, as we have seen, the practice of sophrosyne was one of the ways of becoming like God, but Aristotle cannot ascribe any moral virtue to the Divine, whose activity is pure contemplation. In man, therefore, the godlike element is *Nous* ("reason"), and it is the activity of *Nous,* not the practice of sophrosyne, justice, or courage, that enables him to share the life of God. This contradiction between Plato and Aristotle was not resolved until Plotinus suggested a way in which the moral virtues (regarded as purifications), while admittedly confined to humanity, could yet be used as stages on the road to union with the Divine mind. Since metaphysics and ethics are so distantly related in Aristotle, his version of the doctrine of ὁμοίωσις θεῷ is relevant to sophrosyne at only one point, and here the effect of his new attitude is to undermine an ancient wing of the fortress of sophrosyne.

In the morality of the archaic period, the doctrine of sophrosyne had manifested itself in the proverb "Think mortal thoughts," an idea closely allied with the Delphic maxims, the sayings of the Seven Wise Men, and other admonitions to avoid excess and preserve due measure. Both in its gnomic formulations and in the myths of *hybris* with which the lyric and the tragic poets dramatized the idea, "Think mortal thoughts" involved a recognition of the boundaries that separate man from the gods. When discussing moral virtue, Aristotle upholds the value of measure (*mesotês,* the *metron*) and praises the philosophical content of the Delphic proverb, *Gnôthi sauton,* but when it comes to the intellectual virtues, he breaks sharply with tradition. Guided by his conception of what likeness to God must involve, he denies that man should think

[42] See below, p. 213, and cf. Lucretius 5. 1118 ff.

mortal thoughts and even attacks by name Simonides, who, like Pindar, often employed this theme. Aristotle maintains that man should make himself immortal, so far as possible: that is, he should exercise to the greatest possible extent the faculty of reason which is the Divine element in man.[43] Although he does not refer to sophrosyne in either of the passages in which he recommends that man "become immortal so far as he can" (ἐφ᾽ ὅσον ἐνδέχεται ἀθανατίζειν) they actually mark a moment of crisis in the history of this virtue. To deny that man must think mortal thoughts is to set aside the whole complex of ideas connected with *hybris* and sophrosyne which had dominated Greek morality for centuries. Now begins an entirely new orientation of man in the universe—an orientation that helps prepare for Christianity's ultimate acceptance of Aristotelian theology, since Christianity promises man a destiny so exalted as to justify him in thinking immortal thoughts. That sophrosyne could still play a part in the process by which man makes himself immortal and godlike, in spite of Aristotle's exclusively intellectual approach to the problem, is the result, first, of Plotinus' method of reconciling the Platonic and Aristotelian views and, then, of the great flowering of the whole concept of ὁμοίωσις θεῷ in the thinking of certain Greek Fathers of the Church.[44]

EPICURUS

In separating ethics from metaphysics to a perceptible degree and in completely divorcing ethics from physics, Aristotle set an example that later philosophers (with the important exception of the Stoics) were content in the main to follow. The physics of Epicurus was in any case purely mechanistic and would have offered the virtues no such support as Plato and the Stoa found in cosmology. Epicurus is of all the Hellenistic philosophers—save the Cyrenaics—least significant for the history of sophrosyne. His concept of its function coincides with popular usage, and he assigns it only a secondary role in attaining happiness. While his hedonism is more refined than that of the Cyrenaics,[45] Epicurus nevertheless maintains that pleasure is the beginning and the end of the happy life (Diogenes Laertius 10. 128), the standard by which to judge what to choose and to avoid (D. L. 10. 34; cf. 129). Because his conception of pleasure is not positive enjoyment—the kinetic *hêdonê* of Aristippus

[43] Aristotle's phrase ἀθανατίζειν ἐφ᾽ ὅσον, etc. (*Eth. Nic.* 1177b 33, cf. *Met.* A 2, 982b 30 ff.) recalls, not the key passage in *Theaet.* 176B, but *Tim.* 90B. For the whole history of the concept, consult Merki.

[44] See Chap. IX.

[45] Yet he regards the pleasure of the stomach as the root of all good (409 Usener).

—but freedom from pain and distress (*ataraxia*), Epicurus concedes a certain value to the moral virtues as being necessary to achieve tranquillity. In the *Letter to Menoecus* he says that *ataraxia* results from sober reasoning,[46] which investigates the causes of choice and avoidance and drives out opinions that upset the soul. *Phronêsis* is therefore the greatest good, and from it spring the other virtues (D. L. 10. 131–32). *Phronêsis* teaches that the life of pleasure and the life of virtue are inseparable (D. L. 10. 132). The maxims of Epicurus urge men to be content with little, to limit their desires and thus to outwit fortune; and he was himself famous for his moderation and even abstinence.[47] But virtue, to him, is only the means; pleasure is the goal. Hence the popular embodiment of Epicureanism in the picture described by both Cicero and Seneca: Pleasure surrounded by her slaves, the virtues.[48]

Cicero observes that Epicurus seldom mentioned the names of wisdom, courage, justice, and temperance (*De Finibus* 2. 16. 51); but since, according to Diogenes Laertius (10. 28), he wrote a treatise *On Justice and the Other Virtues,* the likelihood is that he at least recognized the Platonic canon. The value of sophrosyne for Epicurus resides in its connection with the hedonistic calculus, and here he was evidently influenced by Plato's discussions of this subject in the *Philebus* and the *Laws.* The classification of desires according to whether or not they are natural and necessary is a fundamental device in Epicurean ethics. Plutarch, noting the Epicurean limitation of desires, defines sophrosyne as a certain shortening or regulation of the appetites, which does away with alien and excessive desires and imposes moderation and opportuneness on those that are necessary (459 Usener). Cicero further explains the Epicurean attitude when he says that this school seeks *temperantia* because it brings peace and soothes the mind with a certain harmony (*Fin.* 1. 14. 47). He describes the function of *temperantia,* in terms related to the definition current in the Old Stoa, as that which bids us obey reason in choice and aversion. Reason alone is not enough. One may make the proper judgment and yet give way to passion, deceived by pleasures that are neither great nor necessary. *Temperantia* is essential, therefore, to preserve the judgments of reason, so that we will avoid

---

[46] Not *sôphrôn* but νήφων.

[47] Even the Christian Fathers sometimes admit this: see Gregory of Nazianzus *P.G.* 37. 773 ff.

[48] Cicero *Fin.* 2. 21. 61; Seneca *Benef.* 4. 2. 1; cf. Augustine *C.D.* 5. 20. Cicero denies that the Epicurean conception of *temperantia* can be the true one, for no one can at once praise *temperantia* and regard pleasure as the Good (*Fin.* 3. 32. 118–19).

certain pleasures and even endure certain pains, in order to secure the ultimate preponderance of pleasure.

Two points are noteworthy here. One is Cicero's definition of *temperantia* in an etymological sense appropriate to the word sophrosyne, but not to its Latin equivalents.[49] More important is his statement of the special function of sophrosyne according to Hellenistic philosophy: to defend the judgments of reason against the assaults of passion. Aristotle's rejection of the Socratic equation of *aretê* with *epistêmê* had given immense support to the common-sense assumption that something more than reason is needed to produce right conduct. Sophrosyne seemed to many an obvious choice for this "something." Out of the recognition of this function grew the tendency to connect sophrosyne with conversion (*epistrophê*) from Evil to Good, an idea of which there is as yet no trace in Epicurean philosophy, but which was to develop in the ethics of Plotinus and to pass from Neoplatonism to St. Augustine.

It was observed in connection with the *Rhetoric* of Aristotle that in the Hellenistic age sophrosyne enters into a particularly close relation with *tychê* ("fortune"); this is evident in Epicurean doctrine. Hellenistic popular theology makes *Tychê* a goddess, and even those who did not worship at her shrine endeavored, through the philosophical systems that promised *ataraxia* ("tranquillity"), *apatheia* ("impassivity"), and *autarkeia* ("independence") to immunize themselves against her blows. An increasingly important function of sophrosyne was to make the soul impervious to bad fortune. A Fragment of Philodemus shows that the Epicureans specifically assigned this task to sophrosyne: it describes the *sôphrôn* man as one who is not disturbed by the blows of fortune but is prepared by his modest life to meet whatever comes.[50]

THE STOICS

Far more dynamic than the Epicurean school, which seldom deviated in ethics from the doctrines of the founder,[51] is the Stoa with its vigor-

49 Cf. Plato *Crat.* 411E, Aristotle *Eth. Nic.* 1140b 11–12, Chrysippus *SVF* 3. 274, 275. *Temperantia,* which Cicero made the most familiar, although not the sole equivalent, suggests a connection with either time or the action of mixing.

50 Book IX, *Concerning Evils.* Cf. Lucretius 5. 1118 ff. on the folly of avarice and ambition (*vivere parce aequo animo*) and Horace *Odes* 2. 3. 1–3 (*Aequam memento . . . servare mentem . . . temperatam*). For a Stoic version of this commonplace, see Seneca *Ep.* 85. 114, where the fickleness of fortune and the shortness of life are considered an inducement to practice *temperantia.*

51 Hence the absence of development in ethical doctrine and the unscientific acceptance of popular connotations for the words *sôphrôn* and sophrosyne. See, e.g., Metrodorus, Frag. 36 Körte on the duties of a *sôphrôn* wife.

ous, continuing debate on a number of topics connected with the nature and function of sophrosyne. Probably the most far-reaching decision of Zeno and the Old Stoa was to reinstate the Platonic group of four primary virtues, thus guaranteeing the survival of the tetrad in later philosophy. The Stoic theory of a unitary soul implied a unitary *aretê*, and this in fact is what Zeno himself taught, postulating a generic excellence of which the particular virtues were manifestations. If a plurality of virtues was to be admitted, as it was by Chrysippus, the second founder of the school, nothing in the Stoic psychology demanded the limitation of these virtues to four. One of the innovations of Chrysippus indeed was to multiply the virtues far beyond four—"stirring up a swarm," as Plutarch said.[52] Yet even Chrysippus was careful to maintain the primacy of Plato's canon and to subordinate all the other virtues to them as aspects (*eidê*). Zeno accepted the Socratic doctrine that *aretê* is knowledge—*phronêsis*, however ("practical wisdom"), rather than *epistêmê*—but sought to combine this position with a materialistic physics derived ultimately from Heraclitus. This combination led to the apparent contradiction among some writings of the Old Stoa: those that regard virtue as knowledge, and those that make it a tension of the physical *substratum* of the soul. Like the Epicureans, the Stoics regarded the soul as composed of the same stuff as the rest of the universe, and explained its operations in purely physical terms. To account for moral virtue, they had recourse to the phenomenon of tension (*tonos*), which according to its strength or weakness gave rise to virtue or its opposite. Rejecting the Platonic theory of parts of the soul, the Stoics distinguished functions, the most important of which were performed by the ruling element (*hêgemonikon;* Latin *principatus*), usually located in the head.[53] The virtues were traced to a proper tension of the *hêgemonikon.*

In addition to being materialistic, the Old Stoa was also committed to rationalism, even to the point of connecting the passions with the rational soul (the *hêgemonikon*), instead of assigning them to some irrational faculty, as did the Academic and Peripatetic systems. The Stoics vacillated between the theory that passion is the result of a false judgment (*SVF* 1. 209) and the even more rationalistic theory that passion is itself a false judgment (*SVF* 1. 208),[54] but they always insisted on the need for sophrosyne to prevent that domination by the impulses

[52] *SVF* 3. 255.   [53] *SVF* 1. 143.

[54] E.g., avarice is a mistaken supposition that money is good; wantonness, a mistaken assumption that pleasure is good.

(πλεονασμὸς ὁρμῶν) which allows passion to get out of control. As in the Epicurean ideal of *ataraxia*, so with the Stoic *apatheia*, sophrosyne is of all the virtues the one most immediately associated with achieving the *summum bonum*. It differs from the Peripatetic sophrosyne in that it has nothing to do with moderation. Whereas Aristotle required only that the appetites be moderated, the Stoics demanded that passion be extirpated. The difference between *metriopatheia* and *apatheia* became a major obstacle to a synthesis of Peripatetic and Stoic systems in later times.[55]

Moral virtue enjoyed a position of supreme importance in the Old Stoa. Like their Cynic predecessors, the Stoics adopted as their *telos* or *summum bonum* life in accordance with nature, which was identified with life in accordance with virtue (*SVF* 1. 179). Virtuous activity constituted what the Old Stoa called *katorthôma*: everything that the wise man (*sophos, spoudaios*) does in accordance with right reason (*SVF* 3. 501). Since in its earliest stages the Stoa made no essential distinction between intellectual and moral virtue (all *aretae* being aspects of *phronêsis*, or all *aretae* being themselves *epistêmae*), sophrosyne was not assigned to a secondary position, as it was in the Peripatos. The cosmic approach to ethics—the belief in a centralized, teleological universe, every part of which contributes to the perfection of the whole—restored the Platonic justification for the practice of the virtues.[56] The very notion of a cosmic harmony—of order, *philia* ("friendliness"), and *syndesmos* ("unification") coordinating all parts of the universe—recalls the Platonic conception of sophrosyne as *symphônia*, but the early Stoics do not connect the two ideas, because according to their new definition sophrosyne has nothing to do with order.[57]

The definition of sophrosyne ascribed to Zeno is a genuine innovation, reflecting, it is true, earlier ways of looking at the virtue (especially ways attributed to Socrates), but emphasizing an aspect that had never before been so prominent. Zeno defined *aretê* generically as wisdom (*phronêsis*) and explained the other three principal virtues (*prôtae aretae* is the Stoic term) as manifestations of *phronêsis* in different situations:

[55] The Stoics themselves distinguished *apatheia* ("absence of passion") from total lack of feeling, which was considered a fault; but to outsiders the distinction seemed a mere quibble. According to Zeno, passion (*pathos*) is ὁρμὴ πλεονάζουσα (*SVF* 1. 205); Cicero's translation: *appetitus vehementior* (*T.D.* 4. 47). Pleonasmos transformed *hormê* into *pathos*, and it was only the *pleonasmos*, not the *hormê*, that the Stoics sought to extirpate.

[56] See Solmsen, *Theology*, 183, and Joseph Moreau, *L'Âme du Monde de Platon aux Stoiciens* (Paris, 1939), 187.

[57] For Panaetius' revival of the conception of sophrosyne as order, see pp. 222 ff.

justice in rendering others their due, *andreia* in enduring, and sophrosyne in choosing (ἐν αἱρετέοις [*SVF* 1. 201]).[58] The opposite of sophrosyne
is still called *akolasia* (*SVF* 1. 190). Where Plato in the *Republic* had
derived the group of four virtues from his analysis of the soul and the
functions of its parts, Zeno, believing the soul to be unitary, taught the
unity of virtue and justified the various aspects of virtue in terms of
their respective activities. The only organic relation between the Stoic
psychology and the Stoic theory of virtue lies in the doctrine of tension,
which explains how virtue can exist, but not what its function is or how
it should be defined.[59] Sophrosyne, in the definition of Zeno, loses
contact with the ideas of measure, limit, and self-restraint which had
been its province in classical times, but gains authority over the whole
area of moral choice and avoidance.

Zeno's successors in the Old Stoa attempted to clarify what was
obscure in his doctrine, especially the role of *phronêsis*, about which
there was some doubt whether it was only the generic virtue or also a
specific virtue.[60] Cleanthes of Assos made the application of the theory
of *tonos* to virtue explicit by stating that when the tension of the *pneuma*
was sufficiently strong to perform the work of the soul, the result was
strength and power (*ischys* and *kratos*), which, being employed in various
circumstances, took the names of the specific virtues (*SVF* 1. 563).[61]
Elsewhere, however, Cleanthes held that *aretê* can be taught, implying
agreement with Zeno's view of *aretê* as *phronêsis* (*SVF* 1. 567). To remove

[58] The conception of *aretê* as knowledge goes back, of course, to Socrates (Aristotle *Eth. Nic.* 1145b 23 ff.). Both Plato and Aristotle connect moral virtue with choice among pleasures. The Aristotelian antecedents are particularly close; e.g., *Eth. Nic.* 1113a 1–b 2, a fundamental discussion of choice (*proairesis*), which does not mention sophrosyne but concludes with a description of how pleasure deceives the *polloi* into thinking that the pleasant is the good: "They choose the pleasant as if it were the good, and they flee the painful as if it were evil." Cf. *Eth. Nic.* 1116a 11 ff., where *andreia* is defined in terms of choice and avoidance, and 1172b 19, on Eudoxus' theory that pleasure is the Good. See also Plato *Gorg.* 507B (the *sôphrôn* person pursues and avoids ἃ δεῖ), and *Rep.* 618B–C (on the power of *phronêsis* to discern and choose the Good), and Xenophon *Mem.* 3. 9. 4, which equates *sophia* and sophrosyne and ascribes to them the power to choose the Good and to avoid Evil.

[59] Zeno's reputation for sophrosyne is attested by Diogenes Laertius (7. 10. 11). An Athenian decree honored him for exhorting the young to practice *aretê* and sophrosyne, and he was presented with a crown testifying to his own possession of these qualities. His epitaph by Antipater of Sidon says that Zeno scaled heaven by the path of *saophrosynê* (D. L. 7. 29).

[60] Plutarch *Sto. Rep.* 7.

[61] Cleanthes wrote four books on Heraclitus (D. L. 7. 174) and applied the term *pneuma* to the fire that was the physical base of the Stoic cosmos. His concept of Zeus, expressed in his hymn, *SVF* 1. 537, includes the notion of harmony imposed upon the cosmos by God, who understands how to adjust what is excessive and put in order the disorderly (κοσμεῖν τἄκοσμα). Sophrosyne is no part of the vocabulary used to describe this process.

the obscurity of Zeno's arrangement of the four virtues, Cleanthes listed
the manifestations of "strength and power" as *enkrateia, andreia, dikaiosynê,*
and sophrosyne (*SVF* 1. 563). How strong the tradition of four cardinal
virtues must already have been, we may infer from the addition of
a fourth excellence to *andreia, dikaiosynê,* and sophrosyne, when *phronêsis*
was pre-empted as the generic virtue. The elevation of *enkrateia* (usually
a virtue subordinate to sophrosyne) to a position of equality may reflect
the influence of the Cynics or Xenophon.[62] The duplication that might
have resulted from the appearance of both *enkrateia* and sophrosyne in
the canon is avoided by defining sophrosyne as the exercise of *tonos* in
matters of choice, and *enkrateia* as *tonos* in endurance. *Enkrateia* thus
approaches *andreia* (*tonos* in resistance) more closely than it does
sophrosyne.[63]

Ariston of Chios upheld Zeno's theory of the unity of the virtues,
which he distinguished only according to the category of relation. He
taught that *aretê* is one and receives various names only from the variety
of objects with which it deals (just as a knife is one and the same, no
matter what material it cuts). Two accounts exist of the nature of this
unitary *aretê:* Plutarch's report that Ariston believed *aretê* to be health
(*SVF* 1. 375), and Galen's that it was knowledge of Good and Evil
(*SVF* 1. 374). The two accounts reflect the two aspects of Stoic virtue,
the practical and the theoretical. *Aretê* requires knowledge, and this
knowledge must be put into practice, with a resulting condition
of the soul which Ariston, like Plato and the Greeks in general, compared to health. Galen's report further explains that the soul, when
not active in good things or bad, is *sophia* and *epistemê,* but in the
actions of daily life it adopts the names *phronêsis,* sophrosyne, justice
and courage. Ariston found Aristotle's distinction between *sophia*
and *phronêsis* useful as a means of settling the problem of the generic
and the specific. When *phronêsis* resumes its place in the canon with the
three other specific virtues, *enkrateia* drops out. The definition of
sophrosyne that Galen credits to Ariston is the same as that of Zeno
and Cleanthes: when it is necessary to choose the Good and avoid Evil,
aretê is named sophrosyne (*SVF* 1. 374). Plutarch, however, ascribes to
Ariston another definition, which includes several traditional elements
and restores to sophrosyne what Zeno had taken away: when virtue

[62] See Adolf Dryoff, *Die Ethik der alten Stoa* (Berlin, 1897), 70 ff.

[63] Sophrosyne and *andreia* more than once overlapped in Stoic ethics of a later period. Cf.
the definition of *phobos* in Stobaeus 2. 7. 10, p. 90, 11; and consult Gred Ibscher, *Der Begriff
des Sittlichen in der Pflichtenlehre des Panaitios* (Munich, 1934), 71–73.

regulates desire and defines the moderate and the seasonable in pleasures, it is called sophrosyne (*SVF* 1. 375). Again, the two definitions are not contradictory but complementary.

Chrysippus reacted against the unitarianism of Zeno, Cleanthes, and Ariston and maintained that the virtues differ according to the category of essence, not merely that of relation. Instead of saying, with Zeno, that virtue is knowledge (*phronêsis*), he taught (*SVF* 3. 95, 264) that all four primary virtues are *epistêmae* ("wisdom") and *technae* ("science"). The individual virtues, all stemming from the generic *epistêmê*, each add something peculiar and thus produce four different *aretae*. They are inseparable because they share common principles, and each has as its secondary object the accomplishment of the objects of other three.[64] Thus the primary object of *phronêsis* is to contemplate and put into practice what must be done, but it also aims to contemplate and put into practice what must be awarded to others (justice), what must be chosen or avoided (sophrosyne), and what must be endured (*andreia* [*SVF* 3. 280]). Two accounts of Chrysippus' definition of sophrosyne survive, and as in the case of Ariston, they reflect the theoretical and the practical aspects of Stoic ethical theory. One says that sophrosyne is knowledge (*epistêmê*) of things to be chosen and avoided or neither; its antithesis, *akolasia*, is the ignorance of these matters (*SVF* 3. 262, 266). In the other definition its chief function is to render the impulses steady and to achieve theoretical knowledge of them, while its secondary function is to contemplate and put into practice the objects of the other three virtues (*SVF* 3. 280).[65] By recognizing that the impulses (*hormae*) constitute the field of activity of sophrosyne (as in *SVF* 3. 264), Chrysippus provided a bridge between the Old Stoa and Panaetius, whose interpretation of sophrosyne rejected the intellectual rigor of Zeno and based itself on a consideration of the role of the impulses and appetites in moral action.

Most of the doctrine about the virtues in the Old Stoa comes from Chrysippus. He taught, for example, that virtue is the same wherever found (a consequence of the closely integrated system that applied the same laws to microcosm and macrocosm).[66] *Aretê* is identical for gods and

---

[64] The inseparability of the virtues is a doctrine of Plato, but the technical term *antakolouthia* is linked with the Stoics and may have originated with Chrysippus; see *SVF* 3. 295.

[65] Chrysippus (*SVF* 3. 274, 275) defines sophrosyne as a *hexis* in choice and avoidance which preserves the judgments of reason (*phronêsis*). Cf. Cicero *T.D.* 4. 9. 22: *temperantia* quiets the appetites and causes them to obey right reason, and it preserves the *considerata iudicis mentis*.

[66] According to Cicero (*Nat. Deor.* 2. 14. 37), Chrysippus based his ethical system on the study and imitation of the universe.

mortals, for men and women (*SVF* 3. 245, 246, 253, 254)—a return to the Socratic position which Aristotle had rejected. It is significant that moral virtue is again ascribed to the divine. The theme of ὁμοίωσις θεῷ does not appear in the Old Stoa, but when it emerges in the next period, the moral virtues are once more a bond between man and God.[67]

Chrysippus was also responsible for the proliferation of virtues in the Old Stoa, a result perhaps of his effort to systematize what was traditional in popular morality. To each of the four *prôtae aretae* he subordinated a group of secondary virtues (*SVF* 3. 264). In the case of sophrosyne these are *eutaxia* ("proper arrangement"), *kosmiotês* ("orderliness"), *aidêmosynê* ("sense of shame"), and *enkrateia* ("self-restraint"). As the common element in all four secondary virtues suggests, sophrosyne is thought of as controlling or ordering the impulses. The doxographers preserve several Stoic lists of the primary and secondary virtues. Andronicus adds (*SVF* 3. 272) to the family of sophrosyne *austêria* ("severity"), *euteleia* ("frugality"), *litotês* ("simplicity"), and *autarkeia* ("independence"), all of which bring within the orbit of sophrosyne the qualities that had comprised the *telos* of the Cynics and were destined to supply one of the major themes of Stoic popular philosophy. Another list, preserved by Clement of Alexandria, adds *eulabeia* (an "avoidance that accords with reason" [*SVF* 3. 275]); this virtue, which is not a traditional attribute of sophrosyne, is the only one that recalls Zeno's definition of sophrosyne as *phronêsis* in matters of choice. It is noticeable that all these secondary virtues are divorced from any political or social background and have to do only with the ethics of the individual. This divorce is marked in the case of *kosmiotês* and *eutaxia,* which are defined respectively as "knowledge of decorous and indecorous movements" and "knowledge of when and in what order to perform actions" (*SVF* 3. 264). The position that both had formerly enjoyed in the city-state is entirely forgotten.[68]

After the time of Chrysippus, Zeno's definition of sophrosyne gave way before the more traditional motive of control of the passions, largely because of the increasing prominence of the *hormae* ("impulses, appetites") in later Stoic psychology. Chrysippus himself maintained in all its rigor the Stoic principle that passion is a mistaken judgment of the ruling element in the soul (the *hêgemonikon*), which when overmastered by the power of impulse is swept along to something contrary to reason.

[67] See Merki, 8.

[68] The persistent alliance of *kosmiotês* and sophrosyne finds a new expression in a Stoic doctrine recorded by Diogenes Laertius (7. 100). The four species of the beautiful (*kalon*) are the just, the brave, the orderly (*kosmion*), and the wise. The traditional association of order with beauty accounts for the substitution of *kosmion* for *sôphron,* when *kalon* replaces *agathon* as the generic excellence.

Passion is defined as wicked and wanton reason (*ponêros kai akolastos logos*), arising from a perverse judgment that has gained force and power (*SVF* 3. 459). As the use of the key word *akolastos* suggests, even this view of passion gives great weight to sophrosyne, and it was a Stoic proverb that intemperance is the mother of passion (Cicero, *Tusculan Disputations* 4. 9. 22). When the interest of the Stoics shifted from reason to the impulses, still further attention was given to sophrosyne. The inconsistency of Chrysippus' psychology was criticized, especially by Poseidonius,[69] and Chrysippus was in fact the last influential Stoic to insist on such extreme rationalism. With Panaetius passions ceased to be judgments and became once again only the results of judgments, while Poseidonius restored them to the irrational faculties of the soul.[70] The shift of emphasis was related, not only to the influence of Plato and Aristotle on Panaetius and Poseidonius, but also perhaps to the concern of these philosophers for the "probationer"—the man who was not a sage but was trying to become one—and to their desire to adapt Stoic ethics to the practical requirements of Rome.

Panaetius brought numerous and radical innovations to his concept of sophrosyne. Some of them amount virtually to a conflation of Stoic doctrine with that of Aristotle or the Academy. For example, contrary to the belief of the Old Stoa that all *aretê* is *epistêmê*, Panaetius distinguished theoretical from practical virtue (D. L. 7. 92) and located sophrosyne in the second of these categories.[71] If we accept at face value a statement of Aulus Gellius (12. 5), he also rejected Stoic *apatheia*. Cicero seems to support this view when he speaks in *De Officiis* (2. 5. 18) of the need to control (*cohibere*) the passions, instead of extirpating them.[72] Moreover, Panaetius denied that *aretê* by itself is sufficient for happiness; he recognized the need for health, affluence, and strength as well as virtue (D. L. 7. 128). A prominent feature of his ethics is the doctrine of the *prepon* (*decorum*, "what is fitting"); this principle was borrowed from the Peripatetics, but from their rhetoric, rather than their ethics. The *prepon*, as we shall see, is inseparable from Panaetius'

---

[69] See Galen, *De Placitis Hippocratis et Platonis;* ed. Kühn (Leipzig, 1823), IV. 377–79; ed. Müller (Leipzig, 1874), 348, 5–350, 13. Consult Gerhard Nebel, *Hermes* 74 (1939), 36–40.

[70] Panaetius, *ap.* Cicero, *T.D.* 2. 47–48; and see Max Pohlenz, *Antikes Führertum* (Leipzig, 1934), 55 ff.; Poseidonius, *ap.* Galen, *op. cit.:* Kühn V. 429; Müller 405, 5–14.

[71] It does not, however, follow that the theoretical virtue of Panaetius is identical with Aristotle's *aretê dianoêtikê*. For sophrosyne as a practical virtue, see Cicero *Off.* 1. 5. 17 and *Part. Or.* 76–78.

[72] But in *Off.* 1. 20. 69, he implies, contrary to Gellius, that Panaetius agreed with the Old Stoa on this subject. Van Straaten (183) questions whether Gellius understood the true meaning of *apatheia*.

concept of sophrosyne. His single most important innovation—the one that dominated his entire approach to morality—was his view that the appetites or impulses are the source of virtue (*Off.* 1. 4. 11–14). While he accepted the traditional psychology of the Old Stoa—the principle that passion is a *perturbatio animi* (*Off.* 1. 20. 69; cf. 2. 5. 18)—he altered its emphasis: where Zeno and Chrysippus had stressed the responsibility of the *logos* in attaining *aretê,* Panaetius considered the impulses of greater significance. For the life according to reason, he in effect substituted the life according to feeling or instinct and defined the virtues in terms of the basic impulses of human nature, rather than as knowledge or wisdom applied to different situations. Each virtue arises in a desire natural to man: wisdom in the desire for truth, justice in the social instinct, courage in the desire to protect the family and achieve independence, and sophrosyne in the feeling for order, propriety, and moderation (*Off.* 1. 4. 11–14).

Furthermore, Panaetius assigned great importance to individual differences; herein lies another significant innovation, decisive for his conception of the *telos* or *summum bonum.* For the Old Stoa the *telos,* as we have observed, was life in accordance with nature (*SVF* 1. 179, 180–81),[73] which was always identified with life in accordance with virtue, and was equated with both happiness and the Good. Panaetius now required conformance, not only to nature in general (obtaining throughout the cosmos and including human nature), but, beyond this, to *natura propria nostra* (*Off.* 1. 30. 110–11), that nature peculiar to the individual.[74] The special qualities, even the special ambitions and circumstances, of a particular person determine what is morally good in his case. The *telos* therefore consists in life according to the appetites of one's own individual nature, as regulated and controlled by reason (*Off.* 1. 28. 101). From this doctrine follows inevitably the need for the *prepon.*

In rhetoric the *prepon* constitutes the fourth Peripatetic virtue of style.[75] Essentially æsthetic, it became, in the system of Panaetius, the external manifestation of what is morally good—in Greek, *kalon;* in Cicero's translation, *honestas* or *honestum* (*Off.* 1. 27. 94–95). *Honestum* and *decorum,* like health and beauty, their physical counterparts, can be distinguished only in theory, not in fact. In *De Officiis* the *prepon* or *decorum* is mentioned first in connection with the fourth division of virtue, which

---

[73] See Van Straaten (139–58) for a detailed exposition of the *telos*-doctrine of the Stoa and its development by Panaetius.

[74] Clem. Alex. *Strom.* 2. 21: ζῆν κατὰ τὰς δεδομένας ἡμῖν ἐκ φύσεως ἀφορμάς.

[75] See Johannes Stroux, *De Theophrasti Virtutibus Dicendi* (Leipzig, 1912).

is sophrosyne. Cicero says (1. 5. 17): "If we bring a certain amount of measure and order into the affairs of daily life, we shall preserve *honestas* and *decus*," and he postpones his discussion of *decorum* until he expounds the duties prescribed by sophrosyne. *Decorum*, we then learn, is twofold: there is *decorum generale*, found in moral goodness as a whole; and there is *decorum speciale*, which belongs to all the subdivisions of *honestum* but is especially manifest in the fourth. In this *decorum speciale* reside *moderatio* and *temperantia*, together with what Cicero calls a *species liberalis*, a gentlemanly appearance (1. 27. 96). The emphasis on outward appearance, which dictates many of the *officia* connected with the fourth virtue, is consistent with Panaetius' aesthetic approach to morality and with his ideal of the harmonious personality.

The relation of the two kinds of *prepon* or *decorum* to each other and the relation of the second to sophrosyne may be summarized briefly. *Decorum generale* belongs to every action that is morally good, that, in other words, arises from and is in harmony with one of the appetites of human nature, controlled by reason. Since, however, human nature possesses many appetites and impulses, differing with the individual concerned, it is necessary to adjust and harmonize them, so as to create order and beauty, what Plato called a *symphônia* in the soul. When such a harmony exists, *decorum speciale* is present; and since it is the function of sophrosyne to produce this order and equilibrium among the appetites, *decorum speciale* is inseparable from the fourth virtue.[76]

This conception of sophrosyne involves a complete departure from the definition established in the Old Stoa. Zeno's "*phronêsis* in matters of choice" has been replaced by the moral perfection of the basic human desire for order, measure, beauty, and harmony in deeds and words (*Off.* 1. 4. 14). The restraint of appetite is still a function of sophrosyne, as in traditional Greek morality (*Off.* 1. 28. 101, 1. 29. 102), but is now subordinated to the aesthetic function. The triumph of the latter is evident from the comparison between the beauty of a body whose parts are harmoniously arranged and the *decorum* that shines forth (*elucet in vita*) when *ordo, constantia,* and *moderatio* exist in every deed and word (*Off.* 1. 28. 98). One result of this æsthetic approach to sophrosyne is a new emphasis on what Cicero translates as *approbatio* ("approval").[77] Just as

[76] On *prepon* or *decorum*, see Van Straaten (160–63) and consult Lotte Labowsky, *Die Ethik des Panaitios* (Leipzig, 1934); Max Pohlenz, *op. cit.;* and Pohlenz, *To Prepon, Nach. Gött. Gesellsch.* (1933).

[77] Another result of the radical shift in the scope of sophrosyne is the transfer to *andreia* of certain functions that the Old Stoa had assigned to sophrosyne. See Gred Ibscher, *op. cit.,* 71–73, and Van Straaten, 180 ff.

physical beauty combined with harmony gives pleasure (*delectat*), so *decorum* wins approval—*movet approbationem* (*Off.* 1. 28. 98). Panaetius shows more concern for the outward aspects of *sôphrôn* behavior than had any previous philosopher. It is perhaps for this reason that *De Officiis* emphasizes *verecundia,* the virtue that causes us to avoid offending our fellow men. In *verecundia* (the sense of shame, decency, Greek αἰδημοσύνη) the essence of *decorum* is especially evident (*Off.* 1. 28. 99; cf. 1. 28. 100, where precisely the same statement is made about *temperantia*). Consequently, when the duties prescribed by sophrosyne are discussed, serious consideration is given to such matters as controlling the movements of the body, so as to achieve *verecundia* and *pulchritudo* (*Off.* 1. 35. 126–1. 41. 149), and avoiding the unpleasant physical appearance of those who are overcome by passion (1. 29. 102). That *verecundia* has deep roots in Roman ethical tradition no doubt strengthened its claim to a prominent place in the Romanized Stoic *êthos.*

The *officia* of sophrosyne (for which Cicero could find no single Latin rendering) reflect Panaetius' concern for individual differences. *Decorum* is attained only if we obey both the universal laws of nature and the special requirements of our own nature, including those imposed by chance (such as birth and wealth) and those that we ourselves have chosen (like the various professions). The concept of the Mean is also involved in the *officia* that produce *decorum.* Panaetius observes that appetite must be subjected to reason, neither running ahead nor lagging behind (*Off.* 1. 29. 102), and in connection with specific duties he often refers to the need for moderation. His ideal of outer and inward harmony leads him to prescribe a multitude of *officia* which will make *sôphrôn* behavior manifest to the observer; and in the performance of these *officia,* *mediocritas* or *moderatio* will often be the guide. It is in details such as the relevance of the Mean to the domestic arrangements of a gentleman (1. 39. 138 ff.) or to his outward appearance and dignity (1. 39. 141) that Panaetius expresses his fundamentally æsthetic approach to morality and reveals, without a doubt, the influence of the Roman ruling class, whose interest lay chiefly in the practical applications of philosophy.[78] These are the passages in which it is particularly difficult to distinguish between the principles of Panaetius and the interpretations supplied by Cicero.

[78] Doubtless it was as a concession to the demand for relaxation of the Old Stoic rigor that in the Middle Stoa the moral virtues became the concern of the *kathêkon* (Latin *officium*)— which is within the grasp of the probationer— rather than of the *katorthôma* ("right action"), which is possible only for the sage. This development is discussed by E. V. Arnold, *Roman Stoicism* (Cambridge, 1911), 301–2.

The status of sophrosyne in Panaetius' system depends in part on his strong feeling for measure and harmony; in part also on his belief that this excellence, like wisdom, has its origin in an instinct that is uniquely human. While courage and justice spring from desires common to the lower animals, even the basic appetites in which wisdom and sophrosyne originate are exclusively human. Only man has foresight, memory, and the power of reasoning, from which wisdom is developed; and only man has a sense of the beauty and harmony in the visible world, by analogy with which nature and reason develop in him a feeling for beauty and harmony in thought and action (*Off.* 1. 4. 14). Sophrosyne becomes, for Panaetius, the psychological prerequisite for any virtuous activity; as such it achieves *de facto* primacy among the cardinal virtues and provides a new basis for the Stoic doctrine of *antakolouthia* (the "inseparability of the virtues" [1. 27. 94–96, 28. 100]). Since, however, its primacy is largely dependent on the doctrine of the *prepon*, which later Stoics virtually ignored, it was not sustained in the philosophy of Poseidonius or the other successors of Panaetius in the Middle Stoa.

At the close of Book I of *De Officiis* (1. 45. 159), where he arranges the duties in order of precedence, with justice or *communitas* at the top, Cicero refers to a collection made by Poseidonius of deeds so infamous that the wise man would not commit them even to save his country. In such cases alone would sophrosyne (here called *moderatio modestiaque*) take precedence over the *officia* of justice. This collection is lost, and the Fragments of Poseidonius' ethical treatises cast only indirect light on his view of sophrosyne. Unlike Panaetius, Poseidonius had no special feeling, æsthetic or otherwise, that would lead him to give sophrosyne a preferred status above the other virtues,[79] and in his system it became once more merely the excellence of the appetitive element in the soul. It is perhaps significant that the word sophrosyne does not occur in the extant Fragments.[80]

The position of sophrosyne in the system of Poseidonius may nevertheless be determined through a study of his conception of the soul, the passions, and the *summum bonum*. In contrast to Zeno, Chrysippus, and Panaetius, he maintained that the ruling element in the soul (the *hêgemonikon* or *principale*) is not purely rational but includes irrational

---

[79] Nebel (*loc. cit.*, 57) suggests that Poseidonius' special feeling is for *Tapferkeit (andreia)*. A. D. Nock (*J.R.S.* 49 [1959], 2) comments that the word for Poseidonius is enthusiasm, as *decorum* was for Panaetius.

[80] I am indebted to Professor Ludwig Edelstein for the opportunity to consult his unpublished edition of the Fragments of Poseidonius.

faculties as well.[81] Only the excellence of the rational element (*logikon*) constitutes *epistêmê* (or *phronêsis*) and can be imparted by teaching. The *aretae* of the irrational faculties (described in Platonic terms as *thymoeides* and *epithymêtikon*) are themselves irrational (*alogoi*) and are acquired through habituation.[82] There is every reason to believe that Poseidonius considered the excellence of the appetitive soul to be sophrosyne, although no extant fragment actually attests to this belief.[83] Its function would be to render the *epithymêtikon* obedient to the rational element in the soul— a most essential function, since according to Poseidonius the cause of the passions lies in the failure of the irrational faculties to obey the rational.[84] More original is another statement, preserved by Galen, who reports that Poseidonius held the cause of the passions to be "not following in every respect the *daimôn* in oneself which is akin to and has a nature like that of the *daimôn* which governs the entire cosmos, but following instead the inferior and bestial element." [85] This statement in turn should be taken in conjunction with the doctrine about the *telos* ascribed to Poseidonius by Clement of Alexandria: "To live in contemplation of the truth and order [*taxis*] of the cosmos and to fashion oneself in so far as possible according to this, being led astray in no respect by the irrational element of the soul." [86]

From these three doctrines arose the special importance of sophrosyne

[81] These are called δυνάμεις, rather than μέρη or εἴδη, as in Plato. Galen, *op. cit.*: Kühn V. 454-55, Müller 432, 9-15; and Seneca *Ep.* 92. 8. See Karl Reinhardt, "Poseidonius," P. W., Vol. 22. 1, pp. 739 ff., on Poseidonius' theory of the soul and its faculties, and their relation to the passions.

[82] Galen, *op. cit.*: Kühn V. 466-68, 429, VII. 589; and Müller 444, 11-447, 4; 405. 5-14; 583. 15-584. 10. On methods of imparting virtue, see Seneca *Ep.* 95. 65-66; note especially the use of *exempla* for teaching *temperantia*. Poseidonius refers to the Platonic myth of the charioteer and his two horses in discussing the different ways of instilling rational and irrational virtue (Galen, *op. cit.*: Kühn V. 466-68, Müller 445, 15-446, 3 and 447, 1-3). On the consequences for education of Poseidonius' psychology, see Karl Reinhardt, *Poseidonius* (Munich, 1921), 313 ff.

[83] Reinhardt (P. W. 743), discussing the influence of Poseidonius on later Platonists, cites Albinus' definition of sophrosyne as the virtue of the *epithymêtikon* (*Didask.* 29, see below, n. 105). Poseidonius' principal contribution to the history of this virtue may be that he lent his authority to the interpretation of sophrosyne as the excellence of the appetitive element alone, rather than of the entire soul. As we shall find (n. 105), most of the philosophical schools of the Empire agree on this doctrine.

[84] Galen, *op. cit.*: Kühn IV. 377-79 and Müller 348, 5-350, 13. Cf. also Kühn V. 429 and Müller 405, 5-14. The passions are not judgments of the rational faculty of the soul, nor even consequences of such judgments, as the Old Stoa had taught, but arise in the irrational faculties. Virtue depends on the right understanding of the passions; consult Ludwig Edelstein, *A.J.P.* 57 (1936), 286-325, especially 305 ff.

[85] Galen, *op. cit.*: Kühn V. 469-76 and Müller 448, 11-456, 14.

[86] *Strom.* 2. 21. 129. 1-5 (II. 183, 10 Stählin).

for Poseidonius. If the passions—which are the cause of misery and un-happiness [87]—result from the failure of the soul to bring its irrational faculties into subservience to the rational, sophrosyne is essential for happiness and virtue—although for reasons entirely different from those that gave it value for Panaetius. If, moreover, the soul has for its purpose the imitation of the cosmic *daimôn*, whose special characteristics are truth and order, such imitation will reproduce these qualities in the soul. Although Poseidonius does not describe the cosmic order as *sôphrôn*, the way is open for a return to the Platonic conception of the imitation of God as a source of sophrosyne. The affinity between the *daimôn* in the soul and the *daimôn* in the cosmos—as a link between the human and the Divine—lends support to the doctrine of ὁμοίωσις θεῷ, which is in any case strengthened by the parallel of macrocosm and microcosm in the Stoic system.[88]

One way in which sophrosyne might be affected by this renewed emphasis on the contemplation of the heavens is suggested by a passage in the *Tusculan Disputations* (sometimes regarded as an echo of Posei-donius).[89] The Apolline maxim "Know thyself" is here interpreted in the light of such contemplation. The mind that meditates night and day upon the world order and realizes that it is itself *coniunctam cum divina mente* is filled with joy. When it perceives the bond that unites all things, and when it is fired with the desire to imitate the eternity of the Divine, it is filled with *tranquillitas animi*. From this contemplation come the *cognitio virtutis* and the flowering of all the *genera partesque virtutum* (5. 25. 70–71). "Know thyself" thus becomes part of the complex of ideas re-lating knowledge (*cognitio, gnôsis*) and the imitation of the Divine (ὁμοίωσις θεῷ) to virtue and happiness. Another echo of these ideas, in the *Moral Epistles* of Seneca, shows that the demand for ethical catharsis was not forgotten. Speaking of the kinship between man and God (*socii sumus eius et membra*), Seneca suggests that the *telos* of the soul is to return to the heavens, and he maintains that this return can be accomplished only by renouncing avarice and servitude to the body (*Ep.* 92. 30–31).[90]

Some practical applications of Poseidonius' concept of sophrosyne may be found in the Fragments of his historical work, which frequently com-ment on the virtues and vices of individuals or peoples. Athenaeus, for

---

[87] Galen, *op. cit.*: Kühn V. 469 and Müller 448, 11 ff.

[88] On this subject, see Werner Jaeger, *Scripta Minora* (Rome, 1960), 2. 469–81, and cf. Reinhardt, *Poseidonius* (Munich, 1921), 310.

[89] See, e.g., Merki, 8 ff., and consult Cicero *Nat. Deor.* 2. 153 for the connection among knowledge, contemplation, virtue, and happiness.

[90] Cf. Reinhardt, P. W., 757–58, and Annelise Modrze, *Philol.* 87 (1932), 300–31.

example, drawing upon Poseidonius, describes the sophrosyne of the early Romans and cities Scipio Africanus as an example. Since he praises the simplicity and frugality of Scipio, in contrast to the extravagance of Lucullus, who after his victory over Mithridates abandoned sophrosyne and introduced luxury (*tryphê*) to Rome (6. 105. 274 f.), it is clear that Poseidonius' conception of sophrosyne included moderation and restraint, even though it is impossible to prove that the actual word sophrosyne which appears here and in similar passages goes back to Poseidonius himself.[91]

A similar interpretation of the virtue prevails in the writings of the Later Stoa,[92] whose most notable representatives—Musonius Rufus,

[91] Other passages that reveal Poseidonius' concept of sophrosyne as it affects conduct include Athenaeus 5. 211E–215B (on the behavior of the Peripatetic philosopher Athenion) and Strabo 3. 2. 9 (a diatribe against gold and silver) and 7. 3. 2–7 (on the habits of the Mysians). The last passage, which comments on the relation of justice to sophrosyne, interprets sophrosyne in terms of *autarkeia* and *litotês* and compares extreme self-restraint to the Cynic way of life. For a variety of passages in Cicero, Plutarch, Diodorus, and others that may reflect the views of Poseidonius about sophrosyne and allied virtues in the State or in statesmen, consult Margaret Reesor, *The Political Theory of the Old and Middle Stoa* (New York, 1951), 35 ff. Two further beliefs about virtue ascribed to Poseidonius by Diogenes Laertius affect his view of sophrosyne. Like Panaetius, he denies that *aretê* alone suffices for happiness (on this problem, see Seneca *Ep.* 92 and the comments by Annelise Modrze, *loc. cit.*) and requires in addition health, affluence, and strength (D. L. 7. 128); and he recognizes four divisions of *aretê* (7. 92), probably the four cardinal virtues.

[92] Among the other representatives of the Middle Stoa, Hecato alone possesses some importance for sophrosyne, by reason of his emphasis on *enkrateia* as a virtue parallel to sophrosyne (related to it as *fortitudo* is related to *magnitudo animi*) and his contribution to the Stoic doctrine of theoretical and nontheoretical virtue. For the influence of Hecato on Cicero (especially in *Off.* III), on Seneca (in his lost *De Officiis*), and on Martin of Bracara (in various passages of his *Formula Vitae Honestae* where *continentia* is either added to *temperantia* or takes its place in the tetrad), see Heinz Gomoll, *Der stoische Philosoph Hecaton* (Leipzig, 1933), with the comments of Gauthier, 141 n. 2, 150 n. 1, 161 n. 2. The distinction between theoretical and nontheoretical virtue, ascribed to Hecato by Diogenes Laertius (7. 90), is referred to by Cicero *T.D.* 4. 30 (a discussion of *sanitas animi* and its relation to sophrosyne) and Stobaeus II. 62. 15 (on the distinction between *technae* or *epistêmae*—the cardinal virtues—and *dynameis*, which are beauty, health, and strength of soul). It is important to distinguish Hecato's use of the terms *epistêmê* and *dynamis* from that of Poseidonius: to Poseidonius theoretical virtue (*epistêmê*) is the perfection of the rational faculty of the soul—i.e., *phronêsis*. The virtues of the irrational faculties (*andreia* and sophrosyne) are *dynameis* (nontheoretical). To Hecato all four cardinal virtues are theoretical; the *dynameis* are the counterparts (*simulacra virtutum*) which appear in those whose virtue is not yet perfect. What the Middle Stoa tends to call theoretical and nontheoretical virtue is comparable to the distinction between perfect (*teleiae*) and imperfect (*euphyiae*) virtues found in the Middle Academy and among the later Platonists of the second century after Christ. The relevant passages in Cicero, Stobaeus, and Diogenes Laertius and the differences among members of the Middle Stoa on this doctrine are discussed by Robert Philippson, *Philol.* 85 (1930), 357–413; Dryoff, *op. cit.;* Arnold, *op. cit.,* 105; and Gomoll, 39 n. 1. August Schmekel (*Die Philosophie der mittleren Stoa* [Berlin, 1892], 290) denies that the Stobaeus passage derives from Hecato.

Seneca, Epictetus, and Marcus Aurelius—abandoned any pretence of an interest in the theoretical aspects of *aretê*. Without exception these philosophers were concerned with the practical applications of Stoic philosophy; as a result it is often hard to distinguish their Stoicism from the equally practical morality of Platonic or Cynic philosophers in the first centuries of the Empire. Stoics like Musonius and Epictetus, Platonists like Maximus of Tyre, Cynics like Dio of Prusa, even rhetors like Libanius and Themistius, preached essentially the same ethical doctrine. One of the concepts they share is the definition of sophrosyne as the restraint of the appetites.

Musonius will serve to exemplify the treatment of sophrosyne by these later Stoics; [93] although neither as harsh nor as extreme as some contemporary Cynics, he adopted the Cynic-Stoic approach to morality, with its emphasis on *ponos* ("labor") and *askêsis* ("discipline") in attaining virtue. Those traces of the theoretical approach to ethics that remain in Musonius' treatises are mere commonplaces and had no effect on his rules of behavior. He says, for example, that we philosophize with only a small part of the soul, the intellect (*dianoia* [XVI, p. 87 Hense]); yet to Musonius, as to most of his contemporaries, philosophy was not concerned primarily with the intellect. Philosophy was a matter of correct living—of being just, useful, *sôphrôn*, and good (III, p. 9; XVI, p. 87). When he says that virtue is both theoretical and practical (VI, p. 22), he means only that we must know what is right and do it. If forced to choose between *logos* and *êthos*, Musonius says, he would prefer the second, because it is better to *be* self-controlled and *sôphrôn* than to speak correctly about the virtues (V, p. 21).

Sophrosyne in such a context is bound to show affinities with the Cynic conception of the virtue; and in fact for Musonius it is closer to frugality (*euteleia*) and self-control (*enkrateia*) than to any other qualities, and manifests itself above all in a love of simplicity. The beginning and the climax of sophrosyne are found in self-control with respect to food and drink (XVIII A, p. 94). Frugality is to be preferred because it is more conducive to sophrosyne and more fitting for the good man (XVIII B, p. 104). This precept is applied, not only to food and drink, but also to shelter, adornment, and all other departments of human life.

Sophrosyne (together with the other qualities that conduce to simplicity) receives more frequent and prolonged praise from Musonius than

---

[93] Some contributions of Seneca to the history of sophrosyne will be considered in Chap. VIII.

do any of the other cardinal virtues.[94] It invariably appears as a private, individual excellence, never related to the State except as it is the duty of a ruler to provide his subjects with an example of sophrosyne. Even in this instance the virtue itself remains entirely personal. Thus in the Fragment *That Kings Should Be Philosophers* (VIII), Musonius exhorts the King of Syria to rise above pleasure and self-seeking, to love frugality (*euteleia*) and hate extravagance, to practice *aidôs*, rule his tongue, cultivate order (both *taxis* and *kosmos*), and demonstrate propriety in appearance and action (one of the rare allusions to the *prepon* after Panaetius).[95] Although the allusions to frugality or to *taxis* and *kosmos* may be reminiscent of certain Cynic-Stoic doctrines that constituted an important part of the political philosophy of the Hellenistic and Graeco-Roman eras (especially the philosophy of kingship),[96] most of the Fragment is a tissue of commonplaces, which had been handled and rehandled ever since the *Evagoras* of Isocrates and were destined to become the stock in trade of practitioners of the *basilikos logos* in the Second Sophistic.

[94] The strong emphasis on sophrosyne in all the popular philosophies of the imperial age reflects social conditions of the kind that also produced satire and diatribe and the denunciations of pagan luxury, greed, and sexual immorality by early Christian moralists. For a sketch of the pagan background—religious and philosophical, as well as social—against which the development of Christian asceticism, including sophrosyne, must be seen, consult A. D. Nock, *Early Gentile Christianity and its Hellenistic Background* (New York, 1964).

[95] Cf. also XVIII B, p. 104.

[96] The Stoic doctrines that the wise man, who surpasses his fellows in virtue, therefore has the right to rule over them, and that a world monarchy is justified because it corresponds to the cosmic reign of Zeus (or natural law) gave support to the ruler cult in the Hellenistic age and the Roman Empire. Sophrosyne is concerned in both doctrines, since this excellence is invariably required of the wise man (i.e., the ruler), and in its cosmic form it corresponds to the order that the wise man must create in his own soul. The Fragment of Musonius' advice to the king of Syria typifies Stoic references to sophrosyne in this context, since it takes up this virtue as one of the tetrad and shows how each in turn must be acquired through the study of philosophy. Musonius also refers to the theory that the king is "animate law" (*nomos empsychos*), but does not explain the implications of this phrase, which is usually linked with Neopythagorean theories of kingship (see pp. 235–36). To at least some Neopythagorean theorists, the virtue of a king is different from that of his subjects, but in Stoic writings no such distinction is made; nor does Musonius here seem to imply such a theory, unless it may be extracted from his remark that the king must be *sôphrôn* and σωφρονίζειν his subjects, so that he himself may rule σωφρόνως and they be ruled κοσμίως. There is nothing to support an interpretation that would make sophrosyne the virtue of the king and *kosmiotês* the excellence of his subjects, especially since the effect of sophrosyne on both parties is that they avoid wantonness (μηδέτεροι τρυφῶσι). Musonius concludes his discussion of the qualities allied with sophrosyne by saying that they make the ordinary man *semnos* and *sôphrôn* but render the king godlike and worthy of reverence. Here, too, the difference in the two grades of sophrosyne is one of degree, not of kind.

More peculiar to the Stoa, which was traditionally interested in feminine virtue as part of the doctrine that *aretê* is the same for all—men and women, human and Divine—are Musonius' two treatises entitled *Whether Women Should Study Philosophy* (III, IV) and the essay *On Sexual Indulgence* (XII). In all three, sophrosyne continues to denote the control of the appetites and passions, and it is clear that the primary function of philosophy is to instil this virtue. Since the gods give women the same faculties as men, including the impulse towards virtue, how is it right—Musonius asks—that they are denied the chance to study philosophy? All the qualities proper to a good woman may be learned from philosophy, and the first and most important of these is sophrosyne. Musonius analyzes the duties of a *sôphrôn* woman: to avoid unlawful loves and any kind of incontinence or appetite; to hate strife, extravagance, and ornamentation; to control anger and grief and every other passion (III, p. 10). All these actions are enjoined by philosophy, and all are equally necessary for men and women.[97]

In his discourse *On Sexual Indulgence* Musonius again treats the equality of the sexes, this time from a point of view that emphasizes their common moral responsibilities. He requires a single standard of sexual morality, denying to men any further indulgence of their appetites than is proper for women, and treating this rule as a precept of sophrosyne. It is just as incompatible with this virtue for a master to cohabit with a slave girl as for a mistress to do so with a male slave. The extent to which this precept was, if not practiced, at least preached by pagan moralists of the Empire is a sign of the common attack made by pagans and Christians on social and moral abuses of the day.[98]

[97] As III and IV reflect the traditional Stoic concern for the education of women (consult Dryoff, *op. cit.*, 311 ff.), so XII reflects the special interest of this school in "conjugal philosophy." See Bickel, 191 ff. The position of sophrosyne as the excellence proper to the married state seems to have been established in such treatises, which profoundly influenced both the thought and the vocabulary of Patristic writers on this subject. In IV, Musonius reiterates the identity of the virtues for men and women and enumerates the Stoic tetrad. A new reason for cultivating *andreia* appears in his statement that this virtue is necessary for a woman to protect her chastity (sophrosyne) in the face of threats and torture (IV, p. 15). This topic appears in Patristic writings in connection with the theme of the virgin martyr, who unites sophrosyne with *andreia*.

[98] Cf. Seneca *Ep.* 94. 26; Julian I. 46D; Plutarch *Mor.* 144B–145A. Epictetus and Marcus Aurelius say nothing novel about sophrosyne. Epictetus assumes that the wise man will restrain his appetites in his effort to attain freedom, and a great many of his precepts refer to self-discipline and its rewards. Sophrosyne is opposed to *akolasia* and allied to *enkrateia* (*Discourses* 3. 1. 8; 4. 9. 17–18 Schenkl). Epictetus' standards of sexual morality are less lofty than those of Musonius (he does not advocate a single standard), but he frequently condemns adultery and has much to say about the immorality of Roman matrons. His motto ἀνέχου καὶ ἀπέχου ("bear and forbear" [Frag. X]) suggests that endurance and self-restraint

One further consequence of the Stoic doctrine of the identity of virtue may be mentioned, since it leads Musonius to comment on the moral virtues manifested by God and incidentally reveals the way in which Stoics of the Empire interpreted the *telos* of the Old Stoa (life in accordance with nature) and accommodated it to the doctrine of the imitation of God. Musonius observes that man will live in accordance with nature when he realizes that his nature is to be virtuous. Man is an imitation of God (μίμημα θεοῦ), and we think of nothing in connection with the gods more than wisdom, justice, courage, and sophrosyne. God is *sôphrôn* in that he is not overcome by pleasure or self-seeking (*pleonexia*) and is superior to appetite and envy (XVII, p. 90). If man will imitate God in this respect (ὁμοίως ἔχειν), he will be truly happy.

OTHER PHILOSOPHICAL SCHOOLS

There is no need to catalogue the allusions to sophrosyne in the treatises produced by the Academy, the Middle Platonists, the Peripatetics, and the Neopythagoreans of the Hellenistic and Graeco-Roman periods, for they rarely achieve originality. Eclecticism is the mark of all these schools; not until the coming of Neoplatonism did sophrosyne undergo further significant development. It will suffice to note the chief tendencies of the other schools, as expressed by one or two of their more notable spokesmen.

The eclecticism of the Academy shortly after the death of Plato is already evident in the *Definitions* ascribed to Speusippus, the second head of the Academy. Sophrosyne is defined variously as a mean state of the soul in regard to natural pleasures and desires, as a harmony and order of the soul in respect to pleasures and fears, as an agreement in the soul with regard to ruling and being ruled, as doing one's own work (*autopragia*) according to nature, as a reasonable agreement of the soul concerning Good and Evil, and as a disposition according to which the possessor chooses and rejects what he ought.[99] The first of these

---

form the core of his ethical code. Marcus Aurelius also takes sophrosyne for granted as a virtue that should be sought (3. 2, 3. 6, 4. 49, 5. 12, 8. 1, 12. 27), but he does not speculate about its nature, and he accepts the current definition as restraint of appetite (3. 2) He himself is praised by Dio for his *sôphrôn* and *enkratês* rule of the soldiery (71. 3. 3) and by Herodian for his *sôphrôn bios* (1. 2. 4).

[99] Speusippus, Frag. 24 Mullach. Interest in sophrosyne and the other moral virtues remained strong in the generation just after Plato. Xenocrates wrote a treatise *On Sophrosyne*, and Diogenes Laertius tells an edifying story about his powers of persuasion. Polemo, who was *akolastos* in his youth, became drunk and broke into Xenocrates' lecture room when the philosopher was discussing sophrosyne. Polemo was inspired to become a student, adopted a life of austerity, and ultimately became head of the Academy (4. 12, 16).

definitions has Aristotelian overtones, while the last resembles Zeno's concept of sophrosyne. Xenocrates, who succeeded Speusippus, maintained as the core of his ethical doctrine Plato's teaching that moral perfection depends on the rule of *nous* over the irrational and requires the soul to free itself from the bonds of the senses.[100] His belief that the disentanglement of the soul from the fetters of passion is the primary purpose of philosophy is a step in the direction of Neoplatonism and forecasts the principal importance of sophrosyne for the latter school— its role in achieving catharsis.

The Middle Academy was too much concerned with skepticism to spare much attention for ethics, but the New Academy under Philo and Antiochus returned to the tradition of the founder and restored ethics to a position of supreme importance. Antiochus, whom Cicero calls *germanissimus Stoicus*—the "next thing to a Stoic" (*Academica Priora* 2. 43. 132)—illustrates the eclecticism of the New Academy in regard to sophrosyne. His attempt to mediate between the rival schools is manifest in several of his teachings about *aretê,* as when he maintains that the virtues are individual but inseparable—thus combining Peripatetic pluralism with Stoic unity (*De Finibus* 5. 23. 67); or when he wavers between Stoic *apatheia* and Peripatetic *metriopatheia*.[101] Antiochus also tries to make the best of both schools on the question whether virtue alone suffices for the happy life, as orthodox Stoics maintained and the Peripatetics denied.[102] He agrees with the Peripatos in distinguishing intellectual from moral virtue (*Fin.* 4. 7. 18) and placing sophrosyne in the second category; but in accepting a canon of four virtues, which belong to the dominant part of the soul, the *mens* (*Fin.* 5. 13. 26), he leans towards the Stoa. In the midst of this disposition to accommodate the views of every school except the Epicurean, it is not surprising that Antiochus finds the function of sophrosyne to be resistance to pleasure (*Fin.* 5. 23. 67; cf. *Academica Posteriora* 1. 6. 23); this conception persists in Platonism down to the second century after Christ.

The principal spokesmen for Platonism during the early Empire— Onosander, Plutarch, Maximus of Tyre, Apuleius, Hippolytus, and the

---

[100] See Richard Heinze, *Xenocrates* (Leipzig, 1892), 123 ff., especially 150–51.

[101] Hans Strache (*Der Eklektizismus des Antiochus von Askalon* [Berlin, 1921]) holds that Antiochus reconciled *apatheia* and *metriopatheia*. This view is contested by R. E. Witt (*Albinus and the History of Middle Platonism* [Cambridge, 1937], Chap. V).

[102] Antiochus' solution: virtue alone is sufficient for the *vita beata* but not for the *beatissima,* which requires external goods as well (Cicero *Acad. Prior.* 2. 43. 134). On the ethics of Antiochus, see, in addition to Strache, Georg Luck, *Der Akademiker Antiochus* (Bern, 1953), especially pp. 55 ff.

Commentator on the *Theaetetus*—apply this interpretation of sophrosyne to a great variety of topics; but again, lacking the stimulus of a revolutionary movement in thought, they contribute nothing original to the history of the virtue.[103] Albinus is in many ways typical of the Middle Platonists of the second century. The principal interest of the school was now undeniably religious and theocentric, in some cases mystical; and it would seem natural for sophrosyne to share in the consequences of this shift of emphasis. Philosophy, as defined in the *Didaskalos* of Albinus, is a longing for wisdom or a release of the soul from the body. The combination of the other-worldly orientation of the *Phaedo* with the ὁμοίωσις-doctrine of the *Theaetetus* might be expected

---

[103] Onosander's treatise *The General* applies the doctrine of the virtues to the special requirements of the military life and makes sophrosyne the first commandment so that the general will not be drawn away by pleasures from more important concerns (1. 1–2). Cf. Cicero *De Imp. Cn. Pompei* 14, where Pompey's *temperantia* is commended for precisely the same reason. Plutarch invariably comments on the sophrosyne of generals (e.g., Alexander, Agesilaus, Pompey, Sertorius) or their lack of it (Demetrius, Antonius). For Plutarch's varied use of the concept of sophrosyne in the *Moralia*, see below, pp. 248–49. Maximus of Tyre represents a fusion of rhetoric and philosophy, and some of his comments on sophrosyne belong to the no man's land between the two disciplines. In *Orat.* XXV he applies a canon of four virtues to the various *genera causarum:* he maintains that the orator must be *phronimos* as a counsellor in deliberative oratory, a *dikaios* pleader in the courtroom, a *sôphrôn* orator in panegyric, and an *epistêmôn* teacher in the classsroom. The substitution of *epistêmê* for *andreia* and the creation of a fourth *genus causarum* to keep the traditional number of virtues demonstrate the prestige of the tetrad. *Epistêmê* and the classroom had obvious attractions for a philosopher like Maximus, but one can easily imagine situations during the Empire when *andreia* would be the most essential of all qualities for an orator. Both as philosopher and as rhetor, Maximus is interested in *exempla virtutum,* many of which he finds in Homer (see especially *Orat.* XXXII), although he also employs historical examples. For sophrosyne his models include Hector, Achilles, Patroclus, and Penelope—all represent some aspect of *sôphrôn erôs* (*Orat.* XVIII, XXVI)—and Odysseus, who is *sôphrôn* by virtue of his endurance of suffering (*Orat.* XXVI). Heracles is the model of the *sôphronistês,* who drives out evil (*Orat.* XV, XXVI). Examples of *akolasia* are supplied by Paris, Thersites, Sardanapalus, Critias, and Alcibiades (*Orat.* XV, XVIII, XXVI). The *sôphrôn erôs* of Socrates is the subject of two discourses (XVIII, XIX). A theme that Maximus shares with the Stoic Musonius (XI, p. 60) is the sophrosyne of country life (*Orat.* XXIV). The attention paid to *exempla virtutum et vitiorum* is characteristic of philosophical writings in the second and third centuries of our era. The Neopythagoreans and the Neoplatonists, like the Stoics, delight in the allegorical interpretation of Homer and of myth in general; this predilection leads them to seek *exempla* of virtue and vice in epic and tragic poetry and also to find therein exhortations to moral conduct (just as the Christian Fathers find *exempla* and exhortations in the Bible). Iamblichus (*Vita Pyth.* 11 Deubner) treats Odysseus as a model of conjugal sophrosyne, while his *Letter to Aretê* (Stobaeus III, 5. 45–50, pp. 270 ff.) cites Bellerophon and Perseus as types of masculine sophrosyne (chastity). Their monstrous antagonists, the Chimaera and the Gorgon, symbolize the passions that result when the soul is contaminated with matter. Cf. the Neoplatonist Synesius, *Encomium of Baldness* 1170A. Julian (*Orat.* III) comments on the sophrosyne of Penelope, and Proclus (*In Rempub.* 129 Kroll) defends Homer against the charge that Achilles and Odysseus violate sophrosyne.

to endow sophrosyne with an ascetical cast, and there are indeed traces of this view in the *Didaskalos*. The philosopher, Albinus says, must resist pleasure if he is to become like God, and this resistance is made the task of sophrosyne (1). Yet the doctrine of the virtues in chapters 29 and 30 is for the most part merely the familiar conflation of Peripatetic, Stoic, and Academic commonplaces,[104] according to which sophrosyne is defined as the perfection of the appetitive part of the soul and is described as an orderly arrangement (*taxis*) of the appetites and impulses, and their obedience to the *hêgemonikon*.[105] The natural consequences of the doctrine of the ὁμοίωσις θεῷ were not, in fact, recognized by Albinus. They are more apparent in Apuleius' *De Platone*, especially in the biographical chapters which describe Plato's effort to imitate the Pythagorean *continentia* and *castitas* (1. 3),[106] and in certain treatises of Maximus of Tyre,[107] who was strongly affected by Neopythagorean mysticism; but it remained for Plotinus to define the function of sophrosyne in the purification that is a necessary prelude to the ὁμοίωσις θεῷ.

The Neopythagoreans wrote extensively on the subject of sophrosyne, and while the extant works tend to show special interest in the effect of

[104] E.g., the distinction between dianoetic and ethical virtue; the doctrine of the tripartite soul; the inseparability of the virtues when they are perfect; the existence also of imperfect virtues that are not inseparable; the conception of virtue as a mean, in the sense that it lies between two vices, and as an extreme, in so far as it is perfect. As Hippolytus puts it (*Philosophoumena* 569. 4 ff. Diels), the virtues are extremes *kata timên* (so far as value is concerned), but means *kata ousian* (according to their nature). Cf. Apuleius *De Platone* 2. 5 on the virtues as *medietates* and *summitates*. The vice of excess in the case of sophrosyne is always *akolasia;* but the vice of defect is given various names, doubtless because the Aristotelian *anaisthêsia* did not represent a familiar type: *misadonia* ("hatred of pleasure") by Theages the Neopythagorean, *skaiotês* ("gaucherie") by Hippolytus, *êlithiotês* ("foolishness") by Ammonius. See R. E. Witt, *op. cit.*, chaps. VI and VII, for an analysis of Albinus' debt to Antiochus and Poseidonius by way of the *Epitome* of the Stoic Areius Didymus; and consult J. H. Loenen, *Mnemosyne*, Ser. 4, 9 (1956), 296–319, and 10 (1957) 35–36, for a defense of Albinus against the charge of eclecticism.

[105] It is typical of post-Platonic philosophy to assign sophrosyne to the appetitive faculty of the tripartite soul, rather than to all three parts. As a result, one of the Platonic functions of sophrosyne is transferred to justice, now defined as the agreement of all the parts of the soul (*symphônia, Didask.* 29). Cf. Apuleius *De Platone* 2. 4 (the vice of the third part of the soul is *luxuria*) and 2. 6 (its virtue is *abstinentia*); Theages (Stobaeus III, 117, p. 78); Plotinus *Enn.* 1. 2. 1; Sallustius, Chap. VIII Nock. Proclus (*In Rempub.* p. 212. 12 ff. Kroll) seeks to reconcile Plato's view with that of the later schools.

[106] The Latin equivalents that Apuleius favors for sophrosyne do not include the Ciceronian *temperantia*. In *De Platone* 2. 1 the moral virtues are listed as *prudentia, iustitia, pudicitia,* and *fortitudo;* the most important is said to be *prudentia,* the next *continentia* (cf. 2. 9). In 2. 6, sophrosyne is also rendered by *abstinentia*. In the *Golden Ass,* Venus refers to her worst enemy as *Sobrietas* (*Metam.* 5, p. 127 Helm).

[107] See especially the discourses on demonology (VIII, IX, XIII).

this virtue on married life and the education of children, it is evident
that the school found sophrosyne relevant to every department of human
life, including politics. We have observed that Plato's acquaintance
with Pythagorean communities in South Italy may have affected his
theory of sophrosyne in the State, as it is developed in the *Gorgias* and
the *Republic*.[108] Plato's doctrines in turn dominated the political theories
of later Pythagoreans, both in Hellenistic times and thereafter. The
essence of their political philosophy was the application to the State
of the traditional idea of harmony and the adoption of the Platonic
analogy between the State and the tripartite soul. Iamblichus' *Life of
Pythagoras* is instructive in this connection. From it we learn that
government rests upon a Divine foundation; that the rule of the gods is
justified by man's inclination to *hybris,* which must be corrected by
sôphronismos and *taxis* (30. 174–76 Deubner); that the division between
rulers and ruled is natural; and that sophrosyne is the virtue proper to
the subjects. This one-sided interpretation accords with the current
tendency in ethics to make sophrosyne the perfection of the appetitive
element in the soul, which must be obedient to the intellectual faculty,
and to overlook the sophrosyne of the rest of the soul.

Yet Pythagorean treatises on kingship do not entirely neglect the
sophrosyne of the ruler. The scanty fragments of Old Pythagorean
writings suggest that in the early days of the school a theory already
existed which represented God as king of the universe and required the
earthly ruler to imitate Him.[109] A development of this theory may be
seen in the Fragments of four later treatises preserved by Stobaeus,
probably Neopythagorean in origin,[110] all of which are concerned with
the likeness of the king to God. The treatise by Pseudo-Archytas
(Stobaeus IV. 1. 132 ff.) refers to the king as "animate law" (*nomos
empsychos*) and maintains that he is to the State what the rational element is to the soul. This principle is developed further by Diotogenes in
his discussion of the duties and character of the king: he is to the State
as God is to the universe; and since the State is a harmony of different

---

[108] See above, pp. 163 ff., and consult Morrison, *C.Q.* 8 (1958), 198–218.

[109] See E. L. Minar, Jr. (*Early Pythagorean Politics in Practice and Theory* [Baltimore, 1942])
for an effort to reconstruct the political doctrines of this school, partly from Fragments of
Aristoxenus' writings preserved in Iamblichus' *Vita Pyth.;* and see Armand Delatte, *Essai sur
la politique pythagoricienne* (Paris, 1922), 280, 216.

[110] On the date and philosophical credentials of these fragments, see E. R. Goodenough,
Y.C.S. 1 (1928), 55–102; Louis Delatte, *Les Traités de la royauté d'Ecphante, Diotogène et
Sthénidas* (Liège, 1942); E. H. Kantorowicz, *H.T.R.* 45 (1952), 268; and M. H. Fisch, *A.J.P.*
58 (1937), 144–49.

elements (an imitation of the order and harmony of the universe), the king, as animate law, must bring about this harmony in himself. He will do so by conquering pleasure and ruling his passions (Stobaeus IV. 7. 61–62). Pseudo-Ecphantus (Stobaeus IV. 7. 64) makes it clear that the king has a unique character which enables him to contemplate God directly and imitate His virtues. The king's subjects will in turn imitate his virtues, which are a reflection of the Divine. A Fragment of this treatise discusses specific virtues and emphasizes both the need for *autarkeia* ("independence"), which makes one self-restrained, and the danger of extravagance, which leads to incontinence, the mother of *hybris* (Stobaeus IV. 7. 65). The king's imitation of God depends on his achievement of *autarkeia*.[111]

These Fragments are important, not only because they suggest that for the Neopythagoreans the virtue of the king was somehow different in kind, not just in degree, from that of his subjects;[112] but because they provide further evidence of the relation between sophrosyne (and allied qualities) and the imitation of God.

Abundant proof of the central importance of sophrosyne for Neopythagorean private life is supplied by such documents as Iamblichus' *Life of Pythagoras*, the *Life of Apollonius of Tyana* by Philostratus, Phintys' treatise *On Feminine Sophrosyne,* and the treatise ascribed to Ocellus Lucanus.[113] Iamblichus' *Life* is particularly instructive in that it shows how pervasive the role of sophrosyne in Neopythagorean morality actually was. Pythagoras, upon whom the later school projected its contemporary views, is reported to have described sophrosyne as the

[111] *Autarkeia* replaces sophrosyne, perhaps through Cynic (or Stoic) influence, shown also by the emphasis on the danger of *polyteleia* ("extravagance"). For Cynic views on kingship, see Ragnar Höistad, *Cynic Hero and Cynic King* (Uppsala, 1948).

[112] Contrast the Stoic view, as shown, for example, by Seneca; the ruler is not divine because of his position but has the opportunity, like all men, to become godlike through virtue (e.g., *De Clem.* 1. 5. 7, 7. 1).

[113] Apollonius is portrayed as a teacher of sophrosyne, which is almost always interpreted as the means of controlling appetite and passion. See, e.g., 1. 13, where Apollonius is said to have surpassed Sophocles in the famous anecdote about his escape from the mastery exerted by passion, because Apollonius displayed sophrosyne even in youth; and 1.33, on the difference between the so-called sophrosyne of eunuchs and true sophrosyne. Exceptional are passages in which sophrosyne means the absence of arrogance (2. 20); or the presence of sobriety (3. 18), good sense (5. 34), or moderation in a ruler (5. 29 and 36): Vespasian displayed sophrosyne and *metriotês* in avoiding conduct that was either overbearing or craven. Phintys' treatise, *On Feminine Sophrosyne,* is discussed by Bickel, who suggests that it borrows from Stoic treatises on conjugal philosophy (Stobaeus IV. 23. 61 and 61a, p. 588; Bickel, 204 ff.). Pseudo-Ocellus Lucanus knows sophrosyne exclusively with the meaning *continentia;* his remarks on the *sôphrôn* generation of children are comparable to the doctrines ascribed to Pythagoras by Iamblichus (*Vita* 31. 209 ff.); see 24. 14 Harder.

one virtue suitable to both sexes and all ages (8. 41; cf. 27. 132). Although the meaning "chastity" is prominent in Neopythagorean references to sophrosyne, and writers of the second century were particularly fond of crediting the founder with precepts of sophrosyne designed to achieve a minute regulation of marital relations, the chapter in Iamblichus' *Life* which is devoted to this excellence recognizes a wide range of meaning: the duties prescribed by sophrosyne include the strenuous study of *theôrêmata*, the cultivation of friendship, and the practice of silence as an *askêsis* ("discipline") of sophrosyne, as well as obedience to detailed rules for the intercourse of the sexes and the upbringing of the young (31).[114]

The mysticism that burst out sporadically in the Neopythagorean and Middle Platonic schools found its ultimate expression in Neoplatonism, whose theocentric philosophy triumphed over the materialism of both the Stoa and the Garden at the end of antiquity and smoothed the path leading to a Christian philosophy that would lay great emphasis on the purification of the soul as a means to the imitation of God.[115] Plotinus' signal contribution to the history of the cardinal virtues was his use of Plato's canon in a doctrine of catharsis derived ultimately from the *Phaedo,* but owing much to other sources as

[114] Iamblichus praises Pythagoras for teaching the Greeks sophrosyne and *enkrateia* (6. 32) and describes how he discoursed on this subject to the young, whose appetites place them in special need of these virtues (8. 41); to the people of Croton, who thereupon dismissed all the harlots (27. 132, 31. 195); and to the Crotonian women, whom he persuaded to give up their extravagant ways (11). In the course of the *Life,* sophrosyne is linked with dietary rules (24. 106; cf. Porphyry *De Abstinentia* I. 1), with the need for symmetry in all things (31. 187), and with a host of related qualities and practices, such as abstinence from wine, moderation in eating and sleeping, *aidôs,* and friendly feelings towards comrades. Pythagorean sophrosyne is illustrated by many anecdotes, including the story of the heroine Timyche, who bit off her tongue rather than speak under torture (31. 194). The conversion of a young man from *erôs* to sophrosyne by means of music illustrates the moral efficacy of certain rhythms (31. 195; cf. 25. 112). Sophrosyne is closely related to the central characteristics of Pythagoreanism, as they are portrayed by Iamblichus; the *praecepta coniugalia,* which form a significant part of the province of sophrosyne in the *Life* (see especially 31. 209-11), are omitted from the *Life of Pythagoras* by Porphyry, who—as Bickel points out (199)—devotes more attention to purity (*hagneia*) than to conjugal sophrosyne. In *De Abstinentia,* Porphyry treats ἀποχὴ ἐμψύχων as a means of achieving sophrosyne, which he virtually equates with *hagneia.*

[115] Nothing of significance for sophrosyne emerges from the Fragments of Peripatetic writings shortly after Aristotle, although it is known that treatises on sophrosyne were composed by Theophrastus and others. See Heracleides Ponticus, Frag. 52 Wehrli, Straton, Frags. 138-40 Wehrli. The most influential of the later Peripatetics, Alexander of Aphrodisias, has little to say about the virtues in his treatise *On Fate,* except to deny the same virtues to gods and men (37) and to defend freedom of the will on the ground that to reject it would be to nullify both virtue and vice.

well—including Aristotle's distinction between ethical and dianoetic virtue, the Stoic doctrine of *apatheia,* and Pythagorean theories of transcendence and purification.[116] The virtues, as Plato had said, are purifications (*Phaedo* 69B–C), and both he and subsequent philosophers had recognized levels or stages of virtue. Plotinus employed these levels (*bathmoi*) as stages in the process of unification with, or absorption in, the Divine, which he regarded as the goal of philosophy (*Enneads* 1. 2. 1). His idea of absorption involves, however, not only the purification of the soul, but also the return of the soul to its origin; it is this combination of the upward movement with the notion of purification that marks Plotinus' theory of the virtues. Like rungs in a ladder (the influence of the *Symposium* is evident here), the four virtues—always having the same names but performing a different function at each stage of the upward progress—enable the soul to escape from the material and sensible world and ascend towards the goal of unity with the Divine Mind.

The simplest version of the ladder is given by Plotinus himself in the *First Ennead,* where three stages are described: the civic, the cathartic, and the paradeigmatic. Although Plotinus believes, with Plato, that we may become like God through the practice of the virtues, he does not mean that justice, holiness, *phronêsis,* and sophrosyne are Divine attributes. With Aristotle, he elevates the Divine above moral virtue and assigns to justice, sophrosyne, and the rest (operating on the moral level) only a preliminary function, that of preparing the soul to dispense with moral virtue, as does the Divine (1. 2. 1). The civic *aretae,* Plotinus' lowest *bathmos,* limit and moderate the appetites, while entirely removing passions and false opinions (1. 2. 2). The essence of these *aretae* resides in measure. In Peripatetic terms, they result in *metriopatheia;* at this level all four virtues partake somewhat of the nature of sophrosyne. Sophrosyne itself belongs only to the appetitive part of the soul.[117] It is defined as a kind of agreement and harmony of the appetitive with the rational part (1. 2. 1). The second stage of *aretê* is that which purifies the soul from all taint of matter;[118] hence the name "cathartic." Its result is not *metriopatheia,* but what the Stoics called *apatheia.* If the

---

[116] For a survey of the sources of Plotinus' doctrine of purification, see Jean Trouillard, *Le Purification plotinienne* (Paris, 1955). On the development of the theory of *bathmoi,* consult Otmar Schissel von Fleschenberg *Marinos von Neapolis und die neuplatonischen Tugendgrade* (Athens, 1928).

[117] In this respect Plotinus agrees with the Middle Platonists rather than with Plato himself.

[118] Matter is not intrinsically evil but is evil in so far as it is remote from the Divine and from the One.

soul escapes from the condition that Plotinus describes as being *homopathês* ("suffering in common") with the body, it is practicing sophrosyne at the cathartic level (1. 2. 3). Plotinus observes that it would not be wrong to call this stage of *aretê ὁμοίωσις πρὸς θεόν* ("assimilation towards God"). Only the third of Plotinus' *bathmoi* is positive rather than negative. It is at this stage that the activity and the essence of the Divine—that is, the Divine Mind, *Nous*—are imitated. Although in the Divine there are no moral virtues (1. 2. 3), the imitation of the Divine Mind produces in the soul the virtues that Plotinus calls paradeigmatic (exemplary). At this stage the soul no longer has a twofold nature—rational and irrational—nor is there any need for one "part" to control the other, for they are unified, as is the Divine (1. 2. 6). Sophrosyne now takes the form of a turning (or conversion) towards the Divine Mind (*ἡ εἴσω πρὸς νοῦν στροφή*), for in the Divine Mind itself sophrosyne consists in turning towards itself (*τὸ δὲ πρὸς αὐτόν*).[119] Thus Plotinus intellectualizes the virtues, using them progressively to separate the soul from all that is bodily and to enable it (once every impurity has been eliminated) to contemplate the Divine Mind and, by contemplating, to become one with it.

As the Stoics after Zeno multiplied the subdivisions of the canon of cardinal virtues, so the followers of Plotinus added further rungs to the ladder of the virtues and complicated the process of the soul's ascent; they obscured the dialectical method of Plotinus with mysticism derived both from the Greek mystery cults and from the Orient. Porphyry, for example, lists four stages—civic, cathartic, contemplative (or purified), and paradeigmatic. At the first *bathmos* the virtues produce *metriopatheia;* at the second, *apatheia;* at the third they enable the soul to turn towards the *Nous* and contemplate it, without concern for the passions; and the fourth set of virtues belongs not to the soul itself, but rather to the *Nous* (*Aphormai* 2. 34).[120] Iamblichus adds still a fifth grade: his stages are the

---

[119] It is this definition that Augustine borrows when he wishes to describe *temperantia* as it exists in God.

[120] Macrobius (*In Somn.* 1. 8) defines these four types of virtue neatly: *Has [passiones] primae [virtutes] molliunt, secundae auferunt, tertiae obliviscuntur; in quartis nefas est nominari.* The Neoplatonists vary the treatment of the *bathmoi* in many ways. Proclus associates each of the four virtues with a particular stage of the ascent of the soul; he regards sophrosyne as the characteristic virtue of the ethical stage, justice as the civic virtue, *andreia* as the cathartic, and *phronêsis* as the theoretic (*In Rempub.* 12. 26 Kroll). Olympiodorus also considers sophrosyne the virtue appropriate to the ethical grade (*In Phaed.* p. 46 Norvin), but when he analyzes behavior with regard to pleasure in terms of the four *bathmoi*, he assigns "true" sophrosyne to the cathartic level (p. 119). Olympiodorus (*In Alc. I*) discusses *Gnôthi sauton* in the context of the *bathmoi*. Self-knowledge is connected with sophrosyne by way of the

civic; the cathartic; the theoretic, corresponding to Porphyry's contemplative or purified *bathmos*; the paradeigmatic; and the hieratic, which
consists of the virtues of the One (hence they are also called ἑνιαῖαι
[Olympiodorus *In Phaed.* 2. 138 ff.]). The hieratic virtues can be attained
only through mystical union with the One, not through dialectic.
Olympiodorus in his turn erects a structure consisting of seven steps by
inserting two—the physical and the ethical—below the civic virtues,
with which Plotinus had begun. The physical virtues are instinctive
dispositions;[121] the ethical ones are the virtues of well-brought-up children; then come the political or civic virtues, which require knowledge
in order to harmonize the three faculties of the soul; next the cathartic;
then the theoretical, or purified, *aretae;* then the paradeigmatic, whose
functions are the same as in Iamblichus; and at the top the hieratic,
representing the stage of mystical union to be achieved through the
mystery rites practiced by Proclus and his disciples.[122]

Rather than record the proliferations of the doctrine of the virtues in
the Neoplatonic tradition,[123] we shall select a single example, the *Life
of Proclus* by Marinus of Neapolis, because it shows the use of the *bathmoi*
as a structural principle in biography. Marinus announces that he
intends to avoid the hackneyed topics of the logographers and to arrange
his eulogy according to the categories of the seven stages of *aretê* (2). He
is in fact conflating rhetoric and philosophy by expanding the regular
topic of the virtues in epideictic oratory until it embraces the entire
discourse.[124] Philosophy contributes merely the multiplication of the

---

doctrine of conversion (*epistrophê*), which belongs especially to this virtue. For the interpretation of the civic, cathartic, and theoretical stages of sophrosyne as different kinds of
epistrophê, see 215. 4–12 Westerink (on *Alc.* I. 130D–133C).

[121] Cf. Aristotle *Eth. Nic.* 1144b 8.

[122] See Trouillard, *op. cit.,* 186 ff.

[123] Neoplatonic interest in sophrosyne expressed itself in a variety of ways, in addition to
the theory of purification. Some valuable sources include Iamblichus' *Letter to Aretê*, which
exalts sophrosyne as the source and savior of all the virtues and finds cosmic sophrosyne in the
order of the months and the mixture of the elements (Stobaeus III. 5. 45–50, pp. 270 ff.);
Proclus' commentaries on the dialogues of Plato, which interpret allusions to sophrosyne in
the light of current Neoplatonic or Neopythagorean religious beliefs; Hermias of Alexandria,
In Phaedr., with its analysis of *sôphrôn erôs* (43. 5 ff. Couvreur) and its study of ἡ τεχνικὴ
σωφροσύνη, the excellence that belongs to such men of science and practical wisdom as
Asclepius and Heracles (92. 28); the sophistic *Encomium of Baldness* by Synesius, which associates baldness with sophrosyne and cites a number of mythical and historical exemplars, such
as Silenus and Socrates; the *Orations* of the Emperor Julian, which combine Neoplatonic
doctrine on the virtues with rhetorical commonplaces from epideictic oratory and Cynic-Stoic
topics traditionally connected with the *sôphronizôn logos*.

[124] See Menander Rhetor *On Epideictic* II. IX. p. 222. Spengel.

canon of four virtues by seven, to produce the physical, ethical, political, cathartic, theoretic, theurgic, and "ineffable" virtues; the last are so far beyond man as to be incapable of being named by him.

Marinus' *Life of Proclus* demonstrates the usefulness to rhetoric of the Neoplatonic doctrine of *bathmoi* and occasionally introduces a novel interpretation of one of them. For example, in connection with the first category, that of physical virtues, Marinus differs from others of his school (such as Olympiodorus) [125] in defining the physical *aretae,* not as natural dispositions, but as excellences of the body. *Euaisthêsia* ("excellence of the sense perceptions") is "somatic" *phronêsis,* strength of body is "somatic" *andreia,* beauty is bodily sophrosyne, and health is bodily justice. As sophrosyne is seen in the *symphônia* and *homologia* ("agreement") of the faculties of the soul, so beauty consists in a certain symmetry of the organic parts. Here the traditional analogy between sophrosyne and health is replaced by the more specialized Platonic comparison between sophrosyne and beauty (in the sense of symmetry). As a result, health is now considered analogous to justice. A bizarre aspect of Marinus' biography is his effort to correlate the stages in Proclus' acquisition of the virtues with geographical stops on his journey through life. Thus Byzantium, where he was born, is linked with the physical virtues; Xanthus, where he was consecrated to Apollo, with the ethical *bathmos;* and Athens, where he studied philosophy and came to know the *Politics* of Aristotle and the *Republic* and *Laws* of Plato, with the political *aretae* (6, 14).[126] This device, too, is merely an adaptation of the practice of the rhetors, who used famous cities of the Graeco-Roman world as collective exemplars of the virtues and the vices.[127]

Such a fusion of rhetoric and philosophy is entirely typical of the writers of the third and fourth centuries—pagan and Christian alike—in their discussions of sophrosyne. The speculations of the philosophical schools became the commonplaces of the rhetorically trained historians,

[125] Olympiodorus assigns *physicae aretae* to irrational beasts: lions possess *andreia,* cattle sophrosyne, storks justice, and cranes wisdom (*In Phaed.* 45 Norvin). Other irrational creatures that Neoplatonic writers credited with sophrosyne include the turtledove (Elias *Proleg. Philos.* 19. 30 ff.) and the raven (Joannes Philoponos *Com. in Cat.* 141. 25). Cf. Porphyry *De Abstin.* III. 11 on the sophrosyne of the ringdove.

[126] The process is not, however, carried through for the entire series of *bathmoi.* The later stages are associated with the travels of the mind, under the guidance of Orphic and Chaldaean doctrines.

[127] See also Lucian's account of the life of Nigrinus, which depicts Athens as the home of philosophy and sophrosyne, Rome as the seat of *hêdonê* and vice (B 12–16). The rhetorical *topos* concerned with eulogy and invective about cities is discussed by Quintilian 3. 7. 26; see also Menander Rhetor 3. 359 ff. Spengel.

biographers, essayists, and epideictic orators; and the total interpenetration of the two dominant disciplines accounts for the monotony prevailing in literary references to sophrosyne from the Hellenistic period on. It was only when Christianity infused new life into philosophic and religious thought that the development of the concept of sophrosyne, which had been arrested for centuries, began again. For Patristic writers concerned with this virtue, the most impressive contribution made in the final stages of pagan philosophy was the Neoplatonic association of sophrosyne with the process of catharsis and the consequent assimilation of this excellence to *katharotês, hagneia,* and other qualities related to purity, with which it was only occasionally identified in classical Greek thought.

VII

Literary and Popular Usage after Plato

IF Greek literature after the close of the classical period yields no star-tling development in the concept of sophrosyne, it nevertheless offers a wealth of allusions in poetry, prose, and inscriptions which reveal the pervasive importance of this excellence. The Fragments of New Comedy, elegy, epigram, versified Cynic diatribe, and Theocritean idyll—to mention only those remains of Hellenistic poetry that contain references to sophrosyne[1]—present a remarkably unified view. Sophro-syne is nearly always interpreted as the control of appetite, usually erotic. Menander, for example, normally employs the word *sôphrôn* with the meaning "chaste" and applies it indifferently to men and women.[2] The phrase *kosmios kai sôphrôn* is now entirely devoid of political implications and means only "decent and respectable" (*Samia* 129).[3] The scope of *sôphrôn* in the *Monostichae* is somewhat broader; it includes "modest" or

[1] Several important Hellenistic authors—Aratus, Apollonius of Rhodes, Bion, Moschus, Herondas—ignore sophrosyne. Theocritus uses the word *sôphrôn* only once, to describe a modest and respectable woman (28. 14).

[2] *Epit.* 702, *Samia* 129, Frags. 610, 238. The use of *sôphrôn* in fragments of Middle and New Comedy corresponds to its meaning in a third-century poem in praise of an officer at the court of Alexandria (Page, *Select Papyri,* III, 466, No. 111), where it makes one of a long list of adjectives: some were familiar in classical Attic usage ($\chi\rho\eta\sigma\tau\delta\varsigma$, $\epsilon\dot{\upsilon}\gamma\epsilon\nu\dot{\eta}\varsigma$); while others reflect the Alexandrian background ($\varphi\iota\lambda o\beta\alpha\sigma\iota\lambda\epsilon\dot{\upsilon}\varsigma$, $\varphi\iota\lambda\dot{\epsilon}\lambda\lambda\eta\nu$). Here *sôphrôn* implies the rather vague commendation (like our "decent") so often found in Isocrates. Otto Skutsch (*C.Q.* 13 [1963], 94–95) compares with this fragment a similar list of qualities in Ennius (*Ann.* 234–51), where *prudentem* (250) or possibly *suo contentus* (245) might represent *sôphrôn.*

[3] The proper name Sophrone (Prudence) became a stock name for the old nurse in New Comedy (Menander *Epit.* and *Hero;* Terence *Eunuch*).

"unassuming" (with respect to *tychê,* 189, or to the conduct befitting a stranger, 392) and "law-abiding" (380, 580), but most often here too it means "chaste" or "discreet" (160, 505, 555, 634).

In Alexandrian epigram and elegy the rare allusions to sophrosyne relate it either to chastity or to moderation in food and drink.[4] Callimachus, for example, mentions his inability to maintain a *sôphrôn thymos* under the influence of *Erôs* (*Anth. Pal.* 12. 118), and Meleager confesses that he has been captured by *Erôs,* who has stationed him at the gate of his loved one, like a statue inscribed with the words (12. 23): "Spoils won from Sophrosyne." Leonidas of Tarentum relates sophrosyne to another appetite when he dedicates cauldrons, pots, and pans to Gluttony and Voracity and bids them (6. 305): "Receive these evil gifts of an evil giver, and never grant him sophrosyne." The epigrams of the *Anthology,* whether Hellenistic or later, display two general tendencies in their treatment of sophrosyne, depending on the purpose of the epigram: if they are erotic, they revile sophrosyne as an impediment to pleasure and perpetuate the canard that a *sôphrôn* woman is always ugly;[5] but if they are honorary epigrams, they treat sophrosyne with respect, especially when they make it the virtue of philosophers. Antipater's epitaph for Diogenes the Cynic describes his wallet, cloak, and staff as the weapons of independent (*autarkês*) sophrosyne (7. 65), and Simmias' epigram on Plato (7. 60) refers to his sophrosyne and "just habit of mind" (*êthos dikaios*).[6]

The Cynic-Stoic diatribe, whose avowed purpose was to instil sophrosyne (hence its customary designation as *sôphronizôn logos*), sometimes found expression in verse or contributed moralizing commonplaces to poets who were not themselves Cynics. A fragment of an iambic poem by Phoenix of Colophon, apparently a diatribe against wealth, alludes to the folly of piling up riches if one is not made *sôphrôn* by edifying discourse (Frag. 1 Diehl[3]), while Cercidas of Megalopolis (Frag. 2a Diehl[3]) perverts the normal meaning of sophrosyne in his comment on a line by Euripides which attributes to *Erôs* two gales

---

[4] In the *Anthology* as a whole, allusions to sophrosyne are not infrequent: of some forty-seven references, about thirty have to do with chastity, the rest with some other form of restraint.

[5] E.g., 11. 196. Occasionally a poet defies convention and denies this, as in 10. 56 (cf. Plutarch *Advice to Bride and Groom* 142A). For the hostility to sophrosyne which is part of the warfare of the wine-drinking poets against the water drinkers (the *sôphrones*), see my article, *C.P.* 43 (1948), 12–14.

[6] Cf. the epitaph for Zeno (D. L. 7. 29).

or breezes (*Sthen.* Frag. 16. 22–25 Page).[7] According to the Cynic view, the *sôphrôn* breeze, which blows gently from the right, represents the kind of love that is satisfied by harlots, while the violent blast from the left symbolizes intrigues with married women. Cercidas recommends the voyage with sophrosyne, guided by Aphrodite from the *agora* (Horace's *Venus parabilis*), rather than the dangerous adventure with the wind from the left. This perversion of sophrosyne into mere calculation (recalling the *sôphrôn* nonlover of the *Phaedrus*) not only is typical of the Cynic attitude towards sex but also illustrates that transvaluation of words that was one of the Cynic heritages from Diogenes of Sinope. That sophrosyne in one form or another was linked with this school is evident not only from the epitaph for Diogenes mentioned above, but from the famous elegy by Crates of Thebes in which the Cynic ideal of frugality (*euteleia*) is described as the child of glorious Sophrosyne (Frag. 2 Diehl [3]).[8] Wherever Cynic influence is felt—whether in poetry, oratory, or satire—sophrosyne is close to *euteleia* and has as its antithesis extravagance (*tryphê* or *polyteleia*).

The two major influences on the prose literature of the Hellenistic and Graeco-Roman periods were philosophy and rhetoric, and there is at least one point at which the two streams converge: the cardinal virtues. The Academy and the Stoa had centered their ethical doctrines upon the canon, with the result that from the fourth century B.C. any writers, in whatever genre, who were in contact with either school tended to employ this convenient category for moralizing comments. Plutarch is a notable example, and among the historians, Polybius. But at some unknown moment in the Hellenistic age the rhetorical schools had also made the Platonic-Stoic virtues their own. When Aristotle in the *Rhetoric* applied the topic of the virtues to epideictic oratory

---

[7] J. U. Powell and E. A. Barber (*New Chapters in the History of Greek Literature* [Oxford, 1921], 8 ff.) discuss the relation of these fragments of Cercidas and Euripides. Cynic elements in Phoenix and Cercidas are traced by Gustav A. Gerhard, *Phoinix von Kolophon* (Leipzig, 1909), 36–41, 205 ff.

[8] Cf. *Anth. Pal.* 10. 61, where Pallas calls Poverty the mother of Sophrosyne, an association that goes back at least to Aristophanes *Plutus* 563–64. Plutarch (*On Borrowing* 828D) observes that the sanctuary of Frugality is always open to the *sôphrôn*. The claim of various schools to instil sophrosyne is satirized in a fragment of Lycophron's play *Menedemus* (Frag. 3 Nauck), which describes that philosopher's frugal banquets and says: "After a temperate feast a scanty cup was passed around in moderation, and for dessert those who wished to listen had a *sôphronistês logos*." The twofold meaning of *sôphrôn*—referring both to moderation in food and drink and to the philosophic discourse—lends whatever point there is to the jest. For another attempt to play upon the meanings of *sôphrôn*, see Leonidas of Tarentum *Anth. Pal.* 7. 452.

and ethical persuasion, he did not confine his list to four; and it is uncertain what rhetor was the first to do so. Both Cicero in the *De Inventione* and the anonymous *Auctor ad Herennium,* reproducing what is clearly
the commonplace Hellenistic rhetorical doctrine, use the canon of four
virtues both in epideictic and in the topic of the honorable (*honestum* or
rectum), which belongs to deliberative oratory. The definitions offered in
both treatises seem to be Stoic in origin,[9] but beyond this meager clue
there is no evidence to determine who, after Aristotle and before Cicero's
model in *De Inventione,* took this important step. If we turn back to the
oratory of the fourth century B.C., we find that groups of virtues
are often mentioned, but the Platonic four—just these and no others—
are not common. The sophistic eulogy of *Erôs* which Plato ascribes to
Agathon in the *Symposium,* and the panegyrics of Evagoras and Nicocles
by Isocrates stand almost alone in making specific use of the tetrad.[10]
The loss of so much of Hellenistic rhetoric and the gap in Greek oratory
between the fourth century and the beginning of the Second Sophistic
conceal from our gaze the growth of this *topos.*

When sources once more become available, we find that treatises
concerned specifically with epideictic oratory—such as those of Menander
—and the handbooks that include encomium among the preliminary
exercises (*progymnasmata*)—such as those of Hermogenes, Aphthonius,
Theon, Nicolaus the Sophist, and Aristides—follow a uniform pattern.[11]
The four cardinal virtues are dealt with under the heading of Achievements (*praxeis*), sometimes divided according to war and peace, in
which case *andreia* is naturally considered a warlike virtue, and the
other three are considered the virtues obtaining in time of peace
(Menander 3. 372–73 Spengel). Theon alone goes beyond the Stoic
tetrad and adds piety and Aristotle's two favorites, liberality and
magnanimity. The place of sophrosyne in rhetoric and oratory is a
special topic which cannot be briefly summarized, but it is relevant to
the present discussion of sophrosyne in Hellenistic and Graeco-Roman
literature to point out that the rhetorical treatment of the virtues had
wide influence, especially on the writing of history from the fourth
century on. The special affinity of history to epideictic is shown in
the use of the topics of praise and blame by the historians of Philip and

---

[9] See Wilhelm Kroll, *Philol.* 90 (1935), 206–215.

[10] Xenophon, however, knows and uses the tetrad in both eulogy and historiography. He
begins his praise of Agesilaus with piety (*eusebeia*) and then proceeds to the four cardinal
virtues.

[11] See Georg Reichel, *Quaestiones Progymnasmaticae* (Leipzig, 1909). On epideictic in general,
consult Theodore C. Burgess, *University of Chicago Studies in Classical Philology* 3 (1902), 123 ff.

Alexander, who readily adopted the commonplaces of the virtues and vices by now traditional in Attic oratory. Lucian says that Theopompus was "more an accuser than a historian" (*De Hist. Conscr.* 59);[12] and Ephorus notoriously interrupted his narrative with moralizing platitudes and indulged his taste for panegyric. All the Isocratean historians show a strong belief in moral training as a function of history, while the transmission of ethical precepts as commonplaces in the rhetorical schools led to the convention by which the historian judged leading figures according to the canon of the cardinal virtues and their opposed vices.

Polybius, who frequently criticizes rival historians for confusing history with panegyric, and who himself applied different standards to his discussion of the career of Philopoemen in his *Encomium* and his *History* (10. 21. 6–8), nevertheless castigates Philip V and Agathocles for their licentiousness and other vices in terms appropriate to the rhetoric of the courtroom (for example, 10. 26, 15. 23. 5, 15. 25. 22). The influence of philosophy is even stronger, however, especially in two famous passages involving sophrosyne. The discussion of the mixed constitution in Book VI adapts Plato's remarks in the *Republic* about the need to unite *andreia* and sophrosyne in the soul and the State and, with an echo also of the *Laws*, condemns the Lycurgan constitution in Sparta for failing to make the state as a whole *autarkês* and *sôphrôn*, to match the character of the individual Spartans (6. 48. 4–7). In Book XXXI Polybius describes in detail the origin of his friendship with Scipio Aemilianus and explains in the process how the young Scipio deliberately set out to acquire a reputation for sophrosyne and *megalophrosynê*. The first of these he sought by defeating his appetites and molding his life so that it would be in every way consistent and harmonious. At the end of five years he had established a universal reputation for *eutaxia* ("harmonious character") and sophrosyne (31. 22. 25). Although it has been suggested that the philosophical influence at work here is the *Greater Alcibiades*, the resemblances are at least as great to the ethical terminology of the Middle Stoa, especially to that of Panaetius, another member of the household of Scipio.[13]

---

[12] For examples of Theopompus' censorious attitude towards individuals and states, see Chap. IV above, n. 76. On the moralizing tendencies of Hellenistic historians as a group, consult Laistner, 14–15.

[13] Paul Friedländer (*A.J.P.* 66 [1945], 337–40) points out that the same virtues are mentioned in the Polybius passage and in *Alc.* I. 122C. But they are not mentioned alone, as a single group, in *Alc.* I., and the vocabulary employed by Polybius (ὁμολογούμενον, σύμφωνον, εὐταξία) might equally well be Stoic. Polybius frequently refers to the importance

Plutarch is perhaps the best illustration of a man of letters whose wide familiarity with philosophy, rhetoric, and poetry enriched his concept of sophrosyne with reflections of every stage in its historical development. Himself a Platonist, Plutarch normally reproduces the doctrines of Middle Platonism in the *Moralia*—although he follows Aristotle in many aspects of the system expounded in the treatise *On Moral Virtue.*[14] In both the *Moralia* and the *Lives,* Plutarch makes sophrosyne profoundly important for education and morality. He habitually scrutinizes the record of his biographical subjects for this excellence when estimating their moral character; for example, he describes the austerity of Lycurgus and Numa, both of whom sought to instil *autarkeia* and sophrosyne in their people; the purity of Aristides and the *sôphrôn* ("frugal") way of life of Cato the Elder; the clean-handedness of Coriolanus; and above all the continence of Alexander, whom Plutarch (unlike most of his biographers) hails as a model of sophrosyne.[15] When Plutarch wishes to encourage his readers to live a better life through contemplation of an *exemplum horribile* (as he says in his introduction to the *Life of Demetrius*), he chooses for special emphasis and rhetorical amplification those episodes that will show the degeneration of his subject from sophrosyne to licentiousness.

While the *Moralia* contain no novel interpretation of sophrosyne, they are full of curious and enlightening remarks about its relevance to a surprising variety of problems. These include the relation of *tychê* to the virtues of Alexander, the symbolism of the tortoise in statues of Aphrodite and Athene, the need for a *sôphrôn* woman to cultivate charm, the superiority of rooks and daws to Penelope herself where sophrosyne is concerned, the ruler as an image of God, made like Him by virtue, and the search for *exempla* of sophrosyne in Homer.[16] The wide scope of sophrosyne in Plutarch's usage is betrayed by its numerous

---

of the *prepon* and the *kathêkon* (*decorum, officium*) and often comments on the need for sophrosyne in the character of kings and statesmen, but the word normally refers only to self-control and avoidance of luxury, not to political moderation or prudence. See 7. 7. 8 on the *sôphrôn bios* of Hiero; 18. 41. 8 on the character of Attalus; 8. 10. 10 on the companions of Philip I, who were kingly by reason of their acts of high-mindedness, their σωφροσύναις, and their daring. The use of the plural is unusual at this date.

[14] See R. M. Jones *The Platonism of Plutarch* (Menasha, Wisc., 1916).

[15] Lycurgus: *Life* (Loeb edition) 5. 6, 11. 4, 17. 2, 31. 1. Numa: *Life* 4. 3, 20. 7. Aristides: *Comparison with Cato* 6. 1. Cato: *Life* 1. 3, 5. 1, 19. 3. Coriolanus: *Comparison with Alcibiades* 5. 2. Alexander: *Life* 4. 4, 21. 3, 22. 4, 47. 4.

[16] *Moralia* on *tychê* of Alexander: 97C, 326E ff., 337B, 339A; on tortoise: 142D, 381E; on charm: 141F–142A; on Penelope: 988F ff.; on ruler: 780D; on Homeric *exempla:* 31A–C, 32B ff.

antitheses; in addition to the familiar *akolasia, mania,* and *hybris,* we find *ataxia* ("disorder"), *terpnon* ("sensual pleasure"), *asôtia* ("drunkenness"), *philêdonia* ("love of pleasure"), *erôtikon* ("the erotic"), and many others, mostly connected with the domination of the appetites over the rational element.[17]

One final group of Greek authors may be considered as representing the literary treatment of sophrosyne, before Christianity injected new life into the moribund topics of virtue and vice: the members of the so-called Second Sophistic, who flourished under the Empire. They achieved their greatest prominence from the second to the fourth centuries after Christ and mingled in their ethical discourses and panegyrics the commonplaces about sophrosyne that we have already found in the Hellenistic and Graeco-Roman philosophers. Since there is so little originality to enliven such masses of material, it will be sufficient to glance at one of the more significant members of the group, the Emperor Julian, and note how rhetorical and philosophical influences united to produce his concept of sophrosyne.[18]

Julian reflects the rhetorical technique of the great Sophist Libanius, while his brand of Neoplatonism is derived largely from Iamblichus. Like Iamblichus in the *Life of Pythagoras* (31), he gives to the word sophrosyne a wide range of meaning: mastery of the sensual appetites, moderation, obedience to law, military judgment, prudence, and feminine virtue. His familiarity with classical Greek literature is evident in a host of exemplars of sophrosyne drawn from tragedy or epic poetry: Amphiaraus, by the absence of a device on his shield, exemplifies masculine sophrosyne in the sense of modesty (303D), while Penelope, Evadne, and Laodamia serve as models for women (110B, 127C). The feminine exemplars are cited in three panegyrics of Constantius and Eusebeia, all of which derive from the *basilikos logos* of the rhetorical schools. In the case of the emperor, sophrosyne has two principal facets, moral purity and lack of arrogance (especially moderation shown towards conquered enemies)—[19] both of which were thoroughly famil-

---

[17] Synonyms are the conventional *aidôs, enkrateia, kosmiotês. Eunomia* is no longer related to sophrosyne, which has purely individual connotations (97E). *Mikrologia* ("stinginess") may be termed sophrosyne by flatterers who call sophrosyne itself *agroikia* ("boorishness" [57C]).

[18] Other prominent representatives of the Second Sophistic include Dio of Prusa, Aelius Aristides, Libanius, Themistius, and Himerius; all of them employed many of the same commonplaces of sophrosyne as did Julian, especially in discourses concerned with eulogy and the nature of kingship. Although Lucian of Samosata had the same sophistic background, he was much more than a Sophist and employed the familiar topics only to mock them.

[19] The moral purity of Constantius was so great that he could serve as a model, not just

iar as topics of sophrosyne from the time of Isocrates and Xenophon. Julian contrasts Constantius with Alexander the Great and Cyrus, traditional models of *megalopsychia* and *philotimia,* but lacking in sophrosyne. Constantius is their equal in the heroic virtues, but unlike them he exhibited *enkrateia* and sophrosyne in his relations with his father and brothers (41C) and, after he became emperor, in his treatment of his subjects (45C ff.). In the case of the empress, sophrosyne is even more important, since it is the central virtue to which all other qualities are subordinated. When Julian entered the presence of Eusebeia, he thought that he beheld a statue of Sophrosyne erected in a temple, and when she spoke, it was as though he heard the voice of Sophrosyne herself (123B–C). The benevolence and generosity of the empress and her humane influence on the emperor are the most arresting consequences of her sophrosyne (114B ff.). The words *praotês* and *epieikeia* are often linked with sophrosyne in the eulogies and elsewhere,[20] and it is not unlikely that Julian is here influenced by the Roman concept of *clementia.*

The philosophical treatises dependent on Neoplatonism have little to say about sophrosyne, in spite of Julian's assertion that Iamblichus' teaching rid him of insolence and attempted to make him more *sôphrôn* than he was by nature (235B). Rather it was the Cynic-Stoic diatribe that left the greatest impress on Julian's conception of sophrosyne. An admirer of the early Cynics, he berates the degenerate Cynics of his own time for their lack of the true *autarkeia* and sophrosyne that Diogenes, Crates, and Zeno had possessed (202A–D, 213A). His *Misopôgôn* (Beard-Hater) is a *sôphronizôn logos* in the manner of the Cynic diatribe, a satire on the wanton and undisciplined behavior of the people of Antioch, whom he castigates for their luxury and frivolity, much as his model, Dio of Prusa, the Cynicizing Sophist, castigated the people of Alexandria in his famous *Thirty-Second Discourse,* which aimed

for other men, but even for women (16B, 32C, 46D, 101B). His moderation and clemency towards his brothers is termed sophrosyne (41C; cf. also 94B, 100C, 17A–D, 45C, and the comments on his *sôphrôn* use of victory, 95A). The conformity of Julian's panegyrics to the precepts of Menander Rhetor is discussed by M. Boulanger, *L'Empereur Julien et la rhétorique grecque* (Lille, 1927), 17 ff.

[20] *Praotês* and sophrosyne: 123C, 303D, 343A, 365D; *epieikia:* 356C, 129D. The second panegyric of Constantius refers to the ideal ruler as a *sôphrôn autokratôr* (88A) and describes in detail the emperor's sophrosyne (moderation, clemency, 95A). The *Discourses on Kingship* (*Orat.* I–IV) of Dio of Prusa exemplify the Cynic doctrine of the ideal king upon which Julian drew. See especially I. 15–28 and (on the *sôphrôn* king) II. 71 and IV. 20–23. Consult on this theme Ragnar Höistad, *Cynic Hero and Cynic King* (Uppsala, 1948).

to give the Alexandrians, if nothing else, one hour of sophrosyne (30). The central message of the *Misopôgôn* is the supreme value of sophrosyne, which Julian interprets in the Cynic fashion as frugality, austerity, and the endurance of hardship. A passage of special interest is that in which Julian describes *sôphrôn* conduct by the device of putting into the mouths of the Antiochenes an attack on his own sophrosyne. They maintain that they do not even know what sophrosyne is, but suppose, from the way Julian conducts himself, that it must consist of slavery to the gods and to the laws, fair and gentle behavior towards one's equals, protecting the poor against the rich, enduring every kind of abuse without losing one's temper, and abstaining from pleasures, even from those that are not improper (343A–C). The people of Antioch equate sophrosyne with slavery and oppose to it their ideal of liberty.[21] Julian's sophrosyne in religion is contrasted to the noisy gatherings of the Antiochenes, who throng the temples of the gods merely to flatter the emperor (344B–345B).

Throughout the address Julian accuses himself with heavy irony of boorishness and stupidity. He equates his *semnotês* ("holiness") with *agroikia* ("boorishness") and his sophrosyne with *anaisthêsia* ("absence of feeling," one of the Aristotelian extremes opposed to sophrosyne), while his *andreia* consists of refusing to yield to his appetites (351C). He lays the blame for his austerity on his tutor Mardonius; and to justify his attempts to discipline (*sôphronizein*) Antioch, he appeals to Plato, quoting his advice in the *Laws* that a king should behave with *aidôs* and sophrosyne, in order to instil these qualities in his people (354B). Julian associates himself with the Celts, who share his temperament—even his hatred of the theater (359C–D)—and with the cities of Asia Minor near Antioch which have attacked the Christians (361A); and he announces his intention of departing from Antioch and taking with him his *metriotês* and sophrosyne, which so offend the Antiochenes (364D). He persistently classes under the virtue of sophrosyne certain aspects of his governmental policy, notably his insistence on fair prices in the market (365D) and moderation in the law courts (344A). Other references to the sophrosyne of the ruler occur in the satiric work *The Caesars,* which describes Antoninus Pius as *sôphrôn,* not only towards Aphrodite but

---

[21] Cf. 355B, 356B. Even the very donkeys and camels of Antioch carry *eleutheria* to an extreme, being led along the stoas as if they were brides. Johannes Geffcken (*Kynika und Verwandtes* [Heidelberg, 1909], 139–46) discusses the place of the *Misopôgôn* in the tradition of the Cynic diatribe.

towards the State as well (312A), and terms Probus a *sôphrôn* ("wise") administrator (314B).[22]

A final source of evidence about sophrosyne in the Greek world after the classical period is the corpus of inscriptions, which show that ordinary people laid claim to this virtue in sepulchral inscriptions, that honorary decrees ascribed sophrosyne to benefactors of diverse kinds, that proper names derived from the word *sôphrôn* spread over the Mediterranean world, and that a cult of Sophrosyne existed here and there in Asia Minor. The evidence is abundant, but only a few examples need be selected, since the use of sophrosyne in epitaphs and honorary inscriptions tends to become stereotyped.

We have already observed[23] that Attic epitaphs of the archaic period often bear a terse formula, "In memory of *aretê* and sophrosyne," or merely list a number of excellences, like the fifth-century epitaph: "*Sôphrôn,* clever, prudent, and versed in what is fair" (I.G. 1² 1026, 3), or even more briefly: ἀγαθὸς καὶ σώφρων ἀνήρ (Kaibel 4). In such epitaphs, where sophrosyne is linked with *aretê* or *agathos* (the archaic equivalent of *andreia, andrikos*), it seems to denote the virtue of the citizen in time of peace, while *aretê* still implies excellence in war. The formula *aretê kai sôphrosynê* persists in sepulchral inscriptions down through the centuries[24] long after the independent *polis* that inspired it had ceased to exist; but the epitaphs tend to grow longer and more circumstantial as time goes by. A Delian epitaph (dated by Kaibel after 168 B.C.) praises the threefold *aretê* of a certain Polycleis, to whom his fellow citizens erected a memorial because he was best in council, brave in action for his fatherland, and *sôphrôn* in his private life (854). This inscription effectively demonstrates the restriction of sophrosyne to private morality in the Hellenistic age. Epitaphs for women in the early period often employ the same formula as masculine inscriptions— ἀγαθὴ καὶ σώφρων (Kaibel 51) or σώφρων καὶ χρηστή (Kaibel 60)—but the words undoubtedly refer to the usefulness, excellence, and modesty proper to women, rather than to courage and moderation. In feminine epitaphs of the later centuries, sophrosyne is the virtue most elaborately amplified, doubtless because it had always been the special virtue of women. A certain Cleopatra, who was buried beside the road from Naples to Nola in the first century of our era, had an epitaph (Kaibel

[22] Sophrosyne in some form is also ascribed to Augustus (309C), to Tiberius (309C), to Marcus Aurelius (317C, 333C), and to Trajan (333A).

[23] See Chap. I, pp. 13–14.

[24] E.g., Kaibel 2, 39 (both fourth century), 55 (fourth or third century), and Geffcken 183 (third century).

560) exhorting the passer-by to stop and look at the tomb of one whom

envy, not time, led down to Hades. To her Cypris granted possession of the first place in beauty and Athena the pleasant works of *saophrosynê*, while the Muse gave her both wisdom and the lyre. . . . Even though the tomb hides your young beauty, Cleopatra, and the dust possesses your vanished body, still the goodness of your life remains for ever with the living, disclosing the glorious sophrosyne of your soul.[25]

Sophrosyne is the primary virtue of women in Greek inscriptions, often the only one mentioned, or the only moral virtue amid a list of physical qualities, social attributes, and domestic accomplishments. An example is an inscription in Rome whereon the dead woman, Messia by name, is praised for her youth, beauty, intelligence, accomplishments, and sophrosyne (Kaibel 682). Similarly an epitaph to a woman of Cotiae named Theodora describes her as famous for her beauty, stature, and especially her sophrosyne (Kaibel 368).[26]

But sophrosyne is by no means limited to women, even in the period of the Empire, when its archaic position as a masculine civic virtue had long since been forgotten. A physician of Tricca in the first century before or after Christ is said to have guarded the pure (καθαρά) virtue of sophrosyne (Kaibel 506). A certain Artemidorus of Cyprus is praised for living a holy life (σεμνὸς βίος) and is bidden to rejoice even among the dead by reason of his sophrosyne (Kaibel 288a). In these two epitaphs, sophrosyne unquestionably implies moral purity or continence (as the association with *katharotês* and *semnotês* shows), but in many inscriptions down to the end of antiquity there is no clue to its precise meaning, especially when it stands alone. Since courage largely disappeared from epitaphs after the classical period of the city-state, and opportunities to display justice became rare when democracy died out, while wisdom ceased to be felt as a moral virtue, sophrosyne alone of the traditional canon seemed universally applicable.

A small number of late inscriptions refer to a personified Sophrosyne with cult worship in a few places in the Near East, Asia Minor in particular. Mentioned but rarely in Greek literature and never clearly delineated, she is alluded to on one Attic epitaph of the fourth century B.C.—

[25] Metrical requirements in the pentameter dictate the use of the archaic and the classical spellings in vv. 4 and 12, respectively.

[26] *Exempla* are often mentioned: thus a woman of Naxos is compared to Alcestis and Penelope because of her sophrosyne (Kaibel 277), and a Spartan woman is compared to Penelope (Kaibel 874). See Richmond Lattimore (*Themes in Greek and Latin Epitaphs* [Urbana, 1962], 290–301, 335 ff.) for the virtues referred to in pagan and Christian epitaphs and for the principal themes in epitaphs for women.

"Queenly Sophrosyne, daughter of high-minded *Aidôs*" (Kaibel 34); but there is no suggestion of anything like a cult in Athens or elsewhere on the mainland. It is significant, however, that in this Attic inscription she is linked with *Aretê* "victorious in war" as well as with *Aidôs;* both parts of the archaic formula *aretê kai sôphrosynê* undergo personification. In Pergamum *Aretê* and Sophrosyne had two altars. One was set up in the age of Hadrian by L. Castricius Paulus, who also erected a similar altar to *Pistis (Fides?)* and *Homonoia (Concordia?)*. The other altar to *Aretê* and Sophrosyne was erected by Julia Pia, in honor of her husband Claudius Silanus.[27] It is not surprising that the dedicators of these altars should bear Roman names, since personified abstractions received much more attention in Roman religion than in Greek. Evidently the Romans recognized in *Aretê* and Sophrosyne a pair of virtues as quintessentially Greek as Fides and Concordia were typically Roman.

Another inevitable pairing is that of *Hygieia* and Sophrosyne, health of body and mind. A Phrygian inscription at Synnada honors a high priest, Artemon, who was priest of *Hygieia* and Sophrosyne, and who served as gymnasiarch for two years at his own expense.[28] In this case the choice of personifications is dictated by the obvious connection of health with the gymnasium and of sophrosyne with health. *Hygieia* and Sophrosyne constitute the Greek equivalent of Juvenal's famous *mens sana in corpore sano* (10. 356). Finally, Emesa in Syria yields the tomb of Ammia, a priestess of Sophrosyne, whose grave is said to be blessed in that it contains her holy body.[29]

Honorary tablets fall into several categories, including *ephebica, agonistica,* and dedicatory inscriptions. *Agonistica* rarely refer to sophrosyne,[30] and I know of no inscription recording the triumph of a contestant in one of the feminine contests in sophrosyne mentioned by Athenaeus; he does not explain what form such contests took (VI. 105. 273A–B).[31] The other two classes of inscription have much to say about sophrosyne, especially in connection with the supervision of the ephebes. Athens in

---

[27] *Mitteilungen des deutschen archaeologischen Instituts in Athen* 35 (1910) 459, No. 41. Cf. Max Fränkel, *Altertümer von Pergamon* (Berlin, 1890–1895) No. 310, p. 232.

[28] *Bulletin de correspondance hellénique* 17 (1893), 284, No. 86.

[29] *Inscriptions grecques et latines de Syria, deuxième serie* (Beyrouth, 1907) No. 20. For the association of Sophrosyne with *Tychê* and *Erôs* in Roman prayers on the first of December, according to Johannes Lydus *De Mens.* 4. 154, consult P. W. "Sophrosyne" (Türk).

[30] An exception is Dittenberger, *Sylloge Inscriptionum Graecarum*³ (Leipzig, 1917) 3. 1073, 5, in honor of Rufus of Smyrna, victor at Olympia, *ca.* A.D. 117, who is said to have excelled other contestants in *andreia* and sophrosyne.

[31] Possibly these contests were similar to one reportedly held at St. John's College, Annapolis, Maryland, in April 1962, in order to award the title "Miss Sophrosyne."

the fourth century erected tablets bearing annual lists of ephebes and giving the names of the special officers appointed to superintend their training.[32] The office of *sôphronistês* appears first on an Athenian inscription of the year 334–333 B.C.; the earliest literary reference is in Aristotle's *Constitution of Athens (ca.* 328–325 B.C.), which explains the function and the method of selection of these officers: they were men over forty years of age, and one was chosen from each tribe. The *sôphronistês* bought provisions for all the cadets in his tribe and looked after other business connected with their garrison duty. The name *sôphronistês* indicates the nature of the office, and several inscriptions reveal that the ephebes were expected to learn discipline, orderliness, and self-control during their period of service. An Attic bas-relief represents three *sôphronistae* holding in their hands willow withes, the symbol of their authority (C. I. A. 3. 1152). After 303–302 B.C. these officers disappear abruptly; they are not seen again until the age of Hadrian, when they once more appear on inscriptions as supervisors of the ephebes, often accompanied by lower officials called *hyposôphronistae*. A typical inscription is that of 334–333 B.C., which lists the ephebes and their supervisors, adding that the boys obeyed the *sôphronistês,* and awarding this official a golden crown for looking after the boys of the Cecropian tribe honorably and well (*C.I. Supp.* 4. 2. 563b).[33] Another type of inscription is exemplified by a herm (again in Athens) inscribed with the boast of a *sôphronistês* that he has returned the boys to their parents after performing many works of sophrosyne (Kaibel 973).

The prevalence of names based on the adjective *sôphrôn* is another clue to the importance of this excellence in Greek life. Literary and epigraphic evidence testifies to ten names from this root, including Sophrosyne itself —the name of one of the daughters of Dionysius of Syracuse; her sister was Aretê.[34] The masculine name Sophrosynos appears on an inscription from Mytilene.[35] The best-known names are probably those of

[32] See Kaibel 969, 973, 971, and consult P. W. *"Sôphronistês"* (J. Oehler).

[33] In each of the inscriptions belonging to this type, the *sôphronistês* is rewarded with a golden crown, often of specified value. The last epigraphic allusion to this office is dated A.D. 262–263 (I. G. III. 1199, 1202). An inscription from Tenos (Kaibel 948) describes a gymnasiarch Philiscus as μεδέων σωφροσύνης ("guardian of good conduct"), but the title *sôphronistês* occurs only in Attic records, which also attest the existence of an officer called *kosmêtês* (I. G. III. 1120, 1144). One inscription records a father and son serving as *sôphronistês* and *hyposôphronistês* (I. G. III. 1116). For further inscriptions regarding this office and the changes in the number and duties of the *sôphronistae* under the Empire, see Oehler, *loc. cit.*

[34] Plutarch *Dion* 6.

[35] C. I. G. 2. 2206 (with Aeolic doubling of the sigma, Sophrossynos).

Sophroniscus, the father of Socrates; Sophron, the Sicilian author of mimes; and Sophrone, another name for the nymph Daphne and, as we have noted, the name often assigned to the nurse in New Comedy.[36] Sophronas, Sophronicus, Sophronia, Sophronis, and Sophronius are also attested. Inscriptions indicate that these names were popular in Attica, where Sophron appears often, especially in the Roman period. Sophronius gained favor in the Christian era, as we learn from Fabricius, who lists under this name twelve Fathers of the Church.[37] There was also a martyr Sophronia, whom Eusebius calls "in truth the most chaste (σωφρονεστάτη) of women," [38] leaving no doubt about the popular interpretation of the name.

And yet, in spite of the apparent predominance of the moral nuance of the word *sôphrôn,* there is evidence that the original, etymological meaning "of sound mind" continued to influence popular usage. Pausanias, in his description of Thebes, relates the story (8. 11. 12) told by the natives about a stone, apparently no longer on view, with which Athene forestalled Heracles' maddened attack on Amphitryon. After killing his children, the hero was about to turn on his father, when Athene rendered him unconscious by a blow from a stone, which was thereafter known as the *sôphronistêr lithos,* ("the stone that healed the mind").[39] A stone with the opposite effect was said to exist somewhere on the banks of the Meander River in Asia Minor, at the spot where the eponymous hero Meander slew his wife and children in a fit of madness sent by the Mother of the Gods. At the spot where he threw himself into the river after regaining his senses (σωφρόνησας), there stood a rock called by antiphrasis *sôphrôn,* because anyone struck by it became mad and slew one of his kinsmen.[40]

A more learned use of the concept of sophrosyne in which the intellectual nuance is uppermost is the name for the wisdom teeth—*sôphronistêres*—in the Hippocratic Corpus and in the lexicographers.[41] Presumably the name arose from the common belief that wisdom is the

---

[36] A. E. Housman (*C. R.* 2 [1888], 242 ff.) argues for the existence of a common noun *sôphronê* from which the proper name would be derived.

[37] *Bibliotheca Graeca* 9. 158–59.

[38] Eusebius *Hist. Ecc.* 8. 14. On nomenclature derived from the word *sôphrôn,* see Wilhelm Pape, *Wörterbuch der griechischen Eigennamen* (Braunschweig, 1884), and Friedrich Bechtel, *Die historischen Personennamen der Griechen bis zur Kaiserzeit* (Halle, 1917).

[39] For ancient belief in the therapeutic value of stones, see Ludwig Radermacher, *Rhein. Mus.* 67 (1912), 139–41.

[40] Plutarch *De Fluv.* 9. 2–3 (1153. 30 ff.). Cf. Aristotle *De Mirabil. Auscult.* 846b 26.

[41] Hippocratic Corpus, *Carn.* 13; Rufus Medicus, *Onom.* 51.

fruit of age and experience, although the fourth hebdomad (the time at which the Hippocratic author tells us that the wisdom teeth usually appear) seems too early for the *ergmata sôphrosynês,* to use Theognis' phrase. According to Solon's poem on the ages of man, the fourth hebdomad brings strength and courage to their prime, but the mind is not at its best until the seventh and eighth.[42]

[42] Solon 19 Diehl[3]. According to the *New English Dictonary,* the English term "wisdom teeth" (as well as the Arabic equivalent) was inspired by the Greek *sôphronistêres.*

VIII

Sophrosyne in Rome

OF all the forms of Greek *aretê*, sophrosyne proved the most difficult to assimilate to the *virtus Romana*. In its origins—social and political, as well as temperamental—it was entirely foreign to Rome. At the deepest level, sophrosyne is related to the Greek tendency to interpret all kinds of experience—whether moral, political, aesthetic, physical, or meta-physical—in terms of harmony and proportion. At a level more suscep-tible to historical analysis, it is an expression of the self-knowledge and self-control that the Greek *polis* demanded of its citizens, to curb and counterbalance their individualism and self-assertion. And at a level still more accessible to understanding and imitation, sophrosyne is a quality distilled from many generations of literary and philosophical reflection upon the collective experience of the Greeks. Only this third stratum could easily be adapted by Rome, whose national temperament and historical development had endowed her with quite a different set of values.[1] Among the four Greek cardinal virtues, which became known to the Romans in their earliest contacts with rhetoric and philosophy, only two, courage and justice, were close enough to native Roman values to be readily assimilated. *Sophia,* in so far as it was contemplative rather than practical, was regarded with a degree of suspicion, even by Roman philosophers; and sophrosyne was so intensely Hellenic that in its totality it always remained an exotic in Rome.[2]

[1] Richard Heinze (*Vom Geist des Römertums* [Leipzig and Berlin, 1939]) regards sophrosyne as something opposed to the popular Roman concept of the *bona mens,* which, like good health, is a gift of the gods, not to be striven for. Heinze suggests that *fides, constantia,* and *gravitas* are Roman qualities for which the Greeks have no equivalent, while *eudaimonia* and *aretê* lie at the heart of Greek ethics. Karl Büchner (*Humanitas Romana* [Heidelberg, 1957]) selects as basic Roman virtues *constantia, pietas, fides, auctoritas, dignitas, honos,* and *gloria.*

[2] For some examples of Roman distrust of contemplative wisdom or intellectual activity

Yet, with all these qualifications, it is possible to find in Roman literature, from the second century B.C. to the end of antiquity, repeated attempts to transplant this exotic; and to a remarkable extent it, here and there, took root. The variety of connotations possessed by the word sophrosyne enabled the Romans to select those that most nearly corresponded to traditional values among the *mores antiqui*—notably the frugality, self-control, and feminine chastity which ancient observers, both Greek and Roman, were wont to regard as virtues of the early Republic.[3] It is undoubtedly true that, from the second century B.C. on, the accepted picture of the *mos maiorum* was profoundly affected by acquaintance with Greek ethics, particularly the Stoic, and efforts were made to find *exempla domestica* to match imported theory. As Crassus says in *De Oratore* (3. 137): "We must look to the Greeks for *doctrina*, to the Romans for *virtutes*."[4] But in spite of the radical suggestion that the *mos maiorum* is little more than an invention of the second century, under the influence of Stoic ethics,[5] the traditions preserved by Ennius and still later accepted by Cicero and Livy testify to a deep-rooted and genuinely Roman respect for such qualities as *modestia, pudicitia, abstinentia,* and *frugalitas.*

The authentic ideals of early Rome presumably found expression in ways we can no longer examine. Epitaphs, funeral eulogies, and (if they

---

devoid of practical results, see Cicero *Off.* 1. 19 and 153; Seneca *Ep.* 88. 30 and 111. 2. Only under exceptional circumstances did Cicero regard sophrosyne as the *virtus maxima*, as in *Pro Deiot.* 29, where political considerations govern his choice, or in *De Officiis*, where he follows Panaetius. The hierarchy of the cardinal virtues is repeatedly rearranged throughout its history. Thus during the period of sophistic dominance in Greek thought, courage and cleverness (the products of *physis*) are often preferred to justice and sophrosyne (the results of *nomos*); while in the next century Plato elevates justice and wisdom above the other two, and Isocrates prefers justice and sophrosyne, on the ground that *andreia* and *sophia* may belong even to the base. The author of *Epinomis* sets wisdom at the head of the list (977C–D), and in the Old Stoa this excellence becomes the generic virtue that gives rise to all the others.

[3] Ancient observers: Polybius 6. 53–56; Dionysius of Halicarnassus *Ant. Rom.* 2. 18; Poseidonius *ap.* Athenaeus VI. 105. 273A–B; Cicero *Legg.* 2. 1 (3), *De Sen.* 16 (55); Sallust *Cat.* 9. 105, *Jug.* 41. 2, 9; Livy throughout the *First Decade;* Horace in the *Carmen Saeculare.* Modern commentators find in the Roman character a variety of excellences that are allied with sophrosyne. Einar Löfstedt (*Roman Literary Portraits* [Oxford, 1958], 23–24) notes in Livy's preface a spirit of restraint and moderation closely related to sophrosyne. Erich Burck (*Gymnasium* 58 [1951], 167–74) comments on the moderation shown in Rome's conduct towards the Italian allies, which he regards as the product of a long historical formation. A. J. Vermeulen (*The Semantic Development of Gloria in Early Christian Latin* [Nijmegen, 1956]) discusses *moderatio* as an element in Livy's conception of glory (p. 32) and the combination of *gloria* and *moderatio* in Roman ideals from Decimus Brutus on (p. 128).

[4] Cf. Quintilian 12. 2. 30: "If the Greeks excel in precepts, the Romans excel in *exempla.*"

[5] Skepticism about the authenticity of the *mos maiorum* is expressed by R. L. Henry, *Proceedings of the Classical Association* 34 (1937), 7–28. His views are refuted by Laistner, 92–94.

ever actually existed) those songs sung at banquets which contained *laudes atque virtutes* (Cicero *Brutus* 75, *Tusc. Disp.* 4. 3) were perhaps their most direct expression. We have only comparatively late specimens of epitaphs and *laudationes*, subject of course to the influence of Greek ideas.[6] Since, however, the language of epitaphs tends to be conservative, their testimony is of great value. In the case of prominent men, such as the Scipios, the bare list of offices and achievements was early supplemented by the claim to specific virtues, notably courage and prudence (practical, rather than theoretical, wisdom).[7] In the case of the obscure, for whom no *cursus honorum* existed, it was the more necessary to praise their moral qualities; thus a stereotyped set of attributes developed. Two examples will suffice, one masculine, the other feminine, both from the first century B.C.

The epitaph of Aulus Granius, an auctioneer at Rome, describes him as *pudens homo frugi cum magna fide* ("a decent, upright, thoroughly trustworthy man" [CIL 1. 1210]). That of Sempronia Moschis, also at Rome, employs very similar terms: *Hic est illa sita pia frug[i], casta, pudic[a] Sempronia Moschis* ("Here lies a woman who was devout, upright, chaste, and modest" [CIL 1. 6. 26192]). The words *castus, pudens* (or *pudicus*), *frugi*, and *fidus* described qualities that could be attributed to both men and women;[8] and while the simplicity of the earliest epitaphs gives way to elaborate detail during the imperial age, these *priscae virtutes* continue to be celebrated. Thus the famous conclusion to the epitaph of Claudia, around 135–120 B.C.—*domum servavit, lanam fecit* (CIL 1. 1211)—is echoed in later and longer inscriptions, such as the

---

[6] The earliest *laudatio funebris* was said to be that delivered by Publicola for Brutus, the first consul. The development of such eulogies and of sepulchral inscriptions under Greek influence is discussed by D. R. Stuart *Epochs of Greek and Roman Biography* (Berkeley, 1928), 189–220. The tradition of the banquet songs is attacked by Hellfried Dahlman (*Zur Überlieferung über die altrömischen Tafellieder* [Wiesbaden, 1950]), who regards it as an invention based on the Greek precedents of *skolia* sung at symposia.

[7] The process is clearly demonstrated in the succession of Scipionic epitaphs, which devote increasing attention to moral excellence and, by the time of Cn. Cornelius Hispanus (*ca.* 135 B.C.; Dessau 1. 6), display a consciousness of family tradition (*virtutes*) which the hero must augment by his own *mores*. L. Cornelius Scipio Barbatus is described as *fortis vir sapiensque* (Dessau 1. 1) and L. Cornelius Scipio, son of Scipio Hispallus, is said to have possessed *magna sapientia multasque virtutes* (Dessau 1. 7). *Sapientia* here is practical intelligence, that of the magistrate or general; *fortis sapiensque* is the Roman counterpart of the Attic formula ἀγαθὸς καὶ σώφρων. For the use of *prudens* to describe the *virtus* of a Roman general, see the speech of Decius Mus in Ennius *Annales* 200–202 Warmington. The aristocratic Roman ideal of *virtus*, as revealed by inscriptions and early literary remains, is analyzed by Earl, 18–27; see *Historia* 10 (1961), 235–43, and 11 (1962), 469–85, for *virtus* in Plautus and Terence and its relation to political life.

[8] For *castus* applied to a man, see the epitaph of Q. Brutius (CIL 1. 2. 1259): *frugi castus*.

Laudatio Murdiae, which lists among the virtues *modestia, probitas, pudicitia, opsequium, lanificium, diligentia,* and *fides* (Dessau 8394). The epitaphs of women are not unlike those of their Greek counterparts, although the Roman inscriptions show a greater emphasis on domestic skills.[9] As sophrosyne is the dominant virtue of women in Greek inscriptions, so *pudicitia* and *castitas* are most often ascribed to women in Roman epitaphs. For men who are not of Senatorial rank or Equestrian class, Roman epitaphs reveal a concentration on the virtues of private life which is distinctly different from the classical Greek practice—although it is similar to what we have found in Greek epitaphs of the Hellenistic period and later. Nothing points more reliably to the respect for the virtues of restraint and self-control in Roman popular morality than the prominence of *pudens* and *frugi* in such inscriptions.

The earliest Latin literary remains are already too late to preserve a purely Roman tradition. The first Fragment of the writings of the first Latin author, Appius Claudius Caecus—*Tu animi compote es ne quid fraudis stuprique ferocia pariat* ("Control yourself, lest savage anger give rise to some treachery and disgraceful conduct" [Frag. 1 Morel])—has been pronounced thoroughly Roman in its approval of self-control and its recognition of the moral dangers inherent in the opposing vice, yet in all probability it has antecedents in Greek New Comedy.[10] Later literature is still more thoroughly permeated with Hellenism. Such poets as Plautus and Terence, who adapted Menander, Ennius and Pacuvius, who translated Greek tragedy, or Lucilius, who knew Plato's *Charmides,*[11] had every opportunity to become acquainted with the Greek concept of sophrosyne. And in spite of the familiar complaint of Lucretius about the *egestas patrii sermonis* (3. 260; cf. 1. 136–39), the Latin vocabulary available to translate the various nuances of sophrosyne was extensive and flexible. The Fragments of early Roman literature and the comedies of

[9] Richmond Lattimore (*Themes in Greek and Roman Epitaphs* [Urbana, 1962], 296) observes that the ideal of the good housewife was more prominent in Latin than in Greek epitaphs. See pp. 290 ff. and 335 ff. for the enumeration of virtues in Greek and Roman epitaphs, pagan and Christian. A thesis by Jacob C. Logemann (*De functorum virtutibus in carminibus sepulcralibus Latinis laudatis* [Rotterdam, 1916]) discusses *continentia sive sobrietas, castitas sive pudor,* as well as other virtues (e.g., *clementia*) more tangentially related to sophrosyne. I am indebted to Professor J. W. Zarker of Dartmouth College for calling this thesis to my attention.

[10] Paul Lejay (*Rev. Phil.* 44 [1920], 92–141) sees no Greek influence on the poetry of Appius Claudius and finds the Fragments of his *Sententiae* full of the qualities of the Roman genius: self-mastery, energy, activity. Henri Bardon (*La Littérature latine inconnue* [Paris, 1952], 1. 25) demonstrates the dependence of several of the *Sententiae* on Philemon.

[11] Lucilius (*Sat.* 29. 959–60 Warmington) quotes *Charm.* 154B. See lines 1196–1208 Warmington, for a list of maxims that comprise a definition of *virtus.*

Plautus and Terence abound in the verb *temperare,* the nouns *pudor, modestia, verecundia,* and *pudicitia,* and the adjectives *castus, frugi,* and *sobrius,* with their corresponding adverbs; thus the principal Latin translations of *sôphronein,* sophrosyne, and *sôphrôn* became familiar long before the systematic effort to find philosophical equivalents began in the first century.

Temperare brings to the concept of sophrosyne a whole train of associations absent from the Greek word. Since its basic significance is that of mixing, its natural Greek counterpart is κεράννυμι.[12] The participle *temperatus* may always indicate the results of proper mingling, and the noun *temperantia,* while generally equivalent to sophrosyne (especially after Cicero had made it the preferred translation), is nevertheless a possible translation of *eukrasia* ("proper mixture, harmony of elements"), and these nuances enriched and expanded the Roman concept of sophrosyne. We shall find passages—such as Horace *Odes* 3. 19. 3 and Cicero *Orator* 6. 21, 16. 51, 26. 95—in which the idea of a mixture of opposites is combined with the notion of restraint or moderation, both connotations being present in the word *temperare.* The Romans found this combination of ideas especially helpful in discussions of literary style and the mixed constitution, where *temperare* often has implications not found in the Greek *sôphronein.* Such cognate words as *tempus, temperies, temperamentum,* and *temperatio* also possessed associations lacking in the Greek cognates of sophrosyne. *Tempus* was particularly important in establishing the implications of *temperantia,* when it became for the Romans the usual translation of sophrosyne. Later, in the Middle Ages and the Renaissance, *tempus* helped determine the iconography of the personified virtue, which is often represented with an hourglass or a clock.

As early as the time of the elder Cato the adverb *temperate* conveys the meaning "moderately" in the phrase *temperate tepebit* ("it will be moderately warm" [*R.R.* 69. 2]). Ennius uses *temperare* in the sense of "refrain, forbear" when Priam in the *Alexander* is bidden to refrain from acknowledging Paris as his son (*temperaret tollere puerum* [Frag. 48 Warmington]).

---

[12] Ernout-Meillet, *Dictionnaire étymologique de la langue latine,* s.v. *temperare.* See also the extensive study of *temperare* in relation to the concepts of mixture and harmony by Leo Spitzer (*Traditio* 3 [1945], 318 ff.), which proposes for *temperare* an ultimate derivation from *tempus* (a segment of time) interpreted as "the right time." *Temperare* would signify the intervention at the right time of a wise moderator, who adjusts, adapts, mixes, softens, or hardens a substance (such as wine or iron). See also Édouard des Places, S.J., *Révue de Philologie* 16 (1942), 143–45; E. Benveniste, *Mélanges Ernout* (Paris, 1940), 11–16 (*tempus* is to *temperare* as *kairos* is to *kerannymi*); and Marbury Ogle *A.J.P.* 43 (1932), 55–61, on the use of *temperare* by Horace and Virgil, with the comments by Fraenkel, 344, n. 2. For the interaction of the words *temperare, sôphronizein,* and *kerannuein,* see my article, *C.P.* 43 (1948), 10–12.

Plautus employs the word freely with this significance—*linguae tempera* (*Rud.* 4. 7. 28), *temperes in amore* (*Ep.* 1. 2. 8);[13] and the participle *temperans* appears in Terence with the meaning "self-restrained," notably in a line from the *Self-Tormentor* which speaks of a *homo frugi et temperans* (3. 3. 19), a characteristic combination of epithets.[14] The abstract noun *temperantia* became common in the generation of Cicero, Caesar, and Sallust and was from then on the normal equivalent of the Greek sophrosyne.

The noun *modus* ("limit") and its numerous derivatives—especially *modestia*, a very ancient abstract noun, *moderatio, moderare* and *moderari*—expressed one of the central themes of sophrosyne from the very beginning of Latin literature. Thus Ennius in the *Alexander* (57–58) assigns to Hecuba a speech about Cassandra in which she says: "Where is she who not long ago was in her right mind, with maidenly modesty (*sapiens virginali modestia*)?"[15] Plautus couples *modus* and *modestia* (*Bacch.* 613) and explains *intemperans* as *non modestus* (*Merc.* 54). Both *modestus* and *modeste* occur frequently in the early poets;[16] and while Cicero has been credited with coining the noun *moderatio*,[17] its appearance in the *Rhetorica ad Herennium* 3. 2, where it defines *modestia* (the *Auctor's* translation of sophrosyne in the list of cardinal virtues), suggests that it was current before Cicero had begun his activity as translator of Greek philosophical terms.

Of all the popular renderings of sophrosyne, *pudicitia* probably has the deepest roots in the Roman ethical vocabulary. Livy reports the existence of a shrine of *Pudicitia Patricia* in the Forum Boarium before 296 B.C. (10. 23. 3) and the institution of a cult of *Pudicitia Plebeia* in the Vicus Longus in that year (10. 23. 6–10).[18] Although of first importance

---

[13] The verb *temperare* admits a variety of constructions: the dative or *in* with the ablative, as in these two examples; the infinitive as in *Poen. prol.* 33 and 22; *ne* and the subjunctive in *Stich.* 1. 2. 60.

[14] See also *Phorm.* 2. 1. 40: *famae temperans*.

[15] *Sapiens* and *modestia* render in two words the concept that Greek could express with the one word *sôphrôn*.

[16] *Modestus:* Plautus *Trin.* 4. 1. 12; Terence *Adelphi* 5. 8. 7. *Modeste:* Plautus *Pers.* 3. 1. 18 (*modice et modeste*), *Men.* 5. 6. 5; Terence *Phorm.* 1. 3. 18, *Eun.* 3. 5. 32. *Moderare:* Plautus *Mil.* 2. 2. 115. *Moderari:* Plautus *Curc.* 4. 1, *Truc.* 4. 3. 57. *Modice* (with *verecunde*): Ennius *Hecuba* 214. *Modus:* Plautus *Poen.* 1. 2. 21, *Merc.* 3. 4. 67. In Cato *R.R.* 5, *bono modo* means "moderately."

[17] M. O. Lişcu, *Étude sur la langue de la philosophie morale chez Cicéron* (Paris, 1930), 260 ff.

[18] The cult was originally limited to women who had been married only once. For the special recognition of *pudicitia* or sophrosyne as the virtue of married women, see pp. 307 ff. On the alleged shrine in the Forum Boarium, see also Festus 242, 243; and cf. Platner and Ashby (*A Topographical Dictionary of Ancient Rome* [Oxford, 1929], 433 ff.) who suggest

as a feminine virtue (witness the statement of Verginia in Livy 10. 23. 7–8 that *pudicitia* should be for women what *virtus* is for men), it maintains itself as a masculine virtue also throughout Roman literature, especially in eulogy, where it corresponds precisely to that variety of sophrosyne which is the virtue proper to young men in Greek epideictic oratory. *Pudor priscus*—as Horace calls it (*C.S.* 57–58)[19]—*pudens,* and *pudicus* are also current in early Latin literature: *pudor,* which (like *aidôs* in Greek) suggests a sense of compunction or decency in a variety of situations,[20] is more general in meaning than *pudicitia,* which usually signifies chastity.

To judge by the vocabulary of Roman comedy, a familiar equivalent of *sôphrôn*—as used by Menander and the other poets of New Comedy —is *sobrius* (etymologically the negative of *ebrius,* "drunken"). It is not unlikely that a similarity in pronunciation between *sôphrôn* (the *phi* sounded like an aspirated *p*) and *sobrius* (the *b* approximating a *p* before the *r*) encouraged the tendency to equate the two words, and *sobrius* in both literal and metaphorical senses ("sober" and "sensible") occurs often in Plautus and Terence.[21] As with *modeste ac modica, proba et pudica, sobrius* was inevitably coupled with an alliterative companion of like meaning, often *siccus* or *sanus,* both of which were themselves capable of either literal or metaphorical interpretation.[22] The ultimate in alliterative play on these words is achieved by Afranius with his *sollers, sicca, sobria, sana* (148 Ribbeck).

---

that there was no such shrine, and that the veiled statue of Fortuna in her shrine in this area was mistaken for one of *Pudicitia.* Cf. W. H. Roscher, *Ausführliches Lexikon der griechischen und römischen Mythologie* (Leipzig 1884–1886), 3. 3273–75, and consult Gerhard Radke, P. W. "*Pudicitia.*" The sacellum of *Pudicitia Plebeia* dedicated in the house of Verginia, wife of a plebeian, L. Volumnius, on the Quirinal (Livy 10. 23. 6–10, Festus 236, 237) is referred to by Juvenal 6. 308 as still in existence.

[19] Horace associates *Pudor* with *Fides, Pax, Honor,* and *Virtus* in the *Carmen,* and in *Odes* 1. 24. 6 links it with *Fides* and *Veritas.*

[20] *Pudicitia:* Plautus *Cist.* 1. 1. 90; *Epid.* 3. 3. 24, *Amph.* 929–30; L. Piso, Frag. 38 Peters (*pudicitiam subversam*). *Pudicitia* as an excellence of the young: Cicero *Pro Caelio* 3–6. *Pudor:* Naevius, Frag. 61; Ennius *ap.* Nonius 2. 696. *Pudor* also translates *aidôs* (as in some Latin versions of Herodotus 1. 8; on these, see Bickel, 205, n. 1). *Pudens:* Terence *Heaut.* 1. 1. 78. *Pudicus:* Plautus *Trin.* 4. 2. 104, *Curc.* 1. 1. 51. Manutius (see Fausset on *Pro Cluentio* 12): *pudor animi, pudicitia corporis.* The alliteration common in Roman poetry leads to the coupling of *pudicitia* and *pudor:* Plautus *Amph.* 2. 2. 209. *Proba* is linked with *pudica* by Afranius, Frag. 8 Ribbeck.

[21] Literally: Plautus *Truc.* 4. 4. 2 (opposed to *madens*), *Amph.* 3. 4. 18 (*madidus*). Metaphorically: Plautus *Epid.* 4. 1. 38 (*sobrie et frugaliter*), *Pers.* 4. 1. 1, 4. 5. 2; Terence *Andria* 1. 2. 15, *Heaut.* 4. 3. 27, *Eun.* 4. 4. 36.

[22] Terence's phrase *Satin' sanus es aut sobrius* (*Heaut.* 4. 3. 27) perhaps renders the verb σωφρονεῖς ("are you in your right mind?") in the colloquial usage found in comedy and oratory.

Sobrius, the opposite of *ebrius,* was probably still felt as a negative by the Plautine audiences, but it is doubtful that the Romans felt *castus* ("chaste") as a negative after rhotacism had obscured its relation to *carere* ("to be lacking"). Like *pudicus, castus* translates only one facet of *sôphrôn,* but this facet is an important one, especially in the Hellenistic literature that was closest in time to Roman imitators of Greek culture. *Castus* and *castitas* often appear in lists of Latin equivalents enumerated in the effort to convey the total impact of sophrosyne.[23] As we have noted, these two words are ubiquitous in feminine epitaphs where *sôphrôn* or sophrosyne would appear in Greek. *Continens,* too, is negative in connotation, though not in derivation. Plautus and Terence employ it with the meaning "restrained, self-controlled"[24] and Plautus connects it with *frugi* and *siccus* (*Asin.* 857). The noun *continentia,* which Cicero later associates frequently with *temperantia,* as in *De Inventione* 2. 164, already exists in Terence, who speaks in the *Andria* of a *magnum exemplum continentiae* (92). When a distinction is made, *continentia* usually renders the Greek *enkrateia,* and *temperantia* sophrosyne, but frequently the two Latin words are used as synonyms (as by Cicero in *De Imp. Cn. Pompei* 14. 41).

The interest in finding Latin translations for important Greek ethical terms that is so evident in the first period of assimilation left traces in several passages in Ennius, Afranius, and Plautus which equate *sapientia* with *sophia* or *phronêsis.*[25] Although there is no comparable passage for sophrosyne, it is clear that a long list of possible translations could have been compiled by the time of Terence. The most notable characteristic of the group as a whole is their emphasis on the negative aspects of sophrosyne, the repression of appetites and desires. Either in etymology (*sobrius, castus*) or in meaning (*temperans, moderans, continens*) these terms imply restriction or denial.[26] It was much easier to grasp the

[23] E.g., Cicero *Pro Balbo* 9; Horace *A.P.* 207 (*frugi castusque verecundusque*). Some early appearances of *castus* in Latin literature include Plautus *Poen.* 1186, *Rhet. ad Her.* 4. 16. 23; Catullus 16. 5. The abstract noun *castitas* seems not to appear before Cicero. For its use with a more general meaning ("moderation, temperance") or as the generic virtue of purity (*hagneia*) in Latin Christian writing, see Ambrose *Vid.* 4. 23, *De Virg.* 17. 108; Jerome *Adv. Jov.* 1. 27, *Com. in Eph.* 1. 22–23.

[24] Plautus *Most.* 31; Terence *Eun.* 227.

[25] Ennius *Ann.* 227 Vahlen: *sophia sapientia quae perhibetur* (see Hermann Fränkel, *Hermes* 67 [1932], 303–11); Afranius *Sella,* Frag. 1 Ribbeck: *Usus me genuit, mater peperit Memoria, Sophia vocant me Grai, vos Sapientiam;* Plautus *Truc.* 78: *Phronesis est sapientia.*

[26] *Verecundus* (etymologically "full of compunction," from *vereri,* "to be afraid") is another early synonym for *sôphrôn* whose significance is basically negative. For its importance in Cicero, see p. 282 and n. 64. Like *pudor, verecundia* is also a common translation of *aidôs* or *aidêmosynê.* The antonyms to sophrosyne that appear during this early period include *ferocia* (*orgê*) in Appius Claudius, Frag. 1; *confidentia* (*hybris?*) in Pacuvius Frags. 44, 55; *ignavia*

negative than the positive significance of sophrosyne, just as it was easier to assimilate the concept in a fragmentary way than to embrace its totality. It remained for later generations, more deeply imbued with Hellenism, to develop the possibilities of these same Latin words and endow some of them with a positive significance; or, more radically still, to devise entirely new ways of rendering the Greek word, as Horace does when he asks Apollo for an *integra mens* (*Odes* 1. 31. 18–19), or as Juvenal does in his prayer for a *mens sana* (10. 356). The single exception to the rule is a word that occurs with great frequency on early epitaphs and in comedy, often in association with *pudicus, temperans,* or *sobrius,* one that Cicero selects as the most nearly adequate equivalent to *sôphrôn.* This word is *frugi* ("upright, serviceable").[27] Cicero's attempt to elevate *frugalitas* to the canon of cardinal virtues [28] shows a real sensitivity to the nuances of the Roman vocabulary. Far from being restricted to the narrow scope of its English derivatives, *frugi* has for Rome a status comparable in some ways to that of *sôphrôn* or *agathos* in early Greek inscriptions. Without being precisely equivalent in meaning to either of them, it resembles them both in conveying something essential and highly characteristic in the system of values to which it belongs. Cicero no doubt exaggerates its scope when he seeks to make it include all four cardinal virtues, but his instinct is sound in so far as he recognizes it as a *virtus Romana* with a positive content which embraces some fundamental aspects of sophrosyne.

An illustration of the manner in which Romans of the second century B.C. became acquainted with sophrosyne—not through formal study of philosophy or rhetoric, but through the theater, the great Hellenizing medium of the early period—is provided by the *Mostellaria* of Plautus, a comedy probably derived from the *Phasma* of Philemon. The hero Philolaches sings a charming little song which compares a man to a house, carefully protected by the craftsmen who built it, but subsequently damaged by negligent owners and the violence of the weather. The parallel is worked out in some detail. The parents are the *fabri liberum,* the "builders" of their children (120 ff.), and Philolaches him-

---

(*malakia?*) in Plautus *Most.* 137. *Luxuria* (*akolasia*) and *cupido* (*epithymia*) are frequent in comedy.

[27] E.g., Plautus *Asin.* 5. 2. 9, 1. 3. 23, 5. 3. 12; *Poen.* 4. 2. 27; *Trin.* 2. 2. 39; Terence *Heaut.* 3. 3. 19. *Frugaliter:* Plautus *Epid.* 4. 1. 38; *Poen.* 4. 1. 1. CIL 10. 4327; 11. 6216. *Frugi* is often used to describe a slave as useful: Plautus *Amph.* 959; *Aul.* 587; *Cas.* 255, 268. Its antitheses include *improbus* (*Cas.* 268), *malus,* and especially *nequam,* as in Plautus *Pers.* 454. Cf. Cicero *De. Or.* 2. 248, *T.D.* 3. 8; and Horace *Ser.* 2. 7. 3.

[28] *T.D.* 3. 8.

self was *frugi . . . et probus* ("sound and upright") while he was in their charge. But afterward, he says (133–45):

When I was on my own, I ruined the work of the *fabri*. Idleness [*ignavia*] overcame me; that was my bad weather [*tempestas*]. It upset my modesty [*verecundia*] and virtue's Mean [*virtutis modum*] and ripped off my roof then and there. Afterwards I was too lazy to cover myself. From then on, in place of rain, love came into my heart, it dripped into my breast, and flooded it. Now at the same time my property, my good name [*fides*], my reputation, my virtue, and my honor [*decus*] have abandoned me. I have become completely good-for-nothing.

The following scene is the celebrated one in which Philomatium, that *speculum speculo,* adorns herself in the street before her house, and Philolaches, watching her unseen, exclaims (161 ff.): "This is that storm I spoke of, which ripped off all the *modestia* with which I was covered, when love and desire rained into my heart, and never again can I put on a new roof. Now the walls of my heart are drenched." [29]

Whether or not the Greek original actually referred to sophrosyne, the essence of the situation is the young man's recognition that he has lost this quality, in its typical Hellenistic significance of self-control. There is nothing specifically Greek about this episode. Its very universality has made possible the transfer from the Greek to the Roman

---

[29] Philemon likes to symbolize the loss of sophrosyne by the image of a house damaged by a storm. This image appears also in Plautus' *Trinummus* (from Philemon's *Thesauros*), when the father, Philto, warns his son, Lysiteles, against the example of those who praise the *mores maiorum* yet violate them, and urges him to live according to the *moribus antiquis,* as he himself does. Philto preaches a sermon on self-mastery (305–12), to which the son replies piously that his father's precepts have been an *integumentum* for his youth (313), and that he has kept these precepts in good repair by his own *modestia* (317). Philto reminds him that only one who does not regard himself as *probus et frugi* is genuinely *probus: Bene facta bene factis aliis pertegito ne perpluant* ("Protect good deeds with other good deeds, lest the rain pour in" [321–22]). As Friedrich Leo observes (*Plautinische Forschungen* [Berlin, 1895], 177 ff.), a note of philosophizing runs all through the *Trinummus,* even to the remarks of the slave, Stasimus, on the *veteres . . . mores, veteres parsimoniae* (1028 ff.). The comedies of Plautus and Terence in fact abound in moral commonplaces, some of which impinge on sophrosyne as it was presented in Hellenistic comedy. See e.g., the recommendation of the Golden Mean in Terence *And.* 61 (*ne quid nimis* the most expedient rule of life); the description of a good woman in Plautus *Stich.* 120 as one who, although she possesses the opportunity to do evil, restrains herself (*temperat*); the list of *vitia* that should be expelled from Athens which is put comically into the mouth of the Virgo in Plautus *Per.* 549 ff.; the discussion of education in Terence *Adelphi* (especially the use of the *exemplum,* 412, parodied by the slave, 428); the references to *Fortuna* in Plautus *Pseud.* 678 ff. and the complaint of Palaestra in Plautus *Rud.* that her suffering is undeserved, because she has been careful to do nothing impious—has been, as Leo points out (*op. cit.,* 102), *sôphrôn.* Leo also suggests that in *Rud.* 194 *indecore, inique,* and *immodeste* represent, in the Greek of Diphilus, reproaches to the gods for not being *epieikeis, dikaioi,* and *sôphrones.* A comic reference to self-knowledge occurs in *Pseud.* 974–75.

stage; and it was on the same plane of universality that sophrosyne could be transplanted. The nuance that Rome was able to comprehend at this period of her history was the one least special to Greece—the sophrosyne of Hellenistic poetry and popular philosophy. The next step in the process of naturalization was the systematic attempt to capture the full content of the virtue, although the moral implications would always remain stronger than the intellectual, even to Cicero and Horace.

CICERO

The key figure in the naturalization of sophrosyne—the deliberate process in the first century, after the random assimilation in the second —was of course Cicero. No part of his intellectual achievement was more enduring than his creation of a philosophical vocabulary for Rome, and probably no element in that vocabulary presented greater difficulties than the translation of the word sophrosyne. It is true that in his earliest rhetorical treatise, *De Inventione,* Cicero renders sophrosyne as *temperantia* (2. 59. 177) without comment on the problems involved, thereby strongly suggesting that the equivalence of the two words had already been established in the schools of rhetoric. In 45 B.C., however, after years of grappling with the problems of translation, he candidly admits the absence of a single, precise equivalent. Characteristically, however, he transforms what might have seemed a confession of inadequacy on the part of the Latin language into an implied criticism of the Greek, because it has no word for *frugalitas.* In the *Tusculans* Cicero observes that the Greeks apply the term sophrosyne to the virtue that he calls *temperantia* or *moderatio,* occasionally *modestia,* or even *frugalitas.* He explains that the last word has a wider meaning in Latin than the Greek interpretation would suggest, since the Greeks call the *frugi* χρήσιμοι ("useful, serviceable"),[30] while *frugalitas* is really equivalent to complete self-restraint and clean-handedness (*abstinentia, innocentia*). The Greeks, he maintains, have no name for this concept, although one might render it by the word *ablabeia* ("harmlessness"), since *innocentia* is a disposition to harm no one. *Frugalitas* itself embraces, according to Cicero, not just sophrosyne but the entire canon of cardinal virtues. If its meaning had not been so extensive and if it had been bound by the narrow limits of ordinary usage, it could not have supplied the cognomen for L. Piso, the consul of 133 B.C. Since no one who is cowardly, unjust, or stupid is called *frugi,* Cicero maintains that *frugalitas*

---

[30] χρήσιμος is actually used as a synonym for *sôphrôn* in Attic oratory of the fourth century, where both words (like χρηστός) refer to the useful, public-spirited, democratic citizen. See Demosthenes 38. 26.

may properly include courage, justice, and wisdom, but he adds that it has a special relation to the fourth virtue, for it is the peculiar function of *frugalitas* to rule and subdue the movements of the appetitive soul and always to preserve steadfast moderation (*moderata constantia*) in opposition to *libido*. The contrary vice is called *nequitia* (*T.D.* 3. 8).[31]

This passage in the *Tusculans* lists some of Cicero's favorite renderings of sophrosyne. His consciousness that no single word will really serve leads him often to pile up partial equivalents, as in *De Officiis*, where the fourth virtue receives no specific name but is said to include *verecundia, ornatus vitae, temperantia, modestia, omnis sedatio perturbationum animi, modus rerum*, and one variety of *decorum* (1. 93).[32] *Pudor* and *pudicitia* sometimes appear in these lists also,[33] while *abstinentia* is pressed into service to designate sophrosyne in the comparatively limited sense of "clean-handedness," the special excellence of magistrates.[34]

The third book of the *Tusculans*, which deals with the alleviation of distress and is concerned exclusively with private and personal problems, demonstrates the place of sophrosyne in Cicero's conception of the contemplative life. The person who is *frugi* (or *moderatus et temperans*) is shown to be free from distress and is therefore *sapiens*, a sage.[35] But this

---

[31] For *frugalitas* as a translation of sophrosyne, see also *Pro Font.* 40, *Verr.* 3. 78, *Pro Deiot.* 9. 26. Cicero casts much light on the problems of translating Greek ethical terms, because he so often gives the Greek original (e.g., *Off.* 1. 142 on *ordo* and *modestia* as translations of *eutaxia* in two different senses), and also because he frequently lists the cardinal virtues as a group, so that there can be no doubt about the Greek terms he is translating (e.g., *Off.* 1. 43. 153; *Cat.* 2. 63. 25; *De Inv.* 2. 53). Moreover, he sometimes translates a Greek passage available for comparison (see *T.D.* 5. 34. 101, where he renders *sôphrôn* in Plato *Ep.* 7. 326C as *moderatio*).

[32] Cf. 3. 33. 116, which adds *continentia*.

[33] *Legg.* 1. 19. 50 (*moderatio, temperantia, continentia, verecundia, pudor, pudicitia*) and *Fin.* 2. 22. 73 (*pudor, modestia, pudicitia, temperantia*).

[34] E.g., *Off.* 2. 22. 76. Cicero sometimes links *temperatio* with *moderatio* to indicate proper mixture, due proportion of physical elements (*Div.* 2. 45. 94: *caeli temperatio*). See *T.D.* 4. 13. 30, where *moderatio corporis* is called *sanitas* ("health"), *moderatio animi, temperantia*. For *temperamentum*, see *Legg.* 3. 10. 24. Cicero's choice of Latin words to designate the various nuances of sophrosyne had profound influence on later generations. Apuleius is one of the few subsequent writers to depart significantly from his example of preferring *temperantia* as the normal equivalent. See Chap. VI, n. 109 for Apuleius' preferences in *De Platone;* for his use of *temperantia* in *De Mundo* to describe chemical or medical proportion, see Spitzer, *loc. cit.*, 322. The most notable additions to the Latin vocabulary of sophrosyne after Cicero are *clementia* (see pp. 300 ff.) and *temperies* (used by Claudian and Ausonius for metrical reasons; see below, nn. 130 and 148). The most common antitheses in Cicero are *intemperantia* (*Fin.* 3. 11. 39), *libido* (*De. Sen.* 12. 41, *Fin.* 1. 16. 50), *luxuria* (*Cat.* 2. 26), and *avaritia* (*Verr.* 3. 76). *Intemperies* appears in *Rep.* 2. 27. 63.

[35] See also *T.D.* 4. 16. 36, where Cicero equates *moderatus, modestus, temperans, constans*, and *continens* and derives them all from *frugalitas*. He quotes the proverb *Homo frugi omnia recte facit* and identifies the *homo frugi* with the Stoic sage.

is only one side of Cicero's ideal way of life. There is a deep and permanent chasm between the active life and the contemplative. The sage of the *Tusculans* belongs to the facet of Cicero's nature which yearns for the peaceful satisfactions of the study and is therefore inclined to accept the Platonic and Aristotelian estimate of wisdom as the highest good. But the other side of his nature, the side that longed for glory and sought to win renown in the Senate House and on the rostra, put the social virtue of *communitas* (Cicero's rendering of *dikaiosynê* in his list of the four virtues in *Off.* 1. 153) at the top of the hierarchy and led him to describe *iustitia* as the *regina virtutum* (*Off.* 3. 6. 28).[36] Cicero never succeeded in reconciling these two ideals—the sage and the orator-statesman—and the conflict between the forms of excellence that characterized the two ways of life—contemplative wisdom on the one hand and on the other a combination of justice with the *civilis prudentia* or *providentia* essential to the *princeps* (*Rep.* 2. 25. 45)—remained insoluble, however sincerely Cicero might repeat the Platonic and Stoic doctrine that the virtues are inseparable. It is precisely here that *temperantia* seems to take on special significance for him. Since neither the sage nor the orator-statesman can achieve perfection without subduing his appetites and subjecting impulse to reason, *temperantia* may be regarded as a link between the two ideals. It is the virtue essential to both, although it is first with neither. While *temperantia* remains the same, whether it is concerned with the active or the contemplative life, it manifests itself in different ways, enabling the statesman, for example, to restrain his greed and thus win popularity with the masses, and helping the philosopher to achieve the mental equilibrium that constitutes wisdom. Since, however, in the sum of Cicero's literary achievement, the active life receives more attention than its rival, it is the social aspect of sophrosyne which is more often discussed in his works.

   This aspect is of necessity prominent in the rhetorical treatises and

---

[36] Cf. *Rep.* 3. 3. 4–6 for an expression of Cicero's preference for the life of the statesman over that of the pure philosopher. The division in his own nature is brought out with special force in the discussion (*Off.* 1. 43. 153) of possible conflicts among the duties arising from the four cardinal virtues (here called *cognitio, communitas, magnanimitas, moderatio*). After admitting that *sapientia* (*cognitio, sophia*) is the highest excellence, Cicero insists that the duties prescribed by justice must take precedence because they concern the welfare of our fellow-men, than which nothing is more sacred. Speculation is selfish unless translated into action. It is only fair to point out that even Plato in the *Republic* emphasizes at one point justice, at another, wisdom, as the primary virtue, depending on the context. Although it is an oversimplification for the historian to identify the active life with the Roman and the contemplative with the Greek, poets and orators often used this *topos;* see Eduard Norden, *Kommentar zur Aeneis Buch VI*[3] (Leipzig, 1926), on *Aen.* 847 ff.

the orations, where Cicero (like Aristotle in the *Rhetoric*) emphasizes the effects of sophrosyne that benefit society rather than the individual. *De Inventione*, the work of his youth, reproduces, probably without much originality, the school doctrine of Hellenistic rhetoric, including the instructions for the use of the topic of the virtues which had developed in the period after Aristotle. This handbook and the roughly contemporaneous *Rhetorica ad Herennium* possess great significance as the earliest Latin works to discuss the four cardinal virtues as a group. They differ from the *Rhetoric* of Aristotle, in which numerous virtues are treated among the topics of epideictic oratory (1. 9), by confining themselves to the four Stoic virtues and discussing them in the context of deliberative, as well as epideictic oratory.[37] Cicero calls the fourth virtue *temperantia* and defines it as the unwavering and moderate control (*firma et moderata dominatio*) exercised by reason over lust and other improper impulses of the soul. He lists as its subdivisions *continentia, clementia,* and *modestia* (2. 54. 164), which recall the subsidiary virtues that the Stoics attached to sophrosyne[38]—provided that *clementia* is understood as gentleness or mercy, rather than pity, which is not a virtue according to the Old Stoa. The corresponding passage in the *Rhetorica ad Herennium* uses a different equivalent for sophrosyne (*modestia*) and defines it more succinctly, as the continent control of the appetites (*continens moderatio cupiditatum*), without listing subsidiary virtues.[39]

In his later rhetorical works Cicero relied on Peripatetic, more often than on Stoic, sources for his discussion of the virtues. In *De Oratore*, for example, this topic is considered in relation to the epideictic *genus causarum*, as it was in Aristotle's *Rhetoric*, and the virtues are not limited to four. Cicero now observes that panegyric must deal with the goods of

[37] Wilhelm Kroll (*Philol.* 90 [1935], 206–15) suggests a Stoic source for the definitions of the virtues in both works.

[38] Cf. *SVF* 3. 264, where the subdivisions of sophrosyne are *eutaxia, kosmiotês, aidêmosynê,* and *enkrateia;* see also Stobaeus II. 75. 8 and D. L. 7. 87. In *De Inv., continentia* probably translates *enkrateia; modestia, eutaxia;* and *clementia,* perhaps *praotês* (see *SVF* 3. 71. 22 and 160. 20). According to Cicero's definitions here, *continentia* restrains desire (*cupiditas*), and *clementia,* hatred (*odium*); the function of *modestia* is to allow *pudor* to establish its rule and authority.

[39] The *Auctor ad Herennium* also refers to the virtues in his treatment of epideictic oratory (3. 6. 10; cf. *De Inv.* 2. 59. 177) and links *temperantia cupiditatum* with the praise of good health, a physical advantage (3. 7. 14). It is significant that the *Auctor* uses *modestia, moderatio,* and *temperantia* to translate sophrosyne; all three must have been current in the second decade of the first century B.C. The *Auctor* discusses the use to be made of the topic of *modestia* (3. 3. 5), emphasizing the notion of "limit" implicit in the word, and also tells how to controvert the opponent's use of this topic: what he calls *modestia* you must call *inertia et dissoluta negligentia* (3. 3. 6).

nature and fortune, as well as those of the soul [40] (a tripartite division Platonic in origin), and virtue is of course a good of the soul. Cicero furthermore divides the virtues into two classes, those that benefit society and those that benefit the possessor (2. 84. 343)—a distinction also made by Aristotle (*Rhet.* 1. 9. 1366b)—and, like Aristotle, he assigns sophrosyne/*temperantia* to the first category. In *De Partitione Oratoria*, where the virtues are again treated as a topic of epideictic, Cicero retains the tripartite classification of goods (74) but divides the virtues into two different (though still Aristotelian) categories, the intellectual (*scientia*) and the moral or practical (*actio*, 76). *Temperantia* belongs to the second of these divisions—again a Peripatetic tradition. The definition of *temperantia* as moderation of the appetites and rule over the impulses of the soul (76) would be acceptable to any of the Hellenistic schools of philosophy, but the warning against adjacent vices is basically Peripatetic. In the case of *temperantia*, the adjacent vice is brutishness in despising pleasures (*immanitas in voluptatibus aspernandis*, 81), which is obviously akin to the vicious extreme of *anaisthêsia* ("insensitivity") in Aristotle's *Ethics*.[41]

Nowhere does Cicero specifically discuss the use of the topic of the virtues in juridical oratory, although he does point out that a knowledge of the virtues and vices is valuable in this type of speech (*De Or.* 2. 84. 349). His rhetorical treatises do not, in fact, provide an adequate analysis of his own oratorical technique, for he nowhere discusses in detail that adroit use of the topic of virtue and vice in emotional appeals which is a special strength of his oratory, particularly his invective. The appeal to the emotions had been a feature of Roman oratory from its early days. Acquaintance with Greek *technae* merely made more systematic the devices already in use. It has been demonstrated that Cicero in his earliest orations already went far beyond the stereotyped doctrine of the Hellenistic handbooks and approximated the more analytical approach to emotional persuasion suggested by Plato in the *Phaedrus* and elaborated by Aristotle in the *Rhetoric*.[42] In

---

[40] 2. 84. 341.

[41] A special refinement in *Part. Or.* is the recognition of two functions of *temperantia*, both displayed in good fortune (*res commodae*): not seeking that which is lacking and refraining from the enjoyment of what is in one's power (77). It is noticeable also that *fortitudo* is here virtually an aspect of *temperantia* (shown under adverse circumstances, *res incommodae*). The guardian of all the virtues is said to be *verecundia* (79), whose importance for Cicero is linked with his belief that it is a fundamental excellence of early Rome. Quintilian, the last of the great rhetoricians, also treats the virtues in his discussion of epideictic (3. 7. 15), where his name for sophrosyne is *continentia*. In Book XII. 2. 17 he abserves that the epideictic orator will have much to say about *abstinentia* and *temperantia*.

[42] Friedrich Solmsen, *T.A.P.A.* 69 (1938), 542 ff., and *C.P.* 33 (1938), 390–404. For Cato's appeal to the emotions in oratory, see Frags. 66, 74, 76, 83, and 87 Malcovati.

his speeches, whatever their formal category, the epideictic element of *laudatio* and *vituperatio* is almost always prominent. Thus, for one example, the oration on the Manilian Law, while technically deliberative, actually consists of an elaborate eulogy of Pompey and treats in detail the traditional virtues of the *imperator*. Juridical oratory, by its very nature, relies heavily on praise and blame; and it is here that Cicero makes the most extensive use of the topic of *temperantia* and its opposites.

The oration for Sextus Roscius, for example, seeks to establish the moral purity (*innocentia*) of the defendant. The *Pro Caelio* contrasts the alleged *pudicitia* of Caelius with the *impudicitia* of Clodia. The *Pro Fonteio* insists on the *frugalitas, moderatio,* and *temperantia* of the defendant. The reversal of the topic in *vituperatio* is one of Cicero's strongest weapons, used with sovereign effectiveness in the Verrines, the Catilinarians, and the Philippics, as well as in single orations like the *In Pisonem*. The wide range of *temperantia* becomes apparent through a study of its antitheses—principally *libido, intemperantia, luxuria,* and *avaritia*. The recognition of *avaritia* as a prevailing Roman vice in fact added a new facet to the topic of sophrosyne in oratory. Although Greek orators of the fourth century frequently imputed avarice to their opponents and even connected it with lack of sophrosyne, when they equated failure to perform a "liturgy" with bad citizenship, the topic underwent enormous development in Rome, both because the opportunities for indulging in *avaritia* and *cupiditas* were there much greater than in Athens, and because Cicero made a conscious effort to select those parts of the topic of sophrosyne which could be related to the public welfare. The honesty and integrity of the proconsul or other magistrate were now added to the varied nuances of sophrosyne that had been recognized by the Greeks. Cicero observes significantly in *De Officiis* that Panaetius praised Scipio Africanus Aemilianus for his *abstinentia,* but the praise belonged rather to his times, for in those days extortion was unknown (2. 22. 76). He adds that there is nothing worse than *avaritia* in public life and nothing better than *abstinentia* and *continentia* for winning the good will of the people. His belief that clean-handedness on the part of magistrates was a basic part of the *mos maiorum* gave this aspect of sophrosyne/*temperantia* great significance in both his oratorical and his philosophical writings; this attitude was transmitted to the historians and biographers who followed him.[43]

Certain themes are persistently linked with the topic of *temperantia* in

[43] The recognition of *avaritia* and *cupido* as the cardinal Roman vices is not original with Cicero and is not confined to oratory. Polybius had already isolated greed and luxury as Rome's principal failings (31. 23–30).

Ciceronian oratory—notably those of the *mos maiorum,* the *vita rustica,* and the closely related theme of *degeneratio,* all illustrated by extensive reference to *exempla domestica.* In his lavish appeal to the *mos maiorum* Cicero develops a topic already traditional in Roman oratory.[44] His early speech *Pro Roscio* (delivered in 81 B.C.) handles the theme easily and effectively. Not only Roscius himself, so notable for his *innocentia,* but also his wife, Caecilia, preserves the *vestigia antiqui offici* (10). Their virtue is linked with that simple rustic life which from the time of Cato the Censor had been considered a major source of true Roman integrity. Cicero contrasts the *innocentia* of the country with the vices of the city: in the city is born *luxuria;* from *luxuria* comes *avaritia;* from *avaritia, audacia;* and from this, every crime. Country life, on the other hand, is the teacher of *parcimonia, diligentia,* and *iustitia* (27). Both themes, the *mos maiorum* and the *vita rustica,* have their counterparts in Greek literature. Isocrates, for example, ascribes to Solon and Cleisthenes the sophrosyne that Athens has lost in the fourth century, and one has only to think of the *Clouds* and the *Acharnians* to realize how closely Aristophanes associates the oldfashioned country life of Attica with the cultivation of sophrosyne and *aidôs.*[45] Yet here, too, as with the themes of avarice and luxury, Rome found a special relevance in the threadbare topics. Her exaggerated devotion to her heroic past gave the theme of the *mos maiorum* even greater popularity than it had enjoyed in Greece, and the nostalgia for the country which increases in direct proportion to the size of the metropolis in which one lives now endowed the *vita rustica* with unprecedented appeal. Used with fresh enthusiasm and a wealth of Roman coloring, this topic underwent development, not only in oratory and popular philosophy, but even more memorably in lyric and elegiac poetry, where it continued to embellish the topic of *temperantia.*[46]

The theme of the *mos maiorum* is but a prelude to the topic of *degene-*

---

[44] It appeared in the oratory of the earliest period, that of the *laudatio funebris,* if Polybius 6. 53 is to be trusted.

[45] Isocrates *Areop.* 20. 48–49; cf. Cicero *Verr.* 2. 2. 7. The *Oikonomikos* of Xenophon also reflects the importance of country life for the cultivation of virtue. Cf. Cato *R.R., Intro.;* Varro *R.R.* III, *Intro.;* and the *Adelphi* of Terence.

[46] For *temperantia* and the *vita rustica* in Horace, see pp. 294–95. Among the elegiac poets Propertius applies the theme to erotic contexts; see, e.g., 2. 19. 3: *nullus castis . . . corruptor in agris.* The theme of the *rura* is important in satire: see Horace *Ser.* II. 2 and 6; Juvenal 3 and 6. 1–20 (where the *pudicitia* of the Golden Age is essentially that of the untainted countryside). A variation on this theme is the association of the hunter's life with chastity, a *topos* that goes back to the myths of Atalanta and Hippolytus. Some references to this tradition are discussed by Bruno Snell, *Scenes from Greek Drama* (Berkeley, 1964), 37–38.

ratio, the decline of public and private morality from the early days of the Republic. Cicero, who uses this topic with great virtuosity, often accuses his opponents of greed and corruption (*Pro Cael.* 33–34, *Pro Flac.* 28, *Pro Mur.* 76) and contrasts their baseness with the clean-handedness and integrity of the ancestors. A special development is the appeal to exemplars of the virtues, usually heroes of the early Republic or the Punic wars.[47] Nowhere is this device used to greater effect than in the *Verrines*, where *exempla* constitute a principal means of arousing *indignatio* and *odium*. The chief model of *continentia* and *temperantia* is Scipio Africanus Major, who appears in the speech *De Signis* as a contrast to the rapacity and lust of Verres. Cicero draws attention to the antithesis between the two men by his indignant account of Verres' confiscation of a statue of Diana, the virgin goddess, which had been dedicated to Scipio, a man of the utmost decency and holiness (*temperantissimi sanctissimique viri*).[48] It is an outrage that Verres should adorn his house, full of lust, infamy, and dishonor, with such a monument. A characteristic touch is the statement that Scipio excelled Verres, not merely in *temperantia*, but also in good taste where statues and vases were concerned (5. 38. 44).

It is evident then that Cicero's use of the topic of the virtues goes beyond anything to be found in Greek oratory, but—more than this— it is noticeable that of the four cardinal virtues *temperantia* receives by far the greatest attention in *laudatio* and *vituperatio*. Accusations of *luxuria* and *avaritia* are obviously felt to be more effective than charges of injustice in arousing indignation; and scarcely anyone is accused, except incidentally, of cowardice or folly.[49] Not only do accounts of the vile conduct of the lustful Verres or the drunken Antony possess a dramatic element, but Cicero shrewdly makes use of the tradition we have already mentioned, according to which *luxuria* and *avaritia* are the cardinal sins of Rome. That he is not alone in his emphasis on such themes is suggested in the *Pro Caelio*, where he remarks that the prosecutor has said a great deal concerning intemperance and incontinence (11). Quintilian, too, observes that for Romans of the early days *luxuria* was the *summum crimen* (3. 7. 24).[50] However stereotyped these

---

[47] Rambaud (27–35) provides a tabular view of the *exempla* in Cicero's orations and treatises.

[48] Cicero uses the identical phrase to describe Rutilius Rufus, another model of unimpeachable integrity in public life (*Pro. Font.* 38).

[49] Verres (3. 2. 78) is charged with *inertia* and *ignavia*, but these are comparatively minor accusations.

[50] The satirists single out these vices for persistent attack. To mention only Horace and

topics may have been, it is doubtful that any earlier orator had used them with comparable skill. Cicero adapts his remarks to the circumstances of each case in a way that infuses fresh life into the topic. The use he makes of Clodia's notorious *impudicitia,* especially in the celebrated prosopopoeia where Appius Claudius Caecus confronts his unworthy descendant, shows how adroitly Cicero could underscore contemporary scandal with appeals to the *mos maiorum.* Another opportunity for the effective use of the topic of *luxuria* and *voluptas* presented itself when Cicero prosecuted the Epicurean Piso and made the popular conception of Epicurean hedonism an additional charge against the defendant, denouncing him for his *luxuria* and *libidines* (27) and maintaining that he was attracted to the Epicurean school precisely because it made *voluptas* its goal (28).

The *Pro Fonteio,* a speech unusually rich in Roman color (including the appeal to historical exemplars of *temperantia* and *frugalitas*), shows Cicero adapting yet another time-honored oratorical technique to the topic of *temperantia*—this time a device of the advocate, rather than of the prosecutor. The appeal for pity in the peroration traditionally introduced the aged parents or the little children of the defendant. Cicero uses this device in a uniquely Roman fashion by substituting for these familiar props of the Greek courtroom the sister of Fonteius, who is a Vestal. The fact that she has no husband or son to protect her becomes an argument for the acquittal of Fonteius, her sole kinsman, and Cicero contrives to remind the jury of the sacrifice that her life of chastity requires and of the debt that Rome owes to the Vestals. There is even an element of danger to Rome in the peril of Fonteius: his sister may extinguish the fire of Vesta with her tears (21. 46)! Cicero has already described Fonteius himself as *frugi et in omnibus vitae partibus moderatum ac temperatum, plenum pudoris, plenum offici, plenum religionis* (40). He now strengthens the link between chastity and *religio* by reminding the jury of the prayers by which the Vestals have won Divine help for Rome in various crises (49).

All the great sequences of denunciatory speeches—the Verrines, the Catilinarians, and the Philippics—take special care to relate *temperantia* and its antitheses to the State. The worst of Verres' sins is that he disgraces Rome by his conduct as a magistrate, by his rapacity and

---

Juvenal, we note that Horace castigates *avaritia* in *Ser.* I. 1 and II. 3 and *Ep.* I. 6, and excessive indulgence in various appetites in *Ser.* I. 2 and 3 and II. 4 and 8. Juvenal attacks greed and extravagance in 1. 81–146, 12, and 14, and sexual perversion or excess in 2, 9, and 6; he uses the theme of the *cena* in 5.

brutality towards the provincials as well as towards Roman citizens. It is the appearance of the tribune Antony, drunken and debauched, in the sight of the people that inspires the famous descriptive passage in the *Second Philippic* (25. 63). In the case of Piso, too, it is the combination of drunkenness with the office of consul that Cicero, with special force, condemns (10). But the passage that demonstrates most clearly the link between virtue and the welfare of the State is the description in the *Second Catilinarian* of the virtues and vices fighting respectively for the Republic and for the conspirators, a passage that might well have inspired the *Psychomachia* of Prudentius. Cicero says (2. 25):

> On this side fights *Pudor*, on that *Petulantia*, on this *Pudicitia*, on that *Stuprum*, on this *Fides*, on that *Fraudatio*, on this *Pietas*, on that *Scelus*, on this *Constantia*, on that *Furor*, on this *Honestas*, on that *Turpitudo*. On this, finally, *Aequitas*, *Temperantia*, *Fortitudo*, *Prudentia*, virtues all, struggle against *Iniquitas*, *Luxuria*, *Ignavia*, and *Temeritas*. The very gods will help the glorious virtues to overcome the vices.[51]

Although the negative use of the theme of *temperantia* in public life is unquestionably more dramatic and memorable than the positive, Cicero does not neglect the other side. One prolonged discussion of the virtues with special reference to the behavior of the *imperator*, the Roman general, was destined to linger in the memory of Roman orators and historians from the younger Pliny to the Latin Panegyrists, all of whom adapted the praise of Pompey in the oration on the Manilian Law to the eulogy of the emperor.[52] As we have noted, this speech, although technically deliberative, derives most of its effect from its manipulation of the topics of epideictic, especially the virtues of the general, a commonplace in Greek history from Thucydides and Xenophon on. Not only does Cicero contrast the honesty of Pompey with the *avaritia* of other generals, but he maintains that *temperantia* makes possible the wonderful speed with which Pompey moves on campaign: he is not held back by avarice, lust, pleasure, curiosity, nor even the need for rest (14).[53] So great is Pompey's *continentia* that the provincials actually

---

[51] The first group of virtues includes traditionally Roman qualities, while the second recognizes the Greek virtues.

[52] On the Latin panegyrists, see Édouard Galletier, *Panégyriques latins* (Paris, 1949), especially Introduction, pp. vii–xxxvii.

[53] Cf. *Phil.* 2. 26–28, where the virtuous Pompey is contrasted with the *impudicissimus* Antony. The Greek commonplace that the true *imperator* is he who restrains his desires and scorns pleasure is repeated in *Par. St.* 5. 33. The need for *continentia* and *modestia*, not in the general, but in the legionary soldier, is set forth by Caesar *B.G.* 7. 52, where he interprets these virtues as military discipline and says that they are as essential as *virtus* and *magnitudo animi* (another instance of the tension between sophrosyne and *andreia* and their reconciliation

think him sent down from heaven. The *continentia* of Rome now becomes credible to other peoples, who at last understand that not without reason in the days when Rome had magistrates of such *temperantia* did other nations choose to serve the Roman people, rather than be rulers in their own right (14. 41).

The same view of *temperantia* as an instrument of imperial policy recurs in a letter to Quintus, written in 60 B.C., concerning his conduct as governor in Asia. Here Cicero couples moderation and culture (*moderatio* and *doctrina*) as prime necessities for the Roman who is to govern Greeks, and mentions the special claim of the inhabitants of Asia Minor to consideration, since with them originates *humanitas* (*Ad Q.F.* 1. 1. 22; cf. *Ad Fam.* 13. 65. 1). According to this letter, the first duty of a praetor is to be *abstinens* and to restrain his emotions (32). In the case of Quintus, it is *iracundia* that Cicero especially fears, for *humanitas* vanishes when anger is aroused (37).[54]

Towards the close of Cicero's career the topic of the ruler's *temperantia* takes an ominous turn. The speeches of the year 46 B.C. select for emphasis a new aspect of the virtue, *clementia* or *misericordia* ("mercy" or "compassion"). It will be recalled that in *De Inventione*, *clementia* appears as one of the virtues subordinate to *temperantia*, possibly representing *praotês* in some Stoic source. In the *Pro Sulla* Cicero had praised his own *lenitas* ("mildness") and *misericordia* in dealing with the Catilinarian conspirators (1; cf. 87, 92), and in a letter to Cato he mentioned his *mansuetudo* ("humaneness") and *continentia* in Cilicia (*Ad Fam.* 15. 3. 2; cf. Cato's reply, *Ad Fam.* 15. 5). In the oration on the Manilian Law the *mansuetudo* of Pompey was celebrated (14. 42). Now in the *Pro Ligario*, the *Pro Deiotaro*, and the *Pro Marcello* there suddenly appear many references to the *clementia* or *misericordia* of Caesar.[55] The *Pro Deiotaro* in fact reaches its climax and conclusion with the words *clementiae tuae* (15. 43). The *Pro Marcello* begins with a definition of *mansuetudo* or *clementia* as moderation in all things when one has supreme

---

under ideal circumstances). The topic of *disciplina militaris* is a favorite with Livy; see pp. 289 ff. for his identification of this excellence with the *mos maiorum*. Cf. Sallust *Jug.* 45, where the *temperantia* of Metellus restrains the soldiers' *ignavia* and restores *modus;* and *Jug.* 46, where his *innocentia* frightens Jugurtha himself.

[54] Pliny imitates this letter in *Ep.* 8. 24.

[55] *Pro Lig.* 1. 1; 2. 6; 4. 10; 5. 15, 16; 6. 19; 12. 37–38. *Pro Deiot.* 11. 34; 14. 40, 43. *Pro Mar.* 1. 1; 8. 3; 3. 9, 12; 6. 18. On the *clementia Caesaris*, see M. Treu, *Mus. Helv.* 5 (1948), 197 ff. Cf. Sallust *Cat.* 54 on his *mansuetudo* and *misericordia*, and cf. Suetonius *Julius Caesar* 75 on his *moderatio* and *clementia*. Note also the remark of Caesar himself: "*Haec nova sit ratio vincendi ut misericordia et liberalitate nos muniamus*" (*ap.* Cicero *Ad Att.* 9. 7. 1).

power (*in summa potestate rerum omnium modus* [1. 1]). Even the hackneyed commonplace that the conquest of passion and the moderate use of victory are characteristic of the Divine (3. 8) takes on a new significance in the context of this speech. Granted that Cicero is ironic in his references to the *clementia Caesaris,* eulogists of later Caesars imitate in deadly seriousness, if not sincerity, his apparent adulation. Cicero's speeches of the year 46 mark the beginning of a process that reaches its nadir in Seneca's *De Clementia,* addressed to Nero;[56] and the association of *temperantia* in the use of power, under the name *clementia,* with the divinity of an absolute ruler, becomes one of the orator-statesman's most enduring legacies to subsequent orators and historians.[57]

Cicero's philosophical works, written for the most part close to the year of these final speeches, show his desire to bury himself in study and thus avoid contemplating the effects of the civil war; they also demonstrate his continued concern for the State, which now takes the form of speculation about the history of Rome, the sources of her past greatness, and the best government consistent with her true nature. The two tendencies are the final expression of Cicero's lifelong wavering between his two ideals, the sage and the orator-statesman. His attempts to combine them are perhaps most conspicuous in those treatises that adapt Hellenistic philosophy, largely concerned with the ethics of the individual, to the Roman exaltation of public life and the *mos maiorum.* The treatment of sophrosyne in such works is a fair example of the Ciceronian approach to Hellenistic ethics in general. It is most clearly seen, not in the *Tusculans* or *De Finibus*—important though they are as evidence for Greek views of sophrosyne[58]—but in the works that display the greatest

[56] Chaim Wirszubski (*Libertas as a Political Idea at Rome during the Late Republic and Early Principate* [Cambridge, 1950], 150 ff.) points out that Cicero distinguishes between monarchy and tyranny by the criterion of justice, while for Seneca the criterion has become *clementia.*

[57] The need for sophrosyne in the character of a king is also touched on in *Pro Deiot.,* whose antecedents include Isocrates' *Evagoras* as well as the Hellenistic *basilikos logos.* After extolling the *magnitudo animi, gravitas,* and *constantia* of the king, Cicero mentions his singular and admirable *frugalitas* (29). This is not common praise for kings, he admits, since it is a private virtue, in contrast to such *regiae virtutes* as courage, justice, and the like. Yet *frugalitas* —that is, *modestia* and *temperantia*—is the *virtus maxima.* It is not at all characteristic of Cicero to rank *temperantia* first among the virtues, and it is distinctly sinister that he should do so now, when *temperantia* has been transformed into the virtue of an absolute ruler.

[58] In Ciceronian discussions of individual ethics, sophrosyne plays the same part as in Hellenistic philosophy. It is interpreted as the *moderatrix commotionum* and therefore as the source of tranquillity, the goal of both Stoics and Epicureans. The Stoic view, which makes *intemperantia* the *fons perturbationum,* is seen in *T.D.* 4. 9. 22. *Fortitudo* and *temperantia* are sufficient for happiness (*T.D.* 5. 14. 42). *Fin.* 2. 14. 46–47, a Stoic interpretation of the cardinal virtues, gives an aesthetic bias to sophrosyne and identifies it with *humanitas.* The Epicurean theory that *temperantia* bestows peace of mind is cited in *Fin.* 1. 12. 47–48.

Roman color: *De Officiis, De Senectute,* and *De Amicitia* (all written in 45–44 B.C.), and the earlier *De Republica* (54 B.C.) and *De Legibus* (52–46 B.C.). The effect of this deliberate Romanizing is essentially the same as in the orations: sophrosyne is interpreted as the primary means of restraining *avaritia, luxuria,* and *cupido;* its external manifestations are emphasized, especially in *De Officiis;* [59] the *continentia* of public figures is considered to have enormous effect on the general level of morality (*Legg.* 3. 14. 32); and by associating it with *pudor* and *verecundia,* two of the most firmly established of the *priscae virtutes,* Cicero makes sophrosyne an essential part of the *mos maiorum.*

The link between sophrosyne and the *prepon* (the most original element in the ethical doctrine of *De Officiis*) has been noted in Chapter VI as a contribution of Panaetius. For Cicero himself the treatise is remarkable in three respects. First, only in this one of his philosophical works does he implicitly assign to sophrosyne the dominant place in a system of conduct. Although formally he weighs the claims of justice and wisdom to first place among the virtues,[60] actually, by accepting the view of Panaetius that the virtuous life depends on the proper ordering of the impulses of the soul—an ordering that is the specific function of sophrosyne—he gives primacy to this excellence. Nowhere else in Cicero's philosophical treatises does this situation recur. As is the case with St. Ambrose, when he in turn adapts *De Officiis* to Christian morality, special circumstances produce a unique attitude towards sophrosyne.

Secondly, in *De Officiis* Cicero finds a philosophical justification for his habit of linking sophrosyne with *humanitas*—a habit that deserves to be recognized as his most original contribution to the history of the virtue.[61] This justification is another result of following the lead of Panaetius and basing virtue, not on pure *epistêmê* as had been done by the Old Stoa, but on impulses (*aphormae*) guided by reason (1. 4. 11–14). Two of the cardinal virtues, justice and courage, are developed from instincts that man shares with the lower animals, but wisdom and moderation,

---

[59] See 1. 142 on the power of the fourth virtue to win *approbatio.* Panaetius, whom Cicero follows in the main in books I and II, was himself influenced by conditions in Roman society and paid more attention to law and politics than the Old Stoa considered proper. See S. E. Smethurst, *Phoenix* 9 (1955), 111–21.

[60] E.g., 1. 19; 1. 153; 3. 28.

[61] With *Off.* 1. 4. 14, cf. *Fin.* 4. 7. 16, where only man is *particeps pudoris ac verecundiae;* and *Consolatio,* Frag. 12 (Lactantius 3. 19. 3), where purity (*castitas*) and humanistic culture are cited as two characteristics that enable man to fly to the gods—i.e., *ad naturam sui similem.* In *Som. Scip.* 29, however, it is service to the State combined with purification that accomplishes the assimilation to the Divine. For sophrosyne and *paideia* ("culture") in Isocrates, see Chap. IV, n. 80.

even on the instinctive level, are uniquely human. Man is the only animal that has a feeling for order, propriety, and moderation (1. 4. 14), and
the special connection of sophrosyne with behaving like a human being
(suggested, for example, in 1. 100) is an inescapable consequence. The
emphasis placed on beauty as the outcome of order (1. 4. 14) reinforces
this tendency on Cicero's part, since there is a strong aesthetic element
in his conception of *humanitas*.

Thirdly, *De Officiis* gives expression to sophrosyne in rules for everyday conduct that are specifically designed for Roman rather than Greek
consumption, and the minute consideration of the *officia* suitable to
various age groups, occupations, and types of personality is what gives
such a peculiarly Roman flavor to the treatise. Many details—such as
the relevance of *temperantia* to the choice of a home (1. 138 ff.) and to the
preservation of *dignitas* in outward appearance (1. 130) and conversation
(1. 134), in winning popular esteem (2. 46), and in avoiding the vice of
avaritia in public life (2. 77)—speak clearly of the Roman background
and show in a remarkably specific way what aspects of sophrosyne were
most readily adapted to Roman life among the upper classes.

De Senectute offers an example of the naturalization of sophrosyne by
weaving it firmly into a pattern composed of the most intensely Roman
traits and sentiments. In this essay venerable commonplaces about the
relevance of sophrosyne to old age—such as the famous anecdote about
Sophocles and his release from bondage to *erôs* (14. 47)—are assimilated
to one of Cicero's favorite models of *frugalitas* and *abstinentia*, the Elder
Cato. Throughout the essay Cicero represents *temperantia* as one of the
artes and *virtutes* that equip *senectus* (10. 34), and his choice of a spokesman is peculiarly apt. Plutarch records that as early as 189 B.C. a statue
of Cato erected in the temple of *Salus* (Health) at Rome bore an inscription concerning his sophrosyne (*Cato* 19. 4). The location of the statue
suggests that the Romans even at this period were inclined to exploit the
traditional link between health of mind and health of body. In *De
Senectute* the subject of the *vita rustica* (perhaps the most appropriate of
all topics for Cato to discuss) is connected with self-restraint—in this case
the *continentia* of Manius Curius (16. 55);[62] and the power to enjoy old
age is made to seem a result of both *moderatio* and *humanitas* (3. 7), a very
Ciceronian *iunctura*.

Cato is also prominent as an *exemplum virtutis* in *De Republica*: Book I
opens with a tribute to his admirable *industria* (1. 1. 1), and Book II with

---

[62] Valerius Maximus (4. 3. 5) cites Curius as the *exactissima norma Romanae frugalitatis,
idemque fortitudinis perfectissimum specimen.*

praise of his *modus in dicendo* (2. 1. 1). This dialogue employs to the full the device of idealizing the early Republic and holding up for imitation examples of the virtues drawn from that period; in so doing, it provides the most sustained treatment we have of Roman sophrosyne in the context of the State. Such an approach to the virtue is marked, predictably enough, by two principal techniques: the inclusion of several aspects of sophrosyne among the *priscae virtutes,* and the attempt to relate certain familiar Greek themes of sophrosyne to the dominant Roman idea of service to the State. Among the facets of sophrosyne that Cicero here makes part of Roman morality, *pudor* and *verecundia* are particularly noteworthy. An enumeration of qualities clearly intended to suggest sophrosyne in a list of cardinal virtues names *pudor* and *continentia* (1. 2. 2),[63] while the discussion of moral standards for the young and for women refers to *verecundia* in a sense precisely like that given sophrosyne in comparable Greek passages (4. 4. 4, 4. 6. 6).[64] *Clementia* and *mansuetudo* are also given an honorable place among early Roman values by being ascribed to Numa Pompilius himself (2. 14. 27). A special feature in *De Republica* is Cicero's theory of the ideal *princeps,* modeled perhaps on Numa, perhaps on Scipio Aemilianus, perhaps even on Pompey.[65] Although the *princeps* must possess all four Platonic virtues,[66] he has a unique claim to *moderatio,* because his chief duties are to foresee the cycles in political life and control their course (*moderantem cursum,* 1. 29. 45) and to balance and harmonize all the elements in the State; thus he effects a *concordia* that Cicero, using the familiar Pythagorean and Platonic metaphor, likens to a harmony of dissimilar tones in music (*ex dissimillimarum vocum moderatione, moderata ratione,* 2. 42. 69). Hence Cicero describes the *princeps* not only as *rector* (2. 29. 51) but as *moderator* (5. 6. 8), and the ideal constitution over which he presides is said to be

---

[63] Also included here are the avoidance of disgrace and the search for glory, notable additions to the concept of sophrosyne in a treatise that assigns such importance to *gloria.* Other references to *pudor* include 1. 43. 67, 3. 18. 28, 5. 4. 6. There seems to be a reminiscence of the Greek tension between the active and the passive virtues in the description of Marcellus as *acer et pugnax* and of Maximus as *consideratus et lentus* (5. 8. 10). Cf. Plutarch *Marcellus* 9. 3.

[64] *Verecundia* receives more attention in Cicero's account of early Roman morals than any comparable virtue does in Polybius, but the word is not always to be interpreted as a translation of sophrosyne. The *verecundia* of Book V, which deters the best citizens from wrongdoing (5. 4. 6) is closer to *aidôs,* as is *pudor* in the same passage.

[65] Possible sources are discussed by G. H. Sabine and S. B. Smith, *Cicero on the Commonwealth* (Columbus, Ohio, 1929), 93 ff.

[66] *Rep.* 6. 6. 6 (Macrobius *In Somn. Scip.* 1. 1. 8). See Friedrich Solmsen, *C.P.* 35 (1940), 423–24.

moderatum et permixtum (1. 29. 45), *modice temperatum* (2. 29. 65) and *aequatum et temperatum* (1. 45. 69).

The vocabulary of the ideal state in *De Republica* provides an example of what might be called the linguistic Romanization of sophrosyne. The comparison of the rule of a king to the command of reason over the passions (1. 38. 60; cf. 2. 40. 67) is of course a commonplace in Greek treatises on kingship, but the discussion of the mixed constitution, also Greek in origin, takes on a distinctly Roman air with the terminology derived from *temperare* and *moderari*. Since *temperare* has the etymological meaning "to mix," it is natural for Cicero to describe the mixed constitution as *temperatum* (for example, the draught of liberty which the people drink should be *modice temperatam* rather than *nimis meracam*, 1. 43. 66),[67] just as it is natural for the cognates of *modus* to be used in describing the activities of the *moderator* who presides over the *moderatum et permixtum* constitution. Although it is sometimes implied in Greek discussions of political theory that a mixed constitution is *sôphrôn*,[68] the meaning of *sôphronizein* does not lend itself to the same interpretations as *temperare* and *moderari;*[69] hence in this nuance of the vocabulary of sophrosyne, Cicero shows genuine originality.

Like Isocrates, whose moral approach to politics he shares, Cicero demands that the governing class provide examples of good conduct, especially of self-control.[70] Just as he substitutes the early Roman

[67] An echo of Plato *Rep.* 562C–63E.

[68] Plato normally describes the mixed constitution as moderate, but employs the words *metron, metriotês,* rather than sophrosyne. *Laws* 691E–92A, on the mixture within the executive part of the Spartan constitution, speaks approvingly of mingling the *sôphrôn dynamis* of old age with the headstrong strength of the kings, to produce the *metron*. This passage is recalled by Cicero *Legg.* 3. 7. 17, describing the tribunate in Rome as a *modica et sapiens temperatio* of the power of the consuls. Plato's *sôphrôn* is rendered by *modica et sapiens,* while *temperatio* translates, not any form of sophrosyne, but the idea implied in Plato's μείγνυσι ("mingle"). Later on the Latin philosophical vocabulary employed *temperantia* itself (as well as *temperatio*) to translate Greek words for mixture. See Apuleius *De Mundo* 19. 333, where the mixture of diverse elements in the State is described as *civilis rationis temperantia;* cf. 21. 336 (the mingling of physical elements in the universe compared to a musical harmony: *natura veluti musicam temperavit*) and 22. 337. On the background of the theory of the mixed constitution, including Pythagorean concepts of mixture, harmony, and proportion, consult Glenn Morrow, *Plato's Cretan City* (Princeton, 1960), 521–43.

[69] A like application of *temperare* to literary style occurs in *Orat.* 6. 21, where *temperatus* with its radical meaning is predicated of the *medium genus dicendi*. See also *Orat.* 26. 95 (*modica et temperata*) and 16. 51 (the three styles termed *gravis, tenuis,* and *temperata*). Cicero cites as an example of *temperata oratio* his speech on the Manilian Law (*Orat.* 19. 102). Only in his rhetorical works does he describe as a *temperator* one who mixes (*Orat.* 70); the word does not occur as a synonym for *rector* or *moderator* in the Fragments of the *De Republica*.

[70] A study of Cicero's debt to Isocrates by S. E. Smethurst (*T.A.P.A.* 84 [1953], 262–320) finds among the important similarities the part that each played in creating national myths,

republic for the ideal State of Plato's imagination (2. 1. 3), so he gives to the *exemplum virtutis* the position that Plato in his *Republic* assigns to the Forms: the model to be imitated by the statesman of today, who is in turn a mirror to his fellow citizens (2. 42. 69).[71] Everywhere in *De Republica* (as well as in *De Legibus*) Cicero reveals his conviction that public service is the supreme good. In Book III he pronounces theoretical knowledge insufficient without experience in politics, and in the perennial weighing of the active against the contemplative life he decides for the active life as more deserving of praise and more conducive to fame (3. 3. 6). The effect this decision has on his interpretation of sophrosyne becomes evident in the *Somnium Scipionis*, Cicero's equivalent to the myth of Er, where a special reward is promised to the man who has deserved well of the State (6. 13. 13).

The *Somnium* reinterprets the Platonic theme of ὁμοίωσις θεῷ in an attempt to combine Greek and Roman elements. After discussing the immortality of the soul and the divinity of the *mens* in a thoroughly Hellenic tone, Cicero adds a Roman touch by suggesting that the best use of the soul is to serve the State (6. 24–29). Such service is in fact one source of immortality; another is detachment from corporeal things, especially from bodily pleasures—a fundamental cause of likeness to God in Pythagorean, Platonic, and Middle Stoic thought. The two modes of achieving *homoiôsis* are united without a truly organic relationship. A more successful synthesis is achieved in *De Legibus* where Cicero combines the Greek doctrine that self-knowledge is knowledge of the Divine element in man, with the Roman tradition about the primacy of service to the State. In his analysis of "Know thyself" he first maintains that the proverb requires man to realize his likeness to God and

---

the attempt of each to use the past as a model for the future, and their emphasis on self-control as a primary requirement in statesmen.

[71] The *exempla* favored in Cicero's philosophical works are for the most part identical with those in the orations. Rambaud (45) notes that in oratory Roman models are cited before Greek, but in the philosophical treatises the order is reversed. Scipio Africanus Major, Fabricius, and Piso Frugi exemplify *abstinentia* on the part of the magistrate: the first because of his conduct in Sicily; the second because of his refusal of the bribe offered by Pyrrhus; the third chiefly because of his suggestive *cognomen*. See *Verr.* 2. III. 84. 195; *Font.* 17. 39; *De Or.* 2. 51; *Brutus* 106; *Legg.* 1. 2. 6. In *Par. Sto.* 3. 48 Fabricius is celebrated for his *continentia*. Lucretia and Verginia are always the models for feminine *castitas* and *pudicitia* (*Fin.* 5. 22. 64, 2. 20. 66; *Rep.* 2. 25. 46, 2. 37. 63). *Exempla horribilia* among men are Tarquinius Superbus, Sextus Tarquinius, and Appius Claudius the Decemvir: the first for *insolentia* and *superbia* (*Rep.* 2. 25. 45–46); the second for *stuprum* (*Legg.* 2. 20. 66); and the third for *intemperies* (*Rep.* 2. 27. 63). The role played by *exempla virtutis* in his own life is described by Cicero in the Archias oration (12–14). Consult John H. Taylor, S.J., *A.J.P.* 73 (1952), 62–70, on the relation between this passage and *Ep. Fam.* v. 7.

his place in the cosmos, and then traces the effect of this realization on man's behavior as a citizen of the State.[72] One consequence is law-abiding conduct. It is Divine law, not merely written, positive law, Cicero maintains, that prohibits such behavior as that of the wanton Sextus Tarquin, which threatens the welfare of the political organism (2. 4. 10). In a later book of *De Legibus* Cicero returns to the notion that the dangerous example of public figures corrupts the State more thoroughly than their very crimes bring it harm (3. 14. 31); again the bad example that he singles out is that given by *cupiditates principum*. The corrective virtue is here called *continentia* (3. 13. 30; cf. *Brutus* 329).

THE HISTORIANS

The prominence of the topic of sophrosyne (under whatever Latin name) in Roman historiography is in part a consequence of Cicero's preoccupation with the effect of example in the State and his emphasis on the particular danger presented by the two vices of *avaritia* and *luxuria,* which it is the function of sophrosyne to restrain. Livy is the historian who responded most sympathetically to Cicero's influence and put into operation the orator's suggestions about both the style and the moral framework suitable for composing Roman history. Sallust and Tacitus were so remote from Cicero in temperament, political sympathies, and literary style that they to a larger measure—though not entirely— avoided the Ciceronian impress. Sallust, it is true, often recalls Cicero in his persistent allusions to the moral decline of Rome and his close attention to the corrupting effect of *avaritia* and *luxuria*.[73] Yet these topics had long since been employed by the Annalists, including the Elder Cato, for whom Sallust felt particular admiration. Already in Cato's *Origines* the idealization of the ancestors had led to the praise of the *vita Italica* for its *disciplina* (Frag. 76) and the comparison of Sabine *mores* to those of Sparta (Frag. 51). The same attitude informs the discussion of the *vita* and *victus* of Romulus by Piso Frugi (Frag. 8 Peters), his denunciation of the moral corruption of the young in his own day (Frag. 40), and his comment on the subversion of *pudicitia* after the year 154 B.C. (Frag. 38). Nor were the Roman Annalists the only models available to Sallust: he found congenial a number of Greek

---

[72] I. 22. 59.

[73] The evidence for Cicero's influence on Sallust is presented by Rambaud, 123–34. It consists largely of similar views on the moral character of the leader and its importance to the State, the moral decline of Rome as a result of *cupido,* and the dating of this decline from the reign of Sulla. The various dates for the onset of Rome's *degeneratio,* according to various ancient authorities, are discussed by Earl, 42–44.

writers—Plato, Xenophon, and above all Thucydides—who could show him how to manipulate the topics of ancestral virtue and present-day corruption.[74] Among verbal reminiscences of Thucydides in works ascribed to Sallust is an echo of the famous passage about the trans-valuation of ethical terms (3. 82. 4). Thucydides' τὸ δὲ σῶφρον τοῦ ἀνάνδρου πρόσχημα becomes *pudorem atque modestiam pro socordia aestimant* (*Ep. ad Caes.* 1. 6).[75] *Socordia* and *ignavia,* rather than the Ciceronian *intemperantia,* are the historian's favorite antitheses to the concept of so-phrosyne;[76] while sophrosyne itself is usually rendered by such ancient Latin approximations as *pudor* (or *pudicitia*), *modestia,* or *continentia,* rather than by Cicero's favorite, *temperantia,* which—like *frugalitas*—is virtually ignored.[77]

The relation of sophrosyne to Sallust's concept of *virtus Romana* is explained in the preface to the *Bellum Catilinae,* where we learn that it was *cupiditas* and *lubido dominandi* ("lust for conquest") that put an end to *virtus* in its early, ideal condition (2. 1–2). When *desidia, lubido,* and *superbia* took the place of *labor, continentia,* and *aequitas,* Roman morality was utterly changed (2. 5); and in Sallust's own youth *pudor, abstinentia,* and *virtus* were replaced by *audacia, largitio,* and *avaritia* (3. 3–4). In his character sketch of Catiline, Sallust reveals how, in his view, the lack of sophrosyne may join with other flaws to produce a thoroughly depraved personality. Prominent among Catiline's traits were the failure to moderate his appetites and a passionate lust to seize control of the State (5. 5–6), while his effect on the young men who flocked around him was to destroy their *modestia* (14. 6) and *pudor* (16. 2–3).

---

[74] Specific debts of Sallust to these and other Greek sources are noted by Paul Perrochat, *Les modèles grecs de Salluste* (Paris, 1949).

[75] Thucydides' *pleonexia* and *philotimia* become Sallust's *pecuniae cupido* and *imperi cupido* (*Cat.* 10. 3). Arguments for the genuineness of the *Letters to Caesar* are given by Karl Büchner, *Sallust* (Heidelberg, 1960). For a summary of views on the authenticity of the *Epistles,* see Karl Vretska, *C. Sallustius Crispus, Invektive und Episteln* (Heidelberg, 1961), 1. 41–48. Consult also D. C. Earl, *Mus. Helv.* 16 (1959), 152–58.

[76] Socordia: *Jug.* 31. 2, 55. 1, 85. 22. Ignavia: *Jug.* 2. 4; 44. 5; 85. 14. It will be recalled that *ignavia* is an antithesis to sophrosyne in Roman comedy, but that Cicero tends to make it a vice opposed to *fortitudo* (*Cat.* 2. 25). Sallust also opposes *luxuria* and *avaritia* to sophrosyne, as Cicero had done. Other antitheses include *superbia* (*Jug.* 85. 13), *inertia* (*Jug.* 1. 4), *luxus* (*Jug.* 2. 4), and *lubido* (*Jug.* 3. 4).

[77] *Temperantia* does, however, appear among the virtues of Metellus in *Jug.* 45. 1, where it enables him to restore the *disciplina maiorum* to the Roman army in Africa, which had been entirely devoid of *imperium et modestia* (44. 1–2) and given over to *ignavia luxuriaque* (44. 5). Sallust also has Marius comment on the difficulty of maintaining *temperantia* in the midst of power (*Jug.* 85. 9; cf. *Cat.* 11. 8). Reminiscent of the ethical vocabulary of Roman comedy is Sallust's trick of using alliterative phrases, such as *sine modo modestiaque* (*Jug.* 41. 9) and *licentia atque lascivia* (*Jug.* 39. 5).

After these virtues were gone, there was nothing to restrain the downward progress of Catiline's followers.

A complementary account of the positive effect of virtues allied with sophrosyne in the life of a public figure may be found in Sallust's picture of the younger Cato, whom he portrays both through his speech before the Senate and through contrasting character sketches of Cato and Caesar. In the speech Cato repeatedly castigates *luxuria* and *avaritia* (52. 7, 22), rejects Caesar's pleas for *mansuetudo* and *misericordia* in dealing with the conspirators (52. 11, 27), harks back to the ancestral virtues (*domi industria, foris iustum imperium* [52. 2, 22]), and presents a consistent picture of unwavering *severitas*. In the character sketch Sallust distinguishes Cato from Caesar mainly on the basis of Cato's *modestia, decus, severitas, modestus pudor,* and *innocens abstinentia* (54. 5–6), in contrast to Caesar's restless activity, calculated generosity, and ambition. He concludes the pair of contrasting portraits by applying to Cato the phrase used by Aeschylus of the *sôphrôn* Amphiaraus: "He preferred to be, rather than to seem, a good man." Unlike Caesar, who actively sought military experience in order to display his *virtus,* Cato achieved glory by the very fact that he did not seek it (54. 6). The whole passage is Thucydidean in its use of the traditional contrast between the qualities linked with sophrosyne, the "quiet" virtue, and those allied with the active temperament; yet Sallust avoids any suggestion that Cato and Caesar went to undesirable extremes in pursuit of their respective virtues—as had Nicias and Alcibiades, according to Thucydides.[78]

A much closer approximation to the Ciceronian ethical vocabulary is found in Livy, who in many ways fulfills Cicero's requirements for a historian, as set forth in *De Legibus.* He handles both *narratio* and *exornatio* according to the standards of the orator-statesman, while he follows Cicero with remarkable fidelity in his pragmatic conception of the historian's task, in his belief that history has a moral purpose, in his extensive use of *exempla virtutum et vitiorum,* and in his confidence that a

---

[78] Cato Uticensis is cited as a model of both sophrosyne and *andreia* in Julian's *Misopôgôn* (358A). Caesar, in Sallust's portrait, is devoid of qualities associated with sophrosyne, since there is as yet no well-established connection between this excellence and *mansuetudo.* In the *Jug.* Sallust employs the same ethical vocabulary as in the *Cat.,* assigning to Metellus (44–46) certain aspects of sophrosyne—notably *temperantia* and *innocentia* ("absence of corruption")—and ascribing to Marius others (63. 2)—especially self-restraint (*animus . . . domi modicus, lubidinis et divitiarum victor*). Metellus, at one point a model of *temperantia,* at another point becomes an exemplar of that *hybris* (*superbia, contemptor animus*) that the nobles displayed towards the *homo novus* (64. 1).

great personality has the power to shape the *êthos* of a whole society.

Among the themes that pervade the *History*, one of the most ubiquitous is the condemnation of a small group of *vitia*, including *amor, cupido, libido, avaritia,* and *superbia,* each of which is in some fashion antithetical to sophrosyne. In connection with these *vitia*, Livy makes the greatest use of historical models, elevating the rhetorical *exemplum* to a position of major importance in his didactic approach to his task and perpetuating the method—as well as many of the models—already used by Cicero in his study of the early centuries of the Republic.[79] The preface, which reaffirms the moral purpose of historiography (9) and recognizes *luxuria* and *avaritia* as the special vices of Rome (11), maintains that these vices arose later there than in any other great state but have finally brought about a situation in which the body politic is so diseased that neither the ailment nor its cure can be endured. Livy often applies to the State the metaphor of disease and health; he uses such terms as *contagio, rabies, furor,* and *insania* to censure conduct of which he disapproves. Since sophrosyne even in its Latin translations—especially *sanitas* and *sobrietas,* but also *temperantia*—maintains its traditional connection with health and soundness of mind, the virtues allied with it tend to be prominent as remedies for the ills of Rome, although it would be rash to assert that Livy has this connection in mind whenever he employs the metaphor of health and sickness.[80]

While the historian emphasizes the negative aspects of Roman morality in calling attention to the *exempla vitiorum*, he leaves no doubt about the qualities that he considers necessary for a healthy political organism. These include *moderatio*, especially in the use of power, illustrated by the behavior of the decemvirs in 451 B.C. (3. 33. 9); *temperantia*, which is both restraint of the appetites, as in Scipio's advice to Masinissa (30. 12. 18), and control of the lust for power and office, as in the case of Manlius Torquatus' refusal of a consulship in 211;[81] *pudicitia*, a theme

---

[79] Livy's treatment of the virtues and vices is analyzed by Lydia Halle in her unpublished dissertation "A Study of Moralization in Livy" (Bryn Mawr, 1957). For Livy's interest in certain moral qualities, including *pudicitia, clementia,* and *pietas,* see P. G. Walsh, *A.J.P.* 76 (1955), 369–83, and *Livy: His Historical Aims and Methods* (Cambridge, 1961), 46–81.

[80] *Sanus:* 2. 45. 2, 8. 27. 9 (*sanus animus*); 3. 17. 3 (*sana civitas*); 23. 7. 4, 45. 10. 11, 32. 121. 37, 40. 6. 4 (*sana mens*); 3. 17. 3, 2. 29. 6 (*sanitas in curia*).

[81] Livy's comment on Torquatus' action contains an obvious allusion to the sophrosyne of Plato's philosopher-rulers: not even in a city of philosophers could there be *principes graviores temperantioresque a cupidine imperii* (26. 22. 14). *Temperantia* and *gravitas* are also linked in 3. 22. 14. For Livy's approval of *temperantia* in the use of *libertas,* see 34. 49. 8; for the connection of *moderatio* with *concordia,* 3. 33. 9; and with *gloria,* 3. 68. 6, 26. 26. 9. Further examples of Livy's approval of *moderatio* appear in 24. 25. 8, 30. 17. 5, 28. 24. 1–2, 28. 27. 11, 24. 31. 14.

developed in great detail in the stories of Lucretia and Verginia, both of which are used to illustrate the danger to the State of *libido* and its consequences (3. 44. 1);[82] *disciplina militaris,* which L. Aemilius Paulus is praised for maintaining;[83] and *clementia* towards the conquered enemy, said to be a Roman tradition dating from the time of Camillus' merciful treatment of the people of Tusculum (6. 26. 1).[84]

A single instance of Livy's technique of combining the *exemplum virtutis* with the moralizing speech of exhortation must suffice. This rhetorical method unites the pure *exemplum,* familiar in the oratory of every period, with the fictitious speech composed by the historian to convey his own moral precepts, to which he gives additional *auctoritas* by ascribing them to a figure noted for the very type of moral excellence being discussed. The most elaborate moral lecture delivered by any model of sophrosyne in Livy's *History* is the speech of Scipio Africanus Major to Masinissa, King of Numidia, on the occasion of the king's hasty marriage to Sophoniba, daughter of Hasdrubal and former wife of Syphax, a sermon full of echoes of the Cynic-Stoic diatribe.[85] Scipio's disapproval of the marriage, Livy points out, is the more acute because of Scipio's own record in Spain, where even in his youth he was never overcome by the temptations of lust (cf. 26. 49. 1 and 50). Scipio now tells Masinissa that he prides himself on his *temperantia* and *continentia* more than on the other virtues that Masinissa so much admires in him. The king, too, should acquire these qualities, because no danger is so

---

[82] Sextus Tarquinius and Appius Claudius the Decemvir are the chief exemplars of that *libido* which fosters danger to the State. Cicero had already cited them in this connection in *Fin.* 2. 20. 66.

[83] For this theme in Livy, see Walsh, *loc. cit.,* especially p. 381, nn. 51–54.

[84] *Gravitas, pietas,* and *fides* are the other quintessentially Roman qualities whose absence from contemporary Rome Livy deplores.

[85] Another example of this technique is the speech of the Elder Cato against the repeal of the *Lex Oppia.* He rebukes the women who desire its repeal, charging them with *luxuria* and lack of *pudor* (34. 2. 10), then passes from this charge to a general condemnation of *luxuria* and *avaritia* as the two plagues of empire. He links both vices with Greece and Asia. Like Cicero and Sallust, Livy professes to regard the Roman taste for Greek art as a danger sign and associates pleasure in such importations with scorn for the old religion. The moral threat presented by Asia (34. 4. 3, 25. 40. 1–2, 38. 17. 18) is shared by Capua, whose *voluptas, licentia,* and utter lack of *modus* corrupt impartially both the Romans and the army of Hannibal (7. 31. 6, 7. 32. 7, 18. 10–12, 38. 1). Syracuse, a Greek city, is also a symbol of *luxuria;* the beginning of Rome's admiration for Greek ways is sometimes traced to the plunder of Syracuse (25. 31. 9). Westward the course of sophrosyne took its way. It will be recalled that Aeschylus regarded sophrosyne as Hellenic and its opposite as characteristic of oriental peoples. Now Cato considers moderation and restraint Roman, luxury Greek. Still later Tacitus was to hold up the barbarians in Germany as models of a certain kind of sophrosyne (*pudicitia*) for degenerate Rome. For the rhetorical commonplace based on the virtues and vices of cities, see Quintilian 3. 7. 26.

great as that presented by *voluptas.* He who has bridled and mastered
his appetites by *temperantia* has won a victory greater than the recent
military victory over Syphax (30. 14). Masinissa, deeply impressed by
this admonition, sends Sophoniba a draught of poison. Livy approves
this ruthless solution at least partly because of Sophoniba's reputation
for having incited her first husband, Syphax, against the Romans.
Syphax himself blames her for his own *furor* in deserting Rome (30. 13.
11 ff.) and observes that, in marrying her, Masinissa has behaved more
foolishly and immoderately (*stultius atque intemperantius*) than he himself
had previously behaved.

This episode is perhaps the most striking instance of Livy's condemnation of *amor* or *libido* as a source of political disaster.[86] His most
inclusive designation for the Roman appetite for evil is *cupido*—especially in the Sallustian phrase *cupido regni* or *imperi*—a vice manifested in
Roman society as early as the time of Romulus and Remus (1. 6. 3–4).
Superbia appears most frequently in a military context and is often
ascribed to the enemies of Rome but may sometimes account for a
disaster suffered by the Romans themselves, as in the case of the *superbia*
shown to the Samnites at the Caudine Forks (9. 1. 8) or the arrogance
of Flamininus (22. 3. 4–5). *Superbia* naturally receives special attention
in the story of the Tarquins, which occupies a position in Livy's narrative not unlike that of Croesus in the *History* of Herodotus, standing as
a kind of prologue which embodies the principal moral themes of the
entire work. In the case of the Tarquins *superbia*—accompanied by *cupido
regni, libido, vis,* and contempt for Roman *libertas*—constitutes an archetype of the threats to the welfare of the State that are described in later
books of the *History*.

The themes of *superbia* and *libido* are particular favorites of Tacitus as
well, but although he employs them with great skill in both the
Histories and the *Annals* to enhance his account of the imperial vices,
his methods, like his literary style and his very vocabulary, are for the
most part un-Ciceronian. Tacitus indeed uses recognizable commonplaces of sophrosyne in all his extant works, but he shows increasing
independence as he matures. The topics appear in their most conventional form in the *Agricola,* where the devices of epideictic oratory
provide a framework for the biography of Tacitus' father-in-law, and
various facets of sophrosyne appear in traditional order to create the

---

[86] Other examples are those of Flamininus (39. 42. 5–43), Sextus Tarquinius (1. 58.
5), and Antiochus (36. 11. 1–2), whose marriage to a young girl encourages the spread of
luxuria in his army.

desired impression of Agricola's moderation and integrity.[87] The most original interpretation of sophrosyne in this highly conventional picture comes towards the end, when the *moderatio* of Agricola is contrasted, not only with the *ira* of the jealous emperor, Domitian, but even more pointedly with the useless defiance—*contumacia* and *inanis iactatio libertatis* (42)—of the Stoic martyrs. Agricola proved that *obsequium* and *modestia* ("compliance" and "unobtrusiveness"), no less than *ambitiosa mors,* can win glory. With this observation Tacitus makes his own highly characteristic comment on the antithesis between sophrosyne and *andreia.* It is an intensely Roman observation as well in that the goal of both ways of life, the cautious and the bold, is renown.[88]

Topics traditionally linked with sophrosyne are present also in the *Germania* and the *Dialogus de Oratoribus,*[89] but Tacitus' special touch is most evident in the *Histories* and the *Annals,* where he uses some of these topics to bring out the darker side of imperial history. Although he maintains that the period of the Empire was not barren of virtue and even produced *bona exempla,*[90] although, in fact, he proclaims that the pre-eminent function of the *Annals* is to save *virtutes* from oblivion, as well as to hold up to the contempt of posterity base deeds and words (3. 65. 1), he shows an increasing disposition to treat the topic of the virtues with reserve. Syme calls attention to Tacitus' habit of mentioning only ironically or even ignoring altogether those virtues that had been canonized by writers of the Republican era (especially Cicero) and that were being progressively debased by the imperial propaganda machine.[91] Thus when he speaks of *moderatio* in connection with Tiberius,

---

[87] E.g., the *rara castitas* of Agricola's mother (4) and the *moderatio* (7), *temperantia* (8), and *abstinentia* (9) of Agricola himself under various circumstances, all of them connected with public service as general or governor. Syme (123, 198) comments on the presence of conventional moralizing topics in the *Agricola,* including the Ciceronian *peroratio.*

[88] Cf. Sallust's contrast between the ways in which Cato and Caesar achieved fame (*Cat.* 54. 5–6), where, however, both the *sôphrôn* and the *andrikos* ways of life win the historian's approval.

[89] *Germania:* the contrast between the moral purity of the barbarians and the corruption of Roman society (19). But Tacitus does not make the savage entirely noble. He remarks the lack of discipline and the intemperance in drink characteristic of the Germans (23). *Dialogus:* the topic of *degeneratio* and the vocabulary of *temperantia* applied to the criticism of oratory. Messalla uses the traditional vocabulary when he praises Cicero for *sanitas eloquentiae* (25), accuses Cassius Severus of being the first to disregard *modestia* and *pudor verborum* (26), and traces the decline of oratory to the *oblivio moris antiqui* (28). Cf. Cicero *Orat.* 19. 64 and Seneca *Ep.* 114.

[90] *Hist., Prol.* 1. 3.

[91] Syme (344 ff. and Appendix 66, 754 ff.) enumerates several terms that Tacitus avoids, presumably because of his disgust at their abuse: *iustitia, aequitas, felicitas.*

he at one stroke transforms the virtue into a vice by adding the adjective *adroganti* (*Ann.* 1. 8); and when he quotes the emperor as ascribing *temperantia* to himself, he makes sure that we will interpret it as hypocrisy (*Ann.* 1. 14). *Clementia* is another aspect of sophrosyne which he either pointedly ignores or mentions only in a spirit of irony (*Ann.* 4. 74. 2; 11. 3. 1).[92] The vices that Tacitus ascribes to the various emperors are for the most part those that constitute a threat to the liberty of Rome: they have, that is, a strong political significance, in contrast to the private and personal vices of extravagance and excessive indulgence in appetite which Suetonius chooses to emphasize.

Suetonius, who pictures Caligula and Nero as notably intemperate, especially by reason of their gluttony and lust, and draws unforgettable sketches of other members of the imperial family who depart from traditional Roman standards of *pudicitia*,[93] employs many of the techniques of the satirist, without the satirist's reforming motive. Inevitably his depiction of the licentiousness of the Julio-Claudian emperors recalls those scenes in Roman satire which hold up to ridicule the excesses, follies, and perversions of the rich. Although the Roman satirists from Lucilius to Juvenal were indebted in obvious ways to the Greek Cynic-Stoic diatribe for the theme of *intemperantia* in appetite,[94] they embellished this theme with a multitude of details drawn from native sources, so that the topics of the *cena*, of *avaritia*, and of *impudicitia* came to appear more Roman than Greek, and the *sôphronizôn logos* of the Hellenistic diatribe found a predestined target in Roman society. The satirists themselves show varying degrees of moderation in their treatment of these themes. In the history of satire *saeva indignatio*, whether that of Juvenal or of Swift, has on the whole been more prevalent than the Horatian *risus;* and even Horace in his earlier *sermones* lacks the detachment and stylistic sophrosyne that mark his later satires and all the epistles.[95]

[92] For *clementia* and *moderatio* as imperial virtues, see below pp. 300–7.

[93] E.g., *impudicitia*: Caligula 24, 25, 36; Nero 26–29; *violentia, saevitia, superbia*: Caligula 26–28, Nero 36–38; extravagance: Caligula 37, Nero 30–31. On the *impudicitia, crudelitas,* and *avaritia* of other emperors, see *Julius Caesar* 49, 50–52, Augustus 68–69, 71, Tiberius 60–62, Claudius 33–34, Domitian 10–12, 22.

[94] On the *sôphronizôn logos* of the Cynics and its influence on Hellenistic and Roman poetry, see Gustav Gerhard, *Phoinix von Kolophon* (Leipzig, 1909), 228–84; and Johannes Geffcken, *Kynika und Verwandtes* (Heidelberg, 1909), 1–44. The tradition of the δεῖπνον, the comic treatment of sumptuous dinners, also had great influence on Roman satire dealing with the *cena*. Consult L. R. Shero, *C.P.* 18 (1923), 126–43, and *A.J.P.* 50 (1929), 64–70.

[95] See, e.g., the milder treatment of sexual folly in *Ser.* I. 2 and 8, contrasted with *Ser.* II. 3. 247–80.

HORACE AND VIRGIL

It is in Horace, after all, and to a considerable extent in Virgil, that the Roman effort to transplant sophrosyne came to fruition. Both poets, in the moral content and in the very form of their verse, succeeded where earlier writers, even Cicero, had failed. Both managed to express in Roman terms most of the essential elements of sophrosyne, failing only where radically different political conditions made success impossible.

Both by temperament and by reason of his thorough formation in Greek modes of thought, Horace is easily the most *sôphrôn* of Roman authors.[96] He makes completely his own the themes of Hellenistic philosophy, including the popular conception of sophrosyne, just as he makes completely his own the forms of Greek lyric verse. The union of the personal and the political in early Greek lyric, especially that of Alcaeus, made these forms peculiarly suitable for the expression of Horace's own combination of private and public sentiments. He was more fortunate than Cicero in that the two sides of his personality could be united in the figure of the *vates,* and the convictions expressed in his earliest poetry, concerned chiefly with the problems of private life, could in his maturity be applied with equal fitness to Roman society. The core of Horace's personal philosophy, as has often been pointed out, is contentment with little; [97] and for him the fundamental meaning of sophrosyne is always moderation, to which he gives definitive Roman expression in the *aurea mediocritas* (both the phrase and the idea), which is the keynote of his verse.[98] In the *Sermones,* where the poet is still searching for his authentic voice, this theme has already emerged as one peculiarly congenial to him amid the inherited conventions of Lucilian *satura* and the Cynic-Stoic diatribe. In the *Odes* it remains a dominant concern, treated now with a corresponding sophrosyne of style, which reveals itself in the exquisite wedding of thought, emotion, and diction —that apparently effortless control for which Petronius found the perfect phrase, *curiosa felicitas.*[99]

[96] This is a commonplace of Horatian criticism. See Fraenkel (214) on the combination of the sophrosyne of the private individual and the *sophia* of the *vates* in *Odes* 2. 16. The sophrosyne of Horace's style is analyzed by William Everett, *H.S.C.P.* 12 (1901), 9, 16.

[97] The development of this ideal and its extension from private to public life are discussed by Friedrich Solmsen, *A.J.P.* 68 (1947), 337 ff. On the debt of Horace to the example of Archilochus and Alcaeus in uniting the personal and the political in lyric poetry, see Viktor Pöschl in *L'Influence grecque sur la poésie latine de Catulle à Ovide* (Vandoeuvre-Genève, 1953).

[98] See especially *Odes* 2. 10. 5–8 and *Ser.* I. 1. 106, 2. 25, 6. 68; II. 3.

[99] Consult Solmsen (*loc. cit.*) on the difference in diction between the *Sermones* and the *Odes,*

The degree to which the Horatian theme of moderation is absolutely personal, not acquired, is evident from the ease with which the poet puts his stamp on the worn coinage of the diatribe and the rhetorical schools. The *vita rustica* above all comes to life on the Sabine Farm where the contrast between city life with its vices and country life with its austerity for once carries a measure of conviction.[100] It is in fact the Sabine Farm that unifies and gives point to Horace's use of several topics of sophrosyne, both the negative themes of *degeneratio* and *avaritia* and the positive themes of simplicity, self-knowledge, and contentment with what is at hand. His most impressive treatment of *degeneratio,* for example, occurs in the sixth Roman ode, which contrasts the *luxuria* and *dedecus* of the present with the heroic qualities of the age that stained the sea with Punic blood. The emotional impact of the poem derives chiefly from the two stanzas that suggest the manliness of the early Republic through a vignette of the sons of *rustici milites,* who are trained to till the soil with Sabine hoes and perform other tasks at the bidding of a stern mother—

---

and the way in which the theme of moderation is remolded in accordance with the character of Horace's lyric poetry. It would take too long to discuss in detail the sophrosyne of Horace's personal odes, a subject to which much attention has been directed of late, but the following odes deserve special notice:

1. 31, which combines with the honor paid to Apollo, the god of sophrosyne, Horace's judicious rejection of various ways of life and his final prayer for contentment with what is at hand, an old age *nec turpem nec cithara carentem,* and health of mind and body. *Integra mens* is Horace's most literal translation of sophrosyne.

2. 2, on the *temperatus usus* of money and the need to rule the *avidus spiritus.* The significance of the key word *temperato* in v. 3 is discussed by A. O. Hulton, *C.P.* 56 (1961), 173–75, and William M. Calder III, *C.P.* 56 (1961), 175–78.

2. 3, on the *mens temperata* to be maintained in *res arduae* and *bonae.* It is indicative of the basic likeness of the chief Hellenistic ethical systems that *Odes* 2. 2. and 3 should apply the identical terminology of *temperantia* to both Stoic and Epicurean commonplaces. The past participle of *temperare* occurs at precisely the same place in v. 3 of each ode. Cf. the emphatic position of *temperatam* in 3. 4. 66. On Horace's use of *temperare,* see n. 106.

2. 10, which employs Horace's favorite image of sophrosyne: the voyager who must steer a middle course between the treacherous shore and the perilous deep, and which contains the classical formulation of the theory of the Mean. *Sobrius* in v. 8 recalls the translation of *sôphrôn* favored by the comic poets. See Donald Levin, *C.J.* 54 (1959), 169–71, on the references to all four cardinal virtues in this ode.

3. 1, in praise of the contentment of the man *desiderantem quod satis est.* A favorite Horatian image connected with the antithesis to sophrosyne appears here: the *dominus terrae fastidiosus,* who builds his seaside villa on piles sunk into the sea itself. For other uses of this image, see Commager, 82, on *Odes* 2. 18.

4. 9, in which again the tetrad of Stoic virtues is ascribed to the person addressed, in this case Lollius (34–52).

[100] *Epode* 2; *Odes* 2. 18. 1–4; 3. 1. 45–48; 3. 6. 33–34. For some perceptive comments on Horace's love of simplicity provided it was not accompanied by rigorous austerity, see M. E. Taylor, *A.J.P.* 83 (1962), 23–43.

a *pudica mulier* like the Sabine or Apulian matron of *Epode* 2. 39.[101] The choice of the epithet *Sabellis* to describe the hoes betrays the source of Horace's imagery: some typical scene in his own Sabine district, where the activities that bring the day to a close contrast sharply with those depicted in the preceding nighttime scene of stanzas six to eight, involving the *matura virgo* who delights to learn lascivious oriental dances; the contrasting types of *doctrina* in the two scenes form the moral basis of the ode.

This device of contrasts, so characteristic of Horace, is fully exploited in *Odes* 2. 16 (*Otium divos*), where each set of antitheses contains one term illustrating moderation and one illustrating excess. Contentment with little is opposed to greed for wealth and power; the soul that rejoices in the present is opposed to that which cannot leave care behind; and enormous wealth, represented by the possession of huge herds, swift racing mares, and costly apparel, is contrasted with the poet's own treasures: *parva rura*, the gift of lyric song, and the confidence in his position as a poet which enables him to scorn the envious throng. Nothing is lacking except the application of these themes to public, as well as private, life—the final expression of Horace's mission as a *vates*. This step is actually taken in the preceding ode (2. 15, *Iam pauca aratro*), which protests the conversion of farmland and vineyards to gardens and extravagant villas and sets against a detailed description of such unproductive plots of land the *auspicia* and *veterum norma* of Romulus and bearded Cato.[102] The relation between the theme of moderation and the welfare of the State is presented with great vigor in *Odes* 3. 24 (*Intactis opulentior*), which includes an appeal for someone to check *licentia* and *cupido* (29, 51) with a genuine reform. It was his acceptance, however reluctant, of the Augustan settlement and his deep concern for the destiny of Rome that induced Horace to transfer to the State the principles that guided him in his private life, and to praise the *princeps* for his efforts to restore a higher standard of morality (*Odes* 4. 4, 5, 6, 15, especially).[103]

Yet it is in precisely those odes in which Horace is most concerned to show the need for sophrosyne in the life of the State that we are most aware of the chasm between the Greek and the Roman conceptions of

[101] L. P. Wilkinson (*Horace and His Lyric Poetry* [Cambridge, 1945], 29) has a detailed analysis of this Ode.

[102] Solmsen (*loc. cit.*) points out that Horace uses the very detail selected by Sallust *Cat.* 13–14.

[103] See Burck, *loc. cit.*, on the *moderatio* of the Augustan principate. Horace mentions sympathetically the *princeps'* effort to check extravagant building as well as his attempt to improve family life; *temperantia* offered a cure for both extravagance and sexual promiscuity.

this quality. The nursery of Attic sophrosyne had been the free and
democratic city-state of the sixth and fifth centuries, but the Roman
oligarchy had never experienced the precise combination of circumstances—the interaction between the self-assertion of the individual and
the restraints imposed by a *polis* of equally individualistic fellow citizens
—that had nurtured the sophrosyne of Solon and Aeschylus. Hence the
Roman poet knows only two ways of applying sophrosyne to the problems of the State: he can preach the morality of restraint for the entire
city, concentrating on the themes of *luxuria* and *avaritia* which he had
learned, not from his Greek lyric models, but from Cicero and the
historians; [104] or he can single out the only other aspect of sophrosyne
which carries weight in the principate—namely the moderation of the
princeps himself, which is usually interpreted as restraint in the use of his
power over conquered foes. This is the aspect of sophrosyne—*clementia*—
that Horace celebrates in the fourth Roman ode, *Descende caelo;* here, too,
a debt to Cicero is apparent, for the poet echoes in evident sincerity the
note that we have heard sounded in the speeches of the year 46 B.C.—
the praise of *lene consilium* in an absolute ruler and the implied or
express plea for the merciful use of his power.

This solemn ode, with its Pindaric use of the symbolism of music to
represent the harmony of the State in which warring parties have at last
been reconciled,[105] first establishes Horace's right to speak as a *vates*
(*Musis amicus*), then ascribes to the Muses a love for *lene consilium*, and
after depicting in vivid detail the mythical conflict between the Giants
and the Olympians, sums up the meaning of this ancient story with the
significant words: *Vis consili expers mole ruit sua; vim temperatam di quoque
provehunt in maius* (65–67). The word *consili* echoes the earlier *lene consilium*,
while *vis temperata* describes in a characteristically Horatian phrase
(almost a *callida iunctura*) that blending of *andreia* and sophrosyne which
was the Hellenic ideal. In the context of this ode the chief emphasis falls

---

[104] The influence of Cicero on Horace, especially in the Horatian *Epistles*, is studied
by Walter Wili, *Horaz* (Basel, 1948). Edmund Silk (*Y.C.S.* 13 [1952], 147–58) discusses
specific reminiscences in the *Odes*. See Pöschl (*op. cit.,* 108) for parallels between the second
Roman ode and Cicero's ideal of the statesman.

[105] Fraenkel (280–85) discusses the resemblance of this ode to the first Pythian with its in-
vocation to the lyre, and the eighth Pythian, which contrasts the personified *Hasychia* with
the giants Porphyrio and Typhoeus. See also T. H. Wade-Gery, *J.H.S.* 4 (1932), 214,
and, among many commentaries on *Odes* 3. 4: the explication by Wilkinson, *op. cit.;* the discussions by Steele Commager, *Horace*, 204–8, and *A.J.P.* 80 (1959), 37–55; and Louis
McKay, *C.R.* 46 (1942), 243–45; and the comments by Pöschl, *op. cit.,* 114–15, on music as
a civilizing force in Plato's *Laws* and the frequency with which Horace invokes Apollo
in the *Odes*.

on sophrosyne. The possession of *vis*, by the Giants and the Olympians, Antony and Octavian, is taken for granted; and it is the presence of sophrosyne or *temperantia* [106] that distinguishes the victors—morally— from the vanquished and wins the approbation of the gods. In this belief Horace comes close to the fifth-century Greek conception of sophrosyne as maximum passion under absolute control. The ode also shows Horace to be more sensitive than most Romans to the essential meaning of *hybris*. Whereas his countrymen generally do no more than equate it with *superbia*, Horace perceives that *hybris* in its classical form is the extreme to which the heroic individual goes when he lacks self-knowledge and therefore self-restraint. The phrase *vis consili expers* implies that power or passion, *with* the help of wisdom, might still be transformed into sophrosyne, *vis temperata;* and there is no denying the sympathy with which Horace speaks of *Terra* and her defeated children. It is at this point that the Roman interpretation of sophrosyne is added to the Greek, for the *vis temperata* of the victorious Olympians is, by implication, to take the form of *clementia*, the imperial virtue of Augustus, who is described in the *Carmen Saeculare* as *bellante prior, iacentem lenis in hostem* (51–52).[107]

A close connection between the Roman odes and the speech of Anchises in the *Aeneid* (VI. 847–53) has often been perceived.[108] The parallel between *parcere subiectis et debellare superbos* (853) and the virtues celebrated in *Odes* 3. 4 and 1 is self-evident. Both Virgil and Horace allude to the

---

[106] Horace's use of *temperare* shows the effect of Cicero's equation of *temperantia* with sophrosyne. The poet rarely gives it the etymological significance of "mixture" (exceptions are *Odes* 1. 20. 11 and 3. 19. 6). Normally in Horace as in Virgil (see p. 300) *temperare* is synonymous with *regere;* it can also mean "to moderate," "to forbear," or "to keep in equilibrium." Especially notable is the zeugma in *Odes* 1. 12. 14 where, speaking of Jupiter, Horace says: "*qui res hominum ac deorum/ Qui mare ac terras variisque mundum/ Temperat horis.*" Men and gods he *rules;* the cosmos he also rules, but keeps in a state of balance as well. In 3. 4. 45–48 *temperat* and *regit* (used again of Jupiter) are identical in meaning. Other uses include 1. 8. 7 (*temperare* describes the effect of a harsh curb bit), 4. 12. 1 (the moderating effect of spring breezes on the wintry sea); 2. 16. 27 (*amara lento temperet risu*, said of the *sôphrôn* man who is *laetus in praesens*, 25); 3. 24. 18 (the woman who refrains from harming her stepchildren); and 4. 3. 17–18 (*temperas* describes the action of the Muse who produces a harmonious sound from the golden lyre).

[107] See Commager, *A.J.P.* 80 (1959), 37–55, on the appeal for mercy for the Antonians in *Odes* 1. 2, and Commager, *Horace,* 194–209, on the present ode. Consult also Wilkinson, *op. cit.,* 71. Fraenkel (285) comments on the effect obtained by concluding the list of Giants with the sympathetic figure of the *amator Pirithous* (79–80). See J. P. Elder, *A.J.P.* 73 (1952), 140–58, for a discussion of Horace's admiration for *audacia*, in the midst of his praise of moderation in *Odes* 1. 3.

[108] E.g., by George Duckworth (*T.A.P.A.* 87 [1956], 281–316), who compares the arrangement of the Roman odes and of *Aen.* 6. 760–853. See also Henry Rowell, *M.A.A.R.* 17 (1940), 140 ff., and Walter Wili, *Vergil* (Munich, 1930), 94 f.

combination of power and moderation, *virtus* and *clementia,* which is
hopefully ascribed to Augustus on the *clupeus aureus.* It would not,
of course, be surprising to find Horace and Virgil celebrating the same
themes in lyric and epic poetry. The existence of other Horatian topics
of sophrosyne in the *Aeneid*—such as Evander's praise of simplicity in 8.
327, the eulogy of country life in 9. 603–13, the violation of the Mean
by Turnus, together with the extremely Horatian language in which his
fatal error is described in 10. 501 [109]—and of equally Virgilian motives
in Horace (notably in Book IV of the *Odes*) may be accepted without
dispute. But the sophrosyne of Virgilian poetry goes much deeper than
surface allusions prompted by the political and social problems of the
day. If the *clupeus aureus* had never existed, if Horace and Virgil had not
belonged to a coterie and shared certain ideas, the essential sophrosyne
of the *Aeneid* would have been what it now is. The Virgilian sophrosyne
is fundamentally an expression of the primary theme of all great imagina-
tive literature—the victory of order over chaos; but never before the
Aeneid had the theme been developed in such intricate detail or expressed
so richly and deliberately in characterization and imagery.

The *êthos* of Aeneas himself, whose most memorable traits are *pietas*
and *humanitas,* includes as the necessary foundation of them both a
sophrosyne that is repeatedly tested by the powerful assaults of passion
(*furor, violentia*) and is contrasted at every turning point in the narrative
with the unrestrained and therefore destructive passions of other major
figures, especially Dido and Turnus. Dido's violation of sophrosyne takes
the form of *furor* and leads her to betray *pudicitia.*[110] Turnus gives way to
violentia and *superbia.*[111] Both figures represent threats to the ordered and
civilized world that is to emerge from the triumph of justice and *consilium*
embodied in Aeneas. It is part of Virgil's vision of reality that these
threats are themselves embodied in personalities so attractive and so
sympathetically treated, like Horace's *amator Pirithous* (*Odes* 3. 4. 79–80).
The victory of Aeneas is in neither case an easy one, nor does the hero
remain unmoved. The symbol of his sophrosyne is the image of the

---

[109] *Nescia mens hominum fati sortisque futurae et servare modum, rebus sublata secundis,* compared
with *Odes* 2. 3. See Duckworth, *loc. cit.,* 311–12, on these and other Horatian concepts and on
Virgilian echoes in *Odes* 4. 4, 5, 6, 15. The presence of the Golden Mean ratio in Virgil's
poetry and in Horace's *Sermones* is demonstrated by Duckworth, *T.A.P.A.* 91 (1960), 184–220.

[110] *Furor,* mastered or unmastered, as part of the contrast between Aeneas and Dido,
is discussed by Bernard Fenik, *A.J.P.* 80 (1959), 1 ff.

[111] *Violentia: Aen.* 9. 757–61, 11. 901–5, 12. 735–39. *Superbia:* 10. 445–514, 12. 326. See
Warde Fowler, *The Death of Turnus* (Oxford, 1919), 41, on Turnus' want of *temperantia;* and
see *Aen.* 12. 4–7, 103 ff. for the imagery of the lion and the bull as applied to him.

great oak tree that is shaken to its very roots by the violence of the storm (4. 393–96) yet still resists disaster. *Mens immota manet.*

Repetitions of the pattern in which sophrosyne is contrasted with a contrary quality mark the entire course of the *Aeneid.* Jupiter and Juno in Book I set the pattern initially: he stands for order and ultimate peace; she, for *saeva ira* and its consequences. Latinus and Amata in Book VII (at the beginning of the second half of the poem) symbolize the same opposition: civilization, peace, *consilium* on the one hand; unrestrained emotion, egoism, and selfish claims on the other. The association of sophrosyne with the masculine and of unrestrained passion with the feminine is an unexpected reminiscence of the Aeschylean point of view, expressed in the *Suppliants* and the first half of the *Seven against Thebes.*[112] Book VIII is especially rich in contrasts between sophrosyne and some opposing quality: the conflict between Hercules and Cacus, the warning against *luxuria* implicit in the *paupertas* of Evander, the picture of Cato opposing Catiline on the shield of Aeneas. In the last six books Mezentius by reason of his contempt for the gods and his bestial cruelty towards men emerges as an embodiment of *hybris,*[113] but in his almost unrelieved pride and savagery he is less effective (less Greek certainly) than Turnus, whose courage and heroism are nullified by his lack of self-knowledge and failure to preserve *modus* (10. 501–5).

Pöschl's study of the symbolism used in the *Aeneid* notes the concentration in Book I of images that convey this fundamental contrast between sophrosyne and its opposites.[114] The storm establishes the emotional keynote of the poem, and the *saeva ira* of Juno, in addition to foreshadowing the hatred of Carthage for Rome, symbolizes the destructive passions that are ultimately to yield to order, control, and sophrosyne— all embodied successively in Jupiter, Aeneas, and Augustus.[115] The theme of pacification, which Pöschl locates in the scenes where Aeolus controls the raging winds, Neptune quiets the storm, and *impius Furor* is

[112] See pp. 37–40. Another Aeschylean device, also reminiscent of the *Septem,* is the symbolism of the shield of Turnus (Io and Argus) and his helmet (the Chimaera), 7. 85, contrasted with the shield of Aeneas in Book VIII. Consult Stuart Small, *T.A.P.A.* 90 (1959), 243–57.

[113] He is called *insultans* (7. 570), *contemptor divum* (7. 647), *ardens* (10. 889), *turbidus* (10. 763). We hear also about his *superbum imperium* and *saeva arma* (8. 481) and his boast *dextra mihi deus et telum* (10. 773), which recalls the *hybris* of Ajax.

[114] Pöschl, 22 ff. According to Pöschl, the basic image of the poem is the struggle to subdue the demonic, which takes such forms as civil war, passion, and destruction and death in nature.

[115] Virgil emphasizes *consilium* in the prophecy of Jupiter, 1. 257–96, especially 281: *Iuno . . . consilia in melius referet.* Latinus in Book VII also represents *consilium,* but his is vain (586–600).

enchained in the temple of Janus, is associated verbally with *temperantia.*
The noun cannot be accommodated to the hexameter, but the verb is
applied to the action of both Aeolus and Neptune in Book I. Aeolus
temperat iras (1. 57) and Neptune *temperat aequor* (1. 146). The statesman
who quells the mob *regit dictis animos* (1. 153). *Regere* and *temperare* here,
as in Horace, are identical in meaning—further proof of Cicero's success
in establishing *temperare* and its cognates as the proper Roman dress for
sophrosyne.[116]

THE VIRTUE OF THE EMPEROR

In scenes depicting the Virgilian *vis temperata,* the *princeps* often seems
to hover behind the figure of Aeneas, for the qualities displayed by the
Trojan hero in both conquering and conciliating the Italian tribes are
those urgently needed by the ruler of the Roman Empire. It is not surprising then that in the post-Augustan history of sophrosyne the virtue
of the emperor receives the most marked attention and undergoes the
most significant development. A study of imperial sophrosyne must begin with Augustus' reference in the *Res Gestae* to the shield presented to
him by the Senate: *virtutis clementiaeque et iustitiae et pietatis causa* (6. 16–
21, ch. 34). The possible identification of these famous virtues with the
Platonic canon has often been debated.[117] The right of *pietas* to appear
(in place of *prudentia*) is justified both by the historical position of *eusebeia*
in early Greek canons of excellence and by Augustus' concern for the
revival of religion. The real question is whether *clementia* in some
way represents sophrosyne.

The Greek historians, especially those of the early Empire, clearly felt
uncertain about the proper translation of the Latin word *clementia.* The
renderings most favored seem to have been *epieikeia* (the word actually
used in the Greek version of the *Res Gestae*) and *praotês,* but *philanthrôpia*
sometimes appears and so occasionally does sophrosyne. Since, however,
the most familiar nuance of sophrosyne at this period was restraint
of appetite, it never became a popular Greek translation for *clementia.*
Yet the Emperor Julian uses it, just as he uses *philanthrôpia, praotês,* and

[116] See pp. 268 ff. For Virgil's use of other Latin equivalents of sophrosyne or *sôphrôn,*
consult M. N. Wetmore, *Index Verborum Vergilianus* (New Haven, Conn., 1910), under *pudor,
modus,* and *castus.*

[117] The relevant texts are collected by Hieronymus Markowski, *Eos* 37 (1936), 109–28.
Important discussions of the problem include the following: Otto von Premerstein, *Vom
Werden und Wesen der Prinzipats* (Munich, 1937), which suggests that the virtues are less Greek
than Roman and should be linked with the attempt to represent Augustus as a second
Romulus; Joseph Liegle, *Zeitschrift für Numismatik* 41 (1932), 58–100; and Gerhard
Rodenwaldt, *Abhandlungen der Prüssische Akademie der Wissenschaften* 3 (1935), 6–7.

epieikeia, in praising the mercy of Constantius (*Or.* 2. 100C; cf. *Or.*
1. 48A–49A); [118] and there can be no doubt that, for those Romans
who were acquainted with Greek philosophy, *clementia*—moderation in
the use of power—belonged, as early as the last century of the Republic,
to the province of sophrosyne/*temperantia.* This association was perhaps
a legacy from the Middle Stoa, but in a less formal way Greek writers,
even before the Stoics, had linked sophrosyne with *praotês, epieikeia,* and
other words connoting gentleness or humanity, especially towards conquered enemies.[119] The Old Stoa, as we have seen, excluded pity from
the concept of *aretê,*[120] but the Romans distinguished pity (*misericordia*)
from mercy (*clementia, mansuetudo*) and specifically linked only the second
of these qualities with sophrosyne/*temperantia.* Representatives of the
Middle Stoa such as Panaetius and Poseidonius considered mercy
praiseworthy.[121] Polybius links *praotês, philanthrôpia,* and sophrosyne with
andreia as foundations of the State (6. 48. 7; 10. 17. 15; 15. 17. 4) and
in a passage full of significance for Roman political philosophy recalls the
Hellenic antithesis between the heroic and the gentle principles, saying
(18. 37. 7) that it is necessary to be spirited in war (*thymikos*) but
in victory moderate, gentle, and humane (*metrios, praeis,* and *philanthrôpos*)
—Virgil's *debellare superbos* and *parcere subiectis.* Cicero, as we have noted,
treats *clementia* as a subdivision of *temperantia* in *De Inventione,* and in the
oration on the Manilian Law he praises Pompey's *humanitas* and
mansuetudo in the section of the speech devoted to *temperantia* (14.
40–42).[122]

---

[118] See Jürgen Kabiersch, *Untersuchungen zum Begriff der Philanthropia bei dem Kaiser Julian*
(Wiesbaden, 1960), 15–25, for a discussion of Julian's effort to relate *philanthrôpia* to certain
aspects of *clementia* and for the various Greek words used to translate *clementia* by Plutarch,
Cassius Dio, and others.

[119] Sophrosyne and *praotês:* Plato *Rep.* 375C, *Polit.* 306A–311C; Aristotle *Eth. Nic.* 1103b
15–19; Xenophon *Ages.* 10. 1, 11. 2. Sophrosyne and *epieikeia:* Democritus, Frag. 291 DK,
Hypereides 6. 5 (the first alludes to individual, the second to civic, virtue). Thucydides
occasionally uses *sôphrôn* with a meaning close to "merciful" (e.g., 3. 58. 1, 59. 1).

[120] Zeno: *SVF* 1. 214, p. 52, 15–17. Chrysippus: *SVF* 3. 640, p. 162, 35 ff. On the views of
the Old Stoa and their mitigation by Roman Stoics, see W. C. Korfmacher, *T.A.P.A.* 77
(1946), 44.

[121] For the beliefs of the Middle Stoa, see Cicero *Off.* 1. 11. 35, 25. 88; and consult
Norden, *op. cit.,* on *Aen.* 6. 847 ff. Rodenwaldt (*loc. cit.,* 8) draws attention to the differences
between Greek and Roman artistic representations of war: the Greek places the emphasis
on the warlike action, while the Roman represents the two results—*victoria* and *clementia.*

[122] Cicero's treatment of *clementia* varies with his Greek source. Sometimes he brings it
close to *magnitudo animi* (a Middle Stoic substitute for *andreia*) or even to *iustitia.* Cf. *De Virt.,*
Frags. 6, 8 Knöllinger; and see Gauthier, 159. Plato in *Laws* 854D ff. is inclined to relate
mercy to *dikê* in discussing the educative effects of punishment, but it should not be forgotten
that the reformatory where the re-education takes place is called a *Sôphronistêrion* (908E).

The most substantial theoretical discussion of *clementia* is Seneca's essay on the subject, which, like *De Inventione*, reflects Stoic doctrine. According to Seneca, too, *temperantia* is the basic excellence of which *clementia* is a part. He defines *clementia* as *temperantia* in one who has the power to take vengeance and as *lenitas* shown by a superior towards an inferior when exacting penalties (2. 3. 1; cf. 1. 11. 12). It is the virtue most suitable for a ruler (1. 5. 2), who by exercising it shares the power of the gods (cf. Cicero *Pro Marcello* 3). The practice of *clementia* distinguishes a king from a tyrant (1. 11. 4–12. 3); only in the presence of this virtue can justice, peace, security, and dignity flourish (1. 19. 8). Seneca is careful to separate *clementia* from *misericordia*, which he classifies as a vice because it lacks the element of *ratio* (2. 4. 4).[123] The power to distinguish the curable, to whom mercy should be shown, from the incurable, is assigned to *moderatio*, which is here an intellectual, rather than a moral, virtue and recalls the original Stoic definition of sophrosyne as a faculty of choice. The opposite of *clementia* is *crudelitas* or *intemperantia animi*, exemplified by Alexander the Great (1. 25. 1). Augustus is a type of *clementia* (1. 9. 1), but Seneca observes that he was moderate and merciful only in his maturity, not (like Nero) in his youth. Exhausted cruelty (*lassa crudelitas*) is not identical with *clementia*.[124] As for Nero himself, he is his own exemplar of *clementia*, and Seneca's essay is supposed merely to serve as a mirror for the emperor's virtue (1. 1. 1–6).

At this period in the Empire it had already become conventional to ascribe *clementia* to the ruler. After Cicero's eulogy of the *clementia* and *mansuetudo* of Julius Caesar,[125] the *clementia Caesaris* became a commonplace among historians. The temple dedicated to this virtue in the first Caesar[126] evidently set a precedent, for we hear of an altar to the *clementia* of Tiberius as well as of a coin celebrating his possession of this excellence. Since the coin has a twin that refers to the *moderatio* of the same emperor, it has been conjectured that the Senate presented him with a shield comparable to the *clupeus aureus* of Augustus.[127] Other

---

[123] The transition of *misericorida* from a Stoic *vitium* to a Christian virtue is traced by Hélène Petré, *R.E.L.* 12 (1934), 376–89.

[124] This warning implies that Seneca's conception of sophrosyne is positive, rather than, as in the case of many Romans, merely negative.

[125] See above, pp. 278–79 and n. 55.

[126] Dio 46. 64.

[127] The altar: Tacitus *Ann.* 4. 74. 1–3. The coins: Mattingly and Sydenham, 1. 108 (B.M.C. Tib. 85–90). On the *clementia* of Tiberius, see C. H. V. Sutherland, *J.R.S.* 28 (1938), 129–40; M. P. Charlesworth, *Proc. Br. Acad.* 23 (1937), 105–33; Syme, 414–15; R. S. Rogers, *Studies in the Reign of Tiberius* (Baltimore, 1943), 43–48. The iconography of sophrosyne may perhaps be said to begin with scenes representing *clementia* on Roman sarcophagi and other

emperors to whom ancient sources ascribe *clementia* include Caligula, Nero, Vitellius, Trajan, Constantius, Julian, Gallienus, Jovian, and, as a matter of course, most of the subjects of biographies in the *Historia Augusta* and the Latin Panegyrics.[128] It seems nevertheless that at certain times—during the Augustan age and still later, from Vitellius to Hadrian—the word *clementia* fell into disfavor, first because of its cynical association with Julius Caesar and then because it had been ascribed to the monsters Caligula and Nero. Virgil never refers to *clementia* but transfers much of its content to *pietas;* and Propertius, in praising Rome for achieving power as much through *pietas* as through the sword, explicates the word *pietas* in terms suited rather to *clementia* and actually involving the verb *temperare* (3. 20. 22): *victrices temperat ira manus* ("our anger restrains its victorious hands").[129] This avoidance of a term abused in official propaganda later finds a parallel in the practice of Tacitus.

Clementia and *temperantia* are again linked in a highly unusual passage in Claudian's eulogy of Stilicho, which draws on conventional epideictic theory but also goes beyond it for a conception of *clementia* not unlike the cosmic sophrosyne of Greek philosophy. In the beginning, Claudian tells us, *Clementia* was the *custos mundi,* the "guardian of the world." Her dwelling is in the sphere of Jove, where she keeps the heavens in a state of equilibrium between the Cold and the Hot (*temperat aethram/frigoris et flammae medio*). It was she who first disentangled Chaos, scattered the darkness, and bathed the world in light (2. 6–11). The consequences of

---

monuments, and coins depicting *clementia, pudicitia,* and (rarely) *moderatio.* Rodenwaldt (*loc. cit.,* 6) discusses sarcophagi of a type which has four scenes symbolizing four Roman virtues: a battle (*virtus*), a supplication (*clementia*), an offering (*pietas*), and the clasping of hands (*concordia*). On sarcophagi related to this type, see also P. Barrera, *Studi Romani* 2 (1914), 93–120; Inez Scott Ryberg, *M.A.A.R.* 22 (1955), 163 ff.; and Elaine P. Loeffler, *Art Bulletin* 39 (1957), 1–7 (see plates 1 and 4 for *clementia*). Scenes or figures representing *clementia* also occur on Trajan's column (Rodenwaldt, *loc. cit.,* 8) and on coins, including those of Vitellius, Hadrian, Marcus Aurelius, and Probus. On the Hadrianic coins *Clementia* is portrayed as a Junoesque goddess, standing and holding a *patera* in one hand and a vertical scepter in the other (see Mattingly 3. 270, Nos. 251–55, and plate 51. 13, 14). The coins of Tiberius mentioned above carry inscriptions *Clementiae S.C.* and *Moderationi(s) S.C.* above a small bust of Tiberius, in the center of a shield, surrounded, in the one case by a laurel wreath, in the other by a plain circle. The virtues themselves are not portrayed.

[128] See P. W. *"Princeps"* (Wickert) for the evidence connecting *clementia* with the Emperors from Tiberius to Diocletian; consult also P. W. *"Clementia"* (Aust) and Roscher, *Clementia* (I. 1. 910–12).

[129] I owe these observations on Virgil and Propertius to the presidential address of Professor Inez Scott Ryberg before the American Philological Association, December 28, 1962. The absence of *clementia* from coins between Vitellius and Hadrian is discussed by M. P. Charlesworth, *Proc. Br. Acad.* 23 (1937), 112–13.

Stilicho's possession of *clementia* include pardon for the conquered, just as in conventional eulogy of the ruler, and the personified virtue is equipped with such stereotyped sisters as *Fides* and *Iustitia*,[130] but the cosmic implications of this passage make it worthy of note. *Clementia* is identified with the great ordering power of the universe required by most of the Greek physical philosophies (whether they describe it as *philia*, *nous*, or the *sôphrôn krasis*), and its function is explained with the verb *temperare*, used in a sense like that of Horace when he says that Jupiter keeps the cosmos in a state of balance (*mundum temperat* [*Odes* 1. 12. 14]).

Moderatio is scarcely less notable than *clementia* as an imperial virtue, although its traces are mainly literary, rather than numismatic (as in the case of *clementia*). The only coin bearing this inscription is that of Tiberius mentioned above. For this excellence, too, Seneca is a prime source of information, although the *exempla moderationis* cited by Valerius Maximus (IV. 1) are helpful in determining its scope, as contrasted with *pudicitia* (VI. 1), *continentia* (IV. 3), *verecundia* (IV. 5) and *frugalitas* (II. 5). In *De Clementia* the word *moderatio* and its cognates are so often employed to define the function of mercy or compassion in a ruler (as in 1. 2. 2; 1. 11. 1; 1. 18. 1; 1. 19. 4; 1. 20. 1, 4; and 2. 3. 2, 3) as to make it clear that the two ideas are inseparable, and that *moderatio*, even more than *temperantia*, serves Seneca as the normal translation for sophrosyne. Although in a Ciceronian enumeration of virtues he refers to *temperantia*, along with *iustitia* and *fortitudo*, later adding *prudentia* (*Ep.* 113. 12, 19), he tends to restrict *temperantia* to the control of appetite and passion. Sophrosyne in its broader implications is usually *moderatio*; exceptions are the special treatment of the virtue in *De Clementia* and the semi-technical rendering of sophrosyne as *pudicitia* to designate the virtue of married women.[131] Seneca praises *salubris moderatio* in every

---

[130] *Fides: De Cons. Stil.* 2. 30; *Iustitia: De Man. Theod. Cons.* 166. Professor James Hutton has called these passages to my attention. With the concept of *Clementia* ordering the cosmos, we might compare the coin of Probus which shows the emperor holding a scepter surmounted by an eagle and receiving a globe from Jupiter (a type associated also with *Providentia*); the inscription reads: *Clementia temporum* (Mattingly and Sydenham, 5, 2. 86, No. 643). Claudian translates sophrosyne in its more restricted nuance ("self-control") as *temperies: Temperies instruit . . . ut casta petas* (*De Cons. Stil.* 2. 107). His use of the topic of virtue and vice in *vituperatio* is studied by H. L. Levy, *T.A.P.A.* 77 (1946), 53–65; for sophrosyne and its antitheses, see *In Rufinum* 1. 183–95, 220–29. The virtuous man of Alain de Lille's *Anticlaudianus* (inspired by the vicious Rufinus) possesses the gifts of *Pudor* and *Modestia* (VII. 110–37).

[131] See pp. 307–8. In his versions of Greek tragedy Seneca translates *sôphrôn* and sophrosyne by a variety of Latin equivalents, all entirely traditional. See, e.g., in his *Phaedra: sanus* (212), *castus* (226, 237, 704), *pudor* (595, 920). *Pudor* as usual also renders *aidôs* (141, 430). Bickel (183 ff.) shows that Seneca differs in his use of *castus* and *castitas*, depending on whether

conceivable connection: moderation in the exercise of liberty, in the use of wine, in satisfying desires of all kinds, in the style of philosophical discourse, even in the pursuit of knowledge; and he describes the *animus moderatus* as close to the Divine.[132] The high place accorded moderation in the ethics of Seneca lends support to the tradition that the *Formula Vitae Honestae* by the sixth-century Spanish bishop, Martin of Bracara, actually goes back to the lost *De Officiis* of Seneca. Although Martin renders sophrosyne by *continentia* in the section of the treatise devoted to this virtue, the entire discussion of all four virtues is dominated by the spirit of the Mean.[133]

---

he is writing poetry or philosophy. In philosophy, where he follows the Neopythagorean Attalus, *castitas* always means *abstinentia a venere* (*hagneia*) and is not interchangeable with *pudicitia* (sophrosyne, "conjugal virtue"), but in the tragedies this distinction is not observed. See Chap. II, n. 101, above for Seneca's repeated use of the theme of moderation in tragic poetry, even where it is lacking in his Greek models. E.g., *Oedipus* 882–910 with the imagery of the ship at sea: *temperem zephyro levi vela . . . tuta me media vehat vita decurrens via . . . quidquid excessit modum pendet instabili loco.* Latin words used in Senecan tragedy to denote "control" or "restraint" and the opposite are studied by Norman T. Pratt, *T.A.P.A.* 94 (1963), 199–234.

[132] Praise of *modus* and *moderatio: De Tran.* 17. 2, 9; *De Ben.* 1. 15. 3; *De Ira* 1. 21. 1; *Ad Helv.* 9. 3; *Ep.* 1. 5, 40. 8, 41. 5, 88. 29–30. Seneca is careful, however, to maintain the Stoic opposition to Peripatetic "moderation in vice." See *De Ira* 1. 7. 2; *Ep.* 85. 3–4, 116 *passim*. A Ciceronian list of partial equivalents of sophrosyne occurs in *Ep.* 88. 30, where Seneca maintains that *moderatio, frugalitas, parsimonia,* and *clementia* cannot be instilled by liberal studies. *Ep.* 114. 2–3, 22 discusses literary style as a reflection of character: the *siccus* and *sobrius* style reflects an *animus sanus . . . temperans.* The virtual restriction of *temperantia* to the control of the appetites is illustrated by *Ep.* 120. 11, where Seneca says that this virtue reins in desires, and *Ep.* 88. 29 where it puts to flight some pleasures and regulates others, restoring them to a healthy mean (*sanus modus*). Cf. *De Vita Beat.* 10. 3 and *Ep.* 59. 11. *Temperantia* carries a broader significance in *De Vita Beat.* 16. 3 ff. *De Tran.* 9. 1 ff.; and *Ep.* 18. 4, 78. 20, 88. 36. *Ep.* 108 records the impression made on Seneca by the teaching of the Neopythagorean Attalus; see especially 14, on the praise of *castum corpus, sobriam mensam, puram mentem,* and 15, on Seneca's return to the *civitatis vitam,* in which asceticism was impossible.

[133] See especially 6. pp. 247–49, Barlow, on the danger of allowing any of the four virtues to pass *extra modum suum* (for the Peripatetic echo, cf. Seneca *Ep.* 88. 29: *sanus modus*). The paragraph entitled in some manuscripts *De moderanda continentia* advises the reader to avoid being *parcus* and to preserve *mediocritas* even in his *continentia.* The vicious extremes are *prodigalitas* and *luxuria* on the one side, and on the other *sorditas* and *obscuritas.* (In popular morality the Peripatetic Mean tended to avoid the extremes of prodigality and meanness, rather than wantonness and insensibility; see Horace *Ser.* I. 2 where Tigellius represents prodigality and Fufidius meanness.) For Seneca as Martin's source, see Ernst Bickel, *Rh. Mus.* 60 (1905), 505–51; Claude W. Barlow, *Martini Episcopi Bracarensis Opera Omnia* (New Haven, 1950), 204–8; and Gauthier, 141–42. Martin's choice of *continentia* as a translation for sophrosyne has been traced to the influence of the Stoic Hecato via Seneca. See Chap. VI, n. 92, for the possibility that Hecato substituted *enkrateia* (Latin *continentia*) for sophrosyne in his table of virtues. In *Off.* III. 96, 116, 117, etc., Cicero, too, refers to *continentia* rather than *temperantia* (which is preferred in *Off.* I and II); here also the influence of Hecato has been suspected; consult Bickel, *loc. cit.,* 550, and Heinz Gomoll, *Der stoische Philosoph Hecaton* (Leipzig, 1933).

The *moderatio* that ancient authorities often ascribe to Tiberius is, as Rogers has shown, a word of relatively narrow scope, referring usually to that emperor's deliberate limitation of the honors paid to him and his family.[134] In general, however, *moderatio* as an imperial virtue has a broader connotation, as Pliny's *Panegyric of Trajan* demonstrates.[135] This eulogy follows a chronological sequence, introducing the virtues of Trajan in the context of his life story; but *moderatio* sets the keynote for the entire address, for Pliny announces his intention of suiting his speech to the *modestia* and *moderatio* of the ruler (3. 2). In his discussion of *moderatio* itself he employs a contrast between this excellence and *fortitudo,* which suggests that the traditional Greek antithesis has become a rhetorical commonplace. When Trajan stood on the bank of the Danube, knowing that to cross meant triumph, and yet resisted the temptation, he performed a noble act. To cross would be the proof of *fortitudo;* to restrain himself was the result of *moderatio* (16). The implication is clear: *moderatio* is more difficult and hence more praiseworthy than *fortitudo.* The passage is particularly striking because sophrosyne is rarely cited by ancient historians as a motive for limiting the expansion of an empire, whether that of Athens or Rome or another, although Aeschylus relates the imprudent aggression of Xerxes to his want of sophrosyne and Isocrates blames the fall of both Athens and Sparta on their loss of the sophrosyne that once guided their foreign policies.[136]

Still another antithesis to sophrosyne/*moderatio* appears in Pliny's description of Trajan's refusal to accept honors. The emperor will accept only *modici honores,* but he must accept some, for to refuse all is a sign of *ambitio. Moderatio* requires the choice of the most modest (*parcissimos*) honors. Since *moderatio* with respect to honors is a virtue often ascribed to Tiberius, Pliny's purpose here is no doubt to demonstrate the genuine *moderatio* of Trajan, in contrast to the ostentatious modesty of Tiberius, which merely concealed his real *ambitio.* The implied contrast is not un-

---

[134] Rogers, *op. cit.,* 62–87, cites Tacitus *Ann.* 1. 14. 1–3, 2. 36. 2, 3. 56. 1, 4. 37 f.; Velleius 2. 122. 1 (in courting danger Tiberius *excessit modum,* but in accepting honors *temperavit*); Suetonius 32. 2 and 57. 1 (on Tiberius' pretended *moderatio*). Velleius also refers to *moderatio* in the sense of self-restraint and modesty (2. 130. 1). See Rogers, *op. cit.,* 62, for the vocabulary of moderation, which includes *modus* and *temperare* and their derivatives (note the rare *temperamentum* in Velleius 2. 130. 1 and in Tacitus *Ann.* 3. 12. 1) and *pudor* (Tacitus *Ann.* 1. 11. 1, 1. 12. 1–3).

[135] Studies of the *Panegyric,* its sources, and its rhetorical conventions include J. Mesk, *Wiener Studien* 32 (1910), 230 ff., and *Rh. Mus.* 67 (1912), 569 ff.; Lester K. Born, *A.J.P.* 55 (1934), 2–35; and Marcel Durry, *Pline le Jeune, Panégyrique de Trajan* (Paris, 1938), 28 ff.

[136] Aeschylus, see Chap. II, pp. 33–35. Isocrates, see Chap. IV, pp. 144–45. The conception is not a Roman one.

like that which Tacitus explicitly draws in the *Agricola* between the *moderatio* of his father-in-law and the ostentation of the Stoic martyrs.[137]

Pliny includes in his *Panegyric* several other aspects of sophrosyne and clearly indicates the antithesis of each. *Frugalitas* is opposed to *luxuria, clementia* to *crudelitas, continentia* to *libido,* and *pudor* to *superbia.* Of these terms only *pudor* deviates from normal usage. As Pliny uses it, *pudor* embraces not only the avoidance of haughtiness (24) but also simplicity in the emperor's retinue—*pudor fascibus* (76. 8). So profound is Trajan's simplicity, in fact, that the poor find examples of modesty and sobriety in the palace of the emperor (47). *Frugalitas* now bears a more restricted meaning than in Cicero: as practiced by Trajan it amounts to no more than careful expenditure and deserves mention in the *Panegyric* because the benefactions of the emperor do not impoverish the state (41. 1; cf. 49. 5 and 88, and Pliny *Ep.* 2. 4. 3; 6. 8. 5). Trajan demonstrates *clementia* in his capacity as judge (80. 1); but this virtue is on the whole taken for granted, perhaps because Pliny feels less need to insist on it than Seneca felt in the case of Nero.[138]

The *Panegyric* extends its compliments to the women of the imperial family, mentioning the *verecunditas* of Plotina as a parallel to the *modestia* of her husband (83. 7–8). Both the empress and Trajan's sister also receive praise for their own *modestia,* which in Pliny's vocabulary takes the place of the more usual *pudicitia.*[139] As we have observed, *pudicitia* is one of the most venerable and well-established Roman virtues, already personified in the *Amphitryo* of Plautus and honored with a shrine or *sacellum* in the Forum Boarium as early as the third century B.C. Throughout Latin literature it is the normal rendering of that sophrosyne which is the virtue proper to women, both married and single, and to young people of both sexes; but during the early Empire it achieves a further importance and a new precision in the language of philosophy as part of the vocabulary used in Roman adaptations of Greek treatises on conjugal relations. For this development Seneca may be in large measure responsible, if, as Bickel has suggested, his lost essay *De Matrimonio* made available to Roman readers the content of a Stoic diatribe on marriage, which regarded sophrosyne as the excellence

[137] Some echoes of the *Agricola* in the *Panegyric* are noted by Richard T. Bruère, *C.P.* 49 (1954), 161–79.

[138] See Tacitus *Dial.* 41 (possibly composed in the reign of Trajan, according to Syme, 670–73) for the *clementia* of the judge, which makes prolonged oratory unnecessary under the Empire.

[139] But an altar to *Pudicitia* was erected in honor of Plotina (Roscher 3. 3375). See also CIL VIII. 993 for the inscription on a statue of *Pudicitia Augusta* erected in her honor.

proper to wives.[140] This tradition in turn contributed to the Christian commonplace that there are three grades of purity (*hagneia, castitas*), those of the wife, the widow, and the virgin, which the Greek Fathers designated respectively as sophrosyne, *enkrateia,* and *parthenia,* and the Latin as *pudicitia, continentia,* and *virginitas.*[141] Seneca's essay *De Matrimonio* (fragments of which have been recovered from Jerome *Adversus Iovinianum* I. 41–49) followed the Ciceronian practice of adding Roman color to Greek theory by inserting *exempla domestica.* His *laudatio pudicitiae* lists as models of chastity in marriage the traditional Roman heroines: Lucretia, Bilia, Marcia, Portia (46, pp. 386–87 Bickel), Cornelia (49, p. 394), as well as Persian and Greek exemplars long familiar in Stoic and rhetorical commonplaces.[142]

Pudicitia frequently appears on Roman imperial coins, often those designed to honor women of the imperial family. The type consists of a woman, usually seated, drawing a veil over her face with her right hand and often carrying a scepter. It may be seen on coins of Antoninus Pius, Marcus Aurelius, Commodus, Elagabalus, Philip, and others down to the late Empire.[143] It would be an error, however, to consider *pudicitia* an exclusively feminine quality among the imperial virtues. Manilius

[140] Bickel (288–372) discusses the sources for this lost work and comments on the terminology, both Greek and Latin, used by Stoics, Neopythagoreans, and Christians in treatises on virginity and marriage (see especially 204–10 for a useful summary of pagan and Christian usage of *enkrateia, sôphrosynê, hagneia* and their normal Latin equivalents, *continentia, pudicitia, castitas*). Bickel compares Seneca, Frag. 79 Haase: *Mulieris virtus proprie pudicitia est,* with the statement in Phintys' treatise *On Feminine Sophrosyne* (Stobaeus IV. 23, 61 and 61a, p. 588, 17 ff.): γυναικὸς δὲ μάλιστα ἀρετὰ σωφροσύνα (p. 589. 1), and concludes that both Seneca and Phintys drew upon the same Stoic source (204, 364 ff.). Other allusions by Seneca to *pudicitia* as marital chastity include *Ad Helv.* 16. 3–4, *De Ben.* 3. 16. 3, *Ep.* 49, 12 and 94. 26 (where *pudicitia* is recommended to husbands as well as to wives). Contemporaries of Seneca did not distinguish between *pudicitia* and *castitas* as rigorously as he does in his philosophical works. Bickel cites a discussion by Seneca Rhetor about the scope of *castitas* (*Contr.* 1. 2. 13). On the implications recognized by writers of the imperial age and by Patristic sources, consult *T.L.L., castitas.*

[141] See below Chap. IX, n. 62.

[142] For a conventional list of heroes and heroines of *pudicitia,* see Valerius Maximus, VI. 1; and consult H. W. Litchfield, *H.S.C.P.* 25 (1914), 28–35.

[143] See Michael Grant, *Roman Imperial Money* (London, 1954), 151 ff. and plates xxii. 4, xxiii. 3, xix. 6; and consult Gerhard Radke, P. W., *"Pudicitia."* For the gesture with the veil, see the archaic relief of Hera as the bride of Zeus from the temple at Selinunte; and for the identification of the gesture with sophrosyne, see Julian 3. 127D, where Penelope's action of holding up her veil (Homer *Od.* 1. 334) is interpreted as a symbol of sophrosyne. The increase in devotion to Vesta in the third century has been adduced as a reason for the more frequent appearance of the *Pudicitia*-type in coinage at that time (A. D. Nock, *H.T.R.* 23 [1931], 251–69). The attitude and gesture which constitute the type of *pudicitia* occur also in the plastic arts. A marble head of *Pudicitia* was found in the excavations near the Tomb of St. Peter beneath St. Peter's Basilica; see Jocelyn Toynbee and John Ward Perkins, *The Shrine of St. Peter and the Vatican Excavations* (London, 1956), 95 and plate 30. See also R. Calza,

attributes it to the Emperor Tiberius (*Astron.* 4. 546); it appears on many coins, particularly those of Hadrian, as a masculine excellence; and it is often allied with masculine *temperantia* in panegyric.[144] Ammianus, who includes under the rubric of *temperantia* his encomium of Julian's *castitas* after the death of his wife, quotes in this connection the emperor's own allusion (25. 4. 2–3) to a statement of Bacchylides: "As a distinguished painter renders a countenance good to look upon, so chastity [*pudicitia*] adorns and elevates a life that is already reaching the heights." *Temperantia* and *pudicitia* are again treated as synonyms when Ammianus, embroidering on the theme of *degeneratio,* contrasts the *temperantia* of Julian with the low level of contemporary morality and draws particular attention to his wakefulness in the study of philosophy, poetry, and rhetoric, while others sleep (16. 5. 8): "This is a nocturnal proof of *pudicitia* and the other virtues."[145] Julian possessed sophrosyne in other aspects also. A Greek papyrus fragment uses this term to describe his economical administration (like the *frugalitas* of Trajan in Pliny's *Panegyric*).[146] It will be recalled that Julian himself in his eulogies and other writings evinces considerable interest in sophrosyne

---

Bolletino d'Arte 35 (1950), 201 ff., figs. 1–4, for a *Pudicitia* found at Ostia. The gesture of putting the finger to the lips (seen on coins as early as the reign of Claudius, not limited to the *Pudicitia*-type, but assigned also to *Pax* and *Pudor*) may symbolize silence and restraint, according to Jocelyn Toynbee, *Essays Presented to Harold Mattingly* (Oxford, 1956), 214–16. Cf. Horace *Odes* 3. 2. 25–26: *Est et fideli tuta silentio Merces.*

144 On *Pudicitia* as the holiness of the emperor (as head of the state religion), see Mattingly III. cxxxi, cxxxv. Valerius Maximus refers to *pudicitia* as *virorum pariter ac feminarum praecipuum firmamentum* (VI. 1). Most of his Roman *exempla* are not women but men who protected the purity of their sons and daughters or avenged its loss. *Temperantia* is not among the thirty-eight virtues ascribed to emperors and empresses on Roman coins (see Wickert, *loc. cit.*), but it continues to appear in literary tributes to their excellence. Its omission from the coinage is perhaps the result of its being considered too much a private, individual virtue to be exploited in the imperial propaganda. *Clementia, pudicitia,* and *moderatio* are the masculine aspects of sophrosyne which bore a more direct relation to the State, and *pudicitia* is the overwhelming choice for the *virtus feminarum.* When Dionysius of Halicarnassus describes Romulus as *eusebês, sôphrôn, dikaios,* and *polemikos* (*Ant. Rom.* 2. 18), he means by *sôphrôn* something closer to *pudicus* than to *clemens* or *moderatus.* Cf. 2. 24–25, where sophrosyne clearly denotes chastity and obedience to parents; and see Cassius Dio 72. 45 on Commodus, whose sister Lucilla was in no way more *sôphrôn* than he.

145 *Pudicitia* here has a much wider significance than conjugal fidelity and is probably to be interpreted like the *pudicitia* that so often appears on coins of Hadrian (see Mattingly III. 278, Nos. 309 and 355, Nos. 911–13). Ammianus sometimes equates sophrosyne with *virtus simpliciter,* as in his translation of Democritus, Frag. 210 DK (τράπεϑαν πολυτελέα μὲν τύχη παρατίθησιν, αὐταρκέα δὲ σωφροσύνη): *ambitiosam mensam fortuna, parcam virtus adponit* (16. 5. 1).

146 P. Fay. 20 (an imperial edict; see Moulton and Milligan, *The Vocabulary of the Greek New Testament* [London, 1930], s.v. sophrosyne). With this use of sophrosyne, cf. the edict of Severus Alexander on his accession, which explains his remission of a tax as being in accordance with his policy of sophrosyne and urges provincial governors to emulate the emperor's *kosmiotês, sôphrosynê,* and *enkrateia* (cited by Charlesworth, *loc. cit.,* p. 116).

and gives the word a wide range, including not only restraint of the appetites, but also obedience to the laws, good judgment in military matters, wise administration of the State, and sobriety of diction.[147] It is difficult to find anything specifically Roman in Julian's own references to sophrosyne, except that, as has been suggested above, his tendency to apply this term to the generosity and compassion shown by a conqueror towards his defeated enemy may reflect the Roman concept of *clementia* as an imperial virtue.

The fragmentation of sophrosyne into *clementia, moderatio, temperantia,* and *pudicitia,* each designating a different facet of the emperor's moral excellence, recalls what was said at the beginning of this chapter about Rome's failure to grasp the totality of the Greek concept.[148] Yet at least one powerful force was always at work to remind Rome of the existence of a sophrosyne not to be identified with, nor confined to, any one Roman approximation. This was the canon of Platonic-Stoic virtues, firmly embedded in many philosophical and rhetorical works familiar to all educated Romans. Within the framework of the tetrad, sophrosyne could always maintain contact with the fullness of its meaning for classical Greek thought. So long as this could be recalled, it never— even in Latin—quite lost its identity. By contrast one of the most serious dangers threatening the survival of classical sophrosyne in

[147] See Chap. VII, p. 249.

[148] Space does not permit a thorough discussion of the Latin panegyrics of the third and fourth centuries, which conform closely to the pattern established by Seneca and Pliny; consult Édouard Galletier, *Panégyriques latins* (Paris, 1949), Introduction, xxxi ff. A random sampling of references to virtues allied with sophrosyne in these eulogies would include the following: the *Panegyric of Maximian* (II) maintains the now traditional antithesis between *fortitudo* and *clementia* (4); the *Panegyric of Constantine* (VI) finds the four virtues in this emperor to be a resemblance to his father (3) and treats under the rubric of *continentia* the observance of the laws of marriage from an early age (*novum miraculum . . . iuvenis uxorius,* 4). The *clementia* of Constantine finds frequent mention (IX. 20, X. 8). Julian is praised for his *parsimonia* (XI. 10), his horror of luxury (11), and his purity of life (13; cf. Ammianus 25. 4. 2). The *Panegyric of Theodosius* (XII) follows traditional lines, praising the emperor's freedom from *cupiditas* and *libido* (12), his exemplary *modus* and *frugalitas* (13), and his lack of arrogance (20). A common feature in the rhetors' praise of emperors is the assertion that literature is a source of virtue (e.g., Eumenius, V. 8, on the restoration of the schools of Gaul: *litterae fundamenta virtutum, utpote continentiae, modestiae . . . magistras*). On this subject the point of view of the rhetors naturally differs from that of Cynics like Antisthenes (D. L. 6. 103) or of Stoics like Seneca (*Ep.* 88. 30). Among other late Latin writers who employ the topic of the virtues, see Ausonius in his reminiscences of the professors of Bordeaux. The exigencies of the hexameter led Ausonius, like Claudian, to substitute *temperies* for *temperantia* (*Lib. Protrep. ad Nep.* 77 Schenkl). Jacqueline Hatinguais (*Rev. d. Et. Anc.* 55 [1953], 375–87) finds that *modestia* and *frugalitas* were prominent among the virtues of the professors, then as now. Both terms refer to private life, not to professional qualities.

Christian thought lay in its divorce from the canon and in the determination of Christian moralists, from the very beginning, to identify it
with a set of virtues central to their own ethical and religious beliefs. It
was not a linguistic difficulty, such as affected the Romans, but a
radically altered view of the very nature and purpose of human life that
caused Christian thinkers to give to sophrosyne a whole new range of
implications.

IX

Sophrosyne in Patristic Literature

IF the naturalization of sophrosyne in Rome was difficult and only intermittently successful, its conversion to Christianity involved even greater problems and in the end produced a still more thorough transformation. Among these problems the most serious was that which confronted the early Church at every turn during the first four centuries, when she was attempting to assimilate substantial portions of pagan philosophy—namely the fundamental conflict between faith and reason. To identify moral virtues based on natural reason with virtues originating in Divine Grace and to integrate the Greek concept of *aretê* into Christian morality, required the best efforts of the greatest Fathers of the Church.

During the long period of transition each of the four Platonic virtues suffered radical alteration. For sophrosyne the gravest danger lay in the tendency of many Christian moralists to overemphasize its relation to chastity.[1] They adopted the connotation that was most popular throughout the Greek world in the first century of our era—sophrosyne interpreted as control of the appetites—and still further intensified this concept, claiming sophrosyne (chastity, purity) as a specifically Christian virtue, which distinguished the Christian from his pagan neighbor. As a consequence of this process, which was at work in the first two centuries, the second major development occurred in the third and fourth. By the time Christian asceticism began to concern Origen, the

[1] This tendency is discussed by Joseph Pieper, *Fortitude and Temperance* (New York, 1954), 72.

312

Cappadocians, John Chrysostom, and other influential Greek Fathers, sophrosyne was irrevocably allied with the concept of purity; and, like *hagneia* ("holiness") and *katharotês* ("purity"), it became part of a semi-technical vocabulary that the Fathers employed in discussions of the great moral issues of the day: the imitation of God, the purgation of the soul, and the practice of ascetism.

Most of the other developments in the "Christianization" of sophrosyne are in some fashion the product of this radical shift in emphasis. One such development in both the Greek and the Latin Fathers is a specifically Christian solution to the problem that has appeared at many stages in the history of sophrosyne: how to reconcile it with the opposing principle, variously identified as the heroic virtue, the active principle, *andreia,* or *megalopsychia.* The Christian ideal of the virgin martyr unites in a new synthesis sophrosyne and *megalopsychia,* purity and contempt for death. Although the reconciliation of these opposites had become something of a rhetorical commonplace in pagan *encomium,* the new conditions of Christian life and the new spiritual orientation gave it a fresh meaning, just as the encounter of Greek *aretê* with Judaeo-Christian morality gave new life to sophrosyne. A sign of this new life is the intense concern, which appears as early as Philo Judaeus, for discovering in the Bible evidence that the four cardinal virtues already existed in the Old Testament, that in fact the Greek philosophers were the pupils of Moses. For sophrosyne this meant that innumerable texts, in both the Old and the New Testaments, were interpreted as admonitions or examples intended to instil the virtue. The Ten Commandments and the Beatitudes are the most fruitful sources of such texts, but there is no end to the ingenuity and diversity displayed in this pursuit.[2] Inevitably a host of Biblical models replaced the pagan

---

[2] Since this topic is not extensively dealt with in the present chapter, it may be useful to collect here a list of the Biblical passages most often interpreted as texts of sophrosyne. The most popular is Matt. 5. 28 (*Qui viderit mulierem*), cited by Justin Martyr *I Apol.* 15, Athenagoras of Athens *Supp.* 31–32, Theophilus of Antioch *Ad Autolycum* 13, Ambrose *Ex. Ps. 118* 11. 28, 8. 34, and many others. Among the Beatitudes the following are held to commend sophrosyne: "Blessed are the poor," Luke 6. 20 (Ambrose *Ex. in Luc.* V. 64); "Blessed are the poor in spirit," Matt. 5. 3 (*ibid.*); "Blessed are the meek," Matt. 5. 4 (Gregory of Nyssa *In Beat., P.G.* 44. 1214 ff.); "Blessed are they that hunger and thirst after justice," Matt. 5. 6 (*ibid.*); "Blessed are the clean of heart," Matt. 5. 8 (John Chrysostom *Hom XV in Matt.,* Ambrose *Ex. in Luc.* V. 64). In the Lord's Prayer, "Thy will be done" is a prayer for sophrosyne, according to Gregory of Nyssa (*Orat. Dom., P.G.* 44. 1156A). Other Biblical allusions to sophrosyne include: Matt. 13. 47–48 (Gregory of Nyssa *De Virg.* 321 Cavarnos); Matt. 17. 27 (Clement of Alexandria *Paed.* II. 1. 14, 1); Matt. 19. 12 (Justin Martyr *I Apol.* 15); Luke 12. 35–38 (Methodius *Symp.* III. 10); Acts 6. 2, 15. 23–28 (Clement of Alexandria *Paed.* II. 7. 56, 1); I Cor. 15. 53 (*ibid.* II. 10. 100, 2); II Cor. 4. 16 (Augustine *De Mor. Eccl.*

exemplars, and even though the range of sophrosyne in Christian thought is narrower than it had been in the classical period, it still has several nuances, which require a variety of *exempla.* Still another major development in the first centuries of Christianity is the new interest shown by all the Greek and Latin moralists in the spiritual possibilities of women, who have but a minor place in pagan ethical philosophy. Since sophrosyne had always been, and now continued to be, the *virtus feminarum,* it received greatly increased attention in Christian thought. Finally, the preoccupation of Jewish and Christian thinkers, from Philo on, with the nature of original sin gave great importance to sophrosyne, because both pride and intemperance (specifically, gluttony), the overwhelming favorites in the search for a definition of original sin, are in obvious ways antithetical to sophrosyne/*temperantia.*

The concept of *aretê,* which is absolutely central in Greek ethical thought, is much less conspicuous in the Old Testament; and while it becomes more important in the Gospels, where the virtues of humility, charity, and repentance are prominent, it emerges as a key idea in Christian morality only in the Epistles (even though St. Paul uses the word *aretê* but once). It is Paul who dominates the first stage of the history of sophrosyne as a Christian excellence. Three stages in all may be distinguished: the first two centuries, when Paul's influence, interacting with the pagan environment, led the Apostolic Fathers and the Apologists to consider sophrosyne a virtue that set them off from their non-Christian neighbors; the third century, when the influence of Philo prevailed, especially with the School of Alexandria, and Clement and Origen were already turning to Plato and integrating Greek *aretê* into Christian philosophy; and the fourth century, when the process was completed, most brilliantly by the Cappadocians.

Although a distinctively Christian concept of sophrosyne, supported by philosophical argument, even if still rooted in faith, did not emerge until the time of Clement of Alexandria, the foundations on which he and his successors built deserve at least summary treatment. They include, in addition to Greek philosophy (Platonic, Stoic, and Neo-platonic in particular): the rare allusions to sophrosyne in the Septuagint and the New Testament; the somewhat more frequent references by the Apostolic Fathers of the first century and the Apologists of

---

I. 19. 36); Heb. 13. 14 (Jerome *Ep.* 66. 3). In the Old Testament: Gen. 3. 3 (Ambrose *De Iac.* I. 2. 8, *De Hel.* 4. 7); Gen. 9. 22 (Clement of Alexandria *Paed.* II. 6. 51, 1); Ecc. 31. 19, 32. 15 (*ibid.* II. 7. 55, 1–56, 1); Ps. 35. 12 (Augustine *De Mus.* 6. 16. 53); Wi. 4. 1. 2 (Methodius *Symp.* I. 3); Job 18. 19 (Gregory *Mor. in Job, P.L.* 75. 592).

the second; and, perhaps most influential of all after St. Paul, Philo Judaeus, whose methods of reconciling Jewish and Hellenic thought served as a model for Patristic thinkers.

Among the infrequent references to sophrosyne in the Septuagint,[3] those in the Book of Wisdom clearly reflect Stoic influence,[4] and those in the uncanonical IV Maccabees, which has for its avowed purpose the reconciliation of Jewish belief and Greek philosophy, show both Stoic and Platonic traces.[5] The Book of Wisdom celebrates as the fruits of *Sophia* the four virtues, sophrosyne, *phronêsis, dikaiosynê*, and *andreia* (8. 7) "than which there is nothing more profitable in human life."[6] IV Maccabees, whose enormous popularity with Patristic writers on martyrdom[7] gives special weight to its conception of virtue, also connects sophrosyne with *sophia*—of which it is an *idea,* or type (1. 18)— and equips it with two antitheses, gluttony and lust (1. 3), which define its scope. Presently, however, sophrosyne is further defined as the control (*enkrateia*) of the appetites, whether spiritual or physical, and is for all practical purposes equated with reason (*logismos*), which is also said to control (*epikratein*) both types of desire (1. 31–32). The phrase *sôphrôn nous* is repeatedly used as a synonym for *logismos*,[8] whose domination over the passions is the principal theme of the book. In a comprehensive summary of the function of the *sôphrôn nous* the author assigns to it control over ambition, conceit, boasting, arrogance, envy, and anger (2. 15–17). It is noteworthy that he, like Philo, rejects Stoic *apatheia* and gives the *sôphrôn nous* the task of moderating some passions while depriving others of their force (2. 18). They cannot be extirpated,

---

[3] Septuagint: *sôphrones*, Wi. 9. 11; sophrosyne, Wi. 8. 7; Es. 3. 13; II Mac. 4. 37; IV Mac. 1. 3, 6, 18, 30, 31; 5. 23; *sôphrôn*, IV Mac. 1. 35; 2. 2, 16, 18, 23; 3. 17, 19; 15. 10.

[4] The Platonic and Stoic tendencies of the Book of Wisdom and its probable origin in Alexandria during the Hellenistic age, but before Philo, are discussed by Joseph Reider, *The Book of Wisdom* (New York, 1957), 10–19, 27–28. A date after 50 B.C. is suggested by R. H. Charles, *Apocrypha* (Oxford, 1913), I. 519.

[5] For the date (*ca.* 40 A.D.) and place of origin (Antioch) of IV Maccabees and its debt to Plato, particularly the *Gorgias*, see Moses Hadas, *The Third and Fourth Books of Maccabees* (New York, 1953), 95–118.

[6] Wi. 9. 11 (*Sophia* will guide the author *sôphrônôs*, soberly) represents ordinary Hellenistic usage. II. Mac. attributes to the murdered Onias sophrosyne and *eutaxia* (4. 37; cf. Polybius 32. 11. 8 on the virtues of Scipio Aemilianus). That II Mac. was written in Antioch. *ca.* 42 A.D., is the opinion of Solomon Zeitlin, *The Second Book of Maccabees* (New York, 1954), 27–30. Hadas dates it about a century earlier (*op. cit.,* 96–97), while Charles dates it about 106 B.C. (*op. cit.* 2. 128–29).

[7] Hadas, *op. cit.,* 123–24, mentions Gregory of Nazianzus, John Chrysostom, Ambrose, and Augustine among imitators of IV Mac.

[8] E.g., 1. 35; 2. 15, 18; 3. 19 (*sôphrôn logismos*).

because they were implanted by God (2. 20). The Stoic commonplace of the sage as king appears in the statement that he who obeys the Law will rule over a kingdom that is *sôphrôn,* just, good, and brave (2. 23). The concept of *nomos* ("law"), like that of *logos* (the "word"), serves as a bridge between the Greek and the Hebrew traditions.[9] Later Christian attempts to find exemplars and texts of sophrosyne in the Bible have a precedent in IV Maccabees, where Joseph, who conquered the appetite for pleasure through reason (*dianoia,* 2. 2), David, who poured out in sacrifice the water for which he thirsted (3. 17), Eleazar, the protomartyr, and the Seven Brothers (15. 10) are all models of the virtue, regarded as control of the appetites (5. 23). The source of sophrosyne is found in the Law, specifically in the Tenth Commandment—"Thou shalt not covet thy neighbor's wife nor anything that is his" (2. 5)—and in the dietary laws which Eleazar refuses, at the cost of his life, to violate (5. 17 ff.).

THE NEW TESTAMENT

In the New Testament the concept of virtue (as understood in classical Greek thought) begins to play a larger role than it did in the Old Testament; its appearance in the Apocrypha is usually traceable to Stoic influence on Jewish writers in Alexandria or Antioch. Later Christian teaching about the virtues found two major sources in the New Testament: the Beatitudes, which were sometimes interpreted as specific exhortations to practice the Greek cardinal virtues, and the characteristics of Christ Himself, particularly His humility. The one allusion to sophrosyne in the Greek translation of the Gospels occurs in the versions given by Mark and Luke of the healing of the man possessed by demons which, after being driven out of him, took refuge in the Gadarene swine.[10] Both Evangelists describe the man, after the exorcism, as being clothed and in his right mind (*sôphronounta:* Mark 5. 15, Luke 8. 35)—an instance of the survival of the radical meaning of sophrosyne which has many parallels in ordinary Greek usage throughout the Graeco-Roman period.

It is in the Epistles of St. Paul, however, that sophrosyne first attains a place in Christian ethics and morality. Although its nature is completely

[9] See 5. 23 where Eleazar tells Antiochus that the Law (Jewish Law) teaches sophrosyne (control of all pleasures and appetites), *andreia, dikaiosynê,* and *eusebeia.*

[10] For the appearance of sophrosyne and related words in the New Testament, see Arndt and Gingrich, *A Greek-English Lexicon of the New Testament and Other Early Christian Literature* (Chicago, 1952).

transformed by Paul's conception of Grace (Tit. 2. 12–14), which makes even the virtues derived from Greek philosophy essentially different from their Greek counterparts, its function in the Epistles conforms to contemporary pagan usage. Paul recognizes three aspects of sophrosyne, which may be defined in terms of its antitheses: it is opposed to madness (*mania*), to pride (*hyperphronein*), and to the tyranny of the appetites (*epithymia*); the third interpretation is by far the most common.

The antithesis between madness and sophrosyne, which underlies the two passages in the New Testament mentioned above, becomes explicit in the Acts of the Apostles where Paul's arraignment before Agrippa is described. When Festus charges him with madness, Paul replies (Acts 26. 25): "I am not mad [οὐ μαίνομαι], rather I utter words of truth and sophrosyne [ἀληθείας καὶ σωφροσύνης]." In the Second Epistle to the Corinthians a like contrast is made between the condition of being beside oneself and being *sôphrôn* (5. 13). The opposition between sophrosyne and pride is expressed through a play on the root—*phron*—in the Epistle to the Romans (12. 3), which also recalls such traditional Hellenic commonplaces as self-knowledge and thinking mortal thoughts. Paul exhorts the Romans not to have thoughts above what is proper (μὴ ὑπὲρ φρονεῖν παρ' ὃ δεῖ φρονεῖν), but to think modest thoughts (φρονεῖν εἰς τὸ σωφρονεῖν), in view of the great diversity of gifts with which God has endowed mankind. Sophrosyne is not yet equated with humility, but its connection with self-knowledge suggests a way by which the identification may ultimately be made.

To Paul sophrosyne usually signifies self-control and mastery of the appetites. He associates it with *aidôs* (I Tim. 2. 9), with *enkrateia* (Tit. 1. 8, one of the Gifts of the Holy Ghost, Gal. 5. 23), with sobriety (Tit. 2. 2, 6; I Tim. 3. 2), and in the case of women, with conjugal love (*philandria:* I Tim. 2. 9; Tit. 2. 2, 5). Although, like most moralists in the Greek world, he construes sophrosyne as the essential virtue of women (Tit. 2. 6, I Tim. 2. 9), he also enjoins it upon men of every age (Tit. 2. 2, 6) and specifically lists it among the qualifications of a bishop (Tit. 1. 8, I Tim. 3. 2).

Since the writings of Paul were diligently studied by the Fathers, certain of his references to sophrosyne had great influence on later Christian thought about the virtue. His injunction to women to adorn themselves with *aidôs* and sophrosyne, rather than with elaborate coiffures and costly raiment (I Tim. 2. 9), was often echoed in panegyrics of Christian women and exhortations by St. Gregory of Nazianzus, St.

John Chrysostom, and St. Ambrose; while the statement (I Tim. 2. 15) that woman will find salvation in childbearing was quoted in homilies on the married state. The conclusion to this verse—"If they persevere in *pistis* and *agapê* and *hagiasmos* with sophrosyne"—suggests, by its plural verb, that it refers to husbands as well as wives.[11] The alliance of sophrosyne with two of the three theological virtues, faith (*pistis*) and love (*agapê*), as well as with a word denoting holiness or purity (*hagiasmos*), shows how thoroughly it has been Christianized and also indicates which of its aspects was now prominent. The intrinsically Christian orientation of *hagiasmos* is evident in I Thessalonians 4. 7, where Paul reminds his hearers that God has not called them to impurity (*akatharsia*) but to *hagiasmos*, and where he shows that sanctification is a distinguishing mark of the Christian, in contrast to the lust (*pathos epithymias*) of the pagans who know not God (4. 5). A like opposition between sophrosyne and appetite (*epithymia*), and a similar assumption that escape from the enslavement to lust is the mark of a convert appear in the First Epistle of St. Peter. His warning against the rioting and drunkenness of the pagans concludes with the admonition (4. 7): "Be prudent and sober in prayer [σωφρονήσατε οὖν καὶ νήψατε]."

Paul never refers to the entire canon of Greek virtues and in fact uses the term *aretê* only once (Phil. 4. 8). When in I Corinthians 1. 30 he speaks of four excellences "from God," they prove to be *sophia* and *dikaiosynê*, to both of which he gives a Christian content, and the entirely unclassical *hagiasmos* ("sanctification") and *apolutrôsis* ("redemption"), the first of which becomes a fairly common Christian substitute for sophrosyne. Even in a reference to three traditional Hellenic qualities (such as Tit. 2. 12, where the Grace of God is said to teach us to live modestly—*sôphronôs*—justly, and piously) the presence of Grace as the source of virtue shows that the familiar Greek words are being used in a new way. What remains the same is the feeling that sophrosyne has to do with the restraint of appetite.

In spite of the asceticism evinced in such passages as these, Paul gives no support whatever to later extremists like Origen and Tertullian. He approves of marriage and even urges young widows to remarry (I Tim. 5. 14). While he counsels moderation in the use of the goods of creation (Rom. 14. 17, 21; Phil. 2. 3) and sanctions fasting and morti-

---

[11] T. E. Bird (*Catholic Biblical Quarterly* 2 [1940], 259–63) discusses various interpretations of this passage and the general conception of sophrosyne as a virtue of the priesthood and of married life according to Paul.

fication (I Cor. 9. 27), he avoids fanaticism and establishes the principle that all God's creation is good (I Tim. 4. 3–4).[12]

In view of later attempts by the Greek and Latin Fathers to reconcile the heroic and the gentle elements in the concept of *aretê*, one further passage in the Epistles may be mentioned. In II Timothy 1. 7, Paul admonishes his disciple not to be discouraged by his sufferings and reminds him that God has not given us the spirit of fear, but that of power (*dynamis*), love (*agapê*), and sobriety (*sôphronismos*). The normal significance of *sôphronismos* is "castigation, discipline," but here, as occasionally elsewhere,[13] it implies "moderation, sobriety." Thus Paul, in contrasting it with fear (*deilia*) and linking it with power and love as qualities that enable the Christian to endure suffering, takes the first step towards the concept of the martyr who unites sophrosyne with *megalopsychia*, or, as Cyprian puts it, *pudor* with *robur*.[14]

THE APOSTOLIC FATHERS AND THE APOLOGISTS

Allusions to sophrosyne in the writings of the Apostolic Fathers of the first century are infrequent, but they continue the process begun in the Epistles of assimilating the virtue to Christian morality. There are no references to the entire canon of Stoic virtues—nor could there be until Christian thought became less hostile to pagan morality—but the individual members of the canon are all taking on Christian connotations, none more swiftly than sophrosyne. Clement of Rome (*ca.* 96) singles out sophrosyne, alone among the cardinal virtues, for inclusion in lists of excellences important for the Christian life. In the summarizing paragraph of his First Epistle to the Corinthians (62. 2) and in the prayer for all Christians at the close (64. 1), he mentions sophrosyne in conjunction with faith, repentance, and love, linking it with *enkrateia* in the first passage and with both *enkrateia* and *hagneia* in the second. (In both passages *andreia* is replaced by *hypomonê*, "endurance.") Pope Clement praises the Corinthians for their *sôphrôn* and *epieikês eusebeia* ("sober and reasonable piety" [1. 2]) and describes the representatives whom he has sent to them as *pistous* and *sôphronas* ("full of faith and sobriety" [63. 3]). Sophrosyne is clearly a term of special praise, a

---

[12] The attitude of Paul towards fasting and other types of external austerity is discussed by Musurillo, 47.

[13] E.g., Plutarch *Mor.* 712C. For the usual meaning, cf. Aeschylus *Supp.* 992.

[14] *Ep.* 39. 4.

worthy companion of faith: its association with *enkrateia* is an echo of the past, with *hagneia* a forecast of the future.[15]

Hagneia ("purity") is again linked with sophrosyne in the Epistle to the Ephesians by Ignatius of Antioch (10. 3), but Polycarp associates sophrosyne with wisdom in his Epistle to the Philippians (4. 3). Thus it seems likely that both of the widely accepted connotations of the word, the moral and the intellectual, maintained themselves in Christian circles, as in contemporary pagan usage. The writings of the Apologists of the second century, however, give evidence of a strong impulse to emphasize the moral, rather than the intellectual, aspect of sophrosyne and to select this one of the Greek virtues as a criterion by which to judge the conduct of Christians and to distinguish them from the pagans.

There are several reasons for this. One is that standards of sexual morality were indubitably higher (especially for men) among the Christians than in most of contemporary pagan society. Moreover, differing standards of conduct in this area were probably more noticeable in practice than differences in the concepts of wisdom, justice, or courage. Hence sophrosyne soon came to rival charity itself as the visible mark of the Christian; and it receives even more attention than charity in the works of the Apologists, probably because of the nature of the charges that they were obliged to refute. Athenagoras of Athens, Tertullian, and Minucius Felix make it clear that the enemies of the Christians accused them of indecent and obscene orgies in the course of those rites and ceremonies whose secrecy aroused suspicion. Hence the emphasis on purity and chastity as the signs of Christian morality in the writings of the Apologists, who confined sophrosyne almost completely to this sphere. Here begins what has been called "the stubborn and really quite fanatical preference given to *temperantia,* especially to chastity, which runs through the whole history of Christian doctrine as a more or

---

[15] See Werner Jaeger, *Early Christianity and Greek Paideia* (Cambridge, Mass., 1961), 12–26, for a discussion of the *First Epistle* of Clement, especially the Stoic background to its system of Christian virtues. The *Didachê* and the *Epistle of Barnabas* do not allude to sophrosyne, nor does the *Shepherd of Hermas,* but the *Shepherd* often refers to *enkrateia,* which is the subject of the Eighth Mandate. The vision of seven women who support the tower is important in the history of the iconography of the virtues. The women represent seven virtues, each the daughter of the one before; *Pistis* (Faith), the foundation of all virtues, is first. After her comes *Enkrateia* (Self-control), 3. 8. 1–6. *Enkrateia* and sophrosyne continue to be closely associated in Christian morality, as they had been in pagan thought, with *enkrateia* usually more limited in scope. Paul's inclusion of *enkrateia* among the fruits of the Holy Ghost (Gal. 5. 23) increased its prestige among the Apostolic Fathers and the Apologists.

less hidden undercurrent."[16] This distortion must, however, be connected not only with the reaction to a pagan environment, but also with a strong tendency within the Christian family itself to go to extremes, to adopt a contemptuous attitude towards the sensual part of creation and to reject as sinful all contact with the flesh. This tendency, which had its outcome in Montanism and Manicheeism, can be seen very early in the works of both Greek and Latin apologists. There was no more serious problem in the development of a Christian concept of sophrosyne than how to avoid such distortion and retain the essential moderation that belongs to the classical concept of sophrosyne.[17]

Sophrosyne is recognized as a peculiarly Christian virtue in the work of the first Greek Apologist, Aristides of Athens, whose *Apology to Hadrian* praises the conduct of Christians in general and refers particularly to Christian women as *sôphrones* (the men are *enkrateis: T.u.U.* 4, p. 37 Hennecke). The theme is developed at greater length by Justin Martyr in his *First Apology*, which contrasts the licentiousness of Christian converts before conversion with their subsequent devotion to sophrosyne alone (1. 14). Justin's *Second Apology* gives a specific instance of such conversion. A woman who had been wanton during her life as a pagan became a Christian and began both to be *sôphrôn* herself and to try to persuade her pagan husband, who was still *akolastos* ("wanton"), to become *sôphrôn;* she cited the teachings of Christ and warned her husband that there would be eternal fire for those who fail to live in a *sôphrôn* fashion (2. 2). Justin is the first Christian to cite specific texts in the New Testament as the teaching of Christ on sophrosyne. He quotes Matthew 5. 28–29 and 32, and 19. 12 (1. 15), and thereby initiates a powerful tradition. The first of these texts—"But I say to you that whosoever shall look on a woman to lust after her has already committed adultery with her in his heart"—becomes a special favorite with the Fathers.[18] From these verses Justin draws the conclusion that remarriage is sinful; this idea was developed to the point of heresy by his pupil Tatian, who ultimately became an Enkratist and rejected marriage

---

[16] Pieper, *op. cit.,* 72. Sophrosyne as "sobriety" is also regarded as a distinctively Christian attribute, in contrast to pagan drunkenness. See A. P. McKinlay, *Anglican Theological Review* 30 (1948), 44–54.

[17] The importance of moderation is clearly seen and vigorously expressed by Gregory of Nyssa *De Virg.* 7. 353M, p. 282 Cavarnos, and by Augustine *De Beata Vita* IV. 32–33. Cf. also Clement of Alexandria *Paed.* III. 10. 51, 2.

[18] Matt. 19. 12 ("For there are eunuchs who were born so from their mother's womb") also reappears as a text of sophrosyne in both Greek and Latin Patristic literature.

altogether, as he rejected meat and wine. Justin himself does not go to this extreme, but he shows in a striking manner his belief that sophrosyne, as purity, is at the very center of Christian morality. In his *First Apology* he expands in the following way (1. 15) the Biblical statement that Christ came to call, not the just, but sinners to repentance: Christ came to call, not the just *or the sôphrôn* to repentance, but the unjust, the impious, and the wanton (*akolastous*). Justin is also the first Apologist to make the assertion, already familiar among Alexandrian Hellenized Jews, that Plato had learned from Moses (1. 59). The importance of this fallacy, so enthusiastically adopted by the Fathers, was that it enabled them to make open use of Greek philosophy, on the ground that it had a respectable origin in the Mosaic Law.

The moderate position of Justin is in great contrast to the ferocity of Tatian against everything Greek—whether philosophy, education, rhetoric, or religion—as set forth in his *Oratio ad Graecos* (*T.u.U.* Schwartz 4). According to Tatian, sophrosyne is one of the important areas in which the Christians surpass the pagan Greeks. Generally, like Justin, he contrasts it with wantonness (ἀσέλγεια, 33), but on one occasion he maintains that Christian ethics is *sôphrôn,* while that of the Greeks contains much *mania* (33). Tatian specifically accuses the Greeks of shamelessness (ἀσχημοσύνη) in regard to women, because they erected statues of women who wrote useless poetry, particularly Sappho, who sang of her own wantonness. "But our women are chaste (*sôphrones*), and our girls sing of divine themes" (38).[19]

The tradition of finding texts of sophrosyne in the Bible is continued by Athenagoras of Athens, in his *Supplication for the Christians,* addressed to Marcus Aurelius and Commodus. He, too, cites Matthew 5. 28 as the teaching of Christ on sophrosyne and uses it to refute a pagan charge that the Christians are immoral. How can they for whom a wanton look is adultery fail in sophrosyne (*T.u.U.* 4. 31–32 Schwartz)? Still another influential topic, often connected with sophrosyne in Patristic literature, appears when Athenagoras asserts that many Christians renounce marriage so that they may come closer to God—a Pauline doctrine that the Fathers conflate with the Platonic topic of ὁμοίωσις θεῷ.[20] The most significant original contribution that Athenagoras makes to the developing Christian theory about the virtues appears in his treatist *On the*

---

[19] Tatian maintains that Homer, as well as the Sophists, learned from Moses (35).

[20] Cf. Paul, I Cor. 7. 32–40. Like Justin, Athenagoras emphatically disapproves of remarriage, which he calls genteel adultery (εὐπρεπὴς μοιχεία [33]). He compares pagans to harlots, Christians to *sôphrones* women (34), and describes Christian life as *metrios* and *epieikês.*

Resurrection of the Dead. The question arises whether virtue belongs only to the soul or to the whole man, and Athenagoras, perceiving the philosophical implications of the Resurrection, maintains that it is absurd to ascribe virtue to the soul alone. He illustrates this absurdity with reference to the entire group of Stoic virtues, listing first *phronêsis* and *dikaiosynê* and all virtue (πάση ἀρετή, 15), later *eusebeia* and *dikaiosynê* and the rest of *aretê* (19), then *andreia* and *karteria, enkrateia* and *sophrosyne*, and finally *phronêsis* and *dikaiosynê* once more (22). He asks, for example, how one can think that *enkrateia* and sophrosyne could belong to the soul alone, when there is no desire capable of drawing the soul to voluptuousness, sexual intercourse, and the other forms of pleasure that appeal only to the body. Hence it is not unjust for the soul to be reunited with the body at the Resurrection, for this reunion is necessary in order that the body may be rewarded or punished with the soul (22). This argument has an obvious bearing on the old discussion about the existence of the moral virtues in the afterlife or in the Divine nature.[21] It also proves that Athenagoras was familiar with the cardinal virtues. In referring to them all in close succession, he antedates Clement of Alexandria, who is usually regarded as the first Christian author to mention the entire canon.

Still another Greek Apologist, Theophilos of Antioch, confirms the theory that before the close of the second century sophrosyne, as purity, had become a thoroughly Christian virtue. A chapter in his letter *Ad Autolycum* contrasts pagan licentiousness with Christian purity and associates sophrosyne with a long list of Christian attributes, including *enkrateia, monogamia,* and *hagneia* (3. 15). He, too, refers to Matthew 5. 28 as containing the teaching of Christ on purity (13). The next step in the development of Biblical exegesis involving sophrosyne depended on the wide adoption by Christian writers of the method of allegorical interpretation which they now began to borrow from Philo Judaeus.

PHILO JUDAEUS

After the Bible itself and St. Paul, the principal influence on early Christian thought about the virtues is Philo, who pioneered in the integration of Jewish theology with Greek philosophy and hit upon methods of uniting the two traditions which appealed powerfully to many of the Church Fathers. Philo's three contributions to the history of sophrosyne

[21] An exhaustive list of passages in pagan and Christian writers dealing with this problem is given by A. S. Pease, *M. Tulli Ciceronis De Natura Deorum* (Cambridge, Mass., 1955–1958), II. 1035–36.

are, first, the allegorical interpretation of Scripture; secondly, the identification of the Ten Commandments with Greek ethical teaching; and thirdly, the selection of *exempla virtutum* from the Old Testament to replace the familiar models from Greek myth and history.

The allegorical exegesis of Genesis in Philo's *Legum Allegoria* transfers to the Bible the method already successfully used by the Stoics in their interpretation of Homer and Greek mythology. It also employs transparently Platonic notions, such as the statement that God planted in Paradise earthly virtues that are but copies of the heavenly models (1. 14. 43).[22] The allegories relevant to sophrosyne are three in number, of which the first, the identification of the Rivers of Paradise with the four Stoic virtues, is much the most influential. Philo interprets the chief river, which divides into four streams (Gen. 2. 10–14), as generic virtue, Goodness (*agathotês*). It takes its start from Eden (the wisdom of God). Philo then defines the cardinal virtues in Stoic terms (sophrosyne being concerned with choice) and assigns a river to each, chiefly on the basis of etymology. Pheison represents *phronêsis,* Gehon *andreia,* the Tigris sophrosyne, and the Euphrates *dikaiosynê.* The Tigris, whose course is "over against the Assyrians," symbolizes sophrosyne, the restraint of pleasure (*hêdonê*), which tries to direct the course of human weakness, because the word "Assyrian" in Hebrew means "directing," and also because the tiger, the most untameable animal, represents appetite (*epithymia*). Philo notes that whereas the Pheison and Gehon are said to "surround" their respective territories, the Tigris and the Euphrates do not. The reason is that *phronêsis* and *andreia* can encompass and overcome folly and cowardice, but sophrosyne cannot "encircle" appetite and pleasure. Even those who practice *enkrateia* must resort to food and drink. Hence Philo rejects Stoic *apatheia,* except in the case of Moses, for he was purified by Divine Grace. Ordinary men can expect to achieve only *metriopatheia* (*Vita M.* 2. 68; *Leg. All.* 3. 156, 144). Although the

[22] The comparison of the virtues to trees, and the Tree of Life to generic virtue (I. 17. 56) is noteworthy in view of the mediaeval metaphor of the trees of virtue and vice, the *Arbor bona* and the *Arbor mala,* rooted respectively in humility and pride. Cf. also Philo *De Agr.* 11. 43. The influence of this metaphor is considerable. See, for example, Herrad of Landsberg, *Hortus Deliciarum* (12th century), inspired by the tract *De Fructibus Carnis et Spiritus* ascribed to Hugh of St. Victor (*P.L.* 176. 997 ff.), where the influence of Gal. 5. 22 is strong. Among many examples in art of a tree or a plant from which grow virtues related to sophrosyne, one of the best known is the porch of the Baptistery in Parma (*ca.* 1200), where *castitas* is the source from which flower *patientia* and *humilitas,* while *spes* branches out into *prudentia* and *modestia.* Katzenellenbogen, figs. 64–65, illustrates the *Arbor bona* and the *Arbor mala.* The symbolism of the two trees is discussed by Mâle, 106–8.

identification of the four rivers with the four virtues became very popular with the Fathers, Philo's equation of individual pairs did not win universal acceptance; Ambrose, for example, identifies the river Gehon, rather than the Tigris, with sophrosyne.[23]

Two other allegorical interpretations of the Old Testament have a bearing on sophrosyne. The prayer of Jacob in Genesis 49. 16–18 that Dan may become a brazen serpent biting the horse's heel is explained as a prayer that he may become a lover of sophrosyne, because sophrosyne wounds and destroys the passions. The four Stoic passions are the four legs of the horse, and the horseman himself (according to Philo) symbolizes *nous*, which, falling backward, is saved from the passions that carry it along the road that the soul travels (*Alleg. Int.* 2. 24. 94 ff.). Philo frequently employs the Platonic image of the horse to represent the passions and appetites, but usually pictures someone riding astride, rather than a charioteer. In *De Agricultura* he contrasts the true horseman, who controls his steed, with a mere rider, who is at the mercy of the horse— that is, of *thymos* and *epithymia*. The explication of Jacob's prayer illustrates Philo's allegorical method, which here presents in a complicated, not to say grotesque, visual image the Greek commonplace about sophrosyne as the savior of *phronêsis*.

Philo embarks upon an even more complex exegesis when he interprets the episode in the Book of Numbers in which God sends serpents to destroy the Jews, and Moses heals the sick by making the brazen serpent (21. 6). In this case both sophrosyne and *hêdonê* ("pleasure") are represented as serpents: *hêdonê* because it glides through the senses, bringing death to the soul; and sophrosyne because it is the "counterpart" of *hêdonê*. Moses' serpent (sophrosyne) is bronze because this material is firm and unyielding, but also because the sophrosyne of those who attain the virtue only gradually and with effort is not as fine as that of the *theophilos*, whose sophrosyne would be like gold. In fact, Philo continues,

---

23 The identification of the rivers with the cardinal virtues under the influence of Philo appears in Ambrose *De Par., P.L.* 14. 296 ff., and Augustine *De Gen. contr. Man.* 2. 10. 31–34. In later art this allegory provided an apt motive for the decoration of baptismal fonts, such as that in the cathedral at Hildesheim (*ca.* 1240–1250), where the identification of the Gehon with *temperantia* indicates that the immediate source is Ambrose rather than Philo. See n. 127. In illustrated manuscripts of the *Speculum Virginum* (usually ascribed to Conrad of Hirzau) the rivers of Paradise are often combined with the flowers of virtue. Consult Arthur Watson, *Speculum* 3 (1928), 445–69, and *Journal of the Walters Art Gallery* 10 (1947), 61–74. Philo popularized the mystical significance of the number four, which could be applied to a great many tetrads. For some consequences in art, see George M. A. Hanfman, *The Season Sarcophagus in Dumbarton Oaks* (Cambridge, Mass., 1951), 198 ff.

sophrosyne is not the common property of all men, for God commanded Moses to make a serpent "for thyself." [24]

Philo's equation of the Greek cardinal virtues with the Mosaic Law had vast consequences for Patristic writers, who found in this theory the chief means of bringing together virtues derived from faith and Divine Grace and virtues based on natural reason. Philo identifies the Law of Moses with that law which Greek philosophy, particularly the Stoic, considered the expression of life in accordance with nature. As the *nomos* of Plato and the Stoics led to the practice of the four virtues, so the Ten Commandments aim to instil these same virtues, and Philo analyzes the Decalogue according to these four headings.[25] The first four Commandments instil intellectual virtues, the last six moral virtues, but in fact each Commandment exhorts to all the virtues (*Spec. Leg.* 4. 25. 134). The Sixth and Tenth Commandments have most to do with the control of appetite and therefore with sophrosyne and *enkrateia* (usually synonymous in Philo).[26] Sophrosyne is interpreted narrowly as chastity in Book III of the *Special Laws,* which deals with offenses against the Sixth Commandment, but in Book IV (on sins against the last three Commandments) Philo extends the term to include the control of all appetites. The Tenth Commandment is important in that it prohibits an emotion, not an action. The discussion of *epithymia* in Book IV repeats much of what Philo says in his treatise *On the Decalogue* (28. 142–53), where gluttony is regarded as the form of *epithymia* that leads to all the other appetites, and Moses' hostility to it is thereby explained. The dietary laws are *nomoi sôphrosynês,* "laws of sophrosyne" (*Spec. Leg.* 4. 16).[27] Philo's emphasis on the primary guilt of indulging in gluttony explains the theory, so often expressed by the Fathers, that this form of *intemperantia* was responsible for the Fall. Ambrose, the Philo Latinus, repeatedly makes this assertion; for this reason fasting and sobriety are central in his ethics.[28]

The third element in Philo's treatment of sophrosyne which had

[24] *Alleg. Int.* 2. 19. 77–20. 79.

[25] On Philo's theory of the passions, the virtues, and their relation to the Law, consult Wolfson, II. 302–21.

[26] E.g., *De Vir.* 167, *De Agr.* 21. 98. The opposing vice is *akolasia* (*De Agr.* 21. 98). For personifications of *Pudicitia* and *Temperantia* in connection with the Sixth and Tenth Commandments respectively in art of the twelfth century, consult Katzenellenbogen, 47–48, n. 6.

[27] The prohibition of certain kinds of food is at first explained as the result of their being especially delicious (4. 16. 97), but a more philosophical explanation is later given (106). The laws concerning circumcision and marriage are also laws of sophrosyne (*Spec. Leg.* 1. 2. 8–12, 4. 14. 79–24. 131).

[28] See especially *De Helia* and *De Isaac.*

a pervasive influence in Patristic thought is his choice of *exempla virtutum* from the Bible. He makes Abraham the model of all the virtues, including moderation, which is not, however, called sophrosyne, since this term is usually reserved for the control of the physical appetites. Abraham's resignation at the death of Sarah exemplifies the Mean (*to metron*) between the vicious extremes of *apatheia* and excessive mourning (*De Abr.* 44. 255 ff.). Joseph, who remains a favorite exemplar of sophrosyne in Patristic literature, already appears in this role in Philo's *De Josepho*, which shows special interest in the effect of sophrosyne on affairs of state. Joseph is here treated as a type of the *bios politikos*, and Philo comments that such continence as he showed in his encounter with Potiphar's wife is profitable to society, since history provides many examples of the misfortunes, even wars, that result from incontinence and adultery. The results of incontinence (*akrasia*) are civil strife, wars, and other evils, but the effects of sophrosyne are stability, peace, and the possession and enjoyment of perfect good (11. 57). Philo's familiarity with Hellenistic treatises on kingship is evident here.[29] In these treatises, as we noted in Chapter VI, the sophrosyne, *aidôs* and *enkrateia* of the ruler are cited, not only for their effect in rendering the king himself virtuous, but also for their power to *sôphronizein* the entire kingdom. According to Philo, the sophrosyne of Joseph made the prison in which he was confined in Egypt a *sôphronistêrion* for the other prisoners (86 f.).

It is impossible in a summary treatment of Philo's contribution to the history of sophrosyne to do more than suggest his enormous influence. Among the tendencies in his thought that were continued by the Fathers, we should not overlook his belief that ascetic effort is necessary to overcome the passions.[30] In so far as Christian asceticism came to include the ideas of *ponos* ("labor") and *agôn* ("struggle"), it was indebted to Philo, as it was when it carried on the belief that ὁμοίωσις θεῷ involves the moral virtues, considered to be reflections or imitations of heavenly virtues.[31] Moreover, his synthesis, not only of Jewish and Greek thought, but also

---

[29] Edwin Goodenough (*The Politics of Philo Judaeus* [New Haven, 1938], 22–23) regards Joseph in *De Somniis* 2. 61–66 as a cryptic reference to the despised *praefectus Aegypti*. He is portrayed as an enemy of humility and a type of arrogance. Later in the treatise Joseph's character improves, beginning with his rejection of Potiphar's wife. The interpretation of Joseph in *De Somniis* differs radically from that in *De Josepho*, where the theory of Hellenistic kingship is reflected. On this topic, see Goodenough, *Y.C.S.* 1 (1928), 53–102, with critical comments by H. M. Fisch, *A.J.P.* 78 (1937), 59–82.

[30] See Jean Daniélou, S.J., *Philon d'Alexandrie* (Paris, 1958), 190 ff. on the topics of *askêsis*, *pathos*, and virtue in Philo. In the *Life of Moses* the cardinal virtues are ascribed to the austere life (2. 34. 185).

[31] See Merki, 35–44, for this motive in Philo.

of various elements within the Greek tradition, provided a model for Patristic writers. The presence of Peripatetic, as well as of Platonic and Stoic nuances, in Philo's treatment of sophrosyne is manifest in such statements as that in *Quod Deus Immutabilis Est* which describes virtue as a mean between vicious extremes (34. 162 ff.). To Philo the extremes between which sophrosyne lies are not wantonness and insensitivity but careless extravagance (ῥαθυμία) and stinginess (φειδωλία [34. 164]). It was to be important also for the Fathers that Philo rejected the Stoic teaching that all passions are evil and instead found certain passions, such as righteous indignation, useful. His freedom in mingling Jewish virtues, like faith and repentance, with Greek virtues and in giving new meanings to the Greek virtues also served as a stimulus to the Fathers.[32]

CLEMENT OF ALEXANDRIA

It is no accident that the first systematic attempt to integrate Judaeo-Christian and Greek thought was made by the first Greek Christian who was thoroughly indoctrinated in the writings of Philo. Clement of Alexandria did for the Christian concept of sophrosyne what Cicero did for the Roman. There is a vast difference between his philosophical approach to the virtue and Paul's random adoption of a term familiar in contemporary pagan usage, or the Apologists' impulse to single out so-phrosyne in a limited moral connotation as a peculiarly Christian virtue. Clement, educated in the city where a long tradition of harmonizing various cultures already existed, was inspired not only by the example of Philo, but also by the problem he himself faced—a very different one from that of earlier Christian teachers. Where the Apostolic Fathers and the Apologists had emphasized the difference between Christian and pagan conduct, Clement wrote both for an educated Christian public and (in the *Protrepticus*) for pagan readers; and his writings manifest a deep desire to justify the study of Greek philosophy as a legitimate source from which to select doctrines that support Christian belief. Under the influence of Philo he treats Greek philosophy as parallel to Jewish Law,

---

[32] For Philo's adoption of various elements from different philosophical schools and his mingling of Jewish with Greek virtues, see Wolfson, II. Chap. 12, *passim*. Philo's part in the development of the concept of *sôphrôn mania* ("sane madness") or *methê nêphalios* ("sober drunkenness"), both referring to mystical inspiration, is treated by Hans Lewy, *Sobria Ebrietas* (Giessen, 1929), Chap. 1. Clement, Origen, Gregory of Nyssa, Eusebius, and Ambrose all employ the contrast between the drunkenness or madness that results from natural causes, such as wine, and the "wineless intoxication" or "sane madness" of mystical union.

a preparation for the full revelation of the Gospel; and he repeats Philo's claim that the Greek poets and philosophers learned from the Prophets.[33] Thus what is desirable in Greek philosophy is justified on two grounds: its descent from the Jewish Law and its origin in the Divine gift of *phronêsis,* whose proper function is to speculate about the nature of truth. Sophrosyne is one of the legacies from the Greek tradition which Clement most enthusiastically accepts; he gives it, in fact, a position of special eminence as one of the two effects produced by the study of philosophy. According to the *Paedagogus,* this study has two consequences, intellectual and moral, the first termed *epistemê,* the second sophrosyne. The object of the Christian *Logos* is to make the soul *sôphrôn,* not *epistêmonikos* ("full of knowledge" [I. 1. 1. 4]).[34]

As this statement implies, Clement resembles the Apologists in finding sophrosyne a characteristically Christian excellence—moral, rather than intellectual—but he does not, as they do, isolate it from the other three cardinal virtues. His free use of the entire Platonic canon is a mark of his confident approach to pagan philosophy in general.[35] Among the cardinal virtues, however, it is *phronêsis* whose value for Christians he is most concerned to justify. Sophrosyne has long since been accepted, and Clement finds a place in the history of its development mainly because he extends its function in Christian thought by incorporating certain Platonic doctrines into the concept of the virtue already known to the Apologists. The chief result of his innovations is that sophrosyne as a Christian virtue finds a place in speculations about the assimilation to God and *gnôsis,* two subjects of great interest to Clement in the *Stromateis.*

The three major works of Clement—the *Protrepticus,* the *Paedagogus,* and the *Stromateis*—are addressed to three distinct groups of readers— pagan, Christian, and Christian gnostic; but one basic conception of sophrosyne appears in all three.[36] The word normally indicates control of the appetites, although occasionally it extends to other meanings,

[33] *Strom.* II. 18. 78, 1. The works of Clement are cited according to the edition of Otto Stählin and Ludwig Früchtel (Leipzig, 1909–1960). The four Greek virtues were learned from the Hebrews, *Strom.* VI. 11. 95, 4.

[34] See *Strom.* VII. 3. 20, 2 for the role of Greek philosophy in purging the soul, and consult J. T. Muckle, C.S.B., *Phoenix* 5 (1951), 79–86.

[35] The four virtues: e.g., *Strom.* I. 20. 97, 3; II. 18. 78, 1; VII. 3. 17, 3; *Paed.* II. 12. 121, 4 (where *eusebeia* replaces *phronêsis*), III. 11. 64, 1 (where *aidôs* and *philagathia* are added).

[36] The little homily *Quis Dives Salvetur?* contains nothing of special interest for sophrosyne, except an allusion to the concept of *sôphrôn mania,* when Clement says (38. 1) that one who is filled with *agapê* for his brother "is all aflutter concerning him, is in a sane frenzy about him [σωφρόνως μαίνεται]." The Loeb translation "is chastely wild" misses the point of the oxymoron.

equally traditional in classical literature—sobriety, sanity, moderation.[37] Yet the use made of the concept differs from one work to another, depending on whether Clement is preaching to the converted or to pagan readers. In the *Protrepticus* he contrasts pagan with Christian morality and, like the Apologists, represents sophrosyne as the principal and distinguishing Christian excellence, allying it with *enkrateia* and opposing it to *akrasia*. He attacks the indecent conduct of the pagan gods, especially Zeus's lack of sophrosyne (2. 37, 3), and charges the pagans with accepting these gods because they themselves desire wantonness, and with rejecting the true God because they cannot endure sophrosyne (4. 61, 4). It often seems that Clement regards the process of conversion to Christianity as a matter of substituting sophrosyne for profligacy. He says, for example, that the abandonment of the pleasures of the pagan life is followed by a harvest of the fruits of sophrosyne (11. 117, 5). The persistent identification of sophrosyne with conversion to Christ is nowhere better illustrated than in Clement's exegesis of the *Bacchae* of Euripides, a consummate example of the allegorical method of interpreting poetry which Clement learned from Philo and the Stoics. Commenting on the scene in which Pentheus, dressed in fawn skins like a maenad and mocked by Dionysus, behaves as though intoxicated, Clement contrasts his "drunkenness" with the sobriety of salvation. Pentheus becomes a type of paganism; the rites of Bacchus are contrasted with the mysteries of salvation, and the maenads on Mount Cithaeron are supplanted, in Clement's exhortation, by the daughters of God on the Holy Mountain, who lead the *sôphrôn* chorus of the just (12. 119, 1 ff.).

The *Paedagogus,* addressed to Christian readers, is a kind of Greek Christian *De Officiis* and recalls Cicero especially in the great emphasis placed on sophrosyne as the virtue that should govern each detail of conduct. Turning away from the contrast between pagan licentiousness and Christian purity which fills the *Protrepticus,* Clement now analyzes sophrosyne in its specific effects on many aspects of everyday life—eating, drinking, speaking, sleeping, the choice of dress and adornment, marital behavior, and social intercourse.[38] The outward signs of a

---

[37] Sobriety: *Pro.* 10. 96, 1; *Paed.* II. 2. 19, 2–20, 2. Sanity: *Pro.* 12. 118, 5 and 122, 2. Moderation: *Quis Dives* 26, 6; *Paed.* II. 7. 58, 1. In *Pro.* 10. 109, 2, where the *Odyssey* is subjected to allegorical interpretation, Ithaca becomes a symbol of truth, and the abode of truth is divided into two sections, the women's apartment and the council of elders. The first is *semnê* ("chaste"), the second *sôphrôn* ("prudent").

[38] E.g.: Diet: II. 1. 3, 1; 14, 1 and 6. Drink: II. 2. 20, 2; 30, 2; 32, 3. Music: II. 4. 44, 1–5 (the Psalms are *sôphrôn* music). Speech: II. 6. 49, 1; 52, 1. Sleep: II. 9. 77, 1 ff. (the bed must not be too soft). Marriage: II. 10 *passim;* see especially 97, 2, a warning against

Christian life are moderation and simplicity, especially in food, drink, and clothing. The Cynic-Stoic *euteleia* ("frugality") reappears as a mark of sophrosyne (II. 1. 15, 1) but now has Biblical precedent: the blessing of the loaves and fishes shows Christ's approval of a frugal diet and His command to Peter (Matt. 17. 6) His preference for *sôphrôn* food (II. 1. 13, 2–14, 1).[39] Clement appeals constantly to the example and precepts of Christ; hence the sophrosyne of the *Paedagogus* has much greater inwardness than does the *decorum* of Cicero, and its roots are always in Divine Grace.

Like most Christian writers, Clement displays more concern for the spiritual and moral problems of women than is customary in pagan philosophy (except for certain Stoic and Neopythagorean discourses, whose commonplaces he often, in fact, recalls). Yet with all his attention to feminine sophrosyne (as in *Paed.* II. 7. 54, 1 ff.; 8. 65, 2; 10. 109, 4; III. 2. 4–5, 11), he shows no inclination to treat the virtue as exclusively feminine. He points out that *aretê* is the same for both sexes; there is one sophrosyne, one *aidôs* (I. 4. 10, 2). For both men and women, he repeatedly asserts, the principles of sophrosyne will determine what adornment to wear. Furthermore, true beauty consists in *aretê* (the four virtues, II. 12. 121, 4) or in being adorned by the Holy Spirit with justice, wisdom, courage, sophrosyne, *aidôs*, and love of goodness (III. 11. 64, 1). God rejoices to see us sparkling with intelligence (*dianoia*) and clothed with sophrosyne, the pure garment of the body (III. 1. 1, 1).[40] This commonplace, which can be traced back to Prodicus' Choice of Heracles, was given renewed authority by Paul's injunction to women in I Timothy 2. 9; most of what Clement has to say about modesty and simplicity in external things is an amplification of this familiar topic. What is perhaps most remarkable is his own scrupulous moderation in dealing with a subject that for many Christian moralists presented an irresistible temptation to excess. We must aim at moderation (*ta metria*), says Clement, avoiding both wantonness and its opposite extreme.

---

weaving by day the principles of sophrosyne and then at night raveling them, like Penelope with her web (a reversal of the normal symbolism involving Penelope). Use of scents and ointments: II. 8. 65, 2 (sophrosyne is the only proper chrism for Christian women). Jewelry: II. 12. 121, 1–5. Clothing: III. 2. 13, 2 (barbarian finery and luxury caused the ruin of Greece); III. 11. 53, 4. Hair dyes: III. 2. 6, 2. *Sôphrôn* adornment: III. 11. 64, 1.

[39] See also III. 6. 35, 3 on *euteleia*, the child of sophrosyne; III. 7. 39, 1 on Elias as a model of *euteleia* and on the Christian provision for the journey to Heaven: *euteleia* combined with *semnotês sôphrôn* ("chaste purity"); cf. II. 1. 15, 1: *euteleia sôphrôn*.

[40] Cf. II. 12. 129, 1 on *aidôs* and sophrosyne as collar and necklace; III. 2. 4, 1 on the adornment consisting of *enkrateia*. See also *Strom.* II. 23. 145, 1, where sophrosyne is to the body what the fear of God is to the soul.

Between extravagance (τρυφή) and stinginess (φειδωλία) lies the Mean
—harmonious, *sôphrôn,* and pure (III. 10. 51, 3). The Christian is not
exhorted to a life of austerity in the midst of Alexandrian hedonism; he
is merely expected to use in sensible moderation the good things of the
world and to choose what is simple and natural in preference to what
is excessive and bizarre.

A notable feature of the *Paedagogus* is the appearance of sophrosyne in
connection with the motive of ὁμοίωσις θεῷ ("assimilation to God").
Clement is the first Christian writer to develop in a systematic way this
topic (which Philo had already linked with Genesis 1. 26, 27), and
while he cites *Theaetetus* 176B far more often than any other source for
this idea, he also knows *Laws* 716C–D, which he echoes in the *Paedagogus*
and quotes verbatim in the *Stromateis.* It is owing to the influence of this
passage in the *Laws* that he selects sophrosyne as the virtue through the
practice of which we may become like God (*Paed.* II. 1. 15, 1).[41]
Contrasting human beings to birds and beasts, Clement says that we
are closer to God than are they, to the extent that we are *sôphronesteroi,*
more self-controlled. We are created, not to eat and drink, but to know
God. In the context sophrosyne clearly refers, not to the principle
of measure in general (as it does in *Laws* 716C–D), but more narrowly
to the control of the appetites, Clement's usual connotation for the
word; yet we note that in his interpretation he relates sophrosyne to a
form of *gnôsis.* He gives great weight to his statement about self-control
as a source of likeness to God by putting it close to the beginning of
Book II of the *Paedagogus,* which deals with sophrosyne in the practical
details of everyday life. Book III opens with an equally significant
assertion that the greatest lesson taught by the *Logos* is self-knowledge:
if we know ourselves, we will also know God and be like Him in doing
what is good and having as few needs as possible, and we will please
God by wearing the pure garment of sophrosyne (III. 1. 1, 1).[42]

Thus two of the most familiar aspects of sophrosyne, self-control and

[41] See Ladner, 85, on the meaning of *homoiôsis* in Clement; and cf. Merki, 44–60, and E. F.
Osborn, *The Philosophy of Clement of Alexandria* (Cambridge, 1957), 85–94. For a more detailed
discussion of the doctrine as it relates to sophrosyne, see pp. 347–48.

[42] Ὀλιγοδεία ("needing little"), the human approximation to the Divine quality of being
ἀνενδεής ("in need of nothing"), is here linked with sophrosyne. Doing good (ἀγαθοεργεῖν or
εὐπράττειν) appears in the late Stoa as one of the ways of imitating God (Merki, 14–16).
Strom. II. 19. 97, 1 also discusses *enkrateia* and doing good to others as ways of imitating God.
Other virtues that Clement associates with *homoiôsis* include piety (θεοσέβεια), *philanthrôpia,*
and gentleness (ἡμερότης) in *Strom.* VII. 2. 13, 4–14, 1 (and cf. the concluding discussion in
Pro. 12. 122. 1 ff.); but purification from the passions and appetites is always of primary
importance.

self-knowledge, are allied with the doctrine of ὁμοίωσις θεῷ in the *Paedagogus*. They are not independent of each other, for both are needed to achieve that purification which is the essential first step in the process of *homoiôsis*. In the *Paedagogus* Clement lays more emphasis on self-control than on self-knowledge. He maintains, for example, that the corrupt will become incorrupt when man overcomes his appetites through *enkrateia* and attains eternal sophrosyne; such purity will enable us to live the life of the angels (II. 10. 100, 3). And elsewhere (III. 7. 39, 1): the best preparation for the journey to Heaven is frugality (*euteleia*) combined with chaste purity (*semnotês sôphrôn*). The pagan doctrine that purification from the passions may serve as a means of union with God is here stated in terms that recall the vocabulary of the second-century Apologists. In the *Stromateis* Clement tends to associate sophrosyne with *apatheia*, rather than merely with *euteleia* and *semnotês;* and he also does greater justice to the need for self-knowledge, as is appropriate in a work addressed to the Christian gnostic.

The imitation of God is a major theme of the *Stromateis*. To the original Platonic conditions for ὁμοίωσις θεῷ, as expressed in the *Theaetetus* and *Laws,* Clement, following in the wake of the Stoics, adds *apatheia* (the "state of having overcome the passions") and, like Philo, links the pagan notion of assimilation to God with the passage in Genesis regarding the creation of man in the image and likeness of God. Already in the *Paedagogus* Clement himself has added a new and specifically Christian element, Christ as the model (I. 2. 4, 2; I. 12. 98, 3). The principal way in which man can perfect the image of God in himself is by the practice of virtue (*Paed.* I. 12. 99, 1–2), including the Greek cardinal virtues. In the *Stromateis* (II. 18. 78, 1) Clement justifies the presence of these virtues on the ground that Moses' delineation of the virtues was the source of Greek ethics.[43] Hence the definitions current in the Greek schools are acceptable, and sophrosyne is described in Stoic terms as that habit of choice and avoidance which preserves the judgments of *phronêsis* (*Strom.* II. 18. 79, 5; cf. VII. 3. 18, 2). The virtues are inseparable; he who has one has all, and such a person will achieve salvation (II. 18. 80, 2–3). But in spite of the formal definition of sophrosyne as a habit of choice, Clement reverts to his usual conception of it as control over the appetites when he examines the implications of the theory of *homoiôsis*. Strictly speaking, the Divine, being without

---

[43] Cf. VI. 11. 95, 4–5. Clement lists the cardinal virtues and adds subsidiary qualities; to sophrosyne is subordinated *eulabeia,* defined as an avoidance in accord with reason (II. 18. 79, 5), an echo of the old Stoa.

lack or imperfection and totally passionless (*apathes*), cannot be termed *sôphron* or *enkrates;* but human nature, in its effort to become like God, must practice these virtues (II. 18. 81, 1).[44] Man must have sophrosyne in order to be "deified to the point of *apatheia*" (IV. 23. 152, 1). Whoever imitates God will strive to rid himself of his appetites. He who has felt the promptings of appetite and has yet controlled himself is like a widow who becomes virginal (*parthenos*) again through sophrosyne (VII. 12. 72, 1–2).

These passages, with their emphasis on the need for purification as a prelude to assimilation to God,[45] describe the stage in the spiritual life which is termed *praxis* in the theology of the Cappadocians.[46] It is followed by the stage of *theôria,* an aspect of *gnôsis;* and this stage also is linked with sophrosyne by Clement, who says that in the *theôrêtikos bios* one who is pure beholds God in a pure manner (*hagiôs*), for sophrosyne, being present and surveying itself without interruption, is as far as possible assimilated to God (IV. 23. 152, 3). This passage not only establishes sophrosyne as a requirement at the stage of *theôria* but relates it to the "mirror concept" whereby the pure soul looking into its own purity sees the archetype, the Divine purity. This concept, ultimately derived from the *First Alcibiades*—where self-knowledge is equated with sophrosyne and depends on the soul's seeing itself in its most Divine part, as in a mirror (132D–133C)—is crucial for the *homoiô-sis*-theory of Gregory of Nyssa. Usually in the writings of Gregory sophrosyne gives way to *katharotês* at this stage of the spiritual journey, but Clement maintains sophrosyne even here. His description has analogies to the Neoplatonic definitions of sophrosyne at the level that Plotinus calls paradeigmatic: the stage at which sophrosyne in the human soul takes the form of a turning (*strophê*) towards the Divine

[44] Clement generally treats sophrosyne and *enkrateia* as roughly synonymous, although on occasion he distinguishes them (e.g., *Strom.* II. 18. 80, 4). The two words are interchangeable in the discussion of marriage in *Strom.* III. 1. 4, 1 ff. What is said there of *enkrateia*—as pertaining not just to sexual indulgence, but also to other forms of excess, in speech, the pursuit of wealth, etc—is true of sophrosyne as well. Cf. III. 6. 59, 2 ff.

[45] The need for moderation in food and drink is discussed, both from the positive point of view (as an aid to *homoiôsis*) and from the negative as well, for Clement holds that the angels fell through *akrasia* (III. 7. 59, 2). Important discussions of restraint of appetite include *Strom.* II. 20. 109, 1 ff. on *meletê thanatou* ("preparation for death") and II. 22. 132–33, where Plato (*Laws* 716C–D) is quoted. Married life is a state in which *enkrateia* and sophrosyne should be practiced; see III. 10. 68, 1 ff. for Scriptural citations in support of marriage if accompanied by these virtues, and for a refutation of Tatian's stand against marriage. See also *Strom.* III. 12. 86, 1 ff.; unlike most of the Fathers, Clement regards the married state as superior to virginity (*Strom.* VII. 12. 70, 6–8).

[46] Ladner, 98–99.

mind, since in the Divine mind itself sophrosyne consists in a turning towards itself. In such a context self-knowledge becomes a significant part of the Christian *gnôsis.*

Clement concludes his detailed description of the sophrosyne of the gnostic—largely a matter of quietude, orderliness, and absence of desire —with a definition of *Gnôthi sauton* as "knowing for what we are born" (VII. 3. 20, 7). In this discussion of *gnôsis* he once again echoes the Platonic theme of being dear to God (*Laws* 716C–D) and, in the manner that was to be typical of the Greek Fathers, combines the Platonic allusion with a reference to the Beatitudes, saying that he who becomes pure in heart (Matt. 5. 8) through *gnôsis* is dear to God (VII. 3. 19, 2).

A special and very Platonic feature of Book VII of the *Stromateis* is Clement's examination of the motives for practicing virtue. In the case of sophrosyne, the Christian gnostic must be superior to passion and pleasure, not through love of honor, like an athlete, nor through greed for riches, nor through concern for his own health, nor through boorishness (*agroikia*), as if he had no taste for pleasure, nor because of legal restraints or fear, but solely for its own sake. Sophrosyne will be perfected and become permanent through *gnôsis,* and the gnostic will be *sôphrôn* and *apathês,* unaffected by pleasure and pain (VII. 11. 67, 6–8). It is largely the identification with *apatheia* that distinguishes the sophrosyne of the gnostic from the ordinary virtue described in the *Paedagogus.*[47]

Among Clement's borrowings from Plato, we may note his adoption of the theory that the practice of sophrosyne is a preparation for death: to be content with the natural desires is termed a *meletê thanatou,* as in the *Phaedo* (II. 20. 109, 1 ff.). Still more important as a Christian innovation is Clement's belief that sophrosyne may be a preparation for martyrdom. In discussing the perfection of women, for whom sophrosyne is still the chief excellence, Clement says that they, too, can be martyrs if they are *sôphrones.* One may love wisdom without being learned, whether one is a barbarian, a Greek, or a slave, old, young, or a woman, for sophrosyne is common to all (IV. 8. 58, 2–4).[48] The association of sophrosyne and martyrdom is, however, only at its begin-

---

[47] The relation between *apatheia* in Christian gnostics and the Stoic *apatheia* is discussed by Walther Völker, *Der wahre Gnostiker nach Clemens Alexandrinus* (Berlin and Leipzig, 1952), 188–94, 524–40. See also Merki, 49. In general the Greek Fathers are more favorably disposed towards *apatheia* than are the Latin Patristic writers.

[48] This section of the *Stromateis* deals with the perfection of women and shows, chiefly by examples from the Old Testament, that women are capable of *andreia* and other forms of masculine excellence, and of philosophy and rhetoric, too.

ning in Clement. Origen is the Father who develops it more explicitly, particularly in his belief that the ascetic life, the life of sophrosyne, is a substitute for martyrdom, now that the age of martyrdom is past.

Without pretending to exhaust Clement's contributions to the history of sophrosyne, we may call attention to one further development, in which again he follows Philo—namely, his selection of exemplars from the Bible. Although he cites Penelope as a type of feminine sophrosyne and terms Odysseus *sôphrôn* in another sense for silencing Thersites, Clement prefers models from Scripture and greatly extends the list to be gleaned from earlier Christian writers. Christ Himself is the greatest exemplar of sophrosyne in its connection with food and drink. Elias, with his frugal diet, is a type of *euteleia,* while St. John the Baptist, with his honey and locusts, prepares for the humble and *sôphrôn* life of Christ. Joseph illustrates the sophrosyne that, by accepting bondage, shows itself superior to unrestrained license. Judith, Esther, and Susanna exemplify the increasingly important combination of feminine sophrosyne with courage.[49]

Clement marks the first stage in the philosophical consideration of sophrosyne by Greek Christian thinkers; he introduces or states with new precision a number of the most dynamic theories that were to be linked with this concept in the next century: its special relevance to the imitation of God, its connection with martyrdom and with the ascetic life which becomes a substitute for martyrdom, and its responsibility for maintaining the moderation and simplicity in daily life which were the outward mark of the Christian. None of these is more influential, however, than his example in fitting the ethical precepts of the Greek philosophers into the context of Christian teaching. By his frequent allusions to the entire canon of cardinal virtues he demonstrates his freedom and familiarity in the use of pagan learning. After his time Christian writers no longer felt it necessary to sacrifice the Platonic virtues to the Pauline; many centuries were to pass, however, before the two canons were integrated into a single system.[50]

THE CAPPADOCIANS

In passing from Clement to the Cappadocians, we necessarily omit a number of writers who contribute to the growth of a Christian concept

[49] Penelope: *Paed.* III. 8. 41, 5. Odysseus: *Ibid.* II. 7. 59, 2. Christ: *Ibid.* II. 3. 38. Elias: *Ibid.* III. 7. 38, 1. John the Baptist: *Ibid.* II. 10. 112, 1. Joseph: *Ibid.* III. 11. 68, 3. Judith, Susanna, and Esther: *Strom.* IV. 19. 118, 4–119, 3.

[50] Catherine Haines ("The Four Greek Virtues from Socrates to Bonaventure" [Mt. Holyoke dissertation, unpublished, 1941]) discusses the union of the two groups of virtues

of sophrosyne, but none of these would so richly repay detailed study as Origen. Even so brief a survey as that offered in this chapter cannot ignore one major contribution of Origen: his attention to the ascetical side of sophrosyne. It might be said that Origen was to Clement of Alexandria as Tatian, in an earlier generation, was to Justin Martyr. Clement's conception of sophrosyne as moderation and simplicity in the essentials of life, which could be practiced in any environment and any vocation, is replaced in Origen by a fanatical zeal for asceticism. Clement had taught that virginity is not superior to the married state, which he exalted as an act of co-operation with the Creator (*Paed.* II. 10. 83, 2; cf. *Strom.* III. 10. 68, 1–4; III. 12. 84, 2 ff.; VII. 12. 70, 6–8), but Origen took so literally the text from Matthew (19. 12) that Justin had already interpreted as the teaching of Christ about sophrosyne, that he mutilated himself in order to become a eunuch for the sake of the Lord. Believing the passions to be the source of sin, Origen demanded their extirpation and taught that *apatheia* could be achieved through fasting and celibacy (*In Num. Hom.* 24. 2).[51] The connection of sophro-syne with virginity gives this virtue its importance for Origen, since to him virginity is comparable to martyrdom. He is the transitional figure between the writers of the first two Christian centuries, for whom physical martyrdom was an ever-present possibility, and those of the third and fourth centuries, who formulated the idea that asceticism is a spiritual martyrdom.[52] To be sure, persecutions continued into the third century—and Origen himself was tortured under Decius—but he teaches that the imitation of Christ may equally well be accomplished through the acceptance of the ascetic vocation. His *Exhortation to Martyrdom* mentions all four cardinal virtues as the goal of a struggle (*agôn*),[53] and this notion proved exceedingly influential as Christian asceticism developed. Origen's emphasis on the role of *agôn* (or *ponos*, "toil") in attaining *aretê*—so commonplace a notion in Greek

---

in a sevenfold system, completed by St. Bonaventure in *II Sententiae* 25. 1. Consult also Odon Lottin, O.S.B., *Mélanges Mandonnet* (Paris, 1930), 2. 232–59.

[51] Origen distinguishes Christian from "Pythagorean" fasting on the basis of the motives for each; *Contr. Celsum* 5. 49, Koetschau 2, p. 53. See 4. 46 for the superiority of Joseph to Bellerophon as a model of sophrosyne.

[52] See Edward Malone, O.S.B., *The Monk and the Martyr* (Washington, 1950), and Musurillo, 55–62.

[53] Origen maintains that even the pagans have taken part in the *agôn* to win these four virtues, but only the chosen people have sought piety (*eusebeia*)—*Ad Mart.* 5, Koetschau 1, p. 6; cf. 43, 1. p. 40, where Origen mentions four virtues, two of which are *gnôsis* and *dikaiosynê*, while the other two are Christian substitutes for sophrosyne and *andreia*—namely *hagnotês* ("purity") and *makrothymia* ("endurance").

popular philosophy, especially in the Cynic-Stoic diatribe—introduced into Christian theology a tendency to rely on human effort and responsibility which in turn carried the seeds of the Pelagian heresy.[54]

The contemporaries and successors of Origen shared his view of the struggle for virtue as a contest or *agôn*. His great rival Methodius, in fact, described perpetual virginity as an Olympic contest of chastity, while John Chrysostom often compared the *sôphrôn* person to a victorious athlete who derives eternal pleasure from his triumph.[55] Methodius wrote a Christian adaptation of Plato's *Symposium,* substituting eleven holy virgins for Plato's six convivial banqueters and replacing *erôs* with purity (*hagneia*) as the subject eulogized. Many allusions to sophrosyne in these speeches prove that Methodius interpreted it as chastity, often in a physical sense. Marcella, for example, the second speaker, traces the stages in the history of *parthenia* ("virginity") as it rose from the lowest rung in the ladder (where marriages between brother and sister occur). At the highest rung is the perfection of virtue, which is the true likeness to God. Sophrosyne is the penultimate stage—evidently continence in marriage (1. 2, p. 10–3, p. 11 Bonwetsch). It is not always so identified, however, for Thalia, who expounds St. Paul (I Tim. 2. 15), as a summons to purity (*hagiasmos*) and sophrosyne, insists that marriage is but a substitute for true sophrosyne, which she equates with *hagneia* itself (3. 10, p. 38–11, p. 39).[56]

---

[54] Jaeger (*Two Works,* 106 ff.) discusses the great influence exerted on Gregory of Nyssa by Origen's philosophical treatment of the ascetical life: both his emphasis on the *agôn* by which virtue is achieved, and his theory of perfection as a liberation and purification of the soul from the body and its passions. See also Brooks Otis, *Dumbarton Oaks Papers* 12 (1958), 102 ff., on the effects of the body-soul dualism in Origen's thought and his emphasis on the proverb *Gnôthi sauton.* Gregory Thaumaturgus' *Panegyric of Origen* (*P.G.* 10. 1052 ff.) contains a description of the cardinal virtues in the life of Origen himself and relates sophrosyne to "saving the *phronêsis* of a soul that knows itself" (1084C). Gregory says that while Origen did not render him just, prudent, *sôphrôn,* and brave (for no one may assume these virtues who is not inspired by God), he did teach him to love the virtues. Gregory also describes sophrosyne as stability (εὐστάθεια) of soul which gives peace to all who possess it (1085B), and names *eusebeia* the mother of the virtues (1085C).

[55] Methodius *Symp.* 7, 3, p. 74 Bonwetsch; cf. Philo *De Agr.* 27. 119 ff. Chrysostom, e.g., *In Ep. 1 ad Cor.* Hom. XXXVII, 3, 5 (*P.G.* 10. 320).

[56] Among many other references to sophrosyne in the *Symposium,* those in the eighth *logos,* that of Thecla, are the most notable, because they adapt the Platonic myth of the soul's ascent (*Phaedr.* 247D–E) and conflate with it Christian notions of Heaven. Methodius describes the soul as being borne aloft on the wings of sophrosyne (8. 1, p. 82) and *parthenia* (8. 2, p. 83), and transforms Plato's *hyperouranios topos,* glimpsed by the soul before birth, into the meadows to which virginal souls are conducted after death. There they behold, among other Platonic Ideas, Sophrosyne herself (8. 3, p. 83). Here Methodius adds an element from the Judaeo-Christian Eden—trees of virtue, one of which is the tree of sophrosyne (8. 3, p. 84); the others are the trees of *agapê* ("love") and *synesis* ("knowledge"). The *Symposium*

The identification of sophrosyne with *hagneia* is a doctrine that Gregory of Nazianzus shares with Methodius. The Cappadocians as a group bring to fruition the tendencies that we have traced in the development of a Christian concept of sophrosyne. Broadly speaking, there are two prominent characteristics in their approach to the virtue. First, they integrate it completely into their teaching about Christian morality: accepting it as a fundamental virtue—usually the control of the appetites; recommending its universal practice, through their sermons, eulogies, occasional poetry, and commentaries on Scripture; and finding a multitude of exemplars in the Bible. Thus they accomplish the final assimilation of pagan doctrine about the moral virtues to the Christian view of virtue expressed by St. Paul. Secondly, they define more precisely the function of sophrosyne in the ascetic life, which they regard as the Christian continuation of the theoretical life extolled in Greek philosophy. The first of these achievements may be studied in the writings of Gregory of Nazianzus; the second in those of Gregory of Nyssa.

The total assimilation of sophrosyne and the free use of many topics associated with it in pagan literature mark both the *Carmina Moralia* and the *Eulogies* of Gregory of Nazianzus, to which this discussion will be confined. Sophrosyne is frequently mentioned in Gregory's exhortations to ascetical fasting and celibacy;[57] but it is not identical with either form of self-denial, since it is for Gregory the generic virtue by which all kinds of appetites and pleasures are subdued.[58] It is most often linked

---

contains many references to alleged Scriptural exhortations to sophrosyne, such as Luke 12. 35–38; Cant. 4. 9–12; Apoc. 12. 1–6. Methodius' interpretation of Luke 12. 35–38 (*Sunt lumbi vestri praecincti*) makes the girding of the loins a symbol of sophrosyne. Gregory of Nyssa finds in the lighted lamps rather a representation of the virtue (*Hom.* XI, *In Cant., P.G.* 44. 996C–D; p. 317 Langerbeck). For an analysis of the *Symposium* and its doctrine of purity, see Herbert Musurillo, S.J., *St. Methodius, The Symposium: a Treatise on Chastity* (Westminster, Md., 1958), Introduction, 3–23.

[57] For Gregory's teaching on ascetical fasting, always marked by moderation, see Musurillo, 40, 51. The *Carmina Moralia* contain many discussions of *parthenia* ("virginity"), often associated with *hagneia* and sophrosyne. See *P.G.* 37. 521–73 (praise of virginity) and 578–632 (advice to virgins), where Susanna, the model of chastity in marriage, is termed *hagnê* (v. 194) and is credited with a longing (*pothos*) for sophrosyne. Gregory also gives many examples of sophrosyne in the animal kingdom, a favorite topic of Graeco-Roman moralists, which through the *Physiologus* had great influence on mediaeval and Renaissance iconography. He cites the turtledove as *sôphrôn*, an example for widows (vv. 536–39), and praises certain species of fish as models of conjugal sophrosyne (vv. 543–44). The salamander, which lives unharmed in flames, is still another type of sophrosyne (v. 571). Consult Mâle, 118, for the possibility that the symbol of *Castitas* on the reliefs representing this virtue at Amiens and Chartres and in the rose window of Notre Dame de Paris is a salamander.

[58] In a poem of versified definitions Gregory takes up the cardinal virtues and describes

with *hagneia* ("purity").[59] The close association of these two *aretae* is
guaranteed by the famous poem describing the dream that Gregory had
in boyhood, when he was torn between the demands of the spirit and
the flesh. To support the former, there appear to him two beautiful
women who announce themselves as *Hagneia* and Sophrosyne. They are
alike in every respect—beauty, stature, simplicity of adornment (the
kosmos akosmia to which Gregory often refers with approval), modest
clothing and veils (*P.G.* 37, *Car.* 45, vv. 229 ff.). Both assert that they
are close to Christ the King and rejoice in the beauty of heavenly
celibacy; the effect of the dream is to kindle in Gregory a love for
perpetual virginity.[60]

Another one of the *Carmina Moralia*, entitled "To Sophrosyne," also
proves to be an exhortation to virginity. In this poem Gregory admits
that sophrosyne may be achieved in the married state, but asserts that
virginity is preferable for two reasons; one is the familiar Pauline argument that the virgin is free to devote herself entirely to God, and the
other—the reason that becomes increasingly important for the Apologists
and their successors—is that God and the angels are celibate (*P.G.* 37.
643-48). The effects of sophrosyne on the appearance and conduct of
virgins are described in this poem. They range from merely external
marks—a *sôphrôn* walk, a modest demeanor, the *kosmos akosmia*—to more
inward effects, such as control of anger and of the physical appetites.
Although Gregory nowhere condemns marriage as evil, he warns those
who have accepted the vocation of celibacy to avoid backsliding, which
he compares to escaping the fires of Sodom only to run back into the
flames (vv. 58-59); and he regards the remarriage of a widow as a
transgression against *hagneia* (60-61).

Sophrosyne and *hagneia* are again virtually equated in the poem "On
Purity" (*Peri Hagneias*), which immediately follows that to Sophrosyne
(*P.G.* 37. 648-49). This poem presents in Neoplatonic language a theory

sophrosyne as control over pleasures—ἐπικράτησις ἡδονῶν (*Car.* 34, *P.G.* 37. 945-64, v. 57).
Although in the case of *andreia* he defines in Aristotelian terms the vicious extremes between
which the virtue stands as a *mesotês*, Gregory, like many of his contemporaries, finds only one
antithesis to sophrosyne—wantonness (now called *aselgeia*). He normally assigns a narrow
scope to *enkrateia*, control of the appetites for food and drink.

[59] *Hagneia* and sophrosyne appear in the *Scala Paradisi* of John Climacus on the same rung
of the ladder, *gradus* fifteen (*P.G.* 88. 869). For *hagnotês* and its cognates in pagan and
Christian thought, consult A.-J. Festugière, *La Sainteté* (Paris, 1942), Chap. 2.

[60] M. C. Waites (*H.S.C.P.* 23 [1912], 1-46) traces the philosophical allegory to which this
poem is related, with particular reference to the lineage of Heracles at the Crossroads. *Aretê*
in Prodicus' allegory is adorned with *katharotês*, *aidôs*, and sophrosyne (Xenophon *Mem.* 2. 1.
22), the original of Gregory's *kosmos akosmia*. Cf. D. L. 6. 37 for Crates' contribution.

about the relation of the various stages in the practice of virtue. Briefly, in only ten lines, and rather cryptically Gregory teaches that all *aretê,* in the case of the righteous (*dikaioi*), advances to the extent of one step (*bathmos*), so that one who is celibate is made equal to the angels—that is, to the highest stage of virtue for created beings; one who practices *enkrateia* ("continence") is to be ranked with the celibate; and one who enjoys lawful marriage is to be considered the equal of the continent.[61] "Only practice *to sôphron* [purity], so that you may achieve the next higher stage," Gregory concludes. Sophrosyne is here the generic virtue which manifests itself in all three stages of the life of *hagneia:* virginity, continence, and lawful marriage.[62]

Gregory's fondness for using pagan commonplaces in his poetry is especially evident in the *Comparison of Lives,* which applies topics familiar in the Cynic-Stoic diatribe—particularly the contrast between poverty and wealth—to the comparison of the spiritual life and the worldly life (*P.G.* 37, 649–67).[63] The *vita spiritualis* proves to be the monastic life, which the author, like Gregory of Nyssa, assimilates to the pagan tradition of the theoretical life. Here and elsewhere in the *Carmina Moralia* the Cynics and other pagan moralists are contrasted unfavorably with Christian exemplars of the virtues. A long poem "On *Aretê*" (entitled in some manuscripts "On Humility, Sophrosyne, and Continence") takes up systematically a Stoic canon consisting of *enkrateia, andreia, sophrosyne,* and *phronêsis* (*P.G.* 37. 680–752). Under the rubric of sophrosyne (vv. 773 ff.) Gregory recalls the edifying story of Xenophanes and the harlot, the tradition about the orderly and *sôphrôn* life of Epicurus, the conversion of Polemo, and the anecdotes, familiar to all students of popular philosophy since the Hellenistic age, about the wife of Dion and about Alexander's exemplary treatment of the daughters of Darius. All these Gregory praises, but as being untypical of pagan morality, whose true standards are to be found in the licentious behavior of Zeus, Aphrodite, and the other gods. The chastity of Christ and His followers is adduced in contrast, and the virgin-martyr Thecla

[61] The meaning of the first two lines (ἀρετὴ πᾶσα δικαίοις | ἕνα βαθμὸν προβιβάζει) would be clarified if δικαίοις were emended to δικαίους, making the verb προβιβάζει transitive, as it normally is. The meaning would then be: "*Aretê* advances the righteous by one stage."

[62] See Bickel, 207–8, for references to this doctrine.

[63] H. M. Werhahn (*Gregorii Nazianzeni Σύγκρισις βίων* [Wiesbaden, 1953]) finds the epitome of Gregory's aim in the words spoken by the personification of the spiritual life (v. 175): *sôphronizomai phobô* ("I am disciplined by the fear of God"). *Sôphronizomai* represents the contribution of pagan philosophy, as in the Cynic *sôphronizôn logos,* while *phobos* recalls St. Paul (Phil. 2. 12). Cynic influence on Gregory is discussed by Johannes Geffcken, *Kynika und Verwandtes* (Heidelberg, 1909), 18–38.

appears as a type of purity (*hagneia*, sophrosyne, v. 916). Virginity is praised as the means of restoring that image (*eikôn*) of God which was lost through sin. The climax of the section dealing with sophrosyne is the admonition *Hagnize sauton* ("Purify thyself"), which now replaces the Apolline *Gnôthi sauton* ("Know thyself") as the proverbial expression of sophrosyne (v. 928).

While it is unusual for Gregory to recognize any aspect of sophrosyne that is not connected in an obvious way with purity or the control of the passions, one reminiscence of the ancient contrast between sophrosyne and *hybris* does appear in still another poem "On *Aretê*" (*P.G.* 37. 667–79), which is concerned primarily with the vast difference between merely human excellence and the virtue of Christ and the angels. In this context a warning against presumption is to be expected; and Gregory couches it in terms that would have been natural for Pindar, saying that it is the function of sophrosyne to know one's limitations (v. 113 ff.). Entirely Christian, however, is the parallel warning coupled with this, a warning against excessive humility or lack of hope: λίην . . . τρομέειν, χθαμαλοφρονέειν. Gregory in effect establishes a new, non-Aristotelian set of extremes, presumption and despair, between which sophrosyne stands as a *mesotês*.[64]

The other context in which Gregory's views on sophrosyne may be conveniently studied is in eulogy, where the established topics of epideictic oratory were adapted to Christian uses. The fourth century is the great age of the Second Sophistic, and the two Gregories, Basil, and John Chrysostom were as thoroughly schooled in rhetoric as were their pagan contemporaries Libanius, Themistius, and the Emperor Julian. Hence the encomia composed by the Cappadocians, when contrasted with those of their pagan contemporaries, afford a means of judging the impact of Christianity both on this literary type in general and on the topic of sophrosyne in particular. In pagan epideictic of the period the place of sophrosyne is well defined.[65] It should be praised, first in connection with the parents of the person eulogized (his mother being a model of sophrosyne or *pudicitia*), next in connection with his or her own life. In the case of a woman, sophrosyne is likely to be the principal

---

[64] Cf. Anne-Marie Malingrey, *Jean Chrysostome, Lettres à Olympias* (Paris, 1947), 50–53, on Chrysostom's belief that moderation is needed in order to avoid *athymia* (*accidie, taedium vitae*); and consult Katzenellenbogen, 9, n. 1, for the combat between *Sobrietas* and *Accidia*.

[65] See Menander Rhetor *On Epideictic* 3. 372–73 Spengel, and Theon 2. 12. 4 ff. Spengel, for the eulogy of deeds performed in time of peace that reflect sophrosyne; and consult Theodore Burgess, *University of Chicago Studies in Classical Philology* 3 (1902), 123 ff., and Georg Reichel, *Quaestiones Progymnasmaticae* (Leipzig, 1909), 90–91.

virtue, as in Julian's *Eulogy* of Eusebeia, which reaches its climax with the comparison of the empress to a statue of Sophrosyne (3. 123A–B). In the case of a man, sophrosyne may show greater variety but will for the most part be concerned with the control of the appetites and the passions. It will receive special praise at two points: first, in the description of the subject's youthful career at the university (whether in Athens, Antioch, or Alexandria), when sophrosyne of this kind will seem especially admirable; and secondly, at the apex of the man's career—usually as a ruler of some kind—when his personal sophrosyne serves as an example to his subjects.

Christian epideictic orators differ from the pagan, not in their conception of sophrosyne as such (for both groups, in the fourth century, it is normally the control of the appetites), but in their belief that all virtue is dependent ultimately on Divine Grace and that sophrosyne is essential for the salvation of the soul. The position assigned to sophrosyne in the structure of the eulogy tends to be the same as in pagan encomium, although deliberate variations are not uncommon.[66] Gregory's *Eulogy* of St. Basil (*P.G.* 36. 494–605) illustrates his normal treatment of the topic. In conformity with the principles set forth by Menander Rhetor in the previous century, he praises Basil's parents, describes his education, and then examines in detail the notable events of his adult career, celebrating the virtues displayed in each. These *aretae* include the ones required for pagan eulogy (courage, wisdom, self-control), but others are added which are distinctively Christian, and even the pagan virtues prove to have Christian nuances. Basil's parents, for example, are praised for their continence (*enkrateia*) but also for their performance of the corporal works of mercy. The sophrosyne of Basil, as a student in Athens, is described, but in terms entirely Christian: he renounced carnal loves because only loves that are chaste (*sôphrones*) and pleasing to God are eternal (ch. 19).[67]

The praise of sophrosyne in Basil's mature life is broken up into several categories, all treated in a distinctively Christian way: his

---

[66] See, e.g., the eulogies of Gorgonia by Gregory of Nazianzus and of Basil and Gregory Thaumaturgus by Gregory of Nyssa, in which the pagan topics are ostensibly rejected as unworthy but are actually employed. Th. Payr, "Enkomion" *Reallexikon für Antike und Christentum*, discusses innovations in Christian encomium, including panegyric of the martyrs.

[67] Cf. Gregory's funeral oration for his brother Caesarius (*P.G.* 35. 756–88), who was noted for his sophrosyne while studying in Alexandria (see *Anth. Pal.* 8. 94, an epitaph for the *sôphrôn* Caesarius). On the techniques of epideictic used by Gregory of Nazianzus, see Xavier Huerth, *De Gregorii Nazianzeni Orationibus Funebribus* (Strasbourg, 1907), and M. Guignet, *S. Grégoire de Nazianze et la rhétorique* (Paris, 1911).

conquest of appetite (*enkrateia*), his virginity (*parthenia*), his *philanthrôpia*, and his avoidance of pride. The device of contrast, always prominent in eulogy, appears at frequent intervals; thus Basil is declared superior to the standard pagan exemplars and is equated with heroes of the Old Testament and the New (John the Baptist representing purification and abstinence). It is typical of Gregory that he chooses the Cynics as pagan models of self-restraint, only to deride them for their ostentation. Basil, he maintains, surpassed them, because he never chose to take up residence in an amphora, like Diogenes, and attract attention; he preferred to be, rather than to seem, *aristos* (ch. 60).[68] Humility is a vital part of Gregory's Christian sophrosyne.

The climax of pagan eulogy—that the subject deserves to be imitated for his moral excellence—naturally appears in the Christian counterpart as an admonition to honor the dead not only by imitating, but also by praying to, him.[69] Thus Gregory exhorts his hearers to pray to Basil, each according to his own station in life. Virgins should pray to him as to a *nymphagôgos,* and married women as to a *sôphronistês* (ch. 81)— a further proof that sophrosyne was in a special sense the virtue of the married state.

This conception of the virtue dominates Gregory's *Eulogy* of his sister Gorgonia (*P.G.* 35. 790–818), who, he maintains, excelled all women past and present in sophrosyne. Because she was married, he is obliged to devise a form of encomium that will not seem to disparage her for failing to attain the highest stage of *hagneia*—perpetual virginity. He does so by saying that she combined the sublimity of unmarried life with the stability of marriage, avoiding what is undesirable in each state and choosing what is best. She was *sôphrôn atyphos*—chaste without arrogance (797). Her life proved that neither the unmarried nor the married state is what binds us to God or separates us from Him. It is the mind that is important in either condition and offers material to God, as to a Demiurge, to mold into *aretê*. Gregory describes the sophrosyne of

---

[68] This quotation from Aeschylus *Sept.* 592 is a favorite with Julian also (see e.g., *Letter to a Priest* 303C). Gregory's echo of Thucydides 3. 82 (on the transvaluation of ethical terms) reflects the changed social background affecting the meaning of sophrosyne. Where Thucydides says that sophrosyne is considered a cloak for cowardice, Gregory says that Basil's slanderers who called his integrity arrogance would also call a *sôphrôn* man a misanthrope (64). In connection with the *Eulogy* of Basil it may be noted that an epigram ascribed to Gregory of Nazianzus and located in the Church of St. Basil in Caesarea refers to a statue of the four "life-giving" virtues—Ζωογόνων ἀρετῶν τετρακτύος (*Anth. Pal.* 1. 93)—presumably the Platonic tetrad.

[69] For this admonition in pre-Christian eulogy, see, e.g., Isocrates *Evagoras* 75–76 and Xenophon *Agesilaus* 10. 2; and cf. Aphthonius *Progym.* 8 Spengel 2. 36. 18 f.

Gorgonia in exhaustive detail: her exemplary conduct as a housewife, fulfilling Solomon's ideal in Proverbs 31. 10 ff.; her abstinence from adornment and artifice—the blush of *aidôs* and the pallor of *enkrateia* were ornament enough for her; her preservation of the Mean between austerity and wantonness. Only after doing justice to every category of feminine sophrosyne does Gregory proceed to other virtues, such as prudence, piety, charity, and *megalophrosynê*—manifested in mortification and penance. A specifically Christian note is clearly sounded throughout the *Eulogy*. Even though in many of its facets the sophrosyne of Gorgonia resembles that of pagan women, it is transformed in its essence by being related to Gregory's ideal of *hagneia* and by its ultimate function of leading the soul to God.

The *Eulogy* of Basil by Gregory of Nyssa reveals a like familiarity with the traditional topics of epideictic and an equal determination to show the superiority of Christian to pagan virtue. In this oration (as in the same writer's *Eulogy* of Gregory Thaumaturgus) the conventional topics are considered and rejected as unworthy, but actually they are still used as an organizing principle. Thus the encomium of Basil simply gives a spiritual interpretation to each of the pagan topics: the *genos* of Basil was his nearness to God, his *patris* was his virtue, sophrosyne was his household (*ephestion*), *sophia* his property, while justice, truth, and purity were the adornments of his house (*P.G.* 46. 816).[70] Of more significance, however, is the approach to sophrosyne in the ascetical works and commentaries on Scripture by Gregory of Nyssa, not because the basic meaning of the virtue is different from what it is in the eulogies, but because in these two types of writing he connects sophrosyne with the key doctrine of ὁμοίωσις θεῷ and brings to completion the effort of Patristic writers to assimilate pagan teaching about the virtues, chiefly by finding evidence in Scripture that these virtues were equally important in Jewish and early Christian thought.

In sum, Gregory values sophrosyne because of its relation to *katharotês*, which is the imitation by mankind of the Divine purity, attained

---

[70] See Sister James Aloysius Stein, *The Encomium of St. Gregory on St. Basil* (Washington, 1928), xxxiii, for a discussion of the topics of epideictic in pagan and Christian oratory. In Gregory of Nyssa's *Eulogy* of Gregory Thaumaturgus, sophrosyne is again the virtue most essential in youth (*P.G.* 46. 901D). The encomium *De Vita Sancti Patris Ephraem Syri* (*P.G.* 46. 820–49) abandons the conventional scheme of epideictic altogether and directs attention to the Christian virtues of piety, humility, and love. Several specifically Christian virtues—love, grace, humility—are linked with sophrosyne in a eulogy of Bishop Meletius (*P.G.* 46. 857B–C), when Gregory describes the virtues reflected in his face, which was formed in the image of God. The Church herself is called *sôphrôn* in this panegyric (857B).

by purgation (*katharsis*) of what is evil. *Katharotês* is as important to Gregory of Nyssa as *hagneia* to Gregory of Nazianzus. The aim of the ascetical life, which is the subject of the two important treatises *On Virginity* and the *Life of Moses,* is to restore the image of God in the human soul which has been obscured by sin. Because sin originates in uncontrolled passion and the domination of the soul by pleasure, the process of purification depends on the attainment of *apatheia,* the human imitation of the Divine attribute of freedom from passion.[71] Sophrosyne, defined in *On Virginity* as the orderly regulation (*oikonomia*) of all the movements of the soul, accompanied by *sophia* and *phronêsis* (320. 1–3),[72] enables man to achieve *apatheia.* That Gregory links it closely with *katharotês* is evident from many passages coupling the two words. He speaks, for example, of the *katharos* and *sôphrôn* way of life, which cannot be achieved by one who is overcome by the *pathos* of pleasure (*De Vir.* 283. 21 Cavarnos); and he comments, in connection with the Fourth Beatitude, that he who hungers and thirsts after sophrosyne will be filled with *katharotês* (*In Beat., P.G.* 44. 1245B).[73] As was the case with Clement of Alexandria, *apatheia* and *katharotês* are semi-technical terms in Gregory's vocabulary. Sophrosyne never becomes absolutely rigid in its connotations, probably because of its rich background in classical literary usage. All three concepts derive their meaning from the doctrine of assimilation to God, which Gregory adopted as the aim of the ascetical life. A brief recapitulation of this doctrine, which has already been mentioned in connection with several pagan and Christian thinkers, will make it easier to understand how sophrosyne is connected with Gregory's version of the idea.[74]

---

[71] On the meaning of human *katharotês* and *apatheia* for Gregory, see J. T. Muckle, C.S.B., *Mediaeval Studies* 7 (1945), 55–84, especially 58–59, n. 10. *Katharotês* is freedom from all affection for things not of God. *Apatheia* is freedom from any ill-regulated movement of the passions, which in man cannot be completely eradicated, since they are part of human nature. The relation of these two concepts to *gnôsis* is discussed by Jaeger, *Two Works,* 74 ff. The close kinship of sophrosyne and *apatheia* is symbolized by such illustrations of the *Scala Paradisi* as that in Ms. Vat. gr. 394, where the two virtues help the soul as it climbs the fourteenth and fifteenth steps (Katzenellenbogen, 23, n. 2).

[72] Gregory uses both *akolasia* and *akrasia* as antitheses to sophrosyne (*De Beat.* 1241D, *De Inst. Christ.* p. 57 Jaeger).

[73] See also *De Virg.* 340. 7 and Hom. XI, *In Cant. Cant.* 317. 11–12 Langerbeck. In *Contr. Fornicarios P.G.* 46. 496D, the equivalence of sophrosyne and *katharotês* is emphasized by a chiastic arrangement which places them side by side.

[74] In addition to Merki, consult Werner Jaeger, *Scripta Minora* (Rome, 1960), 2. 469–81; Muckle, *loc. cit.;* Robert T. Casey, *H.T.R.* 18 (1925), 39–101; Jean Daniélou, S.J., *Platonisme et théologie mystique* (Paris, 1944); and Th. Ruether, *Die sittliche Forderung der Apatheia in den beiden ersten christlichen Jahrhunderten und bei Klemens von Alexandrien* (Freiburg, 1949).

The concept of ὁμοίωσις θεῷ shows remarkable adaptability from its earliest formal expression by Plato, through the versions current in the Middle and Later Stoa, to Philo, Plotinus, and the Patristic writers, especially Clement, Origen, and Gregory of Nyssa. In the *Theaetetus* of Plato ὁμοίωσις θεῷ, the goal of philosophy, is the flight of the soul from evil, accomplished by becoming as just and holy and wise as possible (176A). Ethical, religious, and intellectual elements are all implied by the inclusion in the *Theaetetus* passage of the words δίκαιον καὶ ὅσιον μετὰ φρονήσεως, and each of these implications was developed by later philosophers with varying degrees of emphasis. Aristotle, without using the Platonic formula, adopted the theme of man's making himself immortal and found in the use of the intellect the means by which he may become like unto God.[75] The Stoics, too, related *homoiôsis* to various forms of knowledge (of God, of the cosmos, of oneself), assuming the identity of Divine and human reason; but they also introduced the notion that virtuous action, doing good to others, is a way of imitating God.[76] Plotinus intensified the religious implications of the doctrine. To him ὁμοίωσις θεῷ meant actually becoming God (θεὸς γενέσθαι) through absorption in the One by a process of purification in ascending stages, at each of which the four cardinal virtues operate, but with different effects at each stage (*Enn.* I. 2. 1 ff., I. 2. 3. 19). Moreover, Plotinus interpreted the union of the soul with God as a return to its original home (*Enn.* I. 2. 6. 2 f.).[77]

Philo began the conflation of the Platonic ὁμοίωσις θεῷ with the Biblical doctrine of man as the image of God (Gen. 1. 26; *De Op. Mundi* 15 ff.). Generally he interpreted this imitation in an ethical sense: likeness to God depends on the practice of the moral virtues. Clement followed Philo, but added an extremely important new element—the imitation of a model, Christ; and unlike Philo, he bade man strive for

---

No attempt will be made here to discuss the implications of the *homoiôsis* doctrine in the development of sophrosyne as an *aretê politikê*, but it may be noted that Patristic writers employed this concept in eulogies and exhortations addressed to emperors, and that it forms a part of the evolution of the topic of sophrosyne in epideictic going back to Isocrates.

[75] See Jaeger, *loc. cit.*, 472, on the Aristotelian passages (including *Part. An.* 2. 10. 656a 8 and *Metaph.* A2, 982b 30 ff.) that concern this topic.

[76] Knowledge: Cicero *De Nat.* 2. 153; *T.D.* 5. 70, 4. 57; Seneca *De Ira* 2. 16. Benefaction: Seneca *De Mor. Lib.* 47; *De Benef.* 3. 14. 4, 1. 1. 9 (see Merki, 8–14). Jaeger (*loc. cit.*, 473) discusses the role played in the Stoic version of *homoiôsis* by the parallelism between the macrocosm and the microcosm. Merki (15, n. 2) suggests that the addition of *eudaimonia* to the theme was the work of Poseidonius.

[77] Merki, 17–25. Plotinus makes *erôs* and beauty, as well as purification, sources of unity with God.

apatheia, which Philo considered unattainable. Clement admitted other virtues—notably piety and good works—to a role in the process of assimilation to God, but gave supreme importance to such qualities as *enkrateia* and sophrosyne, because of their special kinship with *apatheia.* In his doctrine of Christian *gnôsis* Clement fully recognized the intellectual aspect of ὁμοίωσις θεῷ, which consists in the reflection of the Divine *logos* (*Strom.* II. 19, 102. 6).

Although Plato in the *Theaetetus* and elsewhere was more likely to associate justice than any other moral virtue with the imitation of God, a passage in the *Laws,* where the role of God as the measure of all things is under discussion, makes sophrosyne the virtue by which man becomes like unto God and therefore dear to Him (716C–D). Since sophrosyne is traditionally linked with measure, this variation is natural, and the presence of sophrosyne by no means excludes justice. Later philosophers sometimes recalled the importance of measure in ὁμοίωσις θεῷ (Cicero, for example, in *De Senectute* 77), but on the whole they most often ally a different aspect of sophrosyne with ὁμοίωσις: the control, or even the extinction, of the passions. This interpretation, too, appears in Cicero, when he says, with an obvious reminiscence of the *Phaedo,* that the return to God may be accomplished by keeping oneself *integer* and *castus* and pure of *contagio cum corporibus* (*T.D.* 1. 72; cf. *Phaed.* 69C), and it assumes great significance in Philo, who associates *homoiôsis* with *autarkeia* (*In Virt.* 8), and in Plotinus, with his demand for *katharsis* and *apatheia.* Both elements—purification and *gnôsis* or *cognitio*—are important in the theory of ὁμοίωσις θεῷ at each of its historical stages, but sophrosyne was increasingly limited to purification, although its traditional connection with self-knowledge (one aspect of *gnôsis*) equipped it to share in the task of *gnôsis* as well. In the system worked out by the Neoplatonists, both pagan and Christian, when the ideal of asceticism is united with the ideal of contemplation, sophrosyne usually accomplishes the task of purification which makes *gnôsis* possible, and it is always in connection with *katharsis* that Gregory's ascetical writings discuss sophrosyne.

The earliest of these works, *On Virginity,* contains all the essentials of Gregory's doctrine of sophrosyne, which appears in the *Life of Moses* as well, but is embellished in the later work with more numerous allegorical interpretations and Scriptural allusions. *On Virginity* interprets *parthenia* as a metaphysical rather than a physical concept; it is a manifestation of *katharotês,* a quality of the soul rather than of the body, a species of detachment that enables man to partake of the purity of God. God Himself is completely pure and without *pathos*. To imitate God man must perfect himself through the practice of virtue, particularly those virtues that enable him to bring under control the passions inherent in human nature.[78] Although Gregory sometimes adopts the Aristotelian view of *aretê* as a *mesotês*,[79] and in both *On Virginity* and the *Life of Moses* considers sophrosyne to be a mean between excessive yielding to pleasure and utter contempt for marriage (*De Vir.* 283. 17 ff.; *Vita M., PG.* 44. 420A ff.), he more often refers to the virtues as imitations of the Divine attributes, implanted in man's rational nature by God. These virtues constitute the image of God in man—an image that has been disfigured and obscured by original sin and its consequences.[80] Only when *katharsis* (choosing the real good in preference to the supposed good, pleasure) has freed the soul from the "rust" of evil, can man truly reflect the virtues of God (*De Vir.* 292–93). By contemplating them in the mirror of his own soul, he contemplates God (*De An. et Res., P.G.* 46. 89C; cf. *De Beat., Or.* VI, *P.G.* 44, 1272B). Pleasure was the cause of the Fall; hence the process of retracing the steps by which man fell away from God involves at the outset the conquest of pleasure. Specifically, marriage would never have been instituted but for the Fall. Therefore the first step in the return is to renounce marriage (*De Vir.* 303). Unlike Origen, however, Gregory (himself perhaps a married man) does not condemn marriage as evil. Indeed, he defends it vigorously, denouncing as false and extreme the view that marriage is wrong, and citing Isaac and Rebecca as exemplars of *sôphrôn* and *metrios* marriage (282–84). He holds, however, that marriage is only for the strong, since few can withstand the passions it arouses and still achieve perfection. Legitimate pleasures soon lead to excess; virginity is the safer course (287. 17 ff.).[81]

In the treatise *On Virginity* Gregory mentions sophrosyne in connection with various other pleasures, including those of food and drink. The pleasures of taste he considers particularly dangerous, because they can

---

[78] Jaeger (*Two Works*, 25–33) discusses Gregory's use of the concept of virginity (equivalent to *katharotês* and *apatheia*) to bridge the gap between Christian theology and Greek philosophy. See Ladner (322–30) for a general discussion of Patristic attitudes toward virginity.

[79] E.g., *De Virg.* 283. 17, Hom. IX, *In Cant. Cant.* 284. 5 ff. Langerbeck. Gregory's terminology is mostly Platonic or Neoplatonic, often with Stoic additions. A Stoic element (grafted onto the Peripatetic doctrine of virtue as a *mesotês*) is the theory of *tonos* ("tension") in *De Virg.* 283. 17 ff.: a deficiency in *tonos* is a cause of failure to achieve a pure and *sôphrôn* life. Gregory's normal use of sophrosyne recalls the Platonic "control of the appetites" rather than the old Stoic "knowledge of what to choose"; see n. 82 below for some exceptions.

[80] See Muckle, 69 ff. Cf. *De Beat.* 1272C: καθαρότης and ἀπάθεια constitute θεότης.

[81] On the doctrine that marriage is a compensation for the expulsion from Eden, see Gerhard B. Ladner, *Dumbarton Oaks Papers* 12 (1958), 84 ff.

so easily lead to excessive enjoyment. It is necessary to adhere to a
sôphrôn standard, choosing only what is pure and healthful (329. 9 ff.).
The task of sophrosyne is compared to the action of the fisherman in
Matt. 13. 47–48, who separates the good from the bad (321. 15–20).[82]
Gregory condemns excess in any direction, observing that by extreme
austerity one may weaken himself unduly (329–30). To achieve virginity, which can be of the body or the soul, it is helpful to have a model,
and Gregory sketches the character of such a model (revealed elsewhere
to be Basil himself). In so doing he praises those who have grown gray
in what he calls "the purity of sophrosyne"—ἐν τῷ καθάρῳ τῆς σωφροσύνης
(340. 7). From their youth they loved wisdom alone, and although they
were not less subject to temptation than other men, they listened to Him
who said that sophrosyne is the Tree of Life to those who lay hold of it
(Proverbs 3. 18). Significantly, Gregory substitutes sophrosyne for wisdom
in quoting this verse. He adds that on this "tree of sophrosyne" they
sailed across the billows of youth and anchored in the harbor of the Will
of God. The treatise concludes with the statement that the reward for
living a pure life (the life of spiritual *parthenia, katharotês,* sophrosyne) is
to see God (343).

The model of virtue is even more important in the *Life of Moses*. This
treatise has two parts: the one deals with the actual events of Moses' life;
the other, and longer, interprets them allegorically. Moses is the type of
the ascetical life, the life according to virtue. One of the major achievements of Gregory, as Jaeger has pointed out,[83] is to integrate the concept of the ascetical life, which in the first three centuries of our era had
been increasingly identified with the truly Christian life, into the Greek
philosophical tradition which exalts the contemplative life as the best
and most virtuous. The fundamental symbol that Gregory finds in the
life of Moses is the ascent from earthly passions to heavenly contemplation. At the peak of the climb is *Hêsychia* (Quietness), the teacher
of Divine contemplation. That sophrosyne which effected the choice between necessary and unnecessary pleasures in *On Virginity* is paralleled

---

[82] In *De Virg.* Gregory alludes to several functions of sophrosyne, in addition to the fundamental one of purifying the soul. The *sôphrôn kanón* (329. 9–10) and the *sôphrosynês ergatês*
("craftsman of sophrosyne" [330. 10–14]), who separates the chaff from the wheat (the
unnecessary from the necessary desires), recall the power of choice exercised by the Stoic
sophrosyne. For the colloquial use of *sôphrôn* as "sensible" (precisely equivalent to *euphrôn*), see
326. 13, 16. Chap. 22 (332. 15 ff.) contains one of several adaptations of the myth of
the *Phaedrus:* the charioteer who controls the horses is a symbol of sophrosyne. Cf. *De
Beat.* 1216C.

[83] *Two Works,* 20–24.

here by the *gnôsis* of truth, which is a means of purifying our concepts of being and not-being. Such *gnôsis* leads to the true good, which is freedom and *apatheia*, whereas the striving for apparent good leads only to the tyranny of the passions (cf. *De Vir.* 292–93). Gregory finds hidden references to sophrosyne in several texts in the story of Moses. The ingenuity of his allegories reflects a determination to justify in Scriptural terms his lifelong enthusiasm for Greek ethical philosophy. He suggests, for example, that the purple color in the leather of the tabernacle is meant to represent *sôphrôn aidôs* (385D), and that the girdle that keeps the garment of life from being uncontrolled is sophrosyne (357B).[84]

Such allegories abound in Gregory's exegetical works, among which the commentaries on the Lord's Prayer and the Beatitudes best illustrate his doctrine about sophrosyne: the need of Divine Grace to achieve it, the link between sophrosyne and *katharotês* and *apatheia*, and the essential identity of Biblical morality and Greek *aretê*. The treatise *De Oratione Dominica* connects sophrosyne with the phrase "Thy will be done." Comparing bodily and spiritual health in a manner reminiscent of the Platonic *Charmides*, Gregory equates health with doing the will of God and illness with the victory of appetite over self-control. When God's will is done, sophrosyne quenches the wanton and passionate impulse of the mind, humility destroys conceit, and moderation (*metriotês*) heals the disease of pride. To cure these ills is hard, and we need the help of God. Gregory specifically interprets "Thy will" as referring to sophrosyne. Plunged into the flesh by sin, we pray that this good may be accomplished through the power of God (*P.G.* 44. 1164D–1165A). So, too, justice, piety, and *apatheia* are included in the one word *thelêma* ("will"). The great emphasis on the need for Divine help in attaining virtue balances the emphasis on human effort (*ponos, agôn*) in the earlier treatise, *On Virginity*, and, as Jaeger suggests, enables Gregory to arrive at a kind of *mesotês* in his view of the spiritual life.[85]

Other Patristic commentaries relate sophrosyne in different ways to the Lord's Prayer,[86] and a like diversity is shown in the interpretation

[84] The other ascetical works of Gregory are of little special import for sophrosyne, although all evince a belief in the need for purification from the passions as the first step in the ascent of the soul.

[85] *Two Works*, 89.

[86] Particularly significant, in the light of mediaeval interest in the rhetoric of prayer, are the attempts—especially in Latin Patristic writing—to apply the precepts of sophrosyne/*temperantia* to the voice and gesture of one praying (a special instance of the doctrine of oratorical delivery). See n. 94 below. For an example of mediaeval iconography that links *Et ne nos inducas* with the virtue of *temperantia*, consult Arthur Watson, *Speculum* 3 (1928), 459–61, and Plate I.

of the Beatitudes. For Ambrose, the First Beatitude according to Luke ("Blessed are the poor") is an exhortation to practice sophrosyne, while John Chrysostom interprets the Sixth in Matthew ("Blessed are the clean of heart") in this light.[87] Gregory finds sophrosyne in the Second Beatitude according to Matthew ("Blessed are the meek") and also in the Fourth ("Blessed are they who hunger and thirst after justice"), which in fact he regards as an admonition to practice all four cardinal virtues.

The Neoplatonic notion of progress in virtue as consisting of a series of steps (*bathmoi*) inspires Gregory's interpretation of the Beatitudes as rungs in the ladder of perfection—an idea that was to have considerable influence in Patristic thought. The First Beatitude instils humility, because our downfall was the result of pride.[88] The Second Beatitude leads Gregory to discuss the meaning of *praotês* ("meekness"), which he explains as that which makes us slow to turn towards evil. Man's will can turn towards sophrosyne or wantonness (*P.G.* 44. 1213D). Christ's praise of *praotês* is taken as an allusion to *apatheia*, which cannot be achieved by one living in the flesh. Moderation (*metriotês*) and humility (*tapeinophrosynê*) are also involved in the practice of *praotês* (1216A–B, 1217A–B), but Gregory's chief emphasis is on the control of the passions.

In commenting on the Fourth Beatitude, Gregory asks whether it would be the reverse of blessed to hunger for *sôphrosynê, sophia, phronêsis,* or any other kind of excellence (1241B). The answer is negative, for what is said of one virtue is said of all. No virtue divorced from the rest can be perfect (1241C–D), and all virtues are included under the name of righteousness. Gregory also discusses the psychology of hunger and desire, pointing out that nothing is truly satisfying except *aretê*. We can always practice *sôphrosynê* and *katharotês*, he says, and the practice will bring happiness (1244D). Blessed is he who hungers for sophrosyne, for he shall be filled with *katharotês,* and this satiety will lead not to aversion, but only to greater desire (1245B).

---

[87] Ambrose *Ex. in Luc.* V. 54 ff., 64, *CSEL* 32. 4, pp. 202–7. Chrysostom *In Matt.* XV, *P.G.* 57. 227D ff. According to Chrysostom, the pure are those who have attained complete *aretê* or who are living in sophrosyne, because no other virtue is so needful for seeing God. Augustine explains the Seventh Beatitude in Matthew ("Blessed are the peacemakers") as an injunction to secure peace of soul by subjecting the passions to reason, but he equates this Beatitude with the seventh gift of the Holy Ghost rather than with sophrosyne (*De Serm. Dom.* II. 9, *P.L.* 34. 1229–1308). See Piero Rollero, La *"Expositio evangelii secundum Lucam" di Ambrogio come fonte della esegesi agostiniana* (Turin, 1958), 22–23, for a discussion of Gregory's originality and the probable influence of his ascetical conception of the Beatitudes on Ambrose and through him on Augustine.

[88] Pride is *hyperphania*, not *hybris*. According to his context, Gregory regards sometimes pleasure, sometimes pride as the cause of man's fall. In the case of Lucifer, the cause is always pride.

Unlike Chrysostom, Gregory does not mention sophrosyne in connection with the Sixth Beatitude, but here again discusses *apatheia*. The demand for detachment and for the conquest of the passions dominates the entire treatise. The Eighth Beatitude ("Blessed are they who suffer persecution for justice's sake") is linked in a characteristic way with this demand, for pain and torture are said to be instruments of purification and antidotes to pleasure. As sin enters the soul through pleasure, so it is exterminated through its opposite, and the torments of the martyrs heal the disease caused by pleasure (1297D). Thus Gregory finds philosophical support for the alliance between sophrosyne and martyrdom already suggested by Clement of Alexandria.[89]

THE LATIN CHRISTIAN WRITERS

The history of sophrosyne in Latin Christian thought up to the time of Augustine closely follows its course in the Greek Patristic writers. The same tendencies reveal themselves: the early suspicion of pagan ethical doctrine, the absence of references to the Platonic tetrad as a group until the late third century, the exaggerated regard for sophrosyne (usually *temperantia* or *sobrietas*) as a virtue peculiarly Christian, the frequent

---

[89] The third of the Cappadocian Fathers, Basil of Caesarea, is not without significance for the development of a Christian sophrosyne, although his contribution is less distinctive than are those of the two Gregorys. Basil assisted in the positive development of the ascetical ideal through his *Rules,* which assume the priority of chastity. The mark of the ascetic in the first two Christian centuries had been the practice of celibacy; with the rise of monasticism in the fourth century, the vow of chastity still took precedence as the greatest external renunciation (see Dom David Amand, *L'Ascèse monastique de Saint Basile,* Maredsous, 1949). In the *Rules,* Basil discusses *enkrateia* more often than sophrosyne (*enkrateia* is the mother of sophrosyne, *P.G.* 31. 965) and extends its scope to include all forms of self-denial. The *Rules* throughout are marked by moderation (the best standard of *enkrateia* is the avoidance of excess in either direction, *P.G.* 31. 875); but the vocabulary for describing moderation does not include sophrosyne, which for Basil means the control of passions and appetites (see the *First Ascetical Discourse, P.G.* 31. 872, where *parthenia* and sophrosyne are virtually synonymous and are said to be more than merely physical). One function of sophrosyne is to curb—not extirpate—anger (Hom. X, *In Iratos, P.G.* 31. 369). Hom. XI adds to the canon of virtues *hypomenê* ("endurance") in suffering for the faith (see n. 53 above on Origen's substitution of *hypomenê* for *andreia*). The addition is accounted for by the rich tradition of the Christian martyr, but Basil already accepts asceticism as a substitute for martyrdom (cf. *Ep.* 6, Deferrari 1. 41). Basil's attitude towards classical literature (as shown in *On Reading Greek Literature*) is interpreted as an expression of his sophrosyne by Frederick H. Brigham, Jr. (*Classical Folia* 14 (1960), 35–38), who cites Libanius' praise of Basil's sophrosyne as a young man, in a city of pleasure. John Cassian, who promoted the principles of Eastern monasticism in Gaul, includes in his *Conlationes* and *De Institutionibus Coenobiorum* many reminders of the function of virtues related to sophrosyne in practicing asceticism. In his Latin vocabulary, *castitas* renders *hagneia; continentia, enkrateia* (*Inst.* V. 6); purification is the task of *temperantia* (*Conl.* I. 4); and *discretio* ("moderation") is the *genetrix, custos,* and *moderatrix* of all the virtues (*Conl.* II. 1–4).

limitation of its function to the control of appetite, and the consequent association of sophrosyne with the ascetical life. The systematic integration of the cardinal virtues into a coherent Christian philosophy began, for the Latin Fathers, with Ambrose and reached quick fruition in Augustine. With these two writers *temperantia* achieved a distinctively Christian interpretation, whose origins, however, are clearly traceable to Platonic, Neoplatonic, and Stoic thought, together with the modifications already introduced by Philo and certain Greek Patristic writers.

A brief survey of the tendencies apparent in some of the Latin Apologists will make more comprehensible the achievement of Ambrose and Augustine. It should be noted at the outset that *temperantia* and the other Latin equivalents of sophrosyne never became part of any special Christian language. Even when *pudicitia, castitas,* or *temperantia* was claimed as peculiarly Christian, the basic meaning of each word was the same as in the usage of Seneca, Apuleius, or the Latin panegyrists of the fourth century. The Greek Christian writers, whose language the Latin Apologists translated, were on the whole conservative and so far as possible adopted the ethical vocabulary of their pagan contemporaries. When they began to make use of Platonic and Stoic sources, they had all the more reason for maintaining traditional connotations for such words as sophrosyne and *enkrateia*. With the Latin Christian writers, therefore, as with the Greek, specifically Christian nuances of sophrosyne were more a matter of emphasizing one particular facet of the virtue than of giving the term an esoteric significance that pagan contemporaries would not readily have grasped. Like their predecessors in republican Rome, the Latin Fathers were obliged to choose among many possible ways of translating sophrosyne, and although *temperantia* (which had the authority of Cicero behind it) was the general favorite, *sobrietas* (or *sobria mens*) enjoyed some prestige because of its appearance in Old Latin translations of Wisdom and the New Testament, while *pudicitia* kept its traditional place as the normal translation of sophrosyne when it referred to the virtue of women and young persons of both sexes.[90]

---

[90] *Sobrius* and *sanae mentis* are the usual Latin renderings of σωφρονοῦντα in Mark 5. 15 and Luke 8. 35. See *Old Latin Texts,* No. III (Munich Ms. Lat. 6224), Oxford, 1888; No. V (Codex Corbeiensis), Oxford, 1907; No. VI (Codex Veronensis), Oxford, 1911; and consult Adolf Jülicher, *Itala: das neue Testament in altlateinischer Überlieferung* (Berlin, 1954), on Luke 8. 35. See also *Novum Testamentum Sancti Irenaei Episcopi Lugdunensis* (Oxford, 1923) for various translations of εἰς τὸ σωφρονεῖν in Rom. 12. 3: *ad prudentiam, ad sobrietatem, ad sobrietatem vel sanam sapientiam.* For the translation of sophrosyne and *sôphrôn* in the Latin version of Clement of Rome, Epistle to the Corinthians, see D. Germanus Morin, *Anecdota Maredsolana* 2 (1894): 1. 2: *prudentem;* 62. 2: *sobrietate;* 63. 3: *sobrios;* 64. 1: *sobrietatem.* Bickel, 205–

There was no Christian Latin word for sophrosyne which had not already been used by pagan writers.

Latin Christian writing began with such translations from the Greek as the version of Clement's Epistle to the Corinthians made in the first half of the second century (where *sobrius* or *prudens* renders *sôphrôn* in the Greek); but not until the very end of that century did original works by Latin Christians begin to appear, the earliest perhaps being the apologetic dialogue *Octavius* by Minucius Felix. Composed by an African lawyer who was thoroughly familiar with Cicero and Seneca and adopted their ethical vocabulary, the *Octavius* shows several of the tendencies mentioned above, notably the claim to the virtue of purity as a mark of the Christians. The writer maintains that the Christians recognize one another by their *innocentia ac modestia* (31). Like the Greek Apologists, he castigates the indecency of pagan rites and myths and contrasts them with the *pudor* of the Christians, their monogamy, their *sobrietas,* as shown at their banquets where "we temper gladness with seriousness, with pure conversation" (*gravitate hilaritatem temperamus, casto sermone*), and above all their *castitas,* which often inspires the choice of perpetual virginity (31). Although Minucius nowhere refers to the four cardinal virtues as a group, he discusses in close succession chastity (31), justice (32), fortitude (36), and wisdom (38) and gives to each a distinctively Christian flavor.

Tertullian exhibits in a much more extreme way the exaggerated regard for chastity in the hierarchy of the virtues, as a consequence of his conviction that the sin by which the angels fell was *intemperantia* (*De Orat.* 22. 5, *CSEL* 1. 270). We have already noted in Tatian and Origen among the Greek Christians an extreme hostility to the flesh which caused them to adopt a view of sophrosyne incompatible with moderation. Tertullian's radical dualism resulted ultimately in the Montanist heresy, which regarded marriage as evil, and even in his earlier works some extremist tendencies are manifest. The *Apologeticus* merely claims for Christians (as does the *Octavius*) "the most earnest and faithful *castitas*" (9. 19) and praises the *modestia* and *pudicitia* of their banquets (39. 19); but the semi-Montanist and Montanist treatises, with such revealing titles as *De Cultu Feminarum, De Exhortatione Castitatis, De Monogamia, De Virginibus Velandis,* and *De Pudicitia,* are all marked by a

---

10, briefly discusses Christian Latin translations of sophrosyne. It is important to remember that *pudor* and *verecundia,* which often render sophrosyne, may also translate *aidôs* and *aidêmos-ynê,* and that *continentia* is usually *enkrateia.* See L. R. Palmer, *The Latin Language* (London, 1954), 180–205, on Christian Latin as a special language.

fanatical insistence that fleshly appetites are evil and a corresponding distortion of the virtues of *modestia, pudicitia,* and *continentia. Pudicitia* is called the mark of the true Christian, the doorkeeper and priestess of the temple (*De Cultu* II. 1. 1); woman is the *diaboli ianua* (I. 1. 2); and excessive emphasis is put on the external signs of modesty: the avoidance of cosmetics, hair dyes, and jewelry (I. 2. 1; II. 5. 2), or the wearing of a veil. Like Athenagoras of Athens, Tertullian insists that widows must not remarry, and even suggests that marriage itself is a species of adultery (*De Exhor.* 9).

Tertullian stands halfway between pagan and Christian usage in his choice of *exempla virtutum*.[91] He does not scruple to employ pagan models of chastity, citing Lucretia and Dido, the latter according to that version of her story in which she committed suicide rather than marry a second time.[92] His *exempla vitiorum* include the greatest pagan types of self-control, Socrates and Cato. Tertullian, like Gregory of Nazianzus, challenges the pagan philosophers to a contest of *pudicitia* (*Apol.* 46. 10), since they, in the common view, teach the same doctrines and profess the same virtues as the Christians: *innocentia, iustitia, patientia, sobrietas, pudicitia.* He berates Socrates for corrupting the young (46. 10) and both Socrates and Cato for allegedly exchanging wives with other men (39. 12).[93] In his vocabulary *pudicitia* evidently refers to self-control, while *modestia* is the antithesis of pride, being the virtue ascribed to Christians who do not even aspire to the aedileship, in contrast to the ambition of Pythagoras and Zeno, who sought to become tyrants (*Apol.* 46. 13).

Nothing in Tertullian's treatment of the theme of virtue and vice is of more lasting significance than his use of the method of personification in *De Spectaculis,* his vigorous denunciation of the circus, the amphitheater, and the theater. Condemning attendance at the theater because of the *impudicitia* encountered there (17) and at the amphitheater because of the omnipresent *saevitia* (19), Tertullian contrasts with these wicked pleasures the innocent delights of the Christians, and to the battles and wrestling matches of the arena he opposes Christian combats. Behold, he says, *Impudicitia* defeated by *Castitas, Perfidia* slain by *Fides, Saevitia* battered by *Misericordia, Petulantia* overshadowed by *Modestia*

---

[91] On pagan *exempla* in Christian writings, see Mary Louise Carlson, *C.P.* 43 (1948), 93–104.

[92] *Apol.* 50. 5, *De Exhor. Cast.* 13, *Monag.* 17.

[93] Tertullian confuses the elder with the younger Cato and condemns Socrates because of the community of wives advocated in Plato's *Republic.* For this charge and another of bigamy, see Bickel, 130–31.

(29. 5). Brief though this passage is, its consequences for literature and art are incalculable. The pairs of combatants are not identical with those in the *Psychomachia* of Prudentius, but the germ of that famous battle is here. The comparison of the Christian life to an athletic contest, which was popularized by Paul and led to innumerable references to the *agôn* of the ascetical life in Greek Patristic literature, gives way ultimately in Latin Christian writing to the metaphor of the soldier's mortal combat. Already in Tertullian's *De Spectaculis* the struggle to achieve virtue is a life-and-death battle; by the time of Prudentius the allegory of virtue against vice has become entirely military.

Cyprian, Lactantius, and Jerome all contributed to the development of a Latin Christian concept of sophrosyne; our study will limit itself to what seems most original or influential in each of these writers. For Cyprian's view of sophrosyne the greatest importance probably attaches to his writings about the virgin martyr. He honors virgins next to martyrs (*De Habitu Virginum 21, CSEL* 3. 1) and compares them to angels (22). A close correlation between the virtues of virginity and martyrdom is suggested in *Epistle* 10 which says that every Christian should aim to achieve the white crown of the one or the purple crown of the other (5); it becomes explicit in *Epistle* 38, where Cyprian professes to be uncertain which to praise more highly in the case of Aurelius—the glory of his wounds or the modesty of his demeanor, his *virtus* or his *pudor* (1). Similar is the case of Celerinus (*Ep.* 39. 4), whose *robur* and *pudor* are equally deserving of praise. The classical Attic formula for the epitaph, *aretê kai sôphrosynê*, here undergoes a Christian metamorphosis, employing, however, a Latin phrase already familiar in Tacitus.[94]

The first precise formulation of a generic notion of virtue in Latin Christian thought was the work of Lactantius. He rejects the pagan theory of virtue as knowledge of Good and Evil and regards it rather as a matter of the will (*Inst.* 6. 5, *CSEL* 19. 650–51). Virtue is, however, dependent on true knowledge of God (6. 17), and the motive for its

---

[94] For the word play, see Tacitus *Agr.* 45. 2. E. L. Hummel (*The Concept of Martyrdom according to St. Cyprian of Carthage* [Washington, 1946]) discusses the martyr's death as the perfection of all virtue (132 ff.). Cf. Malone (*op. cit.*, 26–40) on the concept of spiritual martyrdom in Tertullian and Cyprian. Like Tertullian, Cyprian holds in exaggerated regard the external signs of virginity or chastity—modesty in dress, the absence of jewelry and cosmetics (*De Hab. Virg.* 9, 15, 21); and he further resembles Tertullian in emphasizing the practical and external in his comments on the Lord's Prayer. With Tertullian *De Orat.* 17 (modesty and humility in gesture and voice), cf. Cyprian *De Dom. Orat.* 4 (the need for *continentia* and *pudor* in prayer; the *impudens* shouts, the *verecundus* prays modestly). Cyprian himself is praised for his moderation in the *Vita* by Pontius, which mentions his lack of *superbia* and calls him *temperatus et ipse de medio* (6, *CSEL* 3, 3, p. xcvl).

practice is the hope of immortality (6. 10). Lactantius' concept of virtue
often appears to be more negative than positive, as when he observes
that the whole duty of virtue is *non peccare* ("to avoid sin" [6. 5]).
He defines virtue as the checking of anger, appetite, and lust; there can
be no *virtus* without *vitium* (5. 7). God, in fact, implanted the *commotiones
animi* in man and, in so doing, planted the material of the vices in the
passions and that of the virtues in the vices. The crown of virtue is
abstinentia voluptatum (6. 23), since like most Christian writers, Lactantius
equates indulgence in pleasure with the death of the soul and regards
asceticism as the path to immortality (7. 12). Although he precedes
Ambrose in transmitting Ciceronian ethical doctrines to Christian
thought, the Ciceronian element is less important in his treatment of
temperantia than it is for Ambrose.[95] Furthermore, despite his lavish use
of Cicero, Lactantius never refers to all four cardinal virtues together.
When the tetrad does at last emerge in Latin Christian writing, it is a
sign that in the West as in the East the age of defensiveness against pagan
attack and pagan tradition is over. The period of assimilation has begun.

Jerome refers with considerable frequency to the entire group of
cardinal virtues,[96] which he, in fact, is one of the first to call by this
name.[97] Yet despite his free allusion to the canon, he does not integrate
it into a coherent system, and his references are little more than casual
citations, seldom of fundamental importance to his thought. It has been
observed that he refers to the whole group most often in his later work,
from 406 to 416, when he was writing his commentaries on St. Paul; it
is possible that at this time he renewed his acquaintance with Cicero's
philosophical works.[98]

A characteristic allusion to the tetrad—as an embellishment in eulogy
—occurs in an Epistle dealing with the family of Pammachius (66.
3, *P.L.* 22. 640). Recognizing the existence of the Stoic doctrine that the

---

[95] Cicero's equation of sophrosyne with *frugalitas* is recalled in Lactantius' discussion of the
moral choice represented by the allegory of the youth at the crossroads. If he does not meet
a *doctor frugalitatis,* he will take the wrong road (*Inst.* 6. 3). Lactantius outstrips Cicero in his
criticism of Stoic theories about the passions (e.g., *Inst.* 6. 14–15) and goes so far as to
say, with reference to anger: *caret virtute quisquis ira caret.* Cf. Cicero *Ad. Q.F.* 1. 1. 22.

[96] Hagendahl (377–78) lists Jerome's references to the tetrad and comments on the
various ways in which he employs it.

[97] A commentary on Mark, variously assigned to Jerome and Fortunatianus of Aquileia
(Schanz-Hosius, *Gesch. der Röm. Lit.* 4. 1. 399), and the *Ex. in Luc.* of Ambrose (*CSEL* 32. 4)
both speak of "cardinal" virtues. *Ex. in Luc.* is dated *ca.* 390; the commentary on Mark possibly as early as 361. Jerome alludes to the tetrad in commentaries on Ephesians and
Nahum (*ca.* 387–389 and 389–392, respectively). After 406 he cites the virtues frequently in
commentaries on Amos, Isaiah, Ezechiel, and Jeremiah.

[98] Hagendahl, 377.

virtues are inseparable, Jerome holds that one virtue may yet be more notable than the others in a given individual. Thus *prudentia* is the preeminent virtue of Pammachius himself, *iustitia* of his wife, *fortitudo* is supreme in his daughter, the virgin Eustochium, while in the case of his married daughter, *temperantia* is the principal virtue. What, Jerome asks, is more *temperans* than the conduct of this woman, Paulina, who, reading the statement of St. Paul that a spotless marriage is honorable (Heb. 13. 4), did not venture to seek the happiness of her sister, nor the *continentia* of her mother, but preferred to walk safely in humbler ways rather than flounder with uncertain step on the heights? Hence she sought the second grade of *castimonia*. This familiar doctrine appears often in Jerome's letters and treatises on virginity, the married state, and widowhood and is usually illustrated by models for each degree of virtue. Thus in a letter to Eustochium the exemplars of virginity are the Blessed Virgin and Thecla, and the models of chastity in marriage and the widowed state are Sarah and Anna (*Ep.* 22, *P.L.* 22. 423–24). What is unusual in Epistle 66 is Jerome's reference to conjugal chastity as *temperantia*, rather than *pudicitia*, a variation that illustrates the influence of context and source on the choice of a Latin rendering. When Jerome enumerates sophrosyne with the other three virtues, his translation is normally the Ciceronian *temperantia*, occasionally a combination of *temperantia* and *castitas*. Thus in *Epistle* 66, where the effectiveness of his reference to the virtues depends on the presence of all four, he translates sophrosyne as *temperantia*, even though in this case it is specifically identified with conjugal virtue. But apart from the tetrad he feels free to follow another, almost equally strong tradition—going back in all probability to Seneca—which makes *pudicitia* the preferred rendering of sophrosyne in the doctrine of the three grades of chastity.[99]

Jerome regards the four virtues as spiritual ornaments of the soul, willed by God and pleasing to Him.[100] They are opposed to four vices

---

[99] *Temperantia* in lists of the four virtues: *In Ier.* 29. 1 ff., *P.L.* 24. 890, and the passages cited by Hagendahl, 378, and nn. 1–3, 5–6. *Temperantia* and *castitas*: *In Eph.* 1. 22–23, *P.L.* 26. 494. Bickel (205, n. 1) cites two passages in *Adv. Iov.* where Jerome pronounces *pudicitia* equivalent to sophrosyne: I. 35, p. 292D (translating I Tim. 3. 2, a bishop must be *pudicum, hoc enim significat sophrona*) and I. 37. p. 297E (*ad pudicitiam non ad sobrietatem ut male in Latinis codicibus legitur* for εἰς τὸ σωφρονεῖν, Rom. 12. 3), and another (I. 27, p. 281C) in which he rejects *sobrietas* in favor of *castitas* as a rendering of I Tim. 2. 15 (ἁγιασμῷ μετὰ σωφροσύνης, in ...sanctificatione cum castitate). Cf. *Ep.* 107, 6, 1: in...sanctificatione cum pudicitia. See Bickel (185 ff.) on Jerome's debt to Porphyry and Seneca for his ascetical vocabulary in *Adv. Iov.* Other references to the three grades of chastity occur in *Ep.* 22. 15, 41, *Ep.* 49. 11, *Ep.* 66. 2.

[100] *Ep.* 52. 13, *P.L.* 22. 1538 (cited by Hagendahl, 378).

—*stultitia, iniquitas, luxuria,* and *formido*—again a Ciceronian tetrad.[101] As a single virtue, sophrosyne or *temperantia* continues to receive special attention in its relation to the ascetical life, which Jerome defends against the attacks of Helvidius, Jovinian, and Vigilantius. Although he regards marriage as inferior to virginity, he does not exaggerate the merits of physical virginity or of fasting but holds them to be merely stages on the road to sanctification (Ep. 130. 11, *P.L.* 22. 1116). The allegorical interpretation of Scripture attracts Jerome less than it does Ambrose, yet passages may be found in which he resorts to this device in order to find the four virtues in the Old Testament. Thus he identifies the tetrad with the four living creatures in Ezekiel 1. 5 and the four smiths in Zachariah 1. 18–20, giving a powerful impetus to the use of number symbolism in the interpretation of the cardinal virtues, which became one of the favorite devices of moral treatises in the Middle Ages.

ST. AMBROSE

St. Ambrose holds unquestioned primacy in the West, like Clement in the East, for the systematic consideration of the four cardinal virtues,[102] combining theory (derived principally from Cicero) with the Judaeo-Christian tradition of allegorical interpretation. His contributions to the history of sophrosyne in Christian Latinity, extensive though they are, will here be considered under only three categories: his adaptation of Cicero's *De Officiis* to Christian usage, his discussion of sophrosyne in moral and ascetical works and eulogies, and his interpretation of Biblical passages concerned with sophrosyne. The third category again has three subdivisions: the borrowing of Philo's allegory of the four rivers of Paradise, the interpretation of specific texts as exhortations to sophrosyne, and the choice of *exempla virtutis* from the Bible.

If the vitality of the Greek concept of *aretê* is demonstrated by the sequence of treatises on moral virtues by Panaetius, Cicero, and Ambrose, the adaptation of a Stoic essay on conduct to the needs of the Catholic priesthood illustrates the receptivity of the Latin Church towards the close of the fourth century. In general Ambrose's principle of selection is simple: he accepts from Cicero's *De Officiis* only what is immediately applicable to the training of priests, and his alterations and additions are guided by the same purpose. The *officia* of adolescence, which Cicero

---

[101] *In Nahum* 3. 1 ff., p. 565; cf. Is. 55. 12–13, p. 653.

[102] For his use of the term *cardinalis,* see (in addition to *Ex. in Luc.*) *De Exc. Frat. Sat.* I. 57, *CSEL* 73. 239. For the more common term *principalis,* see *De Off. Min.* 1. 24. 115 and *De Cain* 2. 1, *CSEL* 32. 1. 396. *Cardinalis* applied to the gifts of the Holy Ghost: *De Sac.* 3. 2. 9, *CSEL* 73. 42.

discusses only briefly (together with the duties of maturity and old age), are greatly expanded in the Christian version, intended as it is for the spiritual formation of young men. *Verecundia,* which Cicero made a sub-head of *temperantia,* is removed by Ambrose from this context entirely and is developed in its own right and at length, even before he embarks on the topic of the four cardinal virtues, so that its importance is greatly enhanced.[103] The discussion of the *virtutes principales,* less systematic even than Cicero's, derives a Christian color from the insertion of Bibli-cal *exempla* and the interpolation of specifically Christian ideas, such as the supernatural origin and goal of virtue. The statement *"Fundamentum Christus est"* (1. 50. 247) sums up the basic difference between Ambrose's theory of virtue and that of his Stoic model; however close Ambrose comes to Cicero, it should not be forgotten that his frame of reference is utterly different. He often seems to invite attention to his divergence from Cicero, as when he defends his violation of the form of the earlier *De Officiis* by saying that Cicero's method of defining and discussing the *genera virtutum* was mere *ars* ("artifice") and *calliditas* ("cleverness"). Ambrose himself postpones his discussion of the sources of the *officia* until he has given Biblical *exempla,* asserting that these models are a *speculum disciplinae,* not a *commentarium calliditatis* (1. 25). In effect, although his imitation of Cicero bears witness to his respect for the greatest of pagan Roman ethical teachers, Ambrose feels obliged to contrast his own concern for the essential nature of virtue with what he represents as Cicero's preoccupation with mere stylistic excellence.

When Ambrose does arrive at a definition of the *principales virtutes,* he uses an entirely Ciceronian vocabulary but achieves greater simplicity and directness by omitting some of Cicero's complicated subdivisions of the *honestum.* Where Cicero says that the fourth division of the *honestum* contains *ordo, modus, modestia,* and *temperantia* (1. 5. 15), Ambrose merely lists the fourth virtue as *temperantia,* "which preserves *modus* and *ordo* in all that we think should be done or said" (1. 24. 115). A notable addition to Cicero's list of subheads of the fourth virtue is the *studium mansuetudinis* (1. 43. 209).[104] Still another list of Biblical *exempla* inter-venes before Ambrose takes up the virtues separately; now, instead of finding a different exemplar for each virtue as Cicero does, he prefers to show that each model figure displayed all four, like Abraham in the sacrifice of Isaac, or Noah in the Flood. The treatment of *temperantia* is

---

103 Examples of *verecundia* in its various aspects include Isaac, Joseph, Moses, and Jeremiah.
104 In *Inv.,* Cicero recognizes *clementia* as one of the *partes temperantiae.* He discusses *mansue-tudo* in *Off.* 2. 9. 32 but not in connection with *temperantia.*

remarkable for its selectivity, its amplification of points that Cicero includes but does not emphasize, its addition of specifically Christian material (such as a long discussion of *castimonia*), and its use of illustrations from Scripture, instead of from Roman history or legend.[105]

The subject of *ingenium* leads to a brief discussion of the various functions of the clergy, rather than to Cicero's long list of secular talents and professions. It is in this context that Ambrose introduces the topic of *decorum*, a striking proof of his dependence on Cicero, since nowhere else in his ethical treatises does *decorum* play an important part. Although *temperantia*, like the other three virtues, is Christianized in various ways, it remains closer to Cicero than do the others. A striking omission in the section on *decorum* is the absence of any reference to *approbatio*, the approval of one's fellows, which is essential to Cicero's treatment of the subject. Even though Ambrose adopts the Ciceronian vocabulary and compares *decorum* with physical beauty, saying that the *decorum speciale* (that is, *temperantia*) *excellit et elucet*, he omits the next phrase, *movet approbationem* (1. 46. 221; cf. Cicero *Off.* 1. 38. 100). Thus the external manifestations of *temperantia*, highly valued by Cicero, are deliberately diminished by Ambrose, to whom only the approbation of God is significant.[106] He further diverges from Cicero in omitting the discussion of amusements, individual differences, the selection of a career, propriety in outward appearance and speech, and vulgar and liberal occupations; he emphasizes instead the vocation of the Levite, with particular attention to the duty of preserving *castimonia* (1. 50. 247), and concludes with a sweeping application of all four cardinal virtues to the *officia* of the priest.

The concept of *temperantia* in Ambrose's *De Officiis Ministrorum* differs from his treatment of the virtue in his other writings, not only in being dominated by the notion of *decorum*, but also in having somewhat wider scope than is usual elsewhere. Normally in the works of Ambrose, *temperantia* is closely related to asceticism, as we see with special clarity in the series of homilies and sermons on virginity and in *De Helia, De Nabuthe*, and *De Noe*, all of which deal with ascetical fasting and show the influence of Philo rather than of Cicero. In this connection Ambrose does not limit himself to the Latin word *temperantia* as a rendering for

---

[105] Hagendahl (364–71) lists parallel passages in Cicero and Ambrose; see also A. F. Coyle, O.F.M. (*Franciscan Studies* 15 [1955], 224–56) for a detailed comparison of the two treatises. P. Dominikus Löpfe, O.S.B. (*Die Tugendlehre des heiligen Ambrosius* [Freiburg in d. Schweiz, 1951], 133–37) analyzes the concept of *temperantia* according to Ambrose.

[106] See F. Homes Dudden (*St. Ambrose: His Life and Times* [Oxford, 1935], 2. 529) for the transformation of the "*decorum*-motive" in *De Off. Min.*

sophrosyne, but is likely to use *castitas* (*De Virginitate* I. 18 Cazzaniga) or *sobrietas* (varied by *sobria mens*) as well, sometimes explaining that sobriety means abstention, not merely from wine, but from bodily lust and worldly pride, by which we are intoxicated even more dangerously than by wine (*Exhort. Vir.* I. 12. 81).[107] Ambrose preaches asceticism for the same reasons as do Philo and the Greek Fathers: the conviction that *intemperantia* was responsible for the fall of the angels and of man, and that *temperantia* promotes likeness to God, since it is an imitation of the virtue of Christ and His Blessed Mother. Like Gregory of Nyssa, who sometimes adopts the theory that pleasure caused the fall of Adam and Eve (*De Virg.* 303 ff.), and that the serpent in the Garden was the sin of lust (*De Or. Dom., P.G.* 44. 1172), Ambrose regards *voluptas* as the serpent. Adam, he maintains, was deceived by the appetite for pleasure: *voluptas . . . nos paradiso exuit* (*Ep.* 63. 14).[108] Eating and drinking are therefore the *causa peccandi*, and fasting is the teacher of continence, the school of chastity. The close alliance between fasting and chastity is a commonplace illustrated by innumerable examples,[109] among which the story of Judith is a special favorite because this heroine combines the two primary aspects of *temperantia: sobrietas* and *castitas* (*De Vid.* 7. 40). While the *luxuriosus* Holophernes was overcome by drunken slumber, she cut off his head and, as Ambrose puts it, *servavit pudicitiam, victoriam reciperavit* (*De Hel.* 9. 29).[110] Judith is also a model of wisdom and courage, but *temperantia* alone is designated as the *virtus feminarum* (*De Vid.* 7. 40; cf. *Ep.* 63. 29).

The conviction that women can best achieve holiness through asceticism prompted Ambrose to write the homilies and treatises that made him known as the Doctor of Virginity.[111] By his combination of

---

107 Cf. *De Exc. Frat. Sat.* I. 51, *CSEL* 73. 236: *Temperantia morum mentisque sobrietas.*

108 One of the strongest arguments for *temperantia* occurs in *De Iacob* I. 2. 8, *CSEL* 32. 2. 8–9, where Ambrose holds that God enjoined it on our first parents when He bade them refrain from the fruit of the Tree; their disobedience deprived them of immortality (cf. *De Hel.* 4. 7, *CSEL* 32. 2. 416; *Ep.* 63. 26 ff.). For the view that the pleasure of taste is the mother of the vices, see Gregory of Nyssa *De Virg.* 329 Cavarnos.

109 E.g., Christ in the desert, John the Baptist, Peter, Moses, Esther, Anna, Daniel, and Elias.

110 Judith is a favorite symbol of *temperantia* in later iconography. See Emil Mâle, *L'Art religieux de la fin du moyen âge en France*[4] (Paris, 1931), 309; and cf. Frances Godwin, *Speculum* 26 (1951), 609–12. The moral significance of Donatello's Judith is explicated by Edgar Wind, *Journal of the Warburg Institute* 1 (1937–1938), 62–63. In the doctrine of the three grades of chastity, Judith as a widow represents *continentia* (*enkrateia*) rather than *pudicitia* (sophrosyne); see Jerome, *Ep.* 22. 21.

111 Pope Pius XII's encyclical, *Sacra Virginitas*, quotes Ambrose more often than any other source except the Bible.

eloquence and moral authority—not by any originality on his part—he popularized the ideas about asceticism held by earlier Christian writers, such as the doctrine of the three degrees of chastity (Ep. 63. 40; *De. Vid.* 4. 23). To denote this generic virtue Ambrose usually employs the word *castitas*—normally equivalent to the Greek *hagneia*, as used by Gregory of Nazianzus and other Greek Fathers. In *De Virginitate*, however, *castitas* unquestionably serves to translate sophrosyne (I. 17–18 Cazzaniga).[112] The conflation of Plato and Ezechiel in this treatise demonstrates the method Ambrose used in reconciling pagan and Biblical sources, and in fact gives his *apologia* for doing so. With an obvious allusion to the *Phaedrus*, he describes the flight of the soul to Heaven after the *perturbatio equorum* has been quieted.[113] In the region *supra mundum* the soul contemplates eternal virtues—*iustitia, castitas, bonitas, sapientia* (I. 17. 108; cf. *Phaedrus* 247D, where the Forms of *dikaiosynê, sôphrosynê*, and *epistêmê* are seen by the charioteer). Details of the Platonic myth are ingeniously fitted into the Christian context, as when Ambrose says that the soul nourished on heavenly virtues leaves behind envy (*invidia*), which is outside the chorus of angels, and appetites (*cupiditates*), which ought not to defile the temple of God (I. 17. 111; cf. *Phaedrus* 247B on the absence of *phthonos* from the heavenly chorus). Apologizing for his use of material from the pagan philosophers and poets, Ambrose maintains that they rather borrowed from "us," and proceeds to quote Ezechiel and the Psalms on chariots, animals, and the wings of the soul (I. 18. 112–18). The four living creatures of Ezechiel 1. 3–5 (the man, the lion, the calf, and the eagle) are explained as symbols both of the powers of the soul (rational, passionate, appetitive, and *dioratikon* or perceptive)[114] and of the four virtues that belong to these powers (I. 18. 114–15). The definition of *temperantia*, which, as usual in later Platonism, is confined to the appetitive part of the soul, differs markedly from the definitions given in *De Officiis Ministrorum*.[115] In *De Virginitate* it is the virtue that, by the bond of sacred charity and the contemplation of heavenly mysteries, despises bodily pleasures (I. 18. 115). The connection of both charity and contemplation with moral virtue, including *temperantia*, becomes still more significant in the ethical doctrines of St. Augustine.

[112] In *De Isaac* 8. 79, *CSEL* 32. 1. 698, *continentia* and *temperantia* together render sophrosyne in Plotinus *Enn.* I. 6. 9. 2; see Pierre Courcelle, *R.E.L.* 34 (1956), 220–39.

[113] On the use of the *Phaedrus* myth by Gregory of Nyssa and other Fathers, see Musurillo, 40, n. 27.

[114] See Courcelle, *loc. cit.*, 226, nn. 3 and 4, on possible sources of the term *dioratikon* in *De Virginitate* 18. 110 ff.

[115] Yet see *De Off. Min.* 2. 9, where *temperantia* is exercised *in despiciendis voluptatibus*.

De Isaac makes a similar attempt to fuse Platonic and Scriptural elements in a description of the soul as a chariot having either good or bad horses. The good horses are the four virtues, the bad are the four passions—*iracundia, concupiscentia, timor,* and *iniquitas* (8. 65, *CSEL* 32. 1. 688).[116] Again we find the ingenious collocation of allusions to the Bible and reminiscences of Plato. The yoke of the good horses, for example, is the *iugum suave* of Matthew 11. 29 ff. The charioteer must keep the horses together, and if *temperantia* is too gentle, *fortitudo* too stubborn, he must know how to reconcile their discord, so that they will not tear the chariot apart (8. 65). In this passage Ambrose makes still another attempt to harmonize the opposing principles, the gentle and the spirited, this time with a mixture of Christian and Platonic terms.[117]

Although Ambrose regards virginity as the highest form of *castitas,* he does not despise marriage, which is a symbol of the union of Christ and His Church.[118] For *temperantia in coniugis* St. Paul is the principal guide (*De Cain* II. 6. 21; *CSEL* 32. 1, p. 396), and the exemplars include Susanna for women, and for men both Isaac (*De Ex. Fr. Sat.* II. 99; *CSEL* 73. 304) and Abraham (*De Off.* 1. 24. 110). In *De Viduis* Ambrose discusses the relevance of all four virtues to the widowed state and, with Judith as his model, subsumes *sobrietas* and *castitas* under the heading of *temperantia* (7. 39–40).

Temperantia is important as a masculine virtue, too, and Ambrose discusses it in a variety of contexts, not only in *De Officiis,* where he is chiefly concerned with priestly *castimonia,* but also in the treatise *De Joseph* (influenced by Philo), in a number of encomia and consolations, and in the important letter to the church at Vercelli (Ep. 63). This letter was inspired by an attack on the virtues of *abstinentia, frugalitas,* and *virginitas* made by two renegade monks who, having renounced their vows, sought to undermine the faith of other Christians. Here Ambrose expresses the belief that *voluptas* was the serpent in Paradise and that fasting is the means of conquering evil (14). The entire letter is dominated by the concept of *temperantia* and the symbolism of the Neoplatonic ladder of virtue. Ambrose begins with the lowest rung, so to speak, in the scale of *temperantia* and praises *sobrietas* and *abstinentia,* which quiet *luxuria,* the mother of lust (18, 26). He first refers to *temperantia* itself with a meaning akin to sobriety: *temperantia* is suited to nature and to Divine law, which in the very beginning of things gave us the fountains

---

[116] Consult Courcelle, *loc. cit.,* 230–31, and P. Hadot, *R.E.L.* 34 (1956), 202–20, on parallels between Ambrose and Plato.

[117] Cf. Gregory of Nyssa *De Virg.* 332 Cavarnos.

[118] See William J. Dooley, *Marriage according to St. Ambrose* (Washington, D.C., 1948).

to drink and the fruit to eat (27), and after many examples of sanctity attained by fasting, he passes to a higher stage of *temperantia*, that which is *parca concupiscentiae* (32). This aspect of the virtue, too, is fortified by Biblical precedent and leads to the highest stage of all, the *gratia virginitatis* (33). The letter demonstrates in terms applicable to men and women alike the essential importance of *temperantia* and its various manifestations. The ultimate reason for the practice of virginity is that it is the *fons et origo pudicitiae, in quo fonte imago Dei luceat* (36). Like his Greek Patristic models, Ambrose here accepts the doctrine of ὁμοίωσις θεῷ as the goal of human effort and sees in the virtues of renunciation the avenue to this goal.[119] As he points out in *De Fuga Saeculi*—a sermon to the newly baptized which reflects the influence of Philo's *De Profugis*—God is without sin, and man, in order to imitate God as far as possible, must flee from adultery, lust, avarice, and faithlessness, rising to Heaven by the virtues, as by steps (4. 17–22). Perhaps to indicate that there is no distinction between the sexes in the injunction to imitate God, Ambrose cites as models both Paul and Susanna (9. 53–54), as well as Joseph and Sarah (8. 47). Sarah is said to bring forth the *sobria ebrietas* of joyfulness in giving birth to Isaac. Ambrose often employs the Philonian motive of *methê nêphalios* or *sobria ebrietas* ("wineless [or] sober drunkenness"), akin to the *mania sôphrôn* ("sane madness") which goes back at least to the *Phaedrus* and supplies mystical writers, pagan, Jewish, and Christian, with a metaphor to describe the ecstasy that comes of contemplation, rather than Dionysiac frenzy.[120]

Ambrose's funeral orations and consolations show with special clarity his conception of *temperantia* as a masculine virtue; they are important because they deal, not with the clergy, but with laymen of various ages and positions in life: Ambrose's own brother Satyrus and two emperors, the young Valentinian and the older Theodosius.[121] The first of the two orations on the death of Satyrus adapts to a Christian point of view the topic of the virtues in pagan panegyric and consolation. It is organized around a canon of excellences—prudence, piety, courage, temperance, and justice—to which Ambrose adds gratitude to God, the only

---

[119] Cf. *De Fuga Saeculi* 4. 17, CSEL 32. 2. 178, and *De Bono Mortis* 5. 17, CSEL 32. 1. 719. In general, as Ladner, 328, points out, comparatively little "assimilation ideology" is found in the Latin Fathers' treatises on virginity.

[120] Cf. *De Cain* I. 5. 19, CSEL 32. 1. 355, where the *ebrietas* of grace is contrasted with physical drunkenness (*temulentia*).

[121] For the four virtues in Ambrosian panegyric, consult Hagendahl, 378–80, and see Charles Favez, *R.E.L.* 8 (1930), 82–91, for his adaptations of the *consolatio* and the funeral oration.

component of the list absent from pagan encomium (42–62, *CSEL* 73. 232–41). Under the rubric of *temperantia* he includes a mixture of pagan and Christian motives; childlike simplicity (51), *verecundia* and *castimonia* (52–53), *clementia* (54), *parsimonia*, also called *castitas habendi* (55), and spiritual poverty (56).[122] It is not surprising to find Matthew 5. 3 quoted as an injunction to practice *temperantia* in this sense, because in his exegesis of Luke, Ambrose links *temperantia* and the First Beatitude ("Blessed are the poor"), which he equates with the First in Matthew ("Blessed are the poor in spirit").

The second of the two orations on Satyrus, which deals with the subject of death and resurrection, is rich in the doctrine of the *meletê thanatou*, the preparation for death. This topic, allied with sophrosyne since Plato's *Phaedo*, is here entirely Christianized by the assertion that Christ is the death of the body and the life of the soul (II. 40, *CSEL* 73. 270). It is necessary to die with Him if we are to live with Him; this death involves the daily death of the appetites and passions. The importance of sophrosyne/*temperantia* lies in the fact that the virtues within its sphere are the ones specifically charged with producing the *imago mortis* (II. 40).[123]

The oration on the death of the Emperor Theodosius provides a Christian interpretation of another topic that was familiar in pagan eulogy from Isocrates on but was now, under the influence of Christian doctrine and historical conflicts between emperors and bishops, undergoing a process of rejuvenation—the virtues of the ruler. Ambrose resembles the Latin panegyrists in praising the moderation of the emperor, and this is the facet of *temperantia* which receives the greatest emphasis in the oration: forgiveness of those who have angered the emperor (13, 14, *CSEL* 73. 377 ff.) and moderation in the exercise of justice (25).[124] The topic of *temperantia* is introduced, however, with a digression on St. Helen and the finding of the True Cross, one of the nails from which was worked into a bridle and presented to Constantine. Ambrose, who himself set an example for later bishops and popes by acting as *sôphronistês* to the emperor, interprets this as a symbol of the need for the ruler to curb his insolence and restrain his lust (41–51)—a

---

122 Contrast the *partes temperantiae* in *De Off. Min.* 1. 115: *modus* and *ordo.*

123 The doctrine of the three deaths—the spiritual, the natural, and the penal—is also referred to (II. 36–37), as it is in *De Bono Mortis* III. 9 and in *Ex. in Luc.* VII. 35.

124 The emphasis on moderation is partly explained by Ambrose's desire to instil this virtue in the heir of Theodosius, the young Honorius. See also *De Paen.* I. 1. 1–2, *CSEL* 73. 119–20: *Moderatio prope omnium pulcherrima est* [*virtutum*] . . . *debet enim iustitiam temperare moderatio.*

commonplace in the Hellenistic *basilikos logos* and still an important nuance of *temperantia* in Christian panegyric.[125] The *Consolation* on the death of Valentinian II emphasizes still a third aspect of kingly sophrosyne, this time the virtue of adolescence: sobriety, renunciation of the normal pleasures of youth, fasting, and chastity (9, 10, 15–17, *CSEL* 73. 334–39). Ambrose is here describing, it has been suggested, an ideal of *aretê* and sophrosyne, rather than the actual character of Valentinian.[126]

In his effort to integrate the ethical tradition of Greek philosophy, especially the Platonic and Stoic, into Judaeo-Christian religious doctrine, Ambrose follows the method of Philo and the Greek Christian writers, particularly Origen. He accepts without question the theory that the pagan philosophers owed their wisdom to Scripture, and sees no incongruity in combing the Bible for exhortations to the practice of the Stoic virtues or for models of these virtues. He follows Philo in the allegorical interpretation of Genesis, in which the Garden of Eden represents the soul of man, the serpent pleasure, and the four rivers the four virtues, although he differs from Philo in details of the allegory. To Philo, as we have seen, the Tigris represents sophrosyne; to Ambrose, the Gehon (*De Par.* 3. 12–16, *CSEL* 32. 1. 272–75).[127] The four periods

---

[125] For an analysis of this speech, consult Sister Mary Dorothy Mannix, *St. Ambrose: Oratio de Obitu Theodosii* (Washington, D.C., 1925). The metaphor of the bridle appears also in *De Off. Min.* 1. 47–48. 228, *De Nabuthe* 15. 64, and *De Isaac* 8. 65 (*frenis iustitiae, retinaculis sobrietatis*). *De Virginibus* III. 2 converts the story of the death of Hippolytus into an *exemplum horribile* of the destructive effect of unbridled passion. Cf. Gregory of Nyssa *De Beat.*, Hom. II. *P.G.* 44. 1216C, for reason as the bridle of the passions, and see Musurillo, 54, on fasting as the bridle of the monk in Greek ascetical writing. The symbolism is so obvious that we should probably be slow to regard Ambrose (influential though he was where iconography is concerned) as the source of the type so common in Western art: the personified *Temperantia* holding—or even, grotesquely, wearing—a bridle or a bit. Among many examples see Giotto's *Temperanza* in the Arena Chapel in Padua, Agostino Duccio's relief on the façade of San Bernardino in Perugia, and the sepulchral figure on the tomb of Pope Adrian VI, Sta. Maria dell' Anima in Rome. The function of a bishop as *sôphronistês* to an emperor is discussed by Synesius of Cyrene *De Regno* (*P.G.* 66. 1056B), a *sôphronizôn logos* addressed to Arcadius.

[126] Kenneth Setton, *Christian Attitude towards the Emperor in the Fourth Century* (New York, 1941), 132. The emphasis on *sobrietas, castitas, temperantia in iuventute* corresponds to the traditional place of sophrosyne in pagan Greek panegyric.

[127] One reason is that the Jews received the command to leave Egypt and eat the lamb (a symbol of *temperantia*) beside this river (16). Ambrose also brings etymology to bear: Gehon means "hole in the earth," and just as a hole absorbs offscourings and filth, so *castitas* is wont to destroy all the bodily passions. The inscription on the font at Hildesheim echoes this explanation: *Temperiem Gehon terrae designat hiatus.* The personified *Temperantia* is represented on the font mixing water with wine, and the corresponding inscription quotes, not the Bible (as in the case of the other three virtues), but Horace (*Ep.* 2. 3. 243): *Omne tulit punctum,*

of human history embraced in Genesis also have specific links with the virtues. The second period, from the Deluge to the Law, is the age of *temperantia*, according to Ambrose, because the patriarchs of this age, Abraham, Isaac, and Jacob, are noted for this excellence (3. 20). It may be observed that the influence of the Philonian allegories on later art and literature in the West is traceable to Ambrose (and Augustine), rather than directly to Philo's own writings.[128]

Again like one of his Greek sources, in this case Gregory of Nyssa, Ambrose in his longest exegetical work, the Commentary on Luke, interprets the Beatitudes in the light of the cardinal virtues. Holding that the four Beatitudes in Luke include the eight in Matthew, he cites as a parallel the virtues, which are so closely linked that he who has one has them all (V. 63, *CSEL* 32. 4. 207), and he interprets each of the Beatitudes in Luke as an injunction to practice one of the virtues. The First ("Blessed are the poor") represents *temperantia* and includes, not only the First in Matthew ("Blessed are the poor in spirit"), but also the Sixth ("Blessed are the pure in heart"); because the poor, having *temperantia*, despise the world and seek not its temptations, and *temperantia* involves purity of heart and soul (53, 64, 68).[129] It is obvious that Ambrose here understands *temperantia* to be the virtue of renunciation and asceticism. This nuance takes precedence in the treatises on fasting, *De Jacob* and *De Helia*, which regard ascetical fasting as the basis of many other virtues, including chastity, continence, purity, and sobriety.[130] The attitude of Ambrose towards *temperantia* in these treatises is identical with that of the Cappadocians towards sophrosyne and rests in the main

---

qui miscuit utile dulci. In *De Par.* Ambrose further justifies his choice of the Gehon by pointing out that it encompasses Ethiopia, which means "abject and vile" and is black, just as our bodies are black with sin.

[128] On the influence of Ambrose and Augustine, see Mâle, 110, nn. 4, 5.

[129] See also *De Exc. Frat. Sat.* I. 56, where Satyrus' *temperantia* includes his being *pauper spiritu.* The mosaics of the Cupola of the Ascension in St. Mark's, Venice, which portray the cardinal virtues and related excellences (some with allusions to the Beatitudes) include a personified *Modestia*, with a cartel reading *Beati eritis vos cum oderint homines* (Luke 6. 22), which according to Ambrose's system of correspondences refers to *fortitudo*, and a *Castitas* with the words *Beati mundo corde quoniam ipsi Dominum videbunt* (Matt. 5. 8). *Temperantia* has no motto but is readily identified by her action of pouring water from one vessel into another. In most representations of this scene the second vessel is supposed to contain wine, but sometimes in Carolingian art the water is being used to extinguish flames, perhaps under the influence of Pomerius (*Vita Contemplativa* 19, *P.L.* 59. 502B), where one of the functions of *temperantia* is to put out the fire of lust (*ignem libidinosae voluptatis extinguit*). See, e.g., the dedication miniature of the Cambrai Gospels, where *Temperantia* holds a torch and a jug (Katzenellenbogen, Fig. 32).

[130] *De Hel.* 8. 22, *CSEL* 32. 2. 423 ff.; *De Iacob* I. 2. 5, 8, *CSEL* 32. 2. 7–9.

on the assumption that since appetite (*gula*) drove man from Paradise, only *abstinentia* can lead him back.[131] Hence the favorite Ambrosian models of *temperantia* are those associated with fasting: John the Baptist, Moses, Daniel, and Elias; although Joseph, always the *speculum castitatis*, is the favored exemplar of *temperantia* considered as the extinction of lust (*De Joseph* 1. 2, *CSEL* 32. 2, 74). The models of feminine *temperantia* are the familiar representatives of the three stages of *castitas*, taken over unchanged from Greek Patristic writing. Like the Greek Fathers, but unlike most of his Latin predecessors, Ambrose prefers Biblical to pagan *exempla*, even in passages where he is most transparently adapting pagan ethical doctrine. In this preference he is followed by Augustine, especially when, in his sermons, he addresses a popular audience.[132]

ST. AUGUSTINE

St. Augustine fully embraces the doctrine of the four cardinal virtues, and we meet them in the context of his most fundamental beliefs.[133] Although the contributions of Plato, Aristotle, the Stoics, and the Neoplatonists, as well as those of Ambrose and, before him, of Philo and Origen, are readily apparent in his theory of virtue, Augustine, more than any other Latin philosopher, pagan or Christian, succeeded in forming an original and coherent system whose indebtedness to many predecessors merely makes more arresting its own sovereign independence. His definition of virtue as love (*De Mor. Ecc.* 1. 15. 25, *P.L.* 32. 1322) and his insistence on the complete dependence of man on God for the attainment of virtue (*C.D.* 4. 20, *Ep.* 155. 12) are the two foundation stones of his ethics; on these is erected his concept of sophrosyne together with the other cardinal virtues. The importance of sophrosyne in his system results from the relation that he establishes between *temperantia* and three central ideas: *conversio*, *superbia*, and *voluntas*. Although much might be said of Augustine's use of topics concerned with *temperantia* in his discussions of Roman history in the *City of God*,[134]

---

[131] See Musurillo (17, n. 43) for a list of Greek Fathers who regard gluttony as the first sin.

[132] See Mary Louise Carlson, *loc. cit.*, 94.

[133] For a systematic study of the ethics of Augustine, consult Joseph Mausbach, *Die Ethik des heiligen Augustinus* (Freiburg, 1909), especially 2. 258–94; on the cardinal virtues see 1. 207–18. See also Étienne Gilson, *The Christian Philosophy of Saint Augustine* (New York, 1960), 113 ff.

[134] For example, the discussion of Roman models of *pudicitia* (1. 16–19, *CSEL* 40), together with the statement that *pudicitia* has *fortitudo* for her comrade (1. 18); the danger of taking pride in one's *castitas* (1. 28); the growth of *cupido regnandi*, *avaritia*, and *luxuria* in Rome (1. 31, 2. 6, 19); the vanity of compelling the four virtues to serve *voluptas*—as in the

in his allegorical interpretations of Scripture, in his choice of *exempla virtutum*, and in his sermons, consolations, and exhortations to the ascetical life, our study will be limited to the three topics mentioned above, in connection with which his true originality becomes evident. Most of the relevant passages derive from works written shortly after Augustine's conversion, when the influence of Neoplatonism was strong and pure. The concept of sophrosyne developed on the basis of essentially Neoplatonic ideas was not rejected in Augustine's later writings, but the theological, polemical, and ascetical works of his episcopate were concerned with other problems and either took for granted the definitions established in the early writings (wherein the virtues are forms of *amor* or *caritas*) or made use of traditional definitions established by the earlier Latin Fathers.

Among the many definitions of *temperantia* (Augustine's usual rendering of sophrosyne) found in his works, some are patently Ciceronian (and Stoic), such as the exact quotation from *De Inventione* in *De Diversis Quaestionibus* 83. 31.[135] Others have a Peripatetic background, like the discussion in *De Beata Vita* which relates *temperantia* to the concept of measure (2. 32–33); while still others—and these the most significant —reflect Plotinus and the Christian Neoplatonists in linking the moral virtues to purification and love. Through Ambrose, Augustine came under the influence of Greek Patristic writers in whose theories of virtue *erôs* (or *agapê*) and *apatheia* have a prominent place;[136] and the impact of Ambrose himself is felt both in Augustine's interpretation of the Beatitudes and in his discussions of *pudicitia, continentia,* and *castitas*

Epicurean system—or *gloria*—as was done in Rome (5. 20); control of appetite as a virtue of the emperor (5. 24), the model being Theodosius; the practice of *temperantia* by certain *Romani principes,* although Rome never deified this virtue (4. 20).

[135] See Maurice Testard, *Saint Augustin et Cicéron* (Paris, 1958), 2. 1–114, for a list of quotations from Cicero in the writings of Augustine.

[136] Fulbert Cayré (*Initiation à la philosophie de Saint Augustin* [Paris, 1947] 83–92) discusses the influence of Clement and Origen on Augustine through Ambrose. For the link between *agapê* and *apatheia* in the *homoiôsis*-theory of Clement, see Völker, *op. cit.,* 532 ff. Gregory of Nyssa regards *agapê* as the source of virtue; see his encomium of Basil (11), and consult Jaeger (*Two Works,* 76–77) on his adaptation of the Platonic *erôs* (or *pothos*) directed towards the good and the beautiful. Ambrose links charity with *temperantia* in *De Virginitate* 1. 18. 113. For *erôs* and *katharsis* in Plotinus, consult Jean Trouillard, *Le purification plotinienne* (Paris, 1955), 154 ff. Purification is the first stage in the ascent of the soul described in *De Ordine* (II. 18. 48, *P.L.* 32. 1017), yet Augustine rejects *apatheia,* not only for mankind (*apatheia* is a state of stupor, even worse than vice [*C.D.* 14. 9]) but even in the case of Christ, for Whom Clement had worked hard to establish it. Cf. *In Io. Ev.,* tr. 60. 3–5, *P.L.* 35. 1798–99. Pierre de Labriolle (*Mélanges Ernout* [Paris, 1940], 215–23) discusses the tendency of the Latin Fathers to reject *apatheia.*

in exhortations addressed to married women, widows, and virgins.[137]
Augustine, however, gives the ascetical aspect of *temperantia* less attention
than does Ambrose; he has a broader concept of the virtue than any
earlier Latin Christian writer and is especially notable for his insistence
that moderation is essential to it. He deplores, for example, the exaltation
of physical virginity or any other form of ascetical virtue to the point at
which pride in such virtue becomes a more serious sin than impurity
itself.[138]

The most influential of Augustine's definitions of virtue is that which
regards it as a form of *amor* or *caritas*.[139] According to *De Moribus
Ecclesiae Catholicae* (written about 387–389), virtue is nothing other than
summus amor Dei, and the four principal virtues are manifestations of this
love (I. 15. 25; *P.L.* 32. 1322). A quarter of a century later Augustine
still abides by this definition, maintaining in Epistle 155 (*ca.* 414) that
virtue in this life consists in loving what ought to be loved—*diligere quod
diligendum est* (IV. 13)—and again he defines each virtue in relation to
this central concept.[140] The definition of *temperantia* in *De Moribus
Ecclesiae* may be taken as fundamental: it is *amor integrum se praebens ei*

[137] The Beatitudes: *De Serm. Dom.* I. 4. 11; consult Piero Rollero, *Augustinus Magister*
(Paris, 1954), I. 213. *Pudicitia*, etc.: *De Bono Coniugali* XVI. 18, XXI. 25; *De Bono Viduitatis*
IV. 5, XV. 19; *De Sancta Virginitate* XI. 11, XXII; *De Continentia* II. 5, V. 12, 13. A
memorable description of *continentia*, personified as the "Madam of a House of Good Fame,"
occurs in *Conf.* 8. 27; see Maurice Cunningham, *C.P.* 57 (1962), 234–35. *Pudicitia* and *sobrietas*
are among the traditional topics of eulogy applied to the praise of Monica, in *Conf.* 9. 9,
where both words designate aspects of sophrosyne. *Sobrietas* appears as a translation of sophrosyne in Augustine's references to Wi. 8. 7 (*De Mor. Ecc.* 27, *Retr.* I. 26), doubtless under
the influence of the Old Latin translation. In *Sol.* I. 1. 6, *P.L.* 32. 872, where the cardinal
virtues are mentioned, *purus* represents *sôphrôn*, obviously equated with *hagnos*.

[138] E.g., *C.D.* I. 28; *De Sanct. Virg.* XXXIII, XLIII–XLIV. Cf. the praise of Gorgonia by
Gregory of Nazianzus for being *sôphrôn atyphos* ("chaste without arrogance"), *P.G.* 35. 797,
and Jerome's description of the combined *temperantia* and humility of Paulina's character
(*Ep.* 66. 3, *P.L.* 22. 640).

[139] Étienne Gilson (*op. cit.,* 132–42) discusses the relation among love, the will, and moral
virtue in Augustine's philosophy.

[140] See also *Ep.* 167. IV. 15 and *C.D.* 15. 22. Thomas Deman, O.P., discusses the
adaptation of the pagan doctrine of the four virtues to Augustine's theory of virtue as love in
Augustinus Magister (Paris, 1954), 2. 721 ff. The other basic ingredient in Augustine's theory
of virtue is his doctrine that its source is God. Virtue is a charism (*C.D.* 4. 20; *Ep.* 155. III.
12; *Serm.* 150. VIII, *P.L.* 38. 812–13). Therefore pagans cannot possess true virtue (*Contr.
Jul. Pom.* 4. 3. 17, *P.L.* 44. 745: *C.D.* 5. 18. 3). Virtue is given by Divine Grace (*En. in Ps.* 83)
and leads to the state of contemplation, where there is no need for moral virtue. On the
condition of the virtues after death, see *De Trin.* 14. 12, *De Gen. ad Litt.* 12. 54, and *Ep.* 155.
IV. 12: the virtues will survive, but in altered form since there will no longer be temptations
to resist or choices to make. The heavenly virtues will be purified (*De Mus.* 6. 16. 55) and
will be merged into the virtue of contemplation (*Ep.* 155. IV. 12). For the distinction
between "civic" virtue and true virtue, see *C.D.* 19. 25.

quod amatur—"love offering itself in its integrity to that which is loved," that is, to God (1. 15. 25). *Temperantia,* Augustine explains, promises us the integrity and safety of the love by which we are bound to God. Its particular function lies in restraining and quieting the passions by which we lust after those things that separate us from the laws of God and from the enjoyment of His goodness (1. 19. 35). Hence the clue to the value of *temperantia* lies in its relation to *cupiditas* and thus to purification. The ascent of the soul, as described in *De Quantitate Animae* and *De Ordine* (two further products of the early period, *ca.* 387–388), is achieved in three principal stages: the purgative, the illuminative, and the unitive.[141] At the first of these stages the cardinal virtues operate to destroy the love of all that is not God. Although Augustine recognizes the existence of other forces that may separate us from God, *cupiditas,* the *radix malorum* (*De Mor. Ecc.* 1. 19. 35), is more seductive than the others; and *temperantia* is man's chief defense against the desires of the flesh and the spirit. The essential step in the journey towards salvation is the first, the *conversio in Deum* (comparable to the Neoplatonic *strophê*), a turning away from self-love towards the love of God.[142] Each of the cardinal virtues has a part in *conversio,* but as Augustine describes it, *temperantia* is the one that effects the actual turning. *Prudentia* decides what is worthy to be loved, *iustitia* recognizes the need to establish a hierarchy of objects to be loved and to give each its due, *fortitudo* resists all pains and terrors in clinging to the decision made by these two virtues, but *temperantia* has the crucial task of fighting the *cupiditates* and carrying out the *conversio amoris,* putting off the old man and being renewed in God (*De Mor. Ecc.* 1. 19. 35, *P.L.* 32. 1326).[143] It is significant that in *De Moribus Ecclesiae* Augustine treats *temperantia* first among the four virtues and at much the greatest length.

A related discussion of *conversio* and its dependence on *temperantia*

---

[141] *De Quant. An.* I. 33. 70, 35. 79 (*P.L.* 32. 1073–79), gives seven steps, reduced to the essential three in *De Ord.* II. 18. 48 (*P.L.* 32. 1017).

[142] On *epistrophê* and conversion in pagan and Christian thought, see A. D. Nock, *Reallexikon für Antike und Christentum,* under "Bekehrung," as well as Ladner, 49 ff. The relation of sophrosyne to the Neoplatonic *epistrophê* is particularly clear in Olympiodorus *In Alcib.* p. 214–15 Westerink.

[143] In *Ep.* 155. IV. 13, where *prudentia* receives the task of choosing what should be loved, *fortitudo* the task of adhering to it in spite of *molestiae, temperantia* in spite of *inlecebrae,* and *iustitia* in spite of *superbia,* the role of *temperantia* is diminished and made strictly co-ordinate with those of courage and justice. Augustine does not emphasize *conversio* in this passage, and *temperantia* is limited to the control of the fleshly appetites. This narrow definition prevails also in *C.D.* 19. 4, in *De Lib. Arb.* 1. 13. 27 (*P.L.* 32. 1235), and in *Serm.* 150. VIII. 9 (*P.L.* 38. 812); it is common in all the works having to do with virginity and the ascetical life.

occurs in *De Musica* (A.D. 387–391), which like *De Moribus Ecclesiae* is deeply imbued with Neoplatonic theories of virtue. Here Augustine ascribes to *temperantia* the extrication of the soul from the love of inferior beauty, so that it may fly to the safety of God (6. 15. 50, *P.L.* 32. 1189). Again the idea of purgation is intimately associated with that of *conversio amoris,* and this catharsis is shown to be the peculiar function of *temperantia.* If *prudentia* is that by which the soul knows where it must take its stand, it is *temperantia* by which the soul betakes itself thither. This process is further equated with *caritas* and is said to be accompanied by *fortitudo* and *iustitia* (6. 16. 51, *P.L.* 32. 1189). Still another treatise begun soon after Augustine's conversion, *De Libero Arbitrio,* casts additional light on the link between *conversio* and *temperantia.* Augustine shows that he who practices each virtue behaves wisely and is therefore *sapiens.* Justice is said to consist in perceiving what relations exist between objects of love and how to distribute *propria suis; prudentia* consists in choosing the incorruptible and preferring it to corruption; the third virtue (unnamed, but clearly *temperantia*) consists in turning (*convertere*) to that which prudence has chosen, and the fourth (also unnamed, but certainly *fortitudo*) in being deflected by no terrors from the object that has been chosen and turned to (2. 10. 29, *P.L.* 32. 1256–57). Here Augustine's language leaves no doubt that *temperantia* accomplishes the actual *conversio.*

That Augustine recognizes a close connection between *conversio* of any kind and *temperantia* is evident from his discussion of self-knowledge in *De Ordine* (dated 386). Here he mentions the need for the soul to withdraw from things of the senses and concentrate thought on itself, and he asks what *conversio* means except turning to oneself away from the immoderateness of the vices, with the help of *virtus* and *temperantia* (I. 8. 23, *P.L.* 32. 988). The nature of this *conversio* is different, being preliminary to the important *conversio in Deum,* but *temperantia* is again singled out as the specific virtue qualified to perform the task.

In all such discussions Augustine takes a broad view of the scope of *temperantia.* Although he recognizes from experience as well as theory that in human life the battle with the flesh cannot be avoided and in the *City of God* specifically describes this battle as the concern of *temperantia,* "that virtue which the Greeks call sophrosyne" (19. 4. 3), he includes among the *cupiditates* other than fleshly appetites. In *De Moribus Ecclesiae* where the function of *temperantia* is said to be "putting off the old man" and being renewed in God, Augustine explains that this Pauline formula means scorning all bodily temptations and popular praise as well, and turning one's entire affection to the invisible and the Divine (1. 19. 36). The mention of *laus popularis* after the temptations of the flesh is typical of Augustine, who like the Cappadocians regards physical chastity as only a small part of the virtue of sophrosyne. In commenting on Galatians 1. 10 as an admonition to avoid human respect and *curiositas,* Augustine adds that herein lies the *magnum temperantiae munus (De Mor. Ecc.* 1. 21. 38). Pride and the desire for *vana cognitio* must be avoided if the soul is to keep itself *casta* for God.[144]

This passage, which is concerned with the danger to the soul of excessive inquiry into the physical universe if combined with forgetfulness of the nature of God, serves as an introduction to Augustine's view of the relation between *temperantia* and *superbia.* He often makes *temperantia* the antithesis of pride, which is for him the real *initium peccati,* more basic even than *voluptas.*[145] Nothing keeps man from his proper relation to God so much as pride, which gave rise to the sin of Adam. Among the Greek Fathers, Origen, followed by Basil and Gregory of Nyssa, had adopted this view; and Ambrose, although often inclined to give precedence to the sin of *intemperantia,* sometimes recognized *superbia* as the greatest offence (for example, *In Psalm. 118.*). *De Musica,* dating from Augustine's early period, characterizes pride as the vice that makes the soul wish to usurp the place of God, rather than be content to serve Him (6. 13. 40, *P.L.* 32. 1184). *The City of God* owes its organization to the polarity between pride and humility: by their possession of these two antithetical qualities, the mundane and the heavenly cities are distinguished.[146] Although Augustine nowhere specifically discusses the relation of *temperantia* to humility, he takes a long step in the direction of equating them and thus gives a new importance to sophrosyne as a Christian virtue.

In classical Greek morality sophrosyne was early recognized as the antithesis of *hybris,* but humility (*tapeinophrosynê*) was not considered an *aretê* (except in such a rare and prophetic passage as Plato *Laws* 716A), nor was sophrosyne explicitly identified with humility. In the Middle Ages, however, the concept of self-knowledge became a bridge that

---

[144] In *Conf.* 10. 35, *temperantia* limits the desire for knowledge and experience. St. Thomas Aquinas, too, lists *curiositas* as one of the vices opposed to *temperantia* (*Sum. Theol.* II. II. 166; 167).

[145] William M. Green (*University of California Studies in Classical Philology* 13 [1949], 407–31) discusses the sources for this belief in the Bible. Irenaeus, Origen, Basil, and others. If pride is the first sin, lust is its sequel (*Conf.* 7. 7. 11).

[146] Hence the great development in mediaeval moral treatises and iconography of the concept of the two trees rooted in humility and pride; see above, n. 22.

linked humility and *temperantia,* under the inspiration of Aristotle. In
the *Ethics* the man who knows himself and, being of little worth,
recognizes the fact, is called *sôphrôn* (1123b 5). In Christian theology no
created thing possesses independent value, and every man is of little
worth. Hence St. Thomas Aquinas can equate sophrosyne with
humility, commenting that Aristotle describes as *temperatus* such a man
as *nos humilem dicere possumus.*[147]

While Augustine never draws this conclusion, he repeatedly shows
the fundamental opposition of *temperantia* to pride; this, too, is an idea
that appears early in his writings. The Peripatetic *De Beata Vita* cites
superbia as one of the results of lack of moderation in the soul (IV. 33,
P.L. 32. 975). More explicitly, *De Musica* describes *superbia* as that which
causes the soul to fall from the love and contemplation of God into
actiones quasdam potestatis suae and into apostasy from God (6. 16. 53, *P.L.*
32. 1190). The *amor Dei* and the *amor sui* are unalterably opposed. If the
soul scorns the works of pride, it is said to place its *amor in Deo* and to
live *temperatissime et castissime et securissime.* In Psalm 35 (*Dixit iniustus*),
which Augustine in *De Musica* expounds in terms of the four cardinal
virtues and their role in purifying the soul, the verse *Non veniet mihi pes
superbiae* ("Let not the foot of pride come to me" [v. 12]), is interpreted
as an allusion to *temperantia.* The soul, in refraining (*temperando*) from
the errors and offenses of pride, clings to God and thus finds eternal
life (6. 16. 53). Later (perhaps 412) Augustine's *Enarratio in Psalm 35*
interprets this verse entirely in terms of humility, without reference to
any of the pagan cardinal virtues (17, *P.L.* 36. 353).

Closely allied to the subjects of sin, pride, and love is that of the will,
and inevitably *temperantia* is related to the *bona voluntas.* The connection
of these two ideas is developed in the early dialogues but persists into
the later writings as well, notably the *City of God.* In *De Musica,* after
temperantia has been explained as the virtue that prevents the soul from
taking pleasure in acts of pride and restrains it from such actions,
fortitudo is distinguished from it by the statement that as *temperantia* is
effective (*valet*) against the lapses that exist in the free will, so *fortitudo* is
powerful to resist violence, by which the soul might be compelled to do
evil (6. 16. 54). *De Libero Arbitrio* also implies a close relation between
temperantia and the will, in the rhetorical question asking whether a
person possessed of a *bona voluntas* could be separated from *temperantia,*

---

[147] See also Siger de Brabant (*Quaestiones morales,* qu. 1), where humility is identified with
Aristotle's *temperantia circa honorem* (*Eth. Nic.* 1123b 5). On this whole development, consult
Gauthier, 456, 474 ff.

which restrains the appetites. What is so hostile to such a will as lust (1. 13. 27, *P.L.* 32. 1236)? All four virtues are the property of one who has a good will, but because to Augustine sin is essentially the neglect of the eternal for the sake of the temporal—the one enjoyed by the mind, the other by the body (1. 16. 35, *P.L.* 32. 1240)—it follows that *temperantia* has an especially close relation with the good will, since it alone is charged specifically with the rejection of bodily pleasure. In the *City of God* Augustine still makes the same distinction among the functions of the cardinal virtues. *Prudentia* teaches (*docet*) that we should not consent to evil, and *temperantia* causes (*facit*) us to refuse consent (19. 4). The treatise *De Mendacio* (395) employs a different vocabulary but reveals the same attitude, maintaining in a discussion of *pudicitia corporis* and *castitas animi* that the latter consists in *bona voluntas* and *sincera dilectio* (19. 40; *CSEL* 41).

One of the discussions of *temperantia* that most clearly reveals the sources of Augustine's ideas and vocabulary occurs in *De Beata Vita*, where he recalls the association of the virtue with measure and moderation. The passage is of special interest because while Augustine regards *modus* and *ordo* as two of the perfections necessary for all substance,[148] he does not often connect either concept specifically with the word *temperantia*. In *De Beata Vita*, however, where he maintains that happiness consists in wisdom (*sapientia*) and identifies *sapientia* with *moderatio animi* (1. II. 11) or *modus animi*, excluding excess and defect (1. IV. 33), he quotes with approval the popular belief that *frugalitas* is the mother of the virtues and, with Cicero (*Pro Reg. Deiot.* 9. 26), explains *frugalitas* as *modestia* and *temperantia* (31). He derives *modestia* from *modus* and *temperantia* from *temperies* and emphasizes the connection of both words with the Mean (32); thus he restores to the Latinized concept of sophrosyne its link with moderation, always less prominent in Latin than in Greek thought on the subject. The derivation of *temperantia*, moreover, reminds us how different are the results of etymologizing sophrosyne and *temperantia*. The presence of *phronêsis*, ever recognizable in sophrosyne, guarantees that this excellence will always be explained as the savior of wisdom, a recurrent definition in pagan and Christian Greek thought.[149] But the kinship of *temperantia* with a root denoting proper mixture, recalled by Augustine in the derivation from *temperies*, meant that moral rather than intellectual connotations would prevail

---

148 Gilson, *op. cit.*, 144.

149 Plato *Crat.* 411E, Aristotle *Eth. Nic.* 1140b 11–12, Clement of Alexandria *Strom.* VII. 3. 18, 2, Gregory Thaumaturgus, *P.G.* 10. XI. 1084C. See also Philo *De Fortitudine* II, p. 377.

in Latin analyses of the virtue. In iconography the result was the type of *Temperantia* most widespread in Italian art in the Middle Ages and the Renaissance, the personified virtue pouring water into a vessel of wine and mixing them duly. This attitude, in fact, is the one assumed by *Temperantia* on the arca of Augustine himself in the Church of S. Pietro nel Ciel d'Oro in Pavia.[150]

Our study may fittingly conclude with Augustine, for it was the authority and prestige of this Father, supplanting the influence of Origen and the Cappadocians and outstripping that of Ambrose and Jerome, which guaranteed the survival in the West of the tetrad of cardinal virtues and thus preserved some portions of the classical concept of sophrosyne while at the same time completing its transformation into an authentic Christian virtue. Once again, as in several earlier stages of its history (notably the transition from tragedy to philosophy in the fourth century B.C. and the period of Neoplatonic speculation in the third and fourth centuries after Christ), sophrosyne proved amazingly adaptable. If, as Christian thinkers hold, three qualities above all—charity, humility, and purity—wrought the most profound changes in the transformation of pagan society by Christianity, it is remarkable that at the end of the fourth century sophrosyne showed close affinities with the second and third of these three. As we have noted, it was from the beginning especially attractive to Christian moralists, who by a radical shift in emphasis—making purity the dominant connotation of sophro-syne—enabled the concept to survive and even develop with undiminished vigor in Christian thought, long after the pagan society that nourished it had died. By adopting the tetrad as a whole, Clement and the Cappadocians in the East, Jerome and Ambrose in the West, removed the one serious threat to sophrosyne in the first three Christian centuries, the danger that it would develop entirely apart from its Platonic-Stoic companions and thus lose most of its classical identity. And now Augustine, by integrating sophrosyne into his personal system of values and developing those nuances that spoke to his condition, endowed it with fresh life and provided a precedent for later Western

---

[150] The tomb of Augustine (above the crypt where the remains of Boethius are thought to lie) is embellished with both cardinal and theological virtues, the work of Giovanni Balduccio, *ca.* 1362. The element of *tempus* in *temperantia* is usually represented (as we noted in Chap. VIII, p. 262) by the presence of an hourglass or a clock in the neighborhood of the personified virtue. See, e.g., *Temperantia* in Ambrogio Lorenzetti's Fresco of Good Government in the Palazzo Pubblico in Siena, and that in the Rouen Ms. of Aristotle's *Ethics*, which inspired the sepulchral figures by Michel Colombe in Nantes (Van Marle, Fig. 57).

theologians who were to find ever new ways of making this virtue relevant to their own concerns.[151]

Augustine furthermore reminds us of the crucial importance of individual thinkers, as well as of great political, social, or religious forces, in shaping the history of *aretê*. His temperamental affinity for certain nuances of sophrosyne led him, to a degree unmatched by the other Fathers, to think out afresh its meaning for himself, to make it in a special sense his own, and thus to establish its relevance to the concepts we have discussed, particularly humility and the conversion from error to truth. The "oscillation between restraint and excess" noted by a biographer of the young Augustine,[152] while most evident in his own account of his turbulent adolescence and young manhood, affected all his later work as well, because it determined, for life, his moral perspective. When his instinctive feeling for restraint had been reinforced by an extraordinarily powerful revulsion from his youthful excess, there developed in Augustine's soul a climate highly favorable for the mature reconsideration of that virtue which more than any other spoke to him of restraint, purity, and conversion. Like Plato, whose temperamental affinity for sophrosyne (in his case harmony and proportion) contrasts so strongly with Aristotle's relative indifference, or like Panaetius, with his deep, instinctive sympathy for sophrosyne as the *prepon*, in contrast to Poseidonius, Augustine found personal significance in this virtue, far beyond what Ambrose or Jerome had seen. He is one of those for whom, in the words of Blake, the road of excess led to the palace of wisdom.[153]

Something of his feeling colors the apology with which he concludes his discussion of *temperantia* in *De Moribus Ecclesiae* (*P.L.* 32. 1328): *Haec dicta sint de temperantia, pro rerum magnitudine breviter, pro instituto tamen opere fortasse copiosius quam oportebat* ("Let this be said about *temperantia*, little enough when one thinks of the magnitude of the subject, but perhaps too much in proportion to the size of this book"). The present study, which even more than *De Moribus Ecclesiae* may seem to have discussed sophrosyne *copiosius quam oportebat*, can find no more fitting conclusion than Augustine's testimony to the *magnitudo rerum* embraced by *temperantia*.

[151] For some new applications of *temperantia* to special problems of the Middle Ages consult the dissertation by Catherine Haines, *op. cit.* The exposition of the functions of the tetrad in connection with monasticism by Odilo of Cluny (*P.L.* 142. 901) is especially characteristic.

[152] John J. O'Meara, *The Young Augustine* (London, 1954), 44.

[153] "Proverbs of Hell," *The Poems of William Blake* (London, 1931), 161.

Appendix: Imagery Related to Sophrosyne

THE imagery of the bridle or the bit—foreshadowed by Aeschylus' references to bridle or yoke in connection with Prometheus' need to learn moderation (*P.V.* 1009–10)—constitutes the favorite symbol for sophrosyne in ancient literature: the mastery of a wild or unruly beast. I postpone until a later time a discussion of the iconography of sophrosyne/*temperantia* in relation to its literary sources, but it may be helpful to include here a list of the principal types of imagery, without attempting to establish connections between a given passage in literature and later artistic representations. In Greek literature there are seven major categories; only the first three are important in the classical period, when the antitheses to sophrosyne, especially *hybris,* lend themselves to vivid imagery more often than does sophrosyne itself. The categories are these:

1. The imagery of health, or the healing of disease. This metaphor is implicit in the very word sophrosyne, whose etymology suggests saving the reason or keeping it sound. Plato was particularly likely to exploit the parallels between health of mind and body; see, for example, the *Charmides,* with the background of the palaestra and the discussion of how to cure Charmides' headache. When the doctrine of the "goods" of body and soul became a commonplace in Hellenistic philosophy, sophrosyne was regularly defined as health of soul (e.g., Ariston of Chios, *SVF* 1. 375). The metaphor is difficult to convert into a visual image and has no importance for later iconography.

2. The mastery of a beast. This metaphor goes back to Homeric

passages in which it is necessary to restrain one's *thymos*, as if it were a wild animal (for example, in the *Odyssey* IX. 302, XX. 18–24). The most influential such image is the comparison of the soul to a charioteer with two horses, one obedient, the other unruly, in Plato's *Phaedrus* (246A ff.). (The beast representing the passions and appetites is a favorite metaphor in Plato's dialogues; see, for example, *Rep.* 588B, *Tim.* 70D; and cf. Isocrates *Ad. Nic.* 12.) Philo Judaeus employs this type of symbolism in allegorical interpretations of the Bible. See, for example, the exegesis of Genesis 49. 16–18 in *Leg. All.* 2. 24–25, which explains the serpent biting the horse's heel as sophrosyne wounding the passions and thereby saving the rider (*Nous*) from destruction (cf. *De Agr.* 21. 94 ff.). Patristic writers often conflate the myth of the *Phaedrus* with supposed parallels from Scripture, such as Ezech. 1. 3–5 (cf. Jerome, *Ep.* 52. 13, 2 on the *quadriga* of the soul). Greek mythology commonly represents the passions as grotesque animals (such as the Chimaera conquered by Bellerophon) or as monstrous enemies of the Olympian gods (Typhoeus, in Pindar *Pyth.* 8. 11 ff.); and nothing is more familiar in Greek art than the symbolic battle between the human (or the Divine) and the bestial, resulting in a victory of order, civilization, sophrosyne over chaos, barbarism, *hybris*.[1] The pedimental sculpture of the temple of Olympian Zeus and the Pergamene frieze are but the best-known examples of this type. In Renaissance art, where the scope of *Temperantia* was considerably narrower than that of the classical sophrosyne, the allegory is often generalized into a victory of Virtue over Vice: for example, Hercules subduing one of the monsters involved in his Labors, or idealized groups like those by Cellini and Giovanni da Bologna. The symbolism of the wild beast hunt—representing the triumph of reason over passion—is common in late Roman and Byzantine mosaics and Roman sarcophagi.[2] One type of sarcophagus portrays the *sôphrôn* huntsman Hippolytus in the neighborhood of such a hunt.[3] The *Pinax* of Cebes introduces Sophrosyne as one of several sisters of *Epistêmê* in a hunting scene (20–22).[4]

3. Imagery derived from military equipment. An early example is

---

[1] See Eva Matthews Sanford, *C.P.* 36 (1941), 52–57.

[2] Doro Levi, *Antioch Mosaic Pavements* (Princeton, 1947), I. 340.

[3] Cf. *Anth. Pal.* 9. 132 for the personified Sophrosyne and Erôs doing battle through their human representatives, Hippolytus and Phaedra. To Ambrose (*De Virginibus* III. 2) the death of Hippolytus, dragged by his frenzied horses, represents the victory of the passions over reason.

[4] For Cebes as one of the antecedents of Prudentius, see Karl Künstle, *Ikonographie der christlichen Kunst* (Freiburg, 1928), I. 156 ff.

the contrast between the hybristic blazons of the Seven against Thebes in Aeschylus' tragedy and the modest devices on the shields of the defenders. We have observed (Chap. II, n. 17) that only the blazon of Hyperbius, among the defenders, is described. Among the attackers, Amphiaraus has no blazon, and this circumstance, which was for Aeschylus a sign of the hero's preference for reality over appearance in the effort to be *aristos* (592 ff.), became in later literature a symbol of his sophrosyne (Euripides, *Phoen.* 1118, Julian 303C). The breastplate of sophrosyne and the sheathed sword of severity became something of a commonplace in addresses to rulers, both Greek and Roman (see Seneca *De Clem.* 1. 1. 1–4); and, with the increasing tendency to compare the life of virtue to a mortal combat against evil, this symbolism becomes normal. St. Paul (Eph. 6. 14–17) gave impetus to the custom of describing the virtues as parts of a soldier's equipment; the shield was especially popular because it provided a convenient place for attributes or even scenes depicting the virtue in action. Artistic representations of the virtues battling the vices are widespread in Gothic art, but the type derives from the *Psychomachia* of Prudentius rather than directly from ancient literature, and usually involves the personification of the virtues as armor-clad women.[5] Attributes identifying the virtues are often displayed on a shield, as in the reliefs at Notre Dame, Amiens, and Chartres discussed by Mâle.[6] The sheathed sword is an attribute of *Temperantia* in Giotto's fresco in the Arena Chapel at Padua and on the Pisano relief on the south door of the Baptistery at Florence.

4. *The Tree of Virtue*. In classical Greek literature *hybris* is more often described as blossom, fruit, or harvest (Aeschylus *Sept.* 60, *Supp.* 106; Sophocles, Frag. 718), but Democritus (Frag. 294 DK) refers to sophrosyne as the flower (*anthos*) of age. The figure became popular only after the time of Philo, who developed in great detail the allegory of the Trees of Virtue, under the inspiration of the Trees of Life and of the Knowledge of Good and Evil in Genesis. Inevitably sophrosyne and the other cardinal virtues came to be represented as trees in the Garden

[5] For the theme of the *psychomachia* in art, consult Adolf Katzenellenbogen, *Allegories of the Virtues and Vices in Mediaeval Art from Early Christian Times to the Thirteenth Century* (New York, 1964), and Raimond van Marle, *Iconographie de l'art profane au moyen âge et à la Renaissance* (The Hague, 1932), 2. 11 ff.

[6] The vices are often depicted in scenes below the figure holding the shield. Exemplars of the virtues and vices are sometimes introduced into such groups. Holofernes, Epicurus, and Tarquinius Superbus are the favorite exemplars of vices opposed to sophrosyne; Pericles, Scipio Africanus, and Cincinnatus, as well as Judith, Susanna, and Joseph in Egypt represent sophrosyne.

of Eden. See Philo *Leg. All.* 1. 14. 43–45, 1. 17. 56–58. St. Paul (Gal. 5. 22, on the fruits of the Holy Ghost) contributed to the popularity of this symbol. For a conflation of the allegory of the Tree of Sophrosyne in Paradise and the myth of the charioteer from the *Phaedrus,* see Methodius *Symp.* 8. 3. 83. Consult Mâle, 105–8, for the *Arbor bona* in twelfth-century art.

5. The Rivers of Paradise. This allegory, too, was introduced by Philo, who identified the cardinal virtues with the four rivers (*Leg. All.* 1. 19. 63; see 1. 21. 69 for sophrosyne as the Tigris). He was followed by Ambrose (*De Par.* 3. 14 ff.; see 3. 16 for sophrosyne as the Gehon) and Augustine (*De Gen. contr. Man.* 2. 10. 13–14). Ambrose inspired the artist of the baptismal font at Hildesheim; consult Mâle, 110, n. 4, on the influence of this allegory, and see Arthur Watson, *Speculum* 3 (1928), 445–69, for the conflation of the allegories of the Rivers of Paradise and the Trees of Virtue in illustrations of the *Speculum Virginum.*

6. The Ladder of Virtue. This symbolism, too, was a late development in Greek literature, even though the inspiration came largely from Plato's *Symposium.* The Neoplatonists described the ascent of the soul in terms of a ladder, on each rung of which the cardinal virtues operated in a different way (Plotinus, *Enn.* I. 2. 1 ff.) or different virtues drew the soul ever higher and closer to the Divine (Gregory of Nyssa *Vita M.;* see Chap. IX, p. 350). Conflated with the idea of Jacob's ladder, this conception produced the *Scala Paradisi* of John Climacus (imitated in the West by Honorius Augustodunensis, *Scala Caeli Minor*), which assigned different virtues to each rung of the ladder. See Mâle, 105–6, for the consequences of this imagery in art.

7. Jewelry or adornment. This type of symbolism, which regards sophrosyne (often coupled with *aidôs*) as the best or only proper adornment for a woman, took its inspiration from the Choice of Heracles (Xenophon *Mem.* 2. 1. 22), in which *Aretê* was adorned with these two qualities. It was popularized by the Cynics (see D. L. 6. 37 for Crates' contribution to the *topos*) and gained great favor in Patristic literature, especially in eulogies of holy women and the ascetical life; but because of the difficulty of representing the image visually, it is of no importance in art.

In Latin literature most of these symbols continued popular, but Roman authors, especially the poets, made a number of original contributions or varied the Greek types in significant ways.

1. Plautus compares a young man's practice of *modestia, verecundia,* and *decorum* to the condition of a house carefully built and maintained by

the *fabri* (the parents). When the youth breaks away from parental control and violates the commands of sophrosyne, Plautus likens him to a house from which the roof is torn off by a violent storm, so that the rain floods in. The two plays in which Plautus employs this symbol are both derived from Philemon, who may be its true originator (*Most.* 161 ff., *Trin.* 317, 321–22). The metaphor from which the symbolism develops occurs in the classical period; see Xenophon *Mem.* 1. 5. 4 on *enkrateia* as the foundation of the palace of virtue.

2. A favorite symbol of sophrosyne in Horace's *Odes* is the voyage of the sailor who prudently avoids the dangerous shallows too close to shore and the perilous depths too far out at sea (*Odes* 2. 10). This image is a special development of the metaphor of the voyage of life, or the storm-tossed ship at sea, which is found as early as the *Odyssey* and becomes common in Greek poetry from Alcaeus on. The connection of this image with sophrosyne is usually only implied in the classical period but is explicit in later poetry (e.g., Cercidas, Frag. 2 Diehl[3], on the voyage with sophrosyne, or Seneca *Oedipus* 882–910). Horace also uses the image of the merchant who is so avaricious that he makes repeated, dangerous voyages to the ends of the earth in search of gain, in contrast to the poet on his Sabine farm, content with little or with what is at hand (*Odes* 1. 31; 3. 1). Another Horatian symbol of the lack of sophrosyne is the rich man who insists on building his seaside villa on piles sunk into the sea (*Odes* 2. 18; 3. 1). With Horace's *dominus terrae fastidiosus*, compare the moralizing interpretations of Xerxes' bridging the Hellespont, an example of the hybristic violation of the boundaries set by the gods.

3. Virgil symbolizes sophrosyne with many highly effective images: the calming of the storm at sea in *Aen.* I (we have noted on p. 300 the use of the verb *temperare*, 57, 146) and the chaining of *Furor* in the temple of Janus; the oak tree of *Aen.* IV. 393–96, which is storm-tossed but not uprooted; the confrontation of Cato and Catiline on the shield of Aeneas in *Aen.* VIII. The sophrosyne of Aeneas is contrasted with the *furor* and *violentia* of Dido and Turnus. Dido's passion is compared to a wound, a fire, poison, disease, or madness (IV. 2, 69; I. 688; IV, 389, 8, 67, 78, etc.). The imagery used to depict Turnus' violation of *temperantia* is sometimes reminiscent of the technique of Aeschylus in the *Septem;* for example, the shield of Turnus with its blazon depicting Io and Argus, and his helmet surmounted with the Chimaera (VII. 85).

4. The Roman triumphal procession gave rise to an important allegorical adaptation, Ovid's Triumph of Amor (*Am.* I. 2. 25–52) in

which *Mens bona* (Sophrosyne?) and *Pudor* (*Aidôs*) are led captive. The expansion of this motive by Petrarch produced the *Trionfi*, one of which was the Triumph of Chastity. Chastity is attended by symbolic animals (the unicorn, the ermine) and by historical, mythical, and Biblical exemplars (Verginia, Lucretia, Dido, Penelope, Judith).[7]

5. Imagery drawn from the animal kingdom abounds in Latin descriptions of virtue and vice, but here again the antitheses of sophrosyne/*temperantia*, rather than the virtue itself, inspired the greater number of images. Thus Turnus is compared to a lion and a bull (*Aen.* XII. 4–7, 103 ff.) which, like the Chimaera on his helmet, represent his uncontrolled passions. Space does not permit a consideration here of the extensive subject of animal exemplars of the virtues and vices, which were common enough in late antiquity (e.g., Plutarch *Bruta Animalia Ratione Uti*,[8] Aelian *De Nat. Anim.*) but became even more popular in the Middle Ages, in the wake of the *Physiologus* and the *De Imagine Mundi* of Honorius Augustodunensis.[9] The varied aspects of sophrosyne required an unusually large number of animal exemplars; in antiquity the turtledove, the salamander, and the tortoise were familiar symbols of sophrosyne as chastity: the first because of its reputation for monogamy; the second because of its supposed power of surviving unharmed in the midst of flames; the third because, by carrying its house with it, it exemplified the modest seclusion proper to a good woman. Consult Gregory of Nazianzus (see Chap. IX, n. 57) for the first two and Plutarch (see Chap. VII, n. 16) for the first and the third. It is perhaps appropriate to mention here the favorite saying of Augustus, σπεῦδε βραδέως (*Festina lente*, "Make haste slowly"), which sums up with gnomic terseness the need to reconcile the two conflicting temperaments, the *andrikos* and the *sôphrôn*. It came to be illustrated by a dolphin twining itself around an anchor; this symbol appears in the statue of *Temperantia* by Giovanni da Bologna in the courtyard of the Bargello in Florence.

[7] On the illustrations of Petrarch's *Trionfi*, see Van Marle, *op. cit.*, figs. 130–41, 160. The "fettered Cupid" as a symbol of chastity in Petrarch's *Triumphus Pudicitiae* is discussed by Erwin Panofsky, *Studies in Iconology* (New York, 1962), 126, n. 79.

[8] For the sophrosyne of crows, pigs, and goats, see Plutarch, *op. cit.*, 988F–991D. Aristotle (*Hist. Anim.* I. 1 ff.) is the source of much doctrine about approximations to moral virtue in various animals. Cf. Plato *Laches* 196–97 on courage in animals, and see Chap. VI, n. 125 on Neoplatonic theories about the *physicae aretae* in irrational beasts.

[9] Animal symbolism involving the cardinal virtues is discussed by Künstle, *op. cit.*, I. 119–32, and Van Marle, *op. cit.* 2. 445–57. See also E. P. Evans, *Animal Symbolism in Ecclesiastical Architecture* (New York, 1896). The proliferation of animals representing *temperantia, pudicitia,* and *castitas* in baroque art reflects the popularity of the emblem books of Alciati and Ripa.

6. The metaphor, ubiquitous in the erotic poetry of all times, that likens the passion of love to a flame,[10] has as its natural counterpart the comparison of sophrosyne (*pudicitia, temperantia, castitas*) to a force capable of extinguishing the fire. The most influential literary passage employing this image occurs in the *Vita Contemplativa* of the fifth-century Latin Father, Julius Pomerius (3. 19, *P.L.* 59. 502), in which *temperantia* is assigned the task of extinguishing the flame of lust. The Carolingian type of *Temperantia* with a torch in one hand, a jug of water in the other, probably derives from this source.[11] In the *Psychomachia* of Prudentius the torch of *Libido* is extinguished, not by water, but by a stone that *Pudicitia* throws (40–48). The twelfth-century Byzantine poet Eustathius describes an allegorical battle between Sophrosyne and Erôs, in which the vessels of fire kindled by Erôs are sprinkled by Sophrosyne with dew from heaven.[12]

The most wide-spread of all mediaeval and Renaissance types of *temperantia* represents the personified virtue as mixing water with wine, so as to temper or moderate the force of the latter. The etymology of the verb *temperare* is enough to account for this image without recourse to any of the classical or late Latin passages in which *temperantia* is interpreted as an agent of mixture or blending (for this interpretation of *temperantia* in Apuleius *De Mundo,* see Chap. VIII, n. 34). The representation of *Temperantia* with an hourglass (later a clock) seems to be a purely mediaeval development, without classical antecedents in literature or art.

[10] On Dido's love as *ignis* or *flamma,* and on the antededents of this metaphor, consult A. S. Pease, *Publi Vergili Maronis Aeneidos liber quartus* (Cambridge, Mass., 1935), 86.

[11] See, for example, the Rhenish Lectionary and the Cambrai Gospels, and consult Katzenellenbogen, 54–55.

[12] *Hysmine and Hysminias* 4. 23.

Subject Index

Aidôs ("modesty," *pudor*), 5, 6, 7, 18, 49, 52, 65, 77–78, 81, 87, 91–92, 114, 128, 143, 156, 180, 193 and n. 89, 204, 229, 317, 327, 331, 351, 383

Akolasia ("wantonness," *luxuria*), 91, 144–45, 159, 166, 176, 179, 201, 216, 218, 249

Allied virtues to sophrosyne, see *Aidôs, Apatheia, Apragmosynê, Autarkeia, Dikaiosynê, Enkrateia, Eunomia, Eusebeia, Euteleia, Hagneia, Hêsychia, Homonoia, Hygieia, Kairos, Karteria, Katharotês, Kosmiotês, Mesotês, Metriotês, Praotês, Prepon,* and *Tlêmosynê*

Anaisthêsia ("insensitivity"), 201, 251

Andreia ("manliness," *fortitudo*), 16, 92, 97, 169, 170–73, 185, 189–90, 194, 216–17, 251, 313, 319, 324, 341

Animal symbolism, 205 n. 30, 248, 399 n. 57, 385

Antitheses to sophrosyne, see *Akolasia, Anaisthêsia, Aphrosynê, Atasthalia, Epithymia, Hybris, Mania, Orgê, Pleonexia, Polypragmosynê,* and *Tryphê*

Apatheia ("absence of passion"), 215, 232, 238–39, 315, 324, 327, 334–35, 346, 348, 351, 371 n. 136

Aphrosynê ("folly"), 3, 18, 20, 23, 131, 159, 193

Apragmosynê ("aloofness, minding one's own business"), 96–98, 101, 103, 105, 111, 136–37, 156, 158, 184

Aretê politikê ("political excellence"), 12–17, 44–46, 72–73, 86–87, 93, 96, 98–99, 102, 110–14, 117, 121–22, 135–42, 144, 147, 157, 172, 185, 205, 235, 250–51, 282, 367–68

Atasthalia ("arrogance"), 9, 18, 23

Autarkeia ("independence"), 118, 122, 125–27, 133–34, 153, 219, 248, 250, 348

Bathmoi ("stages, steps") in the ladder of virtue, 54, 165, 238, 352, 365, 383

Canon of cardinal virtues, the, 25, 41, 72–73, 88 n. 7, 94, 123, 128, 130, 141, 146–47, 151, 172, 187, 196, 197–98, 215–16, 232, 238, 246, 271, 294 n. 99, 300, 315, 324, 336–37, 355, 358, 360–61, 369, 372, 377–78

Charis ("grace"), *Charites* ("the Graces"), 18, 23, 67, 108 and n. 75, 140 and n. 57

Cosmic sophrosyne, 29, 60, 78 n. 114, 162–64, 167, 181–82, 215, 303

Country life (*vita rustica*), 129, 274 and nn. 45, 46, 294–95, 298

Dikaiosynê, dikê ("justice," *iustitia*), 9, 40, 67, 87, 173 n. 49, 189, 193 n. 89, 204, 315, 318, 323, 324, 364

Education for sophrosyne, 74, 98 n. 51, 120, 123, 126, 129 n. 18, 130–32, 137, 148, 171 n. 43, 174, 190–91, 195–96, 255

Enkrateia ("self-control," *continentia*), 114, 118, 122, 125–31, 133, 146, 153, 203, 217, 219, 228, 308, 320 n. 15, 323, 327, 341, 344

Epithymia ("appetite"), 114, 165, 178, 324–26

Eunomia ("behavior in accordance with custom or law"), 9, 13, 15, 19, 23, 25, 95, 112, 193

Eusebeia ("piety"), 19, 41–42, 47, 52, 64–65, 66–67, 77, 94–95, 125, 319, 323

Euteleia ("frugality," *frugalitas*), 106 n. 69, 133, 219, 228, 245, 333

Index of Ancient Authors